MANAGING STRATEGIC ACTION

Mobilizing Change
Concepts, Readings and Cases

Cynthia Hardy

SAGE Publications
London ● Thousand Oaks ● New Delhi

First published 1994

 SAGE Publications Ltd
6 Bonhill Street
London EC2A 4PU

SAGE Publications Inc
2455 Teller Road
Thousand Oaks, California 91320

SAGE Publications India Pvt Ltd
32, M-Block Market
Greater Kailash - I
New Delhi 110 048

British Library Cataloguing in Publication data

Managing Strategic Action: Mobilizing Change –
Concepts, Readings and Cases
  I. Hardy, Cynthia
  658.4012

  ISBN 0–8039–8914–8
  ISBN 0–8039–8915–6 (pbk)

Library of Congress catalog card number 94–066146

Typeset by Mayhew Typesetting, Rhayader, Powys
Printed in Great Britain by Butler & Tanner Ltd,
Frome and London

MANAGING STRATEGIC ACTION

This book achieved its final form only with the help of many friends and colleagues. Beverly played an instrumental role in this project, from the initial conceptualization of a course on strategic change, to teaching the cases, to commenting on the manuscript. Anne and Dave provided helpful reviews of my initial ideas. Art, Deborah and Anne graciously tackled the many specific challenges I asked of them. Finally, Sue contributed endless encouragement to the creative process, right up to the bitter end.

Contents

Acknowledgements

The author and publishers wish to thank the following for permission to use copyright material.

Academy of Management for Donald C. Hambrick and Albert A. Cannella, Jr. 'Strategy Implementation as Substance and Selling', *The Academy of Management Executive*, 3(4) 1989; and for material from Barbara Gray and Sonny S. Ariss, 'Politics and Strategic Change Across Organizational Life Cycles', *Academy of Management Review*, 10(4) 1985; The Braybrooke Press Ltd for material from John Hassard and Sudi Sharifi, 'Corporate Culture and Strategic Change', *Journal of General Management*, 15(2) 1989, pp. 4–19; The Regents of California Management Review for material from Cynthia Hardy, 'Investing in Retrenchment: Avoiding the Hidden Costs', *California Management Review*, 29(4) 1987. Copyright © 1987 by The Regents of the University of California; and David R. Brodwin and L.J. Bourgeois III, 'Five Steps to Strategic Action', *California Management Review*, 26(3) 1984. Copyright © 1984 by The Regents of the University of California; The Director Publications Ltd for Philip Sadler, 'The Politics of the Corporate Jungle', *Director*, May 1992; The Free Press for adapted material from Michael E. Porter, *Competitive Advantage: Creating and Sustaining Superior Performances*, Fig. 2-2, p. 37, Copyright © 1985 by Michael E. Porter; Harvard Business Review for material from John P. Kotter, 'Power, Dependence, and Effective Management', *Harvard Business Review*, July/August, 1977. Copyright © 1977 by the President and Fellows of Harvard College; Richard D. Irwin, Inc. for material from Kenneth R. Andrews, 'The Strategy Concept' from *Concept of Corporate Strategy*, Second Edn. Copyright © 1980 by Richard D. Irwin, Inc.; and Arthur A. Thompson, Jr. and A.J. Strickland III, *Strategy Formulation and Implementation: Tasks of the General Manager*, Revised Edn, 1983, pp. 318–37, Business Publications, Inc.; McGraw-Hill, Inc. for material from Gregory G. Dess & Alex Miller, *Strategic Management*, 1993, excerpted from pp. 109–39; Robert H. Miles for material from *Coffin Nails and Corporate Strategies*, Prentice Hall, Inc. 1982, pp. 58–70. Copyright © 1982 by Robert H. Miles; John Wiley & Sons, Inc. for material from Heidi Vernon-Wortzel and Lawrence H. Wortzel, *Global Strategic Management: The Essentials*, 1991, pp. 135–49.

Every effort has been made to trace all the copyright holders, but if any have been inadvertently overlooked the publishers will be pleased to make the necessary arrangement at the first opportunity.

INTRODUCTION

As the business world struggles with globalization, deregulation, new technologies, and economic recession, business leaders are demanding a greater capacity for strategic *action* – the ability to forge organizations that are capable of carrying out effective strategies in a sustained and profitable way. Success in today's competitive and complex world depends not only upon finding creative new strategies but also the ability to realize them by making the necessary changes throughout the organization. Managers and employees must be able to think strategically and holistically about the organization and the environment within which it is situated. They must also be able to act effectively within organizational and environmental constraints if they are to combat entrenched thinking, and confront inertia and resistance. When we consider organizations like General Motors, IBM and ICI, we can see how crucial organization-wide change is, and how entrenched ideas, cultures and structures often serve to impede the change process.

Business leaders say they need managers with 'soft' or 'people' skills to galvanize an organization and its members into action.[1] What exactly do these skills comprise? They relate to a variety of complex, organization-wide, change-oriented issues. They involve being able to manage people and understanding organizational politics. They incorporate team building, leadership, and spanning organizational and departmental boundaries. Managers, in addition to having analytic skills, must also possess interpersonal and leadership skills; be able to integrate across functions; adopt a global perspective; be capable of managing technology; and have a sense of social responsibility. Much of this hinges on an understanding of 'how things get accomplished within an organization and how to influence the changes'.[2]

Both business schools and the business literature appear to be struggling to respond to this challenge of providing organizations with the skills and techniques necessary to facilitate change. MBA students have frequently been criticized for their lack of soft skills; their inability to take decisions and demonstrate leadership; and their over-specialization in particular functions which precludes a holistic appreciation of the organization.[3] In addition, many recent techniques designed to facilitate organizational change have, in some cases, failed to live up to expectations. For example, total quality management has been accused of focusing attention on internal processes, at the expense of markets, customers and results, and contributing to cumbersome bureaucracies that increase costs and response times.[4] Employee empowerment programmes have often missed the mark because managers have been reluctant to give away sufficient power to their subordinates and, instead, have used it to increase workloads while reducing career opportunities.[5] Even the new source of salvation, process re-engineering, is starting to be questioned for its over-optimistic expectations that critics say have little chance of being implemented.[6]

Other writers have noted that many of today's solutions have been tried before.[7] Recent calls for empowerment mirror demands for employee participation made in the 1950 and 1960s; the network organization can be traced back to Burns and Stalker's organic form of organization in the 1960s;[8] the transnational organization[9] is the global equivalent of the matrix structure;[10] the need for decentralization was the subject of a twelve-part series in *Fortune* as early as 1955; even the recent interest in core competencies[11] was first mentioned in the late 1950s under the heading of distinctive competencies.[12]

It would seem clear, then, that strategic action and the organizational changes on which it depends are difficult to sustain. There is a variety of reasons that account for the difficulty in bringing about enduring organizational change. First, change, at the very least, involves uncertainty and ambiguity. At the worst, it means disruption and dislocation for the individuals involved. For many organizational members, then, change may not be 'good', it may be downright painful and they are, understandably, likely to resist it. Second, strategic change is complex and there are no simple answers. Individuals who are in different departments, at different levels, with different specializations and training, do not necessarily interpret the underlying problem in the same way. They may also have contradictory ideas about the appropriate solution and how it should be carried out. There is no guarantee of consensus, particularly in a large organization requiring major changes. Third, organizations are large, integrated systems. Fixing one part has implications for other departments or systems. Orchestrating system-wide change is a mammoth task – it does not just happen. For these reasons, then, realizing strategic change is difficult and, more often than not, gets bogged down because of resistance, disagreement, compartmentalization and unforeseen outcomes.

Although everyone agrees that strategic change is difficult, we know little about it. It remains, for the most part, a black box: there is a battery of techniques and a world of advice for managers concerning their strategic intentions, but virtually nothing on how to realize them. Strategic planning has, in particular, come in for criticism because of its failure to deliver on implementation.[13] The business literature is obsessed with strategy, but not strategic change; with making strategy, but not doing strategy. Between 1989 and 1993, over 27,000 articles on strategy were written, but only 110 on strategic change.[14] Over 30 different planning tools exist, with such exotic names as nominal group technique, dialectic inquiry, and metagame analysis, but less than a third give any consideration to the actions that have to be taken to put plans into practice.[15] As a result, estimates suggest that only a small percentage of strategic plans are ever successfully implemented.[16]

It would appear, then, that while business leaders are demanding a greater capacity for strategic *action*, much of the business literature remains preoccupied with strategic planning and formulation. But without action and organizational change, strategies will simply remain an impotent plan on a piece of paper, a footnote in a consultant's report, or a figment of an entrepreneur's imagination. The aim of this book, then, is to redress this imbalance by opening up the black box of strategic change. It focuses on the strategic change process whereby system-wide realignment synchronizes the organization around strategic intent and examines how power drives the organization towards its strategic goals. It is the application of power to the strategic change process that helps to bring about strategic action.

The book starts by revisiting the strategic change process: the path whereby managers translate strategic intent into practice through strategic alignment. The emphasis on aligning organizational parameters with strategic intent is not new.[17] Writers have mentioned the importance of coordinating structure, human resource policies, systems and procedures, culture, etc. in order to realize strategic goals.[18] The complexity of juggling these different organizational parameters may, however, account for why implementation has not received more attention in the literature.[19] Despite the difficulties, alignment must be achieved if strategies are to be realized. If CEOs talk about quality but continue to reward productivity; if mission statements stress innovation, but procedures preclude risk-taking; if restructuring creates divisions, but decision making remains centralized at the corporate level, employees will receive mixed messages concerning strategic initiatives and strategies will not be realized.

The second part of the book tackles the issue of power. Actions that converge around strategic goals do not just 'happen' – they hinge on the use of power to orchestrate, mobilize, contain, and direct them. Discussing power is, however, problematic within the context of management education. Experienced managers may know that organizational life paints a political picture, but are rarely willing to admit it. Words like power and politics seem to create embarrassment in the minds of managers and often evoke disbelief on the faces of students.[20] Despite extensive research that has demonstrated that strategy making is seldom a logical, orderly process, its findings have rarely been incorporated into the prescriptive literature, which has retained a firmly rational stance. Despite this neglect, power is an integral part of strategic action. It involves being sensitive to the dynamics of change, able to appropriate the available levers to shape change, and street-wise enough to know when, why and how people resist.

The cases and readings in the final part of the book address specific predicaments that managers face as a result of their strategic choices. Certain strategic initiatives give rise to particular, predictable problems, some of which are explored here. For example, managers involved in mergers and acquisitions must find ways to deal with the cultural discontinuities that exist when two disparate organizations are brought together. Managing decline means facing employee resistance and learning to leverage scarce resources. Innovation is crucial in creating new businesses as well as revitalizing flagging ones; it frequently fails, however, because individuals in different parts of the organization are unable to work together effectively. Global strategies raise the issue of how organizations can structure themselves to span geographic distances and cultural differences in a way that allows them to capitalize on international opportunities. Sustainable development has brought together stakeholders with disparate views and ideologies, who must overcome their differences to work together effectively. Finally, moves to introduce collaborative strategy making cannot depend on traditional views of power: managers must learn to balance their control needs with inclusive decision making.

The book provides an alternative to that part of the traditional literature which devotes its attention to the rational approach to strategy making and the analytic process associated with formulation, rather than the action-oriented problems of implementation. The aim is not simply to help readers to think about strategic action but also to provide a framework to help bring it about. This book confronts the political challenges inherent in realizing strategic change with the help of material designed to uncover the complexity of change processes and the role that power plays in successful strategy making. The selection of the material has been designed to illustrate some of the more common challenges associated with realizing strategic change. Readers interested in the process of strategic change should consult the first and third parts; those seeking a political framework for organizational change should examine the readings and cases from Part II; students and managers wrestling with a particular strategic context should refer to Part III; while those studying the politics of strategic change can combine readings from all three parts (see Tables 1 and 2).

The readings deliberately reflect a mixture of old and new, classic and custom-made, European and North American articles. The cases have been written to appeal to readers in both North America and Western Europe to reflect the increased interest in the international arena. They include state-owned enterprises and not-for-profit organizations as well as large and medium-sized businesses. In addition to cases that examine strategy making from the CEO's perspective, the book also tackles the strategic issues confronting middle and junior managers, and other employees. This diversity shows those readers, at earlier stages of their careers, how they may influence and be influenced by strategic action. It also helps to redress the balance of many textbooks which view strategy making as the sole prerogative of CEOs, and responds to views that strategy making may be more effective when it is a participative process.

While the names in some of the cases will be familiar, less well-known organizations have also been selected to provide a broader set of examples. The book does not concentrate exclusively on renowned organizations for the simple reason that many people work in organizations that the rest of us have never heard of. Moreover by using smaller organizations, readers are introduced to the complexity of strategic change in contexts that are comprehensible and manageable. Not many of us can fully appreciate the scale

Table 1 *Cases matched to strategic themes*

Case	Strategic intent	Structure & form	People & HRM	Culture	Leadership	Strategic realization
Apple (A)	x	x	x	x	x	x
Apple (B)	x	x	x	x	x	x
Mrs Fields' Cookies	x	x	x	x	x	x
Montreal Trust	x	x	x	x	x	x
Automakers		x	x	x		
ICI	x	x		x	x	x
MSP		x	x	x	x	x
Tobacco Firms	x					x
GM/EDS	x	x	x	x	x	x
AECL			x	x		
Bicycle Components	x			x	x	
Conglom	x	x	x	x	x	x

Table 2 *Cases matched to political themes*

Case	The politics of strategy making	The dimensions of power	Critical views of power and politics
Daniel		x	
Crown Corporation		x	
MSP	x	x	x
Northville & Midville	x	x	x
Tobacco Firms	x	x	x
Apple (A) & (B)	x		
Montreal Trust	x		
Mrs Fields' Cookies		x	x
Automakers	x	x	x
ICI	x	x	
GM/EDS	x		
AECL	x		
Loblaws	x		
Conglom	x	x	x

of General Motors, let alone realistically tackle the task of turning the company around. While there is much to be learned from the giants of the industrial world (which is why cases like Apple, ICI and Electronic Data Systems have been included), readers can also benefit from learning about the nature of strategic change in less imposing settings.

The cases grouped at the end of each part also differ from those in most traditional textbooks because they rely on less information rather than more. Instead of describing how someone else has handled a strategic change, these cases set the stage on which managerial action is required. Readers are then invited to identify the actions they would take to resolve the issues involved. In this way, the pedagogical process becomes far more action-oriented: to tackle the cases, the reader must plunge into the unknown by recommending action. Students of all levels and experience find this approach rewarding, especially when they prepare and present action plans in the classroom, which can then be compared and debated. This process is not unlike reality, where: assumptions have to be made; information is incomplete; managers must rely on imagination and insight; and results can be evaluated only after the changes have taken place. Self-directed readers can emulate this process by thinking through, individually, how they would act to solve the problems raised in the cases.

The philosophy underpinning this book rests on a dialogical model of teaching and learning[21] which is a two-way process in which both student and teacher learn from each other. Graduates and undergraduates are as capable of creativity, ingenuity and insight as more experienced managers. The emphasis on the need for strategic *action* focuses student energy on providing ideas that are realistic and innovative. In so doing, the diversity of alternatives facing managers in these situations is revealed which, in turn, identifies the different barriers to strategic action and how they might be overcome. Since there is no 'right' answer (though, sometimes, a few wrong ones), the learning process hinges on understanding the implications of a variety of actions to ascertain the feasible options for the organization in question.

Those readers considering this book for instructional purposes should not be intimidated by this teaching style since it makes for a particularly rewarding teaching experience. By enabling students to become more actively engaged in the learning process through the development and defence of their action plans, motivation is significantly increased. The role of the instructor changes from the traditional fount of all wisdom to that of arbiter of ideas, facilitator and devil's advocate. The aim of the discussion is to allow students to present their ideas and conduct most of the debate between themselves. The instructor intervenes to challenge students when their proposals are shaky, to fill in the gaps they have neglected to address, and to ensure critical issues are discussed. This format facilitates the learning process much more effectively than a teacher offering his or her view in a more direct fashion. A valuable by-product is the generation of new ideas which helps the instructor to reconsider his or her underlying assumptions. It makes teaching a more vital, vibrant task compared with the repetitions of a more structured format which, after a while, saps both the energy and motivation of even the most dedicated teacher. This teaching style depends on two main abilities: the facility to think on one's feet; and a sensitivity to students' ideas that encourages them, probes them, challenges them and critiques them, but never condemns them. Uncertainty concerning the classroom dynamic can be reduced by using a plan to guide the discussion. Once the instructor has a generalized game-plan, preparation is less onerous than for traditional cases and the resulting discussion far more interesting.

The following chapter presents the model of strategic action that frames this book. The remaining chapters and cases are divided into three parts. Part I describes the strategic change process. Part II examines the role of power in bringing about change. Part III explores some key strategic challenges facing contemporary managers.

Notes

1. See Bruzzese, Anita, 'What business schools aren't teaching', *Incentive*, 19–21, March 1991; Ettore, Barbara, 'The MBA world revisited: What corporations are doing now', *Management Review*, 15–20, September 1992; Linder, Jane C. and H. Jeff Smith, 'The complex case of management education', *Harvard Business Review*, September–October, 70: 16–33, 1992; Foggin, James H., 'Meeting customer needs', *Survey of Business*, 6–9, Summer 1992.

2. Foggin, 1992: 8.

3. For example, Bruzzese, 1991; Linder and Smith, 1992; Foggin, 1992; Linder R., 'A modest proposal for private business schools', *Canadian Business*, April, 66: 11–26, 1993.

4. *Canadian Business*, 'TQM: The mystique, the mistakes', 66: 51, 1993; Chang, Richard Y. 'When TQM goes nowhere', *Training and Development*, 47(1): 22–9, 1993; Harari, Oren, 'Ten reasons why TQM doesn't work', *Management Review*, 82(1): 33–8, 1993; Kordupleski, Raymond E., R.T. Rust and A.J. Zahhorik, 'Why improving quality doesn't improve quality (or whatever happened to marketing)', *California Management Review*, 36: 82–95, 1993.

5. See Kizilos, Peter, 'Crazy about empowerment?', *Training*, 27, 12 (December): 47–56, 1990; Kaplan, Robert E., 'Why empowerment often fails', *Executive Excellence*, 8(12): 9, 1991; Brown, D., 'Why participative management won't work here', *Management Review*, 81(6): 42–6, 1992.

6. McPartlin, John P., 'Reengineering: Just chasing rainbows?', *Information Week*, 1 February: 55, 1993.

7. Eccles, R. and Nohria, N., *Beyond the Hype*. Cambridge, Mass: Harvard Business School, 1993.

8. Burns, T. and Stalker, G.M., *The Management of Innovation*, 2nd edn. London: Tavistock, 1966.

9. Barlett, C. and Ghoshal, S., *Managing Across Borders*. Cambridge, Mass: Harvard Business School, 1992.

10. Galbraith, J.R., *Designing Complex Organizations*. Reading, Mass: Addison-Wesley, 1973.

11. Prahalad, C.K. and Hamel, Gary, 'The core competence of the corporation', *Harvard Business Review*, 68: 79–91, 1990.

12. See Eccles and Nohria, 1993.

13. Kiechel, W., 'Corporate strategies', *Fortune*, 106: 34–49, 1982; Kiechel, W., 'Sniping at strategic planning', *Planning Review*, 8–11, 1984; Business Week, 'The new breed of business planner', *Business Week*, 17 September, 62–8, 1984; Pearce, J.A. Freeman, E.B. and Robinson, R.B., 'The tenuous link between formal strategic planning and financial performance', *Academy of Management Review*, 12(4): 658–75, 1987; Hrebiniak, Lawrence G., 'Implementing strategy', *Chief Executive*, 57: 74–7, 1990.

14. According to a CD-Rom search of ABI-Inform abstracts between January 1989 and May 1993.

15. Webster, James L., Reif, W.E. and Bracker, J.S., 'The manager's guide to strategic planning tools and techniques', *Planning Review*, 17(6): 4–13, 1989.

16. See Kiechel, 1984; also see *Business Week*, 'The new breed of strategic planner', 17 September, 62–8, 1984; Skousen, M., 'Roaches outline elephants: An interview with Peter F. Drucker', *Forbes*, August 19, 72–4, 1991.

17. For example, Miles, R.E. and Snow, C.C., *Organizational Strategy, Structure and Process*. New York: McGraw-Hill, 1978.

18. Peters, T.J., and Waterman, R.H., *In Search of Excellence*. New York: Harper and Row, 1982.

19. Hrebiniak, Lawrence G., 'Implementing strategy', *Chief Executive*, 57: 74–7, 1990.

20. See Kotter, John P., 'Power, dependence and effective management', *Harvard Business Review*, 55, 125–36, July–August, 1977; Pfeffer, Jeffrey, 'Understanding power in organizations', *California Management Review*, 35: 29–50, 1992.

21. See Freire, Paulo, *Pedagogy of the Oppressed*. Harmondsworth, UK: Penguin, 1992.

1 A Model of Strategic Action

Formulating strategy is difficult enough. The more problematic task confronting the CEO, however, is the successful implementation of strategy.[1]

The aim of this introductory chapter is to open up the black box of strategic change to provide a model of strategic action. The process of strategic change encompasses the path from strategic intent to strategic realization via strategic alignment. Strategic intent relates to the way in which managers believe they can establish a competitive advantage in their particular environment. Alignment involves the redesign of key organizational parameters to reconstitute the organization in a way that renders it capable of carrying out the intended strategy. Strategic realization occurs when those plans and ideas are transformed into actions, which means managers must be able to combat any inertial forces in the organization. It is argued here that strategic action depends on the effective deployment of power to propel the organization along this path, which helps to achieve strategic change by dismantling the inertial forces in the system and reconstructing a newly aligned organization around the strategic initiative. Strategic action thus encompasses a process of change which is driven by the energy of power.

The first part of this book examines the strategic change process by reiterating the importance of organizational redesign to align key parameters with strategic goals. These parameters span culture, leadership, training and development, hiring and recruitment, resource allocation, information systems, and more. In discussing strategic alignment, the discussion emphasizes a holistic view of strategic change – strategies will be difficult to realize unless the organization is fashioned in an integrated, aggregated way to support them.

The second part focuses on the force or energy needed to drive the organization from intent through alignment to realization. The mobilization of power is integral to successful strategic change for two reasons. The first reason concerns the inertia that stems from the uncertainties, ambiguities and threats embodied in change. So, uncertainty may cause employees to resist change, regardless of how beneficial it may be; ambiguity produces competing solutions to organizational problems, which are supported and opposed by various individuals; and threats and opportunities induce organizational members to engage in political actions to safeguard their own interests. The second reason concerns the need to employ power as the force behind collective action. Organizations do not just meander nonchalantly through restructuring, new hiring programmes, and cultural change to arrive magically at a desired strategic goal. Similarly, managers do not issue edicts or snap their fingers and find their strategic visions obediently and expertly put into place. Organizational energies must be orchestrated and channelled, through the use of power, to support strategic initiatives.

The final part of the book focuses on strategic predicaments. Some of the problems engendered by strategic choice are predictable – a particular strategy will make certain organizational demands which, in turn, raise common sets of problems that manifest themselves as a strategic predicament. In other words, we can often predict the nature of the inertial forces that stand between strategic intent and realization. By taking a small sample of predicaments that are particularly relevant today, readers can gain added insight into the complexity of strategic change and how it can be managed.

This chapter explores these issues in more detail. It tackles the strategic change process, followed by a discussion of power and, finally, examines some common strategic predicaments.

Understanding the Strategic Change Process

Before we can discuss the process of strategic change, we should clarify what is meant by the term 'strategy'. Definitions of strategy have been subject to great debate concerning whether a strategy constitutes those actions which are planned or those which are realized. For the purposes of this book, strategy is defined as the latter.

> Strategy is realized in practice through consistency in a stream of actions and decisions over time.[2]

The actions in question revolve around the mobilization of organizational resources to exploit environmental opportunities and/or defend against threats.[3] They may have been consciously articulated as a means to achieve stated organizational goals or they may have emerged. The focus on actions, rather than plans, enables us to consider three different situations: deliberate strategies where intentions were successfully realized; emergent strategies which were not intended or articulated beforehand; and unrealized strategies where intentions were not carried out.[4] This book focuses primarily on the realization of deliberate strategy – the transformation of strategic intent into a pattern of actions that constitutes a realized strategy. In accordance with this definition, the strategic change process has three components: intent, alignment and realization (Figure 1.1).

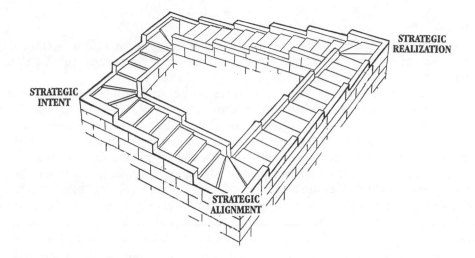

Figure 1.1 *The strategic change process*

Strategic Intent

<table>
<tr><td>

- FORMULATION
- COMPETITIVE ADVANTAGE
- THE ENVIRONMENT

</td></tr>
</table>

Strategic intent is the vision that drives the organization towards a competitive position.[5] It encompasses not only the establishment of strategic goals but the ability to focus attention on, and sustain enthusiasm for, these goals throughout the organization. Strategic intent thus comprises the formation of intentions by organizational members concerning the creation of a competitive advantage in the particular environment in which the business operates. It is those intentions which managers seek to realize through the process of strategic change.[6] It is important to note that, while the business terminology of competitive advantage is used, the process of forming strategic intent – ways of operating successfully within environmental constraints – is equally applicable to organizations outside the business sector.

In order to orient the reader and provide a bridge to other courses on strategy and organization theory, the book starts with a review of strategy, how it is formulated and how it creates competitive advantage. **Formulation** is the process whereby managers analyze the organization and environment in order to select the appropriate strategy. Formulation helps managers decide what to do.[7] It is the choice and elaboration of a particular strategy that constitutes the strategy formulation or planning process which, despite the plethora of techniques, basically revolves around defining the business, conducting a situational analysis (external and internal), establishing planning assumptions or premises, setting objectives and priorities, and developing action plans.[8] Formulation is generally presented as a straightforward, objective task where data and analysis point to a particular strategy. The question of whether commitment to that strategy is shared throughout the organization is seldom considered.

Through formulation, then, managers select the appropriate strategy to achieve **competitive advantage**. Porter[9] is one of the more widely quoted scholars who has provided a framework of the different strategies used by firms to respond to the pressures of their particular environment. He categorizes them according to: cost leadership, which usually translates into lower prices; differentiation, based on such features as image, service, quality, or design;[10] and focus, or market niche.

According to its advocates, formal planning reveals the secret of competitive advantage and identifies the means to achieve it. Critics have, however, questioned the value of planning which, they argue, is a mechanistic process rooted in past practices. They have argued that organizations can no longer afford to follow Porter's advice and focus on cost or differentiation alone. Organizations must achieve both through a continuous process of improvement or through mass customization.[11] Strategic 'thinking', rather than strategic planning, has been called for. It is a more intuitive and creative assessment of both environmental realities and organizational capabilities.[12] Strategy can no longer be thought of as providing a simple and stable 'fit' between the organization and its environment because it focuses on existing resources and opportunities. Strategic 'stretch'[13] is necessary to develop *new* resources and capabilities to deal with future competition and capitalize on future opportunities. Rather than simply allocating resources, strategic stretch leverages resources to ensure the maximum benefit for the minimum investment. So, resources are concentrated around clearly defined, strategic focal points; accumulated from new sources such as employees and alliances; complemented so that different resources reinforce each other; and conserved and recycled.

Another addition to the strategic vocabulary has been the development of core competencies.[14] They represent a form of collective and integrated learning that provides a competitive advantage because the overall 'package' is so difficult to copy. Core competencies incorporate the harmonization of streams of technology; the organization of work; the delivery of value; communication; and strategic commitment that spans boundaries, both internal and external. Resources emanating from a core competence can be easily switched to develop new products, making interdepartmental boundaries more permeable than in the case of divisions or business units. The development by Canon of core competencies relating to precision mechanics, fibre optics and microelectronics led to a variety of products including cameras, video cameras, bubble jet printers, fax machines, copiers, laser imagers and cell analysers.

This new lexicon of strategic stretch, core competencies and strategic thinking reflects a new approach to the **environment**. The traditional literature viewed the environment in terms of a given – an objective, concrete reality that strategy had to accommodate, exploit and make the best of. The task of strategists is, according to this view, to secure as much information as possible to reveal the 'true' nature of the environment and, then develop a strategy to exploit it, relative to other competitors. Critics of formal strategic planning have been demanding a more creative approach to the environment, which is perceived to be requiring more sophisticated strategies.

> So far in the twentieth century, we have already seen the basis of competitive advantage shift at least four times: from price and volume to quality, then to speed, and finally to mass customization. . . . Factors which were once sources of genuine competitive advantage will become simply the minimum entrance requirements for even staying in the game.[15]

Government policies emphasizing deregulation and privatization have affected industries as diverse as airlines and the London Stock Exchange. Trade agreements such as NAFTA, and the dismantling of European Community barriers, have had international repercussions. New technology and globalization have changed market prospects across the world. All these changes are making life more difficult for managers and employees.[16] They demand networking and coalitions instead of hierarchy and competition; alliances instead of mergers and acquisitions; decentralization instead of centralized controls; flexibility instead of scale; quality, customer-orientation *and* low costs instead of a simple choice between cost leadership and differentiation; rewards for performance instead of seniority; global strategies instead of a domestic focus; and more.

This new world order adds to an increasingly voracious business environment that punishes organizations that fail to make the grade. Some of the organizations that have failed to make that grade have been large US and European firms that were previously thought invulnerable. The concomitant success of Japanese competitors has led to questions about whether Western managers can either think or act strategically.[17] These traumatic experiences have led to a re-examination of assumptions and a more creative, proactive approach to strategy, which includes:

> the ability to transcend competition altogether by completely re-defining the rules of competitive engagement in such a way as to provide the reframer with at least a temporary monopoly over the critical success factors of the new game.[18]

Calls for strategic reframing,[19] strategic stretch,[20] and new strategic paradigms[21] demand actions that do not just respond to existing environments but create new ones.

Managers are urged not simply to gather information on environmental characteristics in order to plot a successful strategy; but to develop innovative strategies that create a new environment in which the organization in question has an advantage.

> You've just restructured, you've boosted efficiency heroically, you're dramatically leaner and meaner – but is it enough? Not if you're in an industry where some ferocious competitors aren't just playing the old game better but rewriting the rules from scratch.[22]

Role models who have redefined the rules include Steve Jobs whose visionary insight created the personal computer industry; or Honda's Supercub which changed a market symbolized by Marlon Brando in the film *The Wild Ones* and Peter Fonda in *Easy Rider* to one captured by the advertising campaign: *You meet the nicest people on a Honda.*

In these cases, the environment is enacted or created by the strategies of innovative individuals or organizations. Newly formed or recently shaken-up environments appear most receptive to this proactive use of strategy. As environments mature, the rules of the game become more institutionalized, leaving less room for manoeuvre for strategists and entrepreneurs.[23] There is a greater demand for the collection and analysis of information unless the environment can be shaken up once again and old rules broken, which is what some competitors do.[24]

In summary, strategic intent comprises the formulation of intentions concerning the way in which the organization should secure competitive advantage, and shape or exploit its environment. It is, however, only the first step on the path of strategic action. Moreover, while the formation of strategic intent is usually presented as a rational, orderly process, research indicates that the sharing of strategic intent is problematic. Senior managers often have quite different ideas of what the organization's strategy is. Such disparities in perception and understanding are increased in the case of middle managers who are further away from the strategic apex.[25] In many respects, the lack of agreement should not come as a surprise – strategic change is complex and ideas concerning the correct strategic answer are bound to vary. When we factor in recent views that the environment is not an objective reality, waiting to be revealed, but a social construction of our perceptions and actions, the potential for disagreement increases. What one individual sees as strategic salvation, another may dismiss as a crazy idea. Nevertheless, managers must ensure that strategic intent is shared – by board members who must approve it, employees who must enact it, and even outsiders who must respond to it. Thus the sharing of strategic intent is a political process that involves the persuasion of other organizational members on the basis of tenuous or ambiguous data, and possibly against their better judgement and personal interests.

Strategic Alignment

- STRUCTURE AND FORM
- PEOPLE
- CULTURE
- LEADERSHIP

Strategic alignment starts where strategic intent leaves off. It is the heart of what is known as the implementation process. It is the platform of architecture on which strategy is built. As such it is vital to strategic success – unless the strategy is appropriately underpinned with the right kinds of skills, reward systems, coordination mechanisms, structures, leadership, culture, and control systems, it will fail. Although not a new concept,[26] the issues associated with strategic alignment remain relatively neglected by the management literature which is more interested in formulation.[27] The task of alignment is often either subsumed under the ubiquitous but nebulous term of implementation, or compressed into the straitjacket of organizational structure. Although textbooks on strategy have since extended their horizons and acknowledged that, in addition to restructuring, resources also have to be allocated, commitment secured, progress monitored, and political and cultural barriers dismantled, many continue to dwell on structure with only passing reference to these other organizational parameters.

The complexity of juggling a variety of different organizational parameters to bring them into synch with strategic intent may account for the relative neglect of implementation in the literature. Implementation involves managing complex processes; taking many interrelated decisions; fine-tuning or changing a large number of organizational variables; juggling interdependence; setting up effective control systems; and dealing with the vagaries arising from the human and social aspects of organizations.[28] In spite of the complexity, alignment must be achieved. There is no use publicizing a strategy based on innovation and new product development while retaining a bureaucracy that stifles all initiative; instituting a functional structure that prevents the dissemination of ideas between departments; penalizing people for making mistakes, and using hiring practices that screen out creative researchers. Strategic change is an integrated process[29] in which a number of key organizational parameters are aligned to support the strategy to facilitate its realization.[30]

The starting point is, typically, **structure**. Traditional structures included the entrepreneurial, bureaucratic and diversified forms: as the firm moved through its life cycle and its strategies moved from growth to scale to diversification, the organizational structure was usually changed accordingly.[31] Later the matrix structure [32] and adhocracy[33] were developed to provide an early blueprint for a more innovative organization. Unfortunately, these structures appear to have failed to solve the problems of business. Despite struggling with a series of reorganizations for over a decade, organizations like General Motors and ICI have not yet found a structure to guarantee consistent organizational success.[34] Traditional organizational structures have been criticized for concentrating power in the hands of senior managers which, while guaranteeing managers more control, also disenfranchises and alienates employees who, as a result, fail to identify with corporate goals. Even structures like the matrix, designed to facilitate coordination and innovation by combining functional and divisional structures, have been condemned for bringing about the worst of both worlds instead of the best.[35]

Frustration with the failure of traditional structures to deal with contemporary pressures has led to increased interest in more responsive and flexible organizational **forms**.[36] Empowerment, delegation and participation have been used in organizations like Semco[37] to introduce new perspectives, increase motivation and dismantle departmental barriers. This desire for flexibility has not only been focused on internal structures, it has also permeated barriers between organizations as joint ventures, strategic alliances, and outsourcing have been promoted.

Companies must also have both the mind-set and organizational structures (or, sometimes, the lack thereof) to actively encourage cross-disciplinary teamwork, collaboration, and thus learning. And it is not only interdepartmental barriers which must be demolished; the firm's outer boundaries also need to be radically redefined so that suppliers, customers, and strategic alliance partners can become insiders and be tapped systematically for ideas and insight.[38]

Such developments have led to the modular corporation[39] where all non-core activities are subcontracted to outsiders. Outsourcing has accordingly taken on a new dimension as it has moved from farming out the cafeteria, to handing over the control of all information technology and computer operations to another organization.

Originally, businesses sought to outsource as a way to get the job out the door so they didn't have to worry about it. Today, companies realize the relationship is more complex.[40]

The natural extension of this trend is the virtual corporation[41] that exists only as a temporary network of companies, linked via information technology, which donate their core competences to a transitory collaboration that may span a variety of different countries and cultures.

While the advantages of these new organizational forms include synergy, flexibility, reduced costs and lower investment requirements, they do not come without a price. To be successful, managers must learn to work across, and eventually dismantle, traditional organizational boundaries; develop trust in outsiders; and provide ways of linking different companies together in effective alliances that may span the breadth of the world. Managers can expect to encounter considerable difficulty in mastering these challenges: decentralization and flexibility have remained an elusive goal for more than fifty years. Calls for an end to hierarchy, which can be traced back to the 1920s, have yet to be realized.[42] And, if managers cannot break down interdepartmental barriers, how can they expect to work across inter-organizational boundaries, particularly when they traverse international frontiers and bring together diverse cultures?

Regardless of whether these new organizational forms succeed in revolutionizing the corporate world, organizations are more than structure. They also consist of people, cultures and leaders. These aspects of the organization must also be aligned with the strategic goals of the organization. The following sections discuss each of these organizational parameters in more detail.

One constellation of parameters that is typically ignored in the strategy literature concerns **people**, which refers here to human resource matters. (Other 'people' issues concerning culture and leadership will be dealt with separately below.) This omission probably arises because human resource management is usually considered in a separate course to strategy and thus falls outside the strategic equation. Yet, if people with the appropriate skills are not hired, not trained, not evaluated, not compensated, not promoted and not motivated in ways consistent with strategic aspirations they will only impede the realization of the strategy. It is not enough simply to tell employees and managers what the new strategic directives are – unless the total sum of their organizational experience leads them in the same direction, change will be difficult. Lack of attention to human resource issues is a common cause of strategic failure – senior executives announce a new strategic direction but they continue to reward people for doing things that conform to the old strategy. Employees and managers thus receive a mixed message and revert to the old way of doing things.

Human resource management is, then, a relatively new addition to the strategic agenda[43] and it still receives short shrift by strategists.[44] Some organizations view human resource management only in terms of containing or avoiding problems whereas, ideally, it should be considered as an integral part of strategy, if not a source of competitive advantage in itself.[45] Human resources comprises a number of distinct but related areas, all of which must support the strategic thrust of the organization.[46] Human resource management consists of selection and recruitment; performance evaluation and appraisal; rewards and compensation; and training and development.[47] So, for example, if a company starts to diversify through strategic business units, it will need to develop recruitment procedures to bring new people with different skills into the organization; performance appraisal may have to be modified and delegated to take into account divisional differences; reward systems will have to balance divisional performance with that of the overall organization in order to guard against centrifugal forces; and training programmes may be necessary to enable existing organizational members to adjust. Clearly, then, every strategy makes certain demands of its employees who must be supported by consistent human resource policies.

Each of these human resource areas represents a multi-faceted component of the strategic change process in its own right. First, selection processes must not only match people to jobs in the organization; they must also ensure people are transferred and promoted appropriately, and key executives are chosen who can best promote strategic initiatives. Second, performance appraisal, often one of the least liked tasks on many managers' agendas, is crucial if rewards are to be effectively allocated, and training and recruitment needs are to be accurately forecasted. Measurement methods must be made consistent with the new goals. Third, rewards can take a variety of forms: even the 'simple' matter of payment incorporates salary, bonuses, stock options, benefits and perquisites. Managers must also, however, consider promotion, career opportunities, responsibility and development opportunities as well as praise from superiors, customers and co-workers when rewarding their employees. Managers often fail to use these potential levers and the reward system is 'one of the most underutilized and mishandled managerial tools for driving organizational performance'.[48] Finally management development requires a sustained interest from senior management and the establishment of clear objectives concerning the goals of development programmes; the recruitment and identification of employees with the desired potential for training; comprehensive and systematic rewards that capitalize on training objectives; and effective coaching from superiors.

Unlike human resources, organizational **culture** has been extensively considered in strategic terms.[49]

> A good deal has been written in the last decade about the links between organizational strategy and culture, the problems of strategic inertia in forms, and the need for managers to manage the cultural context of the organization so as to achieve strategic change.[50]

The management of culture has become one of the more fashionable issues in contemporary management theory.[51] The success of Japanese firms led to a search for ways of transplanting this culture into North America and the 1980s were marked by an increasing interest in organizational culture.[52]

Academic debates have raged concerning the definition of culture[53] but as far as business usage has been concerned, the term has been used to signify an invisible (national or organizational) force that either impedes strategy or provides a source of competitive advantage.[54] The term is typically used in business to imply such things as stories and myths, symbols, rituals and routines, power distributions, control systems, and structure, though many anthropologists would categorize these only as the surface trappings of more deep-rooted beliefs, values and assumptions that really constitute culture. This definitional interest in the surface, rather than the submerged, aspects of culture has been attributed to the desire of management theorists to find a concept that can be easily managed to enhance organizational performance.[55]

> The intent [of such definitions] is a promise, namely, that by reinforcing, manipulating, or transforming the culture of their corporations, executives might render the enterprise more effective. They might improve its performance and increase its productivity. They might, to put it bluntly, make it more profitable.[56]

This managerial perspective has led to a hunt for 'strong' cultures[57] such as that which characterized IBM and was believed responsible for the company's success. Unfortunately, as more recent events have shown, a strong culture may be more of a hindrance than a help. The resulting confusion has left managers struggling to change cultures in order to react to new business realities while, at the same time, trying to retain the commitment and loyalty that characterized the original culture.[58] Part of their problem stems directly from the simplification that has occurred in the business literature, which has made it difficult both to appreciate the complex and deeply rooted nature of culture, and to distinguish between aspects of organizational life that can be easily shaped and the fundamental culture which is the result of a complex interplay between all organizational members.

When the term 'culture' is used in this book, it is used advisedly. It refers to the way in which deeply rooted values, beliefs, and assumptions act as a filter on the perception and interpretation of events that often hinders organizational change and reinforces the status quo. A strong culture is formed, not by a few elite members of the organization pressing the right buttons but collectively, in a complex interactive process that involves all members of the organization. It may well prove effective in achieving managerial goals, as long as nothing else changes. A strong culture entrenches both perception and behaviour: ways of seeing and ways of doing. People filter and interpret information according to accepted norms and values. The stronger the culture, the more consistent the filtering and interpretation processes, the more convergent the behaviour, and the more difficult it becomes to perceive, let alone act on, the need for change.

To understand culture in this way, is to acknowledge that it cannot easily be changed, much less tinkered with. Managers cannot expect to dismantle the parts of a culture they consider dysfunctional while retaining the parts they believe to be a source of competitive advantage without a struggle. They must also learn to recognize the existence of powerful subcultures which may not be amenable to assimilation within the context of a larger, homogeneous culture. Managers must, then, understand culture as a deeply rooted phenomenon to appreciate how it impacts upon strategic change; and they should not expect to be able to change it quickly or easily. It takes the use of power to change culture – something often ignored in the literature, but which is discussed in more detail in the following section.

Leadership is another commonly discussed component of strategy making. Indeed, many writers would have us believe that it is the only component. The infatuation of the Western world with great business leaders (and the propensity of many of those great leaders to write autobiographies) has created a leadership myth. It is particularly so in times of crisis, when a charismatic figure such as Lee Iaccoca, John Sculley, Jack Welch, Jan Carlzon or John Harvey Jones is brought in to save the organization from itself. While there may be times when great leaders can be found to do the dirty work, there are other times when there is an unfortunate dearth of visionaries. Even when such a leader exists (and writes a book) what is often omitted is the seemingly boring, mundane organizational adjustments that have to be made to support and realize his or her vision.

Much of the work on leadership and vision represents the 'great man' (and they nearly always are men) theory of management and, as such, glosses over 90 per cent of the strategic task. At the extreme, it simplifies the process of strategic change to: find a great leader; ensure he (*sic*) has both charisma and vision; use the charisma to implement the vision! It is the artist's counterpoint to the science of strategic planning and makes many of the same mistakes by ignoring the myriad of actions that leaders and other organizational members take in order to contribute strategic change. While leaders clearly do help to realize strategic change, it is important to realize that the use of charisma and vision is only one way of doing so. Business leaders have to take many other actions to facilitate strategic change. Even these actions alone will not guarantee success, for a variety of reasons. First, leaders will have to delegate some work to other managers who may or may not carry out their orders in a way consistent with the leader's goals. Second, even if these managers do their duty, other employees will also have to subscribe to the changes. Third, the ripple effect of strategic change causes micro-level adjustments that are crucial to success but of which the leader may never be aware. Finally, if better strategies emerge from broader participation,[59] effective strategic change should not involve just the person at the top of the hierarchy but should engage managers and employees at all levels.

In summary, the preoccupation with leadership and the repackaging of the multi-faceted and complex process whereby strategy is realized under the heading of charisma and vision, is of limited use to managers since it mystifies both the formulation and implementation of strategy. In order to understand how leaders shape strategy, we need a broader conceptualization of leadership style than either the models that emphasize vision and charisma or those that promote a top-down planning approach.

These parameters – structure and form, people, culture, and leadership – must be aligned in the strategic quest. Strategic change often fails because some parameters push energies in one direction while others direct action in another. This process of alignment is, understandably, difficult. The coordination of complicated and often discomforting organizational changes is difficult to orchestrate at the best of times. In many situations, the changes give rise to conflict and resistance. Strategic alignment, like strategic intent, is a political process and, as such, depends on the effective mobilization of power – a matter that will be discussed in more detail in the following section.

Strategic Realization

> • CONVERGENCE

Strategic change is realized as organizational actions **converge** in a new pattern that constitutes a new strategy. It may or may not bear any relation to the original intent, although it is argued here that strategic alignment helps to ensure that the realized strategy approximates the intended one. Example 1.1 illustrates how the realignment of structure, culture, leadership, information, reward system and training provided the convergence necessary for strategic change.

Example 1.1

The new Executive Vice President (EVP) appointed as head of a division of a financial services company was charged with introducing a more aggressive strategy to improve its position in the deregulated financial services industry. This new strategy emphasized new product development, customer orientation, and cost-effectiveness. It marked a big difference from the previous 'laissez-faire' strategy.

The functional structure was reorganized into product groups to stimulate new product development, each headed by a Vice President who reported directly to the EVP. New products were launched and their progress carefully monitored. Two subsequent changes to the structure were made as part of a continuing realignment process.

The EVP engaged in an intensive communication strategy using a variety of media to publicize the new strategy to branches across the country. He increased his direct contact with the branch network and his regional VPs. He also tried to change the culture of his senior management team, which was traditional and hierarchical. It inhibited delegation downwards and made his senior team highly dependent on the EVP's directives. An external consultant was hired to run 'brainstorming' meetings. The EVP stressed a very different leadership style – he was much more of a team player than a commander-in-chief. He wanted all levels of management to exert more initiative.

The EVP also developed an Executive Information System (EIS) which enabled him to assess the profitability of individual products and branches. It was the first time that such comprehensive data had been collected as part of an integrated system which broke down information to the point where the performance of a particular product in a particular branch could be measured. The EIS revealed that new products were being promoted regardless of their profitability. There had been a blitz on promoting VISA cards to existing customers. Unfortunately, since VISA was administered by another bank, it produced minimal profits. Reward systems were changed to ensure that bonuses for branch managers reflected lost as well as new business. In addition, managers received a budget for bad loans – if it was exceeded, the manager's bonus would be affected. The EIS enabled the continuous review of individual branches on a monthly basis to monitor performance.

As delegation and accountability increased, branch managers were required to make three-year budget forecasts against which their performance would be measured and rewarded. The EIS enabled branch managers to track product performance, secure market data, and pinpoint weaknesses and opportunities. These responsibilities required new training programmes to help them make sense of and act on the increasingly sophisticated financial and marketing data.

These were just some of the changes that the EVP made over a three-year period to realign an organization of 2,000 people behind the new strategy.

The term 'convergence' makes it sound as if some form of steady state can be reached when the manager's job is done. If it were only true! Realization is not a fixed, immutable state but a constantly shifting, transient phenomenon as pressures both inside and outside the organization create tensions. Accordingly, when we talk about strategic realization, we must also consider transition as companies grow and change, and new strategies require new ways of doing things. So, for example, the domination of the leader in the entrepreneurial form creates problems as the organization grows; the centralization of the functional form impedes the delegation necessary for diversification; the red tape used to coordinate decentralized decisions brings about bureaucracy ill-equipped to deal with innovation.[60] As a result of these tensions, organizations do not stand still. They may make quantum leaps,[61] followed by periods of convergence where organizational parameters are fine-tuned to support the existing strategy, or they may take incremental steps[62] in their pursuit of strategic change. Whatever the pace of the trajectory, organizational members will struggle to balance the pressures to align the different parts of their organization with those that threaten to tear it apart. Thus, strategic alignment is a balance between convergence and transition, and the realization of a strategy has implications for the formation of subsequent strategic intentions.

Some business writers have argued explicitly against convergence, saying that too much attention to conformity crushes innovation.

> Managerial behavior is predicated on the assumption that we should rationally order the behavior of those we manage. That mind set needs to be challenged. A system requires 'internal variety' to cope with external change. Too often 'internal variety' is perceived within organizations as contention. But internal differences can widen the spectrum of an organization's options by generating new points of view.[63]

According to this view, the inevitable internal tensions within a corporation should not be viewed as pathologies to be eradicated. Instead, 'constructive contention' is a source of dynamism and renewal.[64] Allowing access of a larger number of organizational members to strategic conversations,[65] for example, forces senior managers to re-examine assumptions and introduces creativity to the strategy making process. In this way, organizational learning is supposedly nurtured — by taking in disparate points of view by learning from 'front line troops', as well as people outside the organization, perhaps through temporary personnel assignments on the shop floor, with buyers and suppliers, or overseas. New points of view increase the chances of contradictory opinions which, if constructively managed, can offset the tendency of organizations to follow doggedly the same path long after it has outlived its usefulness.[66]

Summary

This section has described the strategic change process and the role that alignment plays in moving the organization from intent to realization. This continuous process both involves convergence and provokes transition. It is the tension between convergence and transition that underpins the longstanding hunt for the decentralized, flexible organization that is capable of capitalizing on strategic opportunities: a search which has become much like that for the Holy Grail. While change involves new information and ideas, the prevailing bureaucracy, culture, and managerial power mean that new inputs are often limited by senior managers who wish to retain control, thus making the achievement of the truly flexible organization difficult.

For example, Roberts[67] found that the involvement of middle managers in a strategy making was accompanied by a series of meetings to ensure they subscribed to a collective vision. Westley[68] argues that middle managers are most likely to be allowed to participate in strategic conversations, where they might introduce new, contradictory information, when strong cultural norms exercise a *de facto* control and limit their contributions to those that fall within the broad organizational philosophy. One of the reasons, then, why

Japanese companies delegate extensively may lie in the larger, societal culture which ensures a certain degree of conformity and convergence even though employees have a high degree of autonomy.

Accordingly, the tensions involved in the realization of strategic intent embody political overtones: convergence tends to necessitate centralized control, while transition often requires a lessening of control. In fact, all elements of the strategic change process – intent, alignment and realization – have political implications as parts of the organization are dismantled and other are rebuilt. So far, there has been little discussion of how managers might achieve this. The next section tackles this challenge by discussing the role of power in strategic change.

Understanding Power

The first section of the book elaborates the key components of the strategic change process, but has not considered *how* the organization moves from intent, through alignment, to realization. The second component of strategic action concerns the energy that drives the organization through the change process – the mobilization of power.

The traditional literature has tended to neglect power and politics. Still steeped in the rational view of the world, it remains largely committed to the development of analytic and technical skills that do wonders for diagnosis but little for action and practice.[69] As a result, the typical discussion of power in strategy textbooks is brief and simplistic. For example, one 300-page textbook on implementing strategy confined its discussion of power to less then ten pages, most of which were devoted to quotations of Machiavelli who, while providing an insightful examination of power, does not exactly address all the issues facing contemporary managers! Another book aimed at a management audience and devoted to pragmatic and robust action, while admitting that political skills were crucial, spent less than three pages on them.

Researchers have found that strategy making in real life rarely proceeds along the planned, linear route that many business professors (and students) wish it would.[70] But, while drawing attention to the complexity of strategy, this work has stopped short of offering ways to manage the confusion. It has provided insight into how strategy is formed; emphasized the difficulties of implementation; and broken down artificial barriers between it and formulation but, with few exceptions,[71] it has not explained how strategies can be realized. Similarly, work on the politics of strategy making, while richly descriptive, is seldom integrated into the prescriptive and pedagogical literature.[72] So, although more aware of how strategies emerge in real life instead of in the textbooks, managers and students are no nearer to learning how to guide their emergence.

Such neglect probably stems from the high level of discomfort and ambivalence terms like power and politics engender.[73] It is important to realize that power is neither 'good' or 'bad': it all depends on the use to which it is being put. It can be used to further self-interest or it can be used to orchestrate changes that benefit a wide variety of people. Often it represents a mix of both altruistic and selfish motives. For example, a strategic change may bring about improved performance, safeguard jobs, increase shareholder dividends and improve customer service, but it also probably results in a few additional bonuses for the successful strategic architect who brought it about.

Obviously, power is sometimes used to exploit others, but that is no reason to ignore it – mystifying power serves nobody, least of all the people subjected to it. Power will be discussed here to reveal its complexity. It will be argued that power is crucial to collective action, which is why it drives strategic change. At the same time, in order not to ignore the ethical implications, a critical stance will be adopted to reveal the myriad of ways – both constructive and destructive – in which power is used in organizations.

Strategic Change as a Political Process

Power is defined here as a force that affects outcomes; politics is simply the use of power. This deliberately broad, neutral definition is designed to redress the tendency to consider power as a negative, coercive phenomenon – power 'over' others. Power is also a creative and productive force.[74] Organizations consist of both competitive and cooperative elements.[75] They encompass 'contests among interdependent actors operating from different perspectives or frames of reference who are motivated by different self interests' and 'struggles for collaboration among relevant actors in the process of performing organizational work'.[76] Collaboration involves power as much as does conflict. This form of power relates to the Parsonian view of power to achieve system goals and involves power 'to' rather than power 'over'.[77] According to this view, power is not always a zero-sum game but often a synergistic process.

> [Power is the ability of] different parties to achieve something together they could not accomplish individually. This power governs a politics concerned with creating new possibilities in a world where resources may be scarce but some interests may be joined and new resources created. This is win-win politics: victory is only collective, and one party's loss defeats all.[78]

For example, writers have pointed to the necessity of power for innovation.[79] Others have linked political action to the implementation of ethical frameworks.[80] Power can be used for common interest. Even when actors are committed to organization goals, differences of opinion can arise, causing actors to use power either to resolve or avoid conflict, and bring about a solution which they believe is for the common good.[81]

So, power is used both to exploit vested interests and to bring about collective action. Strategic change evokes both these political consequences. Vested interests arise because strategic choices embody opportunities for some organizational members, and threaten others;[82] structural reorganizations involve more resources and authority for some managers and less for others; human resource policies such as appraisal and selection often have political overtones;[83] entrenched cultures reflect existing power distributions that are difficult to change;[84] and leadership battles provoke intense conflicts of personality and style, while new managers have to acquire power.[85] Radical change can be extremely unsettling for organizational members,[86] who may use whatever power they can to resist it. There are, as a result, many instances where strategic change is perceived by managers and employees as a zero-sum game with important consequences for their particular interests. Accordingly, power will be brought to bear by these organizational actors on strategic outcomes to protect those interests.

Even in situations where managers and employees support strategic change, power will still have to be wielded to ensure collective action. First, the costs and benefits of major change are hard to assess. This uncertainty renders the rational–scientific paradigm inappropriate, since with ambiguity comes the potential for conflict.

> Without perfect, unbounded, rationality it is quite feasible that individuals and groups may agree on ends without agreeing on how they are to be pursued. They are likely to perceive the world in terms of their own interests and see their own contribution to values ends as especially significant. Thus, there may well be conflict, and the exercise of power.[87]

Second, the complexity of forming strategic intent, restructuring, instituting new hiring procedures, making new appointments, developing new training programmes, changing information systems and shaping culture require power to orchestrate alignment.

In summary, aligning all the necessary design parameters to support a new strategy is an enormous management challenge. It will not just happen by itself, it requires the use of power, regardless of whether the organization is a political cauldron of conflicting interests and deliberate resistance or whether it is united by common goals. Power and politics thus impinge upon strategy in many different ways: in the boardroom;[88] because of diverging perceptions of strategy;[89] as a result of conflicting interests;[90] or over the choice and outcome of different strategies.[91]

The Dimensions of Power

- RESOURCES
- PROCESSES
- MEANINGS
- THE SYSTEM

So, what does power comprise? The apparently simple definition used here embodies a complex phenomenon which comprises four different dimensions.[92] By acknowledging the multidimensionality of power, we obtain an understanding of a broader array of mechanisms that can be used to effect change. The sooner we peel away the euphemistic wrappers from power, the sooner both managers and employees will be able to understand and influence strategic change.

First, the most common conception of power is exercised by actors to prevail in decision making and bring about specific actions.[93] It has been associated with the possession of objective, structural sources of power such as strategic contingencies[94] and resource dependencies.[95] Power stems from the control of such **resources** as information, expertise, sanctions, political access, credibility, etc.[96] These resources can be used by those who possess and control them to influence directly the behaviour of those who desire them. This phenomenon has also been called overt power[97] and surface power.[98] It is typically used to defeat resistance and is usually clearly visible as competing actors use the power at their disposal to triumph over opponents.

Second, sometimes the use of power is less visible as in the case of non-decision making, where opposition is suppressed and kept out of decision making arenas by confining agendas to 'safe' questions.[99] This form of power resides in the organizational **processes** that incorporate a variety of procedures and routines that can be invoked by dominant groups, working behind the scenes, to prevent subordinates from fully participating in the decision making process. Nondecision making has traditionally been associated with dominant groups and the status quo. The power embedded in processes can, however, also be used to bring about change. Managers may try to end the status quo by *extending* access to decision making arenas and agendas. Processes may be modified to incorporate new committees with new mandates and new members in order to bring change on to the agenda, incorporate new viewpoints, raise awareness, and stimulate new developments. Similarly, new reporting relationships, positions, portfolios, evaluation procedures and budgeting controls can be used to accent new directions and institutionalize new behaviour in a way that does not require repeated applications of resources.

Third, power can also be used to create legitimacy for and acceptance of change through the management of **meaning**.[100] By manipulating symbols and their meanings, reality can be redefined so that the desired strategic change is perceived as legitimate, desirable or unavoidable.[101] Chaffee[102] has referred to the interpretative function of strategy making whereby managers translate the need for change and the form it should take to other organizational members through the use of symbolic communication. In this way, strategic intent is shared among a broader group of organizational members.

A study of hospital and factory closures provides an example.[103] Managers who wanted to secure union and employee support engaged in a complex strategy designed to legitimate the managerial decision to close the unit in question. Their actions included the use of symbols, such as redundancy (severance) compensation and consultation to emphasize managerial credibility and goodwill; and economic reports and presentations of the reasons behind the closure to justify it. In all cases, these actions were symbolic: consultation involved peripheral matters, not the closure decision itself; severance payments did not truly compensate for lost jobs; economic reports justifying the closure were based on confidential figures that were never made public; and the reasons given for the closures were seductive but, in many cases, not the real ones. This form of power may be relatively difficult to observe but it remains, nevertheless, an important way for managers to secure support.[104]

Finally, we must consider the power of the **system**, which confers advantages and disadvantages on certain organizational members *without* being consciously mobilized by them. This power lies in the unconscious acceptance of the values, traditions, cultures, and structures of a given institution. Although these characteristics are often seen as neutral, functional constructs, they usually serve to protect the interests of particular groups.[105] This form of power captures all organizational members in its web. Even those who profit from it find it difficult to change.[106]

The power of the system is the organizational backdrop against which decisions and actions take place. Managers often use the other three sources of power to maintain the status quo and support this system. They can, however, also use them to dismantle parts of the system and release energy for change. Resources can be deployed to change specific actions through rewards and/or punishments. Resources do not, however, make much of a lasting impact since the desired action often rests on the repeated application of either carrot or stick. Processes can be used to institutionalize change in a more enduring and generalized manner if they are modified to embody new behaviours. The changes wrought by new processes are limited, however, to those that conform to existing organizational values and norms since behaviours that clash with the existing system will quickly become marginalized. By manipulating meaning, it may be possible to change these values and legitimate widespread, enduring changes. Table 1.1 and Figure 1.2 illustrate the different dimensions of power.[107]

Table 1.1   Three types of power

	Target: Specific actions	Target: New behaviour	Target: Values, norms
Resource power	principles of behaviour modification used to effect specific actions	insufficient power	insufficient power
Process power	unnecessary use of power	new behaviours are introduced via the process	insufficient power
Meaning power	unnecessary use of power	unnecessary use of power	the management of meaning effects system-wide change

The successful mobilization of power hinges on an understanding of its multidimensionality. The narrow definitions that pervade the literature serve to maintain our ignorance of a complex phenomenon. We are prisoners of our own definitions. If we define power as the ability to influence behaviour for self interest, what do we call the ability to influence behaviour for collective interests? If power is the ability to influence behaviour in the event of resistance, what is the ability to influence behaviour to prevent resistance? If power has to be consciously exercised to influence outcomes, what do we call the advantages that reside in existing structures and systems that benefit certain groups without being actively mobilized by them? In summary, if we fail to include these phenomena in our definitions of power and politics, we relegate them to obscurity: if we do not know what to call them, how can we understand or employ them?

A Critical View of Power

A broad conceptualization of power is important for both pragmatic and ethical reasons. It also represents the means with which to redress the managerialist orientation that has characterized the prescriptive literature which (when it does not ignore power completely) tends to focus on the use of

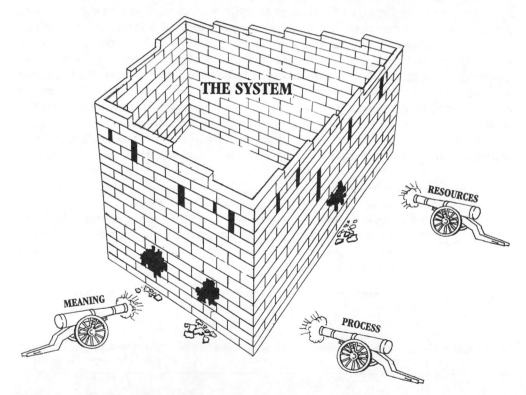

Figure 1.2   *The dimensions of power*

resources. This is not only naive since the above discussion clearly shows that power *is* used in a multitude of ways, it is also unethical. By ignoring the hidden side of power, we are refusing to engage in a debate where ethical issues can surface. In so doing, we prevent the people on the receiving end of power from learning how it works against them and how they might use it.

In revealing the multifaceted nature of power and demystifying the way in which it works, the way is opened up to viewing power as both a coercive and a productive force, and exploring its use by and against managers. Using power against managerial interests is not necessarily 'bad' or misguided. Pretending that power is used only by fair-minded managers in the face of recalcitrant unions or dissident individuals is both idealistic and unrealistic. Power is also used behind the scenes to serve the interests of managerial and other dominant groups and to subjugate other organizational members. Adopting a broader conceptualization of power facilitates a critical view which recognizes both managerial and employee interests. Knowledge of power should not be a managerial prerogative; nor should the darker side of power escape scrutiny.

All too often, resistance to change is dismissed as irrational. The interests of senior managers are assumed to be pure and untainted while those who challenge them are subversive. This view deserves closer examination. For example, consider the case of new organizational forms such as outsourcing and networks which mean that employees, who used to work for and in the particular service company, can look forward to a succession of jobs as they are moved from one client to another. Employees in the client company may be, at worst, laid off and, at best, forced to work with different people from a different company with a different culture. Managers will have to adjust to the loss of control to outsiders and learn how to negotiate who sets the goals; who measures them; who keeps the records; and who does the training.[108]

If resistance does occur, the usual answer is simply to increase communication to provide more information about the benefits of the new arrangements. Such words of wisdom imply that the interests of the various participants are compatible. But, is that always the case? If people are going to be laid off, are not employees and unions right to be concerned?[109] If managers are going to lose control while still being held accountable for getting the job done, is it not surprising that they resist? If one partner is much larger or more powerful than the other, is it not predictable that it tries to exploit that advantage, and is it not sensible for the weaker one to find ways of off-setting its subordination?[110] In other words, the practical problems of creating and sustaining these new organizational forms are not addressed by the simple appeals to improve communication. Managers must realize that the participants' goals are not necessarily going to converge in an obliging harmony. Different individuals and organizations have different goals, regardless of whether they want to work together or not.

The narrower definitions promoted in the literature have served to obscure the true workings of power and depoliticize organizational life.[111] Politics is often defined in terms of the unsanctioned or illegitimate use of power to achieve unsanctioned or illegitimate ends.[112] This approach clearly implies that the use of power is dysfunctional.[113] It ignores the question of: in *whose* eyes is power deemed illegitimate, unsanctioned, or dysfunctional? What one person considers illegitimate, another person may sanction. What penalizes one person, may benefit another. Legitimacy is usually defined by these writers in terms of the 'organization'[114] when they really mean the organizational elites who are able to use their power to legitimate certain actions and discredit others. Thus anyone who contests the managerial prerogative runs the risk of being discredited by the label 'political'.

Other definitions restrict the use of power to situations of resistance.[115] Without opposition 'there is neither the need nor the expectation that one would observe political activity'.[116] This view evokes the idea of a 'fair fight' where one group (usually senior management) is forced to use power to overcome the resistance of another (perhaps unions or intransigent middle managers). It misrepresents the balance of power in the organization – attributing far too much power to subordinate groups who are chastised when they do use it; and ignoring the hidden ways in which managers use power. The idea that management might use power behind the scenes, to further its position by shaping values, using technology and information is conveniently excluded. Thus, the unwillingness to recognize the political aspects of organizational life paints an ideologically conservative picture that implicitly advocates the status quo and obscures the processes whereby organizational elites maintain their dominance.[117]

One example where these shortcomings can be clearly seen is in the management of culture. It is inextricably linked to the use of power since a culture works to the advantage of some groups at the expense of others. Changing culture involves the negotiation of reality between interest groups and, as in the case of most negotiations, the one with the bigger stick usually wins.[118] Shaping culture thus depends on access to political skills and power sources and contributes to the enhancement of power reserves.[119] While advocates of critical research emphasize how power relations are entrenched and reproduced in cultural arrangements,[120] many business writers have, in contrast, been reluctant to acknowledge these political aspects of culture.

Izraeli and Jick[121] point out that many writers on organizational culture have gone to considerable length to avoid any association with power and politics. In fact, it has been argued that some widely cited articles have 'doctored' the definitions of culture to avoid any political connotations.[122] The managerialist work on culture (discussed earlier) sees it as a neutral tool that can be used to enhance organizational performance, and has studiously ignored the political implications. This has led to some serious misperceptions: managing culture is more complicated than the business literature would have us believe; and it is also more political. Cultural change is presented in neutral terms that suggest that it is to everyone's advantage. Those with the power to change culture, however, are those who will gain from doing so. We cannot automatically assume that the changes they propose are going to benefit everyone. For example, calls for cultural change have been subverted to promote anti-union human resource policies.[123] Appeals for 'new management'[124] might be more accurately called 'new unionism' where unions are advised to abandon traditional mandates in order to support organizational interests. We can see, then, that the 'depoliticization' of culture serves no one: managers are deprived of the tools they need to manage effectively; and employees are left in the dark about how power works against them.

Summary

A multifaceted understanding of power is necessary for both pragmatic and ethical reasons. Without it, managers are left without an important means of realizing change. Pfeffer[125] talks about the 'alternative' ways of getting things done in organizations – authority, persuasion and culture. But these particular alternatives all involve an element of power: authority is formal, legitimated power; the persuasion of large numbers of people concerning large-scale, complex changes involves the control of information and the management of meaning; while culture embodies the power of the system. In addition, employees are deprived of understanding how they are subjected to power and how they might employ it to protect themselves.

Strategic Action: Mobilizing Power for Strategic Change

Strategic action requires the active melding of power and process. Most aspects of the strategic change process have political implications. The formation of strategic intent is not simply a rational, objective analysis but a complex process that requires shared perceptions concerning organization, environment and direction. Alignment requires broadsweeping changes that embody not only opportunities but also uncertainty and threats. Realization is the pattern of actions that emerge from the various political influences. This process takes place in a particular system and it is the power embedded in that system which will likely shape strategic outcomes in the absence of any countervailing actions. Since the system is typically vested in the status quo, it is unlikely that the desired strategic change will be realized by default. Managers must, then, mobilize resources, processes and meanings to chip away at the system in an attempt to reconstruct a new one that converges around the new strategy, thereby helping to realize it. They must dismantle those parts of the system which obstruct strategic change and use other parts as the foundation for a new one (Figure 1.3).

The realization of strategic intent usually requires the use of all three sources of power – relying only on one or two is unlikely to provide the necessary energy to drive the organization towards strategic realization. Using only resources to reinforce or punish behaviour is too task-oriented: organizational members will carry out the desired behaviour only with the continual deployment of the necessary resources. Process power helps achieve more enduring changes without continual behavioural reinforcement, but is limited to those change that conform to existing organizational values and norms. By managing meaning, the manager may be able to modify the underlying power of the system, but those changes must be bolstered with appropriate modifications to organizational processes and the deployment of

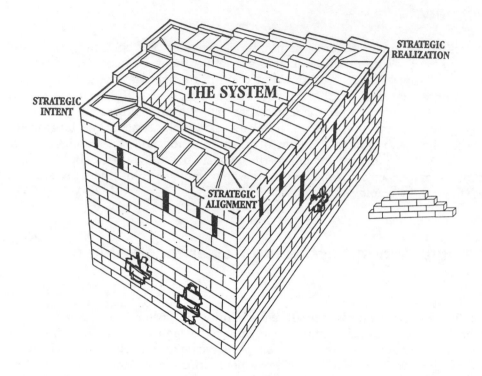

Figure 1.3   Strategic action: applying power to the process

resources if individuals are not to experience confusion concerning the specific changes required of them. By combining the power of meaning, process and resources, managers can redefine the strategic initiative and the changes it embodies as legitimate; facilitate new ideas, people and behaviours through new processes; and control behaviour more directly with the specific deployment of resources. It is the sum of these actions that provides the energy to drive strategic change, as illustrated in Example 1.2.[126]

―――――――――――――――― *Example 1.2* ――――――――――――――――

In response to foreign competition, a US automobile manufacturer decided to introduce a strategy based on quality. As a result of this initiative, the manager of one of its manufacturing plants hired a group of consultants to implement a change programme at managerial levels. Initial findings confirmed that managers wanted a change in the plant's culture, which focused on aggressive, autocratic management and emphasized inter-shift competition and, in the words of the managers themselves, 'lying, cheating, and stealing'. This culture had proven ineffective in meeting the challenges of foreign competition and was widely recognized as being out of step with the larger society. While both managers and consultants agreed that change was necessary, their unspoken assumptions were very different. Management wanted to concentrate on improving quality and reducing costs; while the consultants wanted to change the culture by introducing a participative management style, which would improve quality as a by-product.

The consultants began to implement the change programme by setting up committees to bring together managers in a collective decision making proces and provide a forum where they could learn participatory, problem-solving techniques. The consultants expected the managers to adopt the role of student while learning the new methods. The managers, on the other hand, had a hard time making the connection between these methods and improved quality, particularly since the old pressures continued to haunt them. They were given no extra time to learn new ways of managing; productivity remained the main criterion of success; new behaviour was not rewarded; and when problems arose, individuals reverted to the old management style. As a result, even after two years of meetings, no change had been effected.

The reason for the failure was the following. The consultants wanted to change the existing system, but they used only the power of process – participative committees – which clashed with the values of the underlying macho, competitive culture. Management's emphasis, on the other hand, focused solely on changing behaviour – improving quality while maintaining productivity – but resource power was not used to encourage new behaviour and penalize the old behaviour because reward systems were not changed. The desired change only came about much later when, gradually, a few respected managers started to adopt the new style. They helped to redefine the meaning of a 'good' manager – from one who was macho, aggressive and punitive to one who was democratic and participative. These changes were reinforced by the redeployment of resources to reward both quality and those who adopted the new style, while the new processes continued to facilitate participative decision making. Only when the power of resources, processes, and meaning converged was the power of the system counteracted and the desired strategic change achieved.

Strategic Predicaments

- MERGERS & ACQUISITIONS
- DECLINE
- INNOVATION
- GLOBAL STRATEGY
- SUSTAINABLE DEVELOPMENT
- CONSENSUS

The third section of the book explores a number of strategic predicaments that managers face when they make particular strategic choices. As has been discussed, managers face the inertial forces of the prevailing system that often act as a barrier to strategic change. In some cases, the form that this barrier takes is predictable in the light of the strategic and organizational context in which it occurs. If managers are aware of the nature of the predicament, they are in a better position to address it. This section discusses some common strategic predicaments.

Mergers and acquisitions (M&As) seem to have encountered more than their fair share of problems. Marks and Mirvis[127] maintain that more than two thirds of M&As fail. Financial results are often disappointing.[128] Acquisitions can impede innovation because capabilities are brought in from the outside rather than developed in house.[129] Nonetheless, M&As are expected to remain a popular strategy during the 1990s in areas such as banking and insurance and biotechnology, not to mention the attractiveness of various forms of international cooperation.[130] For these ventures to be successful, writers have stressed the importance of human and organizational issues.[131] These matters are often neglected because of the emphasis on financial considerations in selecting and managing M&As, which has not been accompanied by a similar understanding of human and ethical issues.[132]

Drawing on the model presented in this chapter, the strategic predicament seems obvious – the synchronization of structures, cultures, and human resource systems to allow participating organizations to derive synergy from the partnership. The structures, systems, human resource policies, cultures and leadership styles will have to be modified to support the strategy of the new, combined organization. All too often, the more powerful organization dominates and imposes changes on the weaker one, which is likely to crush the very contribution that the acquired organization was supposed to make. The new 'offspring' of the M&A (or, for that matter, any other collaborative strategy) thus deserves careful attention in terms of clarifying what the strategy is and the creation or dismantling of organizational structures and systems to support it.

Managing decline remains a common managerial challenge, whether due to recession or other competitive adjustments. The recession of the 1990s has been particularly enduring as unemployment levels have remained about 10 per cent in much of Europe and North America. Cutbacks and layoffs have become a fact of life for large numbers of organizations. Previously, manufacturing and blue collar workers bore the brunt of downsizing but, more recently, white collar workers and managerial levels have also been cut.[133] It has been pointed out that anticipated savings often do not materialize and, even when they do, large write-offs are necessary beforehand. So, for example, E.I. du Pont de Nemours took a $125 million one-time charge to gain a $230 million annual after tax savings.[134] IBM's multi-billion dollar loss in 1993 was mainly comprised of massive write-offs related to its massive world-wide restructuring and lay-off programme. Consequently, the effective management of decline requires a long-term perspective that surpasses the financial considerations to incorporate the human resource implications.

Decline is difficult for both managers and employees. Managers appear uncomfortable with their responsibilities for this challenge, which may account for their reluctance to plan for downsizing.[135] The employees who lose their jobs, not surprisingly, are often traumatized by the process, particularly in companies previously known for their life-time employment practices. Even survivors are not unaffected by the turbulence of downsizing.[136] Managing decline represents, perhaps more than any other strategy, a zero-sum game where there is often little to gain and a lot to lose. As one can imagine, it is marked by political battles and resistance. Some of these reactions can be tackled by more attention to the choices that exist within the downsizing paradigm; the selection of strategies that offer more support to employees; and the willingness to confront the human side of downsizing rather than running away from it.

Managing innovation is important if organizations are to renew themselves, transform stagnant businesses, and increase market share.[137] Despite its importance, firms seem to encounter considerable difficulty in developing and marketing successful new products.[138] Part of the problem lies in the simplistic approaches of much of the literature, which attributes innovation to intrepid champions whose support conjures new products out of thin air, or generalized (if innovative) jargon, like 'camping on seesaws', 'jelly moulds', and 'holograms', that offer little, practical help to managers.[139]

One factor that impedes innovation concerns the lack of permeability between departments. New products can only be successfully developed when departments such as marketing, sales, R&D and manufacturing are able to reconceptualize and create knowledge and contribute expertise to processes that cut across departments. Only by focusing on the multifaceted processes necessary to support such an endeavour can innovation be promoted. Massive amounts of resources must also be allocated on the basis of uncertain predictions, and in a way that allows multiple product lines to spread the cost of the investment. This requires a strategy that links innovations to existing products as well as new product lines in order to leverage resources. All these requirements add up to a considerable amount of uncertainty and permeability which must be reflected in and facilitated by organizational parameters.

Managing the global environment has been heralded as the key to corporate success in today's business world. It creates a difficult set of challenges for managers previously used to more local environments. Managers in global organizations must develop efficiencies to enhance the ability to compete in the international arena, built flexibility to capitalize on international differences, as well as create a learning organization that is sensitive and responsive to cultural differences. European firms such as ICI, Unilever, Philips and Nestlé have traditionally relied on multinational strategies, decentralizing operations to respond to national differences. Many US firms (such as Pfizer, Procter & Gamble and General Electric) have adopted international strategies resting on the centralization of operations within the parent country and the transference of new products, processes and strategies to less advanced markets overseas. Japanese companies like Toyota, Canon and Matsushita have adopted classic global strategies to create cost advantages through centralized global-scale operations.[140]

More recently, commentators have advocated a transnational strategy[141] that combines differentiation, innovation and efficiency through the strategic location of resources in different parts of the world. In many cases the organization is supported through international networks of alliances.[142] This approach to globalization represents a formidable structural challenge as complex relationships with different companies, which span both geographical and cultural distances, must be created and managed to achieve both efficiency and flexibility.[143]

Managing sustainable development is a relatively new business challenge. While some firms continue to see it simply as a struggle against more pervasive regulation and harsher penalties, the environment is, nonetheless, topping the agenda of many corporations.[144] It raises three key questions for managers: what products should be brought to market; how much information should be disclosed; and how can companies reduce waste and pollution at source. These are important questions when one considers that, since 1900, the number of inhabitants on the planet has tripled; the world economy has increased twenty times; and the consumption of fossil fuels has increased by a factor of 30 and industrial production by a factor of 50.[145]

The gradual emergence of the environment as a legitimate cause has been stimulated by reports like that of the 1987 Brundtland Commission (set up by the UN under the leadership of Gro Harlem Brundtland, then leader of the opposition and later prime minister of Norway). It helped push the development of strategies for sustainable environment from the backburner to the front. Strategies for sustainable development are complicated, however, because they are formed in the interorganizational domain, and involve businesses, government and environmental activists, as well as both developed and developing countries. Because of the involvement of these different stakeholders, strategy making is fraught with confusion derived from different perceptions of problems and solutions, which are further confounded by the existence of competing interests. To be successful, organizational members have to appreciate the complexity of the domain and learn how to manage a complex set of relationships.

Finally, calls for participation, cooperation and empowerment translate into a need for the **management of collaboration** within the organization. This collegial form of organization has been seen as a factor in strategic success.

> The term 'collegiality' evokes images of warm, supportive relationships and teamwork. Collegial organizations have communal tendencies in the form of coherent social rules and common identities. Highly successful organizations such as Honda derive much of their magic from collegial networks.[146]

This section examines collaboration in the form of the inclusion of middle managers in strategy making.[147] Wider involvement has many advantages: it provides knowledge of operating systems, ensures that strategic vision takes into account organizational reality, and convinces employees to make the necessary changes. The involvement of middle managers (let alone other employees) in strategy making is problematic since most middle level managers appear unaware of what their firms' strategy actually is![148] For their involvement to pay off, they must be both committed and informed about strategic decisions[149] and allowed some influence on those decisions.[150]

The involvement of middle managers in strategy making (or any other form of 'empowerment') has political implications. Senior managers are unlikely to surrender power unless they are sure they can retain control in other ways. Thus, managers typically replace the overt, coercive use of power with more subtle controls. This substitution of power techniques requires a very different approach to management, one on which the traditional literature is unable to shed much light because of its narrow conceptualization of power. This issue of collaboration brings us full circle – back to the issue of strategic intent. For strategic intent to be an effective force in initiating strategic action, it must be shared, and collaboration represents the process through which it is shared. Models that exclude consideration of power are ill-equipped to advise managers on how to collaborate; and those that focus on the visible, coercive face of power are ill-equipped to understand how it represents a force for inclusion rather than exclusion.

Conclusions

This first chapter, which provides the framework of the rest of the book, presents readers with a view of strategic action, whereby strategic intent is realized through the alignment of organizational parameters and the use of power. The different dimensions of power can be employed to dismantle the barriers to change that reside in the existing system, and to realign the organization around strategic intent. Like it or not, strategic change is, then, an inherently political process which lives or dies according to the use of power by the organizational members engaged in and struggling with it.

This emphasis on the implementation, rather than the formulation, of strategy is deliberate. It represents an attempt to redress the prevailing tendency in much of the literature to ignore it. It is not to say that the processes associated with the formation of strategic intent are unimportant; simply that they are one part of the strategic equation. A second, equally important part concerns the realization of intent. This issue has attracted far less attention in the business literature, and the purpose of this book is to offer some insight into what that process looks like and how it might be managed.

The emphasis on power is also intentional, again in reaction to the tendency of the majority of the strategy making literature to ignore it. Power is one, integral component of realizing strategy. This book provides readers with a broad framework that may help them understand how power works. This framework only goes so far however, for two reasons. First, the form in which power manifests itself and the way it is used depends on the particular situation. The specific actions that one individual will take to mobilize resources, change processes and shape meaning will be totally different from another's. As a result, the book does not aim to present a generalized list of recommendations that individuals should follow to realize strategic change; instead, it seeks to sensitize managers and employees to the complex nature of the strategic change process and the multitude of ways in which power operates. Second, because there can be no generalized recommendations, the true test of an effective deployment of power rests with the individual – his or her talent, skills, ingenuity, imagination and intuition in sizing up the political dynamics of a particular situation and in employing power in an effective and ethical way.

Notes

1. Hrebiniak, Lawrence G., 'Implementing strategy', *Chief Executive*, 57: 74–7, April 1990.

2. Pettigrew, Andrew M., *The Awakening Giant: Continuity and Change in Imperial Chemical Industries*, Oxford, England: Basil Blackwell, 1985, p. 438; also see Mintzberg, H., and Waters, J.A., 'Of strategies, deliberate and emergent', *Strategic Management Journal*, 6: 257–72, 1985.

3. E.g. Andrews, Kenneth Richmond, *The Concept of Corporate Strategy*, Homewood, Illinois: R.D. Irwin, 1980.

4. Mintzberg and Waters, 1985.

5. Hamel, Gary and Prahalad, C.K., 'Strategic intent', *Harvard Business Review*, 67(3): 63–76, May–June 1989.

6. This book does not separate formulation from implementation: it simply focuses on the issues associated with the latter. The discussion of power blurs the demarcation between formulation and implementation in a number of ways. First, the political issues raised in the second and third parts of the book help to explain why formulation and implementation are interwoven, by showing how organizational members resist or influence strategic ideas. Second, the discussion helps to explain why managers often form their strategic ideas in response to the political realities that they face. Third, the book discusses why a broader segment of the organizational community, and not simply the upper echelons, should be included in strategy making, and the readings and cases on power provide some idea of how they can. Fourth, the focus on helping managers realize their intentions does not preclude the fact that the strategy may be modified, changed or even abandoned along the path to realization (though the aim is, obviously, to reduce the likelihood of unrealized strategy). Nor does it deny that strategies can emerge in the absence of intent or that they may develop incrementally as vague plans are refined in a step-by-step process. Strategies form and are formed in a number of different ways, with varying degrees of deliberateness.

7. Andrews, 1980.

8. See Webster, James L., Reif, W.E. and Bracker, J.S., 'The manager's guide to strategic planning tools and techniques', *Planning Review*, 17(6): 4–13, 1989.

9. Porter, M., *Competitive Strategy*. New York: Free Press, 1980.

10. See Mintzberg, H., 'Generic strategies: Toward a comprehensive framework', *Advances in Strategic Management*, 5: 1–67, 1988.

11. Davis, S., *Future Perfect*. Reading, Mass.: Addison-Wesley, 1987; and Pine, J., *Mass Customization: The New Frontier in Business Competition*, Boston, Mass.: The Harvard Business School Press, 1993.

12. Mintzberg, H., 'Research on strategy-making', *Academy of Management Proceedings*, 90–4, 1972; Mintzberg, H., 'Crafting strategy', *Harvard Business Review*, July–August, 66–75, 1987; Pascale, R.T., *The Art of Japanese Management: Applications for American Executives*, NY: Simon & Schuster, 1981; Pascale, R.T., 'The renewal factor: Constructive contention', *The Planning Forum*, 17 (6), 1990a; Pascale, R.T., *Managing on the Edge: How the Smartest Companies Use Conflict to Stay Ahead*, NY: Simon & Schuster, 1990b.

13. Hamel, Gary and Prahalad, C.K., 'Corporate imagination and expeditionary marketing', *Harvard Business Review*, 69(4): 81–92, 1991.

14. Prahalad, C.K. and Hamel, Gary, 'The core competence of the corporation', *Harvard Business Review*, 68(3): 79–91, May–June 1990.

15. Kiernan, Matthew J., 'The new strategic architecture: Learning to compete in the twenty-first century', *Academy of Management Executive*, 7(1): 8, 1993.

16. E.g. Whipp, Richard, Rosenfeld, Robert and Pettigrew, Andrew, 'Managing strategic change in a mature business', *Long Range Planning*, 22(6): 92–9, 1989; Boynton, Andrew C. and Victor, Bart, 'Beyond flexibility: Building and managing the dynamically stable organization', *California Management Review*, 34(1), Fall 1991; though Eccles, R. and Nohria, N., *Beyond the Hype*, Cambridge, Mass.: Harvard Business School, 1993, argue that every generation perceives its environment as new, turbulent and difficult to manage.

17. E.g. Hamel and Prahalad, 1989, 1991; Pascale, 1990a, 1990b; Prahalad and Hamel, 1990.

18. Kiernan, 1993: 17.

19. Kiernan, 1993: 17.

20. Hamel, Gary and Prahalad, C.K., 'Strategy as stretch and leverage', *Harvard Business Review*, 71(2): 75–84, March–April 1993.

21. Pascale, 1990a.

22. Magnet, Myron, 'Meet the new revolutionaries', *Fortune*, 24 February 1992: p. 95.

23. E.g. Di Maggio, P., 'Interest and agency in institutional theory', in L.G. Zucker (ed.), *Institutional Patterns and Organizations: Culture and Environment*. Cambridge, Mass.: Ballinger, 1988.

24. Magnet, 1992.

25. Bowman, Cliff and Johnson, Gerry, 'Surfacing competitive strategies', *European Management Journal*, 10(2): 210–19, 1992; Floyd, Steven W. and Wooldridge, Bill, 'Managing strategic consensus: The foundation of effective implementation', *Academy of Management Executive*, 6(4): 27–39, 1992.

26. The 7-S framework, for example, is over ten years old. See Waterman, Robert H., Peters, Thomas J. and Phillips, Julien R., 'Structure is not organization', *Business Horizons*, 23 (3), 1980.

27. According to a CD-Rom search of ABI-Inform abstracts between January 1989 and May 1993, over 27,000 articles on strategy have been written, but only 110 on strategic change.

28. Hrebiniak, 1990: 74.

29. E.g. Carnall, Colin A., 'Managing strategic change: An integrated approach', *Long Range Planning*, 19(6): 105–15, 1986.

30. Miles and Snow introduced this idea in 1978 (Miles, R.E. and Snow C.C., *Organizational Strategy, Structure and Process*, New York: McGraw-Hill, 1978), when they illustrated the link between various organizational features and strategic choice. The defender (which approximates Porter's low-cost strategy) has to ensure the efficient production and distribution of goods and services, which leads to a focus on production processes and economies of scale. A functional organization, formal planning and extensive controls and procedures will feature in this type of organization. The prospector (similar to Porter's differentiation strategy) has to engage in a continuous search for new market and product possibilities. Organizational requirements revolve around environmental monitoring, innovation, and flexibility to allow opportunities to be quickly exploited. The analyser tries to combine both differentiation and low-cost strategies, and must be both responsive and efficient. A matrix structure may be used to emphasize product development and derive some economies and technical specialization from functional groupings.

31. E.g. Chandler, A.D., *Strategy and Structure*. Cambridge, Mass.: MIT Press, 1962.

32. E.g. Galbraith, J.R. *Designing Complex Organizations*. Reading, Mass.: Addison-Wesley, 1973.

33. Mintzberg, H., *The Structuring of Organizations*. Englewood Cliffs, NJ: Prentice-Hall, 1979.

34. Want, J.W., 'Managing radical change', *Journal of Business Strategy*, 15(3): 20–30, 1993.

35. See Eccles, R. and Nohria, N., *Beyond the Hype*, 1993, for a discussion of the dissatisfaction with centralized structures which they trace back to the 1920s.

36. E.g. Dumaine, Brian, 'The bureaucracy busters', *Fortune*, 17 June 1991, pp. 36–50.

37. Semler, Ricardo, 'Managing without managers', *Harvard Business Review*, 67(5): 76–84, 1989.

38. Kiernan, 1993: 9.

39. E.g. Tully, Shawn, 'The modular corporation', *Fortune*, 8 February 1993, pp. 106–15.

40. Winkleman, M., 'The outsourcing source book', *Journal of Business Strategy*, 15(3): 55, 1993.

41. E.g. Byrne, J.A., 'The virtual corporation', *Business Week*, 8 February 1993, pp. 98–102.

42. Bartlett, C. and Ghoshal, S., *Managing Across Borders*. Cambridge, Mass: Harvard Business School, 1993.

43. See Galbraith, J.R. and Nathanson, D., *Strategy Implementation*. St. Paul, Minn: West Publishing, 1978.

44. Fulmer, W.E., 'Human resource management: The right hand of strategic implementation', *Human Resource Planning*, 12(4): 1–11, 1989.

45. Fulmer, 1989.

46. E.g. Miller, D., 'Matching strategy and strategy making: Process, content and performance', *Human Relations*, 42: 241–60, 1989; Cook, Roger and Armstrong, Michael, 'The search for strategic HRM', *Personnel Management*, December 1990.

47. Tichy, Noel, M., Fombrun, Charles J. and Devanna, Mary Anne, 'Strategic human resource management', *Sloan Management Review*, 23(2): 47–61, 1982.

48. Tichy et al., 1982: 410.

49. Lorsch, Jay W., 'Managing culture: The invisible barrier to strategic change', *California Management Review*, 28(2): 95–109, 1986.

50. Johnson, Gerry, 'Managing strategic change: Strategy, culture and action', *Long-Range Planning*, 25(1): 28, 1992.

51. Hofstede, Geert, 'Editorial: The usefulness of the organizational culture concept', *Journal of Management Studies*, 23 (3), 1986.

52. E.g. Ouchi, W.G., *Theory Z*. New York: Avon Books, 1981; Deal, T. and Kennedy, A.E., *Corporate Cultures*. Reading, Mass.: Addison-Wesley, 1982; Peters, T.J., and Waterman, R.H., *In Search of Excellence*. New York: Harper & Row, 1982; Schein, E., 'How culture forms, develops and changes', in R. Kilmann, M. Saxton and R. Serpa (eds), *Gaining Control of Corporate Culture*. San Francisco: Jossey Bass, 1985b; Lorsch, 1986.

53. See Allaire, Yvan and Firsirotu, Michaela, 'Theories of organizational culture', *Organization Studies*, 5(3): 193–226, 1984.

54. See Hollway, Wendy, *Work Psychology and Organizational Behaviour: Managing the Individual at Work*. London: Sage, 1991.

55. Allaire and Firsirotu, 1984; Meek, V. Lynn, 'Organizational culture: Origins and weaknesses', *Organization Studies*, 9(4): 453–73, 1988; Hollway, 1991.

56. Sturm, Douglas, 'Corporate culture and the common good: The need for thick description and critical interpretation', *Thought* 60(237): 142, 1985.

57. E.g. Schein, E., 1985b.

58. Hollway, 1991.

59. E.g. Westley, F., 'Middle managers and strategy: The microdynamics of inclusion', *Strategic Management Journal*, 11, 337–51, 1990.

60. Greiner, L.E., 'Evolution and revolution as organizations grow', *Harvard Business Review*, 46: 37–47, July–August, 1972.

61. Miller, D., and Friesen, P., *Organizations: A Quantum View*. Englewood Cliffs, NJ: Prentice-Hall, 1984; Tushman, Michael, L., Newman, William H. and Romanelli, Elaine, 'Convergence and upheaval: Managing the unsteady pace of organizational evolution', *California Management Review*, 29(1): 29–44, 1986.

62. Quinn, J.B., *Strategies for Change: Logical Incrementalism*. Homewood, Ill.: R.D. Irwin, 1980.

63. Pascale, 1990a: 4.

64. Kiernan, 1993: 12.

65. Westley, 1990.

66. Kiernan, 1993; see Miller and Friesen, 1984.

67. Roberts, J., 'Strategy and accounting in the UK conglomerate', *Accounting, Organizations and Society*, 15: 107–26, 1990.

68. Westley, 1990.

69. E.g. Andrews, 1980; Rumelt, R.P., *Strategy, Structure and Economic Performance*. Boston, Mass.: Harvard Business School, 1974.

70. E.g. Mintzberg, H., 'Research on strategy-making', *Academy of Management Proceedings*, 90–4, 1972; Mintzberg, H., 'Strategy making in three modes', *California Management Review*, 16(4): 44–58, 1973; Mintzberg and Waters, 1985; and Quinn, J.B., *Strategies for Change: Logical Incrementalism*. Homewood, Ill.: R.D. Irwin, 1980.

71. E.g. Quinn, James Brian, 'Managing innovation: Controlled chaos', *Harvard Business Review*, 63(3): 73–84, 1985; Mintzberg, 1987.

72. E.g. Bower, J.L., *Managing the Resource Allocation Process*. Cambridge, Mass.: Harvard University Press, 1970; Allison, Graham T., *Essence of Decision: Explaining the Cuban Missile Crisis*. Boston, Mass.: Little, Brown, 1971; Pettigrew, A.M., *The Politics of Organizational Decision Making*. London: Tavistock, 1973; Narayanan, V.K. and Fahey, L., 'The micro-politics of strategy formulation', *Academy of Management Review*, 7: 25–34, 1982.

73. Pfeffer, Jeffrey, 'Understanding power in organizations', *California Management Review*, 34(2): 29–50, Winter 1992.

74. Clegg, S., *Frameworks of Power*. London: Sage, 1989; Knights, D. and Morgan, G., 'Corporate strategy, organizations, and subjectivity: A critique', *Organisation Studies*, 12(2): 251–73. 1991.

75. Burns, T., 'Micropolitics: Mechanisms of institutional change', *Administrative Science Quarterly*, 6: 257–81, December 1961.

76. Frost, P.J., 'The role of organizational power and politics in human resource management', *Personnel and Human Resources Management*, 1: 2, 1989.

77. Knights, D. and Willmott, H., 'Power, values and relations: A comment on Benton', *Sociology*, 16(4): 578–85, 1982; Knights, D. and Willmott, H., 'Power and identity in theory and practice', *Sociological Review*, 33(1): 22–46, 1985.

78. Baum, Howell S., 'Organizational politics against organizational culture: a psychoanalytic perspective', *Human Resource Management*, 28(2): 195, Summer 1989. Other writers who have emphasized this side of power include Arendt (Arendt, Hanna, 'Communicative power', in Lukes, Steven (ed.), *Power*. Oxford, England: Basil Blackwell, 1986, p. 64.) has spoken of power as the ability to act in concert and people who are 'in power' as being empowered by others to act in their name. Habermas (Habermas, Jürgen, 'Hannah Arendt's communications concept of power', in Lukes, Steven (ed.), *Power*, p.76) argues that power is not 'the instrumentalization of *another*'s will, but the formation of a *common* will in a communication directed to reaching agreement' involving 'the consent of the governed that is mobilized for collective goals'. Giddens (Giddens, Anthony, *The Constitution of Society: Outline of a Theory of Structuration*. Berkeley: University of California Press, 1984, p. 257) has pointed out that power is 'the capacity to achieve outcomes; whether these are related to purely sectional interests is not germane to its definition'. According to Daudi, 'Power is not simply repressive; it is also productive . . . Power subjects bodies not to render them passive, but to render them active' (Daudi, Philippe, 'The discourse of power or the power of discourse', *Alternatives*, 9: 324, 1983.

79. Burgelman, Robert A., 'A model of the interaction of strategic behaviour, corporate context, and the concept of strategy', *Academy of Management Review*, 8(1): 61–70, 1983; Burgelman, Robert A., 'Managing the new venture division: Research findings and implications for strategic management', *Strategic Management Journal*, 6: 39–54, 1985; Kanter, R.M., *The Change Masters: Innovation for Productivity in the American Corporation*. New York: Simon & Schuster, 1983.; Maidique, M.A., 'Point of view: The new management thinkers', *California Management Review*, 26(1): 151–61, 1983; Marcus, Alfred A., 'Implementing externally induced innovations: a comparison of rule-bound and autonomous approaches', *Academy of Management Journal*, 31(2): 235–56, 1988; Feldman, Steven P., 'The broken wheel: The inseparability of autonomy and control in innovation within organizations', *Journal of Management Studies*, 26(2): 83–102, 1989; Frost, Peter J. and Egri, Carolyn P., 'The political process of innovation', in Cummings, L.L. and Staw, B.M. (eds), *Research in Organizational Behaviour*. Greenwich, CT: JAI Press, 1989.

80. Cavanagh, Gerald F., Moberg, Dennis J., and Velasquez, Manuel, 'The ethics of organizational politics, *Academy of Management Review*, 6(3): 363–74, 1981; Velasquez, Manuel, Moberg, Dennis J. and Cavanagh, Gerald F., 'Organizational statesmanship and dirty politics: Ethical guidelines for the organizational politician', *Organizational Dynamics*, 12 (special issue): 65–80, 1983.

81. Hardy, C., Langley, A., Mintzberg, H. and Rose, J., 'Strategy formation in the university setting', *Review of Higher Education*, 6(4): 407–33, 1983.

82. Pettigrew, Andrew, M., 'Strategy formulation as a political process', *International Studies of Management and Organization*, 7(2): 78–87, Summer 1977.

83. Longenecker, Clinton O., Henry P. Sims, Jr. and Dennis A. Gioia, 'Behind the mask: The politics of employee appraisal', *Academy of Management Executive*, 1(3): 183–93, August 1987; Ferris, Gerald R. and King, Thomas R., 'Politics in human resources decisions: A walk on the dark side', *Organizational Dynamics*, 20(2): 59–71, 1991.

84. E.g. Schein, E., *Organizational Culture and Leadership*. San Francisco: Jossey Bass, 1985a.

85. Gabarro, John J., 'When a new manager takes charge', *Harvard Business Review*, 63, 110–23, May–June, 1985.

86. Carnall, 1986.

87. Walsh, Kieron, Hinings, Bob, Greenwood, Royston and Ranson, Stewart, 'Power and advantage in organizations', *Organization Studies*, 2(2): 141, 1981; Frost and Egri, 1989.

88. Schiller, Zachary, 'There's still life in this rust belt relic', *Business Week*, 15 July 1991, pp. 95–101; Sadler, Philip, 'The politics of the corporate jungle', *Director*, May 1992, p. 29.

89. Bowman and Johnson, 1992.

90. Pettigrew, 1977; Watson, T.J., 'Group ideologies and organizational change', *Journal of Management Studies*, 19(3): 259–75, 1982.

91. Gray, B. and Ariss, S.S., 'Politics and strategic change: Across organizational life cycles', *Academy of Management Review*, 10(4): 707–23, 1985.

92. Based on the work of Lukes (Lukes, S., *Power: A Radical View*. London; New York: Macmillan, 1974). For more details see the chapter by Hardy on Power and Politics in the Organization (ch. 13).

93. Clegg, 1989.

94. Hickson, D.J., Hinings, C.A., Lee, C.A., Schneck, R.E. and Pennings, J.M., 'A strategic contingencies theory of intraorganizational power', *Administrative Science Quarterly*, 16(2): 216–29, 1971.

95. Pfeffer, Jeffrey and Salancik, Gerald R., *The External Control of Organizations*. New York: Harper & Row, 1978.

96. E.g. Mechanic, D., 'Sources of power of lower participants in complex organizations', *Administrative Science Quarterly*, 7(3): 349–64, 1962; French, J.R.P. and Raven, B., 'The bases of social power', in Cartwright, D. and Zander, A. (eds), *Group Dynamics*. New York: Harper & Row, 1968; Pettigrew, 1973; Pfeffer, J., *Power in Organizations*. Marshfield, Mass.: Pitman, 1981; Astley, W. Graham, and Sachdeva, Paramjit S., 'Structural sources of intraorganizational power: A theoretical synthesis', *Academy of Management Review*, 9(1): 104–13, 1984.

97. Hardy, C., *Managing Organizational Closure*. Aldershot, England: Gower Press, 1985a; Hardy, C., 'The nature of unobtrusive power', *Journal of Management Studies*, 22(4): 384–99, 1985b.

98. Clegg, S., *Power, Rule and Domination*. London: Routledge & Kegan Paul, 1975.

99. Bachrach, P. and Baratz, M.S., 'The two faces of power', *American Political Science Review*, 56: 947–52, 1962.

100. Pettigrew, A.M., 'On studying organizational cultures', *Administrative Science Quarterly*, 24: 570–81, 1979.

101. Frost, P.J. and Egri, C.P., 'The political process of innovation', *Research in Organizational Behaviour*, 13: 229–95, 1991.

102. Chaffee, E.L., 'Three models of strategy', *Academy of Management Review*, 10(1): 89–95, 1985.

103. Hardy, C., 1985a.

104. Clegg, S., *Power, Rule and Domination*. London: Routledge & Kegan Paul, 1975; Frost and Egri, 1989.

105. Perrow, Charles, *Complex Organizations, A Critical Essay*, second edition. Glenview, Illinois: Scott, Foresman and Company, 1978; Parry, G. and Morriss, P., 'When is a decision not a decision' in Crewe, I. (ed.), *British Political Sociology Yearbook*, 1. London: Croom Helm, 1975.

106. See, for example, Knights and Morgan, 1991; Deetz, Stanley, *Democracy in an Age of Corporate Colonization*. New York: State University of New York Press, 1992.

107. See Hardy, C. and Redivo, F., 'Power and organizational development', *Journal of General Management*, forthcoming.

108. Winkelman, 1993.

109. Watson, 1982.

110. Dent, Harry S. Jr., 'Corporation of the future', *Small Business Reports*, 15(5): 55–63, 1990.

111. E.g. Mayes, Bronston T. and Allen, Robert W., 'Toward a definition of organizational politics', *Academy of Management Review*, 2: 672–8, 1977; Gandz, Jeffrey and Murray, Victor V., 'The experience of workplace politics', *Academy of Management Journal*, 23(2): 237–51, 1980. These calls for scientific neatness reflect the positivist paradigm, with its preference for empirical techniques, quantitative methodologies and causal inferences, that dominates the discipline of management. Thus, a circular relationship emerges. Intellectual traditions that emphasize positivistic research circumscribe definitions which produce a focus on the more visible and measurable aspects of power which, in turn, lend themselves to the quantitative techniques that underpin the positivist orientation.

112. E.g. Mayes and Allen, 1977; Gandz and Murray, 1980; Enz, Cathy A., 'The role of value congruity in intraorganizational power', *Administrative Science Quarterly*, 33: 284–304, 1988.

113. Klein, Jonathan I., 'The myth of the corporate political jungle: Politicization as a political strategy', *Journal of Management Studies*, 25 (1), 1988.

114. E.g. Mayes & Allen, 1977.

115. E.g. Murray, Victor and Gandz, Jeffrey, 'Games executives play: Politics at work', *Business Horizons*, December 1980, pp. 11–23; Pfeffer, 1981; Gray & Ariss, 1985.

116. Pfeffer, 1981: 7.

117. Alvesson, Mats, 'Questioning rationality and ideology: On critical organization theory', *International Studies of Management and Organizations*, 14(1): 61–79, 1984; Deetz, Stanley, 'Critical–cultural research: New sensibilities and old realities', *Journal of Management*, 11(2): 121–36, 1985.

118. Berger, P.L. and Luckmann, T., *The Social Construction of Reality*. New York: Doubleday, 1966.

119. Hofstede, 1986; Clegg, S., 'The language of power and the power of language', *Organization Studies*, 8: 61–70, 1987; Das, Hari, 'Relevance of symbolic interactionist approach in understanding power: A preliminary analysis', *Journal of Management Studies*, 25 (3), 1988; Filby, Ivan and Willmott, Hugh, 'Ideologies and contradictions in a public relations department: The seduction and impotence of living myth', *Organization Studies*, 9(3): 335–49, 1988; Rosen, M. and Astley, W.G., 'Christmas time and control: An exploration in the social structure of formal organization', in Bachrach, S. and DiTomaso, N. (eds), *Research in the Sociology of Organizations*. JAI Press, 1988.

120. E.g. Deetz, 1985; Torgerson, Douglas, 'Interpretive policy inquiry: A response to its limitations', *Policy Sciences*, 19, 397–405, 1986; Mumby, Dennis K., 'The political function of narrative in organizations', *Communication Monographs*, 54: 113–27, 1987; Mumby, Dennis K., 'Ideology and the social construction of meaning: A communication perspective', *Communication Quarterly*, 37(4): 1–15, 1989.

121. Izraeli, Dafna, M. and Jick, Todd D., 'The art of saying no: Linking power to culture', *Organization Studies*, 7(2): 171–92, 1986; also see Smircich, Linda, 'Concepts of culture and organizational analysis', *Administrative Science Quarterly*, 28: 339–58, 1983.

122. Weiss, Richard M. and Miller, Lynn E., 'The concept of ideology in organizational analysis: The sociology of knowledge or the social psychology of beliefs?', *Academy of Management Review*, 12(1): 104–16, 1987; also see Beyer, J.M., Dunbar, R.L.M. and Meyer, A.D., 'Comment: The concept of ideology in organizational analysis', *Academy of Management Review*, 13(3): 489, 1988; Weiss, R.M. and Miller, L.E., 'Response: Ideas, interests and the social science of organizations', *Academy of Management Review*, 13(3): 490–4, 1988.

123. Thompson, P. and McHugh, D., *Work Organizations: A Critical Introduction*. London: Macmillan, 1990; Hollway, 1991.

124. E.g. Lawler and Mohrman, 'Unions and the new management', *Academy of Management Executive*, 1(3): 293–300, 1987.

125. Pfeffer, 1992.

126. Also see Hardy and Redivo, forthcoming.

127. Marks, Mitchell Lee and Mirvis, Philip H., 'Rebuilding after the merger: Dealing with "survivor sickness"', *Organizational Dynamics*, 21(2): 18–32, 1992; also see Porter, M. 'From competitive advantage to corporate strategy', *Harvard Business Review*, 65: 43–59, May–June, 1987.

128. Cartwright, Susan and Cooper, Cary L., 'The role of culture compatibility in successful organizational marriage', *Academy of Management Executive*, 7(2), 1993.

129. Hitt, Michael, A., Hoskisson, Robert E., Ireland, R. Duane and Harrison, Jeffrey S., 'Are acquisitions a poison pill for innovation?' *Academy of Management Executive*, 5(4): 22–34, 1991.

130. Marks and Mirvis, 1992.

131. Hitt et al., 1991; Marks and Mirvis, 1992; Cartwright and Cooper, 1993.

132. Ginter, Peter M., Duncan, W. Jack, Swayne, Linda E. and Shelfer, Jr., A. Gordon, 'When merger means death: Organizational euthanasia and strategic choice', *Organizational Dynamics*, 20(3): 21–33, 1992; Cartwright and Cooper, 1993.

133. Cascio, Wayne F., 'Downsizing: What do we know? What have we learned?', *Academy of Management Executive*, 7(1): 95–104, 1993.

134. Cascio, 1993.

135. Hardy, Cynthia, 'Strategies for retrenchment: Reconciling individual and organizational needs', *Canadian Journal of Administrative Sciences*, 3 (2), 1986; Cascio, 1993.

136. Hardy, 1986; Brockner, Joel, 'Managing the effects of layoffs on survivors', *California Management Review*, 34(2): 9–28, Winter 1992.

137. Kerin, R., Mahajan, V. and Varadarajan, P., *Contemporary Perspectives on Strategic Market Planning*. Boston, Mass.: Allyn and Bacon, 1990; Guth, W. and Ginsberg, A., 'Guest editors' Introduction: Corporate entrepreneurship', *Strategic Management Journal*, 11: 5–15, Summer 1990.

138. Cooper, R. and Kleinschmidt E., 'An investigation into the new product process: Steps, deficiencies, and impact', *Journal of Product Innovation Management*, 3: 71–85, 1986; Dougherty, D. and Heller, T., 'The illegitimacy of successful product innovation in established firms', working paper, Department of Management, The Wharton School, University of Pennsylvania, 1991.

139. See Dougherty, Deborah, 'A practice-centred model of organizational renewal through product innovation', *Strategic Management Journal*, 13: 77–92, 1992.

140. Bartlett & Ghoshal, 1992.

141. Barlett, C.A. and Ghoshal, S., 'Organizing for worldwide effectiveness: The transnational solution', *California Management Review*, 31(1): 54–74, Fall 1988.

142. Ghoshal, S. and Bartlett, C.A., 'The multinational corporation as an interorganizational network', *Academy of Management Review*, 15(4): 603–25, 1990.

143. Bartlett, C.A. and Goshal, S., 'Matrix management: Not a structure, a frame of mind', *Harvard Business Review*, 68(4): 138–45, July–August 1990.

144. Kleiner, Art, 'What does it mean to be green?', *Harvard Business Review*, 69(4): 38–47, 1991.

145. MacNeill, Jim, 'Strategies for sustainable economic development', *Scientific American*, 261(3): 155–65, September 1989.

146. Pascale, 1990a: 12.

147. Floyd, Steven W. and Wooldridge, Bill, 'Managing strategic consensus: The foundation of effective implementation', *Academy of Management Executive*, 6(4): 27–39, 1992; Nichol, Ronald L., 'Get middle managers involved in the planning process', *Journal of Business Strategy*, 13(3): 26–32, 1992.

148. See Reid, 1989; Floyd and Wooldridge, 1992.

149. Floyd and Wooldridge, 1992.

150. Westley, 1990.

PART I   UNDERSTANDING THE STRATEGIC CHANGE PROCESS

Introduction

The strategic change process is the path whereby strategic intent is realized through the alignment of key organizational parameters. The traditional emphasis has always been on the link between structure and strategy; but structure is simply one aspect of a complex network of design factors which span structure, systems, training and development, performance appraisal, hiring, recruitment, culture, and leadership. This first part examines the three components of the strategic change process – intent, alignment and realization – in more detail.

The first three chapters in this section concern strategic intent – they examine strategy formulation, the relationship between organization and environment, and the creation of competitive advantage. The traditional literature emphasizes the conscious **formulation of strategy**, though strategies can also unconsciously emerge. The process of formulation is presented as a rational analytic task whereby environmental opportunities and organizational strengths and weaknesses are assessed in the manner described by Andrews. It is believed that, by undertaking this type of pragmatic analysis, managers are better placed to make an appropriate strategic choice concerning the future direction of their organization and create an effective competitive advantage. As many writers have pointed out, the individual insight which the manager brings to this task can make the difference between a mechanistic understanding of past practices, and a creative move to exploit innovative strategic opportunities.

The chapter by Dess and Miller provides a basic understanding of the different generic strategies – cost leadership, differentiation and focus – and how they create **competitive advantage**. They show how different strategic choices serve to exploit environmental opportunities and, at the same time, place demands on the organization. So, for example, differentiation based on customer service requires extensive databases on customer needs; high quality production; advertising that promotes a quality image; new product development that is linked to a market orientation which, in turn, requires permeable barriers between engineering, research and development, production and marketing departments; and the requisite hiring policies and skill development programmes. Cost leadership, on the other hand, demands (among other things) a flatter structure; effective cost controls; process innovation, which in turn means a hiring policy to attract the necessary expertise and training programmes that provide pertinent skills; and careful consideration of plant size and location to balance economies of scale with transportation costs. This reading makes the bridge between strategic intent and strategic alignment – the nature of the strategic choice requires numerous organizational modifications that are necessary if the strategy is to be realized.

This brings us to the Daft and Weick article, which provides a framework for showing how **the environment** shapes the organization and vice versa. The traditional approach to strategy tends to assume that the environment is an objective, concrete reality. The role of the strategist is to procure as much information as possible about the environment in order to find an undefended niche or an opportunity for competitive advantage. This view often characterizes companies in mature environments where considerable effort goes into collecting and analysing information. Daft and Weick use the term 'discovery' to describe this form of interaction with the environment. Many business writers have been arguing that this form of strategy making is too reactive and what is needed, instead, is a more proactive approach whereby the realization of a strategy creates a new environment in which the organization has a particularly commanding position, at least until other organizations enter and increase the level of competition. Daft and Weick call this process 'enactment'. It tends to characterize younger environments where the 'rules of the game' are not fixed, but it also happens in more mature environments where innovative strategies can rewrite existing rules.

Various aspects of strategic alignment are discussed in chapters 5 to 9. **Structure** is discussed first because it represents an important building block. Readers need to understand the different types of organizational structure that exist and the cost and benefits of structuring an organization in a particular way. The chapter by Thompson and Strickland provides a description of traditional organizational structures – entrepreneurial, functional, divisional and matrix – and discusses the advantages and disadvantages of each.

Designing structure is not just a matter of drawing organization charts. Managers must also identify the critical activities – tasks and functions – associated with a particular strategy; understand the necessary relationships between these activities; group the activities into organizational units in a way that supports those relationships; establish communication channels and coordinating mechanisms between organizational units; devise a distribution of authority; and commit resources to support the integrated structure. Clegg reminds us in his discussion of organizational **forms** that we cannot discuss structure without considering the coordinating mechanisms and systems that hold the organization together. Under the rubric of the postmodern organization, he contrasts more flexible arrangements with the traditional, bureaucratic form. He provides insight into how more flexible organizations can be designed by drawing on the example of Japanese companies.

One area that is typically neglected within the context of strategic change concerns the human resource policies that relate to **people**. Fulmer shows how matters like recruitment, selection, hiring, evaluation, compensation and training must be brought into alignment with the strategic intent. If managers are considering a new strategy they must ensure that people with the appropriate skills are hired and promoted, and that existing organizational members receive the appropriate training. They must also ensure that performance appraisal and compensation schemes are changed so that they revolve around the behaviour necessary to support the new strategy, not the old. Unless people are hired, rewarded, trained and motivated in ways consistent with strategic aspirations they will only impede the realization of the strategy. Lack of attention to human resource issues is a common cause of strategic failure – because senior executives announce a new strategy but continue to reward the behaviour that conforms to the old one.

Hassard and Sharifi show how central **culture** is to the strategic change process. They explain what culture comprises, why it is hard to change, and how it can be changed. Unfortunately, the concept of culture has been simplified in much of the business literature with the result that managers are often unaware of the difficulties involved in trying to change it. When considering strategic change, managers need to be aware of the barriers that exist within the prevailing culture and how they might tackle them. But they must also be realistic: if powerful subcultures exist, they will not easily be absorbed into a one, homogeneous, overarching culture. Even if subcultures can be transformed into a 'strong' organizational culture, managers may be left with such an entrenched, filtered way of viewing the world that makes subsequent strategic change impossible.

The issue of **leadership** is tackled by Brodwin and Bourgeois, who have mapped a variety of different strategy making styles – from top-down to bottom-up. Their work redresses the tendency to view strategy making as the prerogative of senior echelons. The authors draw attention to the fact that the traditional 'commander' approach is only one way to make strategy, despite its pervasiveness in the literature. Moreover, this view of leadership tends to concentrate on formulation and ignore implementation altogether. Other leadership styles delegate an increasing role to lower levels in both formulating and implementing strategy, culminating in the 'crescive' approach where the role of senior management is to orchestrate the strategic initiatives that emanate from throughout the organization. The role of middle and junior managers in strategy making, as well as other employees, has been receiving increasing attention and it is important that readers are aware of a variety of different leadership styles.

Finally, we examine strategic realization. The Hambrick chapter provides an overview of how the convergence of various parts of the organization is necessary to support strategic intent. It is this alignment that helps to realize the strategy. It is important to realize, however, that the strategic task does not stop with convergence. The tensions within the organization and the pressures imposed on it by the environment will, almost inevitably, require further fine-tuning or even revolutionary change at some point. Strategic change is, then, best characterized as a continuing process.

The cases in this part illustrate the diversity of themes that are embedded in the strategic change process and set out in the following list.

Key themes in the strategy making process

Introduction
    What is the strategic intent of the organization?
    What organizational changes are needed to support the strategy?
    What levers exist to shape/promote strategic change?
    What are the main challenges in bringing about strategic change?

Strategic Intent
    What strategic intentions have been formed?
    How have they been formed?
    Who subscribes to them?
    Is the environment enacted or created by strategy?
    Is the environment a constraint on strategy?
    Is the environment a stimulus to strategic change?
    How does the organization 'read' the environment?
    What competitive advantages does the strategy offer?
    What demands does it place on the organization?

Strategic Alignment
    What are the main differences of the traditional structures?
    What are the advantages and disadvantages of each?
    What are the other ways of achieving flexibility and innovation?
    What are the informal aspects of structure?
    What are the systems and coordinating mechanisms?
    How can human resource policies help strategy making?
    How should these policies be changed?
    What is the nature of the existing (sub)cultures?
    What are their implications for strategy?
    What cultural changes are required?
    How can they be carried out?
    Who is the change agent?
    Is there always a change agent?
    If not, how is change orchestrated?

Strategic Realization
    Is the organization aligned around the strategy?
    What elements are misaligned?
    What is the current stage of the organization?
    What future problems can be anticipated?
    How can they be solved?

Summary
    Has strategic intent been realized?

How?

What organizational parameters were changed to facilitate it?

Do organizational parameters still need to be changed?

What changes are likely in the future?

The Apple cases trace the history of this company through its inception to the end of the 1980s, during which time all aspects of the company changed (more than once) to accommodate different strategies, leaders and environments. Apple tracks the development of an entrepreneurial organization whose visionary leader created the personal computer market to a more mature organization that has to compete – and cooperate – with the likes of IBM. It also shows the change from the go-it-alone approach of Steve Jobs, who created an alternative to IBM, to the increasing collaboration that characterizes the industry today. Apple highlights a number of other features: the nature of the entrepreneurial firm; organizational transitions (see the article by Greiner listed in the Further Reading for Part I); different leadership styles; and managing innovation.

Montreal Trust is a division of a Canadian financial services company whose executive vice-president is trying to transform a staid, bureaucratic organization into the innovative, customer-oriented division needed to meet the challenges of a deregulated and increasingly competitive industry. He has to make a series of related changes to all aspects of the organization – structure, systems, people, culture and leadership style – in order to realign the division around its new strategic initiative. Readers should consider how to develop an action plan that will enable him to tackle all these challenges and how these different organizational parameters can be made to converge around the strategic initiative.

Mrs Field's Cookies shows how information systems are an important source of strategic leverage. By using technology in this way, a relatively mundane product was transformed into a nationally successful business. Readers should examine the use of information technology in this company and evaluate how it supported the strategy. They can also compare the strategic advantages of using technology in this way with franchising, which is an alternative strategic weapon that could have been used.

'Automakers' shows how difficult it is to realize strategic change when it involves radical changes to culture. A strongly entrenched macho culture at Automakers represented a major barrier to change which was not helped by misperceptions between the consultants hired to make the change and the managers who were part of the change programme. Readers should consider how they would tackle this culture in the bid to introduce a strategy based on quality, and which other organizational parameters they would modify to support and reinforce the necessary changes. This case also explores the role of consultants in change programmes and illustrates some of the problems that can arise when outsiders are brought into an organization.

Finally, ICI (Imperial Chemical Industries) provides an example of the difficulties involved in changing a previously successful strategy, embedded in a very distinct culture, to meet the challenge of global competition. The role of the CEO and the changes he made to the company's board are particularly important here. This case provides an example of top-down strategic change and, in particular, it draws attention to how a company's board can inhibit change. Readers should consider how they would change the board's membership and composition to facilitate the implementation of a new, global strategy. They should also consider the resistance that is likely to arise and how it could be overcome. Finally, readers should give some thought to the types of changes that will be needed lower down in the company if this strategy is to be realized successfully.

Other cases (from Parts II and III) that can be used to explore the strategy making process include 'Medical Services and Products', which covers the difficulties of making strategic change in the face of resistance from other, senior executives; 'Tobacco Firms', which developed a political strategy to defend their industry in the face of health concerns; General Motors and Electronic Data Systems, whose merger prompted massive growth for the latter; the Bicycle Components Industry, where a viable global strategy must be formulated; and 'Conglom' where strategy making in a divisional organization is discussed.

Further Reading for Part I

Allaire, Y. and Firsirotu, M. (1985) 'How to implement radical strategies in large organizations', *Sloan Management Review*, 19–33, Spring.

Applegate, L.M., James, J.I. and Mills, Quinn D. (1988) 'Information technology and tomorrow's manager', *Harvard Business Review*, November–December, 128–36.

Beatty, Richard W. and Ulrich, David O. (1991) 'Re-energizing the mature organization', *Organizational Dynamics*, 16–20, Summer.

Bowman, C. and Johnson, G. (1992) 'Surfacing competitive strategies', *European Management Journal*, 10(2): 210–19.

Boynton, Andrew C. and Victor, Bart (1991) 'Beyond flexibility: Building and managing the dynamically stable organization', *California Management Review*, 34(1), 53–66, Fall.

Business Week (1985) 'Information power', *Business Week*, 14 October, p. 142.

Byrne, John A. (1993) 'The virtual corporation', *Business Week*, 98–103, 8 February.

Carnall, C.A., (1986) 'Managing strategic change: An integrated approach', *Long Range Planning*, 19(6): 105–15.

Cox Jr., Taylor (1991) 'The multicultural organization', *Academy of Management Executive*, 5(2): 34–47.

Fortune (1994) 'Information technology guide: Special report', 128(7), Autumn.

Gabarro, J.J. (1985) 'When a new manager takes charge', *Harvard Business Review*, 110–23, May–June.

Greiner, L.E. (1972) 'Evolution and revolution as organizations grow', *Harvard Business Review*, July–August, 37–46.

Hamel, G. and Prahalad, C.K. (1989) 'Strategic intent', *Harvard Business Review*, 63–76, May–June.

Hamel, G. and Prahalad, C.K. (1993) 'Strategy as stretch and leverage', *Harvard Business Review*, March–April.

Johnson, Gerry (1992) 'Managing strategic change – Strategy, culture and action', *Long Range Planning*, 25(1): 28–36.

Kanter, R.M. (1991) 'Championing change: An interview with Bell Atlantic's Raymond Smith', *Harvard Business Review*, 119–30, January–February.

Lorsch, J.W. (1986) 'Managing culture: The invisible barrier to strategic change', *California Management Review*, 28(2): 95–109.

McFarlane, W. (1984) 'Information technology changes the way you compete', *Harvard Business Review*, 98–103, May–June.

Mintzberg, Henry (1987) 'Crafting strategy', *Harvard Business Review*, July–August , 66–75.

Mintzberg, H. (1991) 'Five P's for strategy', in *The Strategy Process: Concepts, Contexts and Cases*. Englewood Cliffs, NJ: Prentice Hall, pp. 13–19.

Pascale, R.T. (1984) 'Perspectives on strategy: The real story behind Honda's success', *California Management Review*, 26(3): 47–72.

Prahalad, C.K. and Hamel, Gary (1990) 'The core competence of the corporation', *Harvard Business Review*, 79–91, May–June.

Tushman, Michael L., Newman, William H. and Romanelli, Elaine (1986) 'Convergence and upheaval: Managing the unsteady pace of organizational evolution', *California Management Review*, 29(1): 1–16.

Waterman, R.H., Peters, T.J. and Phillips, J.R. (1980) 'Structure is not organization', *Business Horizons*, 23(3): 14–26.

Whipp, R. et al. (1989) 'Managing strategic change in a mature business', *Long Range Planning*, 22(6) 92–9.

2 Formulating Strategic Intent

Kenneth R. Andrews

The Strategy Concept

What Strategy Is

Corporate strategy is the pattern of decisions in a company that determines and reveals its objectives, purposes, or goals, produces the principal policies and plans for achieving those goals, and defines the range of business the company is to pursue, the kind of economic and human organization it is or intends to be, and the nature of the economic and noneconomic contribution it intends to make to its shareholders, employees, customers, and communities. . . .

The strategic decision contributing to this pattern is one that is effective over long periods of time, affects the company in many different ways, and focuses and commits a significant portion of its resources to the expected outcomes. The pattern resulting from a series of such decisions will probably define the central character and image of a company, the individuality it has for its members and various publics, and the position it will occupy in its industry and markets. It will permit the specification of particular objectives to be attained through a timed sequence investment and implementation decisions and will govern directly the deployment or redeployment of resources to make these decisions effective.

[. . .]

It is important, however, not to take the idea apart in another way, that is, to separate goals from the policies designed to achieve those goals. The essence of the definition of strategy I have just recorded is *pattern*. The interdependence of purposes, policies, and organized action is crucial to the particularity of an individual strategy and its opportunity to identify competitive advantage. It is the unity, coherence, and internal consistency of a company's strategic decisions that position the company in its environment and give the firm its identity, its power to mobilize its strengths, and its likelihood of success in the marketplace. It is the interrelationship of a set of

From Kenneth R. Andrews, *The Concept of Corporate Strategy*. New York: Richard D. Irwin (rev. ed.), 1980.

goals and policies that crystallizes from the formless reality of a company's environment a set of problems an organization can seize upon and solve.

What you are doing, in short, is never meaningful unless you can say or imply what you are doing it for: the quality of administrative action and the motivation lending it power cannot be appraised without knowing its relationship to purpose. Breaking up the system of corporate goals and the character-determining major policies for attainment leads to narrow and mechanical conceptions of strategic management and endless logic chopping. . . .

[. . .]

Formulation of Strategy

Corporate strategy is an organization process, in many ways inseparable from the structure, behaviour, and culture of the company in which it takes place. Nevertheless, we may abstract from the process two important aspects, interrelated in real life but separable for the purposes of analysis. The first of these we may call *formulation*, the second *implementation*. [. . .]

The principal subactivities of strategy formulation as a logical activity include identifying opportunities and threats in the company's environment and attaching some estimate or risk to the discernible alternatives. Before a choice can be made, the company's strengths and weaknesses should be appraised together with the resources on hand and available. Its actual or potential capacity to take advantage of perceived market needs or to cope with attendant risks should be estimated as objectively as possible. The strategic alternative which results from matching opportunity and corporate capability at an acceptable level of risk is what we may call an *economic strategy*.

The process described thus far assumes that strategists are analytically objective in estimating the relative capacity of their company and the opportunity they see or anticipate in developing markets. The extent to which they wish to undertake low or high risk presumably depends on their profit objectives. The higher they set the latter, the more willing they must be to assume a correspondingly high risk that the market opportunity they see will not develop or that the corporate competence required to excel competition will not be forthcoming.

So far we have described the intellectual processes of ascertaining what a company *might do* in terms of environmental opportunity, of deciding what it *can do* in terms of ability and power, and of bringing these two considerations together in optimal equilibrium. The determination of strategy also requires consideration of what alternatives are preferred by the chief executive and perhaps by his or her immediate associates as well, quite apart from economic considerations. Personal values, aspirations, and ideals do, and in our judgement quite properly should, influence the final choice of purposes. Thus what the executives of a company *want to do* must be brought into the strategic decision.

Finally strategic choice has an ethical aspect – a fact much more dramatically illustrated in some industries than in others. Just as alternatives may be ordered in terms of the degree of risk that they entail, so may they be examined against the standards of responsiveness to the expectations of society that the strategist elects. Some alternatives may seem to the executive considering them more attractive than others when the public good or service to society is considered. What a company *should do* thus appears as a fourth element of the strategic decision. . . .

The Implementation of Strategy

Since effective implementation can make a sound strategic decision ineffective or a debatable choice successful, it is as important to examine the processes of implementation as to weigh the advantages of available strategic alternatives. The implementation of strategy is comprised of a series of subactivities which are primarily administrative. If purpose is determined, then the resources of a company can be mobilized to accomplish it. An organizational structure appropriate for the efficient performance of the required tasks must be made effective by information systems and relationships permitting coordination of subdivided activities. The organizational processes of performance measurement, compensation, management development – all of them enmeshed in systems of incentives and controls – must be directed toward the kind of behavior required by organizational purpose. The role of personal leadership is important and sometimes decisive in the accomplishment of strategy. Although we know that organization structure and processes of compensation, incentives, control, and management development influence and constrain the formulation of strategy, we should look first at the logical proposition that structure should follow strategy in order to cope later with the organizational reality that strategy also follows structure. When we have examined both tendencies, we will understand and to some extent be prepared to deal with the interdependence of the formulation and implementation of corporate purpose. [Figure 2.1] may be useful in understanding the analysis of strategy as a pattern of interrelated decisions. . . .

Relating Opportunities to Resources

Determination of a suitable strategy for a company begins in identifying the opportunities and risks in its environment. This [discussion] is concerned with the identification of a range of strategic alternatives, the narrowing of this range by recognizing the constraints imposed by corporate capability, and the determination of one or more economic strategies at acceptable levels of risk. . . .

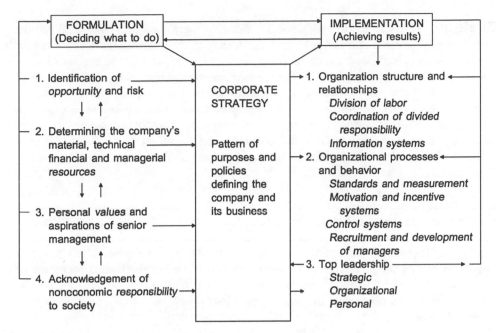

[Figure 2.1]

The Nature of the Company's Environment

The environment of an organization in business, like that of any other organic entity, is the pattern of all the external conditions and influences that affect its life and development. The environmental influences relevant to strategic decision operate in a company's industry, the total business community, its city, its country, and the world. They are technological, economic, physical, social, and political in kind. The corporate strategist is usually at least intuitively aware of these features of the current environment. But in all these categories change is taking place at varying rates – fastest in technology, less rapidly in politics. Change in the environment of business necessitates continuous monitoring of a company's definition of its business, lest it falter, blur, or become obsolete. Since by definition the formulation of strategy is performed with the future in mind, executives who take part in the strategic planning process must be aware of those aspects of their company's environment especially susceptible to the kind of change that will affect their company's future.

Technology From the point of view of the corporate strategist, technological developments are not only the fastest unfolding but the most far-reaching in extending or contracting opportunity for an established company. They include the discoveries of science, the impact of related product development, the less dramatic machinery and process improvements, and the progress of automation and data processing. . . .

Ecology   It used to be possible to take for granted the physical characteristics of the environment and find them favorable to industrial development. Plant sites were chosen using criteria like availability of process and cooling water, accessibility to various forms of transportation, and stability of soil conditions. With the increase in sensitivity to the impact on the physical environment of all industrial activity, it becomes essential, often to comply with law, to consider how planned expansion and even continued operation under changing standards will affect and be perceived to affect the air, water, traffic density, and quality of life generally of any area which a company would like to enter. . . .

Economics   Because business is more accustomed to monitoring economic trends than those in other spheres, it is less likely to be taken by surprise by such massive developments as the internationalization of competition, the return of China and Russia to trade with the West, the slower than projected development of the Third World countries, the Americanization of demand and culture in the developing countries and the resulting backlash of nationalism, the increased importance of the large multinational corporations and the consequences of host-country hostility, the recurrence of recession, and the persistence of inflation in all phases of the business cycle. The consequences of world economic trends need to be monitored in much greater detail for any one industry or company.

Industry   Although the industry environment is the one most company strategists believe they know most about, the opportunities and risks that reside there are often blurred by familiarity and the uncritical acceptance of the established relative position of competitors. . . .

Society   Social development of which strategists keep aware include such influential forces as the quest for equality for minority groups, the demand of women for opportunity and recognition, the changing patterns of work and leisure, the effects of urbanization upon the individual, family, and neighborhood, the rise of crime, the decline of conventional morality, and the changing composition of world population.

Politics   The political forces important to the business firms are similarly extensive and complex – the changing relations between communist and noncommunist countries (East and West) and between prosperous and poor countries (North and South), the relation between private enterprise and government, between workers and management, the impact of national planning on corporate planning, [. . .].

Although it is not possible to know or spell out here the significance of such technical, economic, social, and political trends, and possibilities for the strategist of a given business or company, some simple things are clear. Changing values will lead to different expectations of the role business should perform. Business will be expected to perform its mission not only with economy in the use of energy but with sensitivity to the ecological environment. Organizations in all walks of life will be called upon to be more explicit about their goals and to meet the needs and aspirations (for example, for education) of their membership.

In any case, change threatens all established strategies. We know that a thriving company – itself a living system – is bound up in a variety of interrelationships with larger systems comprising its technological, economic, ecological, social, and political environment. If environmental developments are destroying and creating business opportunities, advance notice of specific instances relevant to a single company is essential to intelligent planning. Risk and opportunity in the last quarter of the twentieth century require of executives a keen interest in what is going on outside their companies. More than that, a practical means of tracking developments promising good or ill, and profit or loss, needs to be devised. . . .

For the firm that has not determined what its strategy dictates it needs to know or has not embarked upon the systematic surveillance of environmental change, a few simple questions kept constantly in mind will highlight changing opportunity and risk. In examining your own company or one you are interested in, these questions should lead to an estimate of opportunity and danger in the present and predicted company setting.

1. What are the essential economic, technical, and physical characteristics of the industry in which the company participates? . . .
2. What trends suggesting future change in economic and technical characteristics are apparent? . . .
3. What is the nature of competition both within the industry and across industries? . . .
4. What are the requirements for success in competition in the company's industry? . . .
5. Given the technical, economic, social, and political developments that most directly apply, what is the range of strategy available to any company in this industry? . . .

Identifying Corporate Competence and Resources

The first step in validating a tentative choice among several opportunities is to determine whether the organization has the capacity to prosecute it successfully. The capability of an organization is its demonstrated and potential ability to accomplish, against the opposition of circumstance or competition, whatever it sets out to do. Every organization has actual and potential strengths and weaknesses. Since it is prudent in formulating strategy to extend or maximize the one and contain or minimize the other, it is important to try to determine what they are and to distinguish one from the other.

It is just as possible, though much more difficult, for a company to know its own strengths and limitations as it is to maintain a workable surveillance of its changing environment. Subjectivity, lack of confidence, and unwillingness to face reality may make it hard for organizations as well as for individuals to know themselves. But just as it is essential, though difficult, that a maturing person achieve reasonable self-awareness, so an organization can identify approximately its central strength and critical vulnerability. . . .

To make an effective contribution to strategic planning, the key attributes to be appraised should be identified and consistent criteria established for judging them. If attention is directed to strategies, policy commitments, and past practices in the context of discrepancy between organization goals and attainment, an outcome useful to an individual manager's strategic planning is possible. The assessment of strengths and weaknesses associated with the attainment of specific objectives [. . .] allows managers to learn from the success or failures of the policies they institute.

[. . .]

Source of Capabilities   The powers of a company constituting a resource for growth and diversification accrue primarily from experience in making and marketing a product line or providing a service. They inhere as well in (1) the developing strengths and weaknesses of the individuals comprising the organization, (2) the degree to which individual capability is effectively applied to the common task, and (3) the quality of coordination of individual and group effort.

The experience gained through successful execution of a strategy centred upon one goal may unexpectedly develop capabilities which could be applied to different ends. Whether they should be so applied is another question. For example, a manufacturer of salt can strengthen his competitive position by offering his customers salt-dispensing equipment. If, in the course of making engineering improvements in this equipment, a new solenoid principle is perfected that has application to many industrial switching problems, should this patentable and marketable innovation be exploited? The answer would turn not only on whether economic analysis of the opportunity shows this to be a durable and profitable possibility, but also on whether the organization can muster the financial, manufacturing, and marketing strength to exploit the discovery and live with its success. The former question is likely to have a more positive answer than the latter. In this connection, it seems important to remember that individual and unsupported flashes of strength are not as dependable as the gradually accumulated product and market-related fruits of experience.

Even where competence to exploit an opportunity is nurtured by experience in related fields, the level of that competence may be too low for any great reliance to be placed upon it. Thus a chain of children's clothing stores might well acquire the administrative, merchandising, buying, and selling skills that would permit it to add departments in women's wear.

Similarly, a sales force effective in distributing typewriters might gain proficiency in selling office machinery and supplies. But even here it would be well to ask what *distinctive* ability these companies could bring to the retailing of soft goods or office equipment to attract customers away from a plethora of competitors.

Identifying Strengths The distinctive competence of an organization is more than what it can do; it is what it can do particularly well. To identify the less obvious or by-product strengths of an organization that may well be transferable to some more profitable new opportunity, one might well begin by examining the organization's current product line and by defining the functions it serves in its markets. Almost any important consumer product has functions which are related to others into which a qualified company might move. The typewriter, for example, is more than the simple machine for mechanizing handwriting that it once appeared to be when looked at only from the point of view of its designer and manufacturer. Closely analyzed from the point of view of the potential user, the typewriter is found to contribute to a broad range of information processing functions. Any one of these might have suggested an area to be exploited by a typewriter manufacturer. Tacitly defining a typewriter as a replacement for a fountain pen as a writing instrument rather than as an input-output device for word processing is the explanation provided by hindsight for the failure of the old-line typewriter companies to develop before IBM did the electric typewriter and the computer-related input-output devices it made possible. The definition of product which would lead to identification of transferable skills must be expressed in terms of the market needs it may fill rather than the engineering specifications to which it conforms.

Besides looking at the uses or functions to which present products contribute, the would-be diversifier might profitably identify the skills that underlie whatever success has been achieved. The qualifications of an organization efficient at performing its long-accustomed tasks come to be taken for granted and considered humdrum, like the steady provision of first-class service. The insight required to identify the essential strength justifying new ventures does not come naturally. Its cultivation can probably be helped by recognition of the need for analysis. In any case, we should look beyond the company's capacity to invent new products. Product leadership is not possible for a majority of companies, so it is fortunate that patentable new products are not the only major highway to new opportunities. Other avenues include new marketing services, new methods of distribution, new values in quality-price combinations, and creative merchandising. The effort to find or to create a competence that is truly distinctive may hold the real key to a company's success or even to its future development. For example, the ability of a cement manufacturer to run a truck fleet more effectively than its competitors may constitute one of its principal competitive strengths in selling an undifferentiated product.

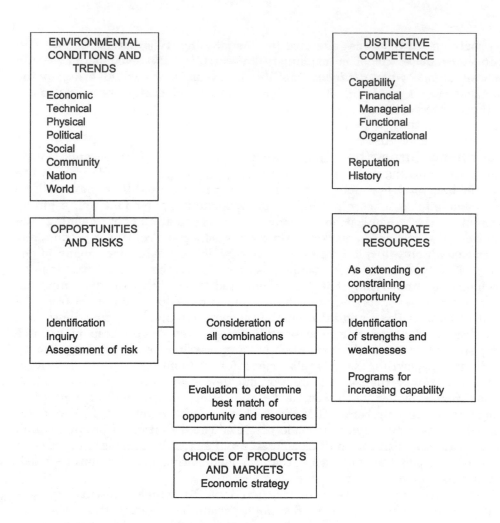

[Figure 2.2]   *Schematic development of economic strategy*

Matching Opportunity and Competence   The way to narrow the range of alternatives, made extensive by imaginative identification of new possibilities, is to match opportunity to competence, once each has been accurately identified and its future significance estimated. It is this combination which establishes a company's economic mission and its position in its environment. The combination is designed to minimize organizational weakness and to maximize strength. In every case, risk attends it. And when opportunity seems to outrun present distinctive competence, the willingness to gamble that the latter can be built up to the required level is almost indispensable to a strategy that challenges the organization and the people in it. [Figure 2.2] diagrams the matching of opportunity and resources that results in an economic strategy.

Before we leave the creative act of putting together a company's unique internal capability and opportunity evolving in the external world, we should note that – aside from distinctive competence – the principal resources found in any company are money and people – technical and managerial people. At an advanced stage of economic development, money seems less a problem than technical competence, and the latter less critical than managerial ability. Do not assume that managerial capacity can rise to any occasion. The diversification of American industry is marked by hundreds of instances in which a company strong in one endeavor lacked the ability to manage an enterprise requiring different skills. The right to make handsome profits over a long period must be earned. Opportunism without competence is a path to fairyland.

Besides equating an appraisal of market opportunity and organizational capability, the decision to make and market a particular product or service should be accompanied by an identification of the nature of the business and the kind of company its management desires. Such a guiding concept is a product of many considerations, including the managers' personal values. . . .

Uniqueness of Strategy   In each company, the way in which distinctive competence, organizational resources, and organizational values are combined is or should be unique. Differences among companies are as numerous as differences among individuals. The combinations of opportunity to which distinctive competences, resources, and values may be applied are equally extensive. Generalizing about how to make an effective match is less rewarding than working at it. The effort is a highly stimulating and challenging exercise. The outcome will be unique for each company and each situation.

3 Creating Competitive Advantage

Gregory G. Dess and Alex Miller

Competitive Advantages

To be successful, a business must hold some advantage relative to its competition. This advantage may take the form of greater differentiation, in which case the customer finds the firm's products or services unique in some way that makes them more attractive and therefore worth a premium price, as in the case of Rolls-Royce automobiles. Alternatively, the firm may have a lower cost position, which allows it to charge similar (or even lower) prices while realizing better-than-average margins. The Wal-Mart chain of retail stores enjoys a low-cost position. These two forms of competitive advantage provide the basis for much of the thinking about business-level strategy in the past decade.[1] [. . .]

In the long run, a business without one or more of these competitive advantages is probably destined to earn no more than what economists call 'normal profits'[2] [. . .]. Normal profits allow investors to earn a return equal to the average return they would expect to receive from any other similar risky investment. Over the long run, firms that perform below this normal profits level will fail to attract or maintain the investments necessary to continue to operate. Performance that yields only normal profits is not particularly noteworthy because normal profits are only average. Businesses usually strive to achieve performance above the level of normal profits, and therefore, the pursuit of competitive advantage has become the central theme of strategic management at the business level. The director of planning at Clark Equipment Company, the leading US firm in the highly competitive forklift industry, explains:

> The process of strategic management is coming to be defined, in fact, as the management of competitive advantage – that is, as a process of identifying, developing, and taking advantage of enclaves in which a tangible and preservable business advantage can be achieved.[3]

From *Strategic Management*. New York: McGraw-Hill, 1993.

Differentiation

In pursuing a competitive advantage based on *differentiation*, firms attempt to create unique bundles of products and/or services that will be highly valued by customers. The value chain in [Figure 3.1] presents some examples of competitive advantage that differentiation can provide. Here are some of the attributes firms use to differentiate their products:

- *Product features*: The physical characteristics and capabilities of a product may be an important form of differentiation. For example, Philips developed a television that can display two channels on the same screen.
- *After-sales service*: Convenience and quality of service may be a critical factor in deciding among alternative products. Sears attracts customers who value an efficient nationwide network of repair services.
- *Desirable image*: This is the obvious basis of virtually all fashion products, ranging from designer blue jeans to furs.
- *Technological innovation*: Technical advances provide the basis of competitive advantage in a broad range of firms. Cambridge Speakerworks patented a stereo speaker system that gives sound quality comparable to giant loudspeakers, but is small enough to fit in any apartment.
- *Reputation of the firm*: A distinguished reputation may be an important source of sales. The saying in the computer industry in reference to IBM's reputation is 'no-body ever got fired for buying from Big Blue.'
- *Manufacturing consistency*: This is especially important in making components that must mesh with others to produce a finished good. This need has given rise to greater emphasis on statistical process control (SPC) and a broad range of quality control techniques aimed at manufacturing.
- *Status symbol*: Cars that cost more than some houses are obviously purchased for reasons other than transportation.

A differentiation strategy can be based on any combination of nonprice attributes such as these. If it is successful in creating some unique and desirable product or service attribute, the firm builds brand loyalty in customers, decreases the number of alternative products the customers are willing to consider, and reduces the customers' sensitivity to prices. These results produce higher profit margins without requiring lower costs. Pursuit of this strategy often involves accepting lower market shares, because mass marketing is usually incompatible with the image of exclusivity associated with premium-priced products. High differentiation may also limit the feasibility of competing on the basis of cost or price, because extra R&D, higher-quality materials, more advertising, and so forth, are often the basis of differentiation.

A successful differentiation strategy allows a business to address the five

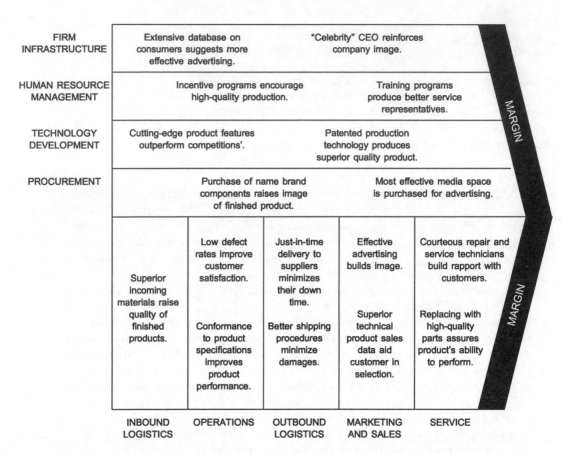

[Figure 3.1]   *Examples of How Firms Achieve* Differentiation *as a Competitive Advantage*
Source: Adapted with permission of The Free Press, a Division of Macmillan, Inc., from Porter, Michael E. (1985). *Competitive advantage: Creating and sustaining superior performance.* New York: Free Press. Copyright ©1985 by Michael E. Porter.

competitive forces [. . .] in such a way that the firm enjoys higher-than-typical returns:

Competitive rivalry may be lessened as firms successfully distinguish themselves. In this way, firms in the same industry may avoid head-to-head confrontations. Jaguar's differentiated products do not compete directly with Hyundai's even though both firms produce automobiles.

Brand-loyal customers are less sensitive to prices. As a result, if a firm's suppliers raise prices, the firm can more easily pass along the resulting cost hike to its customers. In fact, many firms that are successful differentiators are also premium pricers – that is, their customers pay the highest prices in the industry.

New entrants or firms offering product substitutes must overcome this brand loyalty. The customer may feel strongly about a successfully differentiated product. It has proven to be difficult to introduce a new cola-flavored soft drink in the United States, because the existing market leaders have so effectively established the loyalty in their customers. It has been equally difficult to establish a substitute product that would entice customers away from colas.

[. . .]

Cost Leadership

Success with the competitive advantage we call *cost leadership* requires achieving a low-cost position relative to one's competition. Pursuit of this advantage often involves offering a no-frills product aimed at the most typical customer in a large target market. [Figure 3.2] offers some examples of how a competitive advantage can be gained through cost leadership. Because costs can usually be lowered as a product becomes more standardized, low-cost manufacturing firms strive for long production runs, and low-cost service firms tend to offer uniform packages. By targeting broadly defined markets with standard products, such firms hope to gain the greatest possible benefits from economies of scale and experience curve effects. A firm aiming for low-cost production will typically spend less on R&D than competitors following a differentiation strategy. This is especially true of product-related R&D, although a larger portion of the total R&D budget might be directed toward process-oriented R&D intended to make the product easier and cheaper to produce. Advertising will probably be minimal, with promotional efforts stressing price comparisons.

If successful, a low-cost strategy allows a firm to address the five forces in their competitive environment so it can realize higher-than-normal profits:

Holding the low-cost position may convince rivals not to enter a price war. Price wars can be ruinous to all the competitors involved. Thus, a cost advantage great enough to serve as a deterrent may be an important 'peacekeeping' weapon.

Low-cost producers are protected from customer pressure to lower prices. Competitors cannot consistently price below what is known as their survival price. (The survival price allows profit margins just adequate to maintain a business.) By definition, the low-cost leader has a lower survival price than any competitor, so customers will not be able to play one competing supplier against the other to force prices down below a level at which the cost leader can still make profits. To do so would force less efficient suppliers out of business, leaving the low-cost suppliers with a monopoly.

Because of their higher margins, low-cost producers are better able to withstand increases in their costs from suppliers. In some industries, the costs of key supplies are volatile. (For example, a bad crop year can raise coffee production costs dramatically for all competitors in the industry.) In this case, the lowest-cost producer may be the only one that comes near to making a profit.

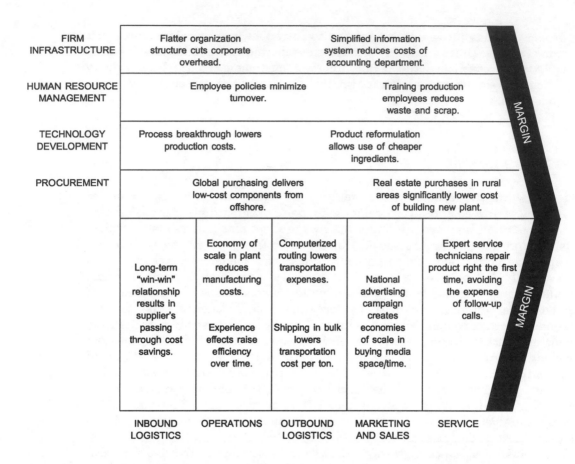

[Figure 3.2]   *Examples of How Firms Achieve* Cost Leadership *as a Competitive Advantage*
Source: Adapted with permission of The Free Press, a Division of Macmillan, Inc., from Porter, Michael E. (1985). *Competitive advantage: Creating and sustaining superior performance.* New York: Free Press. Copyright © 1985 by Michael E. Porter.

New entrants competing on the basis of price must fact the cost leader without having the experience necessary to become efficient. As the cumulative volume of production increases, production costs tend to decrease – the 'experience curve' effect. It is likely that the low-cost leader has already moved far down whatever experience curve is operating in the industry. New entrants lacking this experience are not likely to enjoy comparable efficiency and may be forced to enter the market using some competitive advantage not related to low pricing.

Low-cost producers are in the best position to use pricing to compete with substitute products. As new composite materials continue to chip away at demand for structural steel, the most efficient mills, the minimills [. . .], will be the least-threatened competitors in the industry. The low profit margin usually associated with minimills are the least likely to attract competition from the new substitutes. Furthermore, because of their low-cost position, minimills can remain price competitive with composite materials longer than other less efficient steel producers.

The merits of a cost leadership strategy must be compared to its various risks:

Cost leadership is likely to be an 'all or nothing' strategy. In competitive markets for commodity-like products (those offering little differentiation), the number 1 competitor in terms of low cost may be able to price its products as a level that will not allow less efficient producers to remain in operation. Where product differentiation is not a consideration, customers will naturally seek the lowest price, leaving even the second most cost-efficient producer in an undesirable position.

Cost cutting that leads to loss of desirable product attributes can be ruinous. Watney's Red, a controversial British beer, illustrates this point. The UK beer industry has historically been dominated by ales and bitters, but starting in the 1950s, lagers have taken an increasing share of the market. The makers of Watney's Red mistook this willingness to buy these very different tasting brews to mean that taste was not an important consideration for the customer. Cheaper raw materials, brewing methods, and handling procedures were used to lower the cost of Watney's Red. Not only was the product strongly resisted by the British marketplace, it did much to motivate the creation of CAMRA (the CAMpaign for Real Ales), one of the most vocal consumer advocate groups in Britain today.

Many cost-saving tactics are easily duplicated by competitors. Even competitors pursuing high-differentiation positions for their flagship product line may choose to offer a low-cost line of products, often producing them with the same facilities as their top-of-the-line products. In fact, some generic goods are identical to branded products, but are simply sold with a different label. Such goods are virtual by-products in terms of the minimal incremental investment required to produce them. Therefore, they can provide serious price competition for firms depending on a low-cost position to secure all their sales.

Cost differences among competitors often decline as the market matures. As a product ages, the absolute amount of production required to achieve any given percentage increase in its cumulative volume rises, and consequently, the strength of experience effects declines. When a business begins operation, it may double its cumulative volume in each of the first 2 months, but eventually it will take 3 months to double its cumulative volume, then 1 year, then 2 years, and so on. Once volume reaches high enough levels, further movement along the cost curve is almost imperceptible, because it may take decades to double cumulative volume again. Thus, as the product ages, competitors that once lagged behind are able to catch up.

Dedication to cost cutting often limits a firm's abilities to remain competitive in other ways. In particular, an emphasis on cost control frequently precludes investment in innovation. This leaves the firm vulnerable to technical advances that might make the product obsolete, regardless of any price cuts the firm can offer. An example of this [. . .] was Ford's single-minded pursuit of production efficiencies in producing the Model T. Ford was able to dramatically reduce costs, in part, by refusing to introduce new product features. Meanwhile, GM responded to growing demand for new-product designs and was able to capture a much larger portion of the market.[4]

[. . .]

Market Focus and Competitive Advantage

The extent to which a firm concentrates on a narrowly defined or niche segment of the market is referred to as its *focus*. Focus alone does not constitute a competitive advantage, but it may fundamentally affect a firm's ability to achieve a competitive advantage.

A differentiation strategy is often associated with focusing on a narrowly defined market niche. A broad, mass-market emphasis may be incongruous with some sorts of differentiation, especially those based on status and image. A status symbol loses its effectiveness if shared by all. Additionally, firms that focus on specific segments of the overall market may be in a better position to deliver the forms of differentiation with the most appeal to that segment. [. . .] Tandem successfully used this tactic by focusing on the fail-safe niche within the mainframe computer market.

A cost leadership strategy is often associated with a broadly defined target market. Broadly defined markets typically yield the largest possible volume for any given product line, and this volume results in lower costs through economies of scale and experience curve effects. *Economies of scale* refers to amortizing a given expense or investment over a greater production base. For example, any airline must set up a computer system to handle reservations and flight schedules, but it costs less to do so on a per customer basis for a large airline than a small one. *Experience effects* occur when a task becomes easier as it is repeated until the process is routinized.

[. . .]

Strategic Management in Different Stages of the Market Life Cycle

Here we study how managing for competitive advantage differs across the stages of the market life cycle.[13] The market life cycle is a conceptual model which suggests that markets can evolve through stages typically labeled introduction, growth, maturity, and decline. (As discussed below, we also consider turnaround as a possible stage, but since it is not part of the natural market evolutionary process, it is in a somewhat special category.) As markets move from one life cycle stage to another, strategic considerations change.[14] The changes range from rates of innovation to customer price sensitivity to intensity of competitive rivalry and beyond.[15] [Table 3.1] shows how some important characteristics of markets change over time. As you might expect, strategy must be adjusted to meet the new market conditions from one stage to the next.

In other words, the market life cycle provides a useful framework for studying business-level strategy formulation, because it provides a 'shorthand' for the numerous differences in strategic situations and the behaviour appropriate to each. The product life cycle and technological life cycles are well known and important concepts that we have attempted to build into our consideration of an overall market life cycle. [. . .]

While it is clearly a useful concept, there are two caveats to bear in mind when considering the market life cycle. First, the market life cycle is not intended to be used as a short-run forecasting device. Strategists find it more useful to consider the market life cycle as a conceptual framework for understanding what changes might occur over time rather than when they are likely to occur. Second, industry life cycles are reversible and repeatable. For example, Tide, a synthetic laundry detergent produced by Procter & Gamble, was introduced in 1947, but continues to see strong growth today. The product was significantly modified fifty-five times during its first 30 years.[16] Demand continues to grow as Procter & Gamble makes improvements – offering a liquid form, packaging innovations, and so on. Products such as Tide suggests that a turnaround phase is an appropriate supplement to the traditional life cycle model.

We now look at different strategic management practices within each stage of the market life cycle: introduction, growth, maturity, and decline.

Introduction

The early stages of a market's development establish the climate for much of what is to follow. While firms may enter a market during any stage of its life cycle, studies show that the entrepreneurial pioneers who enter the market first typically gain important advantages.[17] Competitive advantages that are gained because the pioneer was one of the first to enter a market are sometimes called 'first-mover advantages.'[18] First movers are notable for their tendency to hold on to the competitive advantages and market shares they gain as the market matures.[19]

Although market shares tend to become more balanced as markets mature, [. . .] market share gained by successful pioneers during the market's introduction stage are often sustained for many years.[20] One of the reasons pioneers can hold their market share is that they also tend to gain advantages over their competition by being the first to enter a new market.[21] In their early stages, markets begin to establish the 'rules of the game' that often translate

[Table 3.1] *Some Common Characteristics of Market Life Cycle Stages*

Characteristic	Life Cycle Stage			
	Introduction	Growth	Maturity	Decline
Overall market growth	Building rapidly, but on a small base	Faster than GNP	Equal or less than GNP	Decreasing
Product technology	High level of major product innovation, dominant designs not yet established	Dominant design emerges, emphasis placed on product variety	Small incremental innovations, many based on cost savings vs. performance improvements	Little or no change in product
Production technology	Emphasis placed on flexibility, process fixed until dominant design emerges	As dominant design emerges, production process can become more specialized	Emphasis on efficiency, most likely stage for automation	Little or no change in process
Pricing patterns	Prices are high but volatile	Prices decline rapidly as costs fall and competition rises	Prices decline slowly as productivity allows costs to fall	Prices stable
Promotional efforts	Target innovators and try to build awareness of product	Build brand awareness	Tailor promotion to a variety of market segments	Limit market, largely depend on inertia to maintain viable level of sales

Entry and exit	A few pioneers begin to explore the market	Many firms scramble to enter what appears to be a promising market	As market is saturated, growth slows and shakeout begins	A few survivors remain to serve the market
Nature of competition	Limited, focus is often inward, looking toward product rather than toward competitors	Growth may mask success of competitors	Competitive rivalry peaks as competitors try to survive the shakeout	As shakeout is completed, survivors seek to deescalate competition
Capital investment requirements	Substantial, needed to support initial creation of business and/or product	Peak period, needed to fund growth	Reinvestment as needed to maintain viability	Minimal, may in fact "disinvest" by selling off assets
Profitability and cash flow	Unprofitable, substantial negative cash flow	Profitable, but cash flow may still be negative	Profits declining, but larger investment level may mean cash flow is strong	Profits are low, cash flow is small (either negative or positive)

into important competitive advantages.[22] For instance, IBM's success in establishing MS-DOS as an industry standard meant that later entrants in the personal computer market were forced to develop expertise in that operating system or fight the battle of establishing and supporting an alternative one.

There are numerous other means by which pioneers may gain important competitive advantages.[23] By being the first to offer a particular good or service, pioneers often benefit from establishing strong brand recognition. Kleenex and Xerox, both pioneers, were able to establish such strong name recognition that the entire facial tissue and photocopier markets are often identified by their names. Such strong brand recognition may serve as an important switching cost.[24] Pioneers may also be able to differentiate their products or services by marketing their products when there are no countering advertisements being run by competitors.[25] Finally, products and services offered by pioneers may be considered differentiated simply because their products are new.[26]

But the competitive advantages gained by pioneers are not always sustained. Texas Instruments had the expertise in semiconductor design and manufacturing that allowed it to succeed in gaining an impressive market share as a pioneer in the early stages of the digital watch market, while Timex, lacking any competence in the new technology, floundered. However, as the market matured, the basis of competition shifted from electronics design and manufacturing (TI's core competence) to consumer marketing (Timex's core competence). In the end, TI was forced to drop out of the market entirely, taking large writeoffs, while Timex remains a strong competitor. The key to maintaining competitive advantages gained by pioneering a market is to adjust the strategy as required by developments during subsequent market life cycle stages.

Growth

The growth stage of a market's life cycle is often associated with glamour and success. At this stage of the life cycle, demand for the product or service may be growing faster than the industry is able to supply it. There is less price pressure, exciting advances are being made in new technologies, and sales volume (if not profits) soars. Consequently, we often make basic assumptions about the benefits of growth that turn out to be untrue.[27] Consider three of the most common of these assumptions and how each one can be misleading:

One might think it is easier to gain share in growth markets. In the growth stage, customers are less likely to have established strong brand loyalties, making it easier for them to switch suppliers. Because the market as a whole is growing rapidly, competitors are often less likely to retaliate (or, in fact, even notice) when customers are 'stolen.'[28] This reason might be appropriate if the market being considered is for a product or service so radically new that it faces no substitutes from more established industries. Usually, even if new products do not face as much 'in-kind' competition (from the same kind of product), they often face 'functional' competition (from a different product that is used for a similar purpose). For instance, during much of its growth stage, producers in the digital watch market competed with more established mechanical watch manufacturers, which could offer a product that was often more reliable and less expensive. Given this inferiority, gaining share was not merely a process of convincing shoppers to purchase one digital model over another; it involved getting them to shop for a digital watch instead of a mechanical one.

We often assume that there is less price pressure in growth markets. Because products in growth markets often enjoy a demand in excess of supply, many growth markets can support premium pricing. During this stage, young firms are often tempted to price their goods unusually high in order to recoup as much as possible of the heavy investment from their initial startup. However, to the extent that premium pricing at this stage attracts more competitors, the long-run attractiveness of the market to any particular competitor is decreased. Having more competitors is likely to reduce the average profits of all competitors in the industry, create a more traumatic eventual market shakeout, and generally make the market more rivalrous. Thus, managers in this situation must balance the need for short-term returns with the need for long-term viability.

We expect developing critical technical expertise to be easier in the growth phase. During the earliest stages of a market's development, technology generally evolves toward a 'dominant design' – a fairly standard form of the basic product. For example, anyone developing a mass-production car today will design an internal combustion engine fueled with gasoline, because that is the dominant design incorporated into the plans of mechanics, service stations, and so on.[29] But in the earliest days of the automobile industry, many designs called for a steam-powered vehicle that burned wood or coal. Participation in the evolutionary process of defining the dominant design is often viewed as essential to achieving and maintaining a competitive position in terms of technological expertise. However, many followers have outperformed 'cutting-edge' firms whose technology they mimic. By avoiding the expense of pioneering R&D work, these firms are able to invest more in developing efficient manufacturing facilities or strong marketing programs. IBM's entry into personal computers was neither the earliest nor the most technologically sophisticated. In fact, in making its computers, the company largely depended upon components pioneered and produced elsewhere. But IBM's marketing investment far exceeded that of any competitor, and it was able to establish its operating software as a dominant design.

Maturity

More American businesses compete in mature markets than in any other stage of the life cycle. Markets in the mature stage of their life cycle have four characteristics in common. First, a lack of continued growth, which means that not all the firms that entered the market in the growth stage can be supported. Second, most of the key technology no longer benefits from patent protection. Third, cumulative experience can no longer provide an important advantage to any one competitor, since experience has reduced costs to the point that further reductions are difficult. Finally, there are few obvious forms of differentiation that are not already being pursued, so there is a growing trend to compete on the basis of price.

As it enters this phase, the market is beginning to stagnate, and a shakeout looms as a likely possibility.[30] This situation does not allow much opportunity for establishing a strong competitive advantage relative to the competition. It is difficult to gain an advantage that other competitors cannot copy, and the size of any particular competitive advantage is likely to be small relative to differences seen in other stages. As markets mature, the size of pricing and differentiation advantages among competitors typically decreases. Still, there is strong evidence to support the case that if an advantage can be realized, the returns to the competitor in this market can be impressive.

[. . .]

How do firms thrive in such hostile mature markets? As described earlier in the discussion of Du Pont's use of life cycle theories, as markets mature and decline, there is a tendency for the basis of competition to drift away from product differentiation and premium pricing, and toward price competition and commodity-like products. However, moving toward competition on the basis of pricing may not be the best strategy. Research in both the United States and Europe indicates that as markets mature, competition on the basis of differentiation is preferable to price competition.

For instance, a study of survivors and nonsurvivors in the US television market shakeout found that nonsurvivors were notable for placing their primary marketing emphasis on price even though they had no cost or price advantage.[32] Meanwhile, the survivors avoided price competition and instead offered products of superior quality at prices equivalent to the competition's. Studies of the corrugated cardboard and stainless steel industries in Europe produced similar results, leading the researchers to conclude that 'a "total quality" strategy seems to be the best differentiation strategy in stalemate industries.'[33]

Of course, the strongest competitive position is a combination of advantages. But, as data from research on these mature markets indicates, competing on the basis of differentiation achieved by quality alone can lead to good performance levels. It also has the advantage of minimizing the threat of a price war in the market.

Decline

Most markets will eventually be threatened by the development of substitute products, satiated demand, or changing customer needs. Consequently, they will face a period of decline. Often the market virtually disappears, as was the case with wooden power boats, horse-drawn farm implements, and mechanical adding machines. Others survive with a reduced demand, such as the market for home sewing notions or typewriters. In either case, the decline of the market means that the majority of competitors will face curtailed operations and possible shutdown. Yet, there are firms that survive and even thrive against these odds.[34] For example, Jostens, Inc., the maker of school rings, uses a greatly increased diversity of models and features and improved sales training to keep demand for its product growing. As a result, even though the number of high school graduates has been declining since 1976, both Jostens' sales and its profits have increased for 28 consecutive years. James B. Beam Distilling Co. has seen demand for its straight bourbon products fall sharply as the market moved toward white wines and other pale alcoholic beverages, such as gin and vodka. Yet its profits have reached record levels since it responded to this change in the market with the introduction of ZZZingers, a line of canned bourbon mixers.

Such examples are not meant to suggest that it is easy for firms to succeed when the overall market trend is one of decline.[35] In fact, it is rare for more than one or two competitors to survive severe market declines. Strategic management in the decline stage of the market life cycle must accurately assess an individual firm's viability, and this again reduces to an examination of what competitive advantage the firm can maintain. Where that advantage is not capable of supporting a business, the only rational response is to develop a strategy for 'milking' as much as possible from the business before terminating its operations. Where the firm's competitive advantage is sufficiently strong, the appropriate strategy may be one that positions the business as a long-term survivor of an otherwise disappearing market. In considering this range of strategies, four distinct alternatives emerge: divestment, harvesting, niche, and leadership.[36]

Divestment The natural response for many managers facing a declining market is to sell out. This is an appropriate response if it allows them to recover more of the investment than would be available from holding on to the business and implementing one of the other three strategies described below. The decision to divest is complicated by the importance and difficulty of moving quickly. Selling businesses late in a market's decline stage is understandably more difficult, and occasionally corporations will avoid this by selling businesses in mature markets before the 'fire sale' mentality that sometimes comes with the onset of market decline. However, because the market life cycle is notoriously poor at suggesting accurate short-run forecasts, managers run the risk of selling out a business which has a long and profitable life still ahead.

Though it may seem a 'clean' solution, sometimes divestment is not a practical option.[37] Often the present management team is the most knowledgeable available, and savvy new investors may not be attracted to competing in a declining market with an uninitiated management team. Interested buyers for firms in declining markets may already have some sort of association with the business being sold before it is offered for sale. Such buyers would include customers who wish to ensure supplies of key ingredients, employees who think they can save the company, and competitors who wish to consolidate the industry's capacity.

Harvest   Unlike divestment, a harvesting strategy is a process of gradually letting a business wither, in a carefully controlled and calculated fashion. Typically, businesses being harvested are managed in such a way that they produce cash flows that can be diverted to businesses elsewhere in the corporation that have more promising futures. This process typically includes a combination of tactics, such as curtailing any further investment, cutting maintenance expenditure, reducing marketing efforts, halting all R&D, and reducing the size of the managerial work force.

The side effects of this strategy are often problematic. Morale suffers as employees realize that their jobs may not be secure. Suppliers become leery of continued sales to a customer nearing shutdown, and customers become concerned about after-the-sale service. Managing a business through this phase can generate important cash flows, but it is sometimes difficult to get managers to implement a harvest strategy. Few management teams are willing to stake their careers on proving that they can excel at 'killing off' businesses.

Niche   As a market declines, there often remain pockets of demand capable of supporting one or more businesses. For instance, long after the development of integrated circuits brought on the general demise of the vacuum-tube market, there remained a market for replacement parts to service equipment with the older technology. Suppliers of these replacement parts enjoy a strong market position, because they have little competition and the demand for replacement parts is seldom price sensitive. Unfortunately, the low levels of demand typical of these residual markets are usually incapable of supporting more than one business, so it cannot be considered a solution for all competitors.

Leadership   The aim in pursuing this strategic option is to establish a firm in a dominant position so that it will essentially have the declining market to itself. This strategy requires lowering the 'exit barriers' that might keep competitors in the market. [. . .] Exit barriers are the mirror image of this concept, applied instead to competitors' leaving a market.
  [. . .]

Summary

In the long run, a business continues to be successful only if it sustains a competitive advantage over its competitors. Three forms of competitive advantage are differentiation, cost leadership, and quick response. (Though not a competitive advantage in its own right, market focus often impacts heavily on a firm's success in achieving competitive advantages.)

Differentiation, in which firms create products and/or services that customers value, is based on nonprice attributes, such as reputation, innovation, consistency, and service. Cost leadership results from practices, such as standardization and mass production, to operate at lower costs so the firm can realize higher-than-normal profits. The ability to provide a quick response to customer needs is a powerful competitive advantage. From filling an order to answering customer questions, to applying the latest innovations, quick response can deliver a competitive advantage that compares with that of the most differentiated or lower-cost competitors. Besides offering its own potential for competitive advantage, quick response can help make differentiation and cost leadership more effective. A firm that maintains more than one of these competitive advantages simultaneously will enjoy even greater measures of success.

Every business is different, as is the competitive environment it faces and the strategy it pursues. We can effectively capture many of these differences with the market life cycle model. While not a forecasting device, this framework helps to organize our thinking about the competitive environment through the use of chronological stages: introduction, growth, maturity, decline, and turnaround. Appropriate strategies vary according to the current phase of the market life cycle.

In the introduction stage, competitive advantages and market shares are being established that can impact competitors for years to come. In growth markets, shares are easily gained, prices are not under pressure, and foundations for long-term competitive advantages are being formed. In mature markets, patents lose protection, individual firms attempt their own workable forms of differentiation, and prices become more important to the customer. Declining markets are characterized by satiated consumer demand, obsolescence of technologies, and falling total market sales. However, the decline of a market need not signal disaster to a firm. Profitable alternatives including divestment, harvesting, locating a safe niche, and leadership as the sole survivor in the industry are all possible, if the business has the appropriate competitive positioning.

Perhaps the most dramatic of strategies is the turnaround. Determination and careful consideration can lead to comprehensive evaluation of a firm's problems, precise and purposeful cuts in facilities and personnel, and discovery of the appropriate grounds upon which to build a phoenix business. The key to success in formulating a winning turnaround strategy, like any other business-level strategy, rests on understanding, achieving, and maintaining a competitive advantage.

Notes

1. By far the most influential writer on the topic of competitive advantage, and perhaps business-level strategies in general, is Michael Porter. Throughout this chapter, we draw heavily upon his

work, especially in considering the competitive advantages of differentiation and cost leadership. Porter has written two books on the subject of business-level strategy: Porter, M.E. (1980), *Competitive Strategy*. New York: Free Press (in which chapters 2, 8, and 10 to 12 present thinking particularly relevant to this chapter); and Porter, M.E. (1985), *Competitive Advantage*. New York: Free Press (in which chapters 1, 3, and 4 are most relevant).

2. Historically, competitive advantages, such as differentiation and cost leadership, were viewed as incompatible, either-or options. But research has shown that this is not the case. See, for example, Phillips, L.W., Chang, D. and Buzzell, R.D. (1983, Spring), 'Product quality, cost position, and business performance: A test of some key hypotheses' *Journal of Marketing*, 47: 26–43; White, R.E. (1986), 'Generic business strategies, organizational context and performance: An empirical investigation', *Strategic Management Journal*, 7: 217–31; Dess, G.G. and Davis, P.S. (1984), 'Porter's generic strategies as determinants of strategic group membership and organizational performance', *Academy of Management Journal*, 27: 465–88; and Kim, L. and Lim, Y. (1988), 'Environment, generic strategies, and performance in a rapidly developing country: A taxonomic approach', *Academy of Management Journal*, 31: 802–27. For three important theoretical contributions which support the viability of combining business-level strategies, refer to Murray, A.I. (1988), 'A contingency view of Porter's generic strategies', *Academy of Management Review*, 13: 627–38; Hill, C.W.L. (1988), 'Differentiation versus low cost or differentiation and low cost: A contingency framework', *Academy of Management Review*, 13: 401–12; and Jones, G.R. and Butler, J.E. (1988), 'Costs, revenue and business-level strategy', *Academy of Management Review*, 13: 307–21.

3. South, S.E. (1981, Spring), 'Competitive advantage: The cornerstone of strategic thinking', *The Journal of Business Strategy*, 1: 16.

4. Abernathy, W.J. and Wayne, K. (1974, September–October), 'Limits of the learning curve', *Harvard Business Review*, 52, 109–19.

[. . .]

13. Anderson, C.R. and Zeithaml, C.P. (1984), 'Stage of the product life cycle, business strategy, and business performance', *Academy of Management Journal*, 27: 5–24.

14. Hambrick, D.C. and Lei, D. (1985), 'Toward an empirical prioritization of contingency variables for business strategy', *Academy of Management Journal*, 28: 763–88.

15. Hofer, C.W. (1975), 'Toward a contingency theory of business strategy', *Academy of Management Journal*, 18: 784–810.

16. Day, G. (1981), 'The product life cycle: Analysis and applications issues', *Journal of Marketing*, 45(4): 60–7.

17. Strategic implications of entry during other stages of the market life cycle are discussed in Covin, J.G. and Slevin, D.P. (1990), 'New venture strategic posture, structure, and performance: An industry life cycle analysis', *Journal of Business Venturing*, 5: 123–35.

18. Lieberman, M.B. and Montgomery, D.B. (1988, Summer), 'First mover advantages', *Strategic Management Journal*, 9: 41–58.

19. Mitchell, W. (1991, February), 'Dual clocks: Entry order influence on incumbent and newcomer market share and survival when specialized assets retain their value', *Strategic Management Journal*, 12: 85–100.

20. Lambkin, M. (1988), 'Order of entry and performance in new markets' [Special issue], *Strategic Management Journal*, 9: 127–40; Urban, G.L., Carter, T., Gaskin, S. and Muchia, Z. (1986) 'Market share rewards to pioneering brands: An empirical analysis and strategic implications', *Management Science*, 32(6): 645–59.

21. Miller, A., Gartner, W. and Wilson, R. (1989), 'Entry order, market share, and competitive advantage: A study of their relationships in new corporate ventures', *Journal of Business Venturing* 4: 197–209.

22. Robinson, W.T. and Fornell, C. (1985), 'Sources of market pioneer advantages in consumer goods industries', *Journal of Marketing Research*, 22(3): 305–17.

23. Whitten, I.T. (1979), *Brand Performance in the Cigarette Industry and the Importance of Early Entry, 1913–1973*. Washington, DC: Federal Trade Commission.

24. Porter, M. (1980), *Competitive Strategy*. New York: Free Press.

25. Schmalensee, R. (1982), 'Product differentiation advantages of pioneering brands', *American Economic Review*, 72: 159–80.

26. Utterback, J.M.A. and William, J. (1975), 'A dynamic model of process and product innovation', *Omega*, 3: 631.

27. This section is based on work found in Aaker, D.A. (1986, September–October), 'The perils of high-growth markets', *Strategic Management Journal*, 7: 409–21.

28. Miller, A. and Dewhirst, H.D. (1992), 'Technological intensity at a predictor vs. a moderator of the competitive responses to new entrants', *Journal of High Technology Management Research*, 3(1): 39–63.

29. Abernathy, W.J. and Utterback, J.M. (1978), 'Patterns of industrial innovation', *Technology Review*, 80(7): 41–7.

30. Calori, R. and Ardisson, J.M. (1988, May–June), 'Differentiation strategies in "Stalemate Industries"', *Strategic Management Journal*, 9: 255–69.

[. . .]

32. Willard, G.E. and Cooper, A.C. (1985), November–December), 'Survivors of industry shakeouts: The case of the US color television set industry', *Strategic Management Journal*, 6: 299–318.

33. Calori and Ardisson, 1988.

34. The examples given, as well as several others, are discussed in greater detail in Fierman, J. (1985), 'How to make money in mature markets', *Fortune*; 112(12): 40–7.

35. Cameron, K.S., Dutton, R.I. and Whetten, D.A. (1988), *Readings in Organizational Decline*. Cambridge, MA: Ballinger.

36. Discussion of these four types of strategies draws heavily upon Harrigan, K.R. and Porter, M.E. (1983, July–August), 'End-game strategies for declining industries', *Harvard Business Review*, 111–21.

37. Harrigan, K.R. (1984, Winter), 'Managing declining businesses', *Journal of Business Strategy*, 74–8.

4 Strategic Change and the Environment

Richard L. Daft and Karl E. Weick

[. . .] Organizations must make interpretations. Managers literally must wade into the ocean of events that surround the organization and actively try to make sense of them. Organization participants physically act on these events, attending to some of them, ignoring most of them, and talking to other people to see what they are doing (Braybrooke, 1964). Interpretation is the process of translating these events, of developing models for understanding, of bringing out meaning, and of assembling conceptual schemes among key managers.

The interpretation process in organizations is neither simple not well understood. There are many interpretation images in the literature, including scanning, monitoring, sense making, interpretation, understanding, and learning (Duncan and Weiss, 1979; Hedberg, 1981; Weick, 1979; Pfeffer and Salancik, 1978). These concepts can be roughly organized into three stages that constitute the overall learning process, as reflected in [Figure 4.1]. The first stage is *scanning*, which is defined as the process of monitoring the environment and providing environmental data to managers. Scanning is concerned with data collection. The organization may use formal data collection systems, or managers may acquire data about the environment through personal contacts.

Interpretation occurs in the second stage in [Figure 4.1]. Data are given meaning. Here the human mind is engaged. Perceptions are shared and cognitive maps are constructed. An information coalition of sorts is formed. The organization experiences interpretation when a new construct is introduced into the collective cognitive map of the organization. Organizational *interpretation* is formally defined as the process of translating events and developing shared understanding and conceptual schemes among members of upper management. Interpretation gives meaning to data, but it occurs before organizational learning and action.

Learning, the third stage, is distinguished from interpretation by the concept of action. Learning involves a new response or action based on the interpretation (Argyris and Schon, 1978). Organizational *learning* is defined as the process by which knowledge about action outcome relationships between the organization and the environment is developed (Duncan and Weiss, 1979). Learning is a process of putting cognitive theories into action (Argyris and

From 'Toward a model of organizations as interpretation systems', *Academy of Management Review*, 9(2): 294–95, 1984.

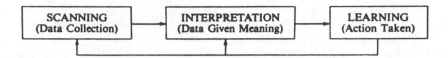

[Figure 4.1]   *Relationships among organizational scanning, interpretation, and learning*

Schon, 1978; Hedberg, 1981). Organizational interpretation is analogous to learning a new skill by an individual. The act of learning also provides new data for interpretation. Feedback from organizational actions may provide new collective insights for coalition members. Thus the three stages are interconnected through a feedback loop in [Figure 4.1].

[Figure 4.1] and the definitions of scanning, interpretation, and learning oversimplify complex processes. Factors such as beliefs, politics, goals, and perceptions may complicate the organizational learning cycle (Staw, 1980). The purpose of [Figure 4.1] is to illustrate the relationship of interpretation to scanning and learning as the basis for a model of organizational interpretation.

Toward a Model of Organizational Interpretation

Two key dimensions are used here to explain organizational interpretation differences. They are: (1) management's beliefs about the analyzability of the external environment and (2) the extent to which the organization intrudes into the environment to understand it. The proposed model provides a way to describe and explain the diverse ways organizations may obtain knowledge about the environment.

Assumptions About the Environment

[. . .] If an organization assumes that the external environment is concrete, that events and processes are hard, measurable, and determinant, then it will play the traditional game to discover the 'correct' interpretation. The key for this organization is discovery through intelligence gathering, rational analysis, vigilance, and accurate measurement. This organization will utilize linear thinking and logic and will seek clear data and solutions.

When an organization assumes that the external environment is unanalyzable, an entirely different strategy will apply. The organization to some extent may create the external environment. The key is to construct, coerce, or enact a reasonable interpretation that makes previous action sensible and suggests some next steps. The interpretation may shape the environment more than the environment shapes the interpretation. The interpretation process is more personal, less linear, more ad hoc and improvisational than for other organizations. The outcome of this process may include the ability to deal with equivocality, to coerce an answer useful to the organization, to invent an environment and be part of the invention.

What factors explain differences in organizational beliefs about the environment? The answer is hypothesized to be characteristics of the environment combined with management's previous interpretation experience. When the environment is subjective, difficult to penetrate, or changing (Duncan, 1972), managers will see it as less analyzable (Perrow, 1967; Tung, 1979). Wilensky's (1967) work on intelligence gathering in government organizations detected major differences in the extent to which environments were seen as rationalized, that is subject to discernible, predictable uniformities in relationships among significant objects. In one organization studied by Aguilar (1967), managers assumed an analyzable environment because of previous experience. Accurate forecasts were possible because product demand was directly correlated to petroleum demand, which in turn was correlated to well defined trends such as population growth, auto sales, and gasoline consumption. However, for a similar organization in another industry, systematic data collection and analysis were not used. Statistical trends had no correlation with product demand or capital spending. Facts and figures were not consistent with the unanalyzable assumptions about the environment. Soft, qualitative data, along with judgment and intuition, had a larger role in the interpretation process.

Organizational Intrusiveness

The second major difference among interpretation systems is the extent to which organizations actively intrude into the environment. Some organizations actively search the environment for an answer. They allocate resources to search activities. They hire technically oriented MBAs; build planning, forecasting, or special research departments; or even subscribe to monitoring services (Thomas, 1980). In extreme cases, organizations may send agents into the field (Wilensky, 1967). Organizational search also may include testing or manipulating the environment. These organizations may leap before they look, perform trials in order to learn what an error is, and discover what is feasible by testing presumed constraints. Forceful organizations may break presumed rules, try to change the rules, or try to manipulate critical factors in the environment (Kotter, 1979; Pfeffer, 1976). A survey of major corporations found that many of them established departments and mechanisms for searching and/or creating environments (Thomas, 1980). These organizations might be called test markers (Weick and Daft, 1983), and they will develop interpretations quite different from organizations that behave in a passive way.

Passive organizations accept whatever information the environment gives them. These organizations do not engage in trial and error. They do not actively search for the answer in the environment. They do not have departments assigned to discover or manipulate the environment. They may set up receptors to sense whatever data happen to flow by the organization. By accepting the environment as given, these organizations become test avoiders (Weick, 1979). They interpret the environment within accepted limits.

Research evidence suggests that many organizations are informal and unsystematic in their interpretation of the environment (Fahey and King, 1977). These organizations tend to accept the environment as given and respond actively only when a crisis occurs. For a crisis, the organization might search out new information or consciously try to influence external events. Other organizations actively search the environment on a continuous basis (Aguilar, 1967; Wilensky, 1967). Organizations thus differ widely in the active versus passive approach toward interpretation.

One explanation of differential intrusion into the environment is conflict between organization and environment. Wilensky (1967) argued that when the environment is perceived as hostile or threatening, or when the organization depends heavily on the environment, more resources are allocated to the intelligence gathering function. Organizations attempt to develop multiple lines of inquiry into the environment. In the corporate world, intense competition or resource scarcity will lead to allocation of more resources into interpretation-related functions. Organizations in benevolent environments have weaker incentives to be intrusive (Child, 1974; Hedberg, 1981). Only rarely do organizations in benevolent environments use their slack resources for trial and error experimentation or formal search. A hostile environment generates increased search because of new problems and a perceived need to develop new opportunities and niches. More exhaustive information is needed.

Another explanation of different levels of intrusion is organizational age and size (Kimberly and Miles, 1980). New, young organizations typically begin their existence as test makers. They try new things and actively seek information about their limited environment. Gradually, over time, the organization interpretation system begins to accept the environment rather than searching or testing its boundaries. New organizations are disbelievers, are unindoctrinated, and have less history to rely on. They are more likely to dive in and develop a niche that established organizations have failed to see. But as the organization grows and as time passes, the environment may be perceived as less threatening, so search will decrease.

The Model

Based on the idea that organizations may vary in their beliefs about the environment and in their intrusiveness into the environment, organizations can be categorized according to interpretation modes. The two underlying dimensions are used as the basis for an interpretation system model, presented in [Figure 4.2], which describes four categories of interpretation behaviour.

The *enacting* mode reflects both an active, intrusive strategy and the assumption that the environment is unanalyzable. These organizations construct their own environments. They gather information by trying new behaviours and seeing what happens. They experiment, test, and stimulate, and

	UNDIRECTED VIEWING Constrained interpretations. Nonroutine, informal data. Hunch, rumor, chance opportunities.	ENACTING Experimentation, testing, coercion, invent environment. Learn by doing.
CONDITIONED VIEWING Interprets within traditional boundaries. Passive detection. Routine, formal data.	DISCOVERING Formal search. Questioning, surveys, data gathering. Active detection.

Unanalyzable

ASSUMPTIONS
ABOUT
ENVIRONMENT

Analyzable

Passive   Active
ORGANIZATIONAL INTRUSIVENESS

[Figure 4.2] *Model of organizational interpretation modes*

they ignore precedent, rules, and traditional expectations. This organization is highly activated, perhaps under the belief that it must be so in order to succeed. This type of organization tends to develop and market a product, such as polaroid cameras, based on what it thinks it can sell. An organization in this mode tends to construct markets rather than waiting for an assessment of demand to tell it what to produce. These organizations, more than others, tend to display the enactment behaviour described by Weick (1979).

The *discovering* mode also represents an intrusive organization, but the emphasis is on detecting the correct answer already in an analyzable environment rather than on shaping the answer. Carefully devised measurement probes are sent into the environment to relay information back to the organization. This organization uses market research, trend analysis, and forecasting to predict problems and opportunities. Formal data determine organizational interpretations about environmental characteristics and expectations. Discovering organizations are similar to organizations that rely on formal search procedures for information (Aguilar, 1967) and in which staff analysts are used extensively to gather and analyze data (Wilensky, 1967).

Organizations characterized as *conditioned viewing* (Aguilar, 1967) assume an analyzable environment and are not intrusive. They tend to rely on established data collection procedures, and the interpretations are developed within traditional boundaries. The environment is perceived as objective and benevolent, so the organization does not take unusual steps to learn about the environment. The viewing is conditioned in the sense that it is limited to the routine documents, reports, publications, and information systems that have grown up through the years. The view of the environment is limited to these traditional sources. At some time historically, these data were perceived as important, and the organization is now conditioned to them. Organizations in this category use procedures similar to the regular scanning of limited sectors described by Fahey and King (1977)

Undirected viewing (Aguilar, 1967) reflects a similar passive approach, but these organizations do not rely on hard, objective data because the environment is assumed to be unanalyzable. Managers act on limited, soft information to create their perceived environment. These organizations are not conditioned by formal management systems within the organization, and they are open to a variety of cues about the environment from many sources. Managers in these organizations are like the ones Aguilar (1967) found that relied on information obtained through personal contacts and causal information encounters. Fahey and King (1977) also found some organizational information gatherings to be irregular and based on chance opportunities.

Examples of conditioned and undirected viewing modes have been illustrated by clothing companies in England (Daft and Macintosh, 1978). These companies developed different interpretation systems over time, although they were in a similar industry. Top management in the conditioned viewing organization used a data collection system to record routinely such things as economic conditions, past sales, and weather forecasts. These data were used to predict sales and to schedule production. These systems had grown up over the years and were used routinely to interpret problems that occurred. The other company gathered information from personal contacts with a few store buyers, salesmen, and informants in other companies. Managers also visited a few stores to observe and discuss in a casual manner what seemed to be selling. This company used undirected viewing. Interpretation was based on a variety of subjective cues that happened to be available.

Another example of interpretation styles is illustrated by the relationship between corporations and their shareholders (Keim, 1981). A few corporations actively influence and shape shareholder attitudes. The enacting organization may try to manipulate shareholder perceptions toward itself, environment issues, or political candidates by sending information to shareholders through various media. Discovery-oriented corporations actively stay in touch with shareholders to learn what they are thinking, and they conduct surveys or use other devices to discover attitudes. A few corporations handle the shareholder relationships through routine data transactions (stockholder voting, mailing and dividend checks), which is typical of conditioned viewing. Finally, some corporations rely on informal, personal contact with shareholders (undirected viewing). Managers use whatever opportunities arise (annual meetings, telephone contact about complaints and questions) to learn shareholders' opinions and to adapt to those opinions.

Other Organizational Characteristics

The model can be completed by making predictions about other organizational characteristics associated with interpretation modes. The predictions pertain

Unanalyzable	**UNDIRECTED VIEWING** Scanning Characteristics: 1. Data source: external, personal. 2. Acquisition: no scanning department, irregular contacts and reports, casual information. Interpretation Process: 1. Much equivocality reduction 2. Few rules, many cycles Strategy and Decision Making: 1. Strategy: reactor. 2. Decision process: coalition building.	**ENACTING** Scanning Characteristics: 1. Data source: external, personal. 2. Acquisition: no department, irregular reports and feedback from environment, selective information. Interpretation Process: 1. Some equivocality reduction 2. Moderate rules and cycles Strategy and Decision Making: 1. Strategy: prospector. 2. Decision process: incremental trial and error.
ASSUMPTIONS ABOUT ENVIRONMENT	**CONDITIONED VIEWING** Scanning Characteristics: 1. Data source: internal, impersonal. 2. Acquisition: no department, although regular record keeping and information systems, routine information. Interpretation Process: 1. Little equivocality reduction 2. Many rules, few cycles Strategy and Decision Making: 1. Strategy: defender. 2. Decision process: programmed, problemistic search.	**DISCOVERING** Scanning Characteristics: 1. Data sources: internal, impersonal. 2. Acquisition: separate departments, special studies and reports, extensive information. Interpretation Process: 1. Little equivocality reduction 2. Many rules, moderate cycles Strategy and Decision Making: 1. Strategy: analyzer. 2. Decision process: systems analysis, computation.
Analyzable		

Passive   Active
ORGANIZATIONAL INTRUSIVENESS

[Figure 4.3]   *Relationship between interpretation modes and organizational process*

to: (1) scanning and data characteristics; (2) the interpretation process within the organization; and (3) the strategy and decision processes that characterize each mode. The predicted relationships with interpretation modes are shown in [Figure 4.3]

Scanning Characteristics

Scanning characteristics pertain to the nature and acquisition of data for top management about the environment. The data may vary by source and acquisition, depending on the interpretation mode of the organization.

1. *Data Sources.* Data about the environment can come to managers from

external or internal sources, and from personal or impersonal sources (Aguilar, 1967; Daft and Lengel, 1984; Keegan 1974). Sources are external when managers have direct contact with information outside the organization. Internal sources pertain to data collected about the environment by other people in the organization and then provided to managers through internal channels. Personal sources involve direct contact with other individuals. Impersonal sources pertain to written documentation such as newspapers and magazines or reports from the organization's information system.

Generally, the less analyzable the perceived external environment the greater the tendency for managers to use external information gained from personal contact with other managers. Organizations characterized as undirected viewing will obtain most of their information from the relationship of senior managers with colleagues in the environment (Keegan, 1974). Managers in enacting organizations also will use personal observations to a large extent, although this information often will be obtained through experimentation and from trying to impose ideas on the environment. When the environment is analyzable, a larger percentage of the data will be conveyed through the management information system. The discovering organization also will use internal, formal reports, although these reports are the outcome of specialized inquiries rather than a routine, periodic reporting system.

2. *Data Acquisition.* Organizational mechanisms for acquiring information and the regularity of acquisition are other distinguishing characteristics of organizational scanning (Fahey and King, 1977). Discovering organizations will allocate many resources to data acquisition. Special departments typically will be used to survey and study the environment. Regular reports and special studies will go to top managers. Conditioned viewing organizations will have regular reports available through the formal information system of the organization. These organizations will devote few resources to external scanning.

Undirected viewing organizations will make little use of formal management information. Data will tend to be irregular and casual. Scanning departments are not needed; formal reports will be ad hoc and irregular. The enacting organization also will use data that are somewhat irregular and will reflect feedback about selected environmental initiatives. The general pattern across organizations is that environmental information is more regular when the environment is analyzable, and more studies and information are available when the organization is active in information acquisition.

Interpretation Process

Interpretation pertains to the process by which managers translate data into knowledge and understanding about the environment. This process will vary according to the means for equivocality reduction and the assembly rules that govern information processing behavior among managers.

1. *Equivocality Reduction.* Equivocality is the extent to which data are unclear and suggest multiple interpretations about the environment (Daft and Macintosh, 1981; Weick, 1979). Managers in all organizations will experience some equivocality in their data. Equivocality reduction will be greatest in organizations characterized as undirected viewing. External cues of a personal nature are subject to multiple interpretations. Managers will discuss these cues extensively to arrive at a common interpretation. Equivocality is reduced through shared observations and discussion until a common grammar and course of action can be agreed on (Weick, 1979). The enacting organization also will experience high equivocality, which will be reduced more on the basis of taking action to see what works than by interpreting events in the environment. Information equivocality generally is lower in the conditioned viewing and discovering organizations. Some equivocality reduction takes place before the data reach managers. Specialists will routinize the data for periodic reports and perform systematic analyses and special studies. The data thus provide a more uniform stimulus to managers, and less discussion is needed to reach a common interpretation.

2. *Assembly Rules.* Assembly rules are the procedures or guides that organizations use to process data into a collective interpretation. The content of these rules and the extent to which they are enforced depend on the organization. Generally, the greater the equivocality in the data, the fewer the number of rules used to arrive at an interpretation. Conversely, the smaller the perceived equivocality of data entering the organization, the greater the number of rules used to assemble the interpretation (Weick, 1979).

Fewer rules are used for equivocal information inputs because there is uncertainty as to exactly what the information means. Only a small number of rather general rules can be used to assemble the process. If the input is less equivocal, there is more certainty as to what the item is and how it should be handled. Hence a greater number of rules can be assigned to handle the data and assemble an interpretation (Putnam and Sorenson, 1982).

The number of information cycles among top management follows a similar logic. The greater the equivocality, the more times the data may be cycled among members before a common interpretation is reached. The lower the equivocality, the fewer cycles needed. The number of assembly rules and cycles tends to be inversely related.

Undirected viewing organizations, which receive equivocal information, will have few rules but will use many internal cycles during the course of assembling an interpretation. By contrast, managers within a directed viewing organization receive unequivocal information that will be handled according to numerous rules, but few cycles are needed to reach a common understanding. The discovering organization also will use many rules, although a moderate number of cycles may be needed because of some equivocality in the reports and data presented to managers. The equivocality in interpreting the success of initiatives in the enacting organization will be associated with the moderate number of assembly rules and information cycles.

Strategy Formulation and Decision Making

The variables described above are directly related to the scanning and interpretation behaviors through which organizations learn about and make sense of the external environment. Two additional variables – strategy formulation and decision making – may be associated with interpretation modes. The hypothesized relationships with interpretation modes also are shown in Figure 4.3.

1. *Strategy Formulation.* Miles and Snow (1978) proposed that corporations can be organized according to four types of strategies: prospector, analyzer, defender, and reactor. Strategy formulation is the responsibility of top management and thus may be related to environmental conditions that are similar to interpretation modes. The prospector strategy reflects a high level of initiative with regard to the environment. The environment is seen as changing and as containing opportunities. The organization develops new products and undertakes new initiatives. This is consistent with the enacting mode of interpretation. The analyzer organization is more careful. It is concerned with maintaining a stable core of activities but with occasional innovations on the periphery if the environment permits. This strategy is consistent with the discovering orientation, in which the organization studies the environment and moves ahead only in a careful, constrained way.

The defender strategy is one in which top management perceives the environment as analyzable and stable and the management is determined to protect what it has. This organization is concerned with maintaining traditional markets and is focused on internal efficiency rather than on external relationships. The defender strategy will tend to be related to the conditioned viewing mode of interpretation. Finally, the reactor strategy is not really a strategy at all. The organization moves along, more or less accepting what comes. This organization will react to seemingly random changes in the environment. Scanning behavior in this organization is based on casual data from personal contact rather than from specialized information systems. The reactor strategy will be associated with the interpretation mode classified as undirected viewing.

2. *Decision Making.* The organizational literature suggests that organizations make decisions in various ways. Organizational decisions may be influenced by coalition building and political processing (Cyert and March, 1963); by incremental decision steps (Lindblom, 1959; Mintzberg, Raisinghani and Théoret, 1976); by systems analysis and rational procedures (Leavitt, 1975); and by programmed responses to routine problems (March and Simon, 1958; Simon, 1960). Decision making generally is part of the information and interpretation processes in organizations; it thus is posed that decision processes may be associated with interpretation modes.

In undirected viewing organizations, the environment is not analyzable. Factors cannot be rationalized to the point of using rational decision models. Managers respond to divergent, personal cues, and extensive discussion and coalition building are required to agree on a single interpretation and course of action. Managers will spend time making sense of what happened and reaching agreements about problems before proceeding to a solution.

In enacting organizations, by contrast, a more assertive decision style will appear. The enacting organization does not have precedent to follow. A good idea, arrived at subjectively, may be implemented to see if it works. Enacting organizations utilize the trial and error incremental process described by Mintzberg et al. (1976). When organizations decide on a course of action, they design a custom solution and try it. If the solution does not work, they have to recycle and try again. Enacting organizations move ahead incrementally and gain information about the environment by trying behaviors and seeing what works.

Discovering organizations also take an active approach, but they assume that the environment is analyzable. Here the emphasis is on rational understanding. Systems analysis will be an important decision tool. Operational researchers and other staff personnel will perform computations on environmental data and weigh alternatives before proceeding. This organization's decision process will be characterized by logic and analysis. Solutions will not be tried until alternatives have been carefully weighed.

Finally, directed viewing organizations may be considered the easiest situation for decision makers. The organization is passive and operates in an analyzable environment. Decision making by managers is programmed. Programs are built into the organization to describe reactions to external events based on previous experience. Rules and regulations cover most activities and are applied unless a genuine crisis erupts. Crises will be rare, but if one occurs, managers will respond with problemistic search (March and Simon, 1958). Problemistic search means that the organization performs a local search through its immediate memory bank for a solution. Only after exhausting traditional responses will the organization move toward a new response of some sort.

Implications

The purpose of this chapter is to present a model of organizations as interpretation systems and to bring together a number of ideas that are related to interpretation behavior. The two variables underlying the model are (1) management's beliefs about the analyzability of the external environment and (2) organizational intrusiveness. These variables are consistent with empirical investigations of interpretation behavior (Aguilar, 1967; Wilensky, 1967), and they are the basis for four modes of interpretation – enacting, discovering, undirected viewing, and conditioned viewing. The model explains interpretation behaviors ranging from environmental enactment to passive observation. The model also makes predictions about scanning characteristics, interpretation processes, and top management strategy and decision behavior.

References

Aguilar, F. *Scanning the Business Environment*. New York: Macmillan, 1967.

Argyris, C. and Schon, D.A. *Organizational Learning: A Theory of Action Perspective*. Reading, Mass.: Addison-Wesley, 1978.

Braybrooke, D. 'The mystery of executive success re-examined', *Administrative Science Quarterly*, 8: 533–60, 1964.

Child, J. 'Organization, management and adaptiveness', Working paper, University of Aston, 1974.

Cyert, R.M. and March, J.G. *A Behavioral Theory of the Firm*. Englewood Cliffs, NJ: Prentice-Hall, 1963.

Daft, R.L. and Lengel, R.H. 'Information richness: A new approach to manager behavior and organization design', in B. Staw and L.L. Cummings (eds), *Research in Organizational Behavior*, Greenwich, Conn.: JAI Press, 4: 141–90, 1984.

Daft, R.L. and Macintosh, N.B. 'A new approach to design and use of management information', *California Management Review*, 21(1): 82–92, 1978.

Daft, R.L. and Macintosh, N.B. 'A tentative exploration into the amount and equivocality of information processing in organizational work units', *Administrative Science Quarterly*, 26: 207–24, 1981.

Duncan, R.B. 'Characteristics of organizational environments and perceived environmental uncertainty', *Administrative Science Quarterly*, 17: 313–27, 1972.

Duncan, R.B. and Weiss, A. 'Organizational learning: Implications for organizational design', in B. Staw (ed.), *Research in Organizational Behavior* (vol. 1), Greenwich, Conn.: JAI Press, 1979, pp. 75–123.

Fahey, L. and King, W.R. 'Environmental scanning for corporate planning', *Business Horizons*, 20(4): 61–71, 1977.

Hedberg, B. 'How organizations learn and unlearn', in P. Nystrom and W. Starbuck (eds), *Handbook of Organizational Design*. New York: Oxford University Press, 1981, pp. 1–27.

Keegan, W.J. 'Multinational scanning: A study of information sources utilized by headquarters executives in multinational companies', *Administrative Science Quarterly*, 19: 411–21, 1974.

Keim, G.D. 'Foundations of a political strategy for business', *California Management Review*, 23: 41–8, 1981.

Kimberly, J.R. and Miles, R.H. *The Organizational Life Cycle*. San Francisco: Jossey-Bass, 1980.

Kotter, J.P. 'Managing external dependence', *Academy of Management Review*, 4: 87–92, 1979.

Lindblom, C. 'The science of "muddling through"', *Public Administration Review*, 19(2): 79–88, 1959.

March, J.G. and Simon, H.A. *Organizations*. New York: Wiley, 1958.

Miles, R.E. and Snow, C.C. *Organizational Strategy, Structure and Process*. New York: McGraw-Hill, 1978.

Mintzberg, H., Raisinghani, D. and Théoret, A. 'The structure of "unstructured" decision processes', *Administrative Science Quarterly*, 21: 246–75, 1976.

Newsweek, 12 March 1979, 62.

Perrow, C. A framework for the comparative analysis of organizations. *American Sociological Review*, 32: 194–208, 1967.

Pfeffer, J. 'Beyond management and the worker: The institutional function of management', *Academy of Management Review*, 1(2): 36–46, 1976.

Pfeffer, J. and Salancik, G.R. *The External Control of Organizations: A Resource Dependence Perspective*. New York: Harper & Row, 1978.

Putnam, L.L. and Sorenson, R.L. 'Equivocal messages in organizations', *Human Communication Research*, 8(2): 114–32, 1982.

Simon, H.A. *The New Science of Management Decision*. Englewood Cliffs, NJ: Prentice-Hall, 1960.

Staw, B.M. 'Rationality and justification in organizational life', in B.M. Staw and L.L. Cummings (eds), *Research in Organizational Behavior* (vol. 2). Greenwich, Conn.: JAI Press, 1980, pp. 45–80.

Thomas, T.S. 'Environmental scanning – The state of the art', *Long Range Planning*, 13(1): 20–8, 1980.

Tung, R.L. 'Dimensions of organizational environment: An exploratory study of their impact on organization structure', *Academy of Management Journal*, 22: 672–93, 1979.

Weick, K. *The Social Psychology of Organizing*. Reading, Mass.: Addison-Wesley, 1979.

Weick, K.E. and Daft, R.L. 'The effectiveness of interpretation systems', in K.S. Cameron and D.A. Whetten (eds), *Organizational Effectiveness: A Comparison of Multiple Models*. New York: Academic Press, 1983, pp. 71–93.

Wilensky, H.L. *Organizational Intelligence*. New York: Basic Books, 1967.

5 Strategy and Structure

Arthur A. Thompson Jr and A.J. Strickland III

[. . .] In a number of respects, the strategist's approach to organization building is governed by the size of growth stage of the enterprise, as well as by the key success factors inherent in the organization's business. For instance, the type of organization structure that suits a small specialty steel firm relying upon a concentration strategy in a regional market is not likely to be suitable for a large, vertically-integrated steel producer doing business in geographically diverse areas. The organization form that works best in a multi-product, multi-technology, multi-business corporation pursuing a conglomerate diversification strategy is, understandably, likely to be different yet again. Recognition of this characteristic has prompted several attempts to formulate a model linking changes in organizational structure to stages in an organization's strategic development.[6]

The underpinning of the stages concept is that enterprises can be arrayed along a continuum running from very simple to very complex organizational forms and that there is a tendency for an organization to move along this continuum toward more complex forms as it grows in size, market coverage, and product line scope and as the strategic aspects of its customer–technology–business portfolio become more intricate. Four distinct stages of strategy-related organization structure have been singled out.

Stage I A Stage I organization is essentially a small, single business enterprise managed by one person. The owner-entrepreneur has close daily contact with employees and each phase of operations. Most employees report directly to the owner, who makes all the pertinent decisions regarding objectives, strategy, daily operations, and so on. As a consequence, the organization's strengths, vulnerabilities, and resources are closely allied with the entrepreneur's personality, management ability and style, and personal financial situation. Not only is a Stage I enterprise an extension of the interests, abilities, and limitations of its owner-entrepreneur but also its activities are typically concentrated in just one line of business. For the most part, today's Stage I enterprise is epitomized by small firms run by 'independent businesspersons' who are 'their own bosses' and, typically, such firms have a strategy which centres around a single product, market, technology, or channel of distribution.

From *Strategy Formulation and Implementation*. Plano, TX: Business Publications (rev. ed.) 1983.

Stage II Stage II organizations differ from Stage I enterprises in one essential respect: an increased scale and scope of operations create a pervasive strategic need for management specialization and force a transition from one-person management to group management. However, a Stage II enterprise, although run by a team of managers with functionally-specialized responsibilities, remains fundamentally a single business operation. This is not to imply, though, that the categories of management specialization are uniform among large, single-business enterprises. In practice, there is wide variation. Some Stage II organizations prefer to divide strategic responsibilities along classic functional lines – marketing, production, finance, personnel, control, engineering, public relations, procurement, planning, and so on. In other Stage II companies functional specialization is keyed to distinct production units; for example, the organizational building blocks of a vertically-integrated oil company may consist of exploration, drilling, pipelines, refining, wholesale distribution, and retail sales. In a process-oriented Stage II company, the functionally sequenced units aim primarily at synchronizing the flow of output between them.

Stage III Stage III embraces those organizations whose operations, though concentrated in a single field or product line, are large enough and scattered over a wide geographical area to justify having *geographically decentralized* operating units. These units all report to corporate headquarters and conform to corporate policies but they are given the flexibility to tailor their unit's strategic plan to meet the specific needs of each respective geographic area. Ordinarily, each of the semi-autonomous operating units of a Stage III organization is structured along functional lines. The key difference between Stage II and Stage III, however, is that while the functional units of a Stage II organization stand or fall together (in that they are built around one business and one end market), the operating units of a Stage III firm can stand alone (or nearly so) in the sense that the operations in each geographic unit are not rigidly tied to or dependent on those in other areas. Characteristic firms in this category would be breweries, cement companies, and steel mills having production capacity and sales organizations in several geographically separate market areas. Corey and Star cite Pfizer International as being a good example of a company whose strategic requirements in 1964 made geographic decentralization propitious:

> With sales of $223 million in 1964, Pfizer International operated plants in 27 countries and marketed in more than 100 countries. Its product lines included pharmaceuticals (antibiotics and other ethical prescription drugs), agriculture and veterinary products (such as animal feed supplements and vaccines, and pesticides), chemicals (fine chemicals, bulk pharmaceuticals, petrochemicals and plastics), and consumer products (cosmetics and toiletries).
>
> Ten geographic Area Managers reported directly to the President of Pfizer International and exercised line supervision over Country Managers. According to a company position description, it was 'the responsibility of each Area Manager to plan, develop, and carry out Pfizer International's business in the assigned foreign area in keeping with company policies and goals.'

Country Managers had profit responsibility. In most cases a single Country Manager managed all Pfizer activities in his country. In some of the larger, well-developed countries of Europe there were separate Country Managers for pharmaceutical and agricultural products and for consumer lines.

Except for the fact that New York headquarters exercised control over the to-the-market prices of certain products, especially prices of widely used pharmaceuticals, Area and Country Managers had considerable autonomy in planning and managing the Pfizer International business in their respective geographic areas. This was appropriate because each area, and some countries within areas, provided unique market and regulatory environments. In the case of pharmaceuticals and agriculture and veterinary products (Pfizer International's most important lines) national laws affected formulations, dosages, labeling, distribution, and often price. Trade restrictions affected the flow of bulk pharmaceuticals and chemicals and packaged products, and might in effect require the establishment of manufacturing plants to supply local markets. Competition, too, varied significantly from area to area.[7]

Stage IV Stage IV is typified by large, multi-product, multi-unit, multi-market enterprises decentralized by line of business. Their corporate strategies emphasize diversification, concentric and/or conglomerate. As with Stage III companies, the semi-autonomous operating units report to a corporate headquarters and conform to certain firm-wide policies, but the divisional units pursue their own respective line of business strategies. Typically, each separate business unit is headed by a general manager who has profit and loss responsibility and whose authority extends across all of the unit's functional areas except, perhaps, accounting and capital investment (both of which are traditionally subject to corporate approval). Both strategic decisions and operating decisions are thus concentrated at the divisional level rather than at the corporate level. The organizational structure of the business unit may be along the lines of Stage I, II or III types of organizations. Characteristic Stage IV companies include General Electric, ITT, Procter & Gamble, General Foods, Textron, and DuPont.

Movement through the Stages From our perspective, the stages model provides useful insights into why organization structure tends to change in accordance with product-market-technology relationships and new directions in corporate strategy. As firms have progressed from small, entrepreneurial enterprises following a basic concentration strategy to more complex strategic phases of volume expansion, vertical integration, geographic expansion, and product diversification, their organizational structures have evolved from unifunctional to functionally centralized to multi-divisional decentralized organizational forms. Firms that remain single-line businesses almost always have some form of a centralized functional structure. Enterprises which are predominantly in one industry but which are slightly diversified typically have a hybrid structure; the dominant business is managed via a functional organization and the diversified activities are handled through a divisionalized form. The more diversified an organization becomes, irrespective of whether the diversification is along either concentric or conglomerate lines, the more it moves toward some form of decentralized business units.

However, it is by no means imperative that organizations begin at Stage I and move sequentially toward Stage IV.[8] US Rubber (now Uniroyal) moved from a Stage II organization to a Stage IV form without ever passing through Stage III. And some organizations exhibit characteristics of two or more stages simultaneously. Sears, at one time, was decentralized geographically for store operations, personnel, sales promotion, banking, inventory and warehousing, and maintenance, yet centralized for manufacturing and procurement of goods, thus overlapping the organization structures of Stage II and III. Furthermore, some companies have found it desirable to retreat into prior stages after entering a particular stage. For example, the DuPont Textile Fibers Department originated out of five separate, decentralized, fully-integrated fiber businesses – rayon, acetate, nylon, 'Orlon,' and 'Dacron.'[9] Many weavers and other industrial users bought one or more of these fibers and used them in significantly different ways that also required different application technologies. According to Corey and Star:

> Customers objected to being solicited by five DuPont salesmen each promoting a different type of synthetic fiber and each competing with the others. Users of synthetic fibers wanted sales representatives from DuPont who understood their product lines and production processes and who could serve as a source of useful technical ideas.[10]

As a consequence, DuPont consolidated all five units into a Textile Fibers Department in an effort to deal more effectively with these customers. The new department established a single multifiber field sales force and set up market programs for four broad market segments – men's wear, women's wear, home furnishings, and industrial products – each of which had a potential demand for all five fibers.

In general, then, owing to the several ways which product-market relationships and strategy may turn, the paths along which an organization's structure may develop are more complex and variable than suggested by a single pattern of moving in sequence from Stage I through Stage IV. Still, it does appear that as the strategic emphasis shifts from small, single-product businesses to large, dominant-product businesses and then on to concentric or conglomerate diversification, a firm's organizational structure evolves, in turn, from one-man management to large group functional management to decentralized, line-of-business management. This is substantiated by the fact that about 90 per cent of the Fortune 500 firms (nearly all of which are diversified to one degree or another) have a divisionalized organizational structure with the primary basis for decentralization being line of business considerations.

One final lesson that the stages model teaches is worth iterating. A reassessment of organization structure and authority is always useful whenever strategy is changed.[11] A new strategy is likely to entail modifications in what the critical tasks and key activities are. If these changes go unrecognized, the resulting mismatch in strategy requirements and organization design creates an opening for strategic performance to be unnecessarily short of its potential.

The Strategy-Related Pros and Cons of Alternative Organization Forms

There are essentially six strategy-related approaches to organization: (1) functional specialization, (2) geographic organization, (3) departmentalization keyed to differences in processing stage, market channel, or customer class, (4) decentralized business/product divisions, (5) strategic business units, and (6) matrix structures featuring *dual* lines of authority and strategic priority. Each form relates structure to strategy in a different way and, consequently, has its own set of strategy-related pros and cons.

The Functional Organization Structure A functional organization structure tends to be effective whenever a firm's critical tasks and key activities revolve around well-defined skills and areas of specialization. In such cases, in-depth specialization and focused concentration on performing functional areas tasks and activities can enhance both operating efficiency and the development of a distinctive competence. Generally speaking, organizing by functional specialities promotes full utilization of the most up-to-date technical skills and helps a business capitalize on the efficiency gains to be had from using specialized manpower, facilities, and equipment. These are strategically important considerations for single-business organizations, dominant-product enterprises, and vertically-integrated firms, and accounts for why they usually have some kind of centralized, functionally specialized structure.

However, just what form the functional specialization will take varies according to customer–product–technology considerations. For instance, a technical instruments manufacturer may be organized around research and development, engineering, production, technical services, quality control, marketing, personnel, finance and accounting. A municipal government may, on the other hand, be departmentalized according to purposeful function – fire, public safety, health services, water and sewer, streets, parks and recreation, and education. A university may divide its organizational units up into academic affairs, student services, alumni relations, athletics, buildings and grounds, institutional services, and budget control. A typical functional structure is diagrammed in [Figure 5.1].

The Achilles heel of a functional structure is proper coordination of the separated functional units. Functional specialists, partly because of their trading and the technical nature of their jobs, tend to develop their own mindset and ways of doing things. The more that functional specialists differ in their perspectives and their approaches to task accomplishment, the more difficult it becomes to achieve both strategic and operating coordination between them. They neither 'talk the same language' nor have an adequate understanding and appreciation for one another's problems and approaches. Each functional group is more interested in its own 'empire' and sets its priorities accordingly (despite the lip service given to cooperation and 'what's

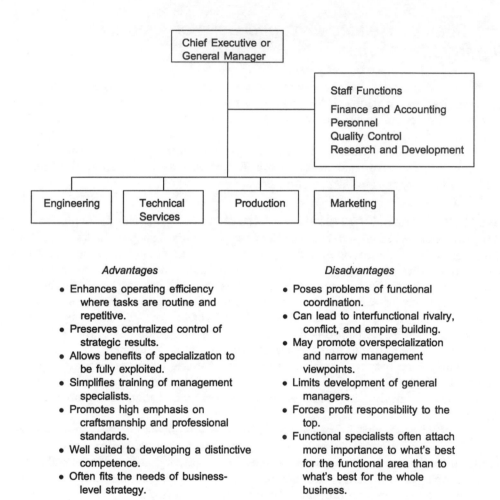

Advantages

- Enhances operating efficiency where tasks are routine and repetitive.
- Preserves centralized control of strategic results.
- Allows benefits of specialization to be fully exploited.
- Simplifies training of management specialists.
- Promotes high emphasis on craftsmanship and professional standards.
- Well suited to developing a distinctive competence.
- Often fits the needs of business-level strategy.

Disadvantages

- Poses problems of functional coordination.
- Can lead to interfunctional rivalry, conflict, and empire building.
- May promote overspecialization and narrow management viewpoints.
- Limits development of general managers.
- Forces profit responsibility to the top.
- Functional specialists often attach more importance to what's best for the functional area than to what's best for the whole business.

[Figure 5.1] *A functional organization structure (manufacturing company)*

best for the company'). This, in turn, can create a time-consuming administrative burden on a general manager in terms of resolving cross-functional differences, enforcing joint cooperation, and opening lines of communication. In addition, as will be discussed below, a purely functional organization is ill-suited for multi-business organizations; it works well within a single business but not across businesses.

Geographic Forms of Organization Organizing according to geographic areas or territories is a rather common structural form for large-scale enterprises whose strategies need to be tailored to fit the particular needs and features of different geographical areas. As indicated in [Figure 5.2], geographic organization has its advantages and disadvantages but the chief

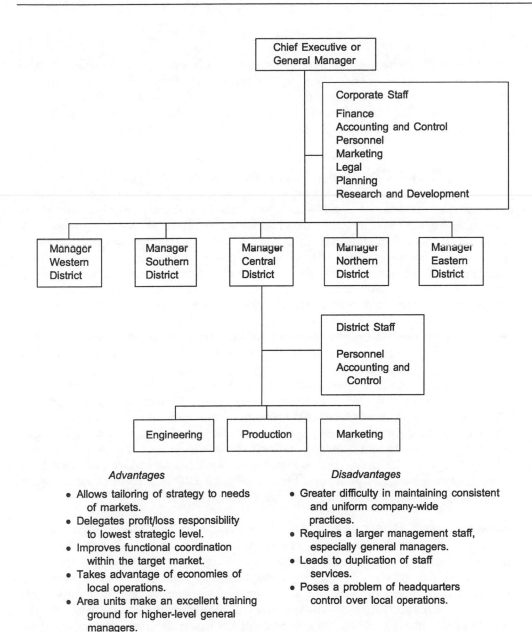

Chief Executive or General Manager

Corporate Staff

Finance
Accounting and Control
Personnel
Marketing
Legal
Planning
Research and Development

Manager Western District

Manager Southern District

Manager Central District

Manager Northern District

Manager Eastern District

District Staff

Personnel
Accounting and Control

Engineering

Production

Marketing

Advantages	*Disadvantages*
• Allows tailoring of strategy to needs of markets.	• Greater difficulty in maintaining consistent and uniform company-wide practices.
• Delegates profit/loss responsibility to lowest strategic level.	• Requires a larger management staff, especially general managers.
• Improves functional coordination within the target market.	• Leads to duplication of staff services.
• Takes advantage of economies of local operations.	• Poses a problem of headquarters control over local operations.
• Area units make an excellent training ground for higher-level general managers.	

[Figure 5.2] *A geographic organizational structure*

reason for its popularity is that, for one reason or another, it promotes improved performance.

In the private sector, a territorial structure is typically utilized by chain store retailers, cement firms, railroads, airlines, the larger paper box and carton manufacturers, and large bakeries and dairy products enterprises; the member companies of American Telephone and Telegraph which make up the

Bell Telephone System all represent geographically decentralized units. In the public sector, such organizations as the Internal Revenue Service, the Small Business Administration, the federal courts, the US Postal Service, the state troopers, the Red Cross, and religious groups have adopted territorial departmentation in order to be directly accessible to geographically dispersed clienteles.

Process, Market Channel, or Customer-Based Organization   Grouping an enterprise's activities according to production stages, market channels, or customer groups fits situations where business strategy is grounded in achieving operating economies or in catering to distinct buyer segments. A metal parts manufacturer may find it operationally efficient to subdivide in series, thus having foundry, forging, machining, finishing, assembly, and painting departments. Firms with a diverse clientele may find it strategically useful to break their distribution and marketing activities down into subgroups to permit different strategic approaches to each buyer/channel category. For example, some years ago Purex Corp. decided that neither product not territorial units were as well-suited to its strategy as was a market channel form of organization because having different units for each channel allowed it to focus separately on selling to supermarket chains and to drug chains. United Way drives are typically organized into a number of individual solicitation units with each assigned to canvass a particular segment of the community – commercial establishments, industrial plants, unions, local schools, county government, city government, hospitals, and agriculture. There are various departments of the federal government set up expressly for veterans, senior citizens, the unemployed, small businesses, widows and dependent children, the poor, and others. [Figure 5.3] illustrates organizing by process, by market channel, and by customer category.

Decentralized Business Units   Grouping activities along business and product group lines has been a clear-cut trend among diversified enterprises for the past half-century, beginning with the pioneering efforts of DuPont and General Motors in the 1920s. Separate business/product divisions emerged because diversification made a functionally-specialized manager's job incredibly complex. Imagine the problem a manufacturing executive would have if put in charge of, say, 50 different plants using 20 different technologies to produce 30 different products in 8 different businesses/industries. In a multi-business enterprise, the needs of strategy virtually dictate that the organizational sequence be corporate to line-of-business to functional area within a business rather than corporate to functional area (aggregated for all businesses). The latter produces a nightmare in making sense out of business strategy and achieving functional area coordination of line-of-business strategy. From a business strategy implementation standpoint, it is far more logical to group all the different activities that belong to the same business under one organizational roof, thereby creating line-of-business units (which, then, can be subdivided into whatever functional subunits that suits the key

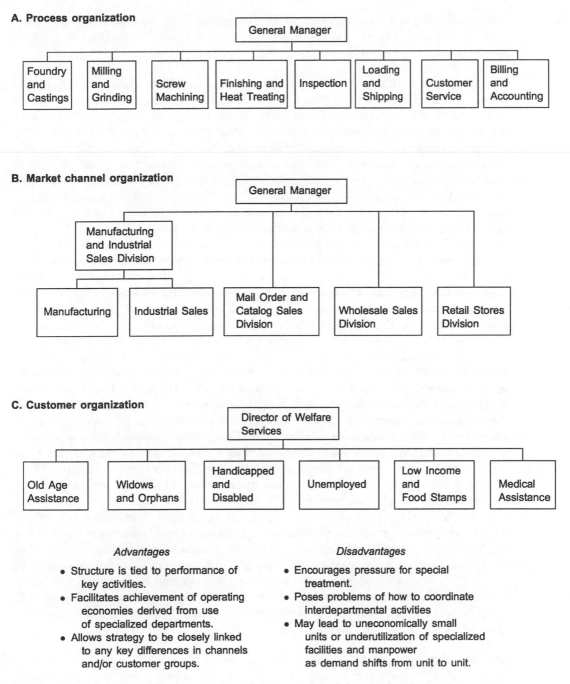

A. Process organization

General Manager

- Foundry and Castings
- Milling and Grinding
- Screw Machining
- Finishing and Heat Treating
- Inspection
- Loading and Shipping
- Customer Service
- Billing and Accounting

B. Market channel organization

General Manager

- Manufacturing and Industrial Sales Division
  - Manufacturing
  - Industrial Sales
- Mail Order and Catalog Sales Division
- Wholesale Sales Division
- Retail Stores Division

C. Customer organization

Director of Welfare Services

- Old Age Assistance
- Widows and Orphans
- Handicapped and Disabled
- Unemployed
- Low Income and Food Stamps
- Medical Assistance

Advantages

- Structure is tied to performance of key activities.
- Facilitates achievement of operating economies derived from use of specialized departments.
- Allows strategy to be closely linked to any key differences in channels and/or customer groups.

Disadvantages

- Encourages pressure for special treatment.
- Poses problems of how to coordinate interdepartmental activities
- May lead to uneconomically small units or underutilization of specialized facilities and manpower as demand shifts from unit to unit.

[Figure 5.3] *Process, market channel, and customer-based forms of organization* activities/critical tasks make-up of the business). The outcome not only is a structure which fits strategy but also a structure which makes the jobs of managers more 'do-able.'

Strategic Business Units   In the really large, diversified companies, the number of decentralized business units can be so great that the span of control is too much for a single chief executive. Then, it may be useful to group those which are related and delegate authority over them to a senior executive who reports directly to the chief executive officer. While this imposes another layer of management between the divisional general managers and the chief executive, it may nonetheless improve strategic planning and top management coordination of diverse business interests. This explains both the popularity of the group vice president concept among conglomerate firms and the recent trend toward the formation of *strategic business units*.

A strategic business unit (SBU) is a grouping of business divisions where the criterion for grouping is based on some important strategic element common to each. At General Electric, a pioneer in the concept of decentralized strategic business units (SBUs), 48 divisions were reorganized into 43 SBUs; in one case, three separate divisions making various food preparation appliances were combined as a single SBU serving the 'housewares' market.[12] At Union Carbide 15 groups and divisions were decomposed into 150 'strategic planning units' and then regrouped and combined into 9 new 'aggregate planning units.' At General Foods SBUs were originally defined on a product line basis but were later redefined according to menu segments (breakfast foods, beverages, main meal products, desserts, and pet foods). These examples suggest that how management chooses to define its SBUs depends largely on managerial judgement and pragmatic considerations. In general, though, the aim is to include within a single SBU those products and activities which share an important strategic relationship – whether it be with regard to similarity in manufacturing, or use of the same distribution channels, or overlap in customers and target markets, or some other pertinent strategic feature.

The managerial value of the concept of SBUs is that it provides diversified companies with a practical rationale for organizing what they do and with a workable approach to staying on top of the strategic performance of diverse operating units. It is particularly helpful in reducing the complexity of dovetailing corporate strategy and business strategy and in developing focused product/market business strategies on a decentralized basis. [Figure 5.5] illustrates the SBU concept of organizing diversification where each SBU is headed by a 'group' vice-president [. . .].

Matrix Forms of Organization   A matrix form of organization is a structure with two (or more) channels of command, two lines of budget authority, two sources of performance and reward, and so forth. The key feature of the matrix is that product (or business) and functional lines of authority are overlaid (to form a matrix or grid) and managerial authority over the employees in each unit/cell of the matrix is shared between the product

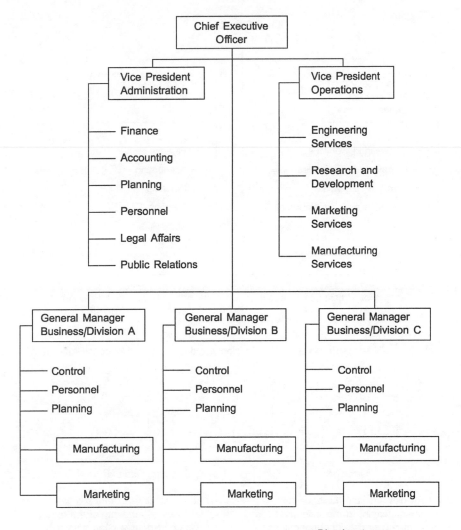

Advantages	*Disadvantages*

Advantages

- Offers a logical and workable means of decentralizing responsibility and delegating authority in diversified organizations.
- Puts responsibility for business strategy in closer proximity to each business's unique environment.
- Allows critical tasks and specialization to be organized to fit business strategy.
- Frees CEO to handle corporate strategy issues.
- Creates clear profit/loss accountability.

Disadvantages

- Leads to proliferation of staff functions, policy inconsistencies between divisions, and problems of coordination of divisional operations.
- Poses a problem of how much authority to centralize and how much to decentralize.
- May lead to excessive divisional rivalry for corporate resources and attention.
- Raises issues of how to allocate corporate-level overhead.

[Figure 5.4] *A decentralized business/division type of organization structure*

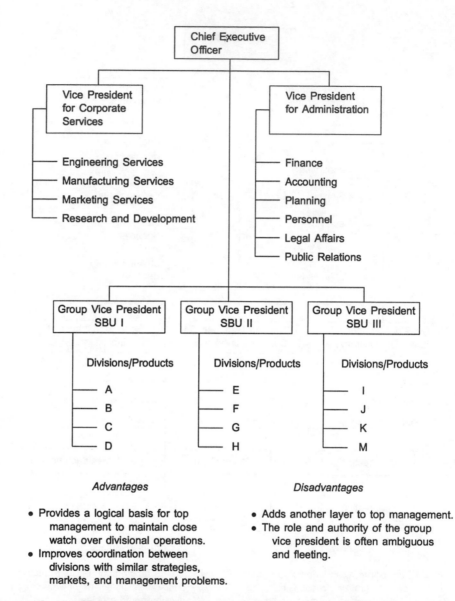

Advantages

- Provides a logical basis for top management to maintain close watch over divisional operations.
- Improves coordination between divisions with similar strategies, markets, and management problems.

Disadvantages

- Adds another layer to top management.
- The role and authority of the group vice president is often ambiguous and fleeting.

[Figure 5.5]   *An SBU type of organization structure*

manager and the functional manager – as shown in [Figure 5.6]. In a matrix structure, subordinates have a continuing dual assignment: to the business/ product and to their base function.[13] The outcome is a compromise between functional specialization (engineering, R&D, manufacturing, marketing, accounting) and product specialization (where all of the specialized talent needed to produce and sell a given product are assigned to the same divisional unit).

A. A defense contractor

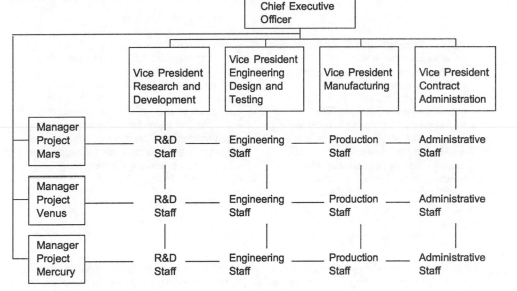

B. A college of business administration

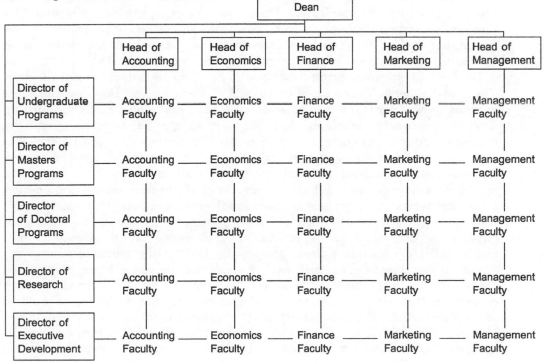

Continued overleaf

[Figure 5.6] *Matrix organization structures*

Editor's Note:

Advantages	Disadvantages
• Permits more attention to each dimension of strategic priority.	• Very complex to manage.
• Creates checks and balances among competing viewpoints.	• Hard to maintain 'balance' between the two lines of authority.
• Facilitates simultaneous pursuit of different types of strategic initiative.	• So much shared authority can result in a transactions logjam and disproportionate amounts of time being spent on communications.
• Promotes making trade-off decisions on the basis of 'what's best for the organization as a whole.'	• It is hard to move quickly and decisively without getting clearance from many other people.
• Encourages cooperation, consensus-building, conflict resolution, and coordination of related activities.	• Promotes an organizational bureaucracy and hamstrings creative entrepreneurship.

[Figure 5.6] *Continued*

A matrix type organization is a genuinely different structural form and represents a 'new way of life'. One reason is that the unity of command principle is broken; two reporting channels, two bosses, and shared authority create a new kind of organizational climate. In essence, the matrix is a conflict resolution system through which strategic and operating priorities are negotiated, power is shared, and resources are allocated internally on a 'strongest case for what is best overall for the unit' type basis.[14]

The list of companies using some form of a matrix includes General Electric, Texas Instruments, Citibank, Shell Oil, TRW, Bechtel, and Dow Chemical. Its growing popularity is founded on some solid business trends. Firms are turning more and more to strategies that add new sources of diversity (products, customer groups, technology) to their range of activities. Out of this diversity are coming product managers, functional managers, geographic area managers, business-level managers, and SBU managers – *all* of whom have important *strategic* responsibilities. When at least two of several variables (product, customer, technology, geography, functional area, and line of business) have roughly equal strategy priorities, then a matrix organization can be an effective structural form. A matrix form of organization allows for the management of multiple sources of diversity by creating multiple dimensions for strategic management, with each dimensional manager being responsible for one dimension of strategic initiative. The matrix approach thus allows *each* of several strategic priorities to be managed directly and to be represented in discussions of how the total enterprise (or business unit) can best be managed. In this sense, it helps middle managers make trade-off decisions from a general management perspective.[15] Further, because a manager is assigned line responsibility for attending to an explicit area of strategic concern, a matrix organization can facilitate management response to a rapidly emerging strategic priority.

Combination and Supplemental Methods of Organization The preceding structural designs are not always sufficient to handle the diversity of situations which complex organizations face. One additional option is to mix and blend the six basic organization forms, matching structure to strategy piece-by-piece and unit-by-unit. Another is to supplement a basic organization design with special-situation devices. Three of the most frequently used ones are:

1. The *project manager* or *project staff* approach, where a separate, largely self-sufficient subunit is created to oversee the completion of a special activity (setting up a new technological process, bringing out a new product, starting up a new venture, consummating a merger with another company, seeing through the completion of a government contract, supervising the construction of a new plant).[16] Project management has become a relatively popular means of handling 'one-of-a-kind' situations having a finite life expectancy and where the normal organization is deemed unable or ill-equipped to achieve the same results in addition to regular duties. On occasions, however, 'temporary' projects have proved worthy of becoming made 'ongoing,' thus resulting in either the elevation of the project unit to 'permanent' status or a parceling out of the project's functions to units of the regular organization.

2. The *task force* approach, where a number of functional specialists are brought together to work on unusual assignments of a problem-solving or innovative nature. Special task forces provide increased opportunity for creativity, open communication across lines of authority, tight integration of specialized talents, expeditious conflict resolution, and common identification for coping with the problem at hand. However, according to Drucker, team organization is more than a temporary expedient for dealing with nonrecurring special problems; he argues that the team is a genuine design principle of organization and is especially good for such permanent organizing tasks as top-management work and innovating work.[17]

3. The *venture team* approach, whereby a group of individuals is formed for the purpose of bringing a specific product to market or a specific new business into being. Dow, General Mills, Westinghouse, and Monsanto have used the venture team approach as a regenesis of the entrepreneurial spirit. One difficulty with venture teams is if and when to transfer control of the project back to the regular organization and the problems of discontinuity and shifting managerial judgements which result.[18]

Perspectives on Matching Strategy and Structure

The foregoing discussion brings out two points: (1) there is no such thing as a perfect or ideal organization design and (2) there are no universally applicable rules for matching strategy and structure. There is room for organizations with similar strategies to have significantly different organization structures. What suits one type of strategy can be totally wrong for another. Structures that worked well in the past may not be as suitable for the future. Experience shows that firms have a habit of regularly outgrowing their prevailing organizational arrangement – either an internal shakeup is deemed periodically desirable or else changes in the size and scope of customer-business-technology relationships make the firm's structure strategically obsolete. An organization's structure thus is dynamic; changes are not only inevitable but typical.

Notes

[. . .]

6. See, for example, Malcolm S. Salter, 'Stages of corporate development', *Journal of Business Policy*, 1(1): 23–7; Donald H. Thain, 'Stages of corporate development', *The Business Quarterly*, Winter 1969, pp. 32–45; Bruce R. Scott, 'The industrial state: Old myths and new realities', *Harvard Business Review*, 51(2): 133–48 [. . .].

7. Raymond Corey and Steven H. Star, *Organizational Strategy: A Marketing Approach*. Boston: Division of Research, Harvard University Graduate School of Business Administration, 1971, pp. 23–4.

8. For a more thorough discussion of this point, see Salter, 'Stages of corporate development', pp. 34–5.

9. Corey and Star, *Organization Strategy*, p. 14.

10. Ibid.

11. For an excellent documentation of how a number of well-known corporations revised their organization structure to meet the needs of strategy changes and specific product/market developments, see Corey and Star, *Organization Strategy*, Chapter 3.

12. William K. Hall, 'SBUs: Hot, new topic in the management of diversification,' *Business Horizons*, 21(1): February 1978, p. 19.

13. A more thorough treatment of matrix organizational forms can be found in Jay R. Galbraith, 'Matrix organizational designs', *Business Horizons*, 15(1): 29–40.

14. An excellent critique of matrix organizations is presented in Stanley M. Davis and Paul R. Lawrence, 'Problems of matrix organizations,' *Harvard Business Review*, 56(3): 131–42, May–June 1978.

15. Ibid., p. 132.

16. For a more complete treatment of project management, see C.J. Middleton, 'How to set up a project organization', *Harvard Business Review* 45(2): 73–82, March–April 1976; George A. Steiner and William G. Ryan, *Industrial Project Management*. New York: The Macmillan Company, 1968; Ivar Avots, 'Why does project management fail', *California Management Review*, 12(1): 77–82, 1969; C. Reeser, 'Human problems of the project form of organization', *Academy of Management Journal*, 12(4): December 1969, pp. 459–67; R.A. Goodman, 'Ambiguous authority definition in project management', *Academy of Management Journal*, 10(4): December 1969, pp. 395–407; and D.L. Wilemon and J.P. Cicero, 'The project manager: Anomalies and ambiguities,' *Academy of Management Journal*, 13(3): September 1970, pp. 269–82.

17. Drucker, *Management*, pp. 564–71.

18. Philip Kotler, *Marketing Management: Analysis, Planning, and Control*, 3rd edn. Englewood Cliffs, NJ: Prentice-Hall, Inc., 1976, pp. 200–1.

6 New Organizational Forms

Stewart R. Clegg

Modernist and Postmodernist Organization

[. . .] Modernist organizations may be thought of in terms of Weber's typification of bureaucratized, mechanistic structures of control, as these were subsequently erected upon a fully rationalized base of divided and deskilled labour. [. . .] These foundations are usually referred to as those of 'Fordism'.
 [. . .]
Fordism was a system of mass production based on both the increases in labour productivity and the wage relation which linked real wage and productivity growth which Taylorism made possible. [. . .]
 Stretching above the organizational base of Fordist enterprises was a pyramid of control, designed in a classically bureaucratic fashion. At its apex this radiated from the product division to the central organs of calculation and control. In the pyramid of control, according to both the formal theory and the practical application of it in organizational design, authority would reside in individuals by virtue of their incumbency in office and/or their expertise. These offices would be organized hierarchically, with compliance being to superordinate instruction expressed in terms of universal fixed rules. Such rules would be formalized so that any appeal against the rules could be expressed in terms of a 'correspondence principle' linking action and formal rules. The day-to-day principles of control, derived from the hierarchy of offices, would reside in direct surveillance and supervision, as well as the standardized rules and sanctions. Employment would be based on specialized training and formal certification of competence, acquired prior to gaining the job. Great care would be taken with the selection of personnel in order to ensure homogeneity in the organization's reproduction. For these upper levels of control (by contrast to the lower levels of those who were far more controlled than controlling), employment could constitute a career in which either seniority or achievement might be the basis for advancement. The

From *Modern Organizations: Organization Studies in the Postmodern World*. London: Sage, 1990.

general formality of relations would be buttressed through the ideal of impersonality such that relations would be role based, segmental and instrumental: the primary sources of motivation would be incentive based. This instrumentalism would be carried over into a principle of differential rewards according to the hierarchy of office, in which prestige, privilege and power would be isomorphic with one another.

At the core of the pyramid there would be a maximal division of labour. Intellectual work of design, conception and communication would be differentiated from manual work. The latter would be the work of so many interchangeable 'hands' executing and making possible the designs of super-ordinate others. These others, the managers, supervisors and administrators of the central work-flow, would be differentiated from the performance tasks. Indeed, in many respects, *differentiation* was the hallmark of the system. There was a maximal specialization of jobs and functions and an extensive differentiation of segmental roles. Forms of expertise would be exclusively held and arranged such that the ideal of the specialist-expert would be the basis for individual or occupational specialist or sub-unit empowerment in the system.

By the 1970s, as Albertsen (1988: 348) puts it, 'the Fordist model began to run out of steam'. [. . .]

Within organizations productivity slowed down, on this view, because Taylorism had reached its limits – there were no new areas left to rationalize; workers had become more resistant, especially during the prolonged period of post-war full employment, and efficiency gains were being outstripped by increasing costs of surveillance and control associated with the rigid separation of menial and managerial labour. [. . .]

Whatever else, it is clear that a modernist representation would not accurately capture the organizational patterns of contemporary Japanese organization, which have served in the 1980s as if they were a very beacon of postmodernity. [. . .] For this reason these are sometimes referred to as 'post-Fordist' or 'Fujitsuist' organizations (Kenney and Florida 1988). [. . .]

Where modernist organization was rigid, postmodern organization is flexible. Where modernist consumption was premised on mass forms, postmodernist consumption is premised on niches. Where modernist organization was premised on technological determinism, postmodernist organization is premised on technological choices made possible through 'de-dedicated' microelectronic equipment. Where modernist organization and jobs were highly differentiated, demarcated and de-skilled, postmodernist organization and jobs are highly de-differentiated, de-demarcated and multi-skilled. Employment relations as a fundamental relation of organizations upon which has been constructed a whole discourse of the determinism of size as a contingency variable increasingly give way to more complex and fragmentary relational forms, such as subcontracting and networking.

[. . .]

Organizational Imperatives

All effective forms of organization must be capable of resolving perennial problems: [. . .]

1. Articulating mission, goals, strategies and main functions.
2. Arranging functional alignments.
3. Identifying mechanisms of co-ordination and control.
4. Constituting accountability and role relationships.
5. Institutionalizing planning and communication.
6. Relating rewards and performance.
7. Achieving effective leadership.

Contemporary Japanese organization can be reviewed under these headings and contrasted with an ideal type modernist, Weberian organization. [. . .]

Mission, Goals, Strategies and Main Functions

With respect to strategy Japanese enterprise groups tend not to adopt the conglomerate model which is more common to large firms in the United States or Britain as the locus of their strategic initiative, preferring instead the *keiretsu* form. This is because Japanese corporations place very little emphasis on merger as a mechanism of growth or diversification of business (Cool and Lengnick-Hall 1985: 8–9; Howard and Teramoto 1981; Kono 1982). As a consequence, as Cool and Lengnick-Hall (1985: 8–9) suggest, organization members *know* what business they are in; they have a deep-rooted and substantive knowledge that a policy of horizontal or vertical acquisitions hardly allows for. One of the reasons why the complex inter-market relations of the *keiretsu* are entered into is to organize those related and ancillary actions which would be internally subject to imperative co-ordination in more typical Western enterprises. In the case of the United States or Britain this centre is likely to be a locus of 'private' calculation which attempts to co-ordinate across a range of economic activities. (Elsewhere in East Asia, such as in the South Korean *chaebol*, the imperative co-ordinator is likely to be the state.) One consequence of having well focused missions, goals, strategies and main functions, it is suggested, is that there usually is a core technology to the organization which is well understood. In consequence, following Emery and Trist (1960) and Tichy (1981), one can propose that 'Since Japanese firms limit their scope to primarily one basic technology, their internal culture tends to be very homogeneous' (Cool and Lengnick-Hall 1985: 9).

De-differentiation of what elsewhere are more likely to be imperatively co-ordinated functions will lead to a lessening of the degree of specialization of functions subordinated to the missions and goals of an organization. Whitley (1990: 64) has suggested that specialization, when associated with relative homogeneity in the nature of employees, will minimize transaction costs. In the Chinese family business this minimization is based upon concentric circles of 'trust' arranged outwards from kin, clan and place. Within Japanese enterprises it is secured through company socialization in the guise of firm-specific training, enterprise unionism and tenure of employment for those in the internal labour market [. . .].

[. . .]

At the centre of de-differentiated specialization of functions and the growth of organizational rather than occupational commitments are technical aspects of production. Technique is not simply a commodity to be bought, but a vital aspect of organization. This is clear in the sense that applied technique includes the human organization or system that sets equipment to work. Equally importantly the concept includes the physical integration of a new piece of equipment into a production process and its subsequent refinement and modification at the hands of the technically skilled workforce. Many manufacturers have come to grief on the belief that technical solutions can be bought pre-packaged. This is to ignore, precisely, that in operation these are always socio-technical solutions. What is at issue is precisely the 'cultural' context in which these solutions have to work. Studies have shown that equipment users rather than makers develop major process innovations (thus stealing a march on their competitors) and that small, imperceptible 'everyday rationalizations' account for the lion's share of productivity gains in an ongoing manufacturing business. Ergas (1987) has referred to this as a 'deepening' model of technological development, in which 'learning by doing; and making the best organizational and technical use of 'what you've got' are far more important than acquiring the latest 'state of the art' process technology (Ewer, Higgins and Stevens 1987: ch. 4). A 'deepening' model of technological development may be contrasted with those discontinuous models of technological development which stress the production of novel technological principles. Discontinuous conceptions of technological change may be termed a 'shifting' model. Kenney and Florida (1988: 140) suggest that in Japan 'the close linkage between production and innovation and a more general legacy of organizational flexibility has resulted in the integration of shifting with deepening'. The achievement of successful integration is very much an institutional question. Where employees have a rooted substantive knowledge of what they are doing, rather than one which is simply a certified mastery of some abstract occupational or analytical techniques, then the institutional conditions appear to be most appropriate for such an achievement.

Japanese organizations achieve integration of research and production through deliberately designed overlapping teams which work in the production complex. Such integration appears to be the key to the simultaneous achievement of 'shifting' and 'deepening'. 'As a result, technologies not only diffuse rapidly and help to rejuvenate mature sectors but large enterprises can quickly penetrate emerging areas either through invention, successful imitation, or knowledge acquisition' (Kenney and Florida 1988: 140). The complex of cross-cutting relations within enterprise groups is used to facilitate this technological innovation. 'Component companies in the corporate family are able to launch joint projects, transfer mutually useful information, and cross-fertilize one another' (Kenney and Florida 1988: 140) using networks which incorporate markets rather than vertical integration.

Deepening requires the combination of technical constraints and complexities, on the one hand, with the constant need to adapt to and anticipate changes in processes and products on the other. One particular organizational feature which facilitates this process is a degree of flexibility in work practices and a skilled and constantly re-skillable workforce (Hoshino 1982). The organization of enterprises dominated by the modernist characteristics of Fordism, in terms of functional specialization, task fragmentation and assembly line production, is inimical to these requirements. The overlapping work roles, extensive job rotation, team-based work units and relatively flexible production lines which characterize Japan are far more facilitative. Flexibility emerged out of the modes of rationality which were constructed during struggles in Japanese enterprises in the post-war era.

At the centre of this emergent mode of rationality was the negotiation of long-term employment tenure in the immediate post-war years. This minimized many of the employment inflexibilities which were endemic to modernist bureaucratic and Fordist organizations. Tenure guarantees reduce the rational basis for worker and union opposition to moves to automation or work re-design by management. Where the jobs of members are guaranteed then the rationality of opposition retreats. In such a context, then, it is not surprising to find that skill sharing will occur more frequently and easily, and that job rotation may be used to facilitate both formal skill sharing and informal learning amongst employees (Koike 1987). Long-term employment also allows management to decide rationally to make large scale investments in upgrading the skills of their workforce and in training them, secure in the knowledge that the investment will earn them a return, rather than accrue to someone else who succeeds in poaching the labour away. Where these guarantees are not in place it is always easier and certainly cheaper not to train and not to rely on a production system which requires highly skilled workers. Instead one would work to the lowest common skill denominator – the basis of modernist organization – and minimize the costs of labour turnover not through minimizing the labour transfers but through minimizing training costs and skills.

Arranging Functional Alignments

Typically, in Weberian bureaucracies, relationships have been settled by hierarchy, giving rise to many of the most characteristic aspects of organizations as they are currently understood. In the case of both the Chinese family business and the Japanese enterprise groups many of these hierarchical relationships are arranged through complex subcontracts and the extensive use of quasi-democratic work teams (in the Japanese case) or personalistic networks (in the Chinese case). Each instance uses horizontal relationships to substitute for functional arrangements which more typically are hierarchical in the modernist bureaucracy.

[. . .]

Unlike a large divisionalized Western corporation, Japanese enterprises are unlikely to practise vertical integration of their component suppliers, in order to minimize transaction costs. Instead, they are likely to use the 'just-in-time' (JIT) system where complex market relations with component subcontractors are used to ensure that supplies arrive on the premises where they are needed at the appropriate time. Large inventory stocks are dispensed with, and the circulation of capital in 'dead' buffer stock is minimized. In Japan there are large JIT production complexes spatially organized so that subsidiary companies, suppliers and subcontractors are in contiguous relationships with each other, extending through to tertiary subcontracting relations. Quoting Cusamano (1985), one may note that with respect to Toyota there are as many as 30,000 tertiary, 5,000 secondary and 220 primary subcontractors. Of the latter, 80 per cent had plants within the production complex surrounding Toyota in Toyota City.

Kenney and Florida (1988: 137) see a number of distinct advantages flowing from the JIT system. One is that it displaces wage costs out of the more expensive core to the somewhat cheaper periphery; another is that it leads to stable long-term relations with suppliers which open up multidirectional flows of information between the partners in the subcontracting network. Personnel as well as ideas are freely exchanged. Innovations can be accelerated through the system.

Japanese work organization is premised on self-managing teams rather than workers striving against each other under an individualistic and competitive payment and production system. In Japanese enterprises the functional alignment of activities is achieved by extensive use of the market principle through subcontracting and a (quasi-) democratic principle through self-managed teamwork. (As it takes place within an overall structure of hierarchy and private ownership it is clear why the principle can only be described as quasi-democratic.) Within the self-managing teams work roles overlap and the task structure is continuous, rather than discontinuous, in which the workers themselves allocate the tasks internally (see Schonberger 1982). [. . .]

[. . .]

Quality circles have been seen as a major achievement of the Japanese system, and not only because they serve as a substitute for quality surveillance as a separate management function. They include both operatives and staff specialists such as engineers in the same circle, oriented towards not only reducing the wastage rate but also making technological and process improvements. Once more this is related to the 'deepening' of technological development. Quality control is not 'externalized', nor is maintenance, to anything like the same degree as in more traditional modernist organizations. Much of the routine preventive maintenance is done by the operatives who use the machines. Kenney and Florida (1988: 132) note that 'downtime' is considerably less on machines in Japan compared to the United States (the figures cited are 15 per cent compared to 50 per cent downtime). This confirms Hayes's (1981) view that the Japanese succeed because of meticulous attention to every stage of the production process.

[. . .]

Mechanisms of Co-ordination and Control

[. . .]

Empowerment on the shop-floor appears to be more widespread in Japanese enterprises than it does in the bureaucratically conceived Fordist structure of Western modernity. This is achieved through mechanisms like extensive firm-specific basic training and learning. In part, this is accomplished through being involved in the work teams with more experienced workers. Job rotation also facilitates this learning. Such rotation takes place not only within the work teams but also more widely in the enterprise.

[. . .]

The empowerment strategies of Japanese enterprises have been identified in a generalized commitment to 'learning by doing' (Kenney and Florida 1988: 133–5). The *kanban* system, which is used to co-ordinate work between different work teams, has been seen as a part of this empowerment. Instead of top-down co-ordination of the workflow in the form of superordinate commands and surveillance, the *kanban* system allows for communication flows which co-ordinate horizontally rather than vertically. Work units use work cards (*kanbans*) to order supplies, to deliver processed materials and to synchronize production activities. Communication is through the cards, laterally rather than vertically, reducing planning and supervision, creating empowerment as workers 'do' for themselves.

Empowerment through widespread use of communication of information has been seen by Clark (1979) to be a key feature of the *ringi-ko* decision-making system, where printed documents circulate widely through the enterprise for comment and discussion. Consequently, when decisions are made after this exposure, snags and sources of opposition will have invariably been 'cooled out', often in ways which are organizationally quite productive. Much the same can be said of the widespread use of 'suggestions schemes', which although not compulsory are so widespread that employees feel obliged to participate in them. [. . .]

Flexibility and empowerment extend throughout the organization structure. There is a far wider use of management 'generalists' than is typically the case under the Weberian model of specialization and credentialization. Managers will not usually be specialists in accounting or finance, for instance, but will more likely be generalists who can rotate between positions (Kagono et al. 1985). 'Management rotation', state Kenney and Florida (1988: 134), 'results in flexibility and learning by doing similar to that experienced on the shopfloor. This blurs distinctions between departments, between line and staff managers, and between management and workers.' Through this rotation the commitment to a tenure principle and the prevention of organizational arteriosclerosis are maintained simultaneously. Managers who never leave do not have to wait for other managers to retire or die so that they can fill their shoes. Typically, the enterprise will always leave some management slots vacant. Nominal subordinates may discharge managerial tasks. Job titles are thus denotive of seniority not function. Because of rotation and the fact that promotion of a subordinate is not threatening to the status of a superordinate, internal managerial competition is far less than in the Weberian bureaucracy. Managers tend to cross boundaries and share knowledge far more in the normal course of doing their work where the quite rational anxieties induced by more explicitly 'face-threatening' systems are present (Kagono et al. 1985: 116).

[. . .]

Japanese enterprises operate under relatively stable capital market conditions compared to the highly volatile share-transactions of bundles of 'ownership' which characterize British, United States and many other Western stock exchanges. (By contrast, family and state ownership consolidates stability of capital formation in the South Korean case.) Surprisingly, perhaps, to advocates of 'free' markets this does not result in a lack of dynamism or a neglect of issues of co-ordination and control at the strategic apices of industry in Japan. In fact, it is the facility to achieve high degrees of such co-ordination and control in its complex inter-market organization and state-facilitated integration which many commentators have seen as the strategic edge of Japanese capitalism. In Japan [. . .] the role of MITI has been of particular importance in vertically co-ordinating enterprises in the achievement of longer-term, macro-economic, industry-wide planning (Dore 1986). Much of the market uncertainty which has to be organizationally buffered in the West is displaced outside the organization in Japan. The system of financial ownership does not generate as much risk in the first place, while the state handles much of what does occur. Consequently there is no necessity to devise strategies to handle risk or to manage uncertainty which is not likely to occur: resources can be better invested in core activities.

[. . .]

Constituting Accountability and Role Relationships

Management involves accountability for role-related actions which it is the manager's responsibility to produce and facilitate in others. The division of labour which achieves this may be more or less complex and more or less individuated. In each of the East Asian economies there is evidence to suggest that both the level of complexity and the degree of individuation of labour are less than is typically the case in a classical Weberian bureaucracy. De-differentiation appears to be operative. Whitley (1990: 65) has suggested that this is in part because of the way skill formation is more intra-organizationally than individually achieved, and thus located in the context of the overall skilling of work groups rather than just the human capital of a competitive individual. Further supporting this sense of group accountability and relationships is a reward system oriented more to teamwork than to individual work. All this is only possible where multi-skilling and flexible skilling are the norm, rather than restrictive skill defensiveness. Where there is a high degree of skill division then more formalized and externalized co-ordination and control will be required. Individual role relationships will tend to be normalized in the calculations which organization agencies make and so management control will be expressed far more in terms of the accountability of individuals.

Institutionalizing Planning and Communication

[. . .] In the manufacturing sectors of Britain, the USA and Australia, conglomerates predominate as a major locus of internalized planning and communication. Whatever the structure, a manufacturing firm's facilities, workforce and distribution network impose their own focus on its technologies and markets, and thus their own limits on rational diversification. Recognizing those limits is a matter of fine judgement; expensive mistakes, resulting from uncoordinated manufacturing strategies and managerial distraction, can occur even in the cases of integration and diversification motivated solely by manufacturing considerations. They occur much more frequently in the case of mergers and takeovers that represent a second best to internal expansion, and the situation is much worse in the usual case where businesses are acquired with no manufacturing rationale at all. Thus arises the typical conglomerate of, say, twenty or thirty unrelated businesses presided over by a single head office which, however, bears ultimate responsibility for their strategic decision-making. Merger and acquisition do not necessarily produce rational reconstruction on divisional lines but can produce conflicting authority structures based on disparate organization cultures and systems resistant to the new locus of control.

In such a situation the head office's necessary lack of insight into the dynamics of the individual businesses is compounded by its over-reliance on the major formally rational means of control over local management and assessment of business prospects – that is, dependence upon financial calculations and accounting techniques premised on the divisional form. The degradation of subsidiary businesses to 'profit centres' in contemporary managerial jargon tells the tale plainly enough. Centralized cost-accounting and capital-budgeting systems are the new organs of control to whose simplistic qualifications all complex technical and organizational questions, as well as future production and marketing imponderables, have to be reduced (Standish 1990). 'Profit-centre' managers in their turn submit to the iron law of quarterly or annual return-on-investment (ROI) calculation, which hardly encourages them to become far-sighted captains of industry. [. . .] Analysts of manufacturing decline almost unanimously pin point the rise to prominence of ROI calculations as the immediate cause of the sharp decline in expenditure on new process technologies, facilities and research and development.

The adoption of one or other accounting convention as the basis for planning has real material consequences (Standish 1990). The most important general example is the use of modified historic-cost accounting in Britain and Australia which systematically overstates profits by understating the value of real capital, and this in turn may lead to inadequate retention of operating surpluses and the winding down of the assets of the business. Another arbitrary – if formally rational – aspect of accounting practice is the choice and weighting of time-frames. Profit is struck on an annual basis, and the time-frame and weighting of anticipated returns can vary greatly. The financial institutions' separation from, and domination of, manufacturers gives yearly accounts a much greater salience than in countries where financial institutions are made more receptive to manufacturers' requirements, and this in turn highlights the artificial distinction between operating costs and capital outlays.

Current ROI calculations and capital budgeting techniques bear a heavy inherent bias to conservative investment behaviour and short-term management of manufacturing enterprise. The quarterly or annual ROI calculation presents an unambiguous case and a very strong influence on local managerial behaviour because it is the main – and often only – form of control of it available, as well as the measure of its success. It is much easier to improve 'performance' on such measures by decreasing the denominator than by increasing the numerator, which can take a long time, involves risk and has to be discounted for taxation. A profit-centre manager can achieve quicker, surer and easier results by delaying replacement of old or worn-out equipment, replacing equipment eventually with technologically dated or inferior substitutes and skimping on maintenance, research and development and personnel development – in other words, by disinvestment and technological stagnation (Hayes and Garvin 1982: 74; Hayes and Wheelwright 1984: 11–13). In the 1970s, for instance, robots did not meet ROI criteria in either Japan or the USA in the car industry. The Japanese introduced them anyway and thereupon gained market dominance through the much higher quality achieved. As a result, robots were paying for themselves within two and a half years (Thurow 1984).

[. . .]

Relating Rewards and Performance

Performance and reward imperatives may be more or less related. Now, this can be achieved in one or other of two contrasting ways. It may be achieved through complex processes of individualization in effort-related bonus systems. Alston (1982), for instance, has noted how these arrangements may give rise to jealousy and rivalry. Alternatively, it may be done through linking rewards not to individual efforts but to organizational success and service. The latter strategy has characterized Japanese management systems. The payment system has been oriented primarily to improving overall organization performance, by tightly coupling length of service to frequent promotion up a ladder of many small gradations. The seniority-based nature of the wages system in Japan, the *nenko* system, has been the major focus of much discussion of the relation between rewards and performance in Japan (see Sano 1977). It should be clear that *nenko seido*, the combination of lifetime employment and seniority-based wages systems, applies only to the core employees, who will be almost entirely males (Matsuura 1981). In common with Matsuura, other writers such as Takeuchi (1982) have argued that the ease of dismissal, low wage and fringe benefit costs and frequent part-time provision of female labour are important in buffering and stabilizing the employment situation of core workers. [. . .] The basis of flexibility is disproportionately shouldered by female patterns of labour force participation.

Wages in Japan are not simply based on age alone. Performance elements do enter into the equation. However, they do so in a distinctive way. Bonuses are related to overall group or organizational performance (Dore 1973: 94–110). It has been suggested, for instance, that wages in Japan are determined by mechanisms based largely on profit maximization, while Matsuzuka (1967) has pointed to the closely related variable of organization size in determining wage disparities, as well as age and duration of employment service. One aspect of this size function seems to be that the *nenko* system is surviving in larger firms while it is being eroded in the smaller ones (Tachibanaki 1982). This stress on organizational aspects in wage determination is picked up by Nakao (1980) in the emphasis given to the correlation between high wages and market share (which is itself related to advertising expenditures).

Alston (1982) has suggested that in practice there are two guidelines or rules at work relating rewards and performance in Japan. First, a single individual is never rewarded alone, but the reward is distributed as equally as possible within the work group. Second, he has pointed to the expressive dimension of the reward system, in addition to its instrumental qualities. Group reward of a symbolic kind like a group photograph or company shield with the group's name on it are important devices used to build up the sense of practical ideological community. However, it is easy to overstress how these rewards relate to job satisfaction. The implicit suggestion is that they do – that non-instrumental rewards are of importance in securing greater commitment, involvement and satisfaction from workers. On these criteria one would anticipate that Japanese workers would exhibit high levels of job satisfaction in comparative surveys. Despite the popular image of Japanese employees as happy and harmonious group workers the reality seems to be that they are not. As Lincoln and McBride (1987: 304) suggest [. . .], a 'particularly perplexing but strong and consistent finding from numerous work attitude surveys is the low level of job satisfaction reported by the Japanese'. This suggests caution in imputing too much in the way of intrinsic superiority from the actor's point of view to Japanese management practices, irrespective of the reasons for this low satisfaction. [. . .]

Achieving Effective Leadership

The global success not only of Japanese enterprise in the 1980s but also of the other NICs of East Asia has been seen by some commentators such as Blunt (1989: 21) as a spur to the renaissance of studies of effective leadership in recent times (for example, Biggart and Hamilton 1987; Conger 1989; Handy 1989; Kotter 1988; Muczyk and Reimann 1987). Leadership is usually defined in terms which relate a 'vision' of the future to some 'strategies' for achieving it, which are capable of co-opting support, compliance and teamwork in its achievement and serve to motivate and sustain commitment to its purpose (after Kotter 1988: 25–6). Hamilton and Biggart (1988) have stressed 'institutional aspects' of leadership – that is, the societal 'principles' or 'values' around which the vision can coalesce.

[. . .]

Organization Imperatives and Organizational Representations

The imperatives of organizations have been discussed in terms of a number of dimensions. Representationally these are arranged as in [Figure 6.1].

[. . .]

The argument of this chapter has been to suggest that a distinctive mode of rationality, which is postmodernist in its opposition to the principles of the Weberian/Fordist organization pattern, may have emerged in some aspects of post-war Japan. [. . .]

If Japan represents one possible path towards postmodernity, it is clear that there have been winners and losers in this development. To recap, the winners have been men who were in internal labour markets in the big name companies and the enterprise group networks. The losers have been women and those, more than two-thirds of all workers, who are outside the core labour market. With respect to women, the loss derives not just from a low level of labour force participation but from the nature of employment practices. Extended service is a key factor in remuneration, as we have seen. Because there are very few women who have extended lengths of continuous employment with a single employer, male–female wage differentials are so large in middle age. It is the nature of the workforce participation which varies, with women's work being largely unskilled because they are not employed in the core enterprises and internal labour market, where continuous training and re-skilling are provided to permanent employees (Koike 1981). The labour market is relatively highly segmented, with comparatively less rights for labour and a more arduous regime of work than in the more social democratic OECD states. Longer hours and shorter recreation are the norm, with the annual average working hours of a Japanese worker amounting to more than 2,100: by

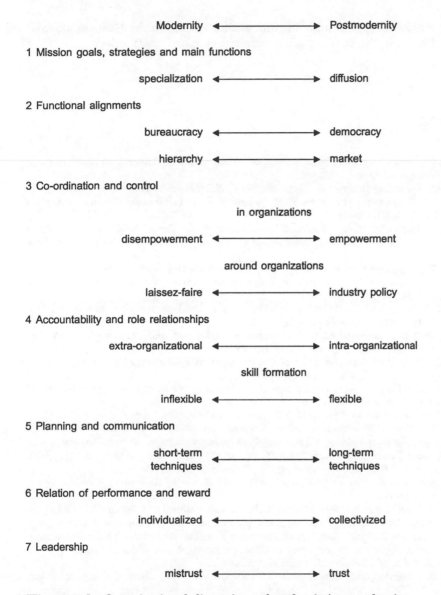

Modernity ←————————→ Postmodernity

1 Mission goals, strategies and main functions

specialization ←————————→ diffusion

2 Functional alignments

bureaucracy ←————————→ democracy

hierarchy ←————————→ market

3 Co-ordination and control

in organizations

disempowerment ←————————→ empowerment

around organizations

laissez-faire ←————————→ industry policy

4 Accountability and role relationships

extra-organizational ←————————→ intra-organizational

skill formation

inflexible ←————————→ flexible

5 Planning and communication

short-term
techniques ←————————→ long-term
techniques

6 Relation of performance and reward

individualized ←————————→ collectivized

7 Leadership

mistrust ←————————→ trust

[Figure 6.1]   *Organizational dimensions of modernity/postmodernity*

contrast, in Britain and the USA the average is 1,800–1,900 hours, with about 1,650 the norm in the Federal Republic of Germany (Deutschmann: 1987). Within the labour market core wages are relatively high, compared internationally – but so are the costs of basic consumer goods and services, with housing, in particular, being inordinately expensive per square metre, compared with OECD averages. Typically, each person occupies far fewer square metres than would be the norm in most other OECD states. Of course, outside Japan, elsewhere in the world, there may also turn out to be losers on a

wider scale, those trapped and organizationally outflanked in modernist organization forms as the leading edge turns ever more postmodern.
[. . .]

References

Albertsen, N. (1988) 'Postmodernism, Post-Fordism, and Critical Social Theory', *Environment and Planning D: Society and Space*, 6: 339–66.

Alston, J.P. (1982) 'Awarding Bonuses the Japanese Way', *Business Horizons*, 25(5): 46–50.

Biggart, N.W. and G.G. Hamilton (1987) 'An Institutional Theory of Leadership', *Journal of Applied Behavioural Science*, 23(4): 429–41.

Blunt, P. (1989) 'Strategies for Human Resource Development in the Third World', opening address to *The International Human Resource Development Conference*, University of Manchester, June 25–8.

Clark, R. (1979) *The Japanese Company*. New Haven, Conn.: Yale University Press.

Conger, J.A. (1989) 'Leadership: The Art of Empowering Others', *Academy of Management Executive*, 3(1): 17–24.

Cool, K.O. and C.A. Lengnick-Hall (1985) 'Second Thoughts on the Transferability of the Japanese Management Style', *Organization Studies*, 6(1): 1–22.

Cusamano, M. (1985) *The Japanese Automobile Industry: Technology and Management at Nissan and Toyota*. Cambridge, Mass.: Harvard University Press.

Deutschmann, C. (1987) 'The Japanese Type of Organization as a Challenge to the Sociological Theory of Modernization', *Thesis Eleven*, 17: 40–58.

Dore, R. (1973) *British Factory, Japanese Factory: The Origins of National Diversity in Industrial Relations*. London: Allen and Unwin.

Dore, R. (1986) *Flexible Rigidities*. Stanford, Calif.: Stanford University Press.

Emery, F. and E.J. Trist (1960) 'Socio-technical Systems', pp. 83–97 in C. Churchman and M. Verhulst (eds), *Management Science, Models and Techniques*, Volume 2. Oxford: Pergamon.

Ergas, H. (1987) 'Does Technology Policy Matter?', pp. 191–245 in B. Guile and H. Brooks (eds), *Technology and Global Industry*. Washington, DC: National Academy Press.

Ewer, P., W. Higgins and A. Stevens (1987) *Unions and the Future of Australian Manufacturing*. Sydney: Allen and Unwin.

Hamilton, G.G. and N.W. Biggart (1988) 'Market, Culture, and Authority: A Comparative Analysis of Management and Organization in the Far East', pp. S52–95 in C. Winship and S. Rosen (eds), *Organizations and Institutions: Sociological Approaches to the Analysis of Social Structure. American Journal of Sociology*, 94, supplement. Chicago: University of Chicago Press.

Handy, C. (1989) *The Age of Unreason*. London: Hutchinson.

Hayes, R.H. and D.A. Garvin (1982) 'Managing as if Tomorrow Mattered', *Harvard Business Review*, 60(3): 70–80.

Hayes, R.H. and S.C. Wheelwright (1984) *Restoring our Competitive Edge: Competing through Manufacturing*. New York: John Wiley.

Hoshino, Y. (1982) 'The Japanese Style of Management; Technical Innovation (Part III Staff Motivation, Job Mobility Are Keys to Japanese Advance', *Sumitomo Quarterly*, 9: 19–22.

Howard, N. and Y. Teramoto (1981) 'The Really Important Difference between Japanese and Western Management', *Management International Review*, 3: 19–30.

Kagono, T., I. Nonaka, K. Satakibara and A. Okumura (1985) *Strategic vs Evolutionary Management: A US/Japan Comparison of Strategy and Organization*. Amsterdam: North-Holland.

Kenney, M. and R. Florida (1988) 'Beyond Mass Production: Production and the Labor Process in Japan', *Politics and Society*, 16(1): 121–58.

Koike, K. (1981) 'A Japan–Europe Comparison of Female Labour-Force Participation and Male–Female Wage Differentials', *Japanese Economic Studies*, 9(2): 3–27.

Koike, K. (1987) 'Human Resource Development and Labor Management Relations', pp. 289–330 in K. Yamamura and Y. Yasuba (eds), *The Political Economy of Japan*. Volume 1: *The Domestic Transformation*. Stanford, Calif.: Stanford University Press.

Kono, T. (1982) 'Japanese Management Philosophy: Can It Be Exported?', *Long Range Planning*, 3: 90–102.

Kotter, J.P. (1988) *The Leadership Factor*. New York: Free Press.

Lincoln, J.R. and K. McBride (1987) 'Japanese Industrial Organizations in Comparative Perspective', *American Review of Sociology*, 13: 289–312.

Matsuura, N.F. (1981) 'Sexual Bias in the *Nenko* System of Employment', *Journal of Industrial Relations*, 23(3): 310–22.

Matsuzuka, H. (1967) 'Industrialization and the Change of Wage Structure in Japan', pp. 111–13 in N. Uchida and K. Ikeda (eds), *Social and Economic Aspects of Japan*. Tokyo: Economic Institute of Seijo University.

Muczyk, J.P. and B.C. Reimann (1987) 'The Case for Directive Leadership', *Academy of Management Executive*, 1(4): 301 11.

Nakao, T. (1980) 'Wages and Market Power in Japan', *British Journal of Industrial Relations*, 18(3): 365–8.

Ramsay, H. and N. Haworth (1984) 'Worker Capitalists? Profit Sharing, Capital Sharing and Juridical Forms of Socialism', *Economic and Industrial Democracy*, 5(3): 295–324.

Sano, Y. (1977) 'Seniority-Based Wages in Japan – a Survey', *Japanese Economic Studies*, 5(3): 48–65.

Schonberger, R.J. (1982) *Japanese Manufacturing Techniques*. New York: Free Press.

Standish, P.E.M. (1990) 'Accounting: The Private Language of Business or an Instrument of Social Communication?', pp. 122–41 in S.R. Clegg and S.G. Redding (eds), with the assistance of M. Cartner, *Capitalism in Contrasting Cultures*. Berlin: De Gruyter.

Tachibanaki, T. (1982) 'Further Results on Japanese Wage Differentials: *Nenko* Wages, Hierarchical Position, Bonuses and Working Hours', *International Economic Review*, 23(2): 447–62.

Takeuchi, H. (1982) 'Working Women in Business Corporations – The Management Viewpoint', *Japan Quarterly*, 29(3): 319–23.

Thurow, L. (1984) 'Revitalizing American Industry: Managing in a Competitive World Economy', *California Management Review*, 27(1): 9–40.

Tichy, N. (1981) 'Networks in Organizations', pp. 386–408 in P. Nystrom and W. Starbuck (eds), *Handbook of Organization Design*. New York: Oxford University Press.

Whitley, R. (1990) 'East Asian Enterprise Structures and the Comparative Analysis of Forms of Business Organization', *Organization Studies*, 11(1): 47–74.

7 Strategic Change and Human Resource Management

William E. Fulmer

Historically the role of the personnel/human resource manager has changed from 'good ol' boy' to personnel specialist to general manager. The first personnel officials were often former first-line supervisors whose primary function was to deal with the new unions of the 1920s and 1930s. It was assumed that because they had worked on the shop floor, they could relate to union problems. From the 1920s to the 1960s, the role of the personnel manager became more complex as labor laws and various forms of protective legislation were passed.

At present, a new shift in the role is occurring. This shift is reflected in the increasing number of companies turning to successful general managers to fill key positions in human resources. Increasingly these managers are moving beyond the traditional *administrative* role of human resources management (HRM) and are developing a more *strategic* role.

These managers, who perform the staff activities traditionally associated with human resource management in large organizations, are beginning to view themselves as *resource* managers, in much the same way that finance people manage the financial resources of the organization. Neither finance nor human resource staffers manage functional areas. It remains for the operations and marketing people to manage the critical functional areas of most organizations. After all, it is those functions that manage the supply and demand for the organization's products or services. This is not meant to denigrate the role of finance and and human resource management. After all, neither marketing nor operations could function without people or money. As Drucker (1983) suggested: 'There are two key areas . . . people decisions and capital-allocation decisions.' (1983: 61).

In recent years there has been growing awareness that human resource management is a 'factor' that can, or at least should, play an important role in the development and implementation of effective strategic plans. It is the latter area where human resource management may be able to play its most significant role.

From 'Human Resource Management: The right hand of strategy implementation', *Human Resource Planning*, 12(4): 1–11, 1989.

This chapter describes several specific human resource elements that strategists should incorporate into their thinking about strategy, especially strategy implementation.

HRM in the Strategic Management Process

[Figure 7.1] presents a diagram of what I consider to be the proper position of human resource management within the broader strategic context. HR forms the foundation for people issues in an organization. Although most capital assets are managed by such groups as finance, marketing, operations, and R&D, HRM can provide great assistance in the management of human assets and can play a role in the leadership of those assets. After corporate leaders have established the strategic direction, it is up to the functional areas of marketing and operations, ideally working together, to develop specific functional strategies that support the company's strategy. In consultation with the functional areas, ideally, the resource areas of finance and human resource management develop their strategies to support the overall business strategy. Ultimately, however, HRM is the very foundation of the organization. The functional areas do not exist, much less 'function' without people. As important as financial resources are to the success of an organization, they are useless unless managed by people.

[. . .]

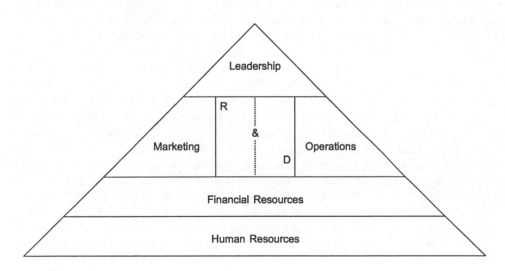

[Figure 7.1]

HRM Implementation Levers

The widely recognized McKinsey 7-S model is a useful framework for addressing the HRM role in strategy formulation and implementation (Pascale and Athos, 1981; Waterman, 1982; and Waterman, Peters and Phillips, 1980). The six S's that need to be considered along with the seventh S of strategy are: structure, systems, staff, skill, style and superordinate or shared values. Although superordinate values and style are areas in which all managers influence the organization, they are sufficiently amorphous that making them operational is very difficult. It is with the remaining four Ss – structure, systems, staff and skill – that the human resource staff can be especially helpful. This chapter considers staff and skill to be areas that HRM systems should address.

Structure

HRM staffs frequently give advice on organizational design questions. Too often this is a relatively nonstrategic activity of merely rearranging boxes to reflect new political realities in the organization, such as who has won or lost the latest management power play, or how to cover up for a manager's weaknesses by assigning certain functions to other managers. There is, however, a significant strategic role that structural design can play. It requires of HRM managers an ability and willingness to take a broader perspective than most traditionally have taken about structure. Only then can they be innovative and identify solutions that give competitive advantage.

There have been several recent developments that illustrate the strategic importance of structure. In 1981 IBM, in an effort to speed up response to a changing field and to reduce competition between sales teams which were marketing overlapping product lines to the same customers, began a massive reorganization effort. Later, in the personal computer industry, IBM established a separate Independent Business Unit (IBU) to compete with more entrepreneurial firms. Some of the problems experienced by Texas Instruments in the home computer market were attributed to their organizational structure. According to some managers, TI's matrix structure fragmented both people and resources. It diffused authority to the point where managers could not carry out their program responsibilities effectively. One manager observed that TI had lost the ability to focus on the right products, for the right growth markets, at the right time (Uttal, 1982; Zipper, 1982). One of the first acts in 1980 of the new CEO of Jaguar Cars, Inc., was to 'straighten out Jaguar's complicated internal organization', and to 'reestablish Jaguar Cars as a single entity, complete with its own sales, marketing and production functions' (Fannin, 1985: 76). Hewlett Packard's growing commitment to the computer industry, as well as Johnson and Johnson's new efforts to serve the hospital market, have necessitated significant organizational changes. These examples illustrate the strategic importance of structure.

Peter Drucker observed that 'Any work on structure must . . . start with objectives and strategy. This is perhaps the most fruitful new insight we have in the field of organization. It may sound obvious, and it is. But some of the worst mistakes in organization building have been made by imposing a mechanistic model of an "ideal" or "universal" organization on a living business' (Drucker, 1974: 525). The critical structural question seems to be 'what is the minimum structure necessary to ensure survival of the organization? That should be the starting point of organizational design' (Sarason, 1972). In the words of Drucker, 'The simplest organization structure that will do the job is the best one. What makes an organization structure "good" are the problems it does not create. The simpler the structure, the less that can go wrong' (Drucker, 1974: 601).

To play a strategic role, HRM managers need skills in the area of organizational design, strong analytical skills, and an ability to think objectively about organizational design and structural issues. Otherwise they cannot deal effectively with the various business functions. They will be unable to understand the needs of the various parts of the organization. They will lack the ability to help integrate the various functions of the organization in a strategically meaningful way.

Systems

Just because the 'structural arrangements are in keeping with the ideal there is no guarantee that the members will have the skills required to function within these structures' (Lodahl and Mitchell, 1980: 197). It remains for the human resource function to help design systems that will enable the organization to obtain and retain the staff with the skills that are needed to successfully implement the strategic plan. As Roger Smith, Chairman of GM remarked while describing the recent strategic changes at GM: 'Changing the boxes was easy. Changing the systems is more difficult' (Smith, 1986).

Recruitment and Selection Systems In a recent study of the competitive advantage of 16 organizations, the authors found a recurring theme: 'at some time or another a company was able to capture or develop the greatest share of critically needed human resource skills, or was able to leverage an existing set of human resource skills to create an enduring competitive advantage' (MacMillan and Schuler, 1985: 24). According to the chairman of Kollmorgen Corporation 'I think success is based more on the quality of the people a business brings on board, and on the way it gets them involved and excited in what's going on than on the quality of the business idea itself' (Bacas, 1985: 62).

The importance of recruiting and selecting managers who are capable of implementing the chosen strategy is obvious. The author of one study asked 'Is it coincidence that Intel, the top performing corporation in our sample, has Ph.D.'s in the top three positions? Combining top technical judgement with business acumen may be an important strategy in the development and selection of corporate officers for high technology firms if the right judgements are to be made' (Schoonhoven, 1984: 14). In a more general sense, Lee Iacocca suggested that a few key managers can make a big difference in the success of a firm: 'the kind of people I look for to fill top management spots are the eager beavers. These are the guys who try to do more than they're expected to. They're always reaching. And reaching out to the people they work with, trying to help them do their jobs better.' He adds, 'So I try to look for people with that drive. You don't need many. With twenty-five of these guys, I could run the government of the United States. At Chrysler I have about a dozen' (Iacocca, 1984: 59–60).

It is important also to be concerned about the quantity and quality of hourly and staff employees needed in the foreseeable future. Too often the focus of manpower planning programs has been on the number of people needed for various jobs in the future. Perhaps more important are the qualitative aspects that cannot be programmed into a forecasting model. One aspect of that quality is whether the person fits the values or style of the organization. In describing firms with an innovation strategy, Lodahl and Mitchell (1980) observe that 'One way of minimizing the difference between innovative ideals and the preexisting ideals of new members is to organize the recruitment process so as to attract those who favor the innovations and to select only those whose ideals are most likely to fit in with the innovative enterprise' (1980: 191–2).

It is not surprising that one of the qualities Delta Airlines uses as a screening and interviewing benchmark is an employee's attitude toward his or her family. As one executive reported to me, 'if they don't think highly of their own family they aren't likely to think highly of the Delta family.' Marriott Corporation has a clearly thought out recruiting system for its new Courtyard division, which takes into account that its strategy for that division is quite different from its more traditional hotels. Electronic Data Systems of Dallas historically has placed great emphasis on recruiting military veterans – partly because of the values of its founder but also because veterans fit well with the strategy of the firm. HRM people need to think through the 'personality' of their company's culture. If that culture contributed to the company's success, select as employees people who will fit and reinforce that culture. To do this will require devising techniques for assuring better 'fit.'

Socialization Systems The recruitment and selection of key human resources is not enough. The retention of key people is essential. In the words of the vice chairman of Chrysler: 'One of the jobs of a CEO is, don't leave behind a bench that can't play the game' (Stavro, 1985: 78). To leave behind the right kind of 'bench' requires an appreciation for how to improve the chances that the right people are developed and retained. One way to do that is through the socialization process, i.e., 'the process by which newly hired employees are made part of a company's culture' (Pascale, 1984: 28). Orientation and training systems can be particularly useful mechanisms or levers of socialization early in an employee's career. Training, broadly defined to include rituals and symbols, can continue to be an effective process of reinforcing the values and skills desired by the organization. Ideally, the values and skills are directly related to the strategic plan, with special emphasis on the key success factors of the organization.

As Pascale observed, many successful companies have an 'obsession with some facet of their performance in the marketplace. For example, McDonalds has an obsessive concern for quality control; IBM for customer service; and 3M for innovation' (1984: 34). Orientation and training programs can be particularly useful mechanisms for reinforcing the values that are critical to the successful implementation of a strategy. Walt Disney Production's orientation and training programs hit hard at the importance of the 'Guest.' Proctor and Gamble is well known for its re-written memos. Tupperware is known for its use of rallies as a way of training and motivating employees to be effective within those organizations. EDS places great emphasis on its training programs. According to one of its managers, 'Other [company] classes are "I'm OK, you're OK." Ours is intensely competitive. It's deliberately intense because we're looking for character. We're not a legion of workaholics, but this is where we drive that part of the culture home' (Gelman, 1985: 68).

One of the concerns that organizations should have about layoff practices is the effect they have on socialization. Instability of employment not only upsets the socialization process but, as Ouchi suggests, 'a disruption of the socialization process will inhibit the passing on of traditions and will result in organizational inefficiency' (Ouchi, 1980: 422).

Reward Systems Reward systems, both positive and negative, can be especially useful as ways of reinforcing the values and behaviors that an organization needs to be successful in implementing its chosen strategy. As Lodahl and Mitchell have pointed out, organization 'members do what they are rewarded for' (1980: 200).

A key step in any reward system is the evaluation system used to measure an individual's performance. Too often evaluation systems and the delivery of rewards are done without much thought to how they relate to the organization's strategic plan. This seems particularly true of highly diversified firms and their heavy reliance on quantitative financial measures (Kerr, 1985). Iacocca placed great emphasis at Chrysler on his 'quarterly review system' for key people and their key people: 'What are your objectives for the next 90 days? What are your plans, your priorities, your hopes? And how do you intend to go about achieving them? (Iacocca, 1984: 47).

Positive rewards can take many forms, from compensation to promotions to various forms of public recognition. In recent years, an increasing number of companies seem to be wrestling with the issue of how to compensate top management in such a way as to reward long-term strategic success, as opposed to short-term financial results ('Executive Compensation,' 1983).

Compensation systems for the majority of employees in some organizations, including unionized workers, are being reevaluated. Driven in large part by foreign competitors with lower labor costs, some firms are reevaluating the criteria for determining compensation (Freedman and Fulmer, 1982; Freedman, 1985). My studies indicate that in successful organizations following a generic strategy of low cost, top management recognizes that the labor intensive nature of their industry requires much tighter controls on labor costs, and in some cases innovativeness in benefits, recruiting and socializing, to offset lower wages, if people are to be retained and motivated to help achieve strategic objectives.

Promotion systems place key people in positions to implement strategic plans. Along with various forms of public recognition, they can clearly signal to the rest of the organization the skills, style and values desired by the organization. 'Negative rewards' also send clear messages. For example, at Procter and Gamble the new hire who does not make brand manager by a certain date is being signalled that he or she is not what the organization is looking for in its management team.

More overt negative actions, such as demotions, discipline and discharge, send very strong signals. Unfortunately too many managers seem to ignore the powerful messages that 'negative rewards' or the absence of 'negative rewards' can send (Fulmer, 1986). The CEO of one company recently commented in my presence: 'If you want to ruin a no-layoff policy, you can't play around with mediocrity.' Thus, organizations should be concerned with the consistency of various HRM practices.

In general, the primary focus of strategically managed HR groups should be the 'people systems' that impact all other areas of the organization [Figure 7.1]. Specifically, HR people must carefully think through the implications of their various 'people systems.' What messages are being sent, either consciously or unconsciously, by the various systems? If the messages are unclear or not supportive of the company's strategy, the systems must be changed. To do this will require an understanding of the company's strategy, willingness to closely examine each system, an ability to read the nuances of the various systems, and an ability to make innovative changes in the systems that are in place.

Leadership

All too often, the role of leadership is ignored in the strategic management process. Although corporate leaders can propose strategies for their organizations, and as such can help shape their companies' directions, perhaps their most significant role in the strategic management process is in the area of implementation.

There is an adage that says 'Things are managed. People are led.' As business becomes increasingly international in scope and as the US grows increasingly pluralistic, with numerous races and ethnicities, leadership will become a requirement for organizational success. Consequently, even though the phenomenon of leadership may not be well understood, it is important to recognize its strategic significance to most organizations.

Leadership cannot be accomplished by a single individual; others must want to follow the lead of the strategic leader. Hence leadership is an organizational task. A strategic leader is required to bring about the needed integrated and coordinated group effort.

Although the precise nature of the leadership role can vary, depending on the personality of each leader and perhaps the nature of the people and organization being led, it is important for leaders to do at least five things very well:

1. Provide a vision, a sense of direction and purpose for the people who make up the organization;
2. Motivate others to think and act strategically;
3. Allocate resources among products, businesses, departments and people;
4. Communicate and protect the corporate values that are key to the organization's success;
5. Assign responsibility to individuals and groups.

In reflecting on his study of leadership, Gluck focuses on two critical factors – vision and leadership – that are the link between 'strategic planning' and 'operational decision making' (Gluck, 1984: 10).

Although the vision and leadership need to come from top management of the organization, if the organization is to successfully develop and implement its strategy, the HRM staff can help in communicating and interpreting the vision and the values of the CEO. At a minimum, this can be reflected in company socialization efforts, especially training programs. Some companies have been innovative in the use of video, including live broadcasting capability, to more effectively communicate with employees. Also, the HR staff can play an important role in monitoring the effect various management actions are likely to have on employees' perceptions of those values and the vision. The skillful use of employee surveys and internal focus groups are two ways of doing this. This is not to excuse top management from being sensitive themselves to such issues, but an effective HRM staff may be more attuned to the employees' needs and concerns than many top line managers.

Conclusions

This chapter has summarized some of the specific ways in which HRM people can contribute to strategy implementation. Clearly, there are a variety of ways in which they can contribute to strategy formulation, especially in helping to understand the structure, systems, staff, skills, style, and superordinate values of both their organization and that of competitors. Also, they can help top management understand human resource environmental and industry trends. But perhaps the greatest contribution is in the design and administration of structures and systems that facilitate the *implementation* of strategic plans, i.e., that use human resources as a strategic weapon to gain competitive advantage.

According to the senior vice president of human resource management for a very successful firm, who claims to have spent considerable time in the last few years 'trying to figure out the function of HRM':

> Business managers have to have a market focus and they are provided with two resources – dollars and people. Managers will tend to focus on the financial side given the score keeping nature of most businesses. The only way to justify human resource activities is if they contribute to improving the relationship between the product and the customer or enhance profit performance of the company.

[. . .] Unfortunately too few general managers understand the role that human resources management can play in strategy formulation and implementation and too few human resource managers and staffers have been trained to play such a role. Perhaps it is time to acknowledge that to date HRM professionals (as well as other business professionals and managers) have not been able to build a convincing case for the strategic contribution of HRM. In other words, they have not been able to show specifically *how* they contribute to the long-term competitive success of their company.

The skills needed to play such a role are both technical and managerial. Technical skills in areas such as compensation, organizational design, training, labour law and negotiations, will continue to be essential. Managerial skills, especially the ability to think and act strategically will become increasingly important.

If the 'profession' is to change, it will require a more managerial focus to our HRM college courses and programs. Students should not only take courses in the various functional areas but also be encouraged to seek work early in their career in key functional areas – not just in HRM jobs. They must develop the ability to communicate effectively with managers outside of HRM and gain their respect.

Companies generally should avoid hiring very many HRM majors for HRM jobs, unless their degree programs are more managerial in focus and unless the students are willing to spend part of their career working in other areas of the company. Hopefully, some of those non-HR assignments come early in one's career.

As 'HR professionals' advance in their career, they should spend more time reading non-HRM journals and attending non-HRM conferences. Hopefully, they will push the HRM journals and conferences, including academic conferences, to become broader in scope and more integrative of other business activities.

Ultimately HR people must stop thinking of themselves as professionals. They are no more professionals than operations or marketing people. They are all managers of a critically important activity – an activity that must contribute to developing a sustainable competitive advantage for the overall organization.

References

Bacas, H., 'Who's in charge here?', *Nation's Business*, May 1985, pp. 57–64.

Drucker, P.F., *Management: Tasks, Responsibilities, Practices*. New York: Harper & Row, 1973.

'Drucker at 73: Revelling in his role as an outsider,' *International Management*, June 1983, 38: 56–61.

'Executive compensation: Looking to the long term again,' *Business Week*, 9 May 1983, pp. 80–3.

Fannin, R. 'Restoring Jaguar's roar', *Marketing and Media Decisions*, June 1985, pp. 75–9.

Freedman, A. and Fulmer, W.E. 'Last rites for pattern bargaining,' *Harvard Business Review*, March–April 1982, 60: 30–48.

Freedman, A. *The New Look in Wage Policy and Employee Relations*. New York: The Conference Board, 1985.

Fulmer, W.E. 'How do you say, "You're Fired?"', *Business Horizons*, January–February 1986, 29: 31–8.

Gelman, E. 'Wheels of the future,' *Newsweek*, 17 June 1985, pp. 64–71.

Gluck, F.W. 'Vision and leadership,' *Interfaces*, 14, January–February 1984, pp. 10–18.

Iacocca, L. *Iacocca*. New York: Bantam Books, 1984.

Kerr, J.L. 'Diversification strategies and managerial rewards: An empirical study,' *Academy of Management Journal*, 1985, 28: 155–79.

Lodahl, T.M. and Mitchell, S.M. 'Drift in the development of innovative organizations,' in J.R. Kimberly and R.H. Miles (eds), *The Organization Life Cycle*. San Francisco: Jossey-Bass, 1980.

MacMillan, I.C. and Schuler, R.S. 'Gaining a competitive edge through human resources,' *Personnel*, April 1985, pp. 24–9.

Ouchi, W.G. 'A framework for understanding organizational failure,' in J.R. Kimberly and R.H. Miles (eds), *The Organizational Life Cycle*. San Francisco: Jossey-Bass, 1980.

Pascale, R.T. 'Fitting new employees into the company culture,' *Fortune*, 1984, May 28, pp. 28–34.

Pascale, R.T. and Athos, A.G. *The Art of Japanese Management: Applications for American Executives*. New York: Simon and Schuster, 1981.

Schoonhoven, C.B. 'High technology firms: Where strategy really pays off,' *Columbia Journal of World Business*, Winter 1984, 19: 5–16.

Smith, R. Remarks to business policy students at the Darden Graduate School of Business, University of Virginia, 3 October 1986.

Stavro, B. 'Is there life after Iacocca?' *Forbes*, 8 April, 1985, pp. 75–8.

Uttal, B. 'Texas Instruments regroups,' *Fortune*, 9 August 1982, pp. 40–5.

Waterman, R.H., Jr. 'The seven elements of strategic fit.', *Journal of Business Strategy*, Winter 1982, 2(3): 69–73.

Waterman, R.H., Jr., Peters, T.J. and Phillips, J.R. 'Structure is not organization,' *Business Horizons*, June 1980, pp. 14–26.

Zipper, S. 'TI scrambling matrix management to cope with gridlock in major profit centers,' *Electronic News*, 26 April 1982, pp. 12–48.

8 Cultural Barriers to Strategic Change

John Hassard and Sudi Sharifi

[. . .]
In recent years, management theory has discovered a new buzz-word – *culture*.
[. . .]
   The concept of culture has become attractive because it offers a new panacea for corporate ills. Management journals document how cultural factors are at the heart of best practice. Human resources experts see cultural norms as the key to the infrastructure of informal organisation. This infrastructure is comprised of the ceremonies and rituals which give meaning to the work environment; it encompasses the core values which leaders and subordinates hold dear. Modern management texts tell managers to create corporate cultures which dovetail with effective corporate strategy. This integration is presented as the main reason for the successes of the 'Excellent' and 'Theory Z' companies.[3] The new axiom of administrative wisdom is that good strategy equals success only when we possess an appropriate culture.
   [. . .]
   In this chapter, then, we will review some recent attempts to use the concept of culture as a tool for business strategy. The literature on corporate culture is examined and some key principles are developed into a strategy for organizational change. [. . .]

When executives say they want cultural change they are generally saying that they want people to *do* things differently; they want tangible, behavioural evidence of change. To achieve this, however, they must realise that change must first be effected in a number of covert and implicit spheres. In particular change must be effected in the types of assumptions and values held by management, employees, and the firm.[4]

[. . .] The first rule of cultural change, therefore, is that it is hard to achieve.[5] Through time, cultures become embedded and entrenched, and form powerful inertial structures. After years with a firm, employees take the cultural artefacts of work, such as the modes of dress, the forms of interaction, the work norms and systems, for granted.

From 'Corporate culture and strategic change', *Journal of General Management*, 15(2): 4–19, 1989.

To this end, when considering cultural change, managers are faced with problems of overcoming employee *resistance* to change; for a new corporate direction can often be both difficult to conceive and demand enormous energy and time to effect.[6] When they are asked to make changes, managers will often discover a bonding within the organisation which serves to reject new initiatives.[7]

[. . .] We should not, however, become too pessimistic about cultural change, for we must remember that organisations are dynamic phenomena: organisations are structures locked in a state of process.

In organisations a cultural identity remains an identity only because it is reproduced over time. Corporate cultures are constructed socially and are reconstructed socially. Assumptions and values are not only learned, they are also re-learned.[8]

[. . .]

[. . .] 'Culture is not the overt behaviour or visible artefacts that one might observe if one were to visit the company. It is not even the philosophy or value system which the founder may articulate or write down in various "charters". Rather it is the assumptions which lie behind the values and which determine the behaviour patterns and the visible artefacts such as architecture, office layout, dress codes, and so on'.[17]

[. . .]

Schein[19] believes that to understand corporate culture it is necessary to analyse the values that govern behaviour and to disclose the underlying assumptions which, although typically unconscious, determine how members perceive, think and feel.

Schein argues that although assumptions are increasingly taken for granted, and indeed tend to fade from consciousness, they nevertheless remain very powerful phenomena. Because of the human need for order and consistency, these assumptions come to form what he calls a cultural paradigm; which is a set of interrelated assumptions about human nature and human activities. Although Schein argues that deciphering this cultural paradigm and uncovering its tacit understandings and intersubjective processes can prove difficult, he believes it is a process which can be achieved.

To this end, Schein offers a four stage approach to understanding how cultural paradigms develop in organisations. The four basic steps of this approach are: analysing the process and content of socialisation of new members; analysing responses to critical incidents in the organisation's history; analysing beliefs, values and assumptions of culture creators or carriers; and jointly exploring and analysing with insiders the anomalies or puzzling features observed or uncovered in interviews. Schein argues that while the first three methods should enhance and complement one another, at least one of them should cover all external adaptation and internal integration issues. To discover the underlying assumptions and eventually to decipher the paradigm, the fourth method is necessary to help the insider surface his or her own cultural assumptions.

Schein suggests therefore that culture is as an adaptive and tangible learning process. His model places emphasis on how organisations communicate their culture to new recruits. It illustrates how assumptions translate into values and how values translate into behaviour. The model explains how cultural codes are transmitted and how new values and behaviours are learned. By outlining these processes, Schein lays foundations for a strategic change programme [. . .].

[. . .]

[. . .] To understand corporate culture and to achieve successful cultural change the management literature suggests that:

- Organisations possess 'assumptions' and 'values' which although largely implicit define what is and what is not appropriate and acceptable behaviour.[30]
- The successful firm will be the one whose assumptions and values fit with the forms of explicit behaviour demanded by its strategy.[31]
- If values and behaviour are incompatible with strategy then successful change may be difficult to achieve.[32]
- When considering change, we need to check first to see whether company strategy demands such a shift: can change be realised by other means?[33]
- Before a major change campaign is commenced, senior management must understand the implications of the new system for their own behaviour: and senior management must be involved in all the main stages preceding change.[34]
- In change programmes, special attention must be given to the company's 'opinion leaders': i.e., those people who at various levels of the organisation have, by virtue of their role, personality or achievements, undue influence on the opinions and behaviour of others.[35]
- When change is needed, we should examine the ways in which the organisation traditionally transmits its values: is this done through, for example, management style, work systems, employment policies, reward systems, or other means?[36]
- To effect change, we must decide how culture channels can be programmed with new messages and also how any old, contradictory messages can be eradicated.[37]
- We must reinforce mass communication campaigns with changes to those structures and processes which threaten to produce contradictory messages: every opportunity must be taken to restate, either formally or informally, the key messages of the new values.[38]
- We must be selective in the new values we select: for maximum impact we should emphasise only one key value.[39]

[. . .] However, the literature also specifies some qualifications to these change principles. It is suggested that:

- The deeper the level at which cultural change is required, then the more difficult and time-consuming the cultural change programme will be.[40]
- The speed at which culture can be changed depends upon whether or not 'multiple' cultures exist.[41]
- Change is easier when the change process involves only surface-level behavioural norms; i.e. because members themselves can suggest what behaviours are required for success today as opposed to those required yesterday.[42]
- Managing the deepest layers of culture requires a participative approach, a derivative of Theory Y: because top management, with or without the help of consultants, cannot dictate changes in assumptions about human nature and the business environment, they can only set appropriate parameters.[43]
- A top-down approach to cultural change may be feasible when either a single corporate culture exists, or where the focus is upon changing norms and not assumptions.[44]
- Top-down approaches yield changes that are relatively easy to bring about, but which are difficult to sustain; these approaches generally result in overt compliance to what is mandated, but not covert compliance.[45]
- Participative approaches – directed at changing underlying assumptions – although difficult and time-consuming to implement, are more likely to result in changes that last: participation yields overt commitment to and covert acceptance of what the group decides.[46]

Therefore, in defining a feasible and realistic approach to cultural change the literature suggests the following process be adopted: First, that we conduct some early cultural change at the norm level. For this we can use a top-down approach if for nothing more than to encourage organisation members to begin behaving in new ways. After the new culture achieves some success, time can be devoted to changing the deeper more fundamental aspects of culture. Here a participative approach can be used to fine-tune the new culture to the unique circumstances of each work unit. Over time, all three levels of culture – assumptions, values and behaviours – can be addressed, and the culture change desired by the organisation can be sustained.[47]

[. . .]

Strategic Re-positioning

The literature suggests that corporate culture can have a major impact on corporate strategy. Culture can affect not only what managers believe, but also the strategic decisions they make about the organisation's relationship with its environment.[48] [. . .]

[. . .]

[. . .] Corporations must realise that in modern markets the need for strategic change will be the only constant.[53] However, commitment to change is meaningless unless the rhetoric can be converted into action, and action which causes managers to examine and challenge their implicit belief systems. Two ways of ensuring this are by making implicit values explicit and by developing a company-wide commitment to innovation.[54]

Corporate Values

Increasingly, corporations are developing cultural statements of intent. Company values are available for employees, customers, and visitors to read in a printed brochure distributed throughout the company's offices, visitors' waiting rooms, etc.[55] Formalized statements remind managers that their decisions are guided by a set of clearly understood principles. The advantage to be gained from this practice is that corporate values are made explicit; for as Lorsch suggests, 'If managers are aware of the beliefs they share, they are less likely to be blinded by them and are apt to understand more readily when changing events make aspects of their culture obsolete'.[56]

Wilkins[57] has argued that in organisations which do not have such explicit statements, senior managers should undertake a form of cultural accounting so that they are aware of their beliefs prior to having to deal with changing events. Such accounting involves senior managers developing a consensus about their shared beliefs. In practice, this process starts with top managers, individually, listing their beliefs and values concerning financial goals/objectives, the prime purpose of the business, the nature of the product market (including quality and service), and the management of employees (including employee needs).[58] The individual answers to these questions can then be compared and form the basis for discussion among top management. Through this process, beliefs which are shared can be identified and codified.

This is a process, however, which cannot be delegated. It must include the company's major decision makers, including the Chairman, Managing Director or Chief Executive Officer.[59] They must be willing to devote the thought and time (perhaps several days) necessary to addressing these questions and to comparing and discussing their individual responses until they reach a consensus. This process should enable top managers gradually to identify a pattern for their culture, and to discover how beliefs/values are related to one another. Again the end product should be that implicit values are made explicit.[60] As many of the barriers associated with implicit cultural beliefs are removed, so management should be able to move rapidly and cohesively in the face of changing demands.

Innovation

As rapid change characterises modern markets, and given the increasing challenge from South East Asia, then as writers such as Kanter[61] and Clark[62] have suggested an innovative culture is a necessity for corporate survival and success.

Many successful companies have indeed made organisational arrangements which ensure their commitment to innovation.[63] One method has been to assign a respected senior manager to a non-portfolio role;[64] that is, to a role in which he or she is free to trouble-shoot – to raise questions, challenge beliefs and suggest new ideas. The person required for such a role must be highly intelligent, with long experience, an inquiring mind, and who has constant interaction with top management and the credibility to challenge beliefs, values and ideas.[65] While committed to the existing culture, he or she serves to keep it fluid and dynamic through their presence in the management group. The increasing presence of such managers, especially in many large American corporations, is testament to the fact that many chief executives understand the value of creative dissent.[66]

Outside directors can also play an important role in maintaining innovation. While they are usually affiliated to firms for long periods of time, they are also far enough removed to provide objectivity and to raise important questions about the appropriateness of the firm's actions.[67] While top managers hold to the view that strategic decisions are the sole purview of management, outside directors can, even with limited time and information, play an important role in keeping managers alert both to the state of the company's culture and to the changing demands being made of the company. Their activities may be conducted on an informal basis or may, as in some companies, be formalized through a Strategy Committee or the Board.[68]

A more orthodox way to ensure innovative actions is to bring in an outside consultant at a senior level.[69] A consultant can bring a new perspective and objectivity to the change situation. However, to be successful the consultant must realise that he or she will arrive with a set of beliefs based on prior experience. What worked for one client may not work for another. To be effective in a new setting, the consultant needs to be aware of the unique culture of the company. If company beliefs have been explicitly stated, then transmission is easier: if they have not, then the consultant will have to be a good detective. A poor understanding of existing beliefs can cause the consultant to step unwittingly on too many sensitive toes, and to be rejected before the ideas for which he or she was hired can be tried out.

Innovation can also be encouraged by allowing dissent at subordinate levels of management.[70] This can assure that succeeding generations of managers will be less blind and less rigid in their adherence to cultural traditions. It can also provide a source of new perspective, as novel ideas bubble up from below. For middle management, Lorsch[71] suggests that two approaches can be used to encourage new thinking. One approach is to stimulate new ideas through organisational means; as, for example, through an in-company programme for middle managers using outside instructors, or through the systematic rotation of managers among functions and/or businesses. This approach has the limitation, however, that new ideas are learned within the context of existing corporate structures.

A second, more radical route is through having managers broaden their perspectives at other institutions. Business School/University-based programmes are but one way of achieving this. Alternatively managers may learn new practices by visiting a range of firms in different countries. A number of companies have used this approach when seeking to widen the experiences of, for example, production managers.[72]

Finally, let us remember that if the corporation decides to broaden managers' experiences, it must, after any broadening experience has occurred, be ready to promote other, similar experiences. Innovation will flourish only if the corporation is committed to experimentation on a long-term basis.

Conclusions

In conclusion, we can say that the concept of culture has *long-term* implications for corporate effectiveness and success. Thus if managers wish to use the concept of culture as a variable for organisational change they must be wary of applying 'quick-fix' solutions. Many companies have been disappointed when failing to emulate the cultural styles of the so-called 'Excellent' companies. A major reason for such failures is that senior managers do not realise that an organisation's culture is based largely on phenomena which are organisation-specific. To achieve successful change, we must not only seek to change the dysfunctional elements of the organisation's culture, we must also seek to preserve and enhance those aspects of its culture which represent distinctive competences. It is here that patience is required, for corporate culture is a deep-seated phenomenon and cultural change can take a long time to achieve.

We can also suggest that awareness of the procedures for achieving cultural change can provide us with new possibilities for strategic decision-making. If culture is at odds with strategy then we have choices of ignoring the culture, managing around it, trying to change the culture to fit the strategy, or changing the strategy to fit the culture. A knowledge of corporate culture and of the processes of cultural change can help us develop a more *proactive* approach to strategic decision-making. We have noted how corporate culture affects various stages of the strategic decision process and consequently the form and content of corporate strategies. With a knowledge of the processes of cultural change we need no longer view culture as merely a constraint on strategy. Instead we can use corporate culture as a variable for developing effective corporate decisions. Only by developing strategies that are informed by an understanding of the corporation's culture will we attain the kind of results we desire.

Notes

[. . .]

3. See Peters, T. and Waterman, R., *In Search of Excellence*. New York: Harper & Row, 1982; and Ouchi, W., *Theory Z*. Reading, Mass: Addison-Wesley, 1978.

4. See Allen, R., 'Four phases for bringing about cultural change' in R. Kilmann *et al*. (eds), *Gaining Control of the Corporate Culture*. San Francisco: Jossey-Bass, 1985; Kilmann, R., 'Five steps to closing culture gaps' in R. Kilmann *et al*. (eds) 1985; Schein, E., 'The role of the founder in creating organizational cultures', *Organizational Dynamics*, 12, 1983, pp. 3–29; and Schein, *Organizational Culture and Leadership*. San Francisco: Jossey-Bass, 1985.

5. See Uttal, B., 'The corporate culture vultures', *Fortune*, 17, 1983, pp. 66–72 and Kilmann, R., *Beyond the Quick-Fix: Managing Five Tracks to Organizational Success*. San Francisco: Jossey-Bass, 1984.

6. See Deal, T., 'Cultural change: Opportunity, silent killer or metamorphosis', in R. Kilmann *et al*. (eds), 1985.

7. See Wilkins, A. and Patterson, K., 'You can't get there from here: What will make culture-change projects fail', in R. Kilmann *et al*. (eds), 1985.

8. See Jelinek, M. *et al*., 'Introduction: A code of many colors', *Administrative Science Quarterly*, 28, 1983, pp. 331–8.

[. . .]

17. Schein, 1985, p. 56.

[. . .]

19. See Schein, 1985.

[. . .]

30. See Schein, 1985.

31. See Davis, S.M., *Managing Corporate Culture*. Cambridge, Mass: Ballinger Publishing Co., 1984; Schein, 1985.

32. See Fombrun, C., 'Corporate culture, environment and strategy', *Human Resource Management*, 22, 1/2, 1983, pp. 139–52.

33. See Sathe, V., 'Some action implications of corporate culture: A manager's guide to action', *Organization Dynamics*, 12(2), 1983, pp. 5–23.

34. See Lorsch, 'Strategic myopia: Culture as an invisible barrier to change', in R. Kilmann *et al*. (eds), 1985.

35. See Davis, T., 'Managing culture at the bottom', in R. Kilmann *et al*. (eds), 1985.

36. See Schwartz and Davis, 'Matching corporate culture and business strategy', *Organizational Dynamics*, 10, 1981, pp. 30–48.

37. See Kilmann, 1984.

38. See Pascale, R., 'Fitting new employees into the company culture', *Fortune*, 28 May 1984, pp. 62–9.

39. See Peters and Waterman, 1982.

40. See Kilmann, 1984

41. See Schein, 1985.

42. See Allen, 1985.

43. See Schein, 1985.

44. See Allen, 1985; and Schein, 1985.

45. See Schein, 1985.

46. See Kilmann, 1984; and Schein, 1985.

47. See Davis, 1984; Kilmann, 1984; and Schein, 1985.

48. See Sapienza, A., 'Believing in seeing: How culture influences the decisions top managers make', in R. Kilmann *et al*. (eds), 1985; and Shrivistava, P., 'Integrating strategy formulation with organizational culture', *Journal of Business Strategy*, 5, 3, 1985, pp. 103–11.

[. . .]

53. See Fombrun, 1983.

54. See Sathe, 1983; Lorsch, 1985, and 'Managing culture: The invisible barrier to change', *California Management Review*, 28, 2, 1986, pp. 95–109; and Clark, P., *Anglo-American Innovation*. New York: De Gruyter, 1988.

55. See Lorsch, 1985.

56. Ibid. p. 97.

57. See Wilkins, A., 'The cultural audit: A tool for understanding organizations', *Organizational Dynamics*, 12, 1983, pp. 24–38.

58. See Lorsch, 1985.

59. See Lorsch, 1985, 1986.

60. See Hickman, C.R. and Silva, M.A., *Creating Excellence: Managing Corporate Culture, Strategy and Change in the New Age*. London: Unwin, 1985; Pascale, 1984; and Lorsch, 1985.

61. See Kanter, R.M., *The Change Masters*. London: Counterpoint, 1985.

62. See Clark, 1988.

63. See Quinn, J., *Strategies for Change: Logical Incrementalism*. Homewood, Ill: Irwin, 1980; Donaldson, G. and Lorsch, J., *Decision Making at the Top: The Shaping of Strategic Direction*. New York: Basic Books, 1983; and Clark, 1988.

64. See Greiner, L., 'Senior executives as strategic actors', *New Management*, 1, 2, 1983, pp. 2–10; and Lorsch, 1985.

65. See Lorsch, 1985.

66. See Kanter, 1985.

67. See Lorsch, 1985.

68. Ibid.

69. See Sathe, 1983; and Lorsch, 1985.

70. See Kanter, 1985; and Davis, 1985.

71. See Lorsch, 1985.

72. Ibid.

9 Leadership Styles

David R. Brodwin and L.J. Bourgeois III

Strategic planning tools have developed enormously over the past 20 years. Such techniques as the growth/share matrix and the experience curve are in widespread use, and other planning techniques allow the manager to evaluate the impact of alternative strategies on the stock price of the corporation. Management consulting firms offer strategic planning on a commodity basis, and any new MBA comes equipped with at least one method for developing such plans.

Unfortunately, the tools for implementing strategies have not developed as quickly as the tools we use for planning. The result of this discrepancy – failed plans and abandoned planning efforts – is all too visible:

> A major diversified manufacturer concluded that a steady stream of new products was the most important factor in improving the stock price, yet the performance measures and management reports imposed on the division heads stress quarterly profit. As a result, division managers don't make the long-term investment required for successful new product development.

> A leading consumer goods company committed itself to strategic planning and built a staff of over thirty planners, many with MBAs and experience in consulting firms. Unfortunately, the expected benefits of planning failed to materialize; in less than two years, the department was disbanded and planning responsibility returned to the operating units.

Recently, business writers have begun to pay more attention to the problems of strategy implementation. Corporate culture is now widely acknowledged as an important force in the success or failure of business ventures; studies of Japanese management practices point out the effectiveness of participative methods in securing wholehearted commitment to new strategies at all levels of the organization.

Despite this interest, three critical questions remain unanswered:

- How can executives be more effective in putting chosen strategies into action?
- How can the planning process be managed so that the strategies which emerge are realistic, not only in terms of the marketplace, but also in terms of the politics, culture, and competence of the organization?

From 'Five steps to strategic action', *California Management Review*, 26(3): 176–90, 1984.

- Research shows that managers do not analyze opportunities exhaustively before taking action; rather, they shape strategy through a continuing stream of individual decisions and actions. How can we reconcile the static academic dogma, 'First formulate strategy, then implement it,' with the dynamic reality of managerial work?

To shed some light on these questions, we studied management practice at a number of companies. We have found that their approaches to strategy implementation can be categorized into one of five basic descriptions. In each one, the chief executive officer plays a somewhat different role and uses distinctive methods for developing and implementing strategies. The approaches differ in a number of other dimensions as well (see Chart 1 [Table 9.1]). We have given each description a title to distinguish its main characteristics.

The first two descriptions represent traditional approaches to implementation. Here the CEO formulates strategy first, and then thinks about implementation later.

1. *The Commander Approach* – The CEO concentrates on formulating the strategy, applying rigorous logic and analysis. He either develops the strategy himself or supervises a team of planners. Once he's satisfied that he has the 'best' strategy, he passes it along to those who are instructed to 'make it happen.'
2. *The Organizational Change Approach* – Once a strategy has been developed, the executive puts it into effect by taking such steps as reorganizing the company structure, changing incentive compensation schemes, or hiring personnel.

The next two approaches involve more recent attempts to enhance implementation by broadening the bases of participation in the planning process:

3. *The Collaborative Approach* – Rather than develop the strategy in a vacuum, the CEO enlists the help of his senior managers during the planning process in order to assure that all the key players will back the final plan.
4. *The Cultural Approach* – This is an extension of the collaborative model to involve people at middle and sometimes lower levels of the organization. It seeks to implement strategy through the development of a corporate culture throughout the organization.

The final approach begins to answer some of the questions posed above, by taking advantage of managers' natural inclinations to develop opportunities as they are encountered. While it has not been widely recognized or studied up to now, we think it may represent the next major advancement in the art of strategic management.

5. *The Crescive Approach* – In this approach, the CEO addresses strategy planning and implementation simultaneously. He is not interested in strategizing alone, or even in leading others through a protracted planning

[Table 9.1]   *Comparison of five approaches*

Factor	Approach				
	Commander	Change	Collaborative	Cultural	Crescive
How are goals set? Where in the organization (top or bottom) are the strategic goals established?	Dictated from top	Dictated from top	Negotiated among top team	Embodied in culture	Stated loosely from top; refined from bottom
What signifies success? What signifies a successful outcome to the strategic planning/implomentation process?	A good plan, as judged on economic criteria	Organization and structure which fit the strategy	An acceptable plan with broad top management support	An army of busy implementers	Sound strategies with champions behind them
What factors are considered? What are the kinds of factors, or types of rationality used in developing a strategy for resolving conflicts between alternative proposed strategies?	Economic	Economic, Political [...]	Economic, Social, Political	Economic, Social	Economic, Social, Political, Behavioral

process. Rather, he tries, through his statements and actions, to guide his managers into coming forward as champions of sound strategies. (Since this involves 'growing' strategies from within the firm, our label comes from the Latin *crescere*, to grow.)

In these five approaches we see a trend toward the CEO playing an increasingly indirect and more subtle role in strategy development. We question the recentralization of strategy-making at headquarters, a trend documented (and encouraged) by some recent writers. We think, at least for some firms, that this might be a mistake.

Our Approach   For clarity, we have reduced the five approaches to their essential elements. This may border on caricature; the Commander Approach, in particular, can be applied with much more subtlety than we have indicated here. Our intent here is not to denigrate any approach but – by exaggerating the differences between approaches – to better identify and analyze the assumptions on which they rest. (To highlight the differences in abbreviated form, [Table 9.2] summarizes the five approaches, showing for each the form of the strategic management question and the CEO's role.)

[Table 9.2]   *The five approaches in brief*

Approach	The CEO's strategic question	CEO's role
Commander	'How do I formulate the optimum strategy?'	Rational actor
Change	'I have a strategy in mind; now how do I implement it?'	Architect
Collaborative	'How do I involve top management to get commitment to strategies from the start?'	Coordinator
Cultural	'How do I involve the whole organization in implementation?'	Coach
Crescive	'How do I encourage managers to come forward as champions of sound strategies?'	Premise-setter and Judge

The Commander Approach

The Scenario   You are the chief executive officer of a large industrial corporation. After six months of study, your consultant hands you a report detailing which businesses the firm should be in and how it should compete in each area. You have studied the report and it supports your own calculations. Now you call all your top managers into a conference room, present the strategy, tell them to implement it, and await the results.

The Approach   The Commander Approach addresses the traditional strategic management question of 'How can I, as a general manager, develop a strategy for my business which will guide day-to-day decisions in support of my longer-term objectives?' The Commander Approach typically employs such tools as experience curves, growth/share matrices, PIMS studies, and industry and competitive analyses.

Strengths and Limitations   In the right company, the Commander Approach will help the executive make difficult day-to-day decisions from a strategic perspective. However, the following conditions must exist for the approach to succeed:

- The CEO must wield enough power to command implementation; or, the strategy must pose little threat to the current management, otherwise implementation will be resisted;
- accurate and timely information must be available and the environment must be stable enough to allow it to be assimilated; and
- the strategist (if different from the CEO) should be insulated from personal biases and political influences which may affect the content of the plan.

An additional drawback of the Commander Approach is that it can sap motivation. People on the firing line tend to withhold strategic alternatives which they think have little chance of acceptance.[1] If the CEO creates the belief that the only acceptable strategies are those developed at the top, he may find himself faced with an extremely unmotivated, un-innovative group of employees.

Why This Approach Persists In light of the limitations of the Commander Approach in its pure form, why is it still prevalent in business schools and among consultants? Several factors account for its popularity. First, despite its drawbacks, it offers a valuable perspective to the chief executive. Second, by dividing the strategic management task into two stages – 'thinking' and 'doing' – the general manager reduces the number of factors he must consider simultaneously. Third, it fits the predisposition common in younger managers toward dealing with the quantitative and objective elements of a situation, rather than with more subjective and behavioral considerations. Finally, the separation between the planner/manager as a thinker and everyone else as a doer fits the view of the boss as an all-powerful hero, shaping the destiny of thousands with his decisions. This somewhat macho view naturally appeals to many aspiring managers.

The Change Approach

The Scenario After receiving your planning group's strategic recommendations, you have reviewed them and have made your strategy decisions. Now you plan modifications to the organization which will support the success of the plan. This includes a new organization structure, personnel changes, new information systems, and revisions to the compensation scheme.

The Approach The Organizational Change Approach extends the Commander Approach by addressing the question 'I have a strategy – now how do I get my organization to implement it?' This approach starts where the Commander Approach ends: with implementation. It assumes that the economic tools described above for strategy formulation have been mastered and adds to the tool kit several behavioral science techniques – including: the use of structure and staffing to focus attention on the firm's new priorities; revising planning and control systems; and other organizational change techniques. The role of the CEO is that of an architect, designing administrative systems to push his recalcitrant company towards new goals.

Structure and Staffing Perhaps the most obvious tool for strategy implementation is to reorganize or to shift personnel in order to lead the firm in the desired direction. The logic behind this approach is that the organization structure should foster the skill-set and outlook needed for the strategy to succeed. For example, a strategy calling for worldwide coordination of manufacturing in order to capture cost efficiencies demands a functional organization for production, while a strategy calling for coordination of marketing (e.g., Proctor and Gamble) calls for a product-oriented organization.

Planning and Control Systems   Planning systems governing capital and operating budgets can be adjusted to encourage decisions consistent with the strategy. For example, if the firm's strategy calls for investing in some businesses while harvesting others, it would be folly to rely on a capital budgeting system which arbitrarily approves every project with a return above a given hurdle rate.

Information systems should translate the strategy into meaningful short-term milestones, so that the progress according to the strategy can be monitored. The key to effective use of information systems in implementing a strategy lies in modern database technology. With traditional systems it was possible to summarize data in only one dimension, usually the line reporting structure. With a database approach, it is possible to track the strategy from multiple perspectives – e.g., division, geography, product line, and type of expense.

The power of such an information system is enhanced considerably when integrated with incentive compensation. Unfortunately, in many cases it isn't possible to translate strategic goals into the clearcut terms needed to support an effective incentive compensation system. At a minimum, however, the general manager must insure that current compensation arrangements don't create an incentive in opposition to the substance of the strategic plan.

Cultural Adaptation   To implement strategy more effectively, the manager can rely on techniques discovered by third world development agencies.[2] These techniques for introducing change in an organization include such fundamentals as: using demonstrations rather than words to communicate the desired new activities; focusing early efforts on the needs that are already recognized as important by most of the organization; and having solutions presented by persons who have high credibility in the organization. These techniques apply equally to the corporate world. For example, the successful introduction of a new technology in one geographic division (a 'demonstration') makes it easier to subsequently obtain organization-wide adoption particularly if the test division shows a significant performance gain.

Strengths and Limitations   With a set of powerful implementation tools at his disposal, the executive using the Change Approach can carry out more difficult plans that would be possible without them. Thus, in a very practical sense, this approach will be more effective than the pure Commander Approach in many organizations.

However, tacking 'implementation' onto 'strategy' doesn't solve most of the problems encountered with the first approach: i.e., the Change Approach doesn't help the CEO and planning staff stay abreast of rapidly changing business conditions; it doesn't deal with situations where politics and personal agendas discourage objectivity among the planners; and, since it still calls for imposing the strategy in top-down fashion, it doesn't resolve the motivational problems created by the first approach.

Finally, this approach can backfire in uncertain or rapidly changing business conditions. The general manager trades off important strategic flexibility by manipulating strategy. Some of these systems, particularly incentive compensation, take a long time to design and install. Should a change in the environment require a new strategy, it may be very difficult to change the firm's course, since all the 'levers' controlling the firm have been set firmly in support of the now-obsolete game plan.

The Collaborative Approach

The Scenario With key executives and division managers, you embark on a week-long planning retreat. Each participant presents his own ideas of where the firm should head. Extensive discussions follow, until the group reaches a consensus around the firm's longer-range mission and near-term strategy. Upon returning to their respective offices, each participant charges ahead in the agreed-upon direction.

The Approach The Collaborative Approach extends strategic decision-making to the organization's top management team in answer to the question 'How can I get my top management team to help develop and commit to a good set of goals and strategies?'

In this approach, the CEO employs group dynamics and 'brainstorming' techniques to get managers with differing points of view to contribute to the strategic planning process in order to extract whatever 'group wisdom' is inherent in these multiple perspectives. The role of the CEO is that of coordinator, ensuring that all good ideas are entertained.

A number of corporations use some type of collaborative approach. General Motors formed 'business teams' in 1980 which consisted of managers from different functional areas. The role of the team was simply to bring different points of view on whatever strategic – usually product-focused – problem was identified. Exxon's major strategic decisions are made by its management committee, which is comprised of all of Exxon's inside directors and is chaired by the board chairman. Every committee member serves as 'contact executive' for the line managers of one or more of Exxon's 13 affiliates and subsidiaries.

Strengths and Limitations The Collaborative Approach overcomes two key limitations inherent in the previous two. By capturing information carried by executives closer to operations, and by engaging several brains at once, it increases the quality and timeliness of the information incorporated in the plan. And, to the extent that participation breeds commitment among the deciders, it improves the probability of successful implementation.

However, what the Collaborative Approach gains in team commitment it may lose in economic rationality. In this approach, strategy is a negotiated outcome among players with different points of view and, possibly, different goals. The negotiated aspect of the process brings with it several risks – that the strategy will be more conservative and less visionary than one developed by a single person or staff team; that the decision-making group may block out bad news, leading to the disorder known variously as 'marketing myopia' or 'groupthink'; and that gaming or fief-building tendencies on the part of senior managers may prevent a consensus from emerging.

A more fundamental criticism of the Collaborative Approach is that it is not 'real' collective decision-making from an organizational standpoint because the managers – the organizational elite – cannot or will not give up centralized control. In effect, this approach preserves the artificial distinction between thinkers and doers and fails to draw upon the full human potential within and throughout the organization. It is the plumbing of this potential that forms the basis of our fourth approach.

The Cultural Approach

The Scenario   Having formulated both a competitive strategy and a long-term 'vision' for your company (either alone or with the collaboration of your senior managers), you proceed to inculcate your entire organization with this vision by molding the organization's culture in such a way that *all* organization members participate in making decisions that will perpetuate the vision. You draft and publish a company creed and song, and create other symbols which, when absorbed by both workers and managers, will ensure singleness of purpose and unity in action.

The Approach   The Cultural Approach extends the Collaborative Approach to lower levels in the organization as an answer to the strategic management question 'How can I get my whole organization committed to our goals and strategies?'

In this approach, the CEO guides his organization by communicating and instilling his vision of the overarching mission for the firm, and then allowing each individual to design his own work activities in concert with that mission. So, once the game plan is set, the CEO plays the role of coach in giving general direction, but encourages individual decision-making to determine the operating details of executing the plan.

To a large extent, the Cultural Approach represents the latest wave of management techniques promulgated to (and, in some cases, enthusiastically adopted by) American managers seeking the panacea to our recent economic woes in the face of successful Japanese competition.

The implementation tools used in building a strong corporate culture range from such simple notions as publishing a company creed and singing a company song to much more complex techniques. These more complex – and usually effective – techniques involve implementing strategy by employing the concept of 'third-order control.'

Since implementation involves controlling the behavior of others, we can think of three levels of control. First-order control involves direct supervision.

Second-order control involves using rules, procedures, and organization structure to guide the behavior of others (as in the Organizational Change Approach described above). Third-order control is a much more subtle – and potentially more powerful – means of influencing behavior through shaping the norms, values, symbols, and beliefs that managers and employees use in making day-to-day decisions.

The key distinction between managers using the Cultural Approach and those simply engaged in 'participative management,' is that these executives understand that corporate culture should serve as the handmaiden to corporate strategy, rather than proselytize 'power equalization' and the like for its own sake.

The Cultural Approach begins to break down the barriers between 'thinkers' and 'doers.' Examples of the successful application of this model are numerous. Hewlett-Packard is a much-heralded example of a company where the employees share a strong awareness of the corporate mission. They all know that the 'HP way' encourages product innovation at every level and at every bench. Matsushita starts each day at 8:00 am with 87,000 employees singing the company song and reciting its code of values.

Strengths and Limitations   Once a corporate culture that supports the firm's goals is established, the chief executive's implementation task is 90 percent done. With a cadre of committed managers and workers, the organization can more or less put itself on 'automatic pilot' with new strategic thrusts being assimilated and implemented at lower levels.

The most visible cost of this system also yields its primary strength. The consensus decision-making and other culture-inculcating activities consume enormous amounts of time, but the pay-off can be speedy execution and reduced gamesmanship among managers. As William Coates, executive vice president of the Westinghouse construction group, described it, 'We spend a lot of time trying to get a consensus, but once you get it, the implementation is instantaneous. We don't have to fight any negative feelings.'[3]

Based on our assessment of the nature of companies which are generally held up as examples of this approach, it appears that the cultural approach works best where the organization has sufficient resources to absorb the cost of building and maintaining the value system. The example firms, Hewlett-Packard, IBM, Matsushita, and Intel, are high-growth firms. Intel, for example, 'promised not to fire any permanent employee whose job was eliminated'. The company's phenomenal sales growth, 29.3% in 1980, helps absorb everyone who wants to stay.[4]

The Cultural Method has several limitations. For one, it only works with informed and intelligent people (note that most of the examples are firms in high technology industries). Second, it consumes enormous amounts of time to install. Third, it can foster such a strong sense of organizational identity among employees that it becomes almost a handicap – that is, it can be difficult to have outsiders at top levels because the executives won't accept the infusion of alien blood.

In addition, companies with excessively strong cultures will often suppress deviance, impede attempts to change, and tend to foster homogeneity and inbreeding.[5] The intolerance of deviance can be a problem when innovation is critical to strategic success. But a strong culture will reject inconsistency.

To handle this conformist tendency, companies such as IBM, Xerox and GM have separated their ongoing research units and their new product development efforts, sometimes placing them in physical locations far enough away to shield them from the corporation's culture.

Homogeneity can stifle creativity, encouraging non-conformists to leave for more accepting pastures and thereby robbing the firm of its innovative talent. The strongest criticism of the Cultural Approach is that it has such an overwhelming doctrinal air about it. It smacks of faddism and may really be just another variant of the CEO-centred approaches (i.e., Commander and Organizational Change Approaches). As such, it runs the risk of maintaining the wall between 'thinkers' and 'doers.'

Preserving that thinker/doer distinction may be the Cultural Approach's main appeal. It affords executives an illusion of control. But holding tight the reins of control (a natural tendency in turbulent times) may result in some lost opportunities – opportunities encountered by line managers in their day-to-day routines.

The next section outlines how some firms capitalize on these opportunities.

The Crescive Approach

The Scenario   As a general manager, you have just received a proposal to pursue continued development of a new product. You evaluate the report, deflate some overly optimistic figures, and consider the manager's track record. The product offers attractive profit potential and seems to fit the general direction you envision for the firm, so you approve the proposal.

The Approach   The Crescive Approach addresses some of the limitations ascribed to the previous approaches by posing the CEO's question as follows: 'How can I encourage my managers to develop, champion, and implement sound strategies?'

The Crescive Approach differs from others in several respects. First, instead of strategy being delivered downward by top management or a planning department, it moves upward from the 'doers' (salespeople, engineers, production workers) and lower middle-level managers. Second, 'strategy' becomes the sum of all the individual proposals that surface throughout the year. Third, the top management team shapes the employees' premises – that is, their notions of what would constitute supportable strategic projects. Fourth, the chief executive functions more as a judge, evaluating the proposals that reach his desk, than as a master strategist.

The Plight of the Chief Executive   At first, the Crescive Approach may sound too risky. After all, it calls for the chief executive to relinquish a lot of control over the strategy-making process, seemingly leaving to chance the major decisions which determine the long-term competitive strength of the company.

To understand the forces which underlie the emergence of the crescive approach, it is necessary to take a fresh look at the task facing the chief executive of large diversified corporations. The CEO faces an unusual dilemma. He is ultimately responsible for the corporation and its divisions, but the size and complexity of the business make it impossible for him to know and understand all the strategic and operating situations facing these divisions.[6] Therefore, if he is to exploit the fact that they can see strategic opportunities which he cannot, he must give up some control over it in order to foster strategic opportunism and achievement. However, this places his career (if not his personal wealth) in the hands of others. How can he manage this?

To answer this question, let's consider five aspects of the strategic management problem:

1. *The chief executive cannot monitor all significant opportunities and threats.* If the company is highly diversified, it is impossible for senior management to stay abreast of developments in all of the firm's different industries. Similarly, if an industry is shifting very quickly (e.g., personal computers), information collected at lower levels often becomes stale before it can be assimilated, summarized, and passed up the ranks. Even in more stable industries, the time required to process information upward through many management levels can mean that decisions are being based on outdated information.

   As a result, in many cases the CEO must abandon the effort to plan centrally. Instead, an incentive scheme or 'free market' environment is established to encourage operating managers to make decisions that will further the long-range interests of the company.

2. *The power of the chief executive is limited.* The chief executive typically enjoys substantial power derived from the ability to bestow rewards, allocate resources, and reduce the uncertainty for members of the organization. Thus, to an extent, the executive can impose his or her will on other members of the organization.

   However, the chief executive is not omnipotent. Employees can always leave the firm, and key managers wield control over information and important client relationships. As a result, the CEO must often compromise on programs he wishes to implement.

   Research indicates that new projects led by managers who were coerced into the leadership role fail, regardless of the intrinsic merit of the proposal. In contrast, a second-best strategy championed by a capable and determined advocate may be far more worthwhile than the optimum strategy with only lukewarm support.

3. *Few executives have the freedom to plan.* Although it is often said that one of the most important jobs of an executive is to engage in thoughtful planning, research shows that few executives actually set aside time to plan. Most spend the majority of their work days attending to short-range problems.[7]

   Thus, any realistic approach to strategic planning must recognize that executives simply don't plan much. They are bombarded constantly by requests from subordinates. So they shape the company's future more through their day-to-day decisions – encouraging some projects and discouraging others – than by sweeping policy statements or written plans. This process has been described as 'logical incrementalism' because it can be a rational process that proceeds in small steps rather than by long leaps.[8]

4. *Tight control systems hinder the planning process.* In formulating strategies, top managers rely heavily on subordinates for up-to-date information, strategic recommendations, and approval of the operating goals.

   The CEO's dependence on his subordinate managers creates a thorny control problem. In essence, if managers know they'll be accountable for plans they formulate or the information they provide, they have an incentive to bias their estimates of their division's performance. A branch of decision science called 'agency theory' suggests how this situation should be handled. First, if the CEO wants his managers to deliver unbiased estimates, he cannot hold them tightly accountable for the successful implementation of each strategic proposal. Without such accountability, he can place great emphasis on commitment as a force for getting things done.

   Second, in order to assess the true ability and motivation of any subordinate, the CEO must observe him over a long period of time on a number of different projects. Occasional failures should be expected, tolerated, and not penalized.

   One means to promote the ongoing flow of strategic information is to establish a special venture capital fund to take advantage of promising ideas that arise after the strategic and operating plans have been completed. Like the IBM 'Fellows' or the Texas Instruments 'Idea' programs, this approach allows opportunities to be seized and developed by their champions at the time they are perceived.

5. *Strategies are produced by groups, not individuals.* Strategies are rarely created by single individuals. They are usually developed by groups of people, and they incorporate different perspectives on the business. The problem with group decisions is that groups tend to avoid uncertainty and to smooth over conflicts prematurely.

   To reduce the distortions that can result from group decision-making, the CEO can concentrate on three tools: first, encouraging an atmosphere that tolerates expression of different opinions; second, using organization development techniques (such as group dynamics exercises) to reduce individual defensiveness and to increase the receptivity of the group to discrepant data; and third, establish separate planning groups at the corporate level and the line organization.

The Responsibilities of the Chief Executive The Crescive Approach for strategic management suggests some generalizations concerning how the chief executive of the large divisionalized firm should help the organization generate and implement sound strategies. The recommendation consists of the following four elements:

- Maintain the openness of the organization to new and discrepant information. This can be done through careful use of staff, external consultants, and market research, and through judicious hiring and rotation policies.
- Articulate a general strategy to guide the firm's growth. This should delineate corporate priorities and shape the premises by which managers at all levels decide which strategic opportunities to pursue.
- Manipulate systems and structures to encourage bottom-up strategy formulation. Critical to this goal is the availability of seed funding for good ideas, unencumbered by bureaucratic approval cycles; tolerance for the inevitable failure when a strong effort has been made; and favorable publicity for the innovators.
- Use the 'logical incrementalist' manner described by James Brian Quinn,[9] to select from among the strategies which emerge.

One of the most important and potentially elusive of these methods is the process of shaping managers' decision-making premises. The CEO can shape these premises in at least three ways. First, the CEO can emphasize a particular theme or strategic thrust ('We are in the information business') to direct strategic thinking. Second, the planning methodology endorsed by the CEO can be communicated to affect the way managers view the business. Third, the organizational structure can indicate the dimensions on which strategies should focus. A firm with a product-divisional structure will probably encourage managers to generate strategies for domination in certain product categories, whereas a firm organized around geographical territories will probably evoke strategies to secure maximum penetration of all products in particular regions.

Conclusion

These five approaches to developing and implementing strategy represent a range of techniques. Through extensive interviews, most managers indicated to us that one of these five approaches predominates in their company, although often one or two of the other approaches may also play a limited role.

The choice of method should depend on the size of the company, the degree of diversification, the degree of geographical dispersion, the stability of the business environment, and, finally, the managerial style currently embodied in the company's culture. Our research suggests that the Commander, Change, and Collaborative Approaches can be effective for smaller companies and firms in stable industries while the Cultural and Crescive alternatives are used by more complex corporations.

In the few cases where two different approaches played equally strong roles in the same company, an explanation could be found in the history and makeup of the company. For example, one company we studied was active in two distinct industries: its aerospace divisions, based in California, used a crescive strategic management process, while its automotive operation, headquartered in the Midwest, used a planning system incorporating elements of both the Commander and the Change Approaches.

Business strategy was once a science of classification: divide the businesses into four piles; get rid of some and nurture others. Now it has become a much more subtle enterprise. Considerations of motivation and the politics of organizations are inescapable. Culture is discovered to have a decisive effect, a finding that should shock no one. It becomes impossible to separate the underlying economic merits of strategy from the drive and dedication of the person who proposes it.

Clearly this situation calls for new approaches. While many observers of the business scene have embraced solutions from overseas, a few companies have been quietly developing a more practical approach. This approach recognizes the need for sound analysis without overlooking the importance of motivation. It acknowledges the chief executive's responsibility for strategy but recognizes his dependence on the eyes, ears, brains, and hands of others in the firm. This approach is crescive management.

Notes

1. Eugene E. Carter, 'The behavioral theory of the firm and top-level corporate decisions,' *Administrative Science Quarterly* 16(4), 1971: 413–28.

2. Conrad M. Arensburg and Arthur H. Niehoff, *Introducing Social Change*, 2nd edn. Chicago, IL: Aldine, 1971.

3. Jeremy Main, 'Westinghouse's cultural revolution,' *Fortune*, 15 June 1981, pp. 74–93.

4. Jeremy Main, 'How to battle your own bureaucracy,' *Fortune*, 29 June 1981, pp. 54–8.

5. William G. Ouchi, *Theory Z: How American Business Can Meet the Japanese Challenge*. Reading, MA: Addison-Wesley, 1981.

6. Norman Berg, 'Strategic planning in conglomerate companies,' *Harvard Business Review*, May/June 1965, pp. 79–91.

7. Henry Mintzberg, 'The manager's job: Folklore and fact,' *Harvard Business Review*, July/August 1985, pp. 49–61.

8. James Brian Quinn, 'Strategic change: "Logical incrementalism",' *Sloan Management Review*, 20(1), Fall 1978: 7–21.

9. Ibid.

10 Strategic Convergence

Donald C. Hambrick and Albert A. Cannella Jr

Today's strategists are at no loss for concepts and techniques to help them formulate strategies. Over the past 15 years, consultants and academic researchers have introduced a variety of powerful and pragmatic tools for answering the question, 'Where and how should we compete?' Tools such as industry and competitor analysis, portfolio models, product life-cycle theory, and internal strength and weakness analysis have gained widespread use.[1] Many executives now express satisfaction with the methods used to derive their business strategies.

But many of these 'best-laid plans' are failing to see the light of day. Plans to innovate fizzle out after a series of task-force meetings; plans to improve quality get no farther than some airy rhetoric and the hiring of a 'quality guru'; and plans to become the low-cost producer bog down when corporate officers balk at expensive outlays for plant modernization. In short, many of our strategies simply aren't happening. Without successful implementation, a strategy is but a fantasy. This problem – how to convert a new strategy into concrete competitive success – is what managers now need frameworks for, and is the focus of our chapter.

Actually, the widespread inability to implement strategy may be a sign that accepted approaches to strategy formulation are not as good as many think they are, for a well-conceived strategy is one that is *implementable*. For that reason, implementation must be considered *during* the formulation process, not later, when it may be too late. A tendency to treat formulation and implementation as two separate phases is at the root of many failed strategies.[2] Regrettably, the recent trend among consultants and business schools to treat strategy formulation as being primarily based on industry and product/market economics exacerbates the schism.

The strategist will not to be able to nail down every action step when the strategy is first crafted – nor, as we will later argue, should this even be attempted. However, he or she must have the ability to look ahead at the major implementation obstacles and ask, 'Is this strategy workable? Can I make it happen?' If an honest assessment yields 'no' or 'only at an unacceptable risk,' then the formulation process must continue. A great strategy is only great if it can actually be carried out. Thus, the guidelines we offer in this chapter about

From 'Strategy implementation as substance and selling', *Academy of Management Executive*, 3(4): 278–85, 1989.

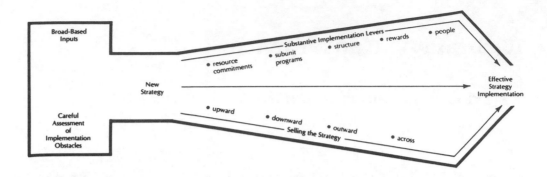

[Figure 10.1]   *The elements of effective strategy implementation*

implementation must be in the mindset of the strategist even at the earliest formulation stages.

Our ideas about strategy implementation have evolved on the basis of situations we have observed in numerous firms, as well as a long and careful reading of the literature on the topic.[3] However, our thoughts have been crystallized and clarified particularly by a recent opportunity to study several successful and unsuccessful implementations of business strategies in a large multibusiness firm. The top management of this company, which we will call Globus, had concluded that the major difference between competitive success and failure for its business units lay more in matters of strategy implementation than formulation, and they sought to understand the common ingredients of their own most effective business strategy implementations. At Globus, we had an opportunity to examine a broad range of plans for strategic change – for achieving low cost position, going global, consolidating, and others. Here, we will draw on one of the businesses we studied – the Bondall Division – to illustrate the very persuasive, recurring themes we observed.

Succinctly put, and portrayed in [Figure 10.1], these were the patterns of behavior for the effective strategy implementers at Bondall and the other units we studied:

1. Obtain broad-based inputs and participation at the formulation stage.
2. Carefully and deliberately assess the obstacles to implementation.
3. Make early, first-cut moves across the full array of implementation levers – resource commitments, subunit policies and programs, structure, people, and rewards.
4. Sell, sell, sell the strategy to everyone who matters – upward, downward, across, and outward.
5. Steadily fine tune, adjust, and respond as events and trends arise.

Background on Bondall

Bondall manufactured several variants of the chemical product ACP, which is used in numerous industrial and consumer product applications ranging from aircraft parts to sporting goods. Bondall had five plants spread across North America, totalling 40 per cent of industry capacity. With these plants located near major customers, Bondall had competed on the basis of price and reliable delivery, emphasizing the commodity segment of the industry; it had always let customers seek out their own applications for ACP. As Will Langston, the division's general manager, said, 'This has always been a tankcar business – we sell carloads full of this stuff. What customers do with it, or might do with it, has never been our concern. The one exception is our New Jersey plant, acquired two years ago, which has a substantial customer application and product R&D section.'

In 1982, two competitors built large plants with a radical new process technology, plunging the industry into dramatic oversupply and pulling down prices for what seemed the long-term future. It became clear that Bondall could no longer be profitable in the commodity segment of the business. Building new plants with the new process technology was out of the question, since Globus (the parent) was not willing to place large investments in mature businesses. After several weeks of analysis and discussion, Bondall management decided on a new strategic direction. Their plan was to deemphasize the traditional commodity segment and largely remake the entire business in the likeness of the New Jersey facility, with a major emphasis on higher value-added, differentiated customer problem solving through the use of ACP.

As part of this plan, management knew the business would have to shrink; in fact, they planned to close the two least efficient plants within a year. They also decided to shift the mix of commodity/speciality business as follows:

[Table 10.1] *Targets under Bondall's new strategy*

	1982	1984	1986
Sales ($ millions)			
Commodity	200	100	60
Specialty	20*	60	100
Total	220	160	160
Number of plants	5	3	3
Return on assets (%) (before taxes)	10	15	22

*All from New Jersey unit

This strategy then fell clearly in line with what Porter[4] called a *differentiation* strategy and Miles and Snow[5] referred to as a *prospector* strategy. From these authors and others, we know what an organization will tend to look like once such a strategy is implemented, but we have little in the way of insights or framework for getting the organization into its new configuration; that is, how does the organization get from here to there?

Langston, following an approach similar to that used by other effective strategy implementers we have observed, met with great success. By the end of 1987, Bondall's sales were $200 million, with about $150 million coming from specialty products. Return on assets that year was 22 per cent. The business developed a highly sophisticated marketing research and customer application capability, identifying and attracting numerous customers that had never used ACP before.

At the outset, Bondall management clearly had a significantly new strategy in mind. The way in which they went on to implement it serves as an archetypal example of the key elements of effective strategic change we observed in our research: astute preliminary groundwork; prompt, broad-gauged, substantive initiatives; and a lot of selling.

Preliminary Groundwork

Broad-Based Inputs on Formulation

One of the most effective aids to implementation is to involve people early on in the development and debate of strategic options. In essence, then, implementation is dependent on the process that is used for formulation. It may not be possible to obtain universal agreement with a new strategic direction, but widespread inputs improve the quality of the choices, raise critical implementation issues, and make the involved individuals more receptive to the new strategy, once chosen. This wisdom is so well known that it requires little elaboration here.[6]

Langston used two major approaches to securing early, broad-based inputs on a new strategy. First, he formed two senior-level, multifunctional task forces to work in parallel (hence, essentially competitively) to analyze the business's strategic situation and make recommendations. His premise, borne out, was that the strategic facts and options were so clear-cut that both groups would arrive at essentially the same broad game plan. However, he felt that wide-spread participation would secure their intellectual and social commitment to the new course of action, as well as highlight the major issues expected to arise during implementation.

The second thing Langston did to secure early input was to meet individually with the 30 people he considered most critical to the success of any new strategy. Langston typically met with these individuals in their offices, with the express purpose of asking them where they thought the business should go and what they saw as the key implications of various approaches he was considering. (There was some overlap between these 30 people and the membership of the task forces.) Even though the one-on-one format was time consuming, Langston considered it critical since it allowed each person to speak his or her mind, conveyed a greater sense of individualism and intimacy, and allowed Langston to close each meeting by securing a commitment: 'Jim, I hear you. Those are legitimate concerns. I'm not sure what we'll decide, but I know for sure that we will need *your* support whichever way we go. Can I count on it?' To a person, all 30 pledged their support to an unknown strategic direction. While not all would be delighted by it when it was finally announced, it would be very difficult, both psychologically and interpersonally, for any one to then block or otherwise sabotage the new direction when it was underway.[7]

Deliberate Assessment of Obstacles

The strategist must comprehend that the implementation setting is not benign. A variety of obstacles – generally known but just as generally overlooked – can and will intervene to prevent the new strategy from unfolding. The effective strategist has a careful understanding of these obstacles. Langston even went so far as to develop a written inventory and analysis of the key barriers his new strategy would face. We will not describe Langston's inventory here, only its three major categories: internal obstacles, external obstacles, and the parent company.

Internal Obstacles The success of a strategy primarily depends on marshalling resources within the business itself. Human and material limitations make this difficult: The business may have the wrong configurations of physical resources, human resources, and systems and procedures. Of equal importance, however, is the fact that there will be internal resistance to correcting these deficiencies. Political resistance arises from individuals who feel they stand to lose something of value if the new strategy is implemented; ideological resistance arises from those who believe the new strategy is ill-fated or in violation of deeply held values; and blind resistance arises from those who are intolerant or afraid of change.

External Obstacles The strategist must also navigate around obstacles outside the business unit. The most obvious counterforce is competition, but the general economic and technological environment can also intervene to impede a new strategy. Less obvious sources of resistance are allies such as suppliers, distributors, and trade associations. These allies often have vested interests in the current strategy of the business and can resist for the same reasons as do those inside the firm.

Parent Company A final potential obstacle is the parent company. Corporate officials can impede implementation, even after approving the strategy in principle. The parent's own grand strategy may change, or it may simply lose patience with or confidence in the new strategy. The strategist must understand that there is nothing unfair about the loss of corporate support: It is a reality. The parent is under its own set of pressures and wants to put its resources where they will do the most good. It is up to the strategist in the business unit to keep corporate executives committed.

A Lot of Substance: Early Use of Implementation Levers

Once the strategist has secured various inputs, settled on the new strategy, and carefully assessed the major obstacles, he or she is ready to start taking substantive implementation actions. Obviously, the number and types of implementation actions depend largely on situational specifics. However, our study of successful and unsuccessful strategy implementation allows some reliable identification of the five major 'make-happen' areas the strategist must consider: resource commitments, subunit policies and programs, structure, rewards, and people. What we have found is that the effective implementer makes significant use of all these levers within the first three months of unveiling a new strategy, without trying to anticipate with precision or detail how all the levers might ultimately be configured. We will inventory the major implementation questions that need to be resolved and give examples of how Bondall dealt with them. Systematically raising these questions brings focus to the battle in developing a well-orchestrated implementation plan.

Resource Commitments

What level of resources should be directed at each product or market? What level of resources should be placed behind each competitive weapon?

Without exception, new strategies will require some type of resource reallocation. Also, many new strategies will have to provide for the acquisition of new resources. However, in addition to placing resources where they are most needed, resource allocation sends signals both inside and outside the firm. These signals provide proof of management's intentions to break with the past and 'get off the dime' under the new strategy.

At the outset of his new strategy, Langston made several major resource allocation decisions: He closed two old, inefficient plants, terminated numerous lower-margin commodity customers, funded marketing research/customer application centers at two of the remaining plants, and funded a major sales-force training program, among others. Naturally, despite Langston's early groundwork, there was some resistance to these decisions since the firm had always been the largest producer of ACP and had served many high-volume (but lower-margin) customers for years. The reallocation of resources signalled a sharp break with tradition at Bondall and caused discomfort, particularly among the salesforce. Some salespeople left the firm voluntarily, some were dismissed as part of the general downsizing of the firm, and some worked hard to develop the competencies required by the new strategy.

Though often painful, the reallocation of resources is crucial to the success of any new strategy. It is in the commitment of resources that the strategy ceases to be merely a paper plan or a gleam in the strategist's eye. As unlikely as it may sound, many strategies fail simply because resources are not decisively reallocated at the outset in line with the new direction's requirements.

Subunit Policies and Programs

What actions will each subunit need to take? According to what timetable and with what outlays?

The strategy of the business must be translated into concrete action plans within the various subunits – be they functional areas, product groups, or regions. Subunit policies and programs form the component pieces of the strategy, serving not just to implement it but also to reinforce and bolster it so that attack from the competition becomes more difficult.

For example, in the marketing function the strategy should be converted into discrete plans and policies in the areas of pricing, promotion, distribution, service, and salesforce development. At Bondall, where a high value-added segmentation strategy was developed, the new pricing policy was to not match competitors' price cuts but rather to keep prices up and sell on the basis of quality, service, and innovation. The new production scheduling policy was that custom orders took precedence and commodity runs were fit in residually, rather than the historical reverse. New salesforce targets were based on profits, not volume. These subunit policies were among the many proposed by department heads in response to Langston's early request for implementation plans from every department. Interestingly, he encouraged each head to implement only about half his or her proposed change initiatives to avoid complete chaos. (We will return shortly to this theme of moderation.) It is clear, however, that strategy implementation occurs largely through the creativity, initiative, and will of mid-level managers.

Structure

How should roles and relationships be organized? How should information flow and decisions get made?

The new strategy will often require a revised physiology for the organization. Groupings may need to be changed, the hierarchy flattened, and more lateral relationships established. The day-to-day way in which information flows and decisions get made may have to change as well.[8]

Langston reorganized Bondall considerably. He created 'customer application teams' oriented toward specific market segments, with each team consisting of sales, marketing, and technical service people. Each team was also supported by a mid-level production manager, who could work with the team on technical issues, production scheduling, and expediting. These teams were liberally sprinkled with (but not dominated by) individuals reassigned from the New Jersey operation who had substantial experience with the customer team approach.

Another major structural initiative was the creation of a product development committee, consisting of application team leaders and chaired by Langston, which met quarterly to exchange reports. The division also developed sophisticated new computer software to analyze a multitude of product/market segments. In short, the business was striving to develop the information system and decision-making protocols that would maximize the likelihood of success for their chosen strategic theme of customized product offerings.

Rewards

What behaviors and outcomes should be rewarded? What should be the types and amounts of rewards?

The impact of incentives and rewards is often overlooked in strategy implementation. This is a substantial oversight since they are a major basis for redirecting the efforts of individuals. Rewards can be formal (incentive schemes, promotions, commissions) or informal (pats on the back, a sense of pride, enthusiasm). The criteria for receiving rewards can and should be tailored to the specific strategic thrust of the business. Sometimes business units must operate within the confines of corporate compensation guidelines, thus reducing the degree of reward discretion available to the general manager. To overcome this restriction, insight and creativity are essential to stimulating key employees to support the implementation process.

At Bondall, requirements from the parent company precluded large changes in the amounts of incentive pay. However, criteria for earning bonuses were shifted dramatically away from volume/market share to margins/profits and, perhaps even more important, away from individual performance to team performance. Assignment to certain desirable application teams and to team leadership posts were held out as important lures to motivate effort, creativity and cooperation. The incentives for production managers at all levels were altered to encourage their willingness to do short, quick production runs instead of the long, efficient runs to which they had been accustomed. New product/market ideas, so central to the new strategy, were not only encouraged but backed with the seed funds and release time needed to try them out.

In the cases of the two plant closings, plant managers were expressly told that they would be evaluated and rewarded in large part on how well they managed the employee and community relations associated with the closings.

This heightened the managers' attention and sensitivity and, when coupled with corporate support for severance and outplacement arrangements, helped minimize the inevitable entanglements and costs associated with the shutdowns.

People

What personal and professional qualities will be needed in the business? How will these qualities be attained?

It is through the aptitudes, values, skills, and contacts of individuals at all levels that strategies become successes. A new strategy will almost inevitably change the optimal mix of human resources for the business. The starting point is to understand the nature of those required changes. Only then can the strategist decide how to bring about the changes. Replacement of individuals, additions to the team, training and development programs, and personal coaching and counseling are among the options available.

For example, at Bondall a number of new people with certain combinations of technical and marketing skills had to be hired or reassigned to staff the newly created market groups. As noted earlier, people from the New Jersey unit who were experienced in the new strategy were liberally seeded into other units. Some new hires with experience in customer application strategies came from other Globus businesses. In addition, intensive training programs were held to help marketing and salespeople develop their skills in market segmentation, marketing of intangibles, and so on.

These five levers – resource commitments, subunit policies and programs, structure, rewards, and people – form the strategist's implementation armament. They are the substance of strategic change. The elements form an intertwined package and must reinforce each other. In fact, among the successful implementations we have observed (including the one at Bondall), the strategist has made at least one significant change in each of the five levers within the first three months of launching the implementation effort.

However, the need for orchestrated action on all five fronts must not delay action until the last detail can be put in place. Such a full-blown implementation plan will take too long to develop and cannot be clearly envisioned at the outset. Therefore, rather than initially exhausting all possible moves, the strategist is better advised simply to be aware of the array of implementation levers at his or her disposal, make early critical changes in the levers, and then be prepared to exercise them in subsequent 'waves.' What we argue for, then, is an initial broad-gauged burst of changes across all the levers, followed by plenty of reinforcing and fine-tuning changes. As shown in [Figure 10.2], this puts us squarely between the 'comprehensive, all-at-once' and the 'incremental' schools of thought about the speed and completeness of strategic change.[9]

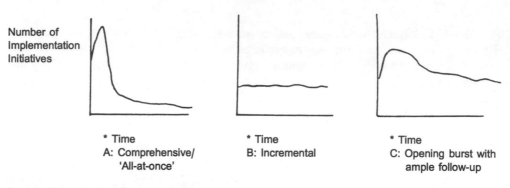

* point of commitment to a new strategy

[Figure 10.2]   *Three approaches to the timing of strategy implementation initiatives*

The Selling of Strategic Change

The new strategy, by its very nature, involves change. The anxiety and resistance provoked by the change will arise from parties who either have a vested interest in the old strategy or cannot envision the yields from the new one. The strategist thus faces a major selling job; that is, trying to build and maintain support among key constituencies for a plan that is freshly emerging. As the very successful Will Langston of Bondall told us, 'We pulled this off by selling, selling and selling some more.' These efforts of persuasion must proceed in four directions: upward to superiors, downward to subordinates, across to other organizational units, and outward to external stakeholders.[10]

Selling Upward

Executives at the corporate level need to be sold on the merits and viability of a strategy. As the stewards of corporate resources, they expect to see careful analysis and supporting data for the strategy, not only at the time it is being proposed but also while it is being implemented.

Langston of Bondall had a very difficult task in selling his strategic plan upward. The strategy called for a substantial infusion of capital and other corporate resources, and it was clearly at odds with the parent corporation's belief that Bondall was stuck in a stagnant, low-margin industry. The proposal for new equipment at two Bondall plants was the first major capital expenditure to be reviewed by the new corporate CEO, who had stated clearly that growth businesses would be favoured in the company's capital allocation. 'We made sure all the i's were dotted and all the t's crossed for this one,' a key

Bondall executive said. 'We also worked hard to pre-sell as many members of the corporate finance committee as we could.'

Not only did the initial approval require careful and complete backup, but maintaining ongoing corporate support was a challenge. Soon after the initial approval of the expansion, competitors caused the already low price of ACP to drop even lower, and corporate officials were inclined to halt the project. Bondall executives, however, developed a computerized decision model complete with price, cost, capacity, and demand variables built in. Using the model, they could show on a day-by-day basis that the new strategy was still a good choice. Their constant readiness to answer questions and qualify options allowed them to maintain credibility and ongoing corporate support for the project.

Selling Downward

Communicating with employees in the business is the type of implementation selling about which we hear most. Employees are the people who will make the strategy work, and their full understanding is required. At Bondall, many members of the management team had to be sold on the new strategy since it meant a complete change of focus and the potential loss of market share leadership. Once commitment was gained, however, the management team worked hard for the success of the overall strategy, and their ideas and efforts were key to making the implementation a success.

How did Will Langston conduct his internal selling effort at Bondall?

I anticipated that there would be four questions people would have on their minds and expect answers for:
- Why do we have to change?
- Why is this the right change?
- Why do you think this organization can handle the change?
- What are you going to do to help me through the change?

I spent a lot of effort working up answers for these questions. When they, or variations of them, were asked, I had a well thought out, and I hoped sincere, response. Even when they weren't asked, I assumed they were still on people's minds, and I would go into my selling pitch.

Of course, the news that must be shared with employees is not always upbeat. Plant closures and employee layoffs are particularly difficult. In closing two plants, Bondall kept employees and community leaders abreast of its plans and put significant outplacement and severance programs in place to help contain what otherwise could have been a very litigious and distracting episode.

Selling Across

A business unit is often dependent on other units of the firm for services or assistance in strategy implementation. For example, sister units that provide raw materials, technology, sales, or services often need to be 'sold' on the new strategy and their role in it.

In addition to its own salesforce, Bondall relied partially on a centralized salesforce, which was not under its direct control, for reaching several specific markets. In the minds of Bondall executives, this salesforce was already giving ACP too little attention compared with other products it handled. Now, with the closing of plants located near customers, the centralized salesforce started expressing a complete disinterest in ACP.

Denise Williams, Bondall's marketing manager, designed and initiated a 'sales' program directed solely at gaining the support of these individuals outside her direct authority. Williams felt that educating the salespeople about ACP and its range of customer applications would be one way to improve their effectiveness with customers. She brought sales personnel to Bondall head-quarters for production seminars, which included introduction to the staff and application team leaders, technical details of the business unit, and explanation of the various marketing and production strategies. The increased attention given to the outside salesforce stimulated them to give more attention to ACP.

Williams was convinced of the importance of calling on customers frequently; however, convincing the outside sales managers to establish a minimum calling rate was no easy task. Looking back, Williams said she was successful in this endeavor by using the same marketing technique internally that she used in the marketplace: She made regular 'calls' on the central sales managers. The payoff was an extra effort on their part in selling ACP.

Selling Outward

The strategist relies on external constituencies for success in implementation. These external parties are no different from insiders in their potential for skepticism and anxiety about the new strategy. The effective implementer will be alert to these problems and develop means for overcoming them.

When Bondall was preparing to close its two outdated plants, executives reassured desired customers about reliable delivery by testing supply lines from the remaining plants. The test convinced customers that delivery from more distant locations would be effective.

A major problem faced by Bondall was to maintain its image as a major producer in the industry in spite of having to close two plants. To address the problem, a two-part campaign was undertaken. First, ads in the print media concentrated on the new initiatives and capabilities at the three remaining plants. Second, an aggressive mail campaign was conducted to reach present and potential customers. As Denise Williams noted, the campaign represented a major change from Bondall's customary reliance on industry journals:

This way, we kept our name on the customers' desks during a difficult time. The information was sent in the form of monthly 'Bondall Newsletters.' This effort, in conjunction with print advertising and stepped up activity from our press people, gave the impression that Bondall was expanding, committed, not cutting back.

Customers are not the only external party that can influence a strategy's chances for success. Regulatory bodies, the media, and suppliers are additional examples. In their plant-closing situations, Bondall's management team was very effective at minimizing the negative fallout. Careful planning of employee relations and community relations resulted in a smooth series of events. Workers, the media, and public officials were kept well informed. In return, the business avoided unfavorable treatment in the media.

Summary, and One More Theme

So far, we have stressed two broad elements of effective strategy implementation. We have examined the substantive levers the strategist draws on to make the strategy happen and we have discussed the active, broad-based selling and communication that must occur to gain support from otherwise resistant or skeptical constituencies. These two elements of implementation could have been drawn from many quarters. The patterns have been supported by examples from the successful experience at Bondall. However, examples are widely applicable, characterizing the options and issues resolved by a number of successful strategists we have observed in various types of organizations.

However, we have seen one additional theme as well, and that is the marked tendency for successful implementers to get on with the implementation process. They are doers, action takers; they are not necessarily impulsive, but they do not attempt to wait until they have identified every potential contingency before beginning to take action. The effective strategist establishes a broad theme and makes several immediate reinforcing decisions across the array of levers we have discussed. Then, he or she vigilantly waits until circumstances unfold to identify other decisions that need to be made. All these later decisions serve to reinforce the original broad theme – be it cost leadership, product innovation, global expansion, or some other basis for competing.

Why is this approach – an opening burst of supporting initiatives with an ample stream of follow-up-actions – a hallmark of effective strategists? Let's turn the question the other way: What are the deficiencies of the alternative approaches? Why is the development of a fully exhaustive and comprehensive implementation plan at the outset of a new strategy usually ineffective? First of all, because it's a stall. Despite the illusion that this approach brings quick action, in reality a quest for an exhaustive implementation plan takes a long time and greatly postpones the changes that are needed. Second, it's unrealistic. All contingencies and eventualities cannot be envisioned at the outset. Finally, a seemingly airtight plan takes on an air of sanctity and authenticity that makes spontaneous correction very difficult for the architect to handle psychologically.

What are the problems with the other extreme, the incremental approach? Its biggest shortcoming is that it does not provide the new strategic thrust with enough early reinforcement. The opportunity to create organizational energy and momentum in support of the new direction is squandered if early initiatives are modest in either scope or magnitude. In fact, an announcement of strategic change without prompt and substantial supporting actions evokes a withering cynicism in an organization, which even artful strategists then have difficulty overcoming.

A close understanding of implementation successes reveals that the strategists set out with broad game plans in mind but were flexible, open-minded, and always on the lookout for the problems the new strategy would be creating and for ways of solving those problems. These strategists were opportunists in the most positive sense of the word. They had broad guidance systems, but were spontaneous and responsive as truly successful strategists must be.

Notes

The authors gratefully acknowledge support from Columbia University's Executive Leadership Research Center and Strategy Research Center.

1. For summaries of leading, widely used strategy formulation concepts and tools, see C. Hofer and D. Schendel, *Strategy Formulation: Analytic Concepts*, St. Paul, MN: West, 1978; and M.L. Porter, *Competitive Strategy*, New York: Free Press, 1980.

2. An eloquent discussion of the pitfalls of conceptually separating strategy formulation and implementation is presented in J.B. Quinn, H. Mintzberg and R.J. James, *The Strategy Process*, Englewood Cliffs, NJ: Prentice-Hall, 1988.

3. Readers interested in other treatments of strategy implementation may wish to see K. Andrews, *The Concept of Corporate Strategy*, Homewood, IL: Irwin, 1971; J. Galbraith and R. Kazanjian, *Strategy Implementation: The Role of Structure and Process*, St. Paul, MN: West, 1985; L.G. Hrebiniak and W.F. Joyce, *Implementing Strategy*, Cambridge, MA: Ballinger, 1982; and D. Nadler and M.L. Tushman, *Strategic Organization Design*, Boston, MA: Scott, Foresman, 1987.

4. See Porter, 1985.

5. R.E. Miles and C.C. Snow, *Organizational Strategy, Structure, and Process*, Englewood Cliffs, NJ: Prentice-Hall, 1978.

6. See various readings in J.R. Kimberly and R.E. Quinn (eds), *Managing Organizational Transitions*, Homewood, IL: Irwin, 1984.

7. W. Guth and I. MacMillan, 'Implementation versus middle management self-interest,' *Strategic Management Journal*, 7, 1989, 313–27.

8. J. Galbraith and R. Kazanjian, *Strategy Implementation: The Role of Structure and Process*, St. Paul, MN: West, 1985.

9. Kimberly and Quinn, 1984; also M.L. Tushman, W.H. Newman, and E. Romanelli, 'Convergence and upheaval: Managing the unsteady pace of organizational evolution,' *California Management Review*, 29, 1986, 29–44; and J.B. Quinn, 'Managing strategic change,' *Sloan Management Review*, 21, Summer 1980, 3–20.

10. To do a good job of selling a strategy requires a well-developed network of contacts. As John Kotter pointed out in his book, *The General Managers* (New York: Free Press, 1982), the effective general manager typically has a network of hundreds or even thousands of individuals through whom he or she can influence others. Obviously, some contacts are more important than others; if the general manager has not established the critical contacts, then the supporting management team must be selected to offset that deficiency.

PART I CASES

Apple (A)

In 1975, Steve Jobs was twenty years old and had dropped out of college to work at Atari on designing arcade games. He was still living with his parents, despite his devotion to counterculture politics that took him on trips to hippy communes like the All-One Farm and the Zen Centre. He had long hair, walked about barefoot, and rarely showered due to the conviction that his fruitarian diet precluded the necessity for doing so. This was the man who founded the Apple computer company.

In the Beginning

About this time, the first computer kit was featured on the cover of *Popular Electronics*. It was a '$495 bucket of parts that had to be soldered, fine-tuned, tweaked and cajoled into operation by someone with a hobbyist's passion, and an excellent grasp of electronics' (Young, 1988: 78). It represented an exciting new development in a world where the only computers available were terminals linked to mainframes. To exploit this new technology, the Homebrew Computer Club was set up to share skills, knowledge and equipment. Steve Jobs attended some of these early meetings with his friend Steve Wozniak. While Woz was interested in creating ever more elegant computer designs, Jobs' initial interest was limited – his engineering expertise was nonexistent compared to the other enthusiasts. As more commercial kits started to appear at the Club, however, Jobs started to think about how he could profit from this new field. He saw that there might be a market for the assembled product, and he took to dropping hints to Woz about the design of the machine that was continually being updated on his kitchen table.

Alex Kamradt, a Lockheed engineer, had also seen the potential of a ready-made computer. He contacted Woz for engineering expertise and Woz brought Jobs along. During this meeting they decided to set up a company to build

---

Case prepared from published material by Professor Cynthia Hardy. Case not to be reproduced without permission.

computers: Jobs was to run the business, Woz was to design the product and Kamradt was to provide the money. The venture ended later that year when Jobs neglected to tell Kamradt that he was taking an extended leave of absence from Atari to stay at the All-One Farm and would not be available for a while.

Jobs and Woz carried on producing personal computers, without Kamradt, as a sideline while continuing with the regular jobs at Atari and Hewlett Packard. On 1 April 1976 they decided to consolidate this partnership with an agreement signed by Jobs (45 per cent), Woz (45 per cent), and Ron Wayne (10 per cent) who also worked at Atari. They planned to make printed circuit boards that could be sold to customers for $50, who would then load them up with components. They called this 'computer' Apple I. When shown to the Homebrew Club, the reaction of other enthusiasts was muted, but a computer retailer (one of the first) told Jobs that while he couldn't sell the naked boards, he was prepared to buy fully assembled Apple computers for around $500 each. The sideline became a business as the partners started to buy components, install them, deliver them to the retailer, and pay suppliers in order to complete a $25,000 contract. They also needed credit which was eventually obtained by Jobs, following many rejections from Kierulff Electronics, a Palo Alto supply house. Despite these developments, the new business remained fairly basic. Friends were called in to assemble the boards in Jobs' family home. The partners settled on a retail price of $666.66 but the release of the movie *The Omen* led to numerous phone calls questioning the significance of the price. The manual put together by Jobs and Wayne was difficult to follow, and the logo – Isaac Newton lost in thought under an apple tree – was reminiscent of the underground press of the 1960s. The first machines also lacked a power supply, a monitor and a keyboard.

At this point, Steve Jobs was more renowned for his abrasive manner and dishevelled appearance than his business acumen. Nevertheless, he continued to obtain credit and loans, secure cheap parts, organize advertising, negotiate sales, and cajole Woz into improving the machine. Gradually sales increased and, by the end of the year, the business had profits of over $40,000. The first product was a success and an improved one was in the pipeline.

Steve Jobs had become a high-tech evangelist, consumed by a single-minded commitment to his new business. As the orders streamed in for the Apple I, the operation moved to Jobs' garage, friends were coopted as employees, and work began on the Apple II. It would use a television for display, have colour, a keyboard, a case and a power supply. The programming language was built into the computer. Woz also developed the idea of expansion slots which would allow the user to buy peripheral, add-on circuit cards to enhance the range of functions the machine could perform. Despite these improvements, a trip to the Personal Computer Festival in the Fall of 1976 showed Jobs that to be competitive, the Apple II would have to be a more sophisticated, self-contained device. The costs involved would require professional help and more investors, but once again Jobs demonstrated his ability to find the right people.

Jobs asked Wayne, who had since opted out of his 10 per cent stake, to design a plastic case for the Apple II, and hired an Atari engineer to design a low-heat power supply that would eradicate the need for a noisy fan. The power supply also reduced the size of the case and was quickly patented. Jobs made arrangements with an electronics firm to manufacture modulators to be sold with, but separate from, the computers. This was to avoid Federal Communications Commission (FCC) regulations that imposed rigid rules on the amount of radio interference generated by computers. The modulator caused the interference and there was no way of reducing it without redesigning the entire circuitry. Jobs realized that if the customer bought the modulator separately, the purchaser rather than the retailer or manufacturer would be responsible to the FCC.

In the 1970s, the personal computer industry was totally new – no one knew what the customer wanted or what the rules of the game were. Jobs realized that it would take media attention to be successful in this fragmented marketplace. He decided to use one of the best advertising agencies – the Regis McKenna agency which specialized in start-up companies. Initially rebuffed, Jobs persisted and persisted, calling the agency every day until they agreed to accept him as a client. Jobs was also able to secure an investment of $91,000 from Mike Markkula, a marketing executive who had recently left Intel. Markkula provided the fledgling company with a business plan and raised $600,000 in venture capital. The new venture was incorporated in January 1977 and Markkula received 20 per cent in equity.

Regis McKenna changed the logo to the multicoloured apple with a bite (byte) taken out of it and developed a marketing campaign consisting of four-page glossy ads. They created an 'image of a $100 million company at a time when it had twelve employees' (Davidson and Colby, 1988: 814). Markkula's business plan relied on independent distribution channels which would be helped by high margins to distributors, dealer naming, cooperative advertising, and point of sales displays. Manufacturing facilities were set up in Dallas. Operations emphasized low costs, quality control, just-in-time inventory control and external suppliers. The Apple II was introduced in May 1977. It was the first computer to have a built-in, user-friendly operating system. It also emphasized user-friendliness by providing accompanying documentation that could easily be understood by non-technical users. The following year, Apple became the first personal computer company to offer a floppy disk drive.

The main barrier to sales had been the lack of software. Jobs solved this problem by a typical counter-cultural move. He published the technical specifications of the Apple II instead of cloaking it in secrecy. New programs and applications started to flood in from programmers who knew exactly how the Apple II worked. Apple assisted some of the more promising program developers which ultimately resulted in over 16,000 software programs, providing customers with a wide range of applications. Another distinctly counter-cultural feature was the lack of compatibility with IBM, which was the major player in the world of computers.

Success

Apple went public in 1980 and, by 1983, had over 3,000 employees. Sales had reached more than $500 million and earnings were over $61 million. The Apple II had the largest installed base of any personal computer priced over $1,000. Over 650,000 units had been sold for around $2,000 each. Analysts estimated that they cost less than $500 to build. Apple's success could be attributed to the user-friendliness of its product which had enabled it to attract large numbers of educational and home users. The company had also benefited from the lack of competition in the embryonic personal computer industry. As a result, growth had continued despite obvious shortcomings with the Apple II: the hardware had not been upgraded in six years; the keyboard was limited to upper case letters, did not contain the full set of characters and had no up and down arrows to move the cursor; and the computer could display only 40 columns on the video monitor compared with the standard 80 columns.

To rectify the problems with the Apple II, the Apple IIe was introduced in early 1983. It offered a large memory capacity, upper and lower case letters, an 80 column screen, and was priced $400 lower than the Apple II. Apple was also attempting to develop a more sophisticated personal computer – the Apple III – to enable it to enter the business market.

At this stage, Apple was organized in a decentralized structure around loose product groupings (Figure 1). The company had developed a unique culture under the tutelage of Steve Jobs. It emphasized individual achievement, entrepreneurialism, and commitment, or perhaps to be more accurate, devotion to the company. An evangelical spirit pervaded Apple coupled with an attitude that was described as 'laid back and cocky . . . Apple employees believe, somewhat self-righteously, that their mission is to bring computer literacy to the masses' (Dreyfus, 1984: 181). A laser disc blasted out Michael Jackson music in the lobby and the staff wore jeans and sneakers. Suits and ties were rarely seen and interaction was informal. Rooms were named after creative artists like Picasso and Rembrandt, and aesthetic values were important – from the design of the product to the design of the working environment.

A Time for Change

In 1983, however, Apple was facing a very different environment than the one conquered by Steve and Woz with their backyard tinkering. In those early days, Apple had had very little competition: Jobs and Wozniak had created a new product and a new industry. Their challenge had been to stimulate primary demand, not fight for market share. Before long, however, competition had started to emerge with more than a hundred manufacturers producing 150 models of personal computers ranging in price from $99 to $37,500. These new competitors had found it relatively easy to enter the personal computer market:

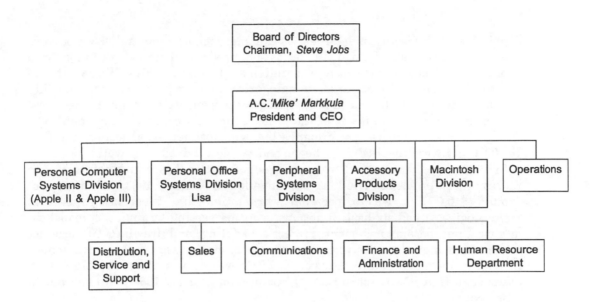

Figure 1 *Apple organization chart, c. 1982 (Adapted from* John Sculley at Apple Computer (A)*, Harvard Business School Case # 9-486-001)*

the technology was not particularly sophisticated, capital was available and distribution channels – the biggest barrier to entry – were expanding rapidly either with the growth of retail chains or the development of in-house sales forces.

As a result, Apple had found itself squeezed on both sides: from both superior proprietary technology and low priced Apple imitations like the Pineapple in the USA, the Lemon in Italy and the Orange in Asia. In the home market, Atari, Commodore and Texas Instruments had surpassed Apple in unit sales. IBM had introduced its Personal Computer in 1983 and was rumoured to be planning production of one million units. It had already secured 19 per cent of the personal computer market while Apple's market share dropped from 29 per cent to 24 per cent. IBM's massive sales force represented a significant advantage in attracting corporate customers – a ready made network existed and IBM was already well established. Apple's use of dealers precluded the company from directly influencing corporate decisions on computer hardware – while businesses may buy goods from dealers they do not use dealers to help them make decisions.

The market was beginning to divide into five broad segments: home, education, small business, corporations, and the professional user. Each had different needs. The professional market (10 per cent of 1983 sales) was relatively sophisticated and required a wide range of options and applications. The corporate market (25 per cent) required communications capabilities and standardization. The small business market (25 per cent) was highly frag-mented and users were typically unfamiliar with computers. The education market (10 per cent) ranged from basic applications in elementary schools to sophisticated users in universities. The home computer market (33 per cent) was the least well defined in terms of needs and price, ranging from professionals' home use to school children's educational toys. While sales of the Apple II covered most of these categories, the company was running into problems: the Apple II was rapidly aging, too expensive for many home users, and unable to meet the needs of the professional and corporate segments. The Apple III offered greater performance but had not met expectations: the first 14,000 units were recalled and the second version did not sell well.

In 1983, Apple announced two new products – the Lisa and Macintosh – to redress these problems. The Lisa was unveiled in January 1983 with a price of around $10,000. It was a personal workstation that incorporated several technologies. It had six basic functions: word processing, graphics, spreadsheet analysis, database management, project scheduling, and drawing. The product had been designed to convert even the most naive user and used a mouse instead of the more familiar keyboard. Little was known about the Macintosh other than that it was scheduled for completion in early 1984 and expected to cost around $2,000.

Apple's product line now consisted of the Apple IIe, the Apple III, the Lisa and the Macintosh. The company now had to address the problem of product overlap and learn how to position its products so that they covered all the market segments but did not compete with each other. Industry analysts also had some concerns about the company. They were worried that the tiny sales force would be insufficient to secure large corporate accounts; that the market and the technology for the 'easy to use' Lisa was too small to justify its price tag; that the Macintosh would steal Lisa's market; that there would be insufficient software support for the Lisa: that large companies would not want to use dealers; that dealers had become disillusioned as a result of reduced margins as Apple IIs and IIes had been discontinued in the face of heavy competition; and that the announcement of the Mac and the Lisa at the same time had confused buyers.

The Lisa quickly ran into problems and sold fewer than 20,000 systems during 1983, less than half of Apple's original forecasts. Apple had no experience in the business market and its counter-cultural image scared many business people who knew, all too well, that 'no one ever got fired for buying an IBM' (*Business Week*, 26 November 1984: 147). Lisa was also criticized for its lack of adequate business software, a shortage of business products to round out its capacity, and its inability to communicate with other computers. Furthermore, Apple had failed to train dealers adequately to sell the product, nor had it developed a direct sales force.

A New Captain at the Helm

On 2 May 1983, John Sculley became President and CEO of Apple. He had spent the last five years as President of Pepsi-Cola Co., Inc. He had a degree in architectural design from Brown University and an MBA from the Wharton School at the University of Pennsylvania and had initially worked at Interpublic, a large advertising agency. He then joined Pepsi where he was soon appointed marketing vice-president en route to the position of CEO. He was credited with several innovations such as the large size plastic bottles, the promotion of caffeine-free colas and the development of the 'Pepsi Challenge' advertising campaign. Sculley had had a longstanding interest in technology and engineering. He had applied for a patent on a colour television tube when only 14 years old, only to find that a company had patented a similar idea a few weeks before.

Steve Jobs had personally spent over four months courting him for the position at Apple. When first contacted, Sculley had not been interested. Jobs had told him: 'You can sell sugared water to children the rest of your career or you can change the world a little' (Jobs quoted in *Fortune*, 9 July 1984: 181). The idea of a change, his love of tinkering, and a compensation package rumoured to be close to $2 million finally tempted Sculley. He was brought in as a professional manager to provide the marketing perspective that had been lacking in the launch of Lisa. He was quickly greeted with an 80 per cent drop in profits for the three months ending September 1983.

Questions

- What was Apple's initial strategy and why was it successful?
- What problems started to arise in the 1980s?
- What strategy should John Sculley adopt for Apple in 1983?
- What would you do to implement this strategy if you were John Sculley?

Source Material

Business Week, 'Apple takes on its biggest test yet', 70–9, 31 January 1983.

Business Week, 'Apple reaches out for a marketing pro', 27–8, 25 April 1983.

Business Week, 'Apple's new crusade', 146–56, 26 November 1984.

Davidson, W.H. and Colby, E.E., 'Apple Computer Inc', in S.C. Certo and J.P. Peter (eds), *Strategic Management: Concepts and Applications*. Random House: New York, pp. 812–28, 1988.

Dreyfus, J., 'John Sculley rises in the West', *Fortune*, 181–4, 9 July 1984.

Fortune, 'Apple's bid to stay in the big time', 36–41, 7 February 1983.

Fortune, 'Growing Apple anew for the business market', 36–7, 4 January 1988.

Inc, 'Entrepreneur of the decade', 115–28, April 1989.

Young, S., *Steve Jobs: The Journey is the Reward*. Scott Foresman & Co: Glenview, Ill, 1988.

Apple (B)

John Sculley, the marketing man from Pepsi-Cola, had been hired in May 1983 to introduce the benefits of professional management to Apple, the company founded by the evangelical iconoclast Steve Jobs. By the end of his first year, it was looking like an inspired appointment. Sculley had introduced two successful computers – the Mac and the Apple IIc – and discontinued the disappointing Apple III. The Mac promised to be a major success: it was priced below $2,000 and was a powerful, easy to use machine that was particularly strong in graphics. It had been successfully aimed at small business users and university students. The Apple IIc extended the life of the Apple line which continued to provide more than three-quarters of the company's revenues. Sculley had also successfully consolidated the five original divisions into two product divisions (the Apple II and Mac divisions, the latter headed by Steve Jobs) and eradicated much of the overlap and duplication that had previously existed. Apple announced record earnings for the quarter ending 28 September 1984; sales in 1984 were up 54 per cent; and stock prices, which had fallen from a high of $63 in 1983 to a low of $17, had rebounded to $25 by November 1984.

Problems Resurface

Despite this initial success, competitive pressures continued to affect Apple. IBM's market share rose from 30 to 35 per cent in 1984, while Apple's fell from 21 to 19 per cent. In October 1984, IBM unveiled two new powerful display screens for its personal computer with better graphic capabilities, designed for the scientific and engineering market. It was becoming clear that Apple would have to be more successful in the business sector to sustain growth and maintain market share, yet the company still lacked a coherent strategy for tackling this challenge.

Sculley and Jobs maintained their commitment to being an alternative to IBM, although they promised 'a gateway into the IBM world' (*Business Week*, 16 January 1984: 81). The Mac and Lisa would be able to communicate with IBM and other mainframes, use IBM software, and connect to each other and other peripheral equipment. The technology was promised for the end of 1984, but was pushed back until 1985. The lack of IBM compatibility and its limited communication capabilities continued to hurt sales of the Mac. Jobs' 'go-it-

---

Case prepared from published material by Professor Cynthia Hardy. Case not to be reproduced without permission.

alone' vision was no longer such an effective strategy. The entry of new competitors into the industry had provided customers with a choice – and most of them wanted something that would work with their IBM equipment. Apple also had to start thinking about strategic alliances with other manufacturers and software houses to ensure the availability of peripherals and applications to round out its product line. IBM had tackled this challenge by writing more software programs itself but, as a result, had alienated some of its independent software producers. Apple had scrapped plans for its own software division but had yet to nurture the necessary relationships to secure a wider range of software. One such attempt was a new software program called JAZZ, developed by Lotus. JAZZ would combine five functions: spreadsheets, database management, graphics, word processing and communications in one package for the Mac. Development has been running into problems, however, and the introduction of JAZZ had had to be delayed.

Apple also had yet to develop a strategy for reaching the business market without alienating its more than 2,000 dealers. Apple had a direct sales staff of 60 compared with over 6,000 at IBM. Any attempt to develop a direct sales force would worry dealers who were already upset by the constant discounting of many of Apple's products. On the other hand, Apple's attempts to market directly had proved unsuccessful in reaching the MIS and data processing executives who made the major computer purchasing decisions. Apple's advertising strategy also needed changing. A TV commercial showed a long line of business executives as lemmings blindly jumping off a cliff. Only the last one, presumably an intrepid Mac user, pulled off his blindfold and saved himself. By showing this during the Superbowl, Apple had managed to insult the very people it was trying to reach.

The need to solve these problems became even more critical as the environment grew increasingly hostile in 1985 and the personal computer industry went into a recession. New, low priced products were emerging from Commodore and Atari and threatening the Apple II division. The growth rate for personal computers slowed from 30 per cent in 1984 to 20 per cent in 1985. Layoffs occurred throughout industry. Sales of the Apple II division dropped by 50 per cent, at a time when income was vital to underwrite Mac's entry into the business market.

Apple was also suffering from internal problems. Most of the company's attention was centred on the Mac division, headed by the charismatic Jobs. He perpetuated the unorthodox culture that typified Apple. Employees were young and dress codes unconventional. Rock music was played at night and classical music during the day, fruit juice was provided free to employees, and a masseur was on call. At the annual meeting in January 1985, the Mac team was in the front row seats listening to Steve Jobs announce mainly Mac products. Apple II employees watched on closed circuit TV from another room while virtually nothing was said about Apple II computers or the people who had kept it a top selling product for nearly seven years. During the quarter ending December 1984, the Apple division brought in $500 million of $698 million in revenues. But despite its performance, Jobs was dismissive of the Apple II division. He had once addressed its marketing staff as members of 'the dull and boring product division' (Jobs, quoted by Uttal, 1985). The head of the Apple II division – Del Yocam, a softly spoken 41-year-old who had worked his way up through the more mundane manufacturing side of the operation – found it difficult to compete with a manager who had 12 per cent of Apple's shares. 'We used to say that the Mac people had God on their team' said an employee of the Apple II division (quoted in *Fortune*, 5 August 1985).

1985 also saw the departure of a number of key personnel. The most dramatic was the departure of Steve Wozniak who left in February following a well-publicized row with Steve Jobs. Woz left to form a new company and took the designer of the new Apple IIc with him. At least six other key personnel also left in early 1985. Most were from the Apple II division and had become increasingly disenchanted with the lack of attention and a culture that they perceived to be becoming increasingly corporate in nature. In addition, Mac was behind schedule and its product development in disarray; and, despite a glitzy launch, JAZZ had done little to speed up the Mac's sales.

A Coup d'Etat?

Relations were also starting to sour between Jobs and Sculley. While their friendship had started out well, a rift had grown as business pressures mounted: each advocated different strategies for placing Apple on a firmer footing. The recession changed the focus for John Sculley from 'how fast can we build them' to 'how quickly can we bring down inventories and control expenses' (Sculley quoted in *Inc*, October 1987: 56). Jobs, on the other hand, wanted the original orientation to continue. Sculley was finding this dissension problematic since he was 'sandwiched' between Jobs' two positions as Vice-president of the Mac Division and Chairman of the Board. It was compounded by the increase in Jobs' scope of operational responsibilities. When Sculley had joined Apple in 1983, Jobs was leading a Mac project team of less than 100 people. By 1985, Jobs was responsible for more than 1,000 people.

> [Jobs] never wanted to become an administrator or a manager. Yet that is exactly what happened. A move that had initially seemed logical in consolidating the company's operations was now clearly a mistake. I had given Steve greater power than he had ever had and I had created a monster. (Sculley, quoted in *Fortune*, 14 September 1987: 109)

Sculley asked Jobs to step down as Vice-president. Jobs refused and the rift between them widened at a Board meeting on 11 April 1985. Sculley told directors that he was asking Jobs to relinquish control of the Mac division. Sculley believed that Jobs could no longer work effectively and if the Board would not back him, Sculley would resign. At the end of a two-day meeting, the Board decided unanimously to ask Jobs to step down as executive Vice-president. Jobs saw this as a surprise attack on him by Sculley and it marked the end of their friendship.

No schedule had been set for the change in Jobs' responsibilities, however, and he was still holding both positions six weeks later. The Board was becoming increasingly impatient with Sculley's inaction. So, Sculley brought in Jean-Louis Gassée, head of Apple France, to replace Jobs by first making him marketing director in preparation for his appointment as general manager of the Mac division. When Gassée was named marketing director, Jobs began testing the loyalty of his colleagues to plan a challenge to Sculley. When Sculley heard of his actions, he immediately informed the senior management team. In a difficult three-hour meeting Sculley forced his senior managers to choose between him and Jobs. Eventually, Jobs agreed to take a vacation and return after the reorganization was complete. The details of the reorganization were worked out in meetings on 29 and 30 May and, on 31 May 1985, Sculley signed the paperwork removing Steve Jobs from his position of Vice-president. Six weeks later, Apple recorded its first loss as a public company and saw its stock hit a three-year low of less than $15.

Initially, Board members had hoped that Jobs would stay with the company in some capacity following the reorganization. In September, however, Jobs announced his plans to start a new venture that would not compete with Apple. The Board considered purchasing a 10 per cent stake in the new enterprise but on learning that he was taking five key employees with him, decided that Jobs had been planning the move while still Chairman. The Board immediately demanded his resignation and Steve Jobs left the company he had founded.

Questions

- What do you think of the way in which John Sculley handled Steve Jobs?
- What strategy should John Sculley adopt now?
- How should he implement it?

Source Material

Business Week, 'Apple Computer's counterattack against IBM', 78–81, 16 January 1984.
Business Week, 'How Apple is bullying IBM's PCjr', p. 124, 16 April 1984.
Business Week, 'Apple's new crusade', 146–56, 26 November 1984.
Business Week, 'A split that's sapping morale at Apple', 106–8, 11 March 1985.
Business Week, 'Software for the common man', 94–100, 18 March 1985.
Business Week, 'High anxiety at Apple over a late start at Lotus', p. 114, 6 May 1985.

Business Week, 'Apple's growth could stay stunted for a while', 113–16, 10 June 1985.
Business Week, 'Steve Wozniak is tired of all play and no work', 67–70, 7 October 1985.
Business Week, 'Those vanishing high-tech jobs', 30–1, 15 July 1985.
Business Week, 'The palace revolt at Apple Computer', p. 38, 17 June 1985.
Business Week, 'Can John Sculley clear up the mess at Apple?', 70–1, 29 July 1985.
Business Week, 'Steve Jobs vs Apple: What caused the final split', p. 48, 30 September 1985.
Business Week, 'Apple, Part 2: The no-nonsense era of John Sculley', 27 January 1986.
Dreyfus, J., 'John Sculley rises in the West', *Fortune*, 181–4, 9 July 1984.
Fortune, 'Apple changes strategy', p. 75, 17 October 1983.
Fortune, 'Growing Apple anew for the business market', 36–7, 4 January 1988.
Fortune, 'Sculley's lessons from inside Apple', 108–20, 14 September 1987.
Inc, 'Corporate antihero: John Sculley', 49–59, October 1987.
Inc, 'Entrepreneur of the decade', 115–28, April 1989.
Kessler, K. 'Apple's pitch to the *Fortune* 500', *Fortune*, 53–6, 15 April 1985.
Morrison, A., 'Apple bites back', *Fortune*, 86–100, 20 February 1984.
Uttal, B., 'Behind the fall of Steve Jobs', *Fortune*, 5 August 1985.
Uttal, B., 'The adventures of Steve Jobs', *Fortune*, 119–24, 14 October 1985.

Montreal Trust

Montreal Trust was formed in 1889 when Sir Donald Smith and Joseph Hickson created the Montreal Safe Deposit for guarding cash, jewellery and valuable documents. By 1899 it had diversified into fiduciary activities and become known as Montreal Trust. The next ten years saw expansion to Toronto, Halifax, Winnipeg and Vancouver and, in 1909, it was acquired by the Royal Bank of Canada. After nearly sixty years of joint activities, Montreal Trust became a subsidiary of the Financial Power Group in 1967. A strategic reorientation in the 1980s led to the diversification of Montreal Trust's financial services and substantial growth through the acquisition of such companies as RoyNat and Crédit Foncier. In 1989, Montreal Trust was acquired by BCE Inc. – a highly profitable, $18 billion (Canadian) enterprise based in telecommunications and related areas. The acquisition was BCE's first venture into the financial services area.

The Canadian financial services industry consists of those companies that lend money, accept deposits, provide insurance, sell securities and transfer funds. Until recently, government legislation ensured the complete separation of the 'four pillars': banking, trust companies, insurance companies and securities firms. Deregulation eliminated many of the divisions between these four groups by allowing companies to provide a wider range of customer services. So, for example, in 1990 Citibank announced that it was streamlining its corporate banking business and concentrating, instead, on building a network of consumer services including loans, credit cards, banking, insurance and investments. Changes in the customer base produced a growing population between 45 and 60 years old with an interest in personalized services. At the same time, technological advances provided opportunities for new products and services. These changes led to an increasingly competitive and consumer-oriented industry in 1990. Further legislation was expected to continue these trends.

Montreal Trust offered a range of financial services including personal services, real estate, corporate services, and investment management (Figure 1). In 1988, a group of external consultants had been commissioned to provide an analysis of the changing environment and recommended a viable strategy for Montreal Trust. They determined that the Corporate Services Division, previously the major source of revenue, was in the mature stage of the product/service life cycle and further growth would be limited. The greatest

Case prepared by Professor Cynthia Hardy, Faculty of Management, McGill University, from original research. The author would like to acknowledge the support of Serge Leclaire in preparing this case. Case not to be reproduced without permission.

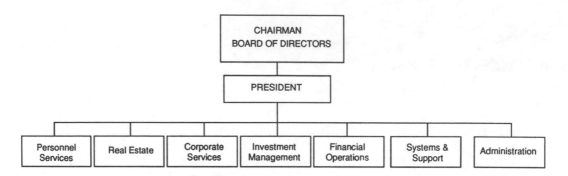

Figure 1 *Montreal Trust: Organization chart*

opportunity for growth lay in the personal financial services provided by the Personal Services Division (PSD); it would, however, require a significant amount of investment. It was at this point that Montreal Trust was sold to BCE Inc.

The Personal Services Division

PSD was structured along the lines of three main functions (Figure 2): branch operations; product and market development; and administrative services. These three areas had been considered key to PSD's success. Of particular importance was the position of Senior Vice-President (Branch Operations). It had been created to oversee the growth of PSD's branch network and, in particular, the integration of Crédit Foncier's branches. Ninety per cent of the 2,000 personnel, including all the regional vice-presidents, reported to this position. The individual concerned – previously a regional branch manager himself – had been selected by the Executive Vice-President. Both these men had risen to the senior levels through the branch network. The success of PSD had been attributed to its steady growth of branches and the careful administration of those branches by their managers. The new environment would require a greater emphasis on sales and marketing to maintain existing customers and attract new ones.

To compete effectively in this new environment, Montreal Trust had to focus on a market niche since it was a relatively small player with only 65 branches across the country (compared with Canada Trust's 300 and Royal Trust's 160 branches; the Royal Bank had some 1,400 branches and over two thousand automated banking machines). It was decided to focus on high-income, urban customers in highly populated areas by providing them with a full line of customer services. Montreal Trust maintained its competitiveness by offering competitive rates for its products, free use of the Interac system (where customers of one bank or trust company use the automated banking machines network to withdraw money from another institution), keeping branches open

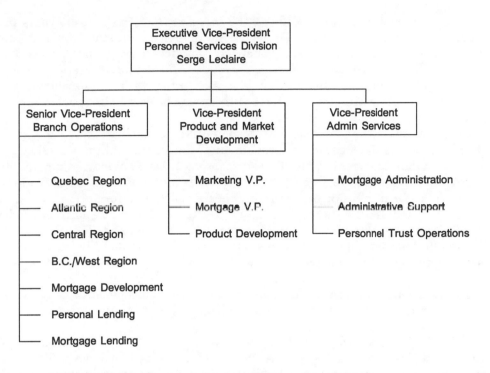

Figure 2   *Montreal Trust: Personnel Services Division, May 1990*

during extended hours, and providing free information services, computerized facilities, courier service, etc. It offered a full line of products whenever possible. In cases where low volume made it unprofitable to offer the service itself, Montreal Trust entered into joint ventures with other companies such as purchasing the administrative capability for its Visa credit card from the Royal Bank.

In May 1990, Serge Leclaire became Executive Vice-President of PSD. His predecessor had been close to retirement and had not introduced any significant changes in response to the environmental pressures. Leclaire had been hired by the previous CEO of Montreal Trust in 1987 as Senior Vice-President for the Systems and Support Services Division. His appointment to PSD was made by the new CEO (head of RoyNat until six months earlier). Leclaire knew something of PSD from his previous position. He knew that the key to success was a strategy that emphasized new products, the customer, and cost-effeciency (since Montreal Trust was a relatively small player).

Leclaire began to promote the idea of more effective *cross-selling* (selling more than one product to a customer) and establishing relationships with a complete household rather than an individual client. He developed the idea of the *Household Relationships Profile*. It provided mortgages and credit to younger customers (20 to 35 years old) during the *lending* stage; mutual funds and retirement savings plans during the *investment* stage (30 to 65 years old); Registered Retirement Income Funds during the *retirement* stage (over 65 years old) and trust management and beneficiary services during the *Estates* stage (death and the introduction of a new cycle at the lending/investment stage). The target group was the growing 50+ age group with the development of more investment/retirement products with an emphasis on client retention and selling multiple products and services.

Leclaire knew that to exploit this potential, a comprehensive marketing database would be needed to provide up-to-date information on clients. It would enable Montreal Trust to target promotions and marketing, making them more cost-effective. Some progress towards a database had been made but Leclaire knew it was not being used properly and that information was either missing or incorrectly duplicated. To rectify this problem, Leclaire started to develop an Executive Information System (EIS). It was modelled on a similar system he had developed in his previous position. It enabled him to assess the profitability of individual products and branches. It was the first time that such comprehensive data had been collected as part of an integrated system which broke down information to the point where the performance of a particular product in a particular branch could be compared with similar branches in the same region.

The EIS produced some startling findings. For example, Leclaire discovered that 65 per cent of bad loans were the result of using mortgage brokers who provided only 25 per cent of total business. Leclaire immediately considered the introduction of policies that would restrict the use of brokers although, since some branches received as much as 50 per cent of their business through brokers, it would represent a significant loss of income in the short term. Since branch managers were paid a bonus based largely on *productivity* (the amount of new business they brought in), it would cut into their earnings. Leclaire found that this emphasis on new business resulted in not only a high percentage of bad loans, but also the loss of existing clients since they did not factor into bonus calculations. He also discovered an unexpected by-product of the focus on cross-selling: the promotion of new products had not been accompanied by any evaluation of their contribution to profitability. For example, there had been a blitz on promoting Visa cards to existing customers by branch personnel. Unfortunately, since Visa was administered by another bank, it produced minimal profits for Montreal Trust.

Leclaire was also able to use the EIS to follow up on performance. The data showed that one month after Leclaire had asked managers to promote more aggressive telemarketing, 40 of the 65 branches had not responded. A follow-up on a promotion of RRSPs (Registered Retirement Savings Plans – where investments reduce taxable income up to certain limits set by the government) showed that only three branches had made any significant increase in sales. These findings reaffirmed Leclaire's realization that the emphasis on products and customers was new to branch managers, branch personnel and regional managers. It represented a dramatic change in culture and many were finding it difficult to adopt more aggressive selling tactics. In addition, employees were unfamiliar with the continuous array of new products they were expected to sell. Moreover the functional structure meant that no one at the senior management level was responsible for coordinating individual products.

Questions

- What is Serge Leclaire's strategy and how will it help PSD?
- Serge Leclaire has asked you to provide him with an implementation plan. What are your recommendations? Include advice on personnel, structure, information systems, and procedures. You should also consider how Leclaire is going to motivate employees to accept his ideas.

Mrs Fields' Cookies

Debbi Fields got the idea to sell her homemade cookies from her husband's clients, who could not resist the batches that she sent to his office daily. She decided to turn her baking skill into a business and with $50,000 that she borrowed from her husband, she opened her first store in Palo Alto, California in 1977. She was 20 years old. Debbi Fields baked her cookies daily, so they could be sold warm and fresh. When business was slow, she would go out into the street and give away free samples to lure customers into the store. Once they were in the store, she would help them decide both the kind and quantity of cookies they would buy. Her emphasis was on making the cookie buying experience a pleasant one, hence all customers were greeted in a warm and friendly manner.

By the end of 1983, Debbi Fields had 160 company owned and operated stores in 13 states, employed 1,000 people, and had an estimated revenue of $30 million. She had no plans to franchise or license her product. However, she did plan on opening 140 new stores in 1984 and expected revenue of $45 million. By this time, she was 27, still married, and a mother of three.

The phenomenal success of Mrs Fields' Cookies can be directly attributed to Debbi Fields and her off-beat 'California' style philosophy: 'We're a people company and what we're really selling a customer is a feel-good feeling' (Debbi Fields).

This philosophy can be seen in her Headquarters in Park City, Utah (ski country) where she works with her staff of 25. Everyone there is involved in every aspect of the business, from overseeing operations to handling customer complaints. Everyone wears more than one hat. All the people in the organization talk about 'feel-good feelings', or make statements like 'We're high on energy here'. Another corporate aphorism is 'Good enough never is'. When employees eat a cookie they are having a 'Mrs Fields' experience'. Mrs Fields' Cookies does little advertising, and no market research. The only new cookies introduced to the stores are the ones Debbi Fields creates herself, usually in her home at 2.00 am. Her test market is her family. Debbi Fields wants to project her personality and philosophy into every aspect of the business. She wants every Mrs Fields' Cookies store to be run in the same way that she ran her first store in Palo Alto.

The 'feel-good feelings' start with the cookies themselves. Unlike most of its competitors, Mrs Fields' does not have a central plant that makes and ships cookies to its outlets. Instead, the cookies must be baked daily on the premises,

Case prepared by Beverly Poisson, Faculty of Management, McGill University, from published material. © Beverly Poisson 1994. Case not to be reproduced without permission.

so they can be served warm and fresh. In fact, the shelf life of a Mrs Fields' cookie is only 2 hours. If it is not sold within that time, it is taken off the shelf and donated to the local Red Cross to be given to blood donors.

Having store employees, most of whom are part-time and earn a minimum wage, responsible for the output would drive David Liederman of David's Cookies (Mrs Fields' competitor) crazy:

> I am terrified of sending anything out there where an employee has to do anything to the food. . . . You have to think at the lowest common denominator. One of the reasons we do so well in the cookie business is that a chimpanzee could take cookies out of that bag and more often than not put them on the tray properly. (David Liederman)

But at Mrs Fields' the employees are responsible not only for mixing the ingredients – shipped by independent distributors to each store – they also have to know when the cookies are ready, as they do not have automatically timed ovens. 'I don't know how long they bake', says an employee who works at a Salt Lake City store, 'you just know when they're done'.

Debbi Fields also trusts her employees to project the image and spirit that she wishes to maintain in all her stores. She expects all employees to look happy, greet customers, and make the cookie-buying experience a pleasant one. Customers must not only walk out with cookies, they have to walk out feeling happy. Hence, Mrs Fields' looks for employees who are going to relate well to the customer.

Being interviewed at Mrs Fields' can be an experience in itself. Prospective candidates not only get the customary interview, they frequently have to audition before other candidates and employees. Natural clowns have the edge.

> We want people to be outrageous. We want people to be themselves. We don't tell people that they have to be pleasant. We tell them that we want them to have fun. We tell them that they have to greet customers. We don't tell them how they have to greet customers. (Debbi Fields)

Putting this much trust in employees is almost unheard of in the industry. David Liederman's philosophy on store employees could not be further from Debbi Fields'.

> The realities of the retail business in any typical urban environment are not wonderful: the external robberies, the internal robberies, the motivation. You're dealing with kids who really are just passing through. The kids are the Achilles' heel of retailing. (David Liederman)

Obviously, putting that much trust in your employees, and getting consistent results, requires strong communication and support. Which is exactly what Debbie Fields provides. She sees her main role as communicating with her people and giving them the support they require to carry out her vision of the company. All full-time personnel (including staff, store managers, and region managers) receive training in Park City, Utah. Debbi visits the stores regularly, logging over 300,000 commercial air miles a year. When she goes into a store she chips in and works with the store employees if they are busy. Store managers can communicate directly with her and her staff by phone or memo

'Mrs Fields' Cookies is an extension of how I see the world. I believe people will do their very best, I really do, provided they are getting proper support' (Debbi Fields).

If she goes into a store and actually finds something wrong, such as crunchy, non-fresh, cold cookies, she has been known to close down the store for a few hours. 'I assume that there's been some reason why the people are not taught what the standards of the company are'. She then takes the time to actually show them how it should be done and what she expects.

The structure of the company is quite simple. Two Vice-Presidents of Operations at the corporate level oversee six regional managers. Each regional manager is responsible for 30 stores. Each store has a store manager, though in some cases these individuals are responsible for two or three locations. In addition, there is a headquarters staff of 25 people.

Store managers are responsible for the daily operations of each store. Each location generates close to $200,000 in sales per year, and requires between two and five employees to run it during any given period of the day. Store managers are responsible for hiring and managing employees, producing work schedules, ordering supplies, estimating baking requirements throughout the day, and ensuring the equipment is maintained. Store managers get support from team leaders, often chosen from the hourly employees. Above and beyond these tasks, store managers are also responsible for keeping both the employees and customers happy.

Randi Fields, Debbi Fields' husband, was involved in the company on a temporary basis from the beginning, but in 1984 he gave up his job as a financial consultant to become Chairman of Mrs Fields' Cookies.

After the opening of the second store Randi has implemented a system that generates a daily profit and loss statement for each location, to give head-quarters control over operating activities and results. Store managers, however, do not see this report, as Randi does not want them to be driven by profit. If they were, Randi believes they would have little incentive to take the cookies off the rack after two hours. Instead, managers are paid salaries, and receive bonuses based on store sales and individual performance. Hourly employees participate in a staff commission fund based on store sales that is paid monthly.

Randi Fields' main contribution to Mrs Fields' Cookies is an understanding of technology and how it can be used to help them achieve their business objectives. His vision is to automate as many of the functions and processes as possible, while maintaining control over the stores on a daily basis. His goal is to free up his store managers' time so they can deal with people, and to have his corporate staff solving problems, not processing information: 'The objective is to leverage people, to get them to act when we have 1,000 stores the same way they acted when we had 30' (Randi Fields).

Randi wants to start by automating as many of the store functions as possible. His plans are described below:

1   *Day Planner*: The first system called the Day Planner will be an expert

system based on historical sales data, that will automatically schedule daily cookie production on an hour-by-hour and product-by-product basis. The system will tell the store manager what to mix and bake, at what time of the day, how many customers are needed per hour, and how many cookies each customer will have to buy for the store to make its sales projections. As the day goes on, the system will update its projections based on the actual results of the day.

2 *Scheduling*: This system will be used to help the store manager schedule the workforce. Based on a two-week sales projection, the system will estimate personnel requirements and produce work schedules detailing both the number of people and skills required.

3 *Employee applications*: This automated interviewing system allows candidates to answer a series of computer-generated questions. The system will then suggest which candidates will succeed or fail as Mrs Fields' Cookies employees.

4 *Maintenance support*: This system will provide support in maintaining and fixing store equipment. If a piece of equipment has failed, the system will produce a list of things to do to try to get it working again (is it plugged in? . . .). If these fail, the system will send a repair request to Park City, telling them which machine is broken, its maintenance history, and which vendor to call.

5 *Communications system*: Randi Fields wants to implement a corporate-wide computerized Phone-Mail message system so Debbi Fields can keep in constant contact with her store managers, and vice-versa.

At the end of each business day, the system will automatically send sales data, forecast data, and inventory levels for each store to Park City store controllers.

Managing 160 stores is already a strain on Mrs Fields' personal and personnel-oriented management style. Randi hopes his technological contribution will solve that problem and allow the company to grow.

Questions

- What is Debbi Fields' strategy? How will Randi's systems allow her to achieve it?
- What effect will these systems have on the company? What areas will they affect the most? Will they allow Mrs Fields' Cookies to grow without changing?
- Compare this method with the franchise system. What are the advantages and disadvantages of each?
- How will employees, especially store managers, react to these new systems?

Automakers of Canada

Automakers of Canada is the Canadian subsidiary of a large US automobile manufacturer. This case concerns one of its automobile assembly plants – T Plant – which employed some 1,300 people. Increased competitive pressures had prompted the corporation's headquarters in Detroit to implement a company-wide participative management programme, which focused on quality. In response to the corporate initiative, a team of five consultants had been hired by the plant manager in 1980 to help implement a Quality of Working Life (QWL) programme.

The entire North American automobile industry was facing increasing competition in the late 1970s and early 1980s. The numbers of imports had risen to over 25 per cent of domestic sales which, coupled with a recession, had made 1980 one of the worst years ever for the North American auto industry. Combined losses of the domestic manufacturers exceeded $4 billion. Studies showed that Japanese cars had at least a $2,000 cost advantage and were of higher quality than most North American cars. In addition, the auto companies were facing increasing government regulations that affected emission control, safety, and fuel economy. They required substantial modification in manufacturing operations and a higher emphasis on quality and safety. In response to these pressures, management at Automakers' US corporate headquarters had embarked on a strategy to improve quality and productivity. The overall company was relatively centralized and the strategy was imposed on Canadian management, which was expected to initiate the necessary changes in individual plants.

The consultants had been hired as a direct result of the company-wide strategy. They first interviewed 90 individuals across the plant which revealed the following.

1 Workers felt severely threatened because of the industry wide layoffs, cutbacks and belt tightening.
2 Union leaders were vigorously opposed to pressure to make 'concession' contracts, as had been done in other companies.
3 The need to reduce costs, improve quality and fight the challenge of imports translated into significant day-to-day pressures on each employee.

Against this backdrop, the consultants set out to design a QWL programme.

Case prepared by Cynthia Hardy, Faculty of Management, McGill University, from published material. All quotations taken from Frances Westley, 'The eye of the needle: Cultural and personal transformation in a traditional organization', *Human Relations*, 43(3): 273–93, 1990. Case not to be reproduced without permission.

At this point, the goals of both consultants and management were vague and no specific productivity or quality targets had been set. The consultants wanted to improve quality and increase motivation and job satisfaction through a participative management programme. Managers wanted to respond to the demands of their corporate bosses. The union refused to participate directly in the QWL scheme, though it raised no objections to a programme centred on managerial ranks. Plant management decided to go ahead with the programme from the level of first line supervisor (foreman) up to plant manager.

The Structure at T Plant

T plant was functionally organized (Figure 1) headed by the plant manager and his assistant plant manager. The functional departments – industrial relations, quality, operations, manufacturing, and engineering – each had their own manager. The departments were of different sizes and contained a number of employee levels. The majority of workers were employed in production – on the assembly line. The plant ran two shifts each headed by a production manager who reported to the operations manager. Managerial levels in production included eight superintendents, 22 general supervisors, and 66 foremen. The foremen each supervised between 10 and 50 hourly paid, unionized workers on the shop floor.

The Culture at T Plant

The culture of T Plant was distinctive even in the estimation of the managers who worked there. It comprised three components: aggression; competition; and lying, cheating and stealing.

Aggression: 2×4 Management

The aggressive, macho management style was termed *2×4 management*. It consisted of reprimands in the form of intensive verbal abuse (*yelling and screaming*), dramatic confrontations and figuratively *beating up* on offenders. Extreme examples of this behaviour had become myths in the organization and perpetrators were spoken of as folk heroes. It was believed that to be promoted, one had to be a 2×4 manager.

> In the old days here, there used to be a lot of a grandstanding, but a lot of it was for show. I can remember one day, [X] came out on to the floor and he saw a piece that he did not like, and he started jumping up and down on it and he bashed it all in, yelling and screaming. And then he said, 'now throw it out, because it is not good for

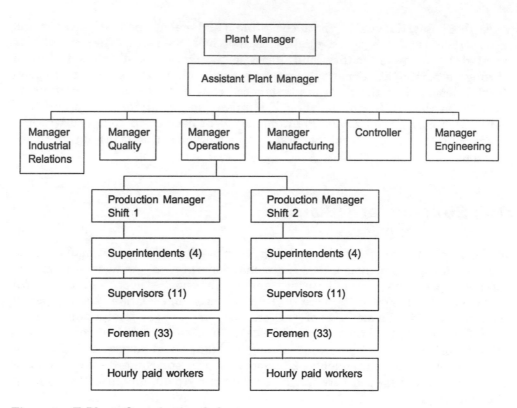

Figure 1   *T Plant: Organizational chart*

anything' and when he turned around, he winked at me. It was a show, it was fun, it was a game. It was just like a John Wayne movie, as soon as the movie was over with, they became human again.

If your boss catches you out, catches something wrong with the product in your area, you can respond in one of two ways. You can say, 'OK, I'll find out what's wrong', or you can say, 'God dammit, it's John Smith. I'm going to call him in here and chew him out.' The second way looks much better, more glory in it.

This macho style was seen as being specific to the factory and quite distinct from the managers' family lives. Some were even embarrassed to describe their work to outsiders:

My brother, who is an accountant, says he cannot believe this place, that it is like a game instead of a workplace. He thinks everything about this place is ridiculous.

Even the worst 2×4 managers were recognized as being quite different away from work.

Mind you, he was a fine fellow outside. He used to tell me that he kept his leopard skin suit in the guard house and would put it on when he came in.

While managers referred to extreme 2×4 type managers as 'monsters', many nonetheless found the management style appealing.

I prefer the straightforward approach. I don't like the foul language. But I do not think people listen to you if you are a nice guy . . . People are scared of someone who chews them out.

Competitiveness: Shiftitis and Empire Building

Another salient characteristic of the T Plant culture was an intense competitiveness which manifested itself in two forms of behaviour – competition between shifts (*shiftitis*) and lack of cooperation between functions (*empire building*). Both were highly valued. Shiftitis was defined by one manager as 'we do not like to see the other shift run as well as we do'. The two shifts were constantly compared to encourage people to work harder. At times, it got out of hand.

> It is a big game, to get the other guy. There is a lot of resentment and competition. We base everything on results and so people will resort to things like counting back on the line, to get a better count for their shift. Sometimes the foreman will lock up his tools so that the other people on the next shift will not get them. We have to . . . make sure things like tools and materials are exchanged, otherwise people start breaking into each other's lockers. Rivalry is good but you have to keep the lid on.

Despite the damage and waste, shiftitis had its defenders: those who felt that it fostered 'good, clean competition'; and others who felt that part of the fun of working at T Plant was its macho, competitive, street-fighting world.

Functional loyalty – empire building – was also very strong in T Plant and permeated all levels of the organization:

> I knew everything about the machines in my area and I used to turn up the speed on the line for brief periods of time so that my boys could produce more units than the other shift. Sometimes the foreman from the other shift would sneak in early to make sure I was not going on overtime. But I just knew how to regulate the line and get things done faster and I had everyone behind me, my boys loved to do it that way. They loved to shove it in [the other shift's] face.

> It is really incredible how one unit pits itself against another in this place. It is as if there is a wall at the end of each unit, and anything that passes through that wall is no longer a problem for that unit. People pass things along because there is always pressure. There is always pressure to deliver the numbers. Despite all the lip service about quality being most important, if you do not get the numbers, you get nothing.

Lying, Cheating and Stealing

The 2×4 management and competitiveness translated, at the individual level, into a set of interconnected assumptions about behaviour which were widely recognized as dysfunctional: 2×4 management led to considerable fear of being exposed and humiliated, and forced people into a self-defensive mode termed *covering ass*.

I've had it solid, with that 2×4 style, it nullifies you. You just start covering ass and playing your cards close to the vest. You collect a lot of excuses and you are ready to hand them out if anything comes up. So the problems never get solved.

Shifts and departments worked actively to pass the buck: passing poor quality products from one department to another; failing to take responsibility for product defects; and rushing faulty products out the door in an effort to beat the other shift in a race for numbers. Such activities were known as *shipping shit.*

The biggest problem around here is that there is no trust, no one wants to get blamed for anything. So say the sealer goes bad and you know how to fix it, but you do not fix it. What you do is call maintenance or call industrial engineering. That way they get stuck with the problem and you do not get chewed up for it. It could be that it was your fault, that you guys screwed up the gun, but you try to cover that up and get it pinned on maintenance and engineering. For example, if you had a big hole, it might be something you could fix, but if you fixed it too many times, then it would become your responsibility, you would pick up the job and you can't hold that job.

The need to hide personal and functional problems and failures, fuelled by the desire to be competitive and to win, combined with the fear of retaliation, resulted in tacit acceptance of all kinds of rule breaking which managers in T Plant called *lying, cheating and stealing* – concealing (stockpiling) parts, hiding personnel, and falsifying reports concerning injuries, defects and man-power.

The book records say that we have a million dollars of obsolete material. But before the last launch, we shipped it out and it turned out to be two million dollars worth. There are kitties all over the place. Foremen squirrel things away that they think they need. Foremen get hit over the head all the time for scrap, so it is better to hide it away and call it lost stock. I think I would do the same thing. But it makes for a lot of waste in the system. Another example is, if you are running rough on certain parts of the line and defects come up, someone will stamp it off so that it does not show up as a loss for our department. That is dangerous, it is just bad for the company. We are more concerned about covering ass than quality or quantity. We would rather run with one man less than we need to do the job properly. We expect the repairmen to pick up the slack. If the repair does not get it, it goes out and the warranty gets it.

Some managers, however, saw these behaviours as necessary to get the job done. Others perceived it as part of the fun of T Plant culture. It represented a kind of freedom to wheel and deal, to live by your wits – a game with its own challenges and satisfactions for those that survived. Many managers liked the excitement and the subterfuge: they had survived in T Plant because they were good at playing a game that required considerable skill and personal toughness.

We all fight to keep down costs, but maybe we are not fighting hard enough, because costs are still way out of control. But you know, it is mostly the new supervisors whose budgets are way over. If they understood the system better, they maybe would lie, cheat and steal a little and would be better off. Old supervisors who know the ropes – his budget will always be under. The words make it sound bad, but lying, cheating and stealing is a system which has worked. Everyone watched what they spend and they stayed on their toes. I do not see that the issue has to be changed unless it is hurting the plant. Most seasoned supervisors can keep it within limits.

In summary, life at T Plant, for workers and managers alike, was rooted in 2×4 management and fierce competition. In perpetrating and defending these values an informally sanctioned system of lying, cheating and stealing had evolved. Managers were ambivalent about this culture. On the one hand, it undoubtedly caused problems for both individuals and the company; on the other, it was well understood and contained elements of excitement and fun.

Changing the Culture

The consultants felt that this culture had to be fundamentally changed: it did not reward members for a job well done; and success was determined by the ability to be aggressive and competitive, rather than through finding innovative ways to cut costs or improve quality. Moreover, the culture did not reward those who asked too many questions, communicated problems, or accepted blame.

The consultants designed a multi-level committee structure to orchestrate the change in management style.

1 Level 1 included all the ten managers (plant manager down to production manager) who already met weekly as members of the management committee.
2 Level 2 included all eight superintendents and four representatives of their direct subordinates – the supervisors.
3 Level 3 consisted of eight committees involving the foremen and members of different functional units in the form of quality circles.

The overall object of this structure was to increase participation at all levels of management by bringing them together in regular, frequent meetings. It was to be followed by a training programme to help members operate in a participatory, problem-solving mode within these committees by training volunteers from the various levels in how to facilitate meetings.

The changes envisaged by the consultants would require managers to go back to basics: reviewing how they carried out their job and learning new ways of managing. In addition, each level had a more specific mandate: Level 1 managers were to delegate authority down the line; Level 2 managers were expected to carry out a socio-technical analysis of the production process to determine where problems arose and to find ways of fixing them; the Level 3 committees were expected to resolve multi-functional problems where possible or pass them up to Level 2 managers to follow up on.

In some respects, the senior (Level 1) managers in T Plant were supportive of the attempt to change their management style. They knew that their behaviour was out of sync with the larger society. Less 'ranting and raving' would make them more 'like managers . . . my idea of managers'. In other respects, however, they remained suspicious of a participative management programme that had been foisted on them by a corporate-level decision. Their chief concern was to reduce costs and improve quality and they felt that the old culture had some merits in this respect: it provided a system that embodied high expectations of performance, punished failure, and rewarded competition and a tough management style. Despite their ambivalence, the Level 1 managers started the change programme with enthusiasm. First, they immediately withdrew from any involvement in the running of the shop floor. They cancelled the traditional morning meeting in which they outlined the day's problems and priorities to their subordinates, and eliminated the radios they used to issue orders directly to the shop floor. Second, they redoubled their efforts to conduct themselves in a more participatory fashion: less screaming and yelling and more listening.

Questions

- What strategy are managers trying to bring about at Automakers?
- What would you do to realize this strategy?
- What problems would you expect the consultants to encounter with their programme?
- What would you do to resolve them?

A New Strategy at ICI

It is 1973, and John Harvey-Jones has just been promoted from division chairman to executive director of the Main Board after more than 20 years as a manager in one of ICI's divisions. ICI is one of the world's largest multinational chemical companies and has sales of over £2 billion, 199,000 employees, and 350 subsidiaries in 40 countries.

Despite its worldwide activity, the company's culture and management style is almost entirely British. 132,000 of the employees are based in Britain. UK sales contribute nearly two-thirds of total worldwide revenues, and almost one-third of the company's overseas sales are exported from the UK. Senior managers are almost all British. The headquarters are in London, within a ten-minute walk of Parliament and Whitehall. Chairmen of the company are usually knighted. When directors leave, they become chairmen of other large UK companies, or play prominent roles in employers' organizations such as the Confederation of British Industry. The financial fortunes of the company are regarded as a barometer for the stock market. It is a British *institution*, and must behave, or at least must be seen to behave, in an ethical, regulated and stable fashion.

ICI is conservative and characterized by a complex management hierarchy and extensive bureaucracy:

> If you have an organization which has been by and large successful, it's 50 years old, it's hierarchical, it's almost totally inbred, it advances layer by layer, rank by rank, it has to be very, very conservative . . . (Director)[1]

The tradition of recruiting first class scientists and turning them into managers reinforces the conservatism. It has led to a tendency to 'over-intellectualize' and has produced a 'smoothing rather than problem-solving culture'.

> The line of succession has been 90 per cent technologists of one sort or another, all coming out of the same kinds of schools, playing rugby together at the same kinds of places, and having the same kinds of orientations to life. The marketing free-swinging businessman or the very innovative science type, as distinct from the good scientific analyst – the free-swingers, and entrepreneurs have been in a minority . . . (Director)[2]

The Main Board (Figure 1) is comprised of 18 people: a chairman; 11 executive directors, including three deputy chairmen who represent a distinct level in the Board's hierarchy; and six non-executive (outside) directors. It

Case prepared by Professor Cynthia Hardy, Faculty of Management, McGill University, from published material. All quotations taken from Pettigrew, A.M., *The Awakening Giant: Continuity and Change in Imperial Chemical Industries*. Oxford, England: Basil Blackwell, 1985. Case not to be reproduced without permission.

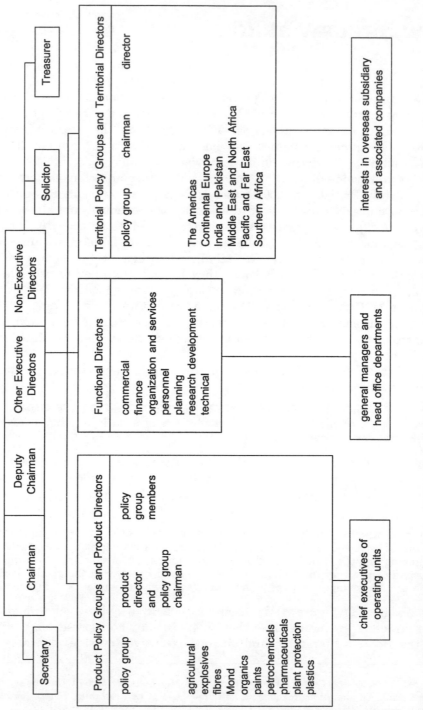

Figure 1 *ICI Board of Directors, April 1974 (Adapted from Pettigrew, A.M., The Awakening Giant: Continuity and Change in ICI, Oxford: Basil Blackwell, 1985: 382)*

operates on a matrix principle where responsibilities are divided by product, function and territory. Each executive director looks after a staff function (e.g. personnel), a geographical region (e.g. Africa) and a business sector (e.g. petrochemicals). In the last capacity, the director is overseer and adviser to the relevant UK division, but not personally responsible for divisional performance. Directors for related businesses (e.g. plastics and fibres) come together in a Policy Group, headed by a deputy chairman, which sets profit targets and approves capital expenditures subject to the approval of the Main Board. In these Groups, each director tends to protect the interests of 'his' division. Since the emphasis is on consensus rather than overt conflict, these arrangements lead to a preoccupation with maintaining existing operations rather than exploiting new opportunities. Decisions regarding investment overseas, especially in the case of technology transfer from the UK, involve several directors, Policy Groups, and Territorial Groups, which makes decisive action even more difficult to achieve. Despite extensive portfolios and committee membership, the existence of the deputy chairmen and consensus decision making style has left the executive directors with little to do. As one director describes it:

> It was the nearest thing to Devil's Island I'd known, boredom not brutality . . .. Ritual dancing time and time again, failure to take the decision, walking away from decisions. Continual frustration where one or two strong and opinionated voices could stop the whole thing stone dead.[3]

The operating units are clustered into nine divisions, some of which are substantial businesses in their own right. One of the largest employs 17,000 people and has sales of £340m – ranking it 32nd among Britain's largest companies. The Main Board monitors the divisions through a system of central planning and budget controls, and two mechanisms in particular: it has the final say over investment decisions; and is the arbiter of personnel policy. Links between the operating divisions and the Main Board are relatively limited due to several layers of staff management between the two levels. Theoretically, divisional chairmen are accountable for the performance of their operations, but the complexity and bureaucracy of the hierarchy had led to a lack of clear-cut responsibilities. (The same is even more true of overseas subsidiaries.) Recently, UK division chairmen have started to meet together informally to defend against the increasingly centralized control of personnel policies.

The Board functions by consensus and the Chairman acts as a first among equals instead of assuming decision making responsibility like the typical chief executive officer. The Chairman's authority is limited to chairing Board meetings, setting agenda, and allocating portfolios to executive directors. He has little influence over appointments to the Board or his successor, whose choice is effectively confined to one of the deputy chairmen who will be elected in a secret vote by directors. The powers of individual executive directors are also limited: important decisions are a matter for the Board as a whole, not an individual. This 'carefully nurtured collectivism' (*Management Today*, January

Table 1   *Financial statistics, millions of pounds*

	Sales	Net income
1970	1,462	86.7
1971	1,524	19.9
1972	1,694	75.5
1973	2,166	177.4

Source: *Moody's Investors Services, Inc.,* 1975, vol. 1

1987: 39) reflects the general culture of the company. It also stems from the last 'strong' chairman whose power had grown to the point where he was effectively able to make appointments to the Board and impose his personal strategy on the company. Unfortunately, his maxim of growth eventually led to a cash crisis in 1966. Subsequent chairmen have been limited to one three- or four-year term to constrain their ability to take unilateral action.

> If you have a chairman who has a three year stint in office, the first year he's not going to lash about him too much because he wants to establish himself. The second year is a year when he can lash about, but the third year he's already saying, 'I don't want to prejudice the position of my successor', and guys on the Board are not wanting to take big risks because there's always one or two competing to be the next chairman. So if you analyse the thing you find that you only have one year in three – rather like elephants – when you can mate and make it happen. (Director)[4]

A further reason for the short tenure of chairmen is that by the time an individual has worked his way up through the hierarchy of divisional chairman, executive director and deputy chairman, he has only a short time before having to retire at 62 years old.

Despite respectable, if not brilliant, financial results (Table 1), the company faces major problems because of (a) its dependency on the UK market, which is rapidly eroding; (b) increasing foreign competition; and (c) a preoccupation with technology rather than markets. Nearly two-thirds of ICI's assets and sales are in commodities (also known as bulk, heavy or mainstream chemicals), such as agricultural products, fibres, explosives, and petrochemicals. These products have low margins and are vulnerable to cyclical fluctuations as opposed to speciality chemicals such as pharmaceuticals, where there is more opportunity to add value and engage in premium pricing. Unfortunately, the Main Board has become more and more preoccupied with monitoring the operating units' capital expenditures and less with the long-term strategy of the company as a whole.

> There were two obsessions, one the obsession with fixed capital and the other . . . was a fear of running into another cash crisis like the one in 1966. There was an enormous cultural force pressing people's minds onto fixed capital and cash management. Anything very quickly boiled back again to the capital programme and what are we going to do in 6 months hence. And when you'd had that capital expenditure, the 6 months after that. The key constraint was how much money would it be prudent to spend in the ensuing 12 months . . . (Director)[5]

Harvey-Jones believes a new strategy is required that will both decrease dependency on commodities and the UK, improve efficiency, and exploit new, profitable, high growth opportunities. He is also convinced that the Main Board itself will have to be reorganized if any strategic thinking (let alone action) concerning the company's worldwide interests is to occur. He feels that a different Board structure is needed which is more compatible with a move to develop markets in North America and Europe.

These changes are counter-cultural since there is a strong feeling that individuals should not rock the boat. Harvey-Jones has already been involved in a failed attempt to change the company. Before he formally became an executive director in April 1973, he had been asked to join the 1972 Organization Committee, which had been set up to examine the organization of the Board. The committee consisted of a deputy chairman and three executive directors. It took evidence from directors, division chairmen, and the heads of overseas subsidiaries. The report contained considerable criticism of the company's structure and culture. It recommended: more strategic thinking about the company's worldwide interests; a smaller Main Board; the end of the position of deputy chairman; and the wider involvement of division chairmen.

The recommendations had been presented at a meeting of the Main Board and 'sank at the first shot'.

> [The Committee] had done just about everything you could have done to get it wrong. It had taken massive amounts of evidence and so aroused massive expectations. It had barely reported back to its colleagues, and it had not really carried its Chairman with it . . . also it doesn't take a genius to see that a hell of a lot of executive directors would have been out of a job if this change had gone through . . .[6]

With successful financial results in 1973, there had been no desire to rock the boat.

> People could give lip service to bits of it [proposed change], but when it was put back in terms of prove this is better than what we have, why upset the company? There was no external crisis, no business problems, so it was theory against theory.[7]

Questions

- What is the strategy advocated by John Harvey-Jones and how will it help ICI?
- What would you do to bring about the new strategy if you were John Harvey-Jones?
- How would you secure support from the Board for the new strategy?
- How would you restructure the Board to help realize the new strategy?

Notes

1. *The Awakening Giant: Continuity and Change in Imperial Chemical Industries*, Oxford, England: Basil Blackwell, 1985, p. 388.

2. Ibid.: 387.

3. Ibid.: 389.

4. Ibid.: 388.

5. Ibid.: 389.

6. Ibid.: 392.

7. Ibid.

PART II MOBILIZING CHANGE: THE ROLE OF POWER

Introduction

The strategic change process discussed in the previous part is typically presented as a relatively rational, orderly practice. In reality, however, it is often intensely political as power is brought to bear by organizational actors either to orchestrate strategic outcomes or influence them in a way that is in line with their own interests. Both the limitations to rationality and the political realities of organizational life mean that power is an integral part of the strategic change process. This is not to say that the irresponsible or unethical use of power is advocated; indeed, it is not. Nevertheless, an understanding of power and its relevance to strategic change is essential.

This part is the lynchpin of the book. By understanding power we are in a better position to understand and manage the strategic change process described in the first part and the strategic predicaments presented in the third part. The formulation of strategic intent, the way in which the environment is perceived, the choice of a particular strategy, and the process whereby strategic intent is shared among organizational members all have political implications. Similarly, the way an organization is structured, the nature of human resource policies, the type of culture, and the way in which leaders influence strategy all involve power and help to create a system of advantages and disadvantages which benefit some individuals and penalize others. The realization of a strategy and the relation it bears to the original strategic intent is, as a result, better understood when observers have an idea of the groups that are affected by the strategy, the nature of their interests, and their access to and use of power. As we shall see, the predicaments discussed in Part III also revolve around issues of power.

The readings and cases in this part are, accordingly, designed to explore how power works. They have been selected to reveal the multiple and often hidden layers of power. Much of the management literature has focused only on the visible side of power; the analysis here goes far deeper because, if we do not appreciate fully the complexity of power, we run the risk of ignoring the ethical implications of using it and obscuring our own political biases. The questions we ask and the answers we uncover are influenced by our own political perspectives and biases. Take a relatively simple example – the benefits provided to workers in the event of plant closure. Some people might not see power as an issue here at all and, instead, would focus on the benevolence of employers in compensating workers for the loss of their jobs. Other observers might ask questions about the bargaining and negotiation processes that led to a particular compensation package, reflecting a relatively fair and balanced use of power by both unions and employers. More critical commentators might argue that the power of managers and unions was unequal: they would examine how the compensation helped employers secure acceptance of their decision, allowing them to close the plant without union resistance, even though many people might have lost their jobs and the community lost an important employer. Such differences in ideological perspective are inevitable and it is important for readers to be aware of their particular perspective and how it affects the way they view the world and the actions they take.

Power is defined in this book in broad, neutral terms: as a force that influences outcomes. The aim of the readings is to flesh out what underlies this definition: power is a multi-faceted concept that works in a myriad of different ways. The use of moral terminology is also avoided because, by reducing objectivity, it can inhibit readers from making an insightful study of the phenomenon. The aim is to increase the reader's awareness of power but also ensure that he or she retains an understanding of the legitimacy of the multiple interests that exist in organizations, instead of being focused purely on self-interest (Figure 1). In order to achieve 'wisdom' rather than simply the 'clever' exploitation of power, the cases and readings encompass both a critical and pragmatic approach.

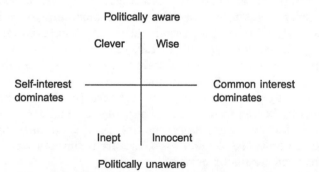

Figure 1   *Political Wisdom (Adapted from S. Baddeley and K. James, 'Political management: Developing the management portfolio,* Journal of Management Development, *9(3): 42–59, 1990.*

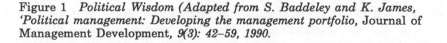

The readings in this part explore the link between power and strategy; provide a deeper understanding of power; and promote a critical framework. The chapters by Kotter and Sadler provide a snapshot of some of the political aspects of strategy making. Kotter demonstrates the dependency which characterizes the day-to-day functioning of a manager's life. With dependency comes power – power over the manager which may hamper his or her ability to do the job. Sadler presents a picture of boardroom politics which shows that securing approval to strategic change is not simply a matter of objective, rational arguments, but also a political process. Thus the use of power becomes important to orchestrating managers' actions and legitimating a particular strategy.

Hardy then provides an overview of power and politics by presenting a four-dimensional model. It shows that power can be used to enforce certain behaviours; prevent decisions from being made; and influence attitudes so that resistance does not arise. These three dimensions represent strategies that managers use to shape organizational outcomes such as strategic change. Hardy adds a fourth dimension – the power that resides in a system and produces certain outcomes without being actively and consciously mobilized by anyone. Gray and Ariss illustrate the different political issues that arise as the organization progresses through the life-cycle starting with the individualistic politics typically associated with entrepreneurial firms, through the bureaucratic politics associated with large-scale organizations pursuing growth, to the politics of declining resources.

The readings then turn to an analysis of two particular issues that frequently surface within the context of contemporary management: employee empowerment and business ethics. The literature advocating empowerment is resurrecting a 'unitary' view of management (see the article by Fox listed at the end of this Introduction). It suggests that management, employees and unions are really working towards the same goals and, if only the latter would cooperate, everyone would benefit. The chapter by Leiba and Hardy takes a closer look at employee empowerment to see if, indeed, this is the case. It challenges the idea that power is given away by managers to their employees and shows that, first, many traditional sources of power such as hiring and firing are retained by managers and, second, where certain forms of power are delegated, they are immediately substituted by other sources of power. In effect, 'empowerment' largely involves substituting formal controls with more sophisticated socialization processes to ensure that employee attitudes are in line with management objectives. This chapter also questions the assertion that management and employee interests converge: empowerment has often been used to facilitate downsizing, which means employees either lose their jobs or receive more work and responsibility for the same (or less) money and reduced promotion prospects.

Bird and Hardy demonstrate that if you want to ensure ethical actions, you need to use power. The article differentiates between ethical objectives that are purely an individual matter and those that require cooperation between organizational members or between the organization and external stakeholders. Power is needed to orchestrate this cooperation. Ethical strategies, just like competitive strategies, require convergence of those key design parameters that lead the organization and its members towards ethical action.

Because of competing pressures, such as profitability and performance, organizations do not just fall into the ethical way of doing things and some may actively resist it. So, power provides the driving force behind ethical action.

The first two cases at the end of this part show how more junior employees are affected by power and some of the things they can do to influence the organization. Both cases will strike a chord with readers who have been in similar situations and will help them to make better sense of the political dynamics that occur in organizations. It is important to start with this individual appreciation of power – if we cannot understand how power impacts upon individuals in the lower echelons, we will be ill-equipped both to deal with the task of orchestrating power at more senior levels and to acknowledge the ethical implications of using power. 'Daniel and the Lions' Den' shows the suppressive effect of power on a newly graduated MBA taking up his first job. Readers might like to ask themselves whether they would have taken this job and what would have been the warning signals that would have made them feel uneasy. They should also consider what Daniel should do now that he has taken the job. 'Crown Corporation' illustrates the links between power and dependency in the case of a new manager. Because managers are always dependent on others to carry out their work effectively, they cannot rely solely on formal authority: in some cases, the manager will be dependent on people over whom he or she has no formal authority; in others, formal authority, without the reinforcement of other sources of power, may prove ineffective. Readers should identify the individuals and groups on whom Antonia is dependent and recommend ways in which she can acquire and use power over them in order to reduce that dependency.

'Northville' and 'Midville' broaden the analysis from individual politics to interest group politics. Although set in the late 1970s, they raise political issues that are equally relevant today. These cases show how different groups are affected by strategic choices and how, as a result, they try to influence strategy making. They also demonstrate how power can be used to shape attitudes as well as behaviour. Readers can devise action plans for both Northville managers, who wish to close the hospital, and the interest groups that are trying to prevent the closure. They can then compare the situation of Northville managers with that of Midville managers to analyse the differences in the political climate.

The last two cases show why power is an integral part of successful strategy making. They make it clear why, without power, strategic realization will remain a fantasy. 'Medical Services and Products' shows how the credibility of a new CEO is inextricably bound up with a new strategy – a strategy that is challenged by a powerful vice-president. Ignoring power in this case will most likely lead to both the failure of the new strategy and the hasty exit of the new CEO. Readers can devise action plans for both Roberta and Donald that address both their strategic and personal goals. They can then review their recommendations from an ethical perspective to ensure they understand all the implications.

The Tobacco Firms provide an example of an overtly political strategy designed to protect the industry against health threats. The case demonstrates pragmatically how power can be used in an extremely effective way, but it also raises many ethical considerations and shows clearly why power is needed to enforce or induce ethical behaviour. Readers should consider both why the actions of the tobacco firms were so successful and, in many respects, so unethical.

Other cases in the book can be used to explore power and politics. In the first part, for example, Apple shows the problems that arise when Jobs and Sculley start to envisage incompatible strategies for the company, and the paralysis that follows from a structure which sandwiches Sculley, as CEO, between Jobs as Vice-president and Jobs as Chairman. At Montreal Trust, a new leader is parachuted in over a vice-president who probably considered the top as his own, and who controls 90 per cent of the division's resources. 'Automakers of Canada' displays the political inertia that can be caused by a deeply entrenched culture, John Harvey-Jones faces similar cultural resistance in forging a new strategy at Imperial Chemical Industries. In Part III, General Motors and Electronic Data Systems illustrate political issues around leadership; Loblaws shows political differences between organizations; and 'Conglom' examines how power is used to create consensus.

Further Reading for Part II

Astley, W.G. and Sachdeva, P.S. (1984) 'Structural sources of intraorganizational power: A theoretical synthesis', *Academy of Management*, 9(1): 104–13.

Bachrach, P. and Baratz, M.S. (1962) 'The two faces of power', *American Political Science Review*, 56: 947–52.

Benfari, R.C. et al. (1986) 'The effective use of power', *Business Horizons*, May–June, 12–16.

Daft, R. (1983) Chapters 10 and 11 in *Organizational Theory and Design*. St Paul: West.

Fox, A. (1973) 'Industrial relations: A social critique of pluralist ideology', in Child, J. (ed.), *Man and Organization*. London: Allen & Unwin, 1973.

Hardy, C. (1985) 'Responses to industrial closure', *Industrial Relations Journal*, 16(1): 16–24.

Knights, D. and Morgan G. (1991) 'Corporate strategy, organizations and subjectivity', *Organization Studies*, 12(2): 251–73.

Longenecker, et al. (1987) 'Behind the mask: The politics of employee appraisal', *Academy of Management Executive*, 1(3): 183–93.

Lukes, S. (1974) *Power: A Radical View*. London: Macmillan.

Martin, N.H. and Sims, J.H. (1956) 'Thinking ahead', *Harvard Business Review*, 25–37, November–December.

Murray, V. and Gandz, J. (1980) 'Games executives play: Politics at work', *Business Horizons*, 11–23, December.

Nota, B. (1988) 'The socialization process at high-commitment organizations', *Personnel*, August, 20–3.

Parry, G. and Morriss, P. (1975) 'When is a decision not a decision?', in Crewe, I. (ed.), *British Political Sociology Yearbook*, 1. London, England: Croom Helm.

Schein, E.H. (1968) 'Organizational socialization', *Industrial Management Review*, 9: 1–15.

Simon, B.L. (1990) 'Rethinking empowerment', *Journal of Progressive Human Sciences*, 1(1): 27–37.

Stewart, T.A. (1989) 'New ways to exercise power', *Fortune*, 52–66, 6 November.

Walton, R.E. (1965) 'Two strategies of social change and their dilemmas', *Journal of Applied Behavioural Science*, 1(2): 167–79.

Wilson J.A. and Elman, N.S. (1990) 'The organizational benefits of mentoring', *Academy of Management Executive*, 4(4): 88–94.

11 Power and the Manager

John P. Kotter

[. . .]

From my own observations, I suspect that a large number of managers – especially the young, well-educated ones – perform significantly below their potential because they do not understand the dynamics of power and because they have not nurtured and developed the instincts needed to effectively acquire and use power.

In this chapter I hope to clear up some of the confusion regarding power and managerial work by providing tentative answers to three questions:

1 Why are the dynamics of power necessarily an important part of managerial processes?
2 How do effective managers acquire power?
3 How and for what purposes do effective managers use power?

Recognizing dependence in the manager's job

One of the distinguishing characteristics of a typical manager is how dependent he is on the activities of a variety of other people to perform his job effectively. Unlike doctors and mathematicians, whose performance is more directly dependent on their own talents and efforts, a manager can be dependent in varying degrees on superiors, subordinates, peers in other parts of the organization, the subordinates of peers, outside suppliers, customers, competitors, unions, regulating agencies, and many others.

These dependency relationships are an inherent part of managerial jobs because of two organizational facts of life: division of labor and limited resources. Because the work in organizations is divided into specialized divisions, departments, and jobs, managers are made directly or indirectly dependent on many others for information, staff services, and cooperation in general. Because of their organization's limited resources, managers are also

From 'Power, dependence, and effective management', *Harvard Business Review*, July–August 1977, pp. 125–36.

dependent on their external environments for support. Without some minimal cooperation from suppliers, competitors, unions, regulatory agencies, and customers, managers cannot help their organizations survive and achieve their objectives.

Dealing with these dependencies and the manager's subsequent vulnerability is an important and difficult part of a manager's job because, while it is theoretically possible that all of these people and organizations would automatically act in just the manner that a manager wants and needs, such is almost never the case in reality. All the people on whom a manager is dependent have limited time, energy, and talent, for which there are competing demands.

Some people may be uncooperative because they are too busy elsewhere, and some because they are not really capable of helping. Others may well have goals, values, and beliefs that are quite different and in conflict with the manager's and may therefore have no desire whatsoever to help or cooperate. This is obviously true of a competing company and sometimes of a union, but it can also apply to a boss who is feeling threatened by a manager's career progress or to a peer whose objectives clash with the manager's

Indeed, managers often find themselves dependent on many people (and things) whom they do not directly control and who are not 'cooperating.' This is the key to one of the biggest frustrations managers feel in their jobs, even in the top ones [. . .].

[. . .]

As a person gains more formal authority in an organization, the areas in which he or she is vulnerable increase and become more complex rather than the reverse. [. . .] It is not at all unusual for the president of an organization to be in a highly dependent position, a fact often not apparent to either the outsider or to the lower level manager who covets the president's job.

A considerable amount of the behavior of highly successful managers that seems inexplicable in light of what management texts usually tell us managers do becomes understandable when one considers a manager's need for, and efforts at, managing his or her relationships with others.[3] To be able to plan, organize, budget, staff, control, and evaluate, managers need some control over the many people on whom they are dependent. Trying to control others solely by directing them and on the basis of the power associated with one's position simply will not work – first, because managers are always dependent on some people over whom they have no formal authority, and second, because virtually no one in modern organizations will passively accept and completely obey a constant stream of orders from someone just because he or she is the 'boss.'

Trying to influence others by means of persuasion alone will not work either. Although it is very powerful and possibly the single most important method of influence, persuasion has some serious drawbacks too. To make it work requires time (often lots of it), skill, and information on the part of the persuader. And persuasion can fail simply because the other person chooses not to listen or does not listen carefully.

This is not to say that directing people on the basis of the formal power of one's position and persuasion are not important means by which successful managers cope. They obviously are. But, even taken together, they are not usually enough.

Successful managers cope with their dependence on others by being sensitive to it, by eliminating or avoiding unnecessary dependence, and by establishing power over those others. Good managers then use that power to help them plan, organize, staff, budget, evaluate, and so on. *In other words, it is primarily because of the dependence inherent in managerial jobs that the dynamics of power necessarily form an important part of a manager's processes.*

[. . .]

Establishing power in relationships

To help cope with the dependency relationships inherent in their jobs, effective managers create, increase, or maintain four different types of power over others. Having power based in these areas puts the manager in a position both to influence those people on whom he or she is dependent when necessary and to avoid being hurt by any of them.

Sense of obligation

One of the ways that successful managers generate power in their relationships with others is to create a sense of obligation in those others. When the manager is successful, the others feel that they should – rightly – allow the manager to influence them within certain limits.

Successful managers often go out of their way to do favors for people who they expect will feel an obligation to return those favors. [. . .] Some people are very skilled at identifying opportunities for doing favors that cost them very little but that others appreciate very much.

[. . .]

Recognizing that most people believe that friendship carries with it certain obligations ('A friend in need . . .'), successful managers often try to develop true friendships with those on whom they are dependent. They will also make formal and informal deals in which they give something up in exchange for certain future obligations.

Belief in a manager's expertise

A second way successful managers gain power is by building reputations as 'experts' in certain matters. Believing in the manager's expertise, others will often defer to the manager on those matters. Managers usually establish this type of power through visible achievement. The larger the achievement and the more visible it is, the more power the manager tends to develop.

One of the reasons that managers display concern about their 'professional reputations' and their 'track records' is that they have an impact on others' beliefs about their expertise. These factors become particularly important in large settings, where most people have only secondhand information about most other people's professional competence [. . .].

[. . .]

Identification with a manager

A third method by which managers gain power is by fostering others' unconscious identification with them or with ideas they 'stand for.' Sigmund Freud was the first to describe this phenomenon, which is most clearly seen in the way people look up to 'charismatic' leaders. Generally, the more a person finds a manager both consciously and (more important) unconsciously an ideal person, the more he or she will defer to that manager.

Managers develop power based on others' idealized views of them in a number of ways. They try to look and behave in ways that others respect. They go out of their way to be visible to their employees and to give speeches about their organizational goals, values, and ideals. They even consider, while making hiring and promotion decisions, whether they will be able to develop this type of power over the candidates.

[. . .]

Perceived dependence on a manager

The final way that an effective manager often gains power is by feeding others' beliefs that they are dependent on the manager either for help or for not being hurt. The more they perceive they are dependent, the more most people will be inclined to cooperate with such a manager.

[. . .]

[. . .] The manager identifies and secures (if necessary) resources that another person requires to perform his job, that he does not possess, and that are not readily available elsewhere. These resources include such things as authority to make certain decisions; control of money, equipment, and office space; access to important people; information and control of information channels; and subordinates. Then the manager takes action so that the other person correctly perceives that the manager has such resources and is willing and ready to use them to help (or hinder) the other person. [. . .]

Generating and using power successfully

Managers who are successful at acquiring considerable power and using it to manage their dependence on others tend to share a number of common characteristics:

1 They are sensitive to what others consider to be legitimate behavior in acquiring and using power. [. . .]
2 They have good intuitive understanding of the various types of power and methods of influence. They are sensitive to what types of power are easiest to develop with different types of people. [. . .]
3 They tend to develop all the types of power, to some degree, and they use all the influence methods. [. . .]
4 They establish career goals and seek out managerial positions that allow them to successfully develop and use power. They look for jobs, for example, that use their backgrounds and skills to control or manage some critically important problems or environmental contingency that an organization faces. [. . .]
5 They use all of their resources, formal authority, and power to develop still more power. [. . .]
6 Effective managers engage in power-oriented behaviour in ways that are tempered by maturity and self-control.[7] They seldom, if ever, develop and use power in impulsive ways or for their own aggrandizement.
7 Finally, they also recognize and accept as legitimate that, in using these methods, they clearly influence other people's behavior and lives. Unlike many less effective managers, they are reasonably comfortable in using power to influence people. They recognize, often only intuitively, what this article is all about – that their attempts to establish power and use it are an absolutely necessary part of the successful fulfillment of their difficult managerial role.

Notes

[. . .]
3. I am talking about the type of inexplicable differences that Henry Mintzberg has found; see his article 'The manager's job: Folklore and fact', *Harvard Business Review*, July–August 1975, p. 49.
[. . .]
7. See David C. McClelland and David H. Burnham, 'Power is the great motivator', *Harvard Business Review*, March–April 1976, p. 100.

12 Power in the Boardroom

Philip Sadler

Scarcely a day goes by without another power struggle at the top, usually ending in what the media love to call a 'boardroom coup.' We like to think that board-level decisions are taken on the basis of rational argument and in the best long-term interests of the stakeholders in the business. In practice, the boardroom is often the arena in which a struggle for power takes place and the principles of management are abandoned in favour of the law of the corporate jungle.

The process of achieving, maintaining and exercising power is what we call politics. It is a subject to which all directors need to be sensitive, yet it does not feature on the curriculum at business schools.

The political use of power comes about in various ways. One of the most common is by forming alliances. This happens when some members of the board meet before a board meeting to agree what line they are going to take to ensure that their interests are safeguarded. Another common political ploy is for an individual director to build a power base within the company centred on a division or a subsidiary, such that the unit is loyal to him personally rather than to the corporation as a whole.

Control over resources – particularly human resources – can be another potent source of power. A divisional chief executive, for example, may refuse to release a young manager of high potential for a developmental appointment elsewhere in the group unless he gains some advantage in return. Information, too, is a frequent source of power as when a director, instead of sharing vital information with board colleagues, uses it to enhance his power and achieve objectives.

The sensitivity of people to political activity going on around them varies quite a lot. Some are politically naive and remain unconscious of the manipulations of those who are engaged in scheming. In consequence, they become easy victims. Others are politically aware but are not skilled enough to handle such situations effectively. To survive in a highly political environment it is important to be politically astute – which means being able to play the political game, even if only defensively. This requires particular kinds of competence:

From 'The politics of the corporate jungle', *Director*, May 1992, p. 29.

- the ability to recognise those who are playing political games despite surface appearances of openness and co-operation;
- identifying the sources and strength of their power;
- building one's own alliances and connections;
- insisting at all times that the proper procedures be followed.

But perhaps the most effective way of dealing with political intrigue is to drag it into the daylight.

Why do directors sometimes engage in political activity? Some feel that it is the only way to achieve outcomes which they sincerely believe to be in the best interest of the firm. Others undoubtedly do it to advance their own personal ambitions. And others simply enjoy playing politics.

Why is it that political activity is more common in some companies than others?

Charles Handy says that there are four basic types of corporate culture. There is the bureaucratic culture, which values procedures and accepts as legitimate the power which comes with holding office. There is the task culture, which values achievement and the power that stems from knowledge or competence. There is the culture which is based on partnership and which values resolving issues through consensus. Finally there is the power culture, which is dominated by one person or a small group. Robert Maxwell's empire was an extreme form of this kind of culture. It is in such an atmosphere, with its focus on power, that political activity is most likely to occur. Indeed in many cases it is indispensable for survival. such a culture attracts those who enjoy the power game. They can even play its most dangerous form – plotting against the throne!

The Maxwell case shows that not all political activity is self-interested or detrimental to the interests of the shareholders. It may be the case that in some situations activities which are at best unwise or at worst illegal can only be stopped by engaging in a political process. To be successful, however, it is vital to be politically astute – there are many 'whistle blowers' without a job.

What should the chairman do if he becomes aware that some members of the board are playing politics? The first thing is to ask himself why. It is possible that it is happening because of deficiencies in the decision-making process. If, however, he is satisfied that this is not the case – and he should consult his non-executive directors to check this out – he should then confront the issue openly at the next board meeting and make it clear that such behaviour is not tolerated.

The best way to forestall scheming in a company is to build a strong cohesive team at board level. Mutual trust and support leave no room for political manoeuvring.

13 Power and Politics in Organizations

Cynthia Hardy

This chapter reviews various models of power and politics and presents a framework applicable to organizational settings. The aim is to offer insight into the scope and diversity of the literature while relating it to the practical issues of management. Power is a complex concept to grasp and has always evoked a considerable amount of controversy around the definition and use of the term (Lukes, 1974). One reason for this is the failure to acknowledge the complexity of the term coupled with attempts to limit what is an inherently general concept (Allison, 1974). Bachrach and Lawler (1980) argue that power is a *primitive* term and, as such, is bound to be vague. These authors suggest that, rather than attempting to pin it down to a precise definition, we should be using the concept of power to reveal the complexity and multi-dimensionality of the phenomenon.

> Extant work on power usually attempts to impose on the concept a level of precision beyond that appropriate for a primitive term. Thus, we must ask not what is power but to what does the notion of power sensitize us. (Bachrach and Lawler, 1980: 14)

This is sound advice: attention should be directed towards asking what power comprises and how it produces results, rather than now neatly it can be defined. Narrow definitions are counter-productive, serving to constrain and restrict subsequent empirical work.

For the purposes of this chapter, a broad definition has been used that equates power with a force that influences outcomes. It encompasses terms such as coercion, manipulation, authority, persuasion and influence as these are, in fact, various forms of power. Politics is defined as the use of power (e.g. Hickson et al., 1986). So, instead of preoccupying itself with neat definitions, the remainder of this chapter concerns itself with examining the complexity of power. It presents four dimensions (Lukes, 1974) of power: decision-making power, nondecision-making, symbolic power, and system power.

A distinction is made between power used in the face of conflict and power used to prevent conflict arising in the first place. This distinction is important since many definitions of power restrict its use to situations where overt resistance has to be overcome (e.g. Pfeffer, 1981a). But power can also be used to ensure that opposition does not emerge. In this case, power is used specifically to prevent conflict from arising. To focus solely on the use of power in the event of conflict is misleading because it totally ignores this important use of power. A second distinction is made between actors who benefit from their conscious mobilization of power through political strategies and those who benefit inadvertently from power that resides in the system. Both these distinctions are significant because they force us to look at the issue of quiescence far more critically: it may not necessarily indicate that people are genuinely satisfied with their lot but, instead, that they have been subjected to political actions or a systemic bias, either of which can render them powerless.

The Sources of Power

The sources of power are manifold and have been traced to a number of distinct resources (e.g. French and Raven, 1968; Pettigrew, 1973; Pfeffer, 1981a). Much of the literature has related power to dependency relations (Emerson, 1962). Power accrues to those who control scarce and valued resources that render others dependent on them (e.g. Hickson et al., 1971; Pfeffer and Salancik, 1974). Power is thus entrenched in the relationship between actors, rather than being an attribute of a particular individual. This issue of resource interdependencies has formed the basis of research to uncover the power resources available to organizational members. For example, because they can restrict access to information and equipment (Mechanic, 1962), lower-level participants can exercise power over members of higher echelons. The control of information has been found to be a particularly important source of power (Pettigrew, 1973; Pfeffer, 1981a). Power has been related to the ability to control uncertainty (Crozier, 1964; Hickson et al., 1971; Pfeffer, 1981a), and to expertise (Pettigrew, 1973). Credibility, stature and prestige can also confer power (Pettigrew, 1973; Pfeffer and Salancik, 1974; Salancik and Pfeffer, 1974). Other power sources include access to and contacts with members of higher echelons and the control of money, rewards and sanctions (French and Raven, 1968; Benfari et al., 1986).

Mere possession of scarce resources does not in itself confer power. Actors also have to be aware of pertinent resources, and control and use them tactically (Pettigrew 1973). Politics thus occurs as actors mobilize power sources.

> Political action takes place when an actor, recognizing that the achievement of its goal is influenced by the behaviour of others' actions in the situation, undertakes action against the others to ensure that its own goals are achieved. (MacMillan, 1978: 8)

Another source of power is legitimacy (Astley and Sachdeva, 1984). Political scientists have long recognized that a regime will be more stable if dominant groups can make the populace believe that existing institutions are best for society (Lipset, 1959; Schaar, 1969; Roelofs, 1976; Rothschild, 1979). Legitimacy can also be created for individual actions, thus reducing the chances of opposition to them. Edelman (1964, 1971, 1977) has pointed out that power is mobilized not only to achieve physical outcomes, but also to give those outcomes meanings – to legitimize and justify them. Political actors use language, symbols, and ideologies to placate or arouse the public on specific issues. Pettigrew (1977) calls this process the management of meaning.

> Politics concerns the creation of legitimacy for certain ideas, values and demands – not just action performed as a result of previously acquired legitimacy. The management of meaning refers to a process of symbol construction and value use designed both to create legitimacy for one's own demands and to 'de-legitimize' the demands of others. (Pettigrew, 1977: 85)

If successful, the process of legitimation prevents opposition from arising and, as such, represents a far safer way of using power then risking confrontation.

> Stable organizing power requires legitimation. To be sure, men can be made to work and to obey commands through coercion, but the coercive use of power engenders resistance and sometimes active opposition. Power conflicts in and between societies are characterized by resistance and opposition, and while the latter occur in organizations, effective operations necessitate that they be kept at a minimum there and, especially, that members do not exhibit resistance in discharging their daily duties but perform them and comply with directives willingly. (Blau, 1964: 199–200)

In this way, language, symbols, structures, rules and regulations embody, institutionalize and legitimate certain power structures. These sources of power translate into a multi-faceted concept which is discussed in more detail below.

The Dimensions of Power

This section extends the work of Lukes (1974) to present four dimensions of power, which reflect some of the developments in the literature that have broadened and extended our understanding of this concept.

The First Dimension: Decision-Making Power

Early studies of community power typically focused exclusively on the decision-making process (see, for example, Dahl, 1957, 1961; Polsby, 1963; Wolfinger, 1971). Researchers analysed key decisions that seemed likely to illustrate the power relations prevailing in a particular community. The object was to determine who made these decisions. If the same groups were responsible for most decisions, as some researchers had suggested, the community could be said to be ruled by an elite. The researchers found, in contrast, that different groups prevailed in decision-making. Such a community was termed *pluralist* and it was hypothesized that America as a whole was a pluralist society (see Lukes, 1974; Parry and Morriss, 1975).

Several assumptions underlay this research. It was believed that political conflict was resolved by political decisions – that power was only exercised in key decisions where conflict was clearly observable. Individuals were assumed to be aware of their grievances and to act upon them by participating in decision-making and trying to influence these key decisions. These researchers saw the decision-making arena as open to anyone with an interest in it, and interpreted an absence of participation as a sign of consensus (see Bachrach and Baratz, 1963; Lukes, 1974; Parry and Morriss, 1975).

Some writers began to question the pluralist assumptions that decision-making processes were accessible and nonparticipation reflected satisfaction. Doubt about the 'permeability' of the US political system was prompted by the civil rights movement and the backlash to the Vietnam War (Parry and Morriss, 1975). The pluralists were criticized for their failure to recognize that interests and grievances might remain inarticulated and outside the decision-making arena. Consequently, conflict might well exist even if not directly observable (e.g. Gaventa, 1980; Saunders, 1980). The focus on formal decision-making was also criticized because of its assumption that the use of power was confined to this arena and that access to it was equally available to all organizational members.

The Second Dimension: Nondecision-Making

Researchers started to examine how full-and-equal participation was constrained. Schattschneider (1960: 105) argued that nonparticipation might be due to:

> the suppression of options and alternatives that reflect the needs of the non-participants. It is not necessarily true that people with the greatest needs participate in politics most actively – whoever decides what the game is about also decides who gets in the game.

Building on this insight, Bachrach and Baratz (1962, 1963, 1970) developed the concept of a second face of power – a process whereby issues could be excluded from decision-making, confining the agenda to 'safe' questions. A variety of barriers are available to the more powerful groups to prevent subordinates from fully participating in the decision-making process through the invocation of procedures and political routines. The use of these mechanisms has been termed nondecision-making, because it allows the more powerful actors to determine outcomes from behind the scenes. This work highlights the fact that power is not exercised solely in the taking of key decisions and the visible decision-makers are not necessarily the most powerful.

Nondecision-making is typically used by dominant groups to protect the status quo because it tends to support and reinforce existing biases in decision-making processes. It is important to note, however, that processes can be manipulated for other purposes. First, less powerful groups are able to use rules and procedures to their advantage. For example, in Canada recently the lone Native member of the Manitoba legislature was able to block the passage of a constitutional agreement between federal and provincial governments (and from which all aboriginal groups had been excluded) by using parliamentary procedures. Second, power-holders may use the process to change the status quo by *extending* access to decision-making arenas and agendas. So, for example, committees may be struck with members of the new guard present in order to produce outcomes that embody change. In other words, while nondecision-making is traditionally associated with dominant groups and inertia, a broader conceptualization of *process power* can be used to associate it with powerless as well as powerful groups; and with change as well as the status quo.

The Third Dimension: Symbolic Power

Some writers argued that while Bachrach and Baratz's work was an improvement on the pluralist model, it did not go far enough because it continued to assume that some form of conflict was necessary to stimulate the use of nondecision-making power (Lukes, 1974). Ranson et al. (1980: 8) remarked that: '[T]he focus [of Bachrach and Baratz] was very much upon "issues" about which "decisions" have to be made, albeit "non-decisions". Power in this view stands close to action, using the bases of power to ensure compliance.'

Parry and Morriss (1975) pointed out that most of the actions that fall under the heading of nondecision-making are, in fact, decisions about which choices have to be made, albeit a decision to do nothing. Actors are aware of grievances and conflict and, as a result, manipulate the process to suppress dangerous issues. By specifying the existence of conflict as a prerequisite of nondecision-making, Bachrach and Baratz ignored the possibility that power might be used to ensure that conflict does not arise. Their assumption (and the assumption of many other writers) was that – if there is no conflict, why would one need to use power? Such a view precludes the idea that power might be used with the specific intention of ensuring that opposition does *not* arise.

Lukes (1974: 24) attempted to correct this deficiency by focusing on how power is employed to shape:

> [people's] perceptions, cognitions, and preferences in such a way that they accept their role in the existing order of things, either because they can see or imagine no alternative to it, or because they view it as natural and unchangeable, or because they value it as divinely ordained and beneficial.

The study of power cannot, then, be confined to observable conflict, the outcomes of decisions, or even suppressed issues. We must also consider the question of political quiescence: why grievances do not exist; why demands are not made; and why conflict does not arise, since such *inaction* may also be the result of power (Lukes, 1974). 'We may, in other words, be duped, hoodwinked, coerced, cajoled or manipulated into political inactivity' (Saunders 1980: 22).

Lukes' third dimension is thus important because it specifically addresses the use of power to pre-empt conflict. The first two dimensions are concerned with power exercised in the face of competition, conflict or opposition. But:

> power is most effective and insidious in its consequences when issues do not arise at all, when actors remain unaware of their sectional claims, that is, power is most effective when it is unnecessary. (Ranson et al. 1980: 8)

The ability to shape values, preferences, cognitions, perceptions means that grievances and issues do not arise or, if they do, they are never articulated or transformed into demands and challenges. Other writers have drawn attention to the more subtle aspects of power. Fox (1973) pointed out that the powerful do not need to make their power visible because their position is rarely challenged. Hyman and Fryer (1975), in their discussion of trade union power, have argued that opposition depends on objective power based on material sources of power – the ability to resist – and subjective power which rests on the awareness of workers that they are in a disadvantaged position and that political issues exist – the will to resist. Lukes' third dimension affects the latter.

Lukes' work focuses on societal and class mechanisms which perpetuate the status quo. It relates to Gramsci's concept of ideological hegemony (Clegg, 1989) – where 'a structure of power relations is fully legitimized by an integrated system of cultural and normative assumptions' (Hyman and Brough, 1975: 199). According to this view, the ability to define reality is restricted solely to dominant classes who use it to support and justify their material domination, thus preventing challenges to their position. Other writers have criticized this 'over-extension' of hegemony (Clegg, 1989) to argue that the third dimension is a viable strategy for specific groups and individuals who wish to legitimate or challenge political outcomes (e.g. Clegg, 1975; Gaventa, 1980; Hardy, 1985a) and, as such, this source of power is not exclusive to the elite.

> All social actors, no matter how lowly, have some degree of penetration of the social forms that oppress. (Giddens, 1979: 72)

We should not assume, then, that dominant groups alone have recourse to the ability to define reality. Instead, we should view ideological and symbolic bases of power as being differentially distributed throughout society, in much the same way as other resources. Some groups may possess more resources but that does not render other groups totally defenceless – there are often counter-vailing sources of power they can seek out and employ.

In this way, we can move away from the conception of ideological power purely in class terms, and examine its use in other arenas, such as organizations. Thus, the third dimension of power is associated with attempts by interest groups to legitimize their demands and 'de-legitimize' the demands of others by *managing meaning* (Pettigrew, 1979). If successful, dominant actors prevent others from making challenges by legitimating existing power positions, and creating perceptions of outcomes as beneficial, acceptable or inevitable. If subordinate actors use the third dimension, it is to question the status quo and raise political consciousness.

The mechanisms that help actors create legitimacy revolve around the use of symbols, including language, rituals and myths. The important aspect of symbols is that they stand for something other than themselves – the meaning is in society, not in the symbol (Edelman, 1964). Furthermore, they have a multiplicity of meanings which can be useful in politics (Abner Cohen, 1975). Language is an important aspect of symbolic political activity (Pettigrew, 1977, 1979; Pfeffer, 1981a). It can work as a catalyst to mobilize support, or as a device to cloud issues and quiet opposition (Edelman, 1964). Mueller (1973) points out how the obfuscation of political reality can be achieved with the use of a highly evocative language. Language and political consciousness are closely linked. Martin (1977) points out that groups who can perceive their situation experientially but who are unable to translate these specific experiences into general terms will be unable to adequately define their own position. This, in turn, will inhibit political consciousness and activity. Language, therefore, is likely to be an important device in both restricting opposition and rallying resistance.

Myths have been defined as fictional narratives and, more explicitly, as narratives of events which explore issues of origin and transformation (see, for example, Abner Cohen, 1975; Pettigrew, 1977, 1979). Myths can be used to legitimate existing power positions (Abner Cohen, 1975; Anthony Cohen, 1975; Pettigrew, 1977, 1979; Gaventa, 1980), by emphasizing the importance of the past and tradition. They can also be used to question the legitimacy of the status quo and emphasize the importance of change and modernization (Anthony Cohen, 1975). So, myths can be used to both justify or challenge the system. Rituals, ceremonies and settings are the more physical aspects of symbolism. They refer to procedures and ceremonies which convey certain messages and meanings. So, for example, the ceremony of dismissal and replacement might be used to signal change, discredit past practices, warn others. Meetings may take on a ritual character in order to convey messages to the participants. Settings, including the grandeur of rooms and the seating arrangements, can express the importance assigned to meetings and individuals (Peters, 1978).

Culture also embodies potential unobtrusive control mechanisms. The interest in the benefits of a Japanese or 'Type Z' culture (Ouchi, 1982) is a case in point. Behaviour is guided by shared norms and values, instead of traditional formalized bureaucratic controls. Jaeger (1983) has found that the use of indirect cultural mechanisms is a viable alternative to bureaucratic structures. An implicit assumption is that culture is a power mechanism that can be manipulated by political actors. Studies have highlighted the role of the entrepreneur in creating a culture (Lane and Roberts, 1976; Beynon, 1973; Martin and Fryer, 1973). Entrepreneurs create cultures to generate order, purpose, and commitment among organizational members, which in turn facilitate the achievement of their goals (Pettigrew, 1977, 1979). And as a result, organizational cultures embody a political element (Salaman 1979).

Structure is another mechanism of unobtrusive control (Perrow, 1970). It is often considered to be determined by environmental constraints (e.g. Burns and Stalker, 1961; Emery and Trist, 1965; Lawrence and Lorsch, 1967) or other imperatives, such as technology (Woodward, 1965), or size (Pugh et al., 1969). Child (1972) has criticized this functional-determinist approach, however, and argued that the nature of structure is to some extent a matter of choice. Dominant organizational members may be in a position to use this degree of freedom to choose a structure that protects and furthers their power positions. Structure is thus a product of both political processes and contextual constraints as 'economic and administrative exigencies are weighted by the actors concerned against the opportunities to create a structure of their own preferences' (Child, 1972: 16). Structures embody certain assumptions, values, and practices which help to ensure that certain behaviours and actions are carried out without question (Ranson et al., 1980). Senior members thus have a vested interest in shaping the mechanisms that provide them with power.

> The organizational structures within which individuals both contribute to organizational performance and pursue sectional interests are in part the outcome of their own initiatives. (Watson, 1980: 213)

Structure and culture can also be used by senior organizational members to acquire legitimacy in the eyes of individuals *outside* the organization (Dowling and Pfeffer, 1975; Pfeffer and Salancik, 1978) by reflecting the myths and demands of the institutional environment rather than norms of efficiency (Meyer and Rowan, 1977–8).

> By designing a formal structure that adheres to the prescription of myths in the institutional environment an organization demonstrates that it is acting on collectively valued purposes in a proper and adequate manner. The incorporation of institutionalized elements provides an account of its activities that protect the organization from having its conduct questioned. (Meyer and Rowan, 1977–8: 349)

Finally, there are other ways in which conflict can be averted. Potential opponents may be coopted (Selznick, 1949), norms may be manipulated and commitment managed (Kanter, 1972). In some cases, the resource interdependence normally associated with first dimension of power may be used. For example, information may be filtered to provide reports favouring the desired outcome, expertise or credibility may be utilized to create legitimacy (French and Raven, 1968) where the right to influence others is automatically accepted by them.

Defeating and Preventing Opposition

The above analysis of the third dimension of power draws attention to an important distinction. In the first two dimensions, a number of declared and identifiable actors or interest groups exist, between whom there is overt or covert conflict regarding their desired outcomes. As a result of this conflict, each actor purposely uses the available power resources to try to ensure that they are successful. The 'winners' will be those who mobilize their power resources most effectively. In the case of the third dimension, no such conflict exists because some actors have taken steps to ensure potential opponents do not challenge them. Power succeeds by preventing conflict. In this situation, although the powerful will have identified their potential opponents, the latter may be unaware of the use of power in producing their quiescence. This section examines the distinction between these two uses of power in more detail.

Instrumental Power

The ability to secure preferred outcomes in the face of competition and conflict among declared opponents can be termed *instrumental* power (see Pfeffer, 1981b). It encompasses the first two dimensions: power may be exercised in the decision-making arena to produce favourable decisions (the pluralist approach) or to keep dangerous issues out of the arena (nondecision-making). The sources of instrumental power are grounded primarily in the differential access to valuable resources (Ranson et al., 1980), which allows political actors to affect behaviour directly. The aim is to enforce the desired outcome in the face of opposition, regardless of how people feel about it.

Symbolic Power

The ability to secure preferred outcomes by preventing conflict from arising represents an unobtrusive use of power. (Other writers have referred to it as deep structure power, e.g. Clegg, 1975). Political actors have defined success, not as winning in the face of confrontation (where there must always be a risk of losing), but in terms of their ability to section off spheres of influence where their domination is perceived as legitimate and thus unchallenged. This dimension of power revolves around attempts to create legitimacy and justification for certain actions and outcomes so that they are never questioned. In this way, power is mobilized to influence behaviour indirectly by giving outcomes and decisions certain meanings; by legitimizing and justifying them.

> Political analysis must then proceed on two levels simultaneously. It must examine how political actions get some groups the tangible things they want from government and at the same time it must explore what these same actions mean to the mass public and how it is placated or aroused by them. In Himmelstrand's terms, political actions are both instrumental and expressive. (Edelman, 1964: 12)

Pfeffer (1981a) has distinguished between substantive (behavioural) and sentiment (attitudinal) outcomes of power. The former depend largely on resource dependency considerations. The latter refer to the way people feel about the outcomes and are mainly influenced by the symbolic aspects of power

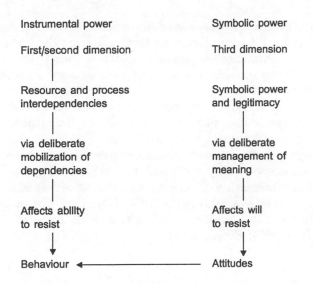

Figure 13.1   *Instrumental and symbolic power*

– the use of political language, symbols and rituals. Pfeffer argues there is only a weak relationship between symbolic power and substantive outcomes: that symbolic power is only used post hoc to legitimize the outcomes already achieved by resource dependencies. If, however, symbolic power is used to legitimize desired outcomes in advance, the use of conventional power sources may not be necessary because the outcome is deemed to be legitimate, and nobody attempts to prevent it. In this way, Pfeffer's model can be expanded to include both uses of power.

Figure 13.1 illustrates these power relationships. Instrumental power is based on the control of resources interdependencies. It encompasses the first two dimensions of power. Through the mobilization of power sources political actors are able to achieve the behavioural or decisional outcomes they desire in spite of opposition and conflict. Symbolic power is derived from sources which are brought into play to legitimize outcomes through the management of meaning. In this way, symbolic power is used to influence attitudes with the use of such mechanisms as symbols, language, rituals and culture. It may be used in conjunction with instrumental power – the one producing the desired substantive outcome, the other producing (post hoc) favourable feelings towards the outcome. But it can also be used *instead* of instrumental power to avoid conflict. In this case, the legitimation and justification of desired outcomes, by producing favourable attitudes, remove the threat of opposition. Steps are taken to 'persuade' other groups to accept certain outcomes although they may be unaware of this.

Other relationships, not highlighted in Figure 13.1, may also exist. There may be a relationship between behavioural outcomes and attitudes – some outcomes may be so unpalatable they automatically produce hostile feelings.

The use of instrumental power itself may influence attitudes if, for example, it is excessively coercive. There will also be feedback from the outcome into the power systems. The existence of certain outcomes and the elevation or diminuation of political consciousness will increase or reduce the power sources of the groups involved.

To sum up, the analysis of power requires an examination of both instrumental and symbolic uses of power. Much of the literature, however, has concentrated solely on the former and, as a result, neglected the use of power to constrain the actions of opponents by influencing their sentiments in such a way that the latter are not fully aware of the political implications of this. Situations of obvious inequality where no conflict would appear to exist are promising venues for study (e.g. Gaventa, 1980; Hardy, 1985b) though, as many writers have pointed out, there are difficulties with empirical verification (Benton, 1981; Lukes, 1974; Clegg, 1989).

The Fourth Dimension: The Power of the System

The three dimensions of power discussed above all involve deliberate, conscious strategies on the part of organizational actors to mobilize power, thereby achieving their objectives either by defeating or circumventing opponents. There is, however, another aspect of power in the way it works to produce certain advantages and disadvantages for organizational members *without* being consciously mobilized. It lies in the power of the system – in the unconscious acceptance of the values, traditions, cultures and structures of a given institution or society. Although these characteristics are often seen as neutral, functional constructs, they also serve to protect the interests of particular groups (Salaman 1979).

> The ideological nature of organizational decisions and events or structure and processes is mystified, disguised and denied by the very structures which advance and perpetuate the oppression of organizational members. For it is often argued that members of organizations are constrained and frustrated not by human agency, or sectional interests, but by neutral technology, inevitable market pressures, unavoidable scientific-technical advances, the need to 'rationalize'. (Salaman, 1979: 181)

So, the very nature of the organization embodies a source of power for some groups, which may not be mobilized by them but which, nevertheless, works to their advantage (Perrow, 1970). While the institutionalization of power within certain structural and cultural arrangements works to the benefit of dominant groups, these groups are not necessarily responsible for establishing the systems from which they benefit (Parry and Morriss, 1975).

This aspect of power represents a fourth dimension in that it acknowledges the fact that some groups are politically disadvantaged as a result of systems which penalize them, without attributing the cause to the conscious use of power by specific groups of individuals. A distinction needs to be drawn between those who mobilize deliberate political strategies to create a system and those who unconsciously and inadvertently derive power from it (Parry and Morriss, 1975), especially since as systems evolve they may become bureaucratic and dysfunctional, serving the interest of no one in particular (Allison, 1971). One writer who has challenged the prevailing conceptualizations of sovereign power is Michel Foucault. His work has recently been applied to studies of organizational power (e.g. Clegg, 1989; Knights and Willmott, 1989; Knights and Morgan, 1991). These writers have drawn attention to a number of contributions from a 'Foucauldian' perspective that have been ignored by more conventional theorists. These points are discussed in more detail below.

Foucault argued that power is a pervasive phenomenon, present in all relations (see Clegg, 1989).

> The modern corporate power is not a monolithic extension of class politics, but more like a web of arbitrary asymmetrical relations with specific means of decision and control. While certain groups benefit from these arrangements, they are in no simple way designed for these gains. The force of these arrangements is primarily in producing order, forgetfulness and dependency. (Deetz, 1992: 35)

The invisible, *disciplinary* form of power is more important than the concepts of sovereign power that dominate the literature. Sovereign power focuses on the control of power by an agent (an individual or interest group) who uses it to produce the desired outcomes. Foucault, in contrast, points out that power has many unintentional effects and is not as predictable or deterministic as others have suggested. Actors may intend to use power in a certain way, but its complexity, invisibility and pervasiveness mean that the actual outcome may be far from the actor's original intentions.

This web of power relations constitutes the identity of individuals which, in turn, confers a positive experience on individuals. Power is not, therefore, as repressive as writers have insisted. This positive experience has a conservative effect in that it leads to the reproduction of the power relations that gave rise to it.

> [S]ubjects come to recognize themselves as discrete and autonomous individuals whose sense of a clear identity is sustained through participation in social practices which are a condition and consequence of the exercise of power. (Knights and Willmott, 1989: 538)

For example, Burawoy (1979) studied how the relaxation of management control and the use of bonus pay schemes were used to increase productivity. They led to a game of 'making out' where workers attempted to maximize bonus pay. Burawoy demonstrated how these games deflected traditional hierarchical and class divisions. Knights and Willmott argue that the games also instilled workers with prestige, a sense of accomplishment, and feelings of pride. In this way, worker identity was constituted by the power relations on the shop floor and, as a result, helped to reproduce them.

These authors also argue that management is subject to similar processes. For example, the concept of corporate strategy which pervades contemporary management, empowers those managers with strategic responsibilities and skills or who form successful strategies by facilitating and legitimating their exercise of power; by providing a rationalization of their successes and failures; and conferring on them a corporate identity and role (Knights and Morgan, 1991). Some groups are disabled by the prevailing set of power relations: managers in personnel management and accounting have not benefited from the focus on strategy. This has led, according to Knights and Morgan (1991), to the transmutation of personnel into human resources management and a stress on the link between strategy and human resources. Similarly, some accounting journals have started to emphasize the role the function can play in strategy making. In other words, groups trying to resist the prevailing set of power relations, or discourse, embodied in strategy may inadvertently reaffirm it.

> [I]ndividuals and groups exercise power to elaborate some and resist other elements of the discourse. They may indeed seek to resist the strategy altogether, but in order to do so, they have to invariably engage with, and be at least partially constituted by, its content . . . both those who embrace and those who resist strategy find themselves caught up in its reproduction. (Knights and Morgan, 1991: 269)

So, although negative effects of power relations provide motivation for resistance, resistance tends to confirm those power relations rather than substitute new ones. This is because the web of power relations is so pervasive, all actors are captured by it. It is not:

> simply a 'way of seeing'; it is always embedded in social practices which reproduce that way of seeing as the 'truth' . . . .. It is for this reason that Foucault emphasizes the inseparability of power and knowledge. (Knights and Morgan, 1991: 262).

The question becomes how can people subjected to the ubiquitous effects of disciplinary power be expected to fight them? Since 'resistance merely serves to demonstrate the necessity of that discipline which provokes it' (Clegg, 1989: 153).

The inclusion of a fourth dimension of power signifies that groups can be subject to power even though it is not actively used against them, in contrast to the other three dimensions where power is consciously mobilized by actors in the form of political strategies designed to achieve certain ends.

> [Disciplinary power is] a way of thinking, acting and instituting. The disciplined member of the organization wants on his or her own what the corporation wants. The most powerful and powerless in traditional terms are equally subjected, though there is no doubt who is advantaged. (Deetz, 1992: 40)

This dimension also reminds us of the limits to power. At some fundamental level, we are all prisoners in its web.

Conclusions

This chapter has tried to clarify the nature of power and politics and the different ways in which they can be used by managers. It has traced the

Table 13.1   *The development of the concept of power (Adapted and extended from Clegg (1989: 182))*

	1st dimension	2nd dimension	3rd dimension	4th dimension
chief advocate	Dahl	Bachrach & Baratz	Lukes	Foucault
challenge to:	elitism: views of power as concentrated in the hands of the few	pluralism: assumption of equal access to decision arenas & agendas	behaviourism: assumption that power is used only in response to conflict	sovereign power: view that power is in the control of actors
focus on:	key decisions	nondecisions	hegemony	disciplinary power
concept of power:	intended deliberate causal visible	intended deliberate causal less visible	intended deliberate causal often invisible	not intended not deliberate arbitrary invisible & pervasive
contribution:	multiple groups in decision-making	use of non-decisions to suppress opposition	use of third dimension to prevent opposition	inability to control power; power embedded in system; problem of resistance

development of the concept as writers have sought to tackle the shortcomings of earlier work (Table 13.1). It has been deliberately integrative in its attempt to reveal the multi-dimensionality of the phenomenon and to show the different ways in which power is used by both dominant and subordinate groups.

As Table 13.2 shows, the study of power is usually focused on its use by dominant groups ('A') to protect or advance their position. Thus, power is embodied in A's control of resources, processes and meaning. Power is not restricted to conscious deployment since it is also entrenched in the prevailing system, where it pervades relationships between the various actors. In this situation, power may advantage certain groups but they neither possess it nor deliberately exercise it over others and, in many respects, are also trapped by it. Disadvantaged groups ('B') do have recourse to some forms of power that can be used to resist dominant groups also through the deployment of resources, processes and meanings. In the case of the first dimension, B is able to get the issue to the decision-making arena. If B loses in this situation, it is due either to the lack of access to resources compared to A, or an inability to mobilize them effectively. Empowerment for B, in this situation, means accumulating more resources and/or learning to use them more expertly. In the case of the second dimension, B loses through being unable to secure access to

Table 13.2 *The dimensions of power*

	1st dimension	2nd dimension	3rd dimension	4th dimension
	decision-making	nondecision-making	unobtrusive	system power
interaction between A & B:	overt conflict	overt or covert conflict	apparent cooperation	submission of B
power of A over B:	resource inter-dependencies	control of processes	control of legitimacy	unconscious beneficiary
action of A:	management of dependencies	management of of process	management of meaning	none
political dynamics:	B is aware of of issue and able to get it to decision arena	B is aware of issue but unable to get it to decision arena	B is unaware of issue and does not resist	B may be aware or unaware but unable to resist
if B loses it is because:	inadequate power, inability to mobilize it	inability to get issues to decision arena	no will to resist	no attempt to resist or resistance reaffirms status quo
empowerment of B requires:	acquisition, use of power in decision arena	ability to gain access to decision process	consciousness raising and de-legitimation strategies	acquisition of power (but prospects limited)

the decision-making arena or being unable to mobilize the power embedded in those processes. For B to prevail against the second dimension, access to and knowledge of decision-making processes must be secured. Fighting against the third dimension means exposing power used unobtrusively through consciousness raising and de-legitimation strategies that unmask the political strategies of A and create a political will to fight. While these actions may bring about some changes, the extent of resistance appears to be limited by the prevailing system – or fourth dimension – which traps advantaged and disadvantaged alike and reduces the chances of radical or revolutionary change. We can see, then, that as we move through the four dimensions, power use becomes less visible and those on its receiving end become more powerless.

It is the contention here that an understanding of these different ways in which power and politics work is important for managers and employees alike. The aim is not to show the former how to exploit the latter, nor to advise the latter on ways of holding the former hostage. Instead, the objective is that by peeling back the layers of power, we are all in a better position to ensure it is used responsibly.

References

Allison, G.T. (1971) *Essence of Decision*. Boston: Little, Brown.
Allison, L. (1974) 'On the nature of the concept of power', *European Journal of Political Science*, 2: 131–41.
Astley, W.G. and Sachdeva, P.S. (1984) 'Structural sources of intraorganizational power', *Academy of Management Review*, 9(1): 104–13.
Bachrach, P. and Baratz, M.S. (1962) 'The two faces of power', *American Political Science Review*, 56: 947–52.
Bachrach, P. and Baratz, M.S. (1963) 'Decisions and nondecisions: An analytical framework', *American Political Science Review*, 57: 641–51.
Bachrach, P. and Baratz, M.S. (1970) *Power and Poverty*. London: Oxford University Press.
Bachrach, S. and Lawler, E. (1980) *Power and Politics in Organizations*. London: Jossey Bass.
Benfari, Robert C., Wilkinson, Harry E. and Orth, Charles D. (1986) 'The effective use of power', *Business Horizons*, 29(3): 12–16.
Benton, T. (1981) '"Objective" interests and the sociology of power', *Sociology*, 15(2): 161–84.
Beynon, H. (1973) *Working for Ford*. London: Allen Lane.
Blau, P. (1964) *Exchange and Power in Social Life*. New York: Wiley.
Burawoy, M. (1979) *Manufacturing Consent*. Chicago: Chicago University Press.
Burns, T. and Stalker G.M. (1961) *The Management of Innovation*. London: Pergamon.
Child, J. (1972) 'Organizational structure, environment and performance: The role of strategic choice', *Sociology* 6: 1–22.
Clegg, S. (1975) *Power, Rules and Domination*. London: Routledge & Kegan Paul.
Clegg, S. (1989) *Framework of Power*. London: Sage.
Cohen, Abner (1975) *Two Dimensional Man*. London: Routledge & Kegan Paul.
Cohen, Anthony (1975) *The Management of Myths*. Manchester: Manchester University Press.
Crozier, M. (1964) *The Bureaucratic Phenomenon*. Chicago: University of Chicago Press.
Dahl, R. (1957) 'The concept of power', *Behavioural Science*, 20: 201–15.
Dahl, R. (1961) *Who Governs*? New Haven: Yale University Press.
Deetz, S. (1992) 'Disciplinary power in the modern corporation', in M. Alvesson and H. Willmott (eds), *Critical Management Studies*. London: Sage.
Dowling, J. and Pfeffer J. (1975) 'Organizational legitimacy', *Pacific Sociological Review*, 18: 122–36.
Edelman, M. (1964) *The Symbolic Uses of Politics*. Champaign, IL: University of Illinois Press.
Edelman, M. (1971) *Politics as Symbolic Action*. Chicago: Markham.
Edelman, M. (1977) *Political Language*. London: Academic Press.
Emerson, R.M. (1962) 'Power-dependence relations', *American Sociological Review*, 27: 31–41.
Emery, F.E. and Trist, E.L. (1965) 'The causal texture of organizational environments', *Human Relations*, 18: 21–32.
Fox, A. (1973) 'Industrial relations: A social critique of pluralist ideology', in J. Child (ed.), *Man and Organization*. London: Allen and Unwin.
French, J.R.P. and Raven, B. (1968) 'The bases of social power', in D. Cartwright and A Zander (eds), *Group Dynamics*. New York: Harper & Row.
Gaventa, J. (1980) *Power and Powerlessness*. London: Oxford University Press.
Giddens, A. (1968) '"Power" in the recent writings of Talcott Parsons', *Sociology*, 2: 257–72.
Giddens, A. (1979) *Central Problems in Social Theory*. London: Macmillan.
Hardy, C. (1985a) *Managing Organization Closure*. Aldershot: Gower Press.
Hardy, C. (1985b) 'The nature of unobtrusive power', *Journal of Management Studies*, 22: 4.
Hickson, David J., Butler, Richard J., Cray, David, Mallory, Geoffrey R. and Wilson, David C. (1986) *Top Decisions: Strategic Decision-Making in Organizations*. San Francisco: Jossey-Bass.
Hickson, D.J., Hinings, C.R., Lee, C.A., Schneck, R.E. and Pennings, J.M. (1971) 'A strategic contingencies theory of intraorganizational power', *Administrative Science Quarterly*, 16: 216–29.
Hyman, R., and Brough, I. (1975) *Social Values and Industrial Relations*. Oxford: Basil Blackwell.

Hyman, R. and Fryer, R.H. (1975) 'Trade unions – sociological and political economy', in J.B. McKinlay (ed.), *Processing People*. London: Holt, Rinehart and Winston.

Jaeger, A. (1983) 'The transfer of organized culture overseas: An approach to control in the multinational corporation', *Journal of International Business Studies*, 14(2): 91–114.

Kanter, R.M. (1972) *Commitment and Community*. Cambridge, Mass.: Harvard University Press.

Knights, D. and Morgan, G. (1990) 'The concept of strategy in sociology', *Sociology* 24(3): 475–83.

Knights, D. and Morgan, G. (1991) 'Strategic discourse and subjectivity: Towards a critical analysis of corporate strategy in organisations', *Organization Studies*, 12: 3.

Knights, D. and Willmott, H. (1989) 'From degradation to subjugation in social relations: An analysis of power and subjectivity at work', *Sociology*, 23(4): 535–58.

Lane, T. and Roberts, K. (1976) *Strike at Pilkingtons*. London: Fontana.

Lawrence, P. and Lorsch, J. (1967) *Organization and Environment*. Cambridge, Mass.: Harvard University Press.

Lipset, S.M. (1959) 'Some social requisites of democracy: Economic development and political legitimacy', *American Political Science Review*, 53: 69–105.

Lukes, S. (1974) *Power: A Radical View*. London: Macmillan.

MacMillan, I.C. (1978) *Strategy Formulation: Political Concepts*. St. Paul, Minn.: West.

Martin, R. (1977) *The Sociology of Power*. London: Routledge & Kegan Paul.

Martin, R. and Fryer, R.H. (1973) *Redundancy and Paternalist Capitalism*. London: Allen and Unwin.

Mechanic, D. (1962) 'Sources of power of lower participants in complex organizations', *Administrative Science Quarterly*, 7(3): 349–64.

Meyer, John W. and Rowan, Brian (1977–8) 'Institutionalized organizations: Formal structures as a myth', *American Journal of Sociology*, 83(2): 340–63.

Mueller, C. (1973) *The Politics of Communication*. London: Oxford University Press.

Ouchi, W.G. (1982) *Theory Z*. New York: Avon Books.

Parry, G. and Morriss, P. (1975) 'When is a decision not a decision?', in I. Crewe (ed.), *British Political Sociology Yearbook*, Vol. 1. London: Croom Helm.

Perrow, C. (1970) *Organizational Analysis*. London: Tavistock.

Peters, T.J. (1978) 'Symbols, patterns and settings', *Organisational Dynamics*, Autumn, 2–23.

Pettigrew, A.M. (1973) *The Politics of Organizational Decision Making*. London: Tavistock.

Pettigrew, A.M. (1977) 'Strategy formulation as a political process', *International Studies of Management and Organizations*, 7(2): 78–87.

Pettigrew, A.M. (1979) 'On studying organizational cultures', *Administrative Science Quarterly*, 24: 570–81.

Pettigrew, A.M. (1985) 'Contextualist research and the study of organizational change processes', in E. Mumford et al. (eds), *Research Methods in Information Systems*. Holland: Elsevier, pp. 53–77.

Pfeffer, J. (1981a) *Power in Organizations*. Marshfield, Mass.: Pitman.

Pfeffer, J. (1981b) 'Management as symbolic action', in L.L. Cummings and B.M. Staw (eds), *Research in Organizational Behavior*, 3: Greenwich, CT: JAI Press, pp. 1–52.

Pfeffer, J. and Salancik, G. (1974) 'Organizational decision making as a political process', *Administrative Science Quarterly*, 19: 135–51.

Pfeffer, J. and Salancik, G.R. (1978) *The External Control of Organizations*. New York: Harper & Row.

Polsby, N.W. (1963) *Community Power and Political Theory*. New Haven: Yale University Press.

Pugh, D., Hickson, D.J. Hinings, C.R. and Turner, C. (1969) 'The context of organizational structures', *Administrative Science Quarterly*, 14: 91–114.

Ranson, S., Hining, R. and Greenwood, R. (1980) 'The structuring of organizational structure', *Administrative Science Quarterly*, 25(1): 1–14.

Roelofs, H.M. (1976) *Ideology and Myth in American Politics*. Boston: Little, Brown.

Rothschild, J. (1979) 'Political legitimacy in contemporary Europe', in B. Denitch (ed.), *Legitimation of Regimes*. Beverley Hills, Calif.: Sage.

Salaman, G. (1979) *Work Organizations: Resistance and Control*. London: Longman.

Salancik, G. and Pfeffer, J. (1974) 'The bases and use of power in organizational decision making', *Administrative Science Quarterly*, 19: 453–73.

Saunders, P. (1980) *Urban Politics*. London: Penguin.

Schaar, J.H. (1969) 'Legitimacy in the modern state', in P. Green and S. Levinson (eds), *Power and Community*. New York: Pantheon.

Schattschneider, E.F. (1960) *The Semi-Sovereign People*. New York: Holt, Rinehart and Winston.

Selznick, P. (1949) *TVA and the Grass Roots*. Berkeley, Calif.: University of California Press.

Watson, T.J. (1980) *Sociology, Work and Industry*. London: Routledge & Kegan Paul.

Wolfinger, R.E. (1971) 'Nondecisions and the study of local politics', *American Political Science Review*, 65: 1063–80.

Woodward, J. (1965) *Industrial Organizations*. Oxford: Oxford University Press.

14 Power and the Organizational Life Cycle

Barbara Gray and Sonny S. Ariss

The case for viewing organizations as political entities has been advanced recently by several organization theorists (Allen and Porter, 1983; Bacharach and Lawler, 1981; Farrell and Petersen, 1982; Mintzberg, 1983; Pfeffer, 1981; Tushman, 1977a). In addition, there has been a growing interest in politics in the business policy literature (MacMillan, 1978; Murray, 1978; Narayanan and Fahey, 1982; Pettigrew, 1977; Quinn, 1980).

The present study links these two streams of research by exploring how politics vary with the strategic changes through which organizations progress during their life cycles. The major thesis is that politics accompanies strategic changes but is manifested differently at each stage of the life cycle of an organization. Generally, the argument for a political theory of strategic change is advanced.

Politics and Strategic Change

[. . .]

Many models of how strategic change occurs portray it as a formal, rational, neatly controlled process. They focus on environmental assessment, opportunity analysis, and logical, orderly planning cycles (Lorange & Vancil, 1977). This rational perspective has been aptly described by Allison (1971). However, Allison also argued that a political perspective was essential in order to gain adequate insight into strategic change. Mintzberg, Rasinghani, and Theoret (1976) and Guth (1976) also showed that politics and coalition dynamics were an essential component of strategy formulation. Indeed, more recent theories on organizational politics can be traced to seminal works on the subject by Weber (1947), Barnard (1968), Cyert and March (1963) and Crozier (1964). The theory that organizations are coalitional in nature (Cyert and March, 1963; March & Simon 1958) was advanced to counter more rational models depicting organizations as profit maximizing entities operating under conditions of perfect knowledge. Instead, organizations are construed as coalitions of

From 'Politics and strategic change across organizational life cycles', *Academy of Management Review*, 10(4): 707–23, 1985.

participants, with differing motivations, who choose organizational goals through a process of continual bargaining.

Four arguments have highlighted the inherent limitations of the rational models and support a political view of strategic change: (1) decision making under uncertain conditions, (2) the role of values and ideology in strategic choice, (3) decision makers' commitments to past strategies, and (4) the multiple goal theories of organizations.

Arguments Favoring a Political Model of Strategic Change

Cognitive Limits to Rationality

Strategic decision making requires the application of judgments to a stream of information. Strategists, however, can pay only selective attention to the barrage of information confronting them (Thompson, 1967; Weick, 1979). Research on perception suggests that people pay attention to what they want to see and hear, that is, to information that is consistent with their own position (Zaskind and Costello, 1962). Moreover, this differential attention to information contributes to political dynamics in organizations. For example, powerful actors in an organization can influence the attention processes of other members (Ranson et al., 1980; Smircich and Morgan, 1982) and advance their own self-interests by getting their point of view accepted (Pfeffer, 1981). Hence, their solution to a problem is most likely to prevail. The biases of top management also may shape the search for information by others in the firm. Because of their own cognitive limits, strategists must rely on staff specialists and line managers to provide additional information. Yet, these individuals need to present information that is both wanted and understood by the top. That is, they need to establish political congruence between the information they gather and the interests of the decision makers to avoid the waste of getting useful information that might be rejected or ignored (Aguilar, 1967). Thus, through establishing political networks, strategists try to make up for their own and organizational limits to rationality and in so doing advance their own views of reality.

Values and Ideology

A second argument supporting a political model of strategic choice is that strategic choice in organizations is inextricably bound up with ideology. Child defined strategic choice as 'a political process in which constraints and opportunities are functions of power exercised by decision makers in light of ideological values' (1972: 11). Beyer (1981) provides a comprehensive argument linking ideology and strategic decision making. Others (Downey and Greer, 1982; England, 1982; Gricar, 1983; Hage and Dewar, 1973) provide empirical evidence that top management ideology shapes strategic decisions and actions.

Ideologies also form the basis for organizational consensus or dissensus. To the extent that an ideology is widely shared, agreement about organizational mission, strategy, and tactics is relatively easy, goals appear singular, and therefore decision making appears rational. However, when ideologies are not widely shared and the dominant coalition cannot sustain enough power to rationalize its ideology, conflicts erupt between coalitions dedicated to differing values (Cyert and March, 1963). What had been brewing as a covert clash of ideologies becomes overt and is labelled politics. This pervasive presence of ideologies, then, suggests that politics, and not rational analysis, undergirds strategic decision making.

Commitment to Past Strategy

An extension of the argument based on the ideology can be found in research on how commitment to past strategy influences strategic decisions. Once committed to a strategy, top managers often find it difficult to recognize its limitations when the environmental context changes. Over time, organizational actions become synonymous with the self-interests of those in power (Culbert and McDonough, 1980). Hence, top managers develop vested interests (psychological and frequently financial) that preserve the status quo (Gardner, 1964; Miller & Friesen, 1980a). Strategists often become bound to past decisions regardless of their effectiveness even when evidence suggests that a decision should be changed (Pfeffer, 1981). Even when a strategy fails to produce the objectives sought, decision makers often increase their commitment to it, persisting because of a general social belief that effective leaders behave in a consistent manner (Staw, 1976; Staw and Ross, 1980). Moreover, they strive to save face and to preserve the image that they are effective leaders. Commitment to past strategies, therefore, only bolsters the power of the dominant coalition (Pfeffer, 1981) by throwing more resources into failing strategies. Wrenching control from such entrenched interests requires a major political revolution (Miller and Friesen, 1980a).

Multiple Goals and Whose Interests are Served

A final argument for a political perspective on strategic changes stems from the theory that organizations have multiple goals. Rational models assume that, given adequate search, managers can have perfect knowledge of alternatives, but they identify a single overriding goal and maximize outcomes with respect to that goal. However, they fail to indicate for whom outcomes are maximized. That is, they do not account for multiple or competing objectives of different organizational members or external stakeholders and how these are reconciled. In sum, the strategic changes result from bargaining among decision makers with differing interests and values and unequal power (Bacharach and Lawler, 1981; Cyert and March, 1963; MacMillan, 1978).

Organizational Life Cycles

Organizational life cycle models claim that all firms pass through predictable stages of growth and that their strategies, structures, and activities correspond to their stage of development. [. . .]
   [. . .]
   The values of life cycle models lie in their acknowledgement of the dynamic, changing nature of organizations as they develop. However, few theories consider how politics change with each stage, and none presents a political model of strategic change over time [. . .].
   [. . .]
   [. . .] The present authors believe that power is wielded differently at each stage of the life cycle. How power is exercised by the dominant coalition varies according to the strategic orientation that dominates each stage.

A Political Life Cycle Model

[. . .] The model suggested here represents a simple integration of other life cycle models (see [Figure 14.1]). It has three general stages of development: (1) birth and early growth, during which the primary political activity, symbolic management, is undertaken by the entrepreneur/founder who serves as chief strategist; (2) maturity, characterized by internal and external scuffles to create programs and standard operating procedures that institutionalize the power of the dominant coalition; (3) a decline or redevelopment stage in which overt politics become rampant as competing interests fight to maintain or reshape the strategic direction of the firm.

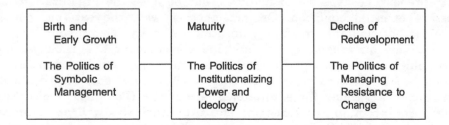

[Figure 14.1]   *A political life cycle model*

Stage 1: Birth and Early Growth

In Stage 1 the firm is typically a single product company with little or no formal structure. Its day-to-day activities and strategic direction are guided by the vision of the entrepreneur who founded the firm (Drucker, 1970). Decisions in this entrepreneurial stage emanate from the entrepreneur's strong sense of purpose (Murray, 1984), his/her high personal need to achieve (Mintzberg, 1973), and fanatical commitment to the idea behind the product (Quinn, 1979). Centralization of power in the entrepreneur is characteristic of this stage. Several researchers have pointed out that innovators or prime movers have power and control during this entrepreneurial stage (Downs, 1967; Kimberly, 1979; Mintzberg, 1973; Quinn and Cameron, 1983). Moreover, this distribution of power is consistent with the typical entrepreneurial personality described by Collins and Moore (1970) as autonomous and unwilling to submit to authority. As a result, the firm's strategy at this early stage usually is whatever the entrepreneur wants it to be. His/her ideology provides the rationale by which certain courses of action, and not others, are pursued.

Context and Strategy   The influence of organizational context during the entrepreneurial stage should not be overlooked. Recent studies of entrepreneurial activity suggest that fortuitous configurations of contextual factors enhance the entrepreneur's consolidation of power. For example, Peterson (1980), citing Katz's (1973) study of the diffusion of innovation, indicated that the primary limits to successful entrepreneurship are contextual rather than characterological in nature. Similarly, Roberts (1984) identified a set of structural conditions that support the emergence of charismatic leadership. Peterson (1980) explains Jimmy Hoffa's elevation to power among the Teamsters by virtue of his ability to capitalize on the structural interdependencies within the trucking industry. And Kimberly (1979) attributes the success of a new medical school to its entrepreneurial dean and to the receptive environment at the time of its birth. In light of this evidence, it seems important to acknowledge the context within which an entrepreneurial strategy and its concomitant political dynamics can emerge.

Mintzberg (1984) refers to this phase as the autocracy, not because the entrepreneur behaves as an autocrat, but because the organization faces a passive external coalition. Or, put another way, the external context is potentially favourable to the organization's activity. This favourable context can include an expanding and underdeveloped market, a rapidly changing technology, or the emergence of a market niche ignored by competitors. For example, stultification of research by firms in a mature or stagnant industry can create a vacuum for entrepreneurial activity (Pennings, 1980a; Scherer, 1967). And according to Peterson, 'entire industries as well as organizations operate to periodically generate the demand and opportunity for entrepreneurship' (1980: 73). An excellent case in point is Celestial Seasonings, which captured an undeveloped market niche for herbal teas and quickly became a million dollar business.

Market conditions during the entrepreneurial stage typically are characterized by high levels of uncertainty (Kimberly, 1979; Miller and Friesen, 1980b). For this reason, market forecasts are of limited use (Quinn, 1979), and very little long range planning is undertaken (Deeks, 1976). Mintzberg (1973) describes firms as making 'bold leaps in the face of uncertainty' in order to pursue new opportunities for growth during this stage. Still, according to Deeks (1976), the dominant tendency in a small firm is to modify its internal structures in accordance with external changes rather than to seek control over its environment (as in managing the external environment, Pfeffer & Salancik, 1978). This is consistent with Mintzberg's (1984) observation that in the early stage firms have few connections to external agents and, hence, are not in a position to exert control over them. It is concluded, then, that during the entrepreneurial stage a firm may be strategically proactive in carving out a market niche for itself, but it is basically reactive in its response to other environmental pressures.

The strategic postures recommended for success during the entrepreneurial stage include clearly defining the scope of the business, distinguishing one's product from competitors, and learning the nature of the business (McNichols, 1983). It is precisely in the creation and maintenance of these 'distinctive' characteristics for the firm that the entrepreneur has a critical political role to play.

Politics Politics in this stage consists of the entrepreneur's effort to shape the organization in his/her own image. He/she exercises power primarily through two political maneuvers: (a) control of the decision premises and (b) symbolic management (Pfeffer, 1981). By being involved in virtually all aspects of the business during its early development, the entrepreneur maintains a pulse on incoming information and retains close control over resource allocations. In this way he/she controls the premises within which decisions must be made.

> Choices can be affected if the social actor can affect the decision premises or the basic values and objectives used in making the decisions. Choices can also be affected if the actor can control the alternatives considered in the choice process, or can impact the information about each of the alternatives that is used in making the decision. (Pfeffer, 1981: 115)

Hence, by retaining control of the choice of strategic alternatives and by interpreting information in light of his/her own personal values, the entrepreneur aligns the firm's goals with his or her self-interest (Culbert and McDonough, 1980). The political trappings of such behaviour, however, are subtle. The entrepreneur's motives likely will be submerged within an overt appearance of organizational rationality. Pfeffer (1981) refers to this legitimation of action as symbolic management. According to Pfeffer, decisions rooted in a given ideology have the semblance of rationality when they follow conventional, traditional, and institutionalized processes of decision making. The entrepreneur's presence in operating decisions effectively renders those decisions functional and political simultaneously. Moreover, subordinates who may have different ideologies or alternative interpretations (e.g., about market opportunities) are unlikely to raise them in opposition during this stage because they lack control of the resources necessary for upward influence (Porter et al., 1983). Hence, in the early stage, it is the entrepreneur's values that are maximized under the guise of organizational rationality.

Furthermore, as a symbolic manager, the entrepreneur must create an image of rationality to which others can subscribe. A successful strategist will create meaning for others in the organization through the use of language, symbols, and rituals (Eoyang, 1983; Huff, 1983; Pondy, 1983; Smircich and Morgan, 1982; Wilkins, 1983). Thus the entrepreneur develops and uses political language to justify and legitimate his/her value positions.

> Creation of the impression that behavior is legitimate (or nonexistent) may be accomplished by acting in ways that make reliable attributions difficult. Some of the 'smokescreen' tactics aimed at manipulating observers' attribution might include making certain that there is a reasonably credible organizational rationale for one's actions, by acting so enigmatically that observers lose confidence in their attributions, or by publicly advocating a 'version' or interpretation of organizational goals that actually serves personal objectives. (Porter et al., 1983: 412).

In order to legitimize the new gestalt (Miller and Friesen, 1980a) proposed for the organization, the entrepreneur must create the impression that everyone's goals are being served by the new strategy.

In summary, at this early stage there is likely to be significant trust and respect for the entrepreneur's overall goal of profit maximization (Pfeffer, 1981). Because the entrepreneur controls the decision premises and the creation of meaning within the firm, entrepreneurial decisions are seldom challenged. Therefore, conflict and political bargaining are likely to be sub-merged or non-existent during Stage 1. Through subtle information control, the entrepreneur's use of power remains unobtrusive, and the politics which establish a strategic direction for the firm are less salient (Pfeffer, 1981), albeit nonetheless real. The present authors' observations about the political tactics used during the birth and early growth stage are summarized in several descriptive propositions (Propositions 1 through 5 in [Table 14.1].

Stage 2: Maturity

The transition to Stage 2 can be difficult to pinpoint if it is the result of gradual sustained growth through new product development or acquisition of other firms. However, if such a transition occurs through merger or acquisition by another firm, the transition may be extremely abrupt and disruptive. Mintzberg (1984) refers to such transitions as periods of confrontation or shaky alliance. He notes three possible changes that firms in the autocracy stage may undergo, depending on the duration of the entrepreneur's term of office and the

[Table 14.1] *Propositions summarizing political tactics at each life cycle stage*

Birth and early growth stage

Proposition 1:	The entrepreneur builds a symbolic reality for others that subtly advances his or her self-interests.
Proposition 2:	The entrepreneur constructs a rational view of organizations by controlling the premises of decisions and managing the flow of information.
Proposition 3:	Resource allocation decisions are guided by the entrepreneur's ideological views.
Proposition 4:	Subordinates strive to maintain a favourable image in the entrepreneur's eyes; opinions contrary to the entrepreneur's ideological views tend to be supressed.
Proposition 5:	A low level of bargaining occurs among subunits.

Maturity stage

Proposition 6:	Powerful individuals institutionalize their ideology by establishing formal policies and procedures that support their self-interests.
Proposition 7:	Subunits try to influence strategic decisions and advance their own goals through the budget allocation process.
Proposition 8:	Subunits try to control critical environmental contingencies by managing uncertainties and by making their activities central and nonsubstitutable.
Proposition 9:	Powerful subunits structure information systems to restrict organizational attention to information that they feel is important.
Proposition 10:	Individual managers or subunits select objective criteria favorable to their own interests to evaluate performance and alternative strategies.
Proposition 11:	Subunits mobilize coalitions to advance their unit goals along with those of other units when they don't have sufficient power to do so on their own.
Proposition 12:	Powerful subunits distribute small rewards and favors to co-opt competing interests.
Proposition 13:	A moderate level of bargaining occurs among subunits.

Decline or redevelopment stage

Proposition 14:	Proponents of the status quo preserve their self-interest by indifference to environmental changes.
Proposition 15:	Proponents of a new strategy try to get key people behind their new concepts of strategy by using co-optation to neutralize serious opposition.
Proposition 16:	Proponents of a new strategy search for 'zones of indifference' in which the new strategy will not be seriously opposed.
Proposition 17:	Change will be resisted by subunits or individual managers who see their interests or power bases threatened by the change.
Proposition 18:	In order to minimize opposition to a new strategy, proponents may (a) try to introduce it incrementally, (b) take advantage of a crisis to introduce the changes, or (c) create the perception that a crisis exists.
Proposition 19:	A high level of bargaining occurs among subunits.

accompanying development of administrative structure. (For details about the contextual factors leading to each transition, see Mintzberg, 1984.) For purposes here, it is sufficient to recognize that the replacement of the entrepreneur with a second generation of leadership appears to be both a necessary and problematic transition prompted by various factors including: acquisition or merger; the reduction of uncertainty (Kimberly, 1979); the delegation of responsibility (Greiner, 1972); and increased boundary spanning activity required to respond to an increasing number of publics associated with product diversity (Miles and Randolph, 1980; Mintzberg, 1984; Tushman, 1977b). Replacement of the entrepreneur with a leader skilled at administration typically accompanies the transition from Stage 1 to Stage 2.

[. . .]

Context and Strategy   By Stage 2 the company has become larger and is managed bureaucratically. The organization depends on hierarchy and specialization in order to achieve efficiency in accomplishing its goals. In Stage 2, technologies found to be effective during Stage 1 become routinized as standard operating procedures. The primary organizational task is organization-building in service of the strategy.

The primary strategic objective of business units during maturation is maintenance and strengthening of market share (Hofer, 1975; McNichols, 1983; Porter, 1980), accomplished through product improvements, pricing and promotional tactics. By this stage the firm has likely diversified into several product divisions, each with its own strategic objectives that must be reconciled at the corporate level in order to allocate corporate resources.

The external environment characterizing the maturity stage is relatively benign. In their study of archetypical transitions, Miller and Friesen (1980b) note that environmental turbulence is lowest during three archetypes (formalization and stability, maturation, and consolidation), all of which are encompassed within this definition of the maturity stage. This is consistent with Mintzberg's claim that at this stage the organization 'faces no focused power in its environment; its external influencers tend to be dispersed and unorganized' (1984: 210). This may be because effective firms have learned to manage environmental uncertainties (Salancik and Pfeffer, 1977). For example, successful market leaders tend to form oligopolies that effectively dictate market conditions for suppliers, competitors, and customers (Pennings, 1980b). To the extent that uncertainty does exist for mature firms, it becomes a catalyst for internal political bargaining and the redistribution of power within the firm (as well as among firms in the industry).

Politics   There is widespread agreement among life cycle models about the increasing institutionalization present at this stage, but the role politics plays in this process has been overlooked. Yet politics at this stage is precisely the ability of those in power (often a successor to the entrepreneur or a dominant coalition) to recast the symbolic rationalizations made during Stage 1 into concrete policies and standardized procedures that reflect and support their own self-interests. Indeed, power is most effective when power-holders have constituted and institutionalized their provinces of meaning in the very structuring of organizational interactions (Ranson et al., 1980). The primary political activity, then, becomes formalizing rules and standard operating procedures that guarantee that power remains in the hands of the dominant coalition. One critical vehicle for exercising and maintaining power is the budget. Through the budgetary process resource allocations are controlled so that some units become dependent on others. When resources are allocated to a subunit, its decision maker will obtain political power from that transaction and subsequently will be in a better position to bargain for additional resources and to influence future strategic choices.

Dependence of certain subunits on others also is created by the design of the flow of work and by management of uncertainty. Power accrues to those subunits that can cope with critical uncertainties plaguing the organization, and, in particular, to those subunits whose expertise is critical and for which substitute sources do not exist (Hickson et al., 1971; Landsberger, 1961). Hence, subunits try to gain control over resources needed by other units and try to develop and maintain a critical expertise that renders them unique.

Powerful subunits also manage information to preserve their power. Because organizational members can pay only selective attention to the plethora of information that bombards them, by structuring the flow of information within the organization, powerful members can restrict others' attention to activities they deem important and keep them dependent on the powerful for critical information. For example, boundary spanning units frequently are powerful because they have access to novel information that is inaccessible to other units (Tushman, 1977b).

Control of performance criteria is another means of politically managing information. Powerful subunits are in a position to propose criteria for evaluating progress toward strategic objectives. By advancing 'objective' criteria for evaluation and then selectively using those that are consistent with their strengths and self-interests, these subunits ensure themselves the rewards that accrue for successful performance (Pfeffer and Salancik, 1978).

Although the formalization and specialization of the bureaucratic stage lead to increased productivity and efficiency, they also create conflict among specialized units, which works to the detriment of the overall profit maximizing goal of the organization (Lawrence and Lorsch, 1967). Interdependence among subunits results in conflict because subunit goals and values may not be consonant (Pfeffer, 1981). Subunit leaders will exercise whatever power they can garner to superimpose the specialized goals of their subunit on overall organizational goals; in addition, they will represent the subunit's goals as in the best interest of the organization as a whole and attempt to minimize their parochial interests. To the extent necessary, subunits mobilize coalitions to advance their unit goals in conjunction with those of other units (Bacharach and Lawler, 1981; Cyert and March, 1963; Narayanan and Fahey, 1982). More powerful subunits are able to build support for their proposals by meting out small rewards and favors to co-opt competing interests.

Strategic change, then, during Stage 2 depends on the success of various coalitions to influence the allocation of critical organizational resources. Narayanan and Fahey (1982) argue that coalitions and strategy formulation are interactive, and the residue left by redistribution of resources and quasi-resolution of conflict may precipitate further coalition formation in the future. Additionally, they note that strategic failures during this stage of an organization's life are directly related to the inability of certain coalitions to garner sufficient power to influence strategic decisions. This was precisely the problem at Ford Motor Company when Lee Iacocca was unsuccessful in convincing Henry Ford to begin production of a small, fuel efficient car in 1975, a year ahead of Chrysler and General Motors (Meadows, 1980).

In summary, the political tactics associated with Stage 2 are designed to solidify and institutionalize the distribution of power that emerged in Stage 1. Several political tactics during the maturity stage serve these ends, including managing critical contingencies, structuring the flow of information, and the use of coalitional politics. Collectively, these tactics constitute a moderate level of bargaining during Stage 2. These political tactics appear as Propositions 6 through 13 in [Table 14.1].

Stage 3: Decline or Redevelopment

This model argues that all organizations face the possibility of decline. Although the maturity stage can be lengthened through management action, internal and external factors or both working simultaneously may force the organization at any time to enter the decline stage (McNichols 1983; Mintzberg 1984; Whetten, 1980).

Context and Strategy   At the end of the maturity stage and the beginning of the decline or redevelopment stage, although past strategies have been very successful and have enabled the firm to grow and mature, the current context in which the firm operates has become increasingly hostile. Typically, it is characterized by an increase in turbulence and heterogeneity (Miller and Friesen 1980b). The firm is largely diversified and caters to different markets. Competition increases as markets become saturated. Products may become obsolete because of changing customer tastes, buying habits, or because of a technological advancement. Therefore, the incentives for change are significant. Greiner (1972) argues that past strategies and behavior become inappropriate to the organization when new stages of development occur. McNichols (1983) argues that strategic planning requires adopting alternatives when the organization is still viable and has the resources to develop new products and services to keep the company healthy and competitive.

Under competitive conditions, Cyert and March (1963) and Ansoff (1970) argue that a decline in revenues triggers a revitalization stage in the organiz- ation. This revitalization (or redevelopment) stage can be described as a dramatic shift away from past traditions, conservatism, and rigidity and toward adaptiveness (Miller and Friesen, 1980b). Consequently, faced with a highly competitive marketplace, dwindling resources, acceleration of new technologies, or other detrimental changes in its external environment, the organization must seek new challenges and new growth opportunities (Lippitt and Schmidt, 1967) in order to survive. Thompson claims that 'survival rests on the coalignment of technology and task environment with a viable domain, and of organization design and structure appropriate to that domain' (1967: 147).

Different strategies are appropriate for coping with the decline stage. They range from a cut-losses early-exit strategy to an aggressive strategy of increased investments, depending on the customer traits, product traits, supplier behavior, competitor traits, and exit barriers. These strategies are illustrative of a more comprehensive list of strategies for firms in declining industries, a discussion of which is beyond the scope of this paper (cf. Harrigan, 1980; Hofer, 1980; Porter, 1980). Such strategic redevelopment disrupts the political relationships among subunits and alters the distribution of power, authority, and responsibility established among coalitions during the maturity stage (Leavitt, 1965).

Politics   Politics during the decline stage tend to be the most overt and possibly the most intense of the three stages. This can be expected because during decline slack resources are depleted in the face of declining revenues and shrinking markets. But cutbacks in slack create personal costs for some managers and departments (Williamson, 1964). As managers struggle to preserve their current levels of resource allocation in the face of decline, political maneuvering increases (Bourgeois and Singh, 1983; Moch and Pondy, 1977; Pfeffer, 1981). Mintzberg goes so far as to call the decline stage a political arena in which there is 'conflict among a wide variety of insiders and outsiders who wish to use the organization for their own purposes' (1984: 221). This politicized environment typically can result from an increasingly indifferent attitude toward change on the part of top management and from a desire to preserve the status quo (Pennings, 1980a) or to perpetuate the organization for its own sake (Mintzberg, 1984). Given such circumstances,

> Divisions may become independent fiefdoms. As a result they are more likely to pursue mutually conflicting strategies since the leadership vacuum reduces the amount of coordination and guidance from the top. (Miller and Friesen, 1980b: 283)

Such political upheaval can ultimately precipitate the demise of the organization.

However, if top management pursues a strategy of redevelopment, large scale strategic change leads to political behavior by those subunits that find their interests or power base threatened by the change (Pettigrew, 1977; Quinn, 1980). Kotter and Schlesinger (1979) and Klein (1976) have noted that political behavior often develops before or during organizational change when what is in the best interests of one group or subunit is perceived by another group to be counter to its best interest. Thus, major strategic change elicits overt political behavior and requires considerable political savvy by a strategist to gain acceptance of the changes (Quinn, 1980).

There is some empirical evidence to suggest that politics during decline are more intense than in other stages. [. . .]

This increased propensity for political dynamics in the decline stage necessitates considerable skill to manage strategic redevelopment. Quinn (1980) suggests a political process for the adoption of major strategic changes. He argues that political interactions among key players are important when solidifying progress towards a goal. Strategists usually try to get key people behind their new concepts or strategy by neutralizing serious opposition or searching for 'zones of indifference' in which the new strategy would not be disastrously opposed (Quinn, 1980). Because no one decision maker has all the power, regardless of that individual's skill or position, the final action taken over time will differ greatly from the intentions of any of the decision makers involved (Allison, 1971). The result tends to be an accumulation of partial decisions on limited strategic issues made by constantly changing coalitions of the critical power clusters (Lindblom, 1954). Managing these shifting coalitions and building commitment to the new strategic direction, then, are the essential political tactics of Stage 3. However, under certain circumstances this incremental process may not be necessary. External events may create a crisis situation for the organization. By taking advantage of the crisis, those introducing new strategies can reduce opposition to and facilitate adoption of the changes they propose. That is, the more organizational members recognize that a crisis exists and believe that it threatens the survival of the entire firm, the less likely they are to resist the proposed changes. Shrewd strategists might even create the perception of a crisis in order to get away with introducing some radical changes. Propositions 14 through 19 of [Table 14.1] summarize the political tactics expected during the demise or redevelopment stage of the life cycle.

Conclusions and Implications of the Model

Politics is an important social influence process in organizations and one that architects of strategic change should be well equipped to handle. Yet the actual processes by which politics imbue strategic change have not been well articulated. The relationship between politics and strategic change within the context of a three-stage model of organizational growth and development has been explored. The model argues that politics is ever present but is manifest differently at each stage of a firm's life cycle. That is, the predominant political tactics needed to manage the organization effectively vary with each stage of the cycle.

In Stage 1 the primary political activity centers around symbolic management in which the entrepreneur instills a vision rooted in his or her own ideology about what the firm should be. During Stage 2 this imprint of the founder is formalized into policies and standard modes of conducting business. An organizational ideology rooted in the institution itself replaces the ideology embodied by the founder during Stage 1. To the extent that institutionalization begins, the ideological imprint of the founder usually remains, even if he or she is soon replaced by another executive (Kimberly, 1979; Miller and Friesen, 1980a; Trice and Beyer, 1983). Politics in Stage 2 centers around whose interests become institutionalized and is characterized by struggles for control of resources to carry out organizational programs. The institutionalization process serves the organization well during maturity, but it can work to its detriment in Stage 3 by restricting the organization's ability to sense and respond to changing environmental conditions. Stage 3 involves power struggles between those who want to preserve the status quo and those who want to reorient the firm's strategy. Hence, politics in Stage 3 revolves around overcoming resistance to strategic change.

[. . .]

Implications for Practicing Managers Several implications for practicing managers and for future research emanate from this model. First, managers should recognize that political dynamics are largely predictable and, therefore, largely manageable if the firm's stage of life is considered. Quinn and Cameron (1983) point to a consistent pattern of development for organizations over time and argue that different activities and structures are appropriate at each stage of growth. This applies to political dynamics as well. A general manager's success as a strategist then depends on his/her ability to understand organizational actions, and his/her own actions, from a political perspective. Moreover, if politics is handled appropriately, it can lead to improved organizational functioning (Pfeffer, 1981). That is, to manage effectively, managers must respond to the political issues salient for the organization at each stage of its life. For example, if an entrepreneur doesn't eventually institutionalize the processes that he/she manages symbolically during the first stage of growth, the organization will become too dependent on his/her judgment and unable to respond expediently to further growth. Such 'routinization of charisma' is necessary for growth (Martin et al., 1983; Trice and Beyer, 1983). Failure to transfer the rationality of the entrepreneur into rules for coordinated action leaves the organization floundering for a basic identity (Ranson et al., 1980).

A second implication concerns leadership. As an organization grows, the nature of the political leadership needed shifts. This may necessitate a concomitant shift in leaders. Kotter (1978) argues that it is useful to match individual decision makers to positions according to their skills and styles. Leaders have different political skills and influence styles, and some may be more suited to the particular stage of organizational growth than others. Hence the model provides justification for replacing chief executives when a major shift in strategy occurs. Such a replacement may, indeed, be warranted if the strategic change represents a move to a new stage in the firm's life cycle and necessitates a different set of political skills for managing the new strategy. Graceful exit by an entrepreneur may be organizationally healthy if he/she is unable to shift from close personal control over operating practices to implementing routine operating procedures for managing coalitional politics and permitting more decentralized control.

A third implication derives from commitment to one's past strategy. Strategists may be unable to conceptualize vital new directions because the existing power structure is too well entrenched. A manager who is successful at building a bureaucracy to support a long term strategy may be unable to recognize an opportunity for redevelopment in Stage 3. Certainly Henry Ford's refusal to bankroll an economical front wheel drive car in 1975 is illustrative (Meadows, 1980). When Lee Iacocca presented Ford this opportunity to get the jump on competitors, Ford refused in the interest of preserving third quarter profits. Yet a change in strategy to respond to increasing environmental pressures (foreign competition, gasoline shortages, and government regulations) was imminent and ultimately necessary for Ford. Henry Ford's commitment to past strategy blinded him to the politics needed to remain competitive.

[. . .]

References

Aguilar, F. (1967) *Scanning the Business Environment*. New York: Macmillan.

Allen, R.W., Madison, D.L., Porter, L.W., Renwick, P.A. and Mayes, B.T. (1979) 'Organizational politics: Tactics and characteristics of its actors', *California Management Review*, 21(1): 77–83.

Allison, G. (1971) *Essence of Decision: Explaining the Cuban Missile Crisis*. Boston: Little, Brown.

Ansoff, I.H. (1970) 'Toward a strategic theory of the firm', in I.H. Ansoff (ed.), *Business Strategy* (pp. 11–40). New York: Penguin.

Bacharach, S.B. and Lawler, E.J. (1981) *Power and Politics in Organizations*. San Francisco, CA: Jossey-Bass.

Barnard, Chester I. (1968) *The Functions of the Executive*. Cambridge, MA: Harvard University Press.

Beyer, J.M. (1981) 'Ideologies, values and decision making in organizations', in P.C. Nystrom and W.H. Starbuck (eds), *Handbook of Organizational Design* (vol. 2, pp. 166–202). New York: Oxford University Press.

Bourgeois, L.J., III and Singh, J.V. (1983) 'Organizational slack and political behavior among top management teams', *Proceedings: Academy of Management*, Dallas, pp. 43–7.

Chandler, A.D. (1962) *Strategy and Structure*. Cambridge, MA: MIT Press.

Child, J. (1972) 'Organization, structure, environment and performance: The role of strategic choice', *Sociology*, 6, 1–22.

Collins, O. and Moore, D.G. (1970) *The Organization Makers*. New York: Appleton-Century-Crofts.

Crozier, M. (1964) *The Bureaucratic Phenomenon*. Chicago: University of Chicago Press.

Culbert, S.A. and McDonough, J.J. (1980) *The Invisible War: Pursuing Self-interests at Work*. New York: Wiley.

Cyert, R. and March, J. (1963) *A Behavioural Theory of the Firm*. Englewood Cliffs, NJ: Prentice-Hall.

Deeks, J. (1976) *The Small Firm Owner-manager: Entrepreneurial Behavior and the Practice of Management*. New York: Praeger.

Downey, H.K. and Greer, C.R. (1982) 'Compliance and social legislation affecting industry: A preliminary investigation of decision criteria', *Proceedings: American Institute for Decision Sciences*, pp. 459–61.

Downs, A. (1967) 'The life cycle of bureaus', in A. Downs (ed.), *Inside Bureaucracy* (pp. 296–309). San Francisco: Little, Brown and Rand Corporation.

Drucker, P.F. (1970) 'Entrepreneurship in the business enterprise', *Journal of Business Policy*, 1(1): 10.

England, G. (1982) 'Managers and their value systems: A five-country comparative study', in W.R. Allen and K. Bragaw (eds), *Social Forces and the Manager* (pp. 89–99). New York: Wiley.

Eoyang, C. (1983) 'Symbolic transformation of belief systems', in L.R. Pondy, P.J. Frost, G. Morgan and T.C. Dandridge (eds), *Organizational symbolism* (pp. 109–21). Greenwich, CT: JAI Press.

Farrell, D. and Petersen, J. (1982) 'Patterns of political behavior in organizations', *Academy of Management Review*, 7: 403–12.

Gardner, J.W. (1964) *Self-Renewal: The Individual and Innovative Society*. New York: Harper & Row.

Greiner, L. (1972) 'Evolution and revolution as organizations grow', *Harvard Business Review*, 50(4): 37–46.

Gricar, B.G. (1983) 'A preliminary theory of organizational compliance with OSHA regulations', in L. Preston (ed.), *Research in Corporate Social Performance* (vol. 5, pp. 121–41). Greenwich, CT: JAI Press.

Guth, W.D. (1976) 'Toward a social system theory of corporate strategy', *Journal of Business*, 49: 374–88.

Hage, J. and Dewar, R. (1973) 'Elite values vs. organizational structure in predicting innovation', *Administrative Science Quarterly*, 19: 279–90.

Harrigan, K.R. (1980) 'Strategy formulation in declining industries', *Academy of Management Review*, 5: 599–604.

Hickson, D.J., Hinings, C.R., Lee, C.A., Schneck, R.E. and Pennings, J.M. (1971) 'A strategic contingencies theory in intraorganizational power', *Administrative Science Quarterly*, 16: 216–29.

Hofer, C.W. (1975) 'Toward a contingency theory of business strategy', *Academy of Management Journal*, 18: 784–810.

Hofer, C.W. (1980) 'Turnaround strategies', *Journal of Business Strategy*, 1(1): 19–31.

Huff, A.S. (1983) 'A rhetorical examination of strategic change', in L.R. Pondy, P.J. Frost, G. Morgan and T.C. Dandridge (eds), *Organizational Symbolism* (pp. 167–83). Greenwich, CT: JAI Press.

Katz, E. (1973) 'Differential factors in the diffusion of innovation', *International Social Service Review*, 32: 9–28.

Kimberly, J.R. (1979) 'Issues in the creation of organizations: Initiation, innovation and institutionalization', *Academy of Management Journal*, 22: 437–57.

Klein, D. (1976) 'Some notes on the dynamics of resistance to change: The defender role', in W. Bennis, K.D. Benne, R. Chin and K.E. Corey (eds), *The Planning of Change* (3rd edn. pp. 117–24). New York: Holt, Rinehart & Winston.

Kotter, J. (1978) 'Power, success and organizational effectiveness', *Organizational Dynamics*, 6(3): 27–40.

Kotter, J.P. and Schlesinger, L.A. (1979) 'Choosing strategies for change', *Harvard Business Review*, 57: 106–14.

Landsberger, H. (1961) 'The horizontal dimension in bureaucracy', *Administrative Science Quarterly*, 6: 299–322.

Lawrence, P.R. and Lorsch, J.W. (1967) *Organization and Environment: Managing Differentiation and Integration*. Boston, MA: Harvard University, Graduate School of Business.

Leavitt, H. (1965) 'Applied organizational change in industry: Structural technological and humanistic approaches', in J. March (ed.), *Handbook of Organizations* (pp. 1145–70). Chicago: Rand McNally.

Lindblom, C.E. (1954) 'The science of muddling through', *Public Administration Review*, 19: 79–88.

Lippitt, G.L. and Schmidt, W.H. (1967) 'Crisis in a developing organization', *Harvard Business Review*, 45: 102–12.

Lorange, P. and Vancil, R. (1977) *Strategic Planning Systems*. Englewood Cliffs, NJ: Prentice-Hall.

MacMillan, I. (1978) *Strategy Formulation: Political Concepts*. St. Paul, MN: West.

March, J.G. and Simon, H.A. (1958) *Organizations*. New York: Wiley.

Martin, J., Hatch, M.J., Kosnik, T. and Sitkin, S. (1983) 'Entrepreneurial control of the culture creation process'. Paper presented as part of the Symposium on Organizational Culture and the Institutionalization of Charisma, Academy of Management Meeting, Dallas, August.

McNichols, T.J. (1983) *Policy Making and Executive Action*. New York: McGraw-Hill.

Meadows, E. (1980) 'Ford needs better ideas – fast', *Fortune*, 16 June, pp. 82–6.

Miles, R.H. and Randolph, W.A. (1980) 'Influence of organizational learning styles on early development', in J.R. Kimberly and R.H. Miles (eds), *The Organizational Life Cycle* (pp. 44–82). San Francisco: Jossey-Bass.

Miller, D. and Friesen, P.H. (1980a) 'Momentum and revolution in organizational adaptation', *Academy of Management Journal*, 23: 591–614.

Miller, D. and Friesen, P.H. (1980b) 'Archetypes of organizational transition', *Administrative Science Quarterly*, 25: 268–99.

Mintzberg, H. (1973) 'Strategy making in three modes', *California Management Review*, 15(2): 44–53.

Mintzberg, H. (1983) *Power in and around Organizations*. Englewood Cliffs, NJ: Prentice-Hall.

Mintzberg, H. (1984) 'Power and organization life cycles', *Academy of Management Review*, 9: 207–24.

Mintzberg, H., Rasinghani, D. and Theoret, A. (1976) 'The structure of unstructured decision processes', *Administrative Science Quarterly*, 21: 246–76.

Moch, M.K. and Pondy, L.R. (1977) 'The structure of chaos: Organized anarchy as a response to ambiguity', *Administrative Science Quarterly*. 22: 351–62.

Murray, E.A. (1978) 'Strategic choice as a negotiated outcome', *Management Science*, 24: 960–72.

Murray, J.A. (1984) 'A concept of entrepreneurial strategy', *Strategic Management Journal*, 5: 1–13.

Narayanan, V.K. and Fahey, L. (1982) 'The micro-politics of strategy formulation', *Academy of Management Review*, 7: 25–34.

Pennings, J.M. (1980a) 'Environmental influences on the creation process', in J. Kimberly and R.H. Miles (eds), *The Organizational Life Cycle* (pp. 135–60). San Francisco: Jossey-Bass.

Pennings, J.M. (1980b) 'Strategically interdependent organizations', in P.C. Nystrom and W.H. Starbuck (eds), *Handbook of Organizational Design* (vol. 1, pp. 433–55). New York: Oxford University Press.

Peterson, R.A. (1980) 'Entrepreneurship and organization', in P.C. Nystrom and W.H. Starbuck (eds), *Handbook of Organizational Design* (vol. 1, pp. 65–83). New York: Oxford University Press.

Pettigrew, A.M. (1977) 'Strategy formulation as a political process', *International Studies of Management and Organization*, 1(2): 78–87.

Pfeffer, J. (1981) *Power in Organizations*. Marshfield, MA: Pittman.

Pfeffer, J. and Salancik, G.R. (1978) *The External Control of Organizations*. New York: Harper & Row.

Pondy, L.R. (1983) 'The role of metaphors and myths in organization and in the facilitation of change', in L.R. Pondy, P.J. Frost, G. Morgan and T.C. Dandridge (eds), *Organizational Symbolism* (pp. 157–66). Greenwich, CT: JAI Press.

Porter, L., Allen, R. and Angle, R. (1983) 'The politics of upward influences in organizations', in R.W. Allen and L.W. Porter (eds), *Organizational Influence Processes* (pp. 408–22). Glenview, IL: Scott, Foresman.

Porter, M.E. (1980) *Competitive Strategy: Techniques for Analyzing Industries and Competitors*. New York: Free Press.

Quinn, J.B. (1979) 'Technological innovation, entrepreneurship and strategy', *Sloan Management Review*, 20(3): 19–30.

Quinn, J.B. (1980) *Strategy for Change: Logical Incrementalism*. Homewood, IL: Irwin.

Quinn, R.E. and Cameron, K. (1983) 'Organizational life cycles and shifting criteria of effectiveness: Some preliminary evidence', *Management Science*, 29: 33–51.

Ranson, S., Hinings, R. and Greenwood, R. (1980) 'The structuring of organizational structures', *Administrative Science Quarterly*, 25: 1–17.

Roberts, N.C. (1984) 'Transforming leadership'. Paper presented at the Symposium on Charisma: Structure, Processes and Consequences. Academy of Management Meeting, Boston, August.

Rumelt, R. (1974) *Strategy, Structure and Economic Performance*. Boston: Harvard Business School, Division of Research.

Salancik, G.R. and Pfeffer, J. (1977) 'Who gets power – and how they hold on to it: A strategic-contingency model of power', *Organization Dynamics*, 5(3): 3–21.

Scherer, F.M. (1967) 'Research and development resource allocation under rivalry', *Quarterly Journal of Economics*, 81: 359–94.

Smircich, L. (1983) 'Concepts of culture and organizational analysis', *Administrative Science Quarterly*, 28: 339–58.

Smircich, L. and Morgan, G. (1982) 'Leadership: The management of meaning', *Journal of Applied Behavioral Science*, 18(3): 257–73.

Staw, B. (1976) 'Knee-deep in the big muddy: A study of escalating commitment to a chosen course of action', *Organizational Behavior and Human Performance*, 16(1): 27–44.

Staw, B. and Ross, J. (1980) 'Commitment in an experimenting society: An experiment on the attribution of leadership from administrative scenarios', *Journal of Applied Psychology*, 65: 249–60.

Thompson, J.D. (1967) *Organizations in Action*. New York: McGraw-Hill.

Toynbee, A. (1957) *A Study of History* (abridged by D.C. Somervell). Oxford, England: Oxford University Press.

Trice, H.M. and Beyer, J.M. (1983) 'The routinization of charisma in two social movement organizations'. Paper presented as part of the Symposium on Organizational Culture and the Institutionalization of Charisma. Academy of Management Meeting, Dallas, August.

Tushman, M.L. (1977a) 'A political approach to organizations: A review and rationale', *Academy of Management Review*, 2: 206–16.

Tushman, M.L. (1977b) 'Special boundary roles in the innovation process', *Administrative Science Quarterly*, 22: 587–604.

Weber, M. (1947) *Theory of Social and Economic Organization*. New York: Free Press.

Weick, K.E. (1979) *The Social Psychology of Organizing* (2nd edn). Reading, MA: Addison-Wesley.

Whetten, D.A. (1980) 'Organizational decline: A neglected topic in organizational science', *Academy of Management Review*, 5: 577–88.

Wilkins, A.L. (1983) 'Organizational stories as symbols which control the organization', in L.R. Pondy, P.J. Frost, G. Morgan and T.C. Dandridge (eds), *Organizational Symbolism* (pp. 81–92). Greenwich, CT: JAI Press.

Williamson, O.E. (1964) *The Economics of Discretionary Behavior: Managerial Objectives in a Theory of the Firm*. Englewood Cliffs, NJ: Prentice-Hall.

Zaskind, S. and Costello, T.W. (1962) 'Perception: Implications for administration', *Administrative Science Quarterly*, 7: 218–35.

15 Employee Empowerment: A Seductive Misnomer?

Sharon Leiba and Cynthia Hardy

In 1990, 200 Fortune 1000 companies were surveyed on the topic of employee empowerment (Messmer, 1990: 25). The study revealed that 88 per cent of the managers believed that they had given employees more authority to make decisions than five years ago. On the other hand, when employees were asked whether management had given them more decision-making authority, only 64 per cent felt they had. Moreover, many employees experienced empowerment not as liberation, but in the form of increased workloads, stress and pressure. Others have complained about companies that pay lip service to the ideals of empowerment, but fail to nurture an environment that truly supports empowered behaviour (Kizilos, 1990). So, empowerment does not seem to be the miracle-worker some advocates would have us believe.

This chapter examines the issue of empowerment more closely. It begins with the management definition of employee empowerment. Next, it describes the organizational changes involved in typical empowerment programmes, and reviews the various objectives and expectations of senior management in implementing these programmes. Then it reviews how empowerment has been defined in the fields of sociology and political science. Finally, management's motives and expectations for employee empowerment are compared with those behind political empowerment. The contrast throws some light on why empowerment programmes sometimes fail and suggests that the term – 'employee empowerment' – may be little more than a seductive misnomer.

Empowerment in the Management Literature

Empowering practices in the business world have been developed to counter feelings of powerlessness which, many theorists believe, are the cause of problems in the work place such as substance abuse, low productivity, low motivation, and stress (e.g. Kizilos, 1990). Traditional, hierarchical organizational structures often disempower a large number of people (Carr, 1991).

[Powerless employees] typically perceive themselves as lacking control over their immediate situation, or lacking the required capability, resources, or discretion needed to accomplish a task. In either case, these experiences maximize feelings of inadequacy. (Conger, 1989: 21)

Organizations with powerless employees are believed to perform sub-optimally because they cannot successfully harness and maximize their human resource potential.

The solution to the problem of employee powerlessness depends on whether one considers the cause to be employees' *actual* inability to act or their *feelings* of inadequacy. The view of powerlessness as the result of a genuine lack of means is embodied in the *relational* approach; while the *psychological* approach regards powerlessness as a perceptual and motivational problem.

The relational approach regards employee empowerment as the exchange of power and responsibility throughout an organization (Goski and Belfry, 1991). According to this view, management must give up some control and employees must accept risk by taking on more responsibility (Foxman and Polsky, 1991). The resulting system of decentralized decision-making, in which employees at all levels are provided with the necessary knowledge and authority to satisfy customers, is expected to be empowering for employees (Penzer, 1991) as employees gain feelings of authority, power, and control when they are given the permission to exercise their own judgements (e.g. Humphrey, 1991; Feldman, 1991).

The psychological approach regards employee empowerment as a system that increases the individual's belief in his/her ability to exercise choice. Empowerment is the process whereby one comes to feel and behave *as if* one has power over significant aspects of one's work, and to develop a sense of dignity in one's job (e.g. Kizilos, 1990; Conger, 1989; Schlossberg, 1991). By informing employees of the importance and meaning of what they do, they develop a sense of pride and ownership in their work and their organization (Feldman, 1991). The psychological view regards employee empowerment as primarily an intra-personal process, rather than an inter-personal one (Hamlin, 1991). 'Management cannot really bestow empowerment, it can only pave the way for people to be empowered; people must assume ownership of their thoughts, feelings, behaviour, and consequences' (Von der Embse, 1989: 27). The psychological approach to employee empowerment thus converges with the motivational assumptions of the job design literature.

> The push of management takes a back seat to the fit between an employee's value system and the intrinsically motivating pull of the task. (Thomas and Velthouse, 1990: 667)

A number of management theorists have combined both psychological and relational approaches by acknowledging the existence of organizational factors that contribute to individuals' feelings of powerlessness (Conger, 1989). They argue that both increased control and a sense of ownership are 'necessary for increased feelings of self-confidence, self-awareness, self-control, and self-efficacy. Thus, the empowerment process must address the reciprocal impact of environmental factors, behaviour, and the individual's cognitive style' (Velthouse, 1990: 15).

In summary, the most comprehensive definition of employee empowerment defines it as an organizational development process that seeks to enhance employees' actual *and* felt self-efficacy by identifying the environmental, behavioural, and cognitive conditions that foster powerlessness, and then removing these conditions via formal organizational practices (Conger and Kanungo, 1988; Velthouse, 1990).

Employee Empowerment Programmes

Empowerment involves a complex set of organizational changes. The methodology described here reflects a compilation of a variety of recommendations from the management literature; many organizations implement a mere fraction of these changes. The articles on employee empowerment agree that the verbal approval of empowerment has to be supported by substantive, formal organizational changes, and recommend a programme that incorporates both relational and psychological approaches.

> Training, teamwork, executive support or reward programs alone will fail to achieve the groundswell of change required for empowerment to succeed. Only by doing all the right things right will you create the synergy needed to release the power of empowerment. (Fleming, 1991: 37)

Empowerment thus requires: alignment to organizational purpose: changes in the organization's management and communication styles; a significant re-design of many organizational jobs; and a complete redesign of many human resource management functions. Each of these areas will now be examined in more detail.

Alignment to Organizational Strategy

Because employee empowerment is such a complex process, it risks becoming unwieldy. Given that top-level managers are usually held responsible for developing strategic goals, they are likely to be very concerned with the outcome of this process, and thus with minimizing its unwieldiness (Schaeffer, 1991). Therefore, it is usually recommended that employees be given the ability to make decisions, but within specified and detailed limits and guidelines, set out by management (Brymer, 1991).

Employees' adherence to these limits and guidelines is referred to as alignment. It involves attuning employees to the organization's strategic goals so that they understand that they have been empowered to make whatever decisions are necessary to reach the goals set out in the mission statement (e.g. Velthouse, 1990; Topaz, 1989/90; Penzer, 1991). At every juncture, aligned employees are expected to ask, 'Is my action in keeping with the vision?' (Belasco, 1989: 12). Alignment is thus facilitated by the communication of a shared vision, clear direction, and well-defined policies, procedures, systems and methods throughout the organization (Humphrey, 1991).

Management Style

Given that upper management sets the alignment boundaries, middle management's responsibility is to know what those boundaries are and to inform subordinates about what is negotiable and what is not (Kizilos, 1990). Managers are supposed to facilitate their subordinates' empowerment by exhibiting trust, encouraging delegation, and offering challenge and encouragement (Velthouse, 1990; Hamlin, 1991). Management's focus should be on coaching people to enhance everyone's abilities to learn, rather than on controlling them (Welter, 1991a). The idea is to lead people to lead themselves (Kaplan, 1991: 9). Some articles have even suggested that managers get into the personal world of each employee to support and encourage them to overcome the fears and self-doubts that block their own growth (Hamlin, 1991: 8).

Organizational Communication

If employees are to perform successfully, they must be able to make informed decisions. The employee-empowered organization must therefore be characterized by timely and accurate information that is shared throughout the organization, rather than one that operates on a 'need to know' basis (Topaz, 1989/90). Communication programmes must be open and ongoing to heighten and maintain employee awareness of strategic business objectives (Fleming, 1991: 36; Velthouse, 1990; Welter, 1991a,b).

Job Re-Design

Job design is another change area often regarded as essential to employee empowerment. The most common recommendation is that jobs be designed to provide feelings of ownership and responsibility (Sheridan, 1991a,b). One way that it has been accomplished is by allowing workers to schedule their own work, and to select or order their own equipment (Welter, 1991a,b).

Hiring and Firing Practices

If empowerment is to be realized, recruitment practices have to be changed to increase employee involvement. For example, hiring procedures should allow employees to interview prospective hires, and influence the final hiring decision (Welter, 1991b; Schaeffer, 1991). Similarly, teams or work groups should be given more responsibility for dealing with discipline and absenteeism problems (Schaeffer, 1991). The rationale is that work teams help maintain order: 'Simple peer pressure often is more effective than managerial threats. Workers are less likely to call in sick if they have to face team members the next morning' (Manz, 1990: 21).

Reward and Appraisal Systems

These systems also have to be modified. Performance appraisals should be preceded by a clear understanding of job responsibilities and measurements for success. Management should solicit employees' input as to what the performance standards should be (Eisman, 1991: 218). The reward system should then incorporate these measurements in a way that promotes pride, self-esteem and trust. For example, by tying performance award to customer satisfaction, workers learn how their job relates to company performance, and build self-confidence (Penzer, 1991).

Examples of other recommendations include supervisor appraisals, peer appraisals, and profit sharing (Beatty and Ulrich, 1991; Schaeffer, 1991). In supervisor appraisals, the employees evaluate their supervisor (Block, 1990). Management's rewards should be based on how well they empower their employees (Topaz, 1989/90) rather than by visible external symbols that differentiate employees by rank (Gonring, 1991). In peer appraisals, co-workers rank each other. Team members provide input to certify that a co-worker has achieved a required skill to qualify for a pay hike (Sheridan, 1991a). In appraisal systems, feedback should be consistent and designed to get 'more of the best rather than less of the worst of people' (Bell and Zemke, 1988: 83).

Training

Training is key to maintaining a sense of control (alignment) in a changing culture (Eubanks, 1991). All employees, regardless of their rank, should be taught:

> not only about their immediate job (i.e. what problems to look for and how to fix them) but the reasons and the processes behind it, and its effect on the bottom line, as well. They must be taught how to approach new situations logically and effectively, so that they will not fear making decisions. (Penzer, 1991: 98)

Teams need to be trained in both technical and group dynamics skills such as interpersonal communication, leadership, group decision-making, and group problem-solving (Carr, 1991; McKenna, 1990; Gonring, 1991; Doyle, 1990).

Managers have to learn how to change relationships based on power and dependency to ones based on influence and trust (Carr, 1991: 39). They need to realize that mistakes sometimes will occur (Austin 1991; McKenna, 1991a,b). They must learn how to handle bad ideas and not penalize employees for making mistakes (Kizilos, 1990; Anderson, 1991). Instead, they should view mistakes as opportunities (Welter, 1991a,b).

> Failure must be acceptable, but it must also be responsible and productive. 'Responsible' means people clean up their mess. 'Productive' means they document what they have learned, and they circulate that document the way one would circulate a document on success. (McKenna, 1991a: 16)

The aim is to stimulate innovation by rewarding success, rather than punishing failure; emphasizing effort rather than discrediting imperfection (Velthouse, 1990).

In summary, the idealized employee empowerment programme involves changes in different parts of the organization to increase the actual autonomy of employees (relational view) which, in turn, increases their perceptions of power (psychological view). However, it is important to note that these recommendations are rarely implemented in their entirety and, more commonly, managers make a few, isolated changes.

Managerial Objectives for Employee Empowerment

Senior managers usually have very specific reasons for wanting to alleviate employee powerlessness. 'People are brought into an organization in order to further its goals. Unless it is a welfare organization, people are hired because of what they can contribute, and only secondarily to meet their needs' (Von der Embse, 1989: 26).

> The purpose of shifting decision-making to the employees is not to remove managers totally from making decisions, or to turn the operation into a democracy. (Odiorne, 1991: 66)

The prime objective, clearly, is to increase competitive advantage (Beatty and Ulrich, 1991). Employees are empowered, not just to enhance morale, but also to improve productivity, lower costs, and raise customer satisfaction (Eisman, 1991).

Employees are expected to perform better because empowerment is supposed to leave them feeling optimistic and involved; committed and persistent; able to cope with adversity; and willing to perform independently and responsibly (Velthouse, 1990; Shelton, 1991; Block, 1990). They are expected to take the initiative and exercise whatever power is necessary to improve performance, whether or not they have official sanction from above (Topaz, 1989/90; Bell and Zemke, 1988; Beatty and Ulrich, 1991). They are also expected to have the organization's best interests in mind (Kizilos, 1990; Block, 1990); perform above and beyond the call of duty; be willing to take risks; and be eager to pursue alternatives (Humphrey, 1991; Velthouse, 1990).

> Employees are not just expected to survive stress, they are expected to thrive on it. (Kizilos, 1990: 51)

Employee empowerment is also instituted to bring about innovation. Change becomes less of a threat because employees are allowed to participate in and to influence it (McKenna, 1991b; Kizilos, 1990). Empowerment is thus expected to move the organization to a system where everyone is continuously involved in improving it (Beatty and Ulrich, 1991). Consequently, empowerment promises businesses longevity in an ever-expanding nationally and internationally competitive marketplace, through improved service and strengthened perform-ance (Goski and Belfry, 1991; Shelton, 1991; Early, 1991; Bell and Zemke, 1988; Schlossberg, 1991).

A somewhat different motive driving some empowerment programmes stems from downsizing. The organization still has to handle the work of managers who have since been terminated which, in turn, may require the empowerment of remaining employees (Brown, 1990). The crumbled career ladder that often follows downsizing may also create a need for empowerment – to compensate for the reduced opportunities for upward mobility and to create loyalty by providing 'growth work environments' (Doyle, 1990: 39).

> Empowerment invites employees to create meaning and challenge for themselves in their current positions. While accepting that they may not become the CEO, they may recognize that personal greatness is achievable where they are. (Macher, 1988: 45)

Organizations thus expect to reap the benefits of high loyalty and a large decrease in employee turnover (Von der Embse, 1989; Eisman, 1991), avoiding the costs associated with traditional ways of building organizational attach-ment, such as pay and benefits (Doyle, 1990). Empowerment programmes may, however, lead to even more cuts: as individuals are empowered to manage themselves, the supervisory role disappears and management layers may be reduced further (Carr, 1991).

Employee empowerment programmes are, then, clearly geared towards the maximization of shareholder wealth. *Employee* empowerment might, then, be more accurately termed *organizational* empowerment. While the former is an appealing term for those alienated by the authoritarian system of management (Welter, 1991a,b), it masks the explicit objectives that underline actions designed to enable the organization to fulfil its traditional mandate.

Empowerment in Sociology and Political Science

This section examines the use of the term 'empowerment' in the socio-political literature. While this literature also equates empowerment with the reduction of powerlessness (Solomon, 1976) it encompasses a somewhat different view compared to the management literature. Empowering activities according to this body of work involve attaining not only a sense of pride, self-respect, and a sense of personal efficacy, but also economic and political influence (Goski and Belfry, 1991; Kizilos, 1990).

> [Empowerment connotes] a spectrum of political activity, ranging from acts of individual resistance to mass political mobilizations that challenge the basic power relations – the social, political, and economic processes and institutions – in our society. (Bookman and Morgen, 1988: 4)

Such empowerment programmes have been applied to a broad spectrum of groups, including women, ethnic minorities, aboriginals, consumers, youths, alcoholics, the poor, among others. In general, such programmes involve a democratization process whereby traditionally powerless groups take control over their lives.

> For women, empowerment begins when they change their ideas about the causes of their powerlessness, recognize the systemic forces that oppress them, and then act to change the conditions of their lives. (Bookman and Morgen, 1988: 4)

Empowerment in this milieu involves a number of key characteristics, which are discussed below. They include alignment to a common purpose, the importance of a grassroots movement, the possibility of conflict, and ownership of key power sources.

Alignment to a Common Strategic Purpose

The social movements of the 1960s and 1970s consisted, for the most part, of persons who belonged to a stigmatized, social category (Solomon, 1976). Empowerment was a popular buzzword of leaders of these movements (Kizilos, 1990). 'Women, African-Americans, and anti-war activists organized and shouted their message to the public' (Goski and Belfry, 1991: 215). The members of these groups shared a common purpose. They wanted control over their lives and to achieve their aspirations (Boyte and Riessman, 1986), both of which required power. Only by taking over the social programmes that determined their well-being could they hope to gain control over their destiny (Bookman and Morgen, 1988; Dacks and Coates, 1988; Kizilos, 1990; Goski and Belfry, 1991). By taking to the streets, they hoped to further their common agendas (Kizilos, 1990; Goski and Belfry, 1991).

A Grassroots Effort

A basic assumption underlying this literature is that empowerment is taken, not given:

> It is usually a self-generated, bottom-up participatory process, the voluntary pursuit of democratic free spaces, in which the idea is for communities to take initiatives. (Boyte and Riessman, 1986: 24)

Individuals seek empowerment because of a belief that only with power are people able to create a better life for themselves (Dacks and Coates, 1988). Empowerment has thus been described as a form of grassroots political activism that a group organizes on its own behalf and for its own benefit (Bookman and Morgen, 1988).

Facilitation

Although it may not be possible to bestow empowerment, some theorists believe that it can be coaxed out of people (e.g. Solomon, 1976) by adopting the appropriate communication style and providing the relevant conditions, language and beliefs to the powerless (Boyte and Riessman, 1986). These conditions refer to access to the resources necessary to achieve collective goals (Solomon, 1976). Language and beliefs provide people with the vocabulary and ideas that foster a change in cognitions, motivations, and feelings from a state of powerlessness to one of control – 'where the community is seen to work for them, not on them' (Boyte and Riessman, 1986: 65).

This view of a facilitated empowerment process requires collaboration between the powerful (usually the professional community) and those desiring empowerment (Boyte and Riessman, 1986). It must, therefore, involve a cooperative outcome, and not involve detriment to the traditional authorities (Dacks and Coates, 1988). Writers acknowledge that even if it is possible for those in power to share it with the powerless, they are only likely do so when it is beneficial to them (Boyd, 1989: 6). This form of collaborative empowerment is possible because there are 'historical moments when the interests of the oppressed and that of the state correspond, and the oppressed can draw advantages from that situation' (Boyd, 1989: 6). In this situation, empowerment offers wider benefits to both powerful and powerless groups: it links 'individual strength and competencies, natural helping systems, and proactive behaviours to social policy and social change, and thereby creates unique sources of democratic energy, experiment, and vision' (Boyte and Riessman, 1986: 314).

> [Empowerment] can be particularly beneficial to organizations because individuals who are psychologically and politically empowered will be able to make choices to effectively engage in conflict and change. (Boyte and Riessman, 1986: 77)

Conflict

Other theorists have questioned this form of collaborative empowerment, where the powerful come to the aid of the powerless. They point out that empowerment may bring into conflict groups that have different relations to the structures and sources of power in society (Bookman and Morgen, 1988). Empowerment, as a process of give and take, suggests a degree of detriment to the giver, and a degree of resentment by the taker, unless the process is seen as positive by both sides (Bookman and Morgen, 1988). These theorists argue that the very act of empowering someone else creates a dependency relationship which, by definition, is disempowering (e.g. Gruber & Trickett, 1987; Simon, 1990). This is particularly true when the facilitator is likely to be a professional with access to sources of power over the 'empoweree'.

Research has illustrated the unwillingness of human service and community development organizations to extend participation to a wider group of individuals, particularly clients, because of the threat to their interests (Warren et al., 1974). Weaker groups may be kept powerless to 'serve as a balancing mechanism for the systems in which they exist. In being excluded and kept separate, and in being the recipients of much of the tension, conflict, contradiction, and confusion that exists within the system, they provide stability for their benefactors' (Pinderhughes, 1983: 333).

> We recognize that such organizations and programs acquire considerable power over their clients, and this power typically is used to ensure the survival and growth of the organization itself or of its key stakeholders at the expense of the clients. (Hasenfeld and Chesler, 1989: 501)

There is, according to this view, an inherent paradox concerning the 'empowerment' of disenfranchised groups by powerful actors since it is in the interests of the latter to control access to decision-making (Gruber and Trickett, 1987; Warren et al., 1974).

Economic and Political Change

Because of the tenuous nature of the relationship between the powerful and powerless (on which both those supportive of and those opposed to facilitation agree), recommendations stress the importance of control over the economic resources and programmes that determine a person's material well-being. Without economic empowerment, individuals will find it difficult to develop the personal confidence and self-esteem necessary to pursue empowerment in other areas of their lives (Dacks and Coates, 1988). Another important aspect of empowerment is allowing people to acquire real power within recognized political structures to provide the tools, the mechanisms, and the resources to make decisions and solve problems (Boyd, 1989).

In summary, empowerment, in the socio-political sense, is a collectivistic strategy intended to improve the quality of people's lives by allowing them the freedom to express and pursue their dreams. It is based on the democratic concept of fair access to society's opportunities. It requires the provision of authority and resources, as well as a certain degree of psychological motivation. Hence, it is both a relational and a psychological process. Increased economic control permits an increased level of participation and ownership in both current and future societal directions and it also provides an enhancement of an individual's sense of self-worth. Empowerment in this sense is usually initiated by those who feel the need to be empowered. While it cannot be 'given', it can be coaxed or encouraged by more powerful groups if interests converge. If, on the other hand, more powerful groups view empowerment as disempowering for them, they will resist it and try to maintain the status quo.

So, What *is* Employee Empowerment?

The definition of empowerment is similar in both management and socio-political literature in that both describe it as a strategy to counter powerlessness by providing psychological and actual power. But that is where the similarity ends. The clearest differences between employee empowerment and socio-political empowerment concern the motives underlying the reduction of powerlessness, the nature of changes in actual power sources, and the acknowledgement of conflict.

Motives

The socio-political literature uses empowerment to describe the process whereby traditionally powerless groups and individuals gain access to their share of society's democratic free space and, in so doing, fulfil their aspirations. This version of empowerment involves striving for increased influence over societal directions and challenging existing power relations in the process. Its use of motivational terminology is designed to heighten the group's awareness of its *own* objectives. Employee empowerment, on the other hand, is a process orchestrated by senior managers and granted to or bestowed on employees that is intended to achieve *organizational* objectives; not to provide an exercise in democracy.

The realities offered by employee empowerment do not measure up to the democratic gains promised by socio-political empowerment. The latter emphasizes increased political influence and choice; it is voluntary, not coercive. Implicit in the employee empowerment model, in contrast, is the message that employees must choose between 'the empowerment way or the highway'. For example, several articles recommend that companies eventually weed out those executives who do not support the new initiative (Eubanks, 1991). A similar fate awaits employees at lower levels who cannot adapt to or do not fit into the new practices associated with empowerment, and whose performance does not improve (e.g. Stewart, 1989).

Control of Resources

Admittedly, employee empowerment may allow more employee influence over current and future operational directions as it grants them increased decision-making autonomy and authority. However, rather than challenging the core power relations, employee empowerment actually maintains the status quo because it leaves the guiding strategy up to senior management and operates within the confines of alignment. Senior management continues to set the direction for the company – 'the future is not participative, but rather dictatorial' (McKenna, 1990: 18). Budgets remain under the control of senior hierarchical levels. In addition, because many organizations fail to implement a complete programme, employees may find that they are actually being asked to accomplish more with less (Welter, 1991a,b).

> Work teams are often told to be self-directing and empowered to improve results while shackled to new, albeit supposedly empowering, systems and structures that do not fit their charge. (Hanna, 1991: 4)

This is particularly true when empowerment occurs in conjunction with downsizing and remaining employees end up working harder (Fisher, 1991; Goski and Belfry, 1991).

> The world is full of 220-volt managers trying to somehow energize 110-volt employees. Call it empowerment, if you will; employees often call it burnout – literally and figuratively. (Von der Embse, 1989: 25)

In other words, the increased economic resources typically promised by socio-political empowerment rarely occur in business. The reality is that while employee empowerment promises increased ownership and remuneration, it does not always offer any tangible reward. Some organizations offer incentives such as team awards and employee suggestion awards, but the value of these awards rarely represents more than a fraction of the productivity gains realized by the empowerment programme. So, the increased productivity gains realized from the employee empowerment effort seldom translate into significantly greater financial compensation for employees.

Conflict

Whereas the socio-political literature acknowledges the conflicting interests of powerful and powerless groups, the management literature seeks to obscure it. The terminology itself is intended to heighten employees' awareness of *business* objectives, rather than their awareness of *employee* objectives. Several management theorists have noted that the term 'empowerment' can be seductive to employees who feel powerless in the stereotypical bureaucratic organizational context (Foxman and Polsky, 1991; Kizilos, 1990; Goski and Belfry, 1991; Velthouse, 1990). This is reinforced by the use of such terms as 'associates', 'team members', 'players', and 'coaching staff' (Welter, 1991a,b; Von der Embse, 1989).

> [The significance behind this terminology is that] different players play different roles. The roles may change from time to time, but the team is in deep trouble unless everyone is a player. (Carr, 1991: 38)

The underlying message of the terminology is that organizational and employee interests are the same. Reality, however, is somewhat different – while employee empowerment presents an image of employee gains, the true objective of organizational empowerment often involves deprivation and sacrifice as work loads increase and career opportunities decline.

> [But while] big companies still demand old-style loyalty . . . they're offering packages to clear out as many people as possible. As companies keep carving layers out of the old hierarchy, empowerment will, for the most part, leave employees . . . with fewer opportunities. (Fisher, 1991: 77)

It is, perhaps, not accidental that the term 'employee empowerment' is used – to obscure reality and promise a collective, democratic gain in power while hiding the true motivations behind empowerment programmes.

Ironically, by downplaying conflict, the literature ignores that empowerment embodies a potential threat to managerial control. Even under conditions of alignment, where subordinates are expected to perform within the negotiable space set out by their managers, 'empowered people can sometimes behave in surprising, unpredictable ways' (Bell and Zemke, 1988: 81).

> [They] discard structure, routing, rules, and accepted procedures. Refusing to be part of a finely tuned orchestra, they occasionally produce noise-cacophony, and substitute effectiveness for efficiency. (Velthouse, 1990: 17)

Empowered employees are able to do things that powerless people find more difficult. As a result, they may take bad decisions, change procedures, break rules or simply be argumentative (Kizilos, 1990: 48).

Management articles tend to offer only simplistic suggestions on how to deal with conflict. They recommend that managers tell employees what is needed, point out employees' abilities, and ask employees what assistance they need to get the job done (Welter, 1991a). This advice not only trivializes resistance, it may even contribute to it. Employees are able to distinguish between a true commitment to empowerment and its use as an excuse or facade. If expectations are not met, trust is lowered, and either the potential for resistance increases among those with the power to do so (Kahnweiler, 1991); or those too powerless to resist experience even greater feelings of helplessness and alienation (Ashforth, 1989).

Conclusions

Organizations that implement empowerment programmes can provide a certain measure of employee satisfaction and organizational empowerment if managers adapt to individual employee's learning styles, and use control in a manner that does not sap employees' energies. Coupled with the use of techniques for improving organizational effectiveness (such as job design, open communication, etc.) employee participation may be increased and feelings of self-efficacy may be enhanced (Macher, 1988). Being able to influence the critical dimensions of one's work can add meaning to employees' careers (Schaeffer, 1991: 9).

Employee empowerment does not, however, offer nearly as much democratic free space as the socio-political term promises. Organizations clearly have different expectations for what empowerment means in practice.

> It is tempting to conclude that many companies are attracted to a fantasy version of empowerment and simultaneously repelled by the reality. How lovely to have energetic, dedicated workers who always seize the initiative (but only when 'appropriate'), who enjoy taking risks (but never risky ones), who volunteer their ideas (but only brilliant ones), who solve problems on their own (but make no mistakes), who aren't afraid to speak their minds (but never ruffle any feathers), who always give their very best to the company (but ask no unpleasant questions about what the company is giving back). How nice it would be, in short, to empower workers without actually giving them any power . . . (Kizilos, 1990: 56)

'Employee empowerment' appears, then, to be a highly seductive misnomer.

References

Anderson, Eric, R. (1991) 'NACM North Central provides "Credit solutions you can trust"', *Business Credit*, 93(10).

Ashforth, Blake, E. (1989) 'The experience of powerlessness in organizations', *Organizational Behaviour and Human Decision Process*, 43(2): 207–42.

Austin, Nancy K. (1991) 'Dr Deming and the "Q" Factor', *Working Woman*, 16(9): 31–4.

Beatty, Richard W. and Ulrich, David O. (1991) 'Re-energizing the mature organization', *Organizational Dynamics*, 20(1): 16–30.

Belasco, James A. (1989) 'Masters of empowerment', *Executive Excellence*, 6(3): 11–12.

Bell, Chip, and Zemke, Ron (1988) 'Do service procedures tie employees hands?', *Personnel Journal*, 67(9): 77–83.

Bennis, Warren (1987) 'Some competencies of great leaders', *Executive Excellence*, 4(12): 14.

Benson, Tracy E. (1991) 'Empowerment: There's that word again', *Industry Week*, 240(9): 44–52.

Block, Peter (1990) 'How to be the new kind of manager', *Working Woman*, 15(7): 51–6.

Bookman, A. and Morgen, S. (1988) *Women and the Politics of Empowerment*. Philadelphia: Temple University Press.

Boyd, Rosalind (1989) *Empowerment of Women in Contemporary Uganda: Real or Symbolic?* Montreal: McGill University Press.

Boyte, Harry C. and Riessman, Frank (1986) *The New Populism: The Politics of Empowerment*. Philadelphia: Temple University Press.

Brown, Thomas L. (1990) 'Fearful of empowerment: should managers be terrified?' *Industry Week*, 239(12): 12.

Brymer, Robert A. (1991) 'Employee empowerment: A guest-driven leadership strategy', *Cornell Hotel & Restaurant Administration Quarterly*, 32(1): 58–68.

Carr, Clay (1991) 'Managing self-managed workers', *Training and Development*, 45(9): 36–42.

Conger, Jay A (1989) 'Leadership: The art of empowering others', *Academy of Management Executive*, 3(1): 17–24.

Conger, Jay A. and Kanungo, Rabindra N. (1988) 'The empowerment process: Integrating theory and practice', *Academy of Management Review*, 13(3): 471–82.

Dacks, Gurston and Coates, Ken (1988) *Northern Communities:: The Prospects for Empowerment*. Alberta: Boreal Institute for Northern Studies.

Doyle, Frank P. (1990) 'People-power: The global human resource challenge for the 90's'. *Columbia Journal of World Business*, Spring/Summer, 36–45.

Early, Virgil (1991) 'Empowering organizations', *Executive Excellence*, 8(2): 13–14.

Eisman, Regina (1991) 'Power to the people', *Incentive*, 165(10): 116, 140, 218.

Eubanks, Paula (1991) 'Employee empowerment key to culture change', *Hospitals*, 65(24): 40.

Feldman, Stuart (1991) 'Keeping the customer satisfied – inside and out', *Management Review*, 80(11): 58–60.

Fisher, Anne B. (1991) 'Morale crisis', *Fortune*, 124(12): 70–80.

Fleming, Peter C. (1991) 'Empowerment strengthens the rock', *Management Review*, 80(12): 34–7.

Foxman, Loretta D. and Polsky, Walter L. (1991) 'Share the power', *Personnel Journal*, 70(9): 116–20.

Gonring, Matthew P. (1991) 'Communication makes employee involvement work', *Public Relations Journal*, 47(11): 38–40.

Goski, Kelly L. and Belfry, Mary (1991) 'Achieving competitive advantage through employee empowerment', *Employment Relations Today*, 18(2): 213–20.

Gruber, J. and Trickett, E.J. (1987) 'Can we empower others? The paradox of empowerment in the governing of an alternative public school', *American Journal of Community Psychology*, 15(3): 353–71.

Hackman, J. Richard, and Oldham, Greg R. (1980) *Work Redesign*. Massachusetts: Addison-Wesley.

Hamlin, Richard (1991) 'A practical guide to empowering your employees', *Supervisory Management*, 36(4): 8.

Hanna, David P. (1991) 'Build integrity into self-directing teams', *Executive Excellence*, 8(12): 4–5.

Hasenfeld, Y. and Chesler, M.A. (1989) 'Client empowerment in the human services: Personal and professional agenda', *Journal of Applied Behavioral Science*, 25(4): 499–521.

Humphrey, John W. (1991) 'A time of 10,000 leaders', *Executive Excellence*, 8(6): 17–18.

Kahnweiler, William M. (1991) 'HRD and empowerment', *Training and Development*, 45(11): 73–6.

Kaplan, Robert E. (1991) 'Why empowerment often fails', *Executive Excellence*, 8(12): 9.

Kaufman, Steven B. (1991) 'Empowerment at Pacific Gas and Electric', *Training*, 28(8): 46–8.

Kizilos, Peter (1990) 'Crazy about empowerment', *Training*, 27(12); 47–56.

Macher, Ken (1988) 'Empowerment and the bureaucracy', *Training and Development*, 42: 41–5.

McKenna, Joseph F. (1990) 'Smart scarecrows: The wizardry of empowerment', *Industry Week*, 239(14): 8–19.

McKenna, Joseph F. (1991a) 'Failure: Managing the last taboo', *Industry Week*, 240(5): 12–16.

McKenna, Joseph F. (1991b) 'America's best plants: SPX', *Industry Week*, 240(20): 49–50.

Manz, Charles C., Keating, David E. and Donnellon, Anne (1990) 'Preparing for an organizational change to employee self-management: The managerial transition', *Organizational Dynamics*, 19(2): 15–26.

Messmer, Max (1990) 'How to put employee empowerment into practice', *Woman CPA*, 52(3): 25.

Odiorne, George S. (1991) 'Competence versus passion', *Training and Development*, 45(5): 61–4.

Penzer, Erika (1991) 'The power of empowerment', *Incentive*, May: 97–138.

Pinderhughes, E.B. (1983) 'Empowerment for our clients and for ourselves', *Social Casework: The Journal of Contemporary Social Work*, 331–8.

Riley, Lorna (1991) 'Increase sales using: The new language in selling', *American Salesman*, 36(10): 16–20.

Rood, Raymond P. and Meneley, Brenda L. (1991) 'Serious play at work', *Personnel Journal*, 70(1): 90–9.

Sargent, Alice G. and Stupak, Ronald J. (1989) 'Managing in the '90's', *Training and Development Journal*, 43(12): 29–35.

Schaeffer, Orville (1991) 'Empowerment as a business strategy', *Executive Excellence*, 8(10): 9–10.

Schlesinger, Leonard A. and Heskett, James L. (1991) 'Enfranchisement of service workers', *California Management Review*, 33(4): 83–100.

Schlossberg, Howard (1991) 'Authors blast those who make excuses for poor business', *Marketing News*, 25(15): 5.

Shelton, Ken (1991) 'People power', *Executive Excellence*, 8(12): 7–8.

Sheridan, John H. (1991a) 'A philosophy for commitment', *Industry Week*, 240(3): 11–13.

Sheridan, John H. (1991b) 'America's best plants: Tennessee Eastman', *Industry Week*, 240(20): 59–60.

Simon, B.L. (1990) 'Rethinking empowerment', *Journal of Progressive Human Sciences*, 1(1): 27–37.

Sirbasku, Jim (1991) 'Powering empowerment', *Manage*, 43(1): 12–13.

Solomon, Barbara Bryant (1976) *Black Empowerment: Social Work in Oppressed Communities*. New York: Columbia University Press.

Stewart, T.A. (1989) 'New ways to exercise power', *Fortune*, 6 November, 52–66.

Thomas, Kenneth W. and Velthouse, Betty A. (1990) 'Cognitive elements of empowerment: An "interpretive" model of intrinsic task motivation', *Academy of Management Review*, 15(4): 666–81.

Topaz, Lionel (1989/90) 'Empowerment: Human resource management in the '90's', *Management Quarterly*, 30(4): 3–8.

Velthouse, Betty A. (1990) 'Creativity and empowerment: A complementary relationship', *Review of Business*, Fall, 13–18.

Verespej, Michael A. (1991) 'No empowerment without education', *Industry Week*, 240(7): 28–9.

Von der Embse, Thomas J. (1989) 'Transforming power into empowerment', *Manage*, 41(3): 25–8.

Warren, R., Rose, S. and Bergunder, A. (1974) *The Structure of Urban Reform*. Lexington, MA: DC Heath.

Welter, Therese R. (1991a) 'A winning team begins with you', *Industry Week*, 240(9): 35–42.

Welter, Therese R. (1991b) 'America's best plants: Lord Corp', *Industry Week*, 240(20): 44–6.

16 Power and Ethical Action

Frederick Bird and Cynthia Hardy

If business people hope to realize ethical objectives, in many cases they will succeed only if they use political means. Many ethical issues arise in settings where actions are determined in part by the exercise of power to obstruct, delimit, or facilitate what people do. Boards, regulatory agencies, creditors, trade unions, managers, operating committees, and interest groups all wield power. Reformers who seek to bring about responsible business practices need more than good intentions and articulate arguments: they need to discover ways of fending off the influence of those who oppose them and to mobilize support for their proposals.

In some settings, ethics and politics have little to do with each other. Moral concerns guide many aspects of our interpersonal interactions without any regard for power or politics. In situations where we are expected to act honestly, with compassion and respect for others, attempts to exert power will be regarded as unethical. In other cases, however, power may be a necessary and legitimate means of securing ethical ends. This chapter does not tackle the topic of the morality and immorality of politics. We inquire here about a more circumscribed issue: the particular ways in which power and political actions can be used to promote ethical concerns in and among businesses, and the ethical criteria that can be used to guide and evaluate those actions. We argue that there is a need to identify those settings where ethical objectives can only be realized by actions that are fittingly described as political. The failure to acknowledge and act on these political features may lead to actions that are ethically inappropriate.

This chapter first examines the arguments used by individuals to decide if an issue has ethical implications. It shows how these arguments produce different ethical challenges which require action in one of three arenas. Finally, it discusses which situations require the use of power.

This chapter is based in part on research funded by the Social Sciences and Humanities Research Council of Canada to F. Bird for a study of how corporations manage moral issues.

Ethical Arguments

As people engage in moral actions, they explain their conduct by giving reasons that constitute the ethical arguments by which people clarify their own impressions, make up their minds, and weigh competing claims. These reasons are cited to explain why an issue has moral implications and defend the evaluation of the issue, assign priorities, justify actions, and persuade others. Individuals may state these arguments overtly or implicitly; with great sophistication or in simple, ordinary terms. Both individuals and (individuals on behalf of) organizations make these arguments whenever they are identifying and acting on moral issues.

People use diverse arguments in support of their moral positions. They cite respected precedents, name widely held principles, demonstrate worthy consequences, invoke the consensus of relevant actors, refer to trusted authorities, or simply confess that, in good conscience, they simply cannot act otherwise (Bird and Gandz, 1991: chapter 6). Despite this variety, it is possible to distinguish three broad categories that are widely used in business: arguments based on utilitarian considerations, social justice and individual rights (see Cavanagh et al., 1981).

Utilitarianism assesses ethical behaviour by considering which action produces the greatest good for the greatest number. Unethical behaviour, according to this approach, falls short of helping the greatest number or represents inefficient means for doing so. For example, a plant closure may be justified on the basis that it will protect the viability of the larger organization. A philosophy based on *individual rights* links ethical behaviour to the protection of certain rights, such as rights of privacy, free consent, freedom of conscience, free speech and due process. So, a plan to test employees for drug use on the grounds it impedes productivity may be rejected as unethical because individual rights to privacy are violated. *Social justice* identifies ethical behaviour on the grounds of fair treatment for all, a fair application of rules, and fair compensation and restitution. Affirmative action and equal pay programmes may, then, be justified on the grounds that all minorities and both genders deserve fair treatment and compensation (see Velasquez et al., 1983).

The utilitarian argument has been found to be the most common among business managers (Stead et al., 1990). This is not to say, however, that other arguments are not used which may produce contradictory assessments, leaving the individual in an ethical quandary. For example, a reluctance to reschedule Third World debt without the imposition of IMF (International Monetary Fund) austerity measures may be justified as ethical on the grounds that the short-term costs will be outweighed by the long-term advantage of placing the economy on a stable footing. Such action may be seen as unethical, however, when other arguments are employed: on the grounds that the individual rights of the poorer sections of an already poor society will be violated; because Westernized countries were irresponsible in lending the money; or social justice dictates restitution in form of more flexible treatment. Similarly, affirmative action legitimated on the grounds of social justice may be countered by arguing that positive discrimination transgresses individual rights. Even a single utilitarian argument can produce contradictory answers: is a plant closure unethical because it will cause unemployment in an isolated community; ethical because it will save the jobs of workers in other towns; unethical because the work will go to non-unionized labour in another country; or ethical because the resulting fall in prices will benefit consumers and protect profitability?

These moral arguments affect how people evaluate a situation and assess its ethical implications. They do not, however, provide a definitive ethical answer and, ultimately, the decision to act or not act is a matter of personal judgement.

Ethical Challenges

While not providing all the answers, the moral arguments above, nonetheless, help individuals decide whether or not an issue has ethical implications. If so, the issue may translate into one of a number of ethical challenges. Actors must understand the nature of these different ethical challenges if they are to identify the appropriate political actions. Broadly categorized, there are three common ethical challenges, described below.

First, ethical actors want other people to *comply* with particular social rules (see Etzioni, 1961). These rules may assume a variety of forms: from professional codes to policies on business conduct; from laws to administrative ordinances; from religious statutes to ethnic customs. These rules define how members within particular groups are expected to act and they are set forth to secure compliance. Organizations may develop new rules regarding, for example, the protection of trade secrets or conflict of interest, if existing rules are not adequate. These rules define standards which are considered to be obligatory, and people who fail to comply will be regarded as acting immorally and may face negative sanctions.

Second, people become concerned with ethics because they hope to secure *commitment* to more idealistic, general principles, such as justice, integrity, social responsibility, and honesty. These terms express ideals to which it is hoped all people will aspire even if they are able to carry them out only in part. The goal is not strict behavioural compliance but a virtuous disposition and the willingness to aspire to ideals which may not be easily attained.

Third, ethical concerns arise because people *crusade* to bring about certain objective conditions. Here the aim is to bring into being something that is not yet a practical reality. Ethicists have campaigned for a myriad of goals from shorter working days to higher wages; from more generous business

Table 16.1   *Examples of ethical challenges*

Type	Examples of actions
Gaining compliance with social rules	Prosecution for embezzling funds
	Instituting a code of ethics
	Rewarding employees with high attendance records
Fostering commitment to ethical principles	Encouraging organizational loyalty
	Fostering executive integrity
	Rewarding acts of conscience
Crusading to bring about unrealized objectives	Campaigning for sustainable development
	Overcoming discrimination

philanthropy to child labour laws; and from the end of glass ceilings to reduced toxic emissions. Crusaders are reformers, seeking to bring about what they consider to be worthy changes.

The distinctions between these challenges are important because they require markedly different actions (Table 16.1). Thus, the effort to gain compliance with social rules, which typically involves some form of monitoring and policing overt conduct, differs from efforts to secure commitment, which are aimed at inspiring identification and idealism. In fact, in organizational settings strong commitment is usually negatively correlated to the close surveillance used to gain compliance (Glisson and Durick, 1988). Similarly, efforts to bring about broadly based commitment differ from the mobilization of support for a particular crusade.

In summary, we have identified three broad ethical challenges: ensuring that behaviour conforms to existing standards; securing commitment to ethical ideals; and campaigning for new, valued objectives. As we shall see, these challenges take place in one of three different arenas.

Arenas of Ethical Action

When people undertake moral actions, they may do so as private individuals interacting with others; as members of a particular organization; or as representatives of organizations in relation to others. We use the term 'arena' to identify where the action is located. In practical terms this typology can be used to identify the extent to which decisive actions with respect to a particular ethical challenge are likely to take place in interpersonal interaction, and interactions within or between organizations.

First, many ethical actions are primarily an *individual* matter. When individuals decide whether to work for a company that manufactures arms or tobacco, they are making private and individual judgements. If they decide to befriend a co-worker that, too, is an individual matter. The extent to which managers are candid, attentive, and loyal to each other is determined, for the most part, by their personal interactions. Organizations may seek out employees who are conscientious, courageous, disciplined, reliable and prudent but the degree to which employees exhibit these traits is the result of their own personal character, formed as a result of their experiences, temperament and upbringing. Similarly, unethical action is sometimes a purely personal matter.

Second, many ethical concerns arise at the *organizational* level, in the context of the relationship of individuals to their organization and the corresponding relationship of the organization to the individuals by which it is constituted. These relationships represent a series of interactions concerning the responsibilities and entitlements of each party as well as activities concerning the organization as a whole. Diverse moral concerns arise at this level – such as the relationships between superiors and subordinates; ways to gain compliance and commitment from organizational members; and the accountability of those making organizational decisions.

Organizations effectively establish ethical expectations for their members – formally, informally, or sometimes, by default. Within this organizational arena, members may fail to live up to normative expectations in the ways described below (Bird and Gandz, 1991: chapter 2).

Non-role acts are inconsistent with organizational definitions of the individual's role. They are not approved by the organization and are often illegal. They include such actions as cheating on expense accounts, embezzling funds, stealing supplies, insider trading, and conflict of interest activities. By engaging in such action, individuals are failing to comply with recognized standards in order to benefit themselves.

Role distortion occurs when individuals distort their role mandates in ways incompatible with broader moral standards in order to benefit the organization. Examples include bribery to secure contracts, pirating computer software, contravening work safety regulations, unjustified differential pricing, falsifying safety and environmental test results, and manipulating suppliers. When such acts of noncompliance are publicized, they receive widespread public condemnation but they are often 'encouraged' by organizational performance pressures and by management turning a blind eye. Even when such acts contravene formal ethical codes of conduct, organizational members may be well aware that to carry out their job successfully, they have to break certain rules and that the 'code' represents the organization's legal safety net if the individual is caught.

Role failure involves the failure to act in accordance with 'ideal' role expectations. Employees and managers may take the easy way out instead of confronting the issue. For example, managers fail: to carry out accurate performance appraisals; to fire incompetent individuals; to take on unreasonable unions demands; or to speak out against proposals in order to avoid conflict, extra work or unpleasant consequences. There is no financial gain, but the organization may suffer as a result of an individual's desire for an 'easy life'. On the other hand, the organization may have contributed to the problem by failing to provide the support necessary to facilitate a problem-solving, proactive response. In the examples above, managers may not act because their experience in the organization indicates one or more of the following: no action will be taken regarding negative performance appraisals; positive performance appraisals may lead to a promotion for the individual concerned but no replacement for the short-staffed department at the losing end; no action has ever been taken to help or get rid of incompetent individuals in the past; senior executives have a track record of caving in to union demands; and criticism of senior management's proposals is rarely taken seriously. Role failure thus represents a lack of commitment to ethical ideals by organizational members.

The third arena of ethical action is *interorganizational*. It concerns the relationships between organizations and their stakeholders – other organizations and groups whose interests influence organizational members (Bird and Gandz, 1991: chapter 3). Included here are ethical concerns that arise as part of a firm's relationship to trade unions, professional associations, trade associations, creditors, investors, shareholders, regulatory agencies, consumer protection groups, customers, suppliers, local and national governments, environmental activists and civil rights groups. Each of these stakeholders makes claims upon an organization which, correspondingly, makes counter-claims on them. Ethical questions arise concerning how these claims are managed in relation to the agreements between the various parties.

Firms may respond in one of several ways to the claims made by stakeholder groups (Bird and Gandz, 1991: chapter 3). In some cases, they may meet those claims in full, but in others they fail to do so, thus raising ethical concerns. For example, it is often in the interests of businesses to **resist** the claims of stakeholders. The US tobacco firms have defended themselves against health concerns by manipulating information to downplay and challenge the evidence linking cancer to smoking. They also directly confronted the regulatory body and stopped its attempt to ban cigarette advertising (see Miles, 1982). As a result, health concerns initially raised in the 1950s did not translate into an advertising ban until 1970 when fragmented opposition groups had sufficiently mobilized to counter the power of the tobacco firms.

Another form of noncompliance arises in the interorganizational arena when organizations simply **avoid** the claims of stakeholders by ignoring any demands for changes in their behaviour. **Tokenism** occurs when organizations make minor concessions to pressure groups in an attempt to avoid larger ones, or try to coopt dissident stakeholders in the hope of heading off confrontation,

Table 16.2 *Ethical challenges in the three arenas*

Ethical challenge	Individual	Organizational	Interorganizational
Compliance	keeping promises	tackling non-role acts and role distortion, e.g. ethical codes, internal audits	tackling resistance and avoidance, e.g. regulations, prosecutions
Commitment	acting with integrity, courage	tackling role failure, e.g. instilling ethical integrity in the organization	tackling tokenism, e.g. ensuring corporate responsibility
Crusades	persuading a co-worker to contribute to a cause	forming a 'glass ceiling' taskforce or a 'green' team	campaign to promote sustainable development

perhaps by allowing representatives of workers or community groups to sit on the board. Such stalling tactics reflect a lack of commitment on the part of the organization to act on the ethical concerns of its stakeholders.

The Ethical Grid

It is possible to combine the distinctions we have made with respect to ethical challenges and arenas for action to identify the varied yet distinctive range of ethical concerns. Challenges concerning compliance, commitment, and crusades can arise in any of the three arenas and necessitate different forms of ethical action (Table 16.2). The ethical grid helps to identify the different settings in which ethical concerns arise and to distinguish the kinds of ethical actions that are called for. This grid provides a backdrop against which we can examine the appropriateness of political means to further ethical concerns.

Power and Political Action

Political action occurs when power is mobilized (e.g. Pettigrew, 1973; Pfeffer 1981; Hardy, 1985; Hickson et al., 1986), in this case, to affect ethical issues. It includes individual and group efforts either to change or maintain the status quo in the form of specific actions and broad policies. Power is defined as a force that influences outcomes. It may be employed in the face of resistance

(Weber, 1978) and it can be used for both moral and immoral purposes. Three sources of power are discussed below.

Resource power: many writers have focused on how the control of scarce resources confers power (e.g. Emerson, 1962; Hickson et al., 1971; Pettigrew, 1973; Pfeffer and Salancik, 1978). The behaviour of others can be influenced by providing or withholding such resources as rewards, punishments, information, expertise, political access, and the ability to deal with uncertainty. It varies from the coercive use of force to avoid and/or punish behaviour to the use of rewards to induce actions. It also includes a less direct manipulation of resources such as using information to present a particular picture or expertise to favour a particular outcome. This form of power corresponds to Lukes' (1974) first dimension of power which is used overtly and directly on behaviour.

Process power is embedded in the administrative and judicial processes that prevail in a society or organization which institutionalize certain behaviours in a less visible way. Bachrach and Baratz (1962) examined this second dimension of power (Lukes, 1974) in the form of nondecision-making, in which access to decision-making arenas and control of agendas is used to screen contentious issues out of the political process and defend the status quo. Process power can also be used proactively – the introduction of new procedures, participants and agendas legitimates and encourages different viewpoints and behaviours; while changing systems and procedures can help to embody new practices and goals. Although the process may be backed up by rewards and punishments, it is the acceptance of and participation in the process that constitutes power.

Meaning power exists in the ability to define the situation (Goffman, 1959) – by managing meaning in such a way that others accept certain priorities (Pettigrew, 1979). It corresponds to Lukes' (1974) third dimension of power. Change often involves redefining reality – raising consciousness – so that the existing state of affairs is no longer taken for granted and individuals become aware of new possibilities (e.g. Freire, 1992). It involves the legitimation of new issues and the delegitimation of existing priorities, through the use of symbols, rituals and myths (see Pfeffer, 1981; Hardy, 1985).

We can, then, identify three ways in which power affects outcomes (which loosely correspond to Lukes' three dimensions). It would be wrong to suggest that they are nice, neat classifications. For example, information can be used both as a resource and to confer legitimacy. Nor are they mutually exclusive: a change may be brought about by redefining reality at the same time as processes are modified to reflect and promote that new reality, and resources are used to bring behaviour into line with the new processes. One source of power that deserves special mention in this regard is people power, which can fall into any or all of the three categories: people represent resources in the event of a strike or boycott; when new individuals and coalitions secure access to decision-making processes, these people constitute process power; and the identification of important individuals with change uses people to influence meaning. So, this categorization is not a taxonomy of power but an indication of its multi-dimensionality.

Table 16.3   *The politics of ethical action: arena of action*

Ethical challenge	Individual	Organizational	Interorganizational
Compliance	apolitical	resource power vs. non-role acts	resource power vs. resistance
		process power vs. role distortion	process power vs. avoidance
Commitment	apolitical	apolitical	apolitical
Crusades	apolitical	meaning power then process power; resource power as a back-up	meaning power then process power; resource power as a back-up

The Politics of Ethical Action

Some forms of ethical action are apolitical. The individual arena is by its nature apolitical: rarely do people use power to persuade friends or sort out personal loyalties. In fact, it has been argued that trying to make this individual arena political constitutes immoral behaviour, and ethics and politics should be clearly separated (e.g. Niebuhr, 1931). In the remaining two arenas, however, we contend that ethical challenges can rarely be met without some exercise of power (see Table 16.3).

In the organizational arena, political action is often required to secure compliance with organizational standards, rules and regulations. Resource power may be used to discourage noncompliance in the form of non-role acts through the punishment of offenders and/or the rewards of adherents. To avoid role distortion, process power must be mobilized in the form of internal audits, performance appraisal, reporting procedures, etc. to ensure that ethical, and not unethical, behaviour is identified and encouraged.

Complete compliance to ethical ideals, on the other hand, involves a personal commitment to organizational values (Westley and Bird, 1992). Rules and regulations often serve only to identify minimum standards. In fact, more coercive measures such as punishments and constraining processes may only alienate employees and provoke strategems designed to conceal instances of noncompliance (Jackall, 1988; Culbert and McDonough, 1980; Waters, 1978). Accordingly, organizations are unlikely to secure total commitment and eliminate role failure through the use of power. Instead they will have to rely on enhancing the ethical integrity of organizational members in other ways, such as more careful screening and hiring practices or by developing mutual trust.

Attempts to bring about ethical crusades necessarily call for the use of power, both to counter the influence of those who might oppose these changes and to mobilize support for them. Crusades for greater employment equity, more responsive environmental policies, higher safety standards, and worker participation encounter resistance for a variety of reasons: from sincere objections to fear of change to concern for vested interests. Successful campaigns are typically associated with organized efforts of groups to push for change even in the face of opposition. As the Organization Development literature will attest, the management of system-wide change in organizations is difficult. It often fails because change agents ignore the political implications of their plans (e.g. Huff, 1980), and change relating to ethical issues is no exception. There is a need, as a result, for the development of a political strategy that makes use of the appropriate power sources. Simply announcing new standards and expecting people to conform to them is unlikely to be the secret of success. First, change agents should consider the power of meaning to legitimate the particular ethical issue and secure support for it. Following a successful redefinition of the situation, new processes can be institutionalized to support the new objectives. Resource power may be necessary to provide an extra motivation for change but, used alone, it will not bring about a successful crusade for new ethical standards.

The interorganizational arena is also often political: stakeholders wishing to ensure compliance or change on the part of a particular organization will have to mobilize power. Noncompliance in the form of resistance can be countered by resource power. Observers debate whether rewards or coercion are most appropriate: rewards elevate the cost of good behaviour; while penalties increase the inclination to find loopholes. Trying to manage meaning is futile in this situation because organizations are actively fighting attempts to define issues as 'non-ethical', as in the case of the tobacco firms mentioned earlier. Organizations engaged in resistance are also unlikely to cooperate willingly with procedures and processes and are, instead, probably looking for ways to circumvent them – as in the case of the tobacco firms refusing to release marketing data to the Federal Trade Commission (Miles, 1982). As a result, resource power is all that is left to modify behaviour. Avoidance, on the other hand, is more passive and can be overcome with new processes that prevent the organization taking the easy way out. For example, Dow Corning did nothing throughout the 1980s in response to safety concerns regarding silicone breast implants. Once these medical devices were brought under the responsibility of the Food and Drug Administration, however, they were required to supply safety data. Unable to do so, the company voluntarily ceased production of the implants.

Commitment problems arise when the organization is following the letter but not the spirit of stakeholder demands: tokenism indicates that the organization is not convinced of the need for a sincere response to stakeholders. As in the case of commitment inside the organization, power can rarely be used to plug all the loopholes, so commitment to broader ethical ideals will ultimately rely on the apolitical goodwill of the organization concerned.

Crusades for change in the interorganizational arena are as problematic as system-wide change inside an organization. Change in an organizational domain often occurs only as new stakeholders are admitted, and the domain becomes more organized, facilitating collaboration. Gray (1989) has shown how a domain organizes as new stakeholders are incorporated, values and objectives are mutually defined and infrastructures are implemented. This process relies first on the management of meaning (Trist, 1983) to define the issue and unite stakeholders, followed by process power to institutionalize interorganizational relations and objectives. Resource power is only used as a back-up to support the joint infrastructure. For example, environmentally responsible behaviour has been brought about as the environment has been redefined as a relevant, societal concern in recent years; as new processes and procedures (such as round tables, 'green' board members) have been put into place; and as both formal and informal (such as bad press) penalties for pollution have been increased.

In summary, while ethics is often considered a personal matter, it is argued here that to understand ethical action or inaction, it helps to examine the distribution of power and political dynamics of the organizational and interorganizational arenas in which the action takes place.

Conclusions: The Ethics of Political Action

While a decision to act ethically is ultimately a matter of personal judgement, many ethical challenges – the successful implementation of ethical action in an organizational or interorganizational arena – are also a political challenge. To engage in effective ethical action, a number of key questions must be addressed and acted upon:

- Is this an ethical issue and, if so, do I want to take ethical action?
- If I want to take action, in which arena should I act?
- What are the political dynamics of that particular arena?
- Which political strategy should I use to act effectively in that arena?
- How do I secure and use power to carry the strategy out?

Up to this point we have primarily analysed the use of political means to realize ethically defined objectives. We will now reverse this analysis to use ethical criteria to evaluate the use of political means. First, the political means ought to be proportionate to the ethical objectives. If we have decided to act because of our concerns about utilitarian objectives, social justice or individual rights then the exercise of power must be judged accordingly. The use of power must be tempered with reference to whether it is beneficial, fair, and does not transgress individual rights. When political means are disproportionately low, actors will be overpowered and unable to realize their objectives. If political means are disproportionately high, actors will overpower others in ways that are unlikely to be inconsistent with their own ethical objectives – that is, they will end up manipulating or coercing others, disregarding their rights and claims to justice.

Second, there is a need to strike a balance between being effective and conscientious, pragmatic and principled. Max Weber (1978) referred to two kinds of political ethics: the ethics of responsibility, which is pragmatic and realistic; and the ethics of ultimate ends, which tends to be utopian and idealistic. He pointed out that the most effective politicians were those who combined both. Political action dominated by pragmatism loses its moral soul: those with power hypocritically cite moral language to legitimate their own interests and manipulate others. Too much emphasis on political idealism can lead to futile, rhetorical goals that are admirable but unattainable.

Political action that is both proportionate and balanced is most likely to be open: actors will be able to learn from their mistakes and adjust their means and objectives in response to changing circumstances. Rarely do people get it right the first time they employ a particular strategy or tactic, and it is difficult to determine the real impact of political action until it has been seen in practice. Ethical actors must be ready to interpret and utilize feedback – political action can and ought to be a way of learning from others.

References

Astley, W.G., and Sachdeva, P.S. (1984) 'Structural sources of intraorganizational power', *Academy of Management Review*, 9(1): 104–13.

Bachrach, P. and Baratz, M.S. (1962) 'The two faces of power', *American Political Science Review*, 56: 947–52.

Bird, F. and Gandz, J. (1991) *Good Management*. Englewood Cliffs, NJ: Prentice-Hall.

Cavanagh, G. et al. (1981) 'The ethics of organizational politics', *Academy of Management Review*, 6(3): 363–74.

Culbert, S. and McDonough, J. (1980) *The Invisible War: Pursuing Self Interests at Work*. New York: John Wiley.

Emerson, M. (1962) 'Power–dependence relations', *American Sociological Review*, 27(1): 31–41.

Etzioni, A. (1961) *A Comparative Analysis of Complex Organizations*. New York: Free Press.

Freire, P. (1992) *Pedagogy of the Oppressed*. New York: Continuum.

Glisson C. and Durick, A. (1988) 'Predictors of job satisfaction and organizational commitment in human services organizations', *Administrative Science Quarterly*, 33(1): 61–81.

Goffman, E. (1959) *The Presentation of Self in Everyday Life*. New York: Doubleday.

Gray, B. (1989) *Collaborating*. San Francisco: Jossey-Bass.

Hardy, C. (1985) 'The nature of unobtrusive power', *Journal of Management Studies*, 22(4): 384–99.

Hickson, D. et al. (1971) 'A strategic contingencies theory of intraorganizational power', *Administrative Science Quarterly*, 16(2): 216–29.

Hickson, D. et al. (1986) *Top Decisions*. San Francisco: Jossey-Bass.

Huff, A. (1980) 'Organizations as political systems: Implications for diagnosis, change, and stability', in T.G. Cummings (ed.), *Systems Theory for Organization Development*. London: Wiley.

Jackall, R. (1988) *Moral Mazes: The World of Corporate Managers*. New York: Oxford University Press.

Lukes, S. (1974) *Power: A Radical View*. London: Macmillan.

Miles, R. (1982) *Coffin Nails and Corporate Strategies*. Englewood Cliffs, NJ: Prentice-Hall.

Niebuhr, R. (1931) *Moral Man and Immoral Society*. New York: Scribners.

Pettigrew, A. (1973) *The Politics of Organizational Decision Making*. London: Tavistock.

Pettigrew, A.M. (1979) 'On studying organizational cultures', *Administrative Science Quarterly*, 24: 570–81.

Pfeffer, J. (1981) *Power in Organizations*. Marshfield, Mass.: Pitman.

Pfeffer, J. and Salancik, G. (1978) *The External Control of Organizations*. New York: Harper & Row.

Stead, W.E. et al. (1990) 'An integrative model for understanding and managing ethical behaviour in business organizations', *Journal of Business Ethics*, 9(3): 233–42.

Trist, E. (1983) 'Referent organizations and the development of interorganizational domains', *Human Relations*, 36(2): 269–84.

Velasquez, M. et al. (1983) 'Organizational statesmanship and dirty politics: Ethical guidelines for the organizational politician', *Organizational Dynamics*, 12: 65–80.

Waters, J. (1978) 'Catch 20.2', *Organizational Dynamics*, Spring, 3–19.

Weber, M. (1978) *Economy and Society*, edited by Roth and Wittich. Berkeley: University of California Press.

Westley, F. (1990) 'The eye of the needle: Cultural and personal transformation in a traditional organization', *Human Relations*, 43(3): 273–93.

Westley, F. and Bird, F. (1992) 'The sociology of organizational commitment', unpublished.

PART II CASES

Daniel and the Lions' Den

Born and raised in Brazil, Daniel had had extensive overseas experience before entering McGill University's MBA programme in Montreal. After an undergraduate degree in engineering in Brazil, he joined a non-profit organization that managed student exchange programmes for three years. During this time, he worked in a variety of different countries, acquired a broad experience in different aspects of international business and perfected his language skills. He spoke English, French, Portuguese, Spanish and Italian. He moved to the headquarters of the organization, where he was responsible for extending the exchange programme to India. In his final year, he decided to take advantage of one of the programmes himself, and was admitted to a three-month internship with the New York office of an international consulting firm – Mitchell & Associates. It turned into a three-year appointment, following which he became a student at McGill University.

During the final year of his studies at McGill in late 1988, Daniel decided to pursue job opportunities in Europe. He did not want to return to Brazil, nor did he particularly want to stay in North America any longer. He felt that his personality, background, languages and business education would fit well in a European context. He decided to arrange an interview at the European office of Mitchell & Associates located in Brussels, which he had learned about while working for Mitchell & Associates in New York, over the Christmas vacation.

Mitchell & Associates had originated in the UK, which remained one of the most important divisions. It now had over 100 offices worldwide, of which more than half covered all the European countries. Offices were organized nationally: Mitchell-UK, Mitchell-US, Mitchell-France, etc. Through his contacts in the New York Office, Daniel knew that the European Office was distinct from the other offices in Europe (including the Belgian Office). It was, in effect, a joint venture of several offices to present a 'common face' and conduct business with the European Commission (EC) in Brussels. It

---

Case prepared from original research by Professor Cynthia Hardy, Faculty of Management, McGill University. All names are disguised. Case not to be reproduced without permission.

originated as an information point for other European offices but had slowly started to deliver services to the European Commission and become an office its own right. It had recently won a contract worth $4 million to create and manage, on behalf of the European Commission, a service that would train and provide information about the upcoming 'Single Market' to small and medium-sized enterprises in the twelve member states. Responsibilities included training and briefing national officers who coordinated 200 centres across Europe, and setting up a centralized structure in Brussels to answer queries and provide information. On the basis of this success, Mitchell-Europe was looking to expand its consulting division.

Daniel received a letter saying that the company would be delighted to meet with him when he was in Brussels. When he arrived at Mitchell-Europe, he found himself being interviewed by an Austrian woman whom he had met while working for the non-profit organization. Bianca had been a close friend in those days and, although they had lost touch in the intervening five years, they immediately felt at ease with each other again.

Bianca explained to Daniel that Mitchell & Associates wanted to extend its European business through more commercial contracts with the Commission and related private companies. The European office was, at this point, a cost centre subsidized by Mitchell-UK, Mitchell-US and Mitchell-France, though it was intended to become a profit centre through the generation of additional business. It had only recently been established as a joint venture with a firm owned by a British lawyer who had been in Brussels for some time. Of the 35 people in the office, 30 were originally from the law firm. Mitchell's aim was to exploit the lawyer's extensive network of contacts to establish a permanent presence in Europe. Bianca and her boss, a Welshman named David, were Mitchell employees responsible for managing the joint venture. Bianca was enthusiastic about the potential of the European office – it was the up and coming place to be. There was lots of flexibility and with Europe 1992 around the corner, it was where the action was. She told Daniel that his international experience and business training might look extremely attractive to Mitchell & Associates. The office was currently dominated by political scientists and lawyers from the law firm: Mitchell wanted both to increase the number of their 'own' people and to place a greater emphasis on a commercial consulting orientation.

She also spoke at length about her boss, David, who had been not only a knowledgeable and exciting colleague but also a protective and effective mentor for her. They were very close since she had gone to Mitchell-Europe with David to set up the joint venture. She respected him professionally and liked him personally. With him in charge, Bianca was convinced that the European Office would be a success and that, if hired, Daniel would also benefit from David's expertise and mentoring.

At the end of the interview, Daniel was excited about the prospect of working for Mitchell & Associates. Having found an old friend to fill in a lot of the information was an added bonus. Daniel trusted Bianca's judgement and he decided this was the job he wanted.

Bianca was also impressed with Daniel – she felt she knew him well enough to guarantee that he would be valuable asset to the company, and his profile was exactly what they were looking for. David was not in Brussels at the time of the interview and so it was impossible to arrange for the two men to meet. Instead, she forwarded a positive report to David's boss – an Englishman called Gerard who was nominally in charge of the European Office but was practically based in the UK most of the time. Gerard knew that it would be best for any new hire to the European Office to be approved by David and he wrote back to Daniel, saying that he should arrange to meet him.

At this point, the informality and uncertainty that characterized the fledgling European Office started to show itself. David seemed to spend most of his time travelling and the company seemed unwilling or unable to organize a formal interview. Growing increasingly frustrated, Daniel decided to take the initiative. He learned that David was scheduled to be in New York. He made an appointment to see him through his secretary and went, at his own expense, to New York. Unfortunately, David was tied up in meetings and Daniel spent the entire day kicking his heels in the New York Office. He despondently flew back to Montreal without having seen David.

Determined not to give up, he called Bianca who spoke to Gerard on his behalf. Speaking to Daniel on the phone, Gerard suggested an alternative route: Daniel would be interviewed by Brendan, another Englishman, who was seconded to the Mitchell Office in Washington, DC for a few years. Gerard trusted Brendan to make a conclusive evaluation of Daniel's potential and, at this point, agreed to cover Daniel's expenses for the trip.

Brendan would return to the UK after his Washington appointment so, if hired, Daniel would not be working for him. The fact that he was in Washington, however, was a sign that he was a 'high flyer' since those destined for the top of the UK hierarchy were typically sent to North America for some North American 'experience'. The two men got on well during the interview and Brendan confirmed much of the same excitement associated with the European operations that Bianca had conveyed. He pointed out, however, that there was a downside to the growth, potential and excitement – there would be a lot of uncertainty as 'things shook down'. He gave Daniel some tips about specific expertise to acquire and also talked about another side to David. Brendan explained that David was a 'hands off' manager, creative and full of ideas but often 'all over the place'. He was absent much of the time due to the extensive travelling he had to do. Brendan also pointed out that while David could be stimulating and energizing, he did not fit the profile of a dependable mentor – he was too busy thinking up new ideas and acting on new initiatives to protect subordinates effectively.

Daniel latched on to the excitement of the European office but dismissed the warnings concerning David's management style. He believed Bianca had more experience of what it was like to work for David than Brendan did. He knew her well enough to trust her judgement over Brendan's whom he had only just met. He also thought that, with two years of MBA training, he would be able to handle most business situations, and did not need much support.

Brendan had been impressed by Daniel and wrote a favourable report on him to Gerard, on the basis of which Daniel received an offer of employment. The contract was very specific about legal details such as holiday allowances, working days and other technical details. Daniel was very pleased with the salary which, at $70,000, was more than 50 per cent higher than the typical MBA salary. The details concerning his specific responsibilities were rather more vague, reflecting the uncertainty of the situation in the office. It stated that he would be based in the European Office working on projects concerning the strategic analysis of European integration and would be reporting to David. The contract he signed on arrival in Brussels had no more detail – it promised a separate annex that would contain information on his responsibilities but Daniel never received it. The contract did, however, specify a six-month trial period. According to Belgian law, Mitchell & Associates were required to provide a six-month probationary period, at the end of which they were obliged to keep Daniel or let him go if he proved unsatisfactory. Daniel was surprised by the trial period – he hadn't been expecting one – but was reassured when informed it was a legal technicality. Besides, he was enthused by the prospects of the new job and confident of his own abilities – he did not anticipate any problems and was convinced a permanent position would be a simple formality.

By the time Daniel arrived in July 1989, however, a number of changes had occurred. First, Mitchell & Associates were trying to buy out the lawyer. The company was uncomfortable with a situation in which they did not have a voting majority and felt that, to exploit the European potential, they needed to have more control. Their aim was to buy out the lawyer; keep the majority of his employees; build up the number of 'Mitchell people' in the office; and concentrate on developing private sector consulting assignments. Daniel felt that this situation would be to his advantage as a newly hired 'Mitchell person' with experience in private sector consulting assignments in the USA. Daniel was immediately incorporated into a number of existing projects. David told him to do his best and, once the situation with the British lawyer was settled, they would talk again about his goals.

Shortly before Daniel's arrival, Panos – a Greek who was part of the European Office as an original employee of the lawyer – had been promoted. For some projects, Daniel was required to report to Panos who, in turn, reported to David. Panos was feeling somewhat threatened by this situation. First, he wanted to ensure his future with Mitchell & Associates which meant 'changing sides' from the lawyer's group to the Mitchell group. Second, while he had some years of experience on the European scene, he did not have an MBA, did not speak as many languages as Daniel, was only a couple of months older, and was being paid about the same salary as Daniel, even after his promotion. Hence, Panos viewed Daniel's appointment with some concern and had not been particularly welcoming or friendly. Daniel had been warned that Panos might find his presence threatening but dismissed it, believing that Panos's behaviour was the result of personality differences. He thought that Panos would be a natural ally, despite these differences, as they both needed to demonstrate their suitability in the new Mitchell environment. He also assumed that David would be looking after his interests.

Questions

- Do you think Daniel is suited to this job?
- Would you have accepted this job?
- How would you handle Panos now?

Crown Corporation

As she prepared to return to work after the New Year's holiday, Antonia was reviewing her first two months at Crown Corporation, and wondering what to do next. She knew she faced some difficult challenges and wanted to take some time to prepare a plan of action.

Crown Corporation was a provincial, state-owned enterprise in one of Canada's provinces. Crown Corporation had been created by an Act of Parliament in the 1960s. The provincial government was Crown Corporation's sole shareholder and it was responsible to the Minister of Consumer Services, though various aspects of its operations fell under the authority of other ministries. The Board of Directors were all appointed by the provincial government, as were the chairman and president. Vice-presidents were appointed by the Board. In 1991, Crown Corporation had over 4,000 employees and a net income of over $200 million on revenues of nearly $2 billion. Return on equity for 1991 was 12 per cent, up from 8 per cent the previous year.

Antonia had joined the Treasury Division of Crown Corporation as manager of Corporate Finance in November 1991, following several years with a major Canadian bank in another province. Her role had been to liaise with the federal government on their banking policies since Canadian banks operate in a highly regulated environment. As a result, she had extensive knowledge of government banking relations at the federal level. As far as Crown Corporation was concerned, however, she was new to the job, the corporation, and the province. It translated into a formidable set of challenges both inside and outside Crown Corporation.

The External Environment

The province operated a relatively centralized model of borrowing on behalf of all its crown corporations and ministries. All debt issued in the province was issued directly by the Provincial Treasury of the Ministry of Finance on behalf of the Province. The Minister then 'onlended' the funds to the crown corporations. The legislation allowed the Finance Minister to exercise direct control over the financial management of its crown corporations beyond

---

Case prepared by Professor Cynthia Hardy, Faculty of Management, McGill University, based on original research. Names and some facts have been disguised. Case not to be reproduced without permission.

borrowing activities. Taken to the extreme, it meant that the Ministry of Finance could act as the 'treasury' for all crown corporations and ministries, though the practice had been to delegate some of these powers to the individual entities.

During the 1970s, Crown Corporation had exercised considerable control over its financial management compared to many other state-owned enterprises because of its large size (representing 50 per cent of all outstanding provincial debt). During this time, Crown Corporation had borrowed under its own name (though under guarantee of the provincial government), and had a large Treasury staff to carry out these functions. During the 1980s, much of the borrowing function had been transferred to the provincial government, and the size of Crown Corporation's Treasury department had decreased accordingly – it became more of a bookkeeping operation with very little emphasis on borrowing and debt management.

In 1987, under a new President and Vice-president (Finance), Crown Corporation started a move to carry out its own borrowing once again. The number and qualifications of treasury staff were increased, and a strategic plan regarding debt management was formulated. A new Treasurer, appointed in 1990 to carry out this strategy, made a number of new appointments. In 1991, Crown Corporation had a Treasury staff of 18, headed by the Treasurer and supported by four departmental managers (one of whom was Antonia). The mandate of the Treasury was to carry out all the analysis and strategy related to borrowing and other Treasury operations. The crucial area of borrowing was carried out in the department of Debt Management, which fell under Antonia's jurisdiction (see the organization chart, Figure 1).

The scope of Crown Corporation's operations were laid out in a *Memorandum of Understanding* between Crown Corporation and the Minister of Finance, which had been signed in 1990. It provided Crown Corporation with some autonomy, but most of this independence resulted from the way in which the Minister implemented the agreement. In other words, should the Minister choose to operate in strict accordance with the agreement, Crown Corporation's autonomy would be severely curtailed. Crown Corporation's aim was to protect the autonomy it had already achieved, and secure additional freedom to extend its Treasury operations, particularly in the area of borrowing and debt management.

In 1991, a new provincial government had been elected, which had two major consequences for Crown Corporation. First, a new Board of Directors had been appointed in early 1992. It involved 14 individuals, many of whom had no previous experience with crown corporations, and included two trade unionists, a professor of women's studies, a real estate proprietor, a former cabinet minister, a retired farmer, a lawyer, and a social worker. The Board had to approve all of Crown Corporation's policies, many of which were reviewed annually, including the overall debt policy. Second, the new government had commissioned an external study of all its crown corporations, which had recommended further centralization of fiscal responsibilities. Crown Corporation was trying to counter this move by arguing the following: due to

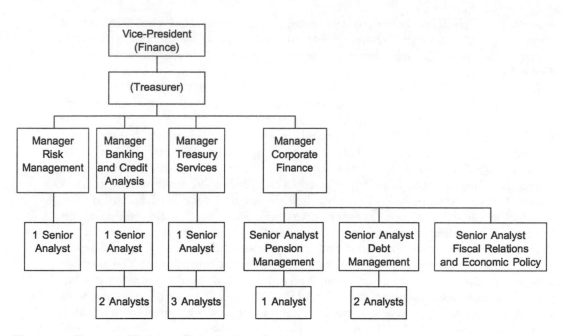

Figure 1   *Treasury Division: Organization chart*

the large and sophisticated nature of its operation, a large and highly qualified staff was required to manage its debt; the Provincial Treasury had over 100 'clients' (ministries and other crown corporations) and could not devote the necessary time to its specialized needs; Crown Corporation was sufficiently large and well recognized to operate independently on financial matters; autonomy in debt management would allow Crown Corporation to add value on its financial transactions which, in turn, would benefit the province through savings and more sophisticated debt management.

The proposed move towards centralization had led to an increase in the tension in the working relationship between government officials and senior management at Crown Corporation. A meeting between the two sides on this issue had recently taken place, which had resulted in an acrimonious encounter between the Deputy Minister of Finance and his assistant deputy, the senior civil servants in the Provincial Treasury, and the Vice-president (Finance) and the Treasurer of Crown Corporation. It had culminated in a shouting match during which the Vice-president (Finance) had antagonized officials by saying he didn't believe they were capable of doing a good job. Antonia knew this was not the way to protect Crown Corporation's financial autonomy, let alone increase it. While she did not normally deal directly with these highest levels of government, she had been hired for her understanding of government relations and so might be able to influence the Treasurer. It was certainly in her interests to do so – if the provincial government decided to centralize financial borrowing, it would mean the virtual annihilation of her department. So far, Antonia had dealt only with civil servants below the level of deputy minister, but had experienced no bad feelings. Nor, as far as she knew, had her staff, who got on well with their provincial counterparts.

Antonia was also aware that the government had created a Secretariat to review its crown corporations. It was engaged in a broad study of all aspects of operations and services. Crown Corporation was currently preparing its brief for the Secretariat.

The Internal Environment

Antonia, as Manager of Corporate Finance, was responsible for assisting the Treasurer in the formulation, development and implementation of a range of Treasury policies, systems, procedures, standards and controls in the area of fiscal relations and economic policy, pension and investment management, and debt management, in accordance with corporate requirements, legislation and generally accepted accounting principles. She was also responsible for liaising with ministerial staff and developing strategies to deal effectively with sensitive and/or politically charged issues. Her subordinates consisted of six professionals – three managers and three analysts. They were highly specialized, technical professionals. Antonia was able to understand the output of their work but was not actually qualified to do it. As a result, she was highly dependent on their analysis to carry out her role of developing general policies. She saw herself as the 'big picture guy' and did not feel it would be effective to become involved in the minute details of her employees' work. Her subordinates were unionized and, as a result, their salaries and working conditions were controlled by labour agreements, over which Antonia had no direct influence. Antonia's appointment had represented the insertion of a new layer between her staff and the Treasurer. Her subordinates had previously reported directly to the Treasurer and Antonia's arrival effectively 'demoted' them, although their job scales had not changed. In fact, while officially above these individuals in the hierarchy, Antonia's position was at an equivalent scale to one of her managers and only one level above the other two.

Antonia had the full backing of her boss – the Treasurer – who had hired her (following a year-long search) for her managerial and people skills both to manage her department, which would increase in importance as the corporation reclaimed its financial autonomy, and to improve government relations in order to secure this autonomy. While the Treasurer was supportive of Antonia, he nevertheless presented one problem – his propensity to 'micro manage' the work of others. His financial expertise equipped him to intervene in much of the technical work of Treasury employees, which often left them frustrated at their inability to do their work for themselves.

Antonia's arrival at Crown Corporation had coincided with a reorganization of the Treasury orchestrated by the Treasurer, who had wanted to 'shake things up'. It had been designed to give added emphasis to certain areas. Of particular importance was debt management, which constituted 80 per cent of Antonia's responsibilities. As a result, Antonia was a visible member of the 'new guard', particularly since she was junior to most of her peers by at least fifteen years. Antonia's extrovert and personable nature had enabled her to establish good relations with her peer managers. Unfortunately, the personal rapport had not produced effective working relationships. Of particular concern was the role of Treasury Services. The reorganization had meant that its mandate as a service department was not clarified. Antonia needed the support of Treasury Services to carry out analysis for Debt Management, which was short on personnel. Attempts to secure such support had proved unsuccessful and had compounded the friction Antonia was encountering with her own staff. As the Treasurer sought to upgrade the activities of the Treasury as part of the move to reclaim responsibility from the government, job definitions were changing and people, especially those in Debt Management, were being asked to do more and different things. The constraints of out-of-date job definitions and resentment at the insertion of a new level in the hierarchy were manifesting themselves in an unwillingness to get the job done.

Questions

- On whom is Antonia dependent to carry out her job effectively?
- What sources of influence does she have?
- What would you advise her to do?

Northville Area Health Authority

In 1977, managers in charge of administering Northville Area Health Authority (AHA), which covered a large city in the north of England, were preparing plans to close Park Road Maternity Hospital. Northville AHA was part of the British National Health Service (NHS), which is a nationalized health care system funded by central government. The NHS structure that existed at that time is summarized in Figure 1.

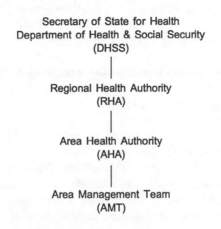

Secretary of State for Health
Department of Health & Social Security
(DHSS)

Regional Health Authority
(RHA)

Area Health Authority
(AHA)

Area Management Team
(AMT)

Figure 1 *The administrative structure of the NHS*

The NHS was responsible to the Department of Health and Social Security (DHSS) whose minister – the Secretary of State for Health – was a member of cabinet. Fourteen RHAs reported to the DHSS, whose members were appointed by the Secretary of State. Each RHA had a number of Area Health Authorities of between 18 and 33 members including 1 medical consultant, 1 general practitioner, 1 trade unionist, 2 health service employees and a number of lay members, who were appointed by the Regional Health Authority. Members of the local (municipal) council made up the remainder. They constituted at least one-third of the membership and were nominated by the local council.

The Area Health Authority was the decision-making body for an Area that included a number of hospitals and medical facilities. It voted on

Case prepared by Professor Cynthia Hardy, Faculty of Management, McGill University, from original research. All names are disguised. Case not to be reproduced without permission.

recommendations made by the Area Management Team, which consisted primarily of professional administrators who did not all have a medical background. In the event of a hospital closure, the procedure required management to make a recommendation to the Area Health Authority. If the decision was affirmed, a consultative document was produced that was supposed to include the reasons for the closure and the implications for patients. This document was then circulated to unions, the Community Health Council, local councils, and staff organizations. Local politicians, the Regional Health Authority and the DHSS were informed and a press statement was issued. Comments from these groups were supposed to be taken into account by the Area Health Authority when making its final decision.

The opinion of the Community Health Council was particularly significant. This body was responsible for protecting the interests of the patients. If it objected to a closure and submitted an alternative plan, the Area Health Authority had to take it into account. If the Area Health Authority still wished to proceed with the closure, it had to refer the decision up to the Regional Health Authority. If the Region would not accept the Community Health Council's proposals then it had to seek the approval of the Secretary of State, who would not necessarily confirm the decision to close. If, on the other hand, the Community Health Council agreed to the closure, then the Area Health Authority could proceed.

The 1970s were notable for a number of incidents where proposed hospital closures sparked orchestrated resistance from doctors, nurses and ancillary workers who took over the hospital in question. These hospital occupations, as they were called, represented a united effort that enabled hospitals to continue to function despite managerial decisions to close them. They had caused the government considerable embarrassment in the light of its attempts to reduce public sector spending.

Park Road Maternity Hospital

Park Road Maternity Hospital was one of the oldest maternity hospitals in the UK, having survived the Blitz during the Second World War. It was also the largest, and many local people had either been born there or had had their babies there. It was devoted to the provision of maternity services and was not part of a larger, general hospital. It had been considered a candidate for closure for a number of years, simply because it was such an old hospital. In 1974, additional factors threatened its survival when it became clear that Northville had an oversupply of maternity beds owing to a fall in the birth rate, coupled with a declining population in the inner city area where Park Road was situated. Park Road Hospital and the maternity wards at King Street and Sackville General Hospitals were all working at about 50 per cent of their capacity.

Northville

Northville was an economically depressed city. It had a high proportion of semi-skilled, unskilled and unemployed workers, elderly people, the homeless, and single parent families. Primary health care services (general practitioners, clinics, etc.) were limited, which had led to a strongly held view that hospital beds were crucial to compensate for the lack of community services and preventative care. However, the city had been experiencing the effects of government spending cuts during the 1970s. In addition, a special fund for bringing new hospitals on-line had been withdrawn. Management had just completed a new general hospital, which it now had to bring on-line with money from its annual budget. It had taken 17 years, over £50 million, and the closure of many small community hospitals to build the 'great white elephant', as it was called. These financial pressures had led to a number of proposals to cut health services in an attempt to balance the budget. Inside eighteen months, two-thirds of the hospitals in the city had been threatened with closure, reduction or redesignation. Staff in the units concerned had not always been consulted on these changes. Allegations had been made that each time a new planning document had appeared, it had been a major headline in the local press before staff were aware of it.

When further cuts were announced in May 1977, there had been an explosion of protest as staff, unions and the Community Health Council tried to resist them. This protest was followed by a deputation to the Secretary of State who agreed to set up a committee of inquiry to look into the matter. The group involved in the resistance were part of a network of local committees, which included tenants' associations, community groups and political parties. Local councillors were active in community affairs – since there was no clear-cut majority in the local council, councillors were keen to champion causes that would win them votes and secure their position on the local council. Different unions represented hospital ancillary workers and nurses. The former were a particularly militant group – there had been eight disputes between October and December 1978 and more than 4,000 working days had been lost in official disputes alone between January and March 1979.

The Proposal

A plan to close Park Road was formally proposed to the Area Health Authority by management in 1976. The initial report met with approval, and in September a consultative document was released to all the relevant groups. It proposed the closure over the following two years, so that wards at King Street and Sackville hospitals could be improved to enable them to cope with any extra demand. Groups immediately expressed concern about the closure. Staff – nurses and ancillary workers – at Park Road set up an action committee to stop the closure. The Community Health Council also opposed the closure, and the National Union of Public Employees (which represented ancillary workers) expressed 'serious concern', arguing that the birth rate would rise again and the Park Road facilities would be needed.

Despite this furore, management pressed on with its proposal. In March 1977, it issued a revised plan that brought forward the closure by a year. This move was, according to management, necessitated by the estimated deficit of £1 million on the annual budget. The new document also mentioned, for the first time, the alternative of closing wards at King Street and Sackville hospitals and retaining Park Road. This alternative was dismissed, however, because the savings would be half a million pounds a year less than closing Park Road. The document also justified the closure by referring to the medical policy of integrating specialist maternity units into a general hospital with all its back-up facilities. The revised plan gave further impetus to the opposition move-ment, however, and the Community Health Council restated its opposition, proposing that the wards at King Street and Sackville hospitals be closed instead.

A special meeting of the Area Health Authority was called in July 1977 to consider the two options – the closure of Park Road, or the wards at Sackville and King Street. Fifteen members (out of 26) had attended but only 9 voted – 5 to 4 in favour of the closure of Park Road. The meeting resolved that the matter should be given further consideration and another meeting would be held to resolve the issue.

Questions

- What would you do, if you were a member of the Area Management Team and wanted to ensure that the closure of Park Road was approved?
- What would you do, if you were a member of the Community Health Council and were determined to prevent the closure?

Midville Area Health Authority

In 1977, managers at Midville Area Health Authority were preparing to close Withybrooke Hospital – a small hospital that had originally been a tuberculosis hospital but, with the virtual eradication of the disease, had catered to chest patients and 'cold surgery' (varicose veins, vasectomies etc.). It was a small cottage hospital with attractive buildings in an idyllic country setting. Patients often enjoyed going there because it was small, friendly and picturesque, and because they were not really ill – either undergoing minor surgery or convalescing. Its medical usefulness was limited, however, because of the lack of support facilities and its distance from the general hospital in town.

Midville Area Health Authority covered the town of Midville – an affluent rural town in the centre of England – and its surrounding villages. It was a relatively prosperous and middle class environment. Relations between management and unions had been peaceful in recent years. Midville managers had recognized the potential for conflict with other interest groups, and had striven to avoid it through dialogue and consultation. Management's medical policy was to concentrate services at the general hospital, which had been greatly enlarged in recent years. A rationalization process was under way, and two geriatric units and a convalescent hospital had already been closed. So far, there had been no major resistance to these closures. This process was, however, being accelerated due to financial difficulties: Midville was under-funded by as much as £1 million per annum, partly as a result of an obligation to cater to the population of a nearby town until its own hospital was built.

In response to the general principle of rationalization and the need to save money, management recommended the closure of Withybrooke in April 1977. It argued that the loss of beds would be compensated for by the opening of a new phase at the general hospital, though there would be a time lag of a couple of years. The Area Health Authority accepted the initial recommendation and a consultative document was prepared and circulated in July 1977.

The Community Health Council called a public meeting in November and, as a result of the strength of feeling there, opposed the closure. It was supported by the local council in the area immediately surrounding Withybrooke, but not by the Midville town council. The union supported the Community Health Council by saying that it 'deplored' the proposed closure. Management was

Case prepared by Professor Cynthia Hardy, Faculty of Management, McGill University, from original research. All names are disguised. Case not to be reproduced without permission.

concerned about the action of the Community Health Council because it would mean that the decision could rest with the Secretary of State, who had grown increasingly nervous about recent hospital occupations.

Questions

- What would you do if you were a manager and wanted to secure the closure of Withybrooke Hospital?
- What would you do if you were a member of the Community Health Council and wanted to prevent the closure?
- What differences do you perceive in the power of these two groups compared with their Northville counterparts.

Medical Services and Products Ltd

Roberta Francis was facing a number of challenges in her new position as CEO of Medical Services & Products Ltd (MSP). First, she was new to both the job and the company. Second, she had a particularly difficult problem with one of her senior executives, Donald Bridges.

Roberta was an established expert in biotechnology. She had been appointed CEO at MSP in 1992. She had started her career in a university research laboratory and, after ten years, had ventured into the business world and, over the following ten-year period, moved from a researcher to vice-president in a US-based biotechnical company. Increasing competition during the 1980s started to shift the emphasis from basic research to commercial applications that would have a better chance of translating into sales. In an attempt to secure financial security and the necessary commercial acumen to compete in this environment, the company had sold out to a large pharmaceutical concern. Roberta decided that she did not want to work in such an impersonal environment and, in 1987, moved back to her native Canada as president of a research laboratory. Her four years with this company had proved successful as profits and sales grew. Her interest in MSP lay in her desire to contribute her technical and research expertise, as well as her management experience. She was also attracted by an organization which, although slightly larger than the one she had left, retained a strong research-driven, collegial culture in which professionals had a great deal of influence.

MSP had provided diagnostic testing and medical equipment to hospitals and physicians since its creation in the early 1960s. A diagnostic testing service was carried out in a number of laboratories and collection centres located across the country. Government regulations determined the fees of all the tests carried out by the company and restricted the type of testing each individual laboratory could do. As a result, while the main laboratory in Toronto (which was also the largest) could carry out all tests, other laboratories were limited. When a specimen was collected by a laboratory not licensed to carry out the test or a collection centre (where no tests were carried out), it had to be shipped to the nearest laboratory licensed to conduct the test. More recently, a mobile diagnostic imaging service which provided specialized equipment and staff to hospitals and clinics had been set up. The company also developed and manufactured medical equipment, including X-ray, ultrasound and spectrometer equipment.

Case prepared by Professor Cynthia Hardy, Faculty of Management, McGill University from original research. All names and some facts have been disguised. Case not to be reproduced without permission.

Three-quarters of MSP's revenues came from diagnostic testing, which represented the cash cow of the business. Growth was, however, constrained since changes in government regulations were effectively decreasing the fees that companies could charge, and the prospects of securing licences to open new laboratories was becoming increasingly bleak. If MSP was to sustain its growth it would have to place more emphasis on new initiatives.

During the 1980s, profits had been boosted by new product developments in medical equipment and instrumentation. Despite the returns generated by these products, they remained expensive products with highly specialized markets, which required significant capital investment. As a result, some board members felt that biotechnology represented a far better opportunity for MSP's continued expansion and growth. Ten researchers had been hired in the late 1980s and a specialist research department had been created. It was felt that 'gene-splicing' (the manipulation of DNA to produce proteins such as insulin) would produce profitable new drugs and treatments. Moreover, there would be some synergy between the expertise of many of the existing professionals in the laboratories and the new biotechnical researchers. Such a move would, however, lead MSP into a completely new field which would probably require some sort of alliance with a larger company to provide the necessary resources. It would also mean a switch from the emphasis on physics and engineering, which had been responsible for the new products in equipment and instrumentation, towards chemistry- and biology-related expertise. Not all the board members were convinced of the need for such a radical reorientation however.

MSP was a company with 2,000 people and $140 million in sales. It was profitable, but the growth of recent years was tailing off. Much of the blame had been pinned on the previous president who had recently been persuaded to step down by the board which considered that his lack of leadership had caused the stagnation. The new research group had so far failed to generate any new, commercial applications and, while these researchers got on well with their 'traditional' colleagues, there was no one at the senior level who could integrate their work into MSP's overall strategy and exploit their potential.

Organizational Structure

The CEO of MSP (see Figure 1) was typically a medical or scientific professional. The previous president had had only nominal qualifications in this area. With a Ph.D. in microbiology, he had spent the last 20 years as a manager, not a researcher. He had been hired in 1980 primarily for his outside contacts with universities, hospitals and the government. At that point, MSP's board had wanted to establish links with outside researchers to develop joint ventures and alliances that might help stimulate new product development.

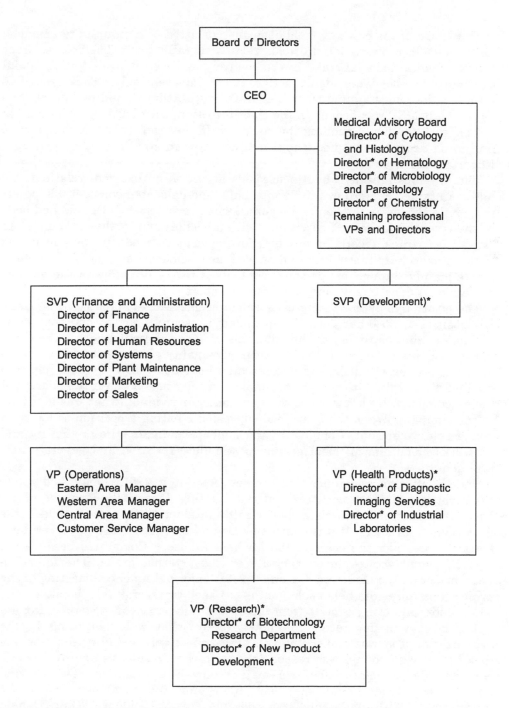

Figure 1 *MSP: Organization chart*

The board of the privately held company consisted of a group of ten medical and scientific professionals in fields related to MSP's core businesses. Since they all had a financial stake in the company and were knowledgeable about the industry, they were highly active, if not interventionist. They tended to form a united view around what the strategic direction should be but, as long as they felt MSP was headed in the right direction, they left the CEO alone to get on with the job of running the company. If, however, they felt things were not going according to plan, they were not slow to step in as they had with Roberta's predecessor.

The previous president had focused his attention on external relations. He had maintained a very low profile internally and delegated considerable power to Donald Bridges – the Senior Vice-president (Development). Donald had been in the company for over 20 years and, with a background in physics, he had an established track record in product development in medical equipment. He took pains to keep himself up to date with new scientific and medical developments mainly through his personal contacts with the directors of the various professional departments and the board members.

The position of Senior Vice-president had been especially created for Donald. His position in 1980 had been Vice-president (Research) but, as had been clear to the incoming president at that time, he was the informal leader – the other vice-presidents deferred to his powerful personality since most of them were younger, less experienced, and impressed by his track record. Donald had also created close links with the professionals and scientists both on the board and in the company. He knew, more than any other individual, what was going on in the company. When the board had suggested creating a position to focus on strategic development, Donald was the logical candidate. His credibility and networks made him an ideal person to stimulate research and generate new products.

Shortly after his appointment to the new position in 1981, Donald had set up the Strategic Action Committee that met monthly. It initially consisted of the Vice-presidents of Research and of Health Products, but he soon added the professional directors. It was chaired by Donald and reported to the President. He also took over the chair of the Medical Advisory Committee because the new President wanted to concentrate on the external arena. The following year, he set up the Directors' Committee – an informal luncheon meeting of the professional directors held each month – to keep track of developments on the 'shop floor' and bring experts from the different departments together. Donald felt that it was imperative to know exactly what was happening in the organization if he was to distribute resources effectively and nurture promising new initiatives. Donald was responsible (with the President's approval which was usually automatic) for two major sources of funding: research and development funds; and equipment funds for the professionals in the laboratories. Both represented considerable sums of money. While Donald frequently cut across lines of authority, it did not cause problems because, with the research mentality and close links to universities, employees were used to operating in a collegial and informal manner.

The Senior Vice-president (Finance and Administration) was a man called Colin Whittington. The position had been upgraded at the same time that the Development position had been created to strike a balance between the professional and nonprofessional sides of the company. While Colin's position looked as if it carried far more responsibility than Donald's, in reality he had none of the power of his colleague. He oversaw most of the company's nonprofessional employees who were treated very much as second-class citizens. They existed to serve the professionals and had none of their status, high salaries, autonomy or perks. Furthermore, research credentials were a passport to respect in the company and while Whittington had 20 years experience at MSP, he had no research background whatsoever. While nominally in control of financial matters, he had little effective power of resource allocation: all the real money was allocated by Donald to fund new developments. Finally, Colin was a timid and low key individual – totally unmatched against the blustery, brusque but nonetheless charismatic figure of Donald Bridges.

The Vice-president (Operations) was in charge of the diagnostic testing operations which comprised the testing laboratories and collection centres, which were divided into three regions. This vice-president and her regional managers were not professionals and were responsible mainly for the administration of the laboratories. The professional side of testing was divided into four disciplinary areas: Cytology and Histology (tests concerning cells and tissue), Haematology (tests concerning the production and function of blood cells), Microbiology and Parasitology (tests concerning microbes and parasites), and Chemistry (the chemical analysis of blood and other body fluids). Actual testing was carried out by professionally registered medical laboratory technologists. A typical laboratory would contain about one half professional and one half nonprofessional staff. Collection centres required no professional staff. The laboratories were effectively self-sufficient as far as testing was concerned, and tests would only be referred elsewhere when the particular laboratory was not licensed to carry it out.

Testing policies and procedures were decided by the Medical Advisory Committee. It consisted of the professional/scientific vice-presidents and directors, and a number of external experts. Each of the four disciplines involved in testing was represented by a 'director' – a senior professional who worked in the main Toronto laboratory. He or she had no line authority, but was expert in the particular discipline. The Committee met once a month to assess new professional developments, and to give advice to the board on policy matters concerning the use of new tests and equipment, and other professional issues. It had a number of sub-committees: Health Products Advisory Committee, Clinical Chemistry Advisory Committee, Haematology Advisory Committee, Microbiology and Parasitology Advisory Committee, Cytology and Histology Advisory Committee, and the Research Committee.

The Vice-president (Research) headed two research departments: Biotechnology, and New Product Development. Nearly everyone in this division was a scientific or medical professional. This individual had replaced Donald when he moved up to the senior vice-presidential position. She was a close ally of Donald and had previously been Director of New Product Development. The Vice-president (Health Products) was in charge of Diagnostic Imaging Services (mobile testing), and Industrial Laboratories (where products and equipment were manufactured).

Roberta's Challenge

When Roberta first took up her position, she received very mixed messages. On the one hand, everyone pointed to the collegial and democratic culture of MSP. On the other hand, it was clear that Donald was an extremely powerful and autocratic figure. His somewhat abrasive style did not seem to cause any problems among the directors or the vice-presidents: they were all in awe of him and clearly basked in his charisma (except for Colin who was intimidated). Donald orchestrated and consolidated his control through the various committees, which not only enabled him to cement his informal networks but also led to the proposal of initiatives that had, in the past, carried a great deal of weight with the previous president and the board. Donald had a considerable amount of talent and research expertise from which the company could clearly benefit. However, his interest was largely confined to the equipment and instrumentation side of the business. He understood little of the potential offered by biotechnology and had made it clear that he preferred a strategy that continued to emphasize MSP's traditional strengths, rather than an over-reliance on a completely new area of research.

It was also painfully clear to Roberta that the nonprofessionals at the head office and in the laboratories, who together constituted two-thirds of the total workforce, were totally demoralized. They knew that their senior vice-president had no power, and were treated as second class citizens in their daily work lives. The latter was not so much the result of individual maltreatment; but the inevitable result of a situation where professionals received all the respect, autonomy and kudos.

Roberta had been hired by the board to solve these problems and put MSP on a sound financial and strategic footing. She was looking forward to the challenge and was confident of her interpersonal skills. The only fly in the ointment was Donald Bridges – due to history, structure, and sheer force of personality, he ran the show at MSP – and he had made it clear that he was not going to give up without a fight.

Questions

- You are Roberta, what strategy do you think MSP should pursue and how do you propose to implement it?
- You are Donald, what strategy do you think MSP should pursue and how do you propose to implement it?
- What are the ethical implications of your answers?

The Tobacco Firms

Robert H. Miles

[. . .]

The Big Six [US tobacco companies] were not unaware of the scattered studies published between 1939 and 1950 linking cigarette smoking to health hazards. Consequently, to a limited extent prior to the 1953 Sloan–Kettering report, research was conducted within at least some of the companies on the physiology of smoking and the pharmacology of smoke, and their relationships to health (e.g., Philip Morris *Annual Report*, 1951; American Brands *Annual Report*, 1954). However, until the early 1950s, the great majority of expenditures on research by the Big Six had been devoted to developing new products, improving quality control of the cigarettes produced, and devising better methods of crop yield and cigarette manufacture. Health-related research was clearly of minor importance. Yet, whereas not one word was mentioned about the smoking-and-health controversy in the annual reports of the Big Six prior to the Sloan–Kettering release, full discussions, all designed to counter this external threat, appeared thereafter in these reports. But the industry's response involved far more than rhetoric. With the publicity devoted to the alleged association between cigarette smoking and health, particularly in regard to lung cancer and heart disease, the industry's traditional orientation toward research shifted dramatically. Focused efforts in the area of research on smoking and health were conducted at both firm and industry levels.

Research Strategies of Individual Firms

At the firm level, major capital expenditure for in-house research facilities were expanded and research sponsored by eminent scientists and medical-research institutions was funded. The traditional section featuring 'tobacco yield and cigarette production research' in the Big Six annual reports was scrapped in 1953. In its place, beginning with 1954, all six firms published lengthy statements on the issue of smoking and health, and without exception, strong arguments were advanced to counter or minimize the conclusions of the antismoking forces. In fact, several of the firms attempted to use their annual reports to persuade their investors that the controversy was only temporary. [. . .]

From *Coffin Nails and Corporate Strategies*, Englewood Cliffs, NJ: Prentice-Hall, 1982.

[. . .]

Despite this apparent nonchalance, strategic choices that altered the focus of tobacco research and the future of the industry were initiated. American Brands declared that the size of its research laboratory 'devoted to the study of what makes up tobacco and tobacco smoke' would be doubled in 1954, and later that a research grant to the University of Virginia Medical College for studies on the physiological effects of smoking had been awarded in September 1954. By 1954, R.J. Reynolds was reporting a doubling of its research-laboratory capacity, adding new radioisotope equipment to make possible 'tracer work' on cigarette smoke. In 1956, Philip Morris announced plans for the construction of a new research laboratory and disclosed an expansion of company grants to higher education to support research in 'health, scientific, and agricultural fields'. Moreover, these efforts by individual firms were being reinforced by similar, concerted research activities at the industry level.

Creation of the Tobacco Research Council

The Tobacco Industry Research Committee, later renamed the Council for Tobacco Research – USA, was created by a coalition of tobacco interests in January of the year following the Sloan–Kettering Report. [. . .] During the decade separating the Sloan–Kettering and Surgeon General's reports (1954–1964), the Tobacco Research Committee awarded grants in excess of $7 million to some 230 scientists in more than 100 hospitals, universities, and research institutions around the country – individuals and organizations that might otherwise have been seeking research funds or working on the payrolls of government regulators and nonprofit antismoking groups.

[. . .]

The Surgeon General's Report marked what many industry observers would characterize as a primary, unequivocal, and direct threat to the legitimacy of the Big Six. The findings and implications it contained, identifying cigarette smoking as a major national health problem contributing to a host of preventable diseases, were decidedly negative for the tobacco industry. The response of the Big Six was stepped-up sponsorship of the Tobacco Research Council and its research-grants activity, as well as separate joint funding by the Big Six of research studies of major gatekeepers and institutions in the medical and scientific communities.

[. . .] Financial support of the Tobacco Research Committee the year after the Surgeon General's Report almost doubled the total cumulative support that this joint venture had received during the previous ten years of its existence; by 1975, its cumulative funding had reached almost seven times the level it had achieved on the eve of the publicized announcement in 1962 of the formation of the Surgeon General's Advisory Committee.

But the Big Six did not rely totally on the research grants awarded by this formal joint venture. In addition, they pooled other resources to make special grants to particular institutions. For instance, in 1963, during the time the FTC was formulating its proposal to require health warning labels on all cigarette packages and advertisements, the Big Six awarded an unrestricted research grant of $10 million (more than its total previous funding to the Tobacco Research Council) to the American Medical Association (AMA). It was not surprising, therefore, according to Fritschler (1975), to find that the AMA was not active in its support of the FTC's initiative during the labeling-regulation hearings that took place early the next year. By 1975, Big Six grants to the AMA had climbed to a total of $18 million (Fritschler, 1975).

In 1971, Washington University Medical School in St. Louis also received a pooled research grant from the Big Six in the amount of $2 million for cancer research, and in 1972, Harvard was granted $2.8 million for cardiovascular and pulmonary research. In 1973, when UCLA was granted $1.7 million for research related to smoking and health, the industry reported that some $48 million had been provided for health research in 'independent' laboratories. That same year, the Big Six announced that not only had they 'funded more scientific research on smoking and health problems than any other source, government or private', but that 'the tobacco industry is now providing more financial support for smoking and health research than all of the private health agencies *combined*' (R.J. Reynolds, *Annual Reports*, 1970, 1972).

[. . .]

Lobbying and Coopting the Institutional Environment[1]

The history of lobbying in the US tobacco industry is rooted in a tradition of joint effort among manufacturing competitors and other industry participants. As early as 1915, the Tobacco Merchants Association was founded by member firms to collect and analyze information about state, federal, and special agency or department reports and activities of relevance to the tobacco industry. Since then, tobacco growers, warehousers, wholesalers, retailers, and manufacturers have often joined forces to anticipate or react to both potential and real environmental threats.

The industry created the Tobacco Tax Council in 1949 to deal with a common concern of members of the tobacco subsystem over continuing federal and increasing state taxation on cigarettes. The council was to report to sponsoring organizations on taxes relating to tobacco products. This organization is currently supported by virtually all the elements of the tobacco industry, and it has lobbied vigorously for a reduction in what it labels 'discriminating taxes on American smokers'.[2] Its existence also serves to remind politicians at all levels of how much their coffers depend on the tax revenues from the sale of tobacco products.

By the late 1950s, however, it had become evident to members of the tobacco subsystem that a far more serious threat to their well-being than taxation was being mounted by certain elements of the federal government in collaboration with other interest groups. By this time, the antismoking forces had begun to coalesce around the mounting evidence linking the tobacco habit to health disorders; and this group was getting enough press and media coverage to raise serious concerns not only in the investment community surrounding the tobacco industry but among smokers and nonsmokers alike. This attention escalated the smoking-and-health controversy from a 'weak signal' to an issue of national prominence, and at least one major administrative agency, the Federal Trade Commission, had taken the ball and was about to make an end sweep with it.

This rather exponential increase in both activity and attention in the industry's institutional environment aroused the latent tobacco subsystem. One of the broadest and wealthiest political subsystems in US history began to stir. In a political system pioneered by the spirit of free enterprise, one of the best indicators of the potential strength of this particular subsystem is financial dependence of many important constituencies on the industry under threat. Another indicator, in this specific case, is human habituation with the primary product of the threatened industry.

US smokers spent an estimated $7 billion on cigarettes during 1963, the year in which the federal government began mounting a campaign to require health warning labels on cigarette packages and advertisements. That same year, more than 34,000 workers were employed in cigarette manufacturing plants, and over 600,000 families, dispersed among 26 states, were dependent upon tobacco farm crops as their primary source of income. By 1967, advertising outlays to promote tobacco products exceeded $300 million (Fritschler, 1975).

Although the Big Six and their lobbying arms have persistently bemoaned the state and municipal tax burdens borne by their cigarette brands, these payments have probably served them well by creating revenue dependencies in legislatures that could potentially do harm to the industry. National, state, and municipal taxes on tobacco retail sales amounted to $3.25 billion per year by the mid-1960s, although this tax revenue dependence is not distributed evenly among the states. For instance, in 1975, ten states collected over $100 million each in cigarette tax revenues.

Tobacco farming has become an institution in the states in which the controversial leaf is grown. Tobacco allotments (parcels of land that carry a license from the US Department of Agriculture to grow tobacco) have become an important part of a farmer's estate, one that the farmer can sell at retirement or pass on to heirs. The rent alone on one acre of tobacco allotment has reached $1,000 a year in some areas, compared to a rent of less than $100 annually for an acre on which soybeans are grown. This extremely high financial yield per acre, combined with the taxes raised from cigarette sales and manufacture in certain states, creates a potentially broad and powerful prosmoking constituency. Indeed, actions taken to outlaw cigarettes by elected officials in North Carolina or Virginia would be about as helpful in ensuring their reelection as outlawing cars, gambling, or sunshine would be to their political counterparts in Michigan, Nevada, and Florida. Members of Congress from tobacco states were in powerful positions in the early 1960s. 'In the Senate, nearly one-fourth of the committees were chaired by men from the six tobacco states. Of the twenty-one committees in the House, tobacco state congressmen chaired seven' (Fritschler, 1975: 26).

What the Big Six needed most as the battle over smoking and health heated up was an organization and a strategy for assembling and orchestrating the mutual interests of all these potential supporters. They first formed a joint lobbying venture to organize these interest groups. Using this joint political venture, they developed a concerted strategy aimed away from the smoking-and-health issue itself and, instead, at the process by which administrative agencies of the federal government were attempting to force it upon the tobacco industry.

Creation of the Tobacco Institute

The creation of the Tobacco Institute, Inc. in 1958 was the industry's response to the need for an organized lobbying effort. The Institute's activities are controlled by the chief executive officers of the sponsoring tobacco companies, who serve on its board of directors. It draws its revenues from participating tobacco companies in exact proportion to the share of the domestic cigarette market held by each in the preceding year. From the time of its creation, the Institute has borne the delegated responsibility for managing the industry's programs on public issues. Its primary activities have involved efforts to deny the cause–effect implications of the Surgeon General's Report and to mount an active campaign against any government legislation and administrative initiatives whose intent is to limit the discretion of the Big Six.

The Institute was headed initially by a former US ambassador, who left to become the director of the Foreign Service Institute. He was succeeded by Earle G. Clements, former US congressman, US senator, and governor of Kentucky, who was close to the Johnson administration in the White House at the time. Indeed, Clements's daughter, Bess Abell, served as Lady Bird Johnson's social secretary (Fritschler, 1975).

The Tobacco Institute had worked for some time to develop the case for smoking by emphasizing the inconclusiveness of the research evidence, the contribution of tobacco products to the national economy, and the individual rights of smokers. But the initial efforts in 1963 of one federal administrative agency to restrict cigarette advertising and label cigarette products with health warnings created the need for an intensified and concerted lobbying effort directed at various instrumentalities of the federal government. The initiative taken by the Federal Trade Commission was the first of its kind for the tobacco industry. If it could not be checked or at least eased at its inception, the prospects for the Big Six were going to be bleak. [. . .]

The Tobacco Lobby: Strategies and Tactics

The Federal Trade Commission announced its proposal to restrict cigarette advertising and to mandate health-warning statements on all cigarette packages in 1963. In doing so, it was operating on its own initiative under the traditional principal of 'delegated authority' as an administrative agency of Congress. Its commissioners believed that such a regulatory move was within the FTC's charter and that the mounting evidence linking smoking to ill health provided sufficient justification for it to proceed against the industry. At the time of their public announcement, the commissioners of the FTC informed interested groups, including the Big Six, that three days of open hearings on the proposed cigarette-and-advertising rule would be conducted in March of the following year.

Former Senator Clements was hired by the Big Six in 1964 to develop and direct, through the Tobacco Institute, the industry's lobbying strategy against the FTC's attempts to initiate and enforce its health-warning labeling rule. Several elements of the strategy developed by Clements warrant special attention.

Switch the Issues   First, Clements directed his lobbying attack away from the smoking-and-health issues, focusing instead on the legitimacy of the FTC's rule-making authority. His tactic was one of having the labeling issue wrestled away from that regulatory agency to be taken up by a more sympathetic Congress. Thus, the earlier public-relations emphasis on the criticism of the correlational findings of medical researchers was played down. Instead, as Fritschler (1975: 54) observed, 'the strategy of the tobacco men was to question Federal Trade *authority to make policy* involving a cigarette health warning and thereby insure that the final policy decision would be made by Congress, not the FTC. Consequently, . . . the tobacco interests raised with skill and eloquence some of the most basic questions that have stalked the growth of agency policymaking powers.'

Under Clements's leadership, the tobacco lobby based its complaints on the clear language of Article I of the Constitution, which states, 'All legislative powers herein granted shall be vested in a Congress of the United States . . .' Accordingly, the tobacco lobbyists argued that a democratic form of government was threatened when nonelected bureaucrats in administrative agencies were permitted to exercise policy-making powers of the government that are constitutionally the responsibility of elected representatives of the people. They argued that those associated with the tobacco interests were being denied participation in policy making that was being proposed by the FTC. And they argued further that, when an administrative agency is permitted to set national policy, there are no electoral means to hold administrative decision makers responsible for their decisions.

[. . .]

Mobilize a Concerted Front To accomplish this strategy, Clements had to organize a united front among all elements of the tobacco subsystem that, according to Fritschler (1975: 4):

> cuts across institutional lines and includes within it all groups and individuals who are making and influencing government decisions concerning cigarettes and tobacco. . . . The tobacco subsystem included the paid representatives of tobacco growers, marketing organizations, and cigarette manufacturers; congressmen representing tobacco constituencies; the leading members of four subcommittees in Congress . . . that handle tobacco legislation and related appropriations; and certain officials within the Department of Agriculture who were involved with the various tobacco programs of the department. This was a small group of people well known to each other and knowledgeable about all aspects of the tobacco industry and its relationship with the government.

In addition, Clements sought to appeal for the sympathetic support, or at least nonopposition, of individual-freedom, pro-private-sector and anti-federal-regulation sentiments of the public at large and of other big businesses in particular. By focusing away from the substance of the smoking-and-health controversy and toward the general legitimacy of policy making by bureaucrats instead of elected representatives, he succeeded in maximizing the breadth and power of his prosmoking lobby while minimizing the opposition of marginally interested groups. [. . .]

[. . .]

Next, Clements rightly sensed that the Big Six were going to have to give up something. The evidence accumulated by the health forces and the media attention it received had generated too much momentum to be dismissed or stonewalled. Therefore, with some difficulty but eventual success, Clements persuaded the Big Six to accept health-warning labels on cigarette packages in exchange for unfettered media advertising and a prohibition against states' developing their own health warnings.

Clements, relying on agreement among his constituencies, focused the attention of Congress, and in particular on the Senate Commerce Committee and the House Interstate and Foreign Commerce Committee that had FTC oversight responsibility. The House Committee was stacked with Southerners, one of the most influential of whom (Kornegay, D., North Carolina) later decided not to run for Congress and assumed, instead, the position of vice-president and general council of the Tobacco Institute (Fritschler, 1975). He later succeeded Clements as head of the Institute.

Finally, Clements was an old friend and political ally of Lyndon B. Johnson, then president of the United States. Indeed, Clements had once served as the executive director of the Senate Democratic Campaign Fund. According to Fritschler, Clements was therefore one of the few people who could keep President Johnson out of the controversy. [. . .]

These were the elements of the Tobacco Institute's lobbying strategy. The tactics employed by the prosmoking lobby accounted for the fact that the strategy of the Big Six was not only successful but actually resulted in what many would describe as a 'limited victory'.

FTC Hearings and Congressional Oversight

On March 16, 1964, the commissioners of the FTC began three days of hearings on the proposed cigarette-labeling and -advertising rule. Only one of the commissioners – MacIntyre, from North Carolina – opposed the rule.

The first witnesses to appear were in favor of the rule. Later came a representative of the Tobacco Institute, who was followed by still others who favored the rule. The second day included the trade interests; advertising and tobacco growers' associations testified. On the third day, congressional and gubernatorial elected officials from the tobacco states vigorously protested the proposal that directly threatened their constituents. They, too, hoped to get the issue transferred from the FTC to Congress.

The Big Six themselves chose to publicly ignore the FTC by not appearing at the hearings. Instead, an attorney named Austern was retained by the Tobacco Institute to represent manufacturers. He avoided the smoking-and-health controversy and focused on the illegality of the general rule-making authority that had been assumed by the FTC. The commissioners, as expected, responded that rule making was in their jurisdiction under the tradition of delegated authority from Congress.

The FTC's cigarette-labeling rule was to take effect nine months after the hearings. But within a month after the conclusion of the hearings, the Big Six created another joint venture, the Cigarette Advertising Code, Inc. The purpose of this association was to establish and maintain a self-policing advertising code. According to Fritschler (1975: 107):

> creation of the voluntary code was intended to signify to Congress and the public that the industry was interested in regulating itself, and that the action of the Federal Trade Commission was an unnecessary obstacle to self-regulation.

To give clout to the Code, the Big Six hired former New Jersey Governor Robert B. Meyner as its administrator and empowered him to levy fines against violators up to $100,000. The Code prohibited advertising targeted at persons under 21 and cigarette-advertising health claims. The Code lasted six years, until the cigarette advertising ban on radio and television.

[. . .]

The cigarette lobby now appeared in full force, with each witness rolling out a broad set of issues at stake: the inconclusiveness of the Surgeon General's Report; the importance to the national economy of unfettered competition; the proper role of Congress in national policy making as outlined in Article I of the Constitution; the contributions of tobacco to everything from employment and tax revenues to the nation's balance-of-payments situation. Scientists and professionals were marshaled by the Tobacco Institute into the hearing room to criticize the evidence linking smoking to health.

The support of 'friends' of the tobacco industry also got into the act. The American Newspaper Publishers Association, the Advertising Federation of America, the Association of National Advertisers, the Radio Advertising Bureau, and the National Association of Broadcasters, all fearing loss of revenues from proposed cigarette-advertising restrictions, aligned themselves with the tobacco interests (Fritschler, 1975). The National Association of Broadcasters, an ally of the smoking lobby, entertained more than 400 of the 535 members of Congress at a reception, held at its annual convention in Washington, DC, during the week of the hearings. Moreover, it has been estimated that at the time, more than one-third of those members of Congress owned major stockholdings in radio and television stations (Parker, 1965). Guiding all these activities was the Tobacco Institute's carefully orchestrated and skillfully played lobbying strategy.

The FTC and its loose confederation of health and special-interest groups were no match for the resources and unity that supported and guided the tobacco lobby. Indeed, the major difficulty that plagued the health groups throughout the congressional hearings was a lack of agreement about what they wanted Congress to do (Fritschler, 1975). All they could seem to agree on was that smoking was harmful to health and that the federal government should do something about it. Their inability to develop an action plan comparable to that of Clements's strategy resulted in a disunity that became evident as the health groups testified before the congressional committee.

For instance, the FTC argued that it was the most appropriate agency to enforce the labeling and advertising rules, whereas the Surgeon General argued that the Department of Health, Education and Welfare was best prepared for this task. The health groups were also in disagreement over the wording of proposed health-warning labels. [. . .]

But disunity was only one of the weaknesses that characterized the health lobby. They also had little or no political support from powerful constituencies, and their financial viability was either uncertain or contingent upon the sympathetic support of the Congress that wanted to wrestle the labeling issue away from them. The FTC, for instance, had virtually no support from the industries it regulated, all of which feared greater policy-making powers on the part of nonelected, career bureaucrats in federal administrative agencies. Moreover, the funding of both federal (e.g., Public Health Service) and nonprofit (e.g., American Cancer Society, American Heart Association, and so on) health groups has always been precarious and to some extent influenced by congressional appropriations and corporate-donation programs. Therefore, when the congressional contest was waged, the smoking forces simply overwhelmed the nonsmoking forces.

[. . .]

The legislation that emerged from hearings in both houses of Congress and was signed by the president specifically voided the Federal Trade Commission's labeling rule and took away for several years its delegated authority to make new regulations relating to cigarette advertising. The commission, other administrative agencies, and individual states were prohibited from requiring or even considering the requirement of a health warning in cigarette advertising for four years. Later, Congress extended this moratorium on the FTC to six years! The diluted label proposed in the bill was to be required only on cigarette packages, not in cigarette advertising in the broadcast and printed media. [. . .]

[. . .]

Media and Advertising Strategies

The congressionally imposed four-year moratorium on the FTC's rule-making authority over the tobacco industry did not prevent that Commission from moving forward with the smoking-and-health issue short of rule making itself. Indeed, in the years following Congress's rebuke, the FTC continued to keep the smoking-and-health issue before the public eye and build support for health warnings in all cigarette advertising even though the four-year moratorium on its rule-making power had been extended by Congress to six years, ending in 1971.

Support of the Federal Communications Commission (FCC), which licensed and regulated broadcasters using the public airwaves, and the US Department of Health, Education and Welfare (HEW) was also enlisted during this period. The FTC quickly set up its cigarette tar and nicotine laboratory and then began to submit a long series of hard-hitting annual reports to Congress. The FTC's 1966 Report to Congress called for a stronger health-warning label and more appropriations for the FTC and HEW so they could step up their public antismoking campaigns. The 1967 report vigorously attacked the advertising tactics of the Big Six, which the FTC argued were misleading to the public. In the 1968 report, the FTC first recommended that cigarette advertising be banned from the public broadcast media entirely. But the most important event during the FTC's state of moratorium was the *unexpectedly sudden* and *unique* entry of the Federal Communications Commission into the smoking-and-health controversy in 1967.

The FCC and the 'Fairness Doctrine'

The FCC was prompted to act when it received a letter from a young attorney, John F. Banzhaf, requesting that the Commission required a New York City television station to give free, to responsible health groups, the same amount of air time as that sold to the Big Six for the purpose of promoting the virtues and values of smoking. In doing this, Banzhaf was requesting that the FCC apply its 'Fairness Doctrine' in an unprecedented manner. The FCC's response did not require that exactly equal time be given to both views, but it did require stations licensed to operate over the public airwaves to provide 'a significant amount of time for the other viewpoint' (Fritschler, 1975: 145).

Heretofore, the Fairness Doctrine had been applied to situations in which expressed viewpoints of a personal nature, particularly statements about politicians, obligated broadcasters to give 'equal time' to opposing points of view. Because only the four-year, congressionally imposed moratorium governed the rule-making authority of the FCC, this commission was not constrained as was the FTC beyond 1968. Its creative application of the Fairness Doctrine to the public broadcast advertisement of a major consumer product caught both the Big Six and Congress off guard. [. . .]

[. . .]

Continued Control over Vital Information   During the years separating the labeling hearings and the eventual broadcast ban, the FTC continued to press for more information from the Big Six regarding both their advertising expenditures and their research on the effects of cigarette advertising – an initiative begun long before the labeling controversy and one not affected by the congressional moratorium. But the FTC had been successful in obtaining only advertising-expenditure data that were broken down by general media categories. HEW had also been active in monitoring the industry's accumulating smoking-and-health research findings. Indeed, it had succeeded in persuading the Big Six to release annual reports summarizing those findings. But during the late 1960s, the FTC filed subpoenas against all members of the Big Six to require them to divulge both more specific data on advertising expenditures and more sensitive marketing-research data on the effects of cigarette advertising on a broad range of consumer behaviors, especially regarding the decision to start smoking. The Big Six responded with litigation that, again, served to postpone a potential threat posed by their institutional environment. They argued that detailed marketing data of the types sought by the FTC were proprietary, and that by seeking to incorporate them in its annual reports to Congress, the FTC could not guarantee confidentiality.

Once again, the joint defensive strategies of the Big Six were successful in delaying a threat to their primary domain, because they controlled access to vital information that federal regulators required in order to proceed against them. It was not until 1977 that a federal judge ruled against the Big Six in favor of the FTC's subpoenas for detailed advertising information; but even that victory was unrealized. The immediate response of the Big Six was to mount an appeal of the court decision that would cause, at the very least, several more years of delay for the FTC.

A New Congress Acts   By the close of the 1970s, the breakdown in the defense of the tobacco subsystem was becoming more visible. The smoking-and-health issue had continued to build momentum, and the growth in the domestic cigarette market had plateaued. Moreover, the FTC and other federal administrative agencies had become smarter. The use of subpoenas and the court system by the FTC, and the FCC's creative application of the Fairness

Doctrine with support, again, from the court system, enabled both agencies to avoid direct oversight by a Congress that had been all too sensitive to the demands of the industry they threatened. By the time the broadcast-advertising ban was proposed as a congressional bill, even the forces within that institution had shifted. Senator Moss (D., Utah), the key antismoking figure who had been outmaneuvered in 1963 with the unusual floor vote on the labeling bill, was now the chairman of the Senate committee having oversight responsibility for the FTC. It was not surprising, therefore, that although the oversight committee in the House of Representatives failed to pass the bill, the Senate committee overruled. At the Senate hearings, the representative of the Tobacco Institute announced that the Big Six were willing to withdraw all radio and television advertising beginning January 1, 1970. In exchange, the tobacco lobby requested that the FTC continued to be required to give Congress six months' notice of any rule-making activity affecting cigarettes. The bill was passed. The ban was to become effective January 2, 1970, and a stronger health-warning label was prescribed.

Broadcast-advertising Ban: A Victory for Whom?

But how serious was the loss of access to the broadcast-advertising media to the Big Six? First, the Big Six's joint defensive strategies had postponed potentially immediate threats for almost a decade. [. . .] This period was sufficiently long to enable the Big Six to engage in the formation and implementation of new strategic directions, involving major reallocations of resources, to ensure their survival. Moreover, subsequent research has demonstrated that the victory for the health forces was more apparent than real and that the tobacco interests, as well as the investment community, recognized the advertising ban as such *before* the fact.

The loss of major advertising media to any consumer-products industry could reasonably be predicted to have severe consequences for the prospects of continued growth and prosperity of member firms. In the present case, approximately 80 percent of the Big Six's advertising expenditures in 1969 had been allocated to the broadcast media (radio and television). [. . .] Moreover, from the mid-1960s until the 1971 broadcast-advertising ban, cigarette companies had been the largest television advertisers in the United States.

Failing to avert the broadcast-media ban, the Big Six reacted with neither resignation nor panic. They adapted to this unprecedented handicap, first by shifting advertising expenditures to formerly minor media. Because they had experienced regulations in several European countries that had prohibited cigarette advertisements in broadcast media for a number of years prior to 1971, the Big Six were already practiced in the use of alternative promotional strategies for introducing new cigarette products. They turned this experience to their advantage after the US ban.

Domestic cigarette-advertising expenditures in printed media (newspapers and magazines) and outdoor media (billboards), for instance, jumped 227 percent between 1970 and 1971. The sponsoring of special events such as the Virginia Slims Tennis Tournament, the Doral Open Golf Tournament, the 'Win With Winston' Sweepstakes, and others, became commonplace. The television advertisement of 'little cigars' between 1970 and 1972 was also an attempt to skirt the cigarette-advertising ban, a tactic that was cut short by Congress's 'Little Cigar Act' of 1973. Several firms even toyed with the idea of introducing pipe tobacco or cigars with the same names as their traditional cigarette brands in order to maintain broadcast-media exposure of these brand images.

Second, the oligopolistic market of the Big Six had locked them into huge outlays for broadcast advertising that for many firms did not substantially alter their market shares. It was conceivable, therefore, that the elimination of access to this medium might result in greatly reduced costs for the Big Six without commensurately affecting any member's competitive strength. Analysis of the annual advertising outlays of the Big Six reveals that substantial cost savings were, indeed, realized from the ban.

From the time of the announcement of the formation of the Surgeon General's Advisory Committee in 1963 until the eve of the broadcast-media ban on cigarette advertising that went into effect on January 1, 1971, the gross domestic expenditure of cigarette advertising increased from $250 million to just under $315 million per year [. . .]. But during the first three years under the ban, gross industry expenditure on cigarette advertising fell back and momentarily stabilized at around $250 million per year. Thus, one of the potential industry benefits of the broadcast advertising ban was a virtual gift of approximately $200 million in reduced advertising expenditure from 1971 to 1973. [. . .]

The reprieve granted the Big Six from a deadlocked broadcast-advertising strategy, although enormous in terms of cash savings, was not long-lived. By the end of the fourth year after the ban, annual cigarette-advertising expenditures had jumped again, from the $250-million range to an all-time high of $330 million. The Big Six had mastered the switch to printed, outdoor, and point-of-purchase advertising, and the early success of innovative low-tar brands (i.e., allegedly 'safer' cigarettes) was creating new opportunities for market-share growth by way of aggressive advertising. [. . .]

A far more serious by-product of the broadcast advertising ban, however, was the fact that it voided the application of the Fairness Doctrine to the promotion of cigarettes. Because there were no more cigarette commercials, no obligation was imposed on broadcasters to air antismoking spots. During the two-year (1969–70) life of the Fairness Doctrine, about 1,200 antismoking messages were aired by the three major US television networks; but during the first two years (1971–72) of the broadcast ban, the number of antismoking messages delivered by these networks totaled less than 250 (Doron, 1979: 17). Hindsight analysis reveals that the flurry of antismoking commercials during the three years preceding the ban had a far more dramatic impact on cigarette consumption than the ban itself. The Big Six, apparently in possession of this foresight, actually *volunteered* to withdraw from broadcast advertising before the ban was to become law.

Through the use of econometric modeling, Doron (1979) has demonstrated that the Big Six were better off after the ban. He estimates that they lost 2.7 billion packages of cigarettes during the three years under the Fairness Doctrine, owing to the combined effect of the antismoking commercials and other antismoking activities, but lost only 1.7 billion during the first five years of the ban.[3] [. . .]

[. . .]

Summary

A number of effective collaborative efforts and formal joint ventures were employed by the Big Six to mount a broad range of anticipatory and reactive strategies whose purpose was to defend the traditional tobacco domain from threats to its legitimacy and efficacy from the broader institutional environment. On the anticipatory side, the defense was mounted with pooled resources and a unified strategy that simply overwhelmed the antismoking forces for a period long enough for the Big Six to develop the longer-term strategies [. . .]. When reaction to unavoidable institutional threats was called for, the joint positions of the Big Six were generally well conceived in advance and resulted in a skillful and orderly retreat that was always accompanied by the negotiation of important regulatory concessions. One cannot help being struck by the political sensitivity of this group of traditional competitors, and in particular by the acute sense of timing that was exhibited in all their efforts to defend a very profitable domain. But vanguard became rear guard as the joint political ventures encountered greater and greater antismoking sentiment during the 1960s and struggled to give the Big Six the time to engage in major organizational adaptations that would ensure their survival. Other strategic behaviors would be required to get the most out of, and to avoid overdependence on, the declining domestic domain.

Questions

- What was the strategy used by the tobacco firms to defend their industry, and why was it so successful?
- Provide a counter-strategy for the anti-smoking lobby at that time (1970s).
- How have the strategies of both the anti-smoking and the tobacco lobby changed since then?
- What are the ethical implications of these strategies?

Notes

1. We have relied primarily on the work of political scientist A. Lee Fritschler (1975) for this account of the tactics used by the tobacco industry to influence its institutional environment.

2. The effectiveness of the Tobacco Tax Council may be judged in part by the fact that the *federal* excise tax of 8 cents per pack of twenty cigarettes has remained unchanged since 1952. This means that the federal tax *rate* on cigarettes has fallen from 35 per cent of the retail price of a pack in the mid-1950s to 15 per cent in 1977 (Warner, 1978).

3. Similar conclusions were reached in an analysis of per capita cigarette consumption by the US Department of Agriculture (Miller, 1974a). This report revealed that actual per capita cigarette consumption lagged behind an estimated path of potential by about 4.5 per cent in 1964–67, widened sharply to a 14–15 per cent lag with the antismoking advertisements on radio and television in 1968–69, and then began to close the gap between actual and forecasted consumption by 1973. Warner (1978) and Hamilton (1972) have reported similar findings.

References

Doron, G. (1979) *The Smoking Paradox: Public Regulation in the Cigarette Industry.* Cambridge: Mass: Abt Books.

Fritschler, A.L. (1975) *Smoking and Politics: Policymaking and the Federal Bureaucracy.* Englewood Cliffs, NJ: Prentice-Hall.

Parker R. (1965) 'Cigarettes have friends in labeling battle', *Raleigh (NC) News and Observer,* March.

Pfeffer, J. and Salancik, G.R. (1978) *The External Control of Organizations: A Resource Dependence Perspective.* New York: Harper & Row.

Riker, W.H. (1979) 'Foreword', in G. Doron *The Smoking Paradox: Public Regulation in the Cigarette Industry.* Cambridge: Mass: Abt Books.

Smith Barney and Company (1968) *The Cigarette Industry.* Topical Research Comment No 97–69, New York.

Part III   Managing Strategic Predicaments

Introduction

If we acknowledge the need and difficulty of strategic alignment, and the political implications of strategic change, it should come as no surprise that implementation is problematic. There are a variety of common strategic predicaments that contemporary managers frequently face in implementing new strategies. To a large degree, these predicaments arise because of the political issues that are embedded in the strategic context. Some, but by no means all, common strategic predicaments facing contemporary managers are presented in this part.

Merger and acquisitions, while having lost some of the lustre they acquired during the 1980s, nonetheless remain a common event in the business world. One of the major challenges of M&As has been the cultural melding that is required to produce strategic synergy, cost efficiency, or financial benefits. The chapter by Fulmer and Gilkey highlights some of the managerial challenges that must be addressed if managers are to merge two cultures in a way that benefits both, instead of allowing one to crush the other. The readings on culture and human resource management are also relevant here: the former because it highlights the difficulties in orchestrating cultural change; and the latter because it emphasizes the importance of synchronizing such matters as compensation across the two companies. This material can also be used to examine other forms of joint venture such as alliances, networks, outsourcing, etc.

With the recession of the early 1990s providing a repeat of many features of the early 1980s, managing decline seems to be a continual, and depressing, feature of the contemporary business world. Even if recession is not the cause, globalization, deregulation and increased competition will continue to make downsizing a fact of life for many managers. There are two aspects of managing decline: the first concerns the business-economic aspect of finding a turnaround strategy that will bring the organization out of decline. While it is an important consideration, it is not the focal point of the material here. The emphasis in this book concerns the management of the people who are affected by retrenchment and cutback strategies. Since declining resources tend to stimulate political activity, managers are faced with political as well as motivational challenges. The chapter by Hardy presents some of the steps managers can take to avoid resistance and protect employees. These actions can also be viewed more critically, however, by examining the way in which managers use power to manage meaning and make unpalatable actions legitimate and acceptable.

Innovation is crucial in both revitalizing flagging businesses and creating new ones. It is, however, a difficult strategy to sustain and many organizations have had problems bringing viable new products to market. The chapter by Dougherty suggests how product innovators might overcome this persistent failure to understand markets for new products. It emphasizes what innovators need to know about markets and technology. It takes a closer look at the content of market–technology knowledge and how it can be developed, and identifies the organizing practices that sustain the continual creation and exploitation of this knowledge. Readers interested in how to design an innovative organization are left with the challenge of deciding how to reconcile the 'needs' of effective product innovation with the 'technology' offered by management and organizational theory.

Globalization is one of the 'hot' new topics in management. More and more organizations are competing within the global marketplace, but they are also struggling with the demands that global strategies place on them. A major dilemma concerns how to balance needs for standardization and cost effectiveness with needs for flexibility and responsiveness. The chapter by Wortzel discusses these strategies in more detail and highlights the assumptions behind them. It argues that organizations do have some choice in the strategy they select, but that the choice must be supported by an organization capable of carrying it out. This, in turn, requires attention to the strategic and geographic location of manufacturing, research and development, and marketing as well as the communication and information flows that provide the linkages between geographically and culturally disparate parts of the organization.

The sustainability of our ecological environment has only recently become a strategic issue for many companies. In so doing, it has created a whole set of new challenges for managers previously unaccustomed to taking environmental concerns into account. The chapter by Westley and Vredenburg shows how it has brought together very different interest groups, such as big business, radical environmental groups, and government, in attempts to develop strategies for sustainable development. In many respects, however, these interest groups remain ideologically distanced, and for any joint initiative to emerge and flourish all sides must be aware of their differences and able to find a way to work through them. Westley and Vredenburg discuss the role of bridging organizations in managing these political differences and forming strategies for sustainable development.

The management of collaboration, fittingly, concludes this book. With the advent of the postmodern organization and the need for collaboration within and between organizations, different styles of management and strategy making – more inclusive than exclusive – are being adopted. Westley's chapter examines collaboration in the form of the inclusion of middle managers in strategy making. While extensive participation has many advantages, it is also very threatening to senior managers who are used to viewing strategy making as 'their' job. As a result, they are unlikely to surrender power to other managers unless they are confident that they can retain some control. The chapter discusses how and when middle managers are likely to be included in strategy making and the costs and advantages of doing so.

The cases in this section have been selected to address the various themes. The example of General Motor's takeover of Electronic Data Systems provides a colourful – and ultimately successful – illustration of how the problems associated with mergers and acquisitions can be resolved, though not without some political upheavals along the way. Readers should consider whether the takeover was a smart strategic move. If not, why not? Given the takeover is not a fact, how should the two companies be merged to maximize synergy and minimize conflict? Equally important, how should General Motors handle Ross Perot?

The case on Atomic Energy of Canada provides some insight into how the difficult task of retrenchment can be accomplished by confronting rather than ignoring the human resource implications of downsizing. Readers should assess where the sources of friction are likely to arise and how they can be addressed. They might also consider whether management and employee interests are compatible in a situation like this. Both the Midville and Northville cases (Part II) can also be used to discuss the problems of managing decline.

The case of 'Machco's New Finishing Machine' shows some of the complex elements of organizational design that are necessary if companies are to innovate effectively. Of particular importance is the way in which individuals in different parts of the firm understand and relate to each other as well as to the overall strategy and capabilities of the organization. Another issue concerns how innovation can be sustained in the long term. Machco succeeded because the project in question was buffered from the stultifying effects of the larger bureaucracy that surrounded it. So, although effective in this particular case, it remains to be seen whether Machco can continue to innovate. Apple can also be used to show how innovation was created in the young organization through its culture, hiring of key individuals, and Steve Jobs' unique personality, and how new leadership and growth served to dampen that creative spirit.

The case on the Bicycle Components Industry illustrates the difficulties inherent in tackling global markets. It shows how the original world leader, an Italian firm called Campagnola, has been increasingly outmanoeuvred by its more flexible, innovative and responsive Japanese competitor. The environment has changed and become more hostile for this Italian firm and many other firms like it. They need to make some significant changes in how they conceptualize the market, the customer and the competition if they are to be successful in this new world order. Readers should devise a viable strategy for Campagnola. They can also compare the development of the two companies to see how their two different business approaches came about. Imperial Chemical Industries (Part I) is another case that can be used to ascertain the organizational implications of global strategies.

The Loblaws case illustrates some of the difficulties in reconciling different stakeholders with opposing views on both the environment and the role of business. The case introduces the concept of 'bridging organizations' and illustrates the necessity for business to be more sympathetic to the goals and fragile structures of these mediating organizations if collaborative alliances are to be successful. It also introduces students to the idea of marketing products from a societal perspective, and facilitates an understanding of how product endorsements can best be used. Finally, the case provides an interesting description of a social movement group and its reactions to some of the developments occurring around issues of sustainability.

The example of 'Conglom' illustrates how power can be used to secure collaboration: by the replacement of the overt, coercive use of power with more subtle controls. This substitution of power techniques thus requires a very different approach to management, one on which the traditional literature is unable to shed much light because of its narrow conceptualization of power. Yet, collaboration involves power as much as conflict does. This issue of collaboration brings us back to the issue of strategic intent and how it is shared, not just by those at the senior executive level but by other organizational members. For strategic intent to be realized, it must be shared and that process often involves the use of power – particularly the management of meaning – to create legitimacy and support for the strategy in question.

Further Reading for Part III

Allio, R.J. (1989) 'Formulating global strategy', *Planning Review*, 17(2): 22–8.

Cascio, Wayne, F. (1993) 'Downsizing: What do we know? What have we learned?', *Academy of Management Executive*, 7(1): 95–104.

Dougherty, D. (1990) 'Understanding new markets for new products', *Strategic Management Journal*, 11: 59–79.

Dougherty, D. (1992) 'A practice-centred model of organizational renewal through product innovation', *Strategic Management Journal*, 13: 77–92.

Floyd, Steven W. and Wooldridge, Bill (1992) 'Managing strategic consensus: The foundation of effective implementation', *Academy of Management Executive*, 6(4): 27–39.

Frost, Peter J. and Egri, Carolyn P. (1989) 'The political process of innovation', in L.L. Cummings and B.M. Staw (eds), *Research in Organizational Behaviour*. Greenwich, CT: JAI Press.

Frost, P.J. and Egri, C.P. (1991) 'The organizational politics of sustainable development', in H. Thomas (ed.), *The Greening of Strategy: Sustaining Performance*, 11th Annual Proceedings of the Strategic Management Society.

Glaister, K.W. (1991) 'International success: Company strategy and national advantage', *European Management Journal*, 9(3): 334–8.

Hardy, C. (1987) 'Investing in retrenchment: Avoiding the hidden costs', *California Management Review*, 29(4): 111–25.

Harshbarger, D. (1987) 'Takeover: A tale of loss, change and growth', *Academy of Management Executive*, 1(3): 337–41.

Hitt, M.A., Hoskisson, R.E., Ireland, R.D. and Harrison, J.S. (1991) 'Are acquisitions a poison pill for innovation?', *Academy of Management Review*, 5(4): 22–34.

Kleiner, A. (1991) 'What does it mean to be green?', *Harvard Business Review*, July–August, 38–47.

MacNeill, J. (1989) 'Strategies for sustainable economic development', *Scientific American*, 261(3): 154–65.

Nichol, Ronald L. (1992) 'Get middle managers involved in the planning process', *Journal of Business Strategy*, May–June, 26–32.

Porter, M.E. (1990) 'New global strategies for competitive advantage', *Planning Review*, 18(3): 4–14.

Ruckelshaus, W.D. (1989) 'Towards a sustainable world', *Scientific American*, 261(3): 166–75.

Schwieger, D.M. et al. (1987) 'Executive actions for managing human resources before and after acquisition', *Academy of Management Executive*, 1(2): 127–38.

17 Managing Mergers and Acquisitions

Robert M. Fulmer and Roderick Gilkey

[. . .]

Five dimensions distinguish the blended corporate families from the 'nuclear' companies (that is, one that has not experienced a major reorganization and still has a direct lint to its original founders). These dimensions include (1) the structure of the system, (2) the purpose of the system, (3) the tasks of the system, (4) the factors influencing managers, and (5) the forces that impinge on the system.[6]

A summary of the conflicts associated with the blended corporate family appears in [Table 17.1].

Managing the Blended Corporate Family

Managing the blended family can be as formidable a task as managing a corporate merger, given the presence of legal constraints, lawyers, ex-spouses, and divergent family histories, rules, rituals, traditions, and ideals. The lack of a shared history with a common vision of both past and future is one of the most difficult challenges that the newly blended family must face. In the following section we will review the major points in [Table 17.1] that apply to uniting both blended families and corporations in postmerger transition.

1. New Structure and Systems In merged organizations, authority structures and systems of control are in flux and unclear. This naturally leads to confusion and anxiety. The lack of historical precedent means that such basic issues as the travel and entertainment policy, or even the more personal issue of dress or grooming standards, may need to be clarified or discussed. At a more fundamental level, the question 'Who decides what?' must be addressed before equilibrium can be restored.

From 'Blending corporate families: Management and organization development in a postmerger environment', *Academy of Management Executive*, 2(4): 275–84.

[Table 17.1] *The differences between the nuclear and blended corporation*

Structural Issues

Nuclear	Blended
People and systems have evolved with the organization.	Previous management systems and personnel exert continued influence on current employees.
Everyone has experienced the same management and management style.	Varied experiences of being managed by different leadership styles, systems, and personnel.
Employees belong to one major system.	Multiple systems are present.
Membership is clearly defined, based on historical continuity, selection procedures and a formal organizational chart – a relatively closed system.	A more open system where personnel comes in the outside organization in roles and relationships that are often initially unclear.
Relationships are clearly defined and reinforced by social networks and systems that offer rites of passage, rituals, and a common history and folklore that support the organization.	Bonds uniting people are sudden, often arbitrary, and ill defined. There is no sense of historical continuity, body of shared experience, or ritual to support the formation of a bonding unit or culture.
Boundaries are clear and based on historical precedent.	Boundaries are fuzzy and there are no precedents.

Purpose of the System

Nuclear	Blended
Clearly defined mission and strategy that comes from within the company, from its own people, past and present.	Sense of mission and understanding of strategy is often unclear and comes in part or whole from 'outsiders.'

Tasks of the System

Nuclear	Blended
Consistent with the overall level of the organization's stage of development.	Often inconsistent and incongruent as different companies in different phases of development must address varying tasks in managing growth/maturity.
Definition of tasks flows from a central management system that has enjoyed continuity. Roles are defined.	Task definition comes from changed and multiple sources. Roles are defined.

Continued overleaf

[Table 17.1]   *Continued*

Factors Influencing Managers

Nuclear	*Blended*
Because of strong internal traditions and shared experiences, 'outside' managerial experience and relationships exert little influence over current performance.	Continuing contact with past systems, practices, and personnel can exert great influence and make the integration process more difficult.
Ideals from the past serve the interest of continuity during times of change.	Ideals from the past, to the extent they have been internalized and lived, are often distracting.
Career paths are stable and perceived as relatively predictable.	Career paths and plans are changed, thus raising concerns about fairness and future memberships.
Geographic location and the need to move seen as relatively predictable.	Location and moving are major, often realistic, concerns.
Patterns and systems for exerting influence are clear and established.	Employee influence systems are disrupted and significant forms or procedures for influencing the company are often lost, thus exacerbating all the previously cited difficulties (loyalty conflicts, loss of purpose, etc.)
The levels of dissent, innovation, and risk taking are relatively clear.	The limits for 'deviant' behavior not defined; risk averse behavior usually prevails, although the system may inadvertently encourage behind-the-scenes rebellions.

Forces that Impinge on the System

Nuclear	*Blended*
External sources of influence on the system are arranged in stable and predictable patterns.	Influence and control are suddenly exerted by new players outside the organization, whose language, methods, and purposes are often unclear and unpredictable.
Locus of expertise is internal and relatively centralized.	Locus of expertise is more external, creating confusion about the locus and nature of power and influence in the system.
Stakeholders are defined and their agendas are usually known.	New stakeholders are present and their agendas are often unknown or unclear.

2. The Power of Outsiders   This problem is exacerbated by the fact that power is exercised by intermediaries and outsiders who ordinarily play a more minor role in the company (if they have a role at all). Like a newly blended family that may have to deal with judges, lawyers, psychiatrists, and social workers, a newly blended corporation has to conduct its business in an arena where investment bankers, brokers, and consultants all exert power and influence. In such an environment, the sources of expertise and authority become more decentralized and diffuse, which can undermine the effectiveness of the management system. Paul Sadler, a manager in an acquired corporate we studied, disdainfully commented,

> Whenever I have to get input from above to deal with a problem, I think about going directly to McKinsey, since those are the guys who are really calling the shots around here now. It was bad enough when you tried to get information from above and you'd have to wait around. Now you wait and when you hear something you're not even sure it's coming from your own organization!

In addition, the appearance of 'outsiders' from the acquiring company disrupts mentoring relationships and career paths, as new structures, demands, and competitors appear. The new managers can come to feel resentment much like that of a parent in a blended family who has to manage someone else's children. The resentment between new managers and employees is often mutual and is apt to arise particularly when the stronger party exercises his or her power in an insensitive manner.

3. Territorial Battles   Previous alliances and power structures persist, often overriding or causing individuals to resist the new authority structure. The party in power before the marriage took place can easily invoke power again and use it to impede the unification of the family. Under such circumstances an informal organization can form, easily thwarting efforts to establish a more formal system of control. The new corporate family needs this control, however, to develop as a consistent and well-defined unit. Questions arise in a merged department as to whether the 'new kids' will do as well as those who have worked with the manager in charge.

4. Who Will Fit In?   Membership in the new family system is no longer clearly defined after a major reorganization. Since conflicts inevitably arise as the company defines its new identity, it is not possible to determine easily who is and who is not meeting the new criteria. Consider that the longer a child has been in one family, the greater the risk that he or she will not be fully integrated into a new one. Adolescents can easily construct a life that is at the fringe of the blended family, either by isolating themselves as much as possible or by making only brief forays into the family to challenge its authority and boundaries. Likewise, adapting to new ways and redefined objectives is hardest for employees with the longest tenure preceding the reorganization. It is somewhat ironic that some of the most loyal employees can most easily become recalcitrant and unproductive in a new environment.

5. Start-up Problems   Immediately after the merger, the blended family must begin to work as a functional unit. There is not enough time, however, to develop sufficient historical precedent so that an operating system can be smoothly established. In addition, there are no culturally transmitted rites of passage to assist in bridging the transition from separate to blended states.[7]

Interventions for Blended Corporate Families

Specific steps can be taken to alleviate some anxieties and concerns associated with the dramatic restructuring of a person's most important relationships. These should be a part of a conscious program of integration, and specific efforts should be made to use these reaffirmations of encouragement and support to facilitate the transition from separate to blended corporate families.

We will now review the parallels between blended families and merged corporations and describe intervention strategies that can be used to alleviate the adjustment pains of employees in a blended corporate family (see [Table 17.2])

1. New Structure and Systems   This predictable and normal crisis can be dealt with through a transition management program that quickly reaffirms basic structures and clarifies the control system and reporting relationships.

It is very important to reaffirm the basic structures that now exist in the organization. Consider that when a parent remarries, children should be reassured that their relationship to their parent is not being challenged, although it may be changed. Likewise, as soon as decisions are made about the 'survivors' of a merger, the change in the organization should be announced so that each employee can begin to work out his or her new role and its expectations. The new parent company should then clarify roles and procedures as quickly as possible. In those situations where more deliberation is called for, the transition managers should make clear when decisions will be made and announced.

Even when bad news has to be shared, a prompt announcement enables people to deal with the situation more effectively than they could if they were forced to 'wait for the other shoe to fall'. Tony Stone, general manager in the Electronics and Instrumentation Sector, felt that

> one of the major successes in Allied's integration activities was the commitment to employees to [let them] know about their status within two months of the merger approval. Although some of the news was not positive, everybody from the corporate staff received written notices about [his or her] future. Within nine months, the integration of the two staffs was largely complete.

As with other blended families, blended corporate families need clear interpretations of their situation so that members can gain an intermediate vision of the future before the consolidation into a functional unit takes place.

[Table 17.2] *Summary of blended corporate family problems and interventions*

Problems	Intervention
New structure and systems	• Reaffirmation of basic structure • Clarify controls and reporting relationships • Active involvement of CEO and others to bridge/facilitate the transition • Active communication
The power of outsiders	• Representative transition team • Participative management • Scheduled candor • Deal with an acquired company as if it were a partner in a merger • Clarify general mission, strategy, and the role of external players
Territorial battles	• Transitional rites to provide social mechanisms to usher in the acceptance of the new state
The question of who fits in	• Clarification of job status, role, and reporting relationships • Reassurance and feedback mechanisms • Positive new practices
Start-up problems	• Building a new culture using key leadership figures, the media, and all available forms of communication • Using management education to disseminate information, socialize, and acculturate

When a company interprets and clarifies the transition process, and outlines the immediate steps and inevitable uncertainties associated with each step, it can offer support and prevent declining morale and postmerger drift.

2. The Power of Outsiders This problems can be alleviated by establishing a transition team comprised of members from both corporate staffs. Choosing individuals from both sides tends to blunt the we/they perspective. The most carefully orchestrated merger/acquisition efforts attempt from the beginning to create a climate of mutuality and cooperation. According to Ed Hennessey, CEO and chairman of Allied-Signal Inc., who has been involved in over 100 acquisitions, 'If you are ever going to make the people part work out, you have to treat the deal as a merger even, maybe especially, if it is an acquisition.'[8] This approach is not intended to be manipulative; rather, it is an attempt to treat everyone with respect and make all individuals feel they are a part of the new corporate family as soon as possible.

One way to do this is through 'scheduled candor'. We have already stressed the need for all individuals to cope with ambiguity; managers need to recognize that when they can provide clarity and candor, it will help ease much of the stress their subordinates may be facing. Vince Bazzaro, a former Bendix staff executive, commented on the importance of the Allied president's attendance at a senior management seminar at the end of a week in which a major merger announcement had been made:

> Personally, Hennessey seemed more distant than Agee did, but when I think about the times I've talked to him, I realize he is actually more candid. You have to respect him for coming out for the last day of the senior management seminar after all the negotiations and meetings associated with the Signal announcement. He looked exhausted, but his willingness to answer lots of questions was the highlight of the program for me.

3. Territorial Battles   Old loyalties persist long after the new organization has been established. While it is easier to redefine jobs than realign loyalties, in time both happen. In the meantime, a struggle during which old allegiances and alliances continue to exert their influence in the political process may occur.

Many employees are likely to be involved in a mourning process, in which lingering attachments imperil the transition to the organization. This is particularly true if the acquired business was previously privately held and individuals are devoted to previous owners. In such cases employees often persistently wish that the old family order would reemerge so that a reunion and reinstatement of the old ways would occur. Similarly, we have found that realigning commitments is easier if the members of the founding family are not visible members of the new corporate hierarchy. This is particularly true if the new corporation is radically different from its predecessor.

In these cases it appears that it is better to have a decisive change in leadership. Employees may be plunged into a sudden state of shock and mourning, but they will also be able to confront the transition in a definite and clear manner. Once they have come to grips with the emotional realities, they can get on with their work and lives without an extended period of emotional turmoil and unproductive postmerger drift. One highly successful corporation we observed actually gathered employees together to hold a ceremony at which they eulogized an old program they were phasing out, and then offered a champagne toast to a new start-up venture.

Founding fathers or entrepreneurs have an important symbolic role, but they can interfere with the processes needed to establish a more highly developed organization. This is not to say that the employees' attachments to the previous organization and its leaders should be casually dismissed and disregarded; in fact, it is sometimes imperative that the new management in a merger/acquisition demonstrate its awareness of the contributions of its predecessors. In one very successful bank takeover we studied, the acquiring bank instructed members of the transition team to spend time in the new bank talking with employees about what it was like formerly to work for the bank (which was then privately held), and to share in the exchange of stories and anecdotes about banking in the 'old days'. The effort here, as it was explained to us, was to provide support to people who had experienced a serious loss and needed the loss to be acknowledged and understood by everyone. As the vice-president of human resources in charge of the transition process stated, 'It was important that all of us demonstrated some empathy and awareness, that we respected what they had accomplished in the bank and also that we understood that sense of loss they were experiencing.'

4. The Question of Who Fits In?   Since membership in the new family is not initially clear or ensured, a period of testing and negativism is a predictable feature of the blended corporate family. While some negativism is inevitable, we believe that much of it is preventable if the proper clarifying and supportive interventions are made – that is, if the firm quickly announces who will be staying and what their status will be. The next step is to provide extra reassurance. The reaffirmation of basic structures, cited earlier, is facilitated by extra reassurance or by the offering of positive new practices by top management. For example, when Ed Hennessey first arrived at Allied, he stayed at a corporate training program about the company. Tom Samuels, one of the executives attending the sessions, recalled,

> I remember the first time he came out to visit one of my plants with John Connor [the previous CEO]. We had always referred to him as Mr. Chairman, but Hennessey made it clear that he wanted to be called Ed. He got rid of 700 people from the corporate staff, but then he raised the salary levels of almost everyone who was left. He's certainly bent over backwards to be fair to the Bendix people. When we did the last morale survey, the results showed that the Bendix crowd had higher morale than the Allied group.

5. Start-up Problems   Since there is insufficient time to develop a culture and history to support the new corporation, transitional ideologies and mediating structures have to be developed. Strong communication efforts sponsored, if not spearheaded, by the CEO seem to be a preferred mode of dealing with this problem in the best corporations. In the case of Allied-Signal, Ed Hennessey oversaw the production of a film that was shown to several thousand employees in an effort to develop a common understanding, or ideological perspective, on the historical events in which they were participating. This self-conscious attempt to develop a common historical perspective and build a new culture is a necessary part of the transition process for the blended corporate family. A variety of means are available for developing a common new culture. Among them is the use of management training to further the socialization and acculturation process.

Several firms have successfully used massive training education programs to bring about a cultural change that emphasizes common objectives and shared values.[9] In addition to the information and education offered, seminars provide an opportunity for managers to meet their counterparts from different parts of the merged organization. Phil Thompson, the Aerospace executive, observed:

> Top-level executive development is an Allied idea that is super. This was the first time I had seen general managers from Allied in a situation where we could chat. Of course, we'd been to the annual management meeting, but with several hundred people there, I always wound up sitting by other Bendix people whom I already knew. Since this senior management seminar was the first one, it was a bit rough in places,

but it still was very useful from the standpoint of both content and getting to know other people throughout the organization. It gave me a much better perspective on how Allied has done things and helped me understand a bit more of that history and culture.

Conclusion

We have reviewed major areas of conflict we have observed in postmerger corporate settings. In discussing these difficulties with numerous managers, we have been struck by their references to family struggles in their attempt to describe the conflicts they observed in the corporate postmerger environment. [. . .]

[. . .]

The proverbs about marriage also apply to mergers. Just as people can 'marry more money in ten minutes than they may earn in a lifetime', firms can achieve increased sales, profits, or market share more quickly through a merger than through internal growth. But the 'Marry in haste, regret at leisure' principle may also apply, suggesting the importance of premerger analysis that looks beyond the romantic dreams of synergy and financial fit to the more elusive goal of day-to-day compatibility.

Notes

[. . .]

6. We wish not only to reference the work of Clifford Sager, Hollis Brown, Helen Crohn, Tamara Engel, Evelyn Rodstein, and Libby Walker (*Treating the Remarried Family*. New York: Brunner/Mazel, 1983), but also acknowledge our debt to these individuals for the considerable assistance their seminal work provided us. We have developed our own adaptation of the problems of the blended corporate family with reference to their framework.

7. Luciano L'Abate and Steven Weinstein, *Structured Enrichment Programs for Couples and Families*. New York: Brunner/Mazel (in press).

8. Allied-Signal Corp. interview, 14 February 1986.

9. Robert M. Fulmer, 'The role of management development in mergers and acquisitions', *Personnel*, February 1986.

18 Managing Decline

Cynthia Hardy

Many companies view retrenchment as an isolated and unpleasant incident, best carried out and forgotten as quickly as possible. This attitude ignores the fact that retrenchment is not purely about disbanding operations: it is often part of a strategy designed to sustain the larger organization. When the global picture is taken into consideration, it becomes clear that the hidden costs are significant and can jeopardize the future survival of the organization. There are a number of factors which give rise to these hidden costs.

Union resistance, regardless of the form it takes, causes major problems for management. A strike weakens the larger organization. Occupations, in which employees take over the factory or hospital in question to prevent the sale of assets or transfer of production, are expensive. Even in North America where such overt resistance is less common, unions can withdraw cooperation, make contract negotiations difficult, initiate grievances, and prevent the smooth transfer of production, all of which represent additional costs to managers wishing to make effective cost savings.

Employers often dismiss the impact retrenchment has on continuing employees, seeing the problem purely in terms of those who leave. Yet the survivors are crucial to the future success of the organization and if they are alienated, productivity will fall; commitment will be reduced and may result in people leaving the organization as soon as the opportunity arises; creativity and innovation will be difficult to foster; and employees will be reluctant to make the concessions and sacrifices integral to future competitiveness. Companies which change policies of job security are particularly vulnerable if employees feel management is reneging on past promises and compromising managerial credibility over the handling of cutbacks. This makes it difficult to foster a creative and effective team spirit at a time when it is most needed.

Unfavorable publicity is another cost. If detailed reports of cutbacks are published, customers may start to worry that the firm is going out of business. Potential new recruits will look elsewhere for jobs if they feel that the organization has a poor record. Union officials and employees in other plants may become interested – and anxious. Community officials will start to question decisions and actions.

From 'Investing in retrenchment: Avoiding the hidden costs', *California Management Review*, 29(4): 111–25, 1987.

Organizations linked to the public sector will want to avoid political intervention. Government officials may have the ability to revoke cutback decisions if they feel that they have been handled in a way that is politically embarrassing. Even where intervention is less direct, the clumsy handling of retrenchment can lead to a series of difficult questions for senior managers. Private organizations are not exempt from political interference: contracts are awarded, subsidies granted, and payments made from government sources – and all of these can be jeopardized by retrenchment actions that meet with government disapproval.

Plant closures, cutbacks, and the rationalization of operations have been and will continue to be one of the major challenges facing contemporary managers. Increasing economic uncertainty and tough foreign competition are making such decisions imperative. Managing them in a way that incurs the costs described above will be expensive – particularly in the long term, as the struggle to restore viability unfolds. For these reasons, *retrenchment must be considered to be an investment in the future*, since contraction is the price paid for future success. Retrenchment deserves the same creative analysis as any other investment decision; otherwise, downgrading – rather than downsizing – will be the result.

[. . .]

[. . .] This chapter, by examining ten Canadian and British organizations, identifies the tasks associated with the successful management of retrenchment. These organizations were part of a study carried out in both public and private sectors [which showed that] organizations incurred some costs, and avoided others, during their experience with retrenchment (see [Table 18.1])

Avoiding the Costs

Many of the costs associated with downsizing can be avoided with the implementation of a retrenchment program that takes into account the needs of both the departing and continuing employees, as well as the unions and other interest groups which are involved. This would allay many of the fears associated with cutbacks and would help employees to view retrenchment as a challenge rather than a threat, enabling them to respond positively to the increased demands and changes required of them. Individuals must be convinced that the cutbacks are a step towards increased profitability and efficiency, that there are opportunities associated with a more streamlined operation, that their increased effort will be rewarded, and that their concerns will not be ignored. The remainder of this chapter addresses the tasks required of management in this respect.

[Table 18.1]　*The Organizations*

The ten organizations referred to in the article are described below. At the request of their respective organizations, the names 'Andersons', 'Whitefields', 'Midville', and 'Northville', have been substituted to conceal their identity.

- Between 1975 and 1980, Imperial Chemical Industries (ICI), the British chemical manufacturer, closed *Mountside* works. The factory, situated in the northwest of England, employed more than 1,000 people.
- ICI closed another plant at *Brookside* in Scotland during the mid-seventies. In this case, local union officials put up considerable resistance, involving the press and political leaders in an effort to prevent the closure. They eventually accepted the decision, but only after national union leaders and the headquarters level of the company had been drawn into the negotiations, despite the fact that there was no enforced redundancy and all employees were given the option of working in another plant on the site.
- '*Andersons*' is an engineering multinational. In 1978, it announced the loss of 1,000 jobs in a Scottish factory. Attempts to bring in a new product to save the remaining 500 jobs failed, and the factory was closed in 1980. The company helped employees to set up a small engineering factory on the site of the old one to save 200 jobs.
- In June 1983, *CIL*, a divisionalized Canadian manufacturer and distributor of chemical and allied products, announced the partial closure of an explosives factory in an isolated community in Northern Ontario. There were 176 people involved, of whom 53 continued to work in the ongoing part of the operation. This, however, was closed in 1985.
- '*Whitefields*', a manufacturing multinational offered, in 1983, an early retirement option to all employees with 25 years service in its Canadian operations. Of more than 1,200 eligible employees, 432 accepted.
- *Air Canada*, the state-owned airline, offered a voluntary severance program to all of its managerial staff in August 1982. Nearly 18%, more than 600 people, took advantage of the program.
- *Atomic Energy of Canada Ltd. (AECL)*, the state-owned nuclear power agency, laid off over 500 people in its manufacturing operations in 1983. [See case at the end of Part III.]
- '*Midville*' and '*Northville*' AHAs (Area Health Authorities) both proposed hospital closures in the mid-seventies in response to funding cuts. At Midville, the proposed closure was implemented. At Northville, however, unions, employees and patient groups united in their opposition to the closure and the recommendation was overruled, forcing management to retain the hospital. [See cases in Part II.]
- *Ville Marie* is a social service agency in Montreal. In 1981, an 11% funding cut was announced by the provincial government of Quebec.

Nearly 200 interviews were carried out with managers, union officials, employees, and representatives of other interest groups in each organization. Documentation – in the form of managerial and union reports, correspondence and memoranda, and newspaper articles – was also analyzed.

The Task: Managing Awareness

We were able to say: let's do it, we have the time to do it; let's not wait until the crisis is so great all we can do is swing the axe. We have the time to do it in a more socially responsible way; in a way that minimizes the hurt on people, so let's do it before it is forced upon us in a more unpleasant way. (Human resource executive)

Once the costs of retrenchment have been ascertained and the larger picture established, the situation of the individual organization can be assessed in terms of whether there is a need to adopt a broader and longer-term view of downsizing. Awareness of this need must be created among the senior level of management for two reasons: to ensure that the necessary cuts are made in a timely and logical manner, avoiding a crisis and allowing for a more humane approach to be put into place; and to secure a commitment among decision makers to a more enlightened approach and the investment which that entails.

A lack of awareness of the need for downsizing will result in counter-productive decisions which worsen an already difficult situation. At Atomic Energy of Canada Ltd (AECL), where more than 500 individuals were laid off in 1983, previously full order-books in the late seventies and early eighties had obscured management's perceptions. Senior management was unwilling to face up to the prospect of layoffs even though the numbers showed that something was 'definitely wrong'. As a result, AECL was hiring new graduates up until 1981 (to arrive in 1982). Before the end of 1981, however, the corporation had been forced to do an about-turn with a hiring freeze, followed by an announcement of layoffs in November 1982. This not only compromised managers' credibility, it left them with the difficulties of laying off additional staff and dealing with a disaffected group of people who had turned down other jobs to work for AECL. As a result, future graduates will look a little more critically at AECL's hiring promises.

Human resource managers at Air Canada, which has undergone a series of cost-cutting measures in recent years, took steps to persuade senior executives of the need for action. The experience of the American airline industry with recession and deregulation was 'powerful ammunition' in this respect. It enabled them to convince senior management that cost cutting should begin as soon as possible while there was time to plan a more humane program than had been the case in most of the American companies.

Difficulties in predicting the future with any degree of certainty can be overcome. Managers at Ville Marie, a Montreal social service agency, knew the government planned to cut their budget in 1981, but not by how much. They responded by planning three scenarios representing cuts of 8 per cent, 10 per cent, and 12 per cent. The knowledge accumulated in the process put them in a good position to effect the 11 per cent cut they ultimately received.

Senior managers will provide the funds necessary to protect and support employees only if they consider it worthwhile. As a result, there is a need to impress upon them the hidden costs of retrenchment. The explosives division at CIL (the Canadian chemical manufacturer) effected the partial closure of a factory in a small town in Ontario. Divisional and human resource managers presented the executive committee with nine reasons why they should handle the closure carefully, ranging from the possibility of sabotage and other potential union problems to the difficulties of finding alternative employment in such an isolated area. The result was that a retrenchment program was approved, as were the funds (nearly $1 million for 123 employees) required to carry it out.

The Task: Managing the Alternatives

> We were prepared to seriously look at [alternative ways of reducing costs] if there was an emotion out there that wanted it. (Manager)

The aim of creating awareness is to buy time and commitment, both of which allow a more flexible approach to downsizing, including the opportunity to consider some of the alternative methods of reducing costs. If action is taken early enough, attrition can be used to reduce personnel. Worksharing, early retirement, and voluntary severance as well as leaves of absence, pay freezes, and redeployments to other locations are other options for cost cutting. Since these methods involve an additional cost to the employer or take longer to have an effect, employers need to be well prepared to be able to make use of them.

Of particular interest to managers wishing to reduce the effect of retrenchment on employees is the question of whether severance can be conducted on a purely voluntary basis. Air Canada, ICI, and Whitefields (a manufacturing multinational which offered an early retirement option to all its Canadian operations staff with 25 years service) all used voluntary programs.

Voluntary severance has been criticized as an expensive method of cutback: employees have to be paid to leave. However, even at AECL – where more than 500 had already been laid off at the height of the recession, and the incentive offer 'was not a rich package' – 80 people took advantage of it.

The concern that the best people leave is not borne out in practice, since people have loyalties which bind them to the organization 'regardless of the job market'. Managers felt it was often the marginal performers who left; perhaps because they were disillusioned with their jobs and voluntary severance provided an opportunity to leave, or perhaps because they feared a less honorable discharge later. Even when experience is lost, the opening up of promotion opportunities more than compensates.

> A lot of people say nobody's indispensable and it seems to be true because [although] I was afraid when I saw the number of people leaving and the quality of those people, it turned out we could do without them ... [and it] certainly hasn't crippled us because what it's done has provided opportunities for people who were waiting. So we haven't really suffered even though we've lost a lot of experience. (Manager)

The company can always protect itself by stating formal conditions. Air Canada reserved the right of refusal in cases where scarce skills would be lost to the competition. Informal persuasion can be used to ease out some of the more marginal performers. However, voluntary programs must be *seen* to be voluntary to be effective. Managers must not be perceived as 'leaning' on people. Nor must there be too many denials: even at Air Canada there was pressure from CEO down to let everyone go unless there were some 'really dire circumstances'. A 'voluntary program' also means accepting the numbers who apply, be they above or below expectations. Managers at Whitefields were willing to cut expenses or carry the extra overhead rather than fire anyone, in the event that an insufficient number of people volunteered.

Voluntary severance provides both the company and the employee with benefits. Employees are given a choice and there is no stigma attached to their dismissal. The company gains credibility by being seen to accommodate employee needs, which translates into commitment and productivity from continuing employees.

The Task: Managing Involvement

[The joint committee] worked well because what it did was keep the company and the union working together, solving the problems. By making them participants I think it was much more successful. (Manager)

Employees will be worried about the impact the cutbacks will have. Involving representatives in at least part of the decision-making process helps to reduce feelings of powerlessness and provides a forum in which employee interests can be protected.

Companies that restricted involvement have met with criticism. Andersons, a multinational which had set up a feasibility study to investigate the closure of a Scottish engineering factory with 1500 employees, refused to allow union participation or to release the figures on which the recommendation for closure was based. The result was a great deal of suspicion concerning the company's motives and an unwillingness to believe that the closure was necessary.

Andersons has a traditional position – they make a decision and the union agrees . . . I think they made a mistake. If they'd come to the same decision with union involvement it would have been easier to accept. (Union official)

Beliefs that effective involvement cannot be created around the issue of cutbacks are unfounded. Mechanisms were established to facilitate employee involvement in most of the organizations. At Mountside, a special committee was set up with union and management representation to secure the cooperation of the senior stewards. It brought together the two sides as a problem-solving group, avoiding the need to resort to the formal negotiating procedure. It made recommendations concerning employee needs to the works manager, who was then able to make decisions fully aware of the likely consequences. He sometimes made concessions, for example, allowing people to leave before their termination date (with full severance pay) if they found another job. This helped win the goodwill of the stewards. They felt they were an active part of the process, able to safeguard their own interests rather than having to watch helplessly from the sidelines. The committee acted as a safety valve, achieving a 'remarkable degree of trust on both sides' and preventing any industrial unrest.

At CIL, placement committees were established with managers and union representatives to consider the issues of retraining, counselling, and out-placement. Federal legislation dictated the establishment of a Joint Planning Committee at AECL with union/employee and management membership and an independent chair. For each of the four employee groups, the corporation also set up Joint Manpower Adjustment Committees (JMACs), with a similar format, to handle the grievances and outplacement needs of the particular group.

The Task: Managing Fair Play

[It's important that the] employee group perceives there's been a lot of fairness, a lot of trust, and the selection process is done fairly objectively; because if it isn't, the more you upset people. (Manager)

Employees were reassured by a sense of fairness in how the process was handled, particularly when managers were forced to undertake enforced dismissals involving some sort of selection process. A perception of fairness prevents the initiation of grievances and provides some security to continuing employees.

Three common selection criteria are seniority, required skills, and perform-ance. Seniority has the advantage of being a criterion that workers 'relate to', helping them to view dismissals 'in a rational fashion' and accept the choices that are made. Some critics argue that it robs the organization of its young blood. However, the problem with the other two criteria is that they are more subjective and decisions may be contested. Unions at AECL disagreed with the selection criteria that were used to protect critical skills, initiating over 100 grievances, some of which they won in arbitration.

On another issue, AECL's sense of fair play was commended: its willingness to handle unionized and nonunionized groups in the same way. Of the four employee groups at the corporation, only two were represented by unions. However, JMACs were set up on the same basis for all these groups, and management established grievance procedures for the nonunionized employees who were not protected by collective agreements.

Discrimination between management and nonmanagement employees creates a sense of injustice. Air Canada ran into this problem: voluntary severance was offered only to managers on the basis that their jobs were being terminated permanently. Other employees were laid off on a temporary basis according to union contracts and did not qualify for the same severance pay. Despite the difference in the nature of the layoffs, union representatives felt that their members were being discriminated against and management had a difficult time explaining the position to them.

The Task: Managing Support

> It's marvellous how it's been done. Every help one could imagine was there. (Manual worker)

A variety of support mechanisms can prove invaluable in helping employees deal with job loss, which enhances managerial credibility in the eyes of both departing and continuing employees and provides a firm foundation for future employee relations. Of particular importance here are attempts to reduce the insecurity of employees, such as with severance pay and help in finding new jobs.

All the firms provided some sort of severance pay. Both Andersons and ICI exceeded the state minimum.[8] Air Canada offered one month per year of service (up to 18 months). Whitefields offered two years' salary over the following four years. CIL instituted a minimum of $4,000 and paid between one and two weeks' pay per year of service. AECL offered one week's pay per year of service with a variety of supplements providing up to an additional 55 days' pay for some employees.

Outplacement also helps employees. ICI advertised on behalf of its employees, appointed a redeployment manager, set up a 'job shop' in which vacancies were posted, provided training in interview skills, and allowed paid time off to attend interviews. CIL provided job search seminars, moving expenses, job search expenses, paid time off, retirement counselling, and financial planning. AECL undertook 'ad tracking' on behalf of employees, posted vacancies, advertised, provided seminars on job search techniques, offered secretarial support, staffed an outplacement center, and organized a job fair in which potential employers were invited on site. This type of aid has a positive impact at a relatively low cost.

> There's no denying that providing that sort of [outplacement] aid helps the acceptance of the pain of workforce reduction. . . . It really doesn't cost you that much. It costs a lot in time and effort in the organizing, but it doesn't cost you in terms of dollars in cash outlay, and in some respects it's more appreciated. (Manager)

Managers at Andersons took a somewhat different approach. First, they tried to save some jobs by transferring a substitute product to the Scottish factory. When that failed, they hired a consultant to conduct an international search for a buyer for the factory and equipment. When this proved unsuccessful, a local search, instigated by the company and its employees, uncovered a demand for the engineering skills of the workforce. As a result, a small subcontracting engineering firm was set up, with the company's help, employing around 200 of the original employees.

The Task: Managing Disclosure

The worst thing is the insecurity of not knowing. (Employee)

Empirical studies agree that it is in the employees' interests if managers disclose as much information as they can, as soon as they can, as often as they can. Advance notice improves morale and enhances the chances of finding another job. The absence of information, on the other hand, leads to rumor, which is usually more pessimistic than reality.

Some managers at Ville Marie withheld information, believing it would add to anxiety to say too much about impending cuts. Employees, however, found that the resulting rumors increased uncertainty and tension.

It was mostly rumor. That's what we found so maddening – that there was nothing we could grasp. It was just rumor and it was very tense. Everyone was concerned that they might be cut and they didn't know whether it was going to be [on] seniority or not. (Employee)

CIL sent specially trained counsellors to the closing plant on the day of the announcement 'to get as much information to all the employees as quickly as possible'. Even though they were not legally required to do so, AECL managers informed individuals of their future at the same time as the announcement of group dismissals (sixteen weeks in advance) to avoid having the entire corporation worry and thus having a detrimental effect on production.

Advance notice does not necessarily result in conflict, sabotage, or declining productivity, as is sometimes charged. The percentage of hours lost due to industrial action fell at Andersons from 18 per cent in 1977 to less than 1 per cent in the first nine months of 1979, after the announcement of redundancies. Absenteeism fell during the rundown process at Mountside, as did the number of customer complaints, while the output per man-weeks remained stable. Productivity actually rose at CIL.

It is not enough simply to inform employees at the beginning of the exercise; information should be updated as the retrenchment program progresses. A weekly bulletin at Mountside was issued both in a newssheet and via the internal telephone. It ran for more than two years and was revised weekly to ensure that employees were aware of what was happening.

Information should be realistic – raising false hopes can backfire. At another closure in ICI, three statements were made shortly before the closure was announced, indicating that there was no threat to jobs. The actual announcement took employees by surprise and they started to question the company's motives, blaming the closure on ineffective planning and accusing it of hiding the real situation from them.

The Task: Managing Understanding

> We spent so much time and effort in trying to get understanding of why it happened
> and how we were going to close it [the factory], and what help we were going to give,
> that acceptance became rather inevitable. (Manager)

From the effective disclosure of information should come an understanding of
why retrenchment is occurring, which is important if union officials and
employees are to accept the cut. Opposition arose at Northville because
medical reasons for the cuts were disputed by medical staff, while the financial
rationale was considered an unacceptable basis on which to cut health
services.

Air Canada took a number of steps to create an understanding of the
corporation's position throughout the organization. An audio-visual program
was created called 'The Air Canada Challenge', which included a film, articles
in the company magazine, and meetings between managers and employees. It
was used to explain what was happening in the industry in terms of costs,
declining markets, and deregulation. Individuals were informed of the steps
being taken to deal with these problems – the marketing efforts to attract new
business, the measures to save gasoline, the steps to increase efficiency.
Finally, it impressed upon employees the need for sacrifices, cost cutting, and
increased productivity.

The Task: Managing Blame

> There has to be a very well argued case for closure – people need convincing. They
> are going to have to be satisfied that the reasons for closure are credible. (Manager)

One issue that will arise from trying to create an understanding of the reasons
behind the cutbacks is the question of who is responsible. Managers have to
choose between accepting responsibility for the current situation and directing
the blame elsewhere. The latter can be a very risky strategy: if employees find
out the reasons for cutbacks are not valid, they will start to question the entire
retrenchment exercise, and management will find itself the subject of a great
deal of suspicion.

Andersons' attempt to blame the closure on falling world demand was
contested by the unions who felt it was a 'cosmetic exercise' designed to
placate financial institutions worried about their investments. The closure was
interpreted as a political move rather than a financial necessity and the unions
felt that they could pressure the company into changing its decision.

Managers can sometimes take advantage of an external scapegoat. Although
the Mountside closure was part of a rationalization plan, managers tended to
blame it on the old age of the plant and the proximity of the potentially
dangerous chemical plant to a hospital and residential area. These reasons

were visible, comprehensible, and had the added advantage of absolving management from all blame. In this case, the 'scapegoating' worked, as did a similar situation at Midville AHA where a proposed hospital closure was blamed on government spending cuts, even though:

> I know darn well that had we had the money we still would have closed it. They [the unions] don't realize that. We were using the financial argument but what we were really after was rationalization. (Manager)

If a clearly visible scapegoat exists, one that does not implicate management and that is easy to understand, managers may choose to use it. If, however, the explanation is complicated or contentious, this strategy may well backfire.

Conclusion: The Task is Managing Survival

> It's like most dollars ahead of people decisions. They are short term in their good effect, and long term in their bad effect; if indeed there is any good effect. (Manager)

Retrenchment should not be viewed as an unpleasant but short-lived affair, to be put to one side and forgotten as soon as possible. It is an investment in the future, the basis on which success depends. Layoffs are the price that a company or institution is prepared to pay. That price will only produce benefits if retrenchment does not hamper the return to viability. For retrenchment to play its part in the performance of the organization, it should be part of an integrated strategy to restore competitiveness, with a focus on all the necessary ingredients for success.

While this article finishes with the larger picture, managers ideally should *start* with it. Managers and employees need to know where the organization is going and how it intends to get there – and whether more cuts are part of that picture. Only in this way can managers assess the hidden costs and design a program accordingly. Moreover, it is only by knowing that retrenchment lies ahead that managers can take timely action, use alternative measures, prevent hiring mistakes, and demonstrate to employees that their sacrifices will indeed produce a more viable organization. The earlier the recognition that retrenchment is part of a survival strategy, the more likely it is to be viewed as an investment rather than a crisis. With this type of forward thinking and proactive planning, managers should be thinking of how to manage *survival*, rather than how to manage retrenchment. [. . .]

[. . .]

Notes

[The NHS structure described in the chapter refers to the situation following the 1974 reorganization.]

[. . .]

8. In Britain, redundancy compensation is mandatory. Minimum requirements are ½ week's pay per year of service while age 18–21; one week's pay per year of service while age 22–41; 1½ week's pay while age 42–65. This is for employees with more than 2 years of service up to a maximum of 20 years of service. The state reimburses 41% of this amount.

19 Managing Innovation

Deborah Dougherty

The ability to develop commercially viable new products is important because product innovation is often a primary means to maintain or build share in mature markets, enter new businesses, exploit technologies more fully, and react to changing customer needs or new competition. Even those organizations which emphasize a defensive strategy based on standardization and quality need to be able to innovate effectively from time to time. We know, however, that established firms have difficulty developing and marketing viable new products. The biggest single cause for failure is that product innovators do not carry out thorough market analyses to identify customer needs and priorities.[1]

This chapter suggests how product innovators might overcome this persistent failure to understand markets for new products. It emphasizes what innovators need to know about markets and technology. The first section defines product concept development as a process of knowledge creation and exploitation, and briefly outlines how knowledge is created. The second section takes a closer look at the content of market–technology knowledge and how it can be developed. In the third section, organizing practices are identified that sustain the continual creation and exploitation of this knowledge. The reader is left with the challenge of combining the 'needs' of effective product innovation with the 'technology' of management and organizational theory to design an innovative organization. There may well be no single ideal type, since different organizations and organizational forms have different mixtures of activities they need to combine.

Product Concept Development: Linking Market and Technology

The first step in product innovation is to develop a comprehensive understanding of the product. This statement perhaps conflicts with our notions that

Adapted from Deborah Dougherty, 'A practice-centred model of organizational renewal through product innovation', *Strategic Management Journal*, 13: 77–92, 1992.

product innovation should be a free, unfettered process of idea creation, but research shows clearly that the sooner a comprehensive understanding of the product is developed, the better the development will go. 'Comprehensive' refers to the idea that a product constitutes the *integration* of market and technology knowledge. For example, laser technology underlies a wide range of products, such as fibre optic networks or cutting tools, which can be marketed to a wide variety of customers, from banks to surgeons. A product 'operationalizes' both market and technological issues into a particular configuration of the 'four Ps' of marketing: product, price, position in the market, and placement in distribution.

A comprehensive definition may be unclear but it frames the development effort, so innovators can fill in the details and operationalize the product into the physical configuration of attributes. This product concept enables them to learn because they can then fine-tune the idea or respond to market shifts or mistakes in earlier knowledge development. Failed innovators work with an incomplete or partial product definition, so they are continually surprised by aspects of the product configuration that they have not conceptualized. With new products, too many factors emerge too quickly for the unprepared to respond to. With a comprehensive product conceptualization, innovators can continually assess the uncertainty of their efforts, at least qualitatively, and make an informed judgement as to whether they should cancel the effort, or shift to another more feasible market or technology.

Developing a commercially viable new product also comprises the *creative* linkage of market and technological possibilities. Customers may not be able to articulate their needs clearly, and those needs may change as they learn to use the product. This means that the product's attributes cannot be specified easily and could change over time. At the same time, the product and/or manufacturing technology may be new, which means that technical problems may crop up unexpectedly, or that certain attributes cannot be delivered after all. Product innovators must experiment with sets of attributes, work closely with customers, pursue multiple paths at once, and make discontinuous leaps in imagination as they craft the comprehensive package of market and technology issues into a viable product. This creative process may continue for years beyond a product's first introduction.

This definition of product concept development does not presume that there is one correct product design. It does presume that there is a feasible set of attributes that a product needs to manifest to be viable. For very innovative products, the feasible set may be nebulous and shifting as the market and the technology emerge interactively over a period of years. For other product ideas there may be no feasible set, and discovering this fact as quickly as possible is also a positive outcome.

The challenge to product innovators is, then, to locate the boundaries of this feasible set quickly – that is, to frame the product concept – and to operationalize it by creating and exploiting the requisite market–technology knowledge. Since an innovation is by definition new, much of this knowledge will be tacit. That is, it will be hard to codify since insights into customer needs and/or what is technologically possible may be rooted in a specific context, and acquired only through hands-on experience, including experience with the firm's capabilities and idiosyncrasies. Some of the knowledge will, however, be articulated: explicit, codifiable, canonical, and transmittable in a formal or systematic language. Tacit knowledge is rich and dense but not easily shared, while articulated knowledge is thin and grainy but easily shared.[2]

Knowledge creation occurs as tacit and articulated insights expand and interact. One important ingredient in knowledge creation is the base of prior knowledge, since the ability to recognize the value of new ideas, assimilate them, and apply them depends partly on what is already known. Using an analogy with memory, the more objects, patterns, and concepts that are stored, the more readily new information about these constructs can be acquired.[3]

Creating concepts is a good way to create knowledge, since concepts condense tacit images into language, drawings, or gestures. For example, a metaphor captures one kind of thing in terms of another, and can articulate tacit knowledge. The qualitative processes of customer focus groups rely heavily on metaphor. From customers' stories about how they work we might conceptualize that they want 'user-friendly' attributes in their voicemail rather than 'power'. Or we might *re*conceptualize the technology underlying voicemail from 'packet switching' to 'networks', which places the notion of 'voicemail' in new technological contexts and widens the range of articulable product concepts. Another way to conceptualize is to recluster information and meanings as they accumulate, which helps to reconceive the essence of elusive phenomena. For example, one firm developed a new mission statement which reclustered the categories of its knowledge base such as fat chemicals and surface active agents into a new dimension of surface active science. This reclustering allowed the firm to conceive of product diversification into their areas where surface science was important, such as floppy disks. Using another metaphor, this firm 'stuck to its knitting' by reclustering the contents of its knitting bag.[4]

The Content and Process of Market–Technology Knowledge Creation

Product innovation comprises the development, integration, and use of tacit and articulated market–technology knowledge over time. The conventional conceptualization of this process, shown in Figure 19.1, is a diagram of the relevant departments intersecting. This conceptualization segments market and technology issues by clustering them into different functional areas and it does not explicate the content of the requisite knowledge. Figure 19.2 suggests a *re*clustering of four types of market–technology knowledge. Their creation

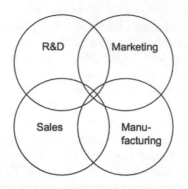

Figure 19.1   *Conventional conceptualization*

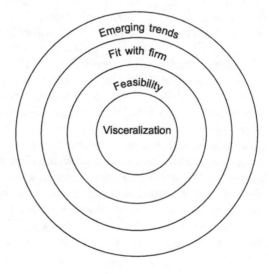

Figure 19.2   *Reconception with recluster of knowledge*

relies on the contributions of expertise such as R&D, marketing, manufacturing, sales and finance, but these functional areas are not emphasized.

Table 19.1 outlines the tacit and the articulable knowledge for each type, and
describes the process by which each can be created metaphorically. Each type
is elaborated below.

Table 19.1

Content: implicit in each function	Content:	Visceralization	Feasibility	Fit with firm	Emerging trends
	tacit	image of product in use	expert insight, judgement of possibilities	deep sense of firm's capabilities	sense of forces of change
	articulated	stories of customers, technology	forecasts, paths of development	core competencies, renewal plan	scenarios of likely events
Process: not described	Process:	Expedition; explorers	Research; scientists	Council of Elders; Councillors	Strategic Scouting; Leaders

Visceralization of the Product in Users' Hands

The core of market–technology knowledge concerns why people want the product, how it fits into the flow of their lives or their work, and how they will evaluate it. Tacit aspects of visceral knowledge include a vivid image of the product in use and a deep sense of the nuances of user problems and how the technology can solve those problems. Articulated aspects of visceral knowledge would comprise stories of customers and technological solutions.

Through visceralization, produce innovators come to imagine the product in use, develop a real sense of the problem that the product will solve for customers, see how customers perceive value, appreciate customers' preferences and decision-making processes, and understand how to specify customer needs in terms of technologies and manufacturing processes. A realistic sense of the customer's actual use contextualizes the product's development. For example, to tell technical people that the product should be 'easy to use' does not provide much insight into how easy, nor what use. Visceralization does. Visceral market–technology insight is where the disparate departmental perspectives regarding customers and products overlap the most, so the joint development of visceral market–technology knowledge may be essential to the development of an innovation team.

Articulating visceral knowledge relies heavily on the art of direct interpersonal relations with potential users, and on the art of recognizing surprising juxtapositions. Notice as well that market and technology issues are inextricably integrated. Interdisciplinary teams can also generate visceral insight by imagining customers. In one new product case, a team for a new consumer product met together in a brainstorming session, and it was the manufacturing engineer who came up with the product concept and advertising campaign that the team ultimately developed.

In contrast, the failure to generate visceral knowledge leads to insurmountable surprises. For example, a chemical product firm cancelled an innovative battery after three years because, according to this product manager, they never learned how batteries fit into the flow of users' work:

> We should have learned more about what went into the design of products that use batteries. We finally realized that users choose what battery to use as an afterthought. Had we known that up front, we might have launched the product differently. You need to consider the procedure that people use to select batteries so you can sell them on yours. All we did was go out and say here's the product and here's what it does, but we never got to the right people.

Effective visceralization relies on people's ability to develop spontaneous experiments, tell stories of possible use, engage in face-to-face interaction, and puzzle out the seeming conflicts between new and established expectations. A metaphor for creating visceral knowledge and transferring tacit visceral insight into articulated knowledge is 'expedition'. An expedition connotes the systematic but aesthetic inquiry into the lives of strangers who would be friends. As members of an expedition, product innovators become explorers. They immerse themselves in the community of their potential customers, but, like anthropologists or dinosaur hunters, they also stand back and make sense of what they see from the perspective of what they already know. Product innovators use their field work to help them conceive of ways in which they can create value for these potential customers by synthesizing the firm's technologies and other know-how into a variety of performance possibilities or other product features.

Customer visits with multi-functional teams are one way to generate visceral insight. Another is 'lead user' analysis, in which innovators look for customers at the leading edge of a market trend who have experience with the problem the product solves, since such experience enables these customers to articulate design needs more readily. Some people are also experimenting with simulations and virtual reality which put potential customers in touch with the product concept so they can react to it immediately. This also generates the tacit, rich insights into user–product interaction early in the conceptual development.[5]

Feasibility

A thorough knowledge of certain customers' needs does not tell you if there are enough customers to make a viable business opportunity, nor if the technology is practicable. Therefore, the 'feasibility' type of market–technology knowledge is also essential. Tacit aspects of feasibility include expert insight into the possibilities of an idea, and professional judgement regarding the keys to market and technological development. Articulated aspects would include demand forecasts, estimates of the market size, and analyses of technological paths to achieve the opportunity. Feasibility assesses whether certain ideas are reasonable to pursue, and provides compelling evidence on the scope of the opportunity.

A product idea may be more feasible if its technology is part of a technology 'regime' or a 'natural trajectory'. Within such regimes or trajectories, technologies can evolve more quickly because complementary technologies are being developed at the same time, so specific problems can be worked out more readily. However, if a technology is in its early stages, fewer problems are solvable, and the product idea is less feasible. Manufacturing competencies may also follow emerging regimes, as a plant learns to evolve from 'job shop' custom production, to high-volume 'continuous flow' production, and ultimately to high-volume 'job shop' production in which multiple products are produced on the same line. Manufacturing competencies can interact with marketability by providing lower costs, higher quality or greater flexibility in design changes.[6]

A number of other issues make certain markets more or less feasible. If the product is different from users' existing patterns of consumption, they may not be able to evaluate the product easily, so the rate of adoption may be very slow. In addition, certain products such as software may require complementary technologies or a dispersion of user know-how before individual users can benefit from the products. What the competition might do also affects a product's feasibility. Strong competitors with 'deep pockets' who are entrenched in a market may respond to a new entry by cutting their prices, filling out their product line, or investing heavily in advertising. Entry might be ill-advised. Limited investments in R&D on the part of competitors, however, might signal a market that is ripe for development by a firm with the necessary capability. In addition, competition may be limited if the prospective market is characterized by diverse segments and unstandardized technology.[7]

Creating the feasibility type of market–technology knowledge relies heavily on the tacit skill and experienced insight of experts. For example, a marketer who developed the initial market assessment for a successful new computer explained:

> Bob walked into my office in Atlanta and said: 'I need you to estimate the size of the XX computer market.' I never did anything like that before. I had a rough idea of [an early entrant in the emergent market], but I started from scratch and read everything I could find. I talked to a lot of people in the company, to consultants, and went to computer stores and talked to them too. What I remember most was seeing an ad for Visicalc, and thinking to myself: 'Aha! Software is holding up the development of the market. Software is the key in the lock.'

Notice how she wove data together with imaginative insight to create an informed and expert opinion. She explained that her final 'numbers' were still an opinion, but her analysis provided senior management with enough understanding of the opportunity to authorize entry into the market, an authorization they had been holding back on for several years.

In contrast, the failure to assess feasibility can leave too many possibilities open to fantasy. In one example, the initial plan for a very new electronic product was to let 'the market' decide which segments were best:

> There is little basis for identifying the prime target now, so we will go wide. We will build awareness, let the customers select themselves, and then focus our marketing and sales efforts on those customer segments who demonstrate the greatest acceptance of the service.

Within this lack of framework, a year-long test market produced mostly surprises, not a coherent understanding of the opportunity. The failure to create feasibility knowledge left the product innovators and their managers with no basis for judging subsequent investments or redesign choices.

While visceral knowledge is richly grounded in intense interpersonal relations and action research, feasibility knowledge is richly grounded in expertise and professional know-how. A metaphor for creating this cluster of knowledge is 'research', or 'doing science'. A good scientist creates insight by applying both knowledge and know-how, and by systematically exploring and testing hypotheses. Innovators as scientists need to create heuristics to judge what elements of a feasibility question to sample first, to assess what is being learned, and to apply what has already been learned. Innovators also need the expertise to assess the current state or trajectory of a technology or market, and to make choices among alternate possibilities.

Fit with the Firm

Product innovators need another kind of market–technology knowledge to address the product's fit with the firm – its 'synergy', how the product might combine resources and skills, and know-how to enhance the firm's competitive strength. Tacit aspects of fit with the firm consist of a deep, almost intimate sense of the firm's capabilities. Such knowledge depends on experience with its businesses, a sense of its history and extensive insight into its culture. The articulated aspects of fit with the firm include an identification of key areas of the firm's competence and technology that will or ought to be developed, a description of how the specific new product fits with those competencies and technologies, and specific product attributes that reflect them, such as a certain kind of quality, service arrangement and price.

Knowledge of how a product fits with the firm frames and focuses product innovators' efforts. It enables people to commit scarce resources (time, money, attention) to an uncertain activity, because fit points to a longer term sense of what is valuable to the firm. Generating this knowledge is a creative process. For example, in one successful case the mission of the division in which the innovators were located was to provide high-quality commodity chemicals. The innovators developed a product that fit with the quality and commodity mission, but also extended the array of chemicals the division provided. One explained that they could work out the fit with the firm because they sought to determine *how* their idea fitted with the mission, not whether it did.

If an appreciation for how a product fits with the firm is not developed, then the innovation does not become part of the firm during its development. In other words, it is like a tumour that is continually at risk of being excised. For example, in a communications firm an innovative use of networking was developed for large industrial customers, based on extensive market research and technical development. Both visceralization and feasibility were well developed, considering the novelty of the product. But the product innovators did not articulate the product's relationship to the firm in a way that made sense to others, so when the vice-president who was sponsoring the project left, his replacement quickly cancelled the project.

Research suggests that 'old timers' are a vital resource to new product efforts because, in the words of project managers, they know 'the system', know 'where the skeletons are buried', and know how to 'make things happen'. Therefore a metaphor to conceptualize the creation of knowledge of fit with the firm is a 'council of elders'. The council needs a 'renewal strategy' as the template of its discourse. A renewal strategy identifies the directions for innovation based on the firm's core competencies, the amounts of resources to be devoted to innovation, and objectives that innovators should address, such as further development of a particular technology, protection or expansion of market share in certain businesses, and exploration of possibilities in an emerging market area.[8]

The 'council' would consider the relationship between the renewal strategy and the new product. The relationship may be discontinuous with current practice, so the councillors must engage in active discourse to ferret out whether and how the product idea and the firm go together. New products can also provide the insights for reconceiving of the renewal strategy. The metaphor of a council of elders is not intended to invoke 'old fuddy-duddies', but rather the 'wise heads' who have the capability to work out the complex strategic issues that new products inevitably raise. The actual councillors might be quite young and from any location in the hierarchy.

Emerging Trends

Fit with the firm must be complemented with knowledge that is externally oriented. What is valuable to customers changes as their needs and problems change, and as new technologies significantly increase capability and performance. Trends in taste such as a preference for fresh foods may reduce the demand for prepared foods and open up new opportunities; rising concern over environmental damage may force producers to redesign their products; the persistent failure of an interest in home networked computing to emerge in the USA has frustrated many would-be innovators in banking and computing; and US automobile makers' penchant to eschew trends in product quality may have lost them market share for good. Tacit aspects of trend knowledge include a feel for the currents in markets and technologies, a sense of those forces of change that are most important, and an ability to navigate among them.

Articulated aspects of trend knowledge include forecasts of product and technology life cycles and scenarios of likely events.

Trend analyses go beyond any specific product, but they help bring closure to the search for the feasible set of attributes that any new product should embody. Trend knowledge bounds the choices of attributes by pointing to the direction(s) in which a product category might evolve over time. In an example of a new medical product, innovators and their managers could not make sense of the emerging field of cancer care (for which the product was intended). Rather than articulate that emergence and then think how this area's evolution might affect the firm's plans in the biological sciences, they simply put the underdeveloped product out, to search for markets that might be interested in its rather higgedly-piggedly package of attributes. Trend knowledge creates a vital thought space for envisioning the evolution of a product category, and for anticipating the necessary evolution of the firm in order to maintain the product's value to both the customers and the firm. Without the capability to understand trends and apply them in practice, firms risk becoming static and outdated.

An important source of trend knowledge is immersion in the ongoing flow of events in a field of endeavour. Technologists can stay up with potential breakthroughs if they are encouraged to monitor outside events and keep up with colleagues. Marketing and sales people can gather insights into emerging opportunities by tracking customers' new needs and problems. Purchasing people can track emerging suppliers, and manufacturing managers can stay up with new techniques for quality and process speed. All other areas of expertise likewise have their own trends to monitor.

The metaphor of 'strategic scout' conceptualizes the creation of knowledge of external trends and how they affect both the innovation and the firm. A strategic scout pays close attention to emerging possibilities, searches out a direction for the firm within the nexus of trends, and energizes people toward that direction. Trend assessments happen in all parts of the firm, so scouting for trend knowledge needs to happen in all parts of the firm. A strategic business-level scout needs to articulate the nature of the business overall in terms of key opportunities and to focus the energy of the people within. A strategic product-level scout needs to articulate the nature of a product *vis-à-vis* key trends, shape others' understandings of the product's possibilities, and involve others in the enactment of the opportunity.

To conclude this section, it is important to recognize that an organization that can create all four knowledge types more generally would have an advantage over one which had to create the knowledge anew for each innovation. While the development of each product requires some unique visceral insight, firms whose people are already practised at understanding what is valuable to customers, ferreting out unmet needs, appreciating how the firm's technological capabilities might meet those needs, and working with fellow explorers from other areas of expertise, could develop visceral insight more quickly. Assessing the feasibility of a particular product also relies heavily on existing knowledge. A product does not arise in a vacuum, so an organization that has a baseline of technology and marketing know-how which can be applied to more than one product would be able to generate feasibility knowledge more quickly for specific products. Developing fit with the firm knowledge takes considerable practice as well, since considerable judgement is required. Organizations can do so more readily if their employees are experienced with considering whether and how a new product might build on the firm's competencies, exploring possible reconfiguration of assets, and examining the implications the new product might have for existing businesses.

Organizing Principles for Effective Product Innovation

It is premature to leap from the *what* of product innovation to particular structures and practices for *how* to carry it out. While it seems reasonable that effective innovation requires interdisciplinary teams, champions, sponsors, phase review processes, and so forth, three more general attributes of the organizational infrastructure are necessary to assure that people are capable of developing, exploiting, and continually maintaining this market–technology knowledge.

A New Sense of Roles and Responsibilities

First, being adept with and competent in visceralization, feasibility, fit, and trend assessment needs to be a legitimate part of people's jobs. Being 'market oriented' or 'responsive to the environment' does not just happen. People who develop new products must be practised at the particular activities and skills described above in order to be responsive. In most established organizations operating on bureaucratic principles, work is broken down into narrow functional specialities that are based on internal, not external, workflows. Thus, people are expected to be competent in market research, industrial engineering, design or sales, but not necessarily in the externally oriented skills described here. With these kinds of narrow jobs, an industrial engineering (IE) person assigned to a new product might represent IE (and protect IE's interests), rather than contribute IE expertise to the design. To innovate effectively, people need to be competent at both sets of skills; the industrial engineer needs to understand tooling design *and* how such tooling might relate or not to a particular product. Indeed, the striking and persistent failure to be able to incorporate customer needs into the innovation process may be caused by this lack of external skill. One might argue that marketing people should handle 'market' knowledge. However, the argument here has been that this knowledge needs to be linked with technology, and thus created and maintained by all areas of expertise.

To support this broadened job definition, people need to take on a complete role, which is not the usual practice in organizations that break work down into narrow pieces that have been 'abstracted' from the overall task of the enterprise. Successful innovators need to feel committed to and responsible for the entire product effort, and cannot simply execute a separate portion of the overall task. For example, a packaging expert explained how a broadened role on a successful new product enabled him to see and understand more, without in fact expanding his workload. In contrast, his usual narrow role of being the packaging person gave him too much to do:

> What you lose [in the usual process] is contact. Because we were dedicated in a team, we got involved and spent time in other areas like market research and plant engineering . . . Because I was more involved, I could ask marketing about the questions they ask in focus groups or surveys. Prior to this, no one ever said to me: 'We're running a focus group. What questions would you like to have asked?' This generated a lot of synergies . . . Now I am back [in the usual organization] and I have 30 or 40 products to look at . . .

Roles which encompass the whole task cannot be implemented, however, unless people acquire new skills and competencies. People first need to know how to develop the four clusters of market–technology knowledge, and how to be competent at exploring, doing research, serving as councillors, and scouting. Hands-on experience such as expeditions to existing as well as new customers, feasibility conferences over the business domain and its various product areas, fit with firm councils, and scouting, is necessary to build up people's experience base. In addition, people need to maintain the various areas of expertise that are vital to a firm's businesses, such as core and applied sciences, manufacturing design and engineering knowledge and know-how, marketing, sales and distribution, finance and accounting, programming, and so forth. A system of continued formal training, sabbaticals and development of two or more areas of competence would enhance such expertise.

The infrastructure in the organization needs to support broader roles. If people are expected to maintain skills which are often tacit, they cannot be assigned to a plethora of projects. Human resource management systems must track people's assignments and development of skills and competencies to assure that they are given an adequate exposure to a variety of market–technology knowledge creation efforts without being assigned to too many projects. The reward system needs to reward the development of expertise, skills and competencies. Career progression based on a person's breadth and depth of competencies and practised experience, rather than movement through a hierarchy of contrived jobs, would both fulfil people's needs for development and the organization's needs for realistic, complete work roles.

Work as Collaboration

The organization needs to incorporate the principle that work is inherently collaborative. The locus of the full array of market–technology knowledge is in the work group. No one person could fully comprehend all of the issues. Research shows that successful product innovators always developed effective collaboration across the departments. Often, by first learning about each other, members of a team can work effectively alone because they *know* each other's constraints and needs. Collaboration helps everyone to 'calibrate' what they know and where they are going. By relying on joint customer visits and informal but regular interaction, a team can work without formal meetings, because everyone has an active sense of the whole project. Collaboration also gives everyone a sense that their input matters, which helps people understand choices even when their recommendations are not used.

To enable collaborative work, organizations need to define work in collaborative terms. This may seem silly, but if we stop and think about it, work is often defined in individual terms. Managers need to carve the work to be done into bounded wholes or action domains, set forth expected accomplishments and milestones, and then delegate. Instead of defining oneself as a market researcher or accountant or sales rep, people need to see themselves as helping to run the polypropylene business by contributing their particular expertise, for example. Quality based manufacturing, networking programs, venture units, and vendor–customer organizations are a few of the many structures that are both widely used and premised on collaborative rather than individual work.

People also need skills and competencies to work in a collaborative mode. First, training in everyday skills for collaboration such as running meetings, listening, leading, and making group decisions should be a prerequisite for all employees. Innovators often note how vital such training is to their ability to work effectively on a project, even though these skills seem rather 'obvious' after the fact. Another collaborative skill is to be able to appreciate the perspectives of people in the different departments, who inhabit disparate 'thought worlds' regarding customer needs and new products. A third collaborative skill is the ability to anticipate what people in another department need to know or do in order to carry out their part of the work. Such anticipatory insights enable interdepartmental teams to quickly diagnose and resolve problems, and keep the development moving.

Strategizing for Product Innovations

An ongoing process of strategizing provides the shared cognitive map that enables the development of market–technology knowledge for new products. Both the innovations themselves and the relationships between them and the rest of the businesses in the organization need to be directed, bounded and defined. The organization cannot be all things to all people, and cannot develop unique resources and competencies if it tries to be. Research suggests that organizations that are competent with innovations have clear and simple strategies which frame the market–technology connections. A strategy sets the initial direction and guides the development of competencies that enable continued market–technology knowledge creation. The strategy also enables innovators with a particular product develop the fit-with-firm category of product attributes.

Finally, a strategy that is closely connected to innovation may also enable the organization overall to reconceive and reformulate some of its businesses in response to changes in customer needs or technological possibilities. Individual innovations represent experiments with new possibilities that may open up new or redefine old competencies, provided this insight can be captured. The continuing process of market–technology knowledge creation provides the grist for strategic redirection, as new trends are noted, or current trajectories are exhausted, or new market possibilities are discovered.

Notes

1. This is not to say that 'marketing' should dominate new product development, only that the failure to understand what customers are really interested in can result in commercial failure. See early work by Rothwell, R.C. Freeman, A. Horsley, V. Jervis, A. Robertson and J. Crawford (1974) 'SAPPHO updated: project SAPPHO Phase II', *Research Policy*, 32: 58–291. In addition, William Souder (1987) *Managing New Product Innovations*. Boston: Lexington Books; and Robert Cooper and Elko Kleinschmidt (1986) 'An investigation into the new product process: Steps, deficiencies, and impact', *Journal of Product Innovation Management*, 3: 71–85.

2. For elaborations on the difference between tacit and articulated knowledge see Polyani, M. (1966) *The Tacit Dimension*. New York: Doubleday; Nonaka, I. (1990) 'The learning organization', *Harvard Business Review*; and Brown J. and Duguid, P. 'Organizational learning and communities of practice: Toward a unified view of working, learning, and innovation', *Organization Science*, 2: 33–48.

3. See Cohen, W. and Levinthal, D. (1990) 'Absorptive capacity: A new perspective on learning and innovation', *Administrative Science Quarterly*, 35: 128–52.

4. Nonaka has developed many of these ideas about using metaphors to help create knowledge.

5. For ideas on lead user analysis, see Urban, G. and von Hippel, E. (1988) 'Lead user analysis for the development of new industrial products', *Management Science*, 34: 569–81. For customer visits, see McQuarrie, E. and McIntyre, S. (1990) 'Implementing the market concept through a program of customer visits', Marketing Science Institute Working Paper #90-107, Cambridge, Mass.

6. These interactions are discussed by Kotabe, M. (1990) 'Corporate product policy and innovative behavior of European and Japanese multinationals', *Journal of Marketing*, 5: 19–34.

7. Diana Day develops various issues of competition in 'Research linkages between entrepreneurship, strategic management, and general management', in D.L. Sexton (ed.), *State of the Art in Entrepreneurship Research*. Boston: PWS-Kent Publishing, 1992.

8. The idea of renewal strategy is developed from George Day's discussion of growth strategy in his 1990 book, *Market Driven Strategy: Processes for Creating Value*. New York: Free Press.

20 Managing the Global Environment

Lawrence H. Wortzel

Strategic management involves identifying and responding to opportunities as well as threats. Increasingly, both can originate from outside a firm's domestic market. More and more manufacturers in any country/market must now not only go head to head with domestic competitors, but must also face up to foreign multinationals. Furthermore, most of today's products have potential markets in several countries. Many argue, therefore, that markets and competitors are now global, and that firms should develop global strategies to survive and grow. People, however, disagree about what a global strategy should actually look like.

[. . .] Firms of one kind or another have been operating across country borders for hundreds of years. Marco Polo was in the import/export business, and his writings are a by-product of his business travels. The current era of international business, marked by the burgeoning of multinationals, began after World War I, was interrupted by World War II, and accelerated rapidly when the war ended in 1945.
 [. . .]
 [. . .] By the late 1960s, European and Japanese multinationals had begun competing with US multinationals in such industries as chemicals, automobiles, and consumer electronics. By the 1980s, multinational firms from the newly industrializing countries had entered the world market. And by mid-1988 the 500 largest non-US multinationals included 11 firms from South Korea, three from Taiwan, and six from Brazil.
 [. . .]

From Multinational to Global

Although their businesses were expanding horizontally into more and more markets, most European and US multinationals managed their business

---

From Wortzel, L.H., 'Global strategies; standardization versus flexibility', in H. Vernon-Wortzel and L. Wortzel, *Global Strategic Management: The Essentials*. New York: Wiley, 135–49, 1991.

vertically, that is, coordinating the production, distribution, and marketing functions primarily within countries (or, less frequently, regions). Typically, they managed their business as a collection or portfolio of individual domestic entities, each with self-contained marketing and, often, manufacturing facilities. In many cases, national management led to significant differences in product lines across countries, as individual country managements reacted to specific threats and opportunities within their particular domestic markets.

By the 1980s, the competitive advantages that had produced success in the early post-World War II period were no longer sufficient. Technological leads became much harder to sustain. Competitors became much more adept at copying each other's new products. An expanding number of firms across a wider spectrum of countries could be cost-competitive in manufacturing standardized products. Many more firms had the ability to promote brand names. And consumers had become much more receptive to new brands. Firms had to search for new sources of competitive advantage.

Many suggested that the multinational, with its vertical, country-focused management, inevitably faced a competitive disadvantage. They believed there were potentially important competitive advantages available to firms as a result of their being multinational. But multinationals, because of their country-focused organization and management, were not seizing these opportunities. While firms might be optimizing their businesses in terms of domestic market opportunities in each country, their country-by-country actions, taken together, were not optimal for the whole corporation. Critics pointed to the success of the leading Japanese multinationals in penetrating foreign markets. These Japanese firms employed large, highly coordinated, centralized manufacturing facilities located in Japan, from which they fanned out their products around the world.

Out of such arguments were born the concepts of the global firm and the global industry. Simply stated, a global industry is one in which a firm's activities in one country market can affect its competitive position in other country markets. A global firm is one that is organized and managed to take advantage of whatever synergies are available across country markets. The global firm, many argue, will render both the multinational and the domestic firm obsolete by gaining insurmountable competitive advantage. The differences they envision between the multinational and the global include the following:

- The global firm, like its predecessor the multinational, markets its products in many countries, and might also manufacture in many countries.
- Unlike the typical multinational, the global firm offers a standardized product in all country markets, perhaps also standardizing brand name, positioning, and advertising content.
- The global firm manufactures at whatever sites, and utilizes whatever plant sizes, that will minimize the cost of the delivered products across its country markets.

- The global firm organizes itself in a way that facilitates the efficient marketing, manufacture, and distribution of its standardized products.

In sum, a global firm has one global strategy rather than a series of national strategies.

Global Firms, Global Industries, and Global Strategies

The notion of globalization – a global firm pursuing a global strategy – is very appealing to managers. In many industries, there are potential synergies in managing horizontally – that is, coordinating activities and functions across national boundaries. In these industries, global strategies – strategies that capitalize on the potential for synergy – offer the possibility of greater competitive advantage than national strategies. The easiest way to achieve the synergies is to standardize everything, and standardization is naturally attractive to managers. Standardizing the product makes it easy to standardize manufacturing and control systems, thus making the business easier to run and more amenable to control from headquarters.

Global standardization has its critics as well as its proponents. Proponents correctly perceive that the weakness in the country-specific strategies most multinationals pursue is that they may not be optimal for the corporation as a whole. But their critics say the proponents do not give enough weight to the greatest strength inherent in national strategies – the ability to tailor product, product line, and marketing efforts country-by-country to take best advantage of opportunities in each market. Flexibility, not standardization, the critics of standardization say, is the key to a successful global strategy.[8]

Critics of standardization believe that Japanese firms' successes were not due simply to the low-cost position they attained through long, high-volume production runs of standardized products. They note that many Japanese firms customize their products – autos and consumer electronics included – as necessary to best fit the requirements of specific country markets. Japanese firms have pioneered flexible manufacturing techniques that give them the ability to customize products and to quickly introduce new models in small quantities without incurring a significant cost penalty. Japanese firms' ability to identify opportunities to customize, and then to deliver to the market customized products at more or less the same cost, has sustained their success in world markets.

The major premises behind the argument for global standardization are that it has the potential for providing a cost advantage over both domestic firms and vertically managed multinationals, and that such cost advantages are an essential determinant of competitive advantage. The firm with a cost advantage can then either pass its cost savings on to customers in the form of lower prices or use the extra margin its low costs provide to enhance its R&D or marketing activities.

Implicit in these premises is the idea that cost savings are upstream (procurement, manufacturing) rather than downstream (distribution, marketing) activities. Firms can consolidate their upstream activities, but they must perform downstream activities country-by-country. Thus, a firm can best achieve cost savings by consolidating and rationalizing its upstream activities. The key to realizing these cost savings is producing standardized products and then marketing the same standardized products in each country.

Given the competitive situation that most firms face, no one can argue strongly against the importance of a favorable cost position as a key component in any strategy designed to produce significant volumes. What is questionable, however, is the viability of competitive strategies based on product standardization.

Critics argue that a global strategy based simply on offering a standardized product worldwide will not in all cases lead to a significant sustainable competitive advantage.[9] Global standardization, in fact, may result in a penalty rather than a bonus, because it locks the firm into a particular competitive posture, while sources of competitive advantage continually change. Where the sources of competitive advantage keep changing, sustainable competitive advantage is produced by flexibility, not standardization. The key is to constantly identify and capitalize on new sources of competitive advantage, and to be faster and more adept at identifying and implementing opportunities for change. Taking advantage of the opportunities requires a far more sophisticated and flexible strategy than simply standardizing.

Assumptions behind the Debate

The major reason for the standardization/flexibility debate is that proponents of each strategy start from a different set of assumptions in three critical areas: country/market and product characteristics, determinants of a favorable cost position, and trade and investment barriers. [Table 20.1] identifies the key differences in the assumptions behind the standardization and flexibility strategies. To highlight the differences, I have drawn the characterization of each position as sharply as possible. Simply stated, the assumptions behind a standardization strategy are these:

- 'One size fits all': the global consumer. Due mainly to technological advances in transportation and communication, consumers worldwide – or at least in many countries – have become similar enough in their tastes and preferences that the same product will satisfy all of them. Where the standardized product might not be a consumer's ideal choice, if its price is sufficiently lower than that of the ideal product, the consumer will buy it.

[Table 20.1] *Global strategy assumptions*

Areas of assumption	Assumptions behind	
	Standardization	Flexibility
Country market and product characteristics	Similar: not highly segmented. Stable: few changes or new products.	Different: highly segmented. Dynamic: constant change. New products.
Keys to favorable cost position	Manufacturing costs are significant. Economies of scale in manufacturing. Experience-curve effects resulting from long runs of few products. Choice of production location(s) critical. Scale of economies of R&D	Marketing costs are significant. Significant economies of scope as well as scale in manufacturing. Economies of scope in marketing and distribution. Market stimuli critical for new product development.
Trade and investment barriers	None. Invest, manufacture, procure where most advantageous. Ship anywhere.	Foreign direct investment regulated: nonregulatory investment barriers erected by host governments. Tariff and nontariff barriers to trade. Protectionism: nationalism; regionalism.

- Product standardization leads to economies based on size. There are economies available in one or more of the business functions – manufacturing, procurement, distribution, R&D, management – as a result of marketing a standardized product across countries. Larger unit sales of the standardized product result in scale economies.
- Minimal trade barriers. Firms can freely ship merchandise across borders, tariffs are low or nonexistent, and nontariff barriers such as quotas or red tape do not exist, so a firm can manufacture wherever it is most advantageous.

In contrast, the assumptions behind a flexibility strategy are:

- Consumers in different country markets have different preferences, and if their preferences can be met without incurring a large cost penalty, customers will prefer a customized product.
- Manufacturing flexibility makes up for scale. By adopting flexible manufacturing techniques, the firm can produce small quantities of a wider

range of products at costs approaching those obtained for a long run of a single product.

- Trade barriers exist that preclude freedom in choosing manufacturing sites.

Choosing the Right Global Strategy

Simply stated, setting a global strategy is a matter of adjusting as much as possible the business functions – manufacturing, procurement, marketing, distribution, and R&D – within the constraints of trade and investment barriers in a way that provides the best possible product/market fits. In some cases, the best fit is a standardized product; in others a customized product fits best. Setting a global strategy often involves following a zig-zag line between standardization and flexibility, trading off the costs and benefits of one against those of the other.

To identify the best product/market fit, first we have to identify salient product characteristics and then classify products according to these characteristics. Simply rating products as candidates for standardization (or for customization) is not sufficient. A second dimension – rate of change – is equally important.

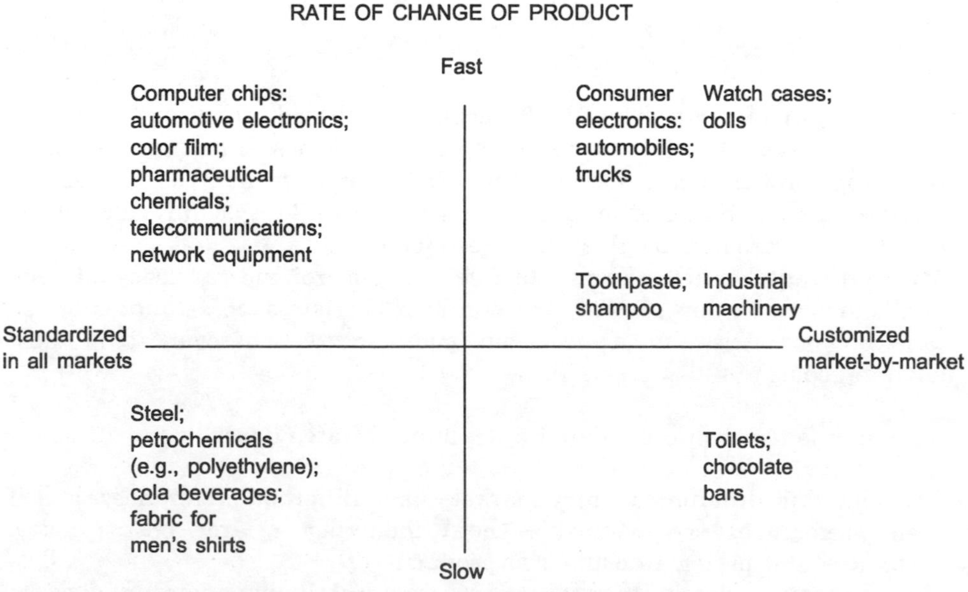

RATE OF CHANGE OF PRODUCT

Fast

Computer chips:
automotive electronics;
color film;
pharmaceutical
chemicals;
telecommunications;
network equipment

Consumer   Watch cases;
electronics: dolls
automobiles;
trucks

Toothpaste; Industrial
shampoo   machinery

Standardized
in all markets

Customized
market-by-market

Steel;
petrochemicals
(e.g., polyethylene);
cola beverages;
fabric for
men's shirts

Toilets;
chocolate
bars

Slow

[Figure 20.1]   *Market requirements and product characteristics*

[Figure 20.1] arranges a sample of products along these two dimensions. The horizontal dimension, the consumers' preferred product, classifies products along a continuum from standardized to customized. The vertical dimension, rate of change in product, covers a spectrum from fast to slow. Let's examine some of the product examples in each of the four quadrants.

Standardized Products

Many of the successful efforts at producing and marketing a standardized product across country markets have resulted from customers who demanded a standardized product. When customers demand standardization, standardizing does not lead to a competitive advantage; it is simply a competitive necessity. There are other cases in which standardization has come about through the efforts of marketers. We shall examine both cases.

Rapidly Changing Standardized Products

The clearest cases of customer-demanded standardization occur where the customer is a multinational firm. Examples of standardized products include many OEM auto parts and telecommunications equipment used in trans-border data networks. Although auto manufacturers may tailor the appearance and features of their cars to specific markets, many of the working parts they use are standardized. The objective is to use the identical part in every country in which they assemble autos. Multinational firms that have trans-border communications networks want standardized equipment at all sites to ensure network compatibility. To retain multinational customers, a supplier must not only offer a standardized product, but must be able to provide it globally, wherever its customers have operations.

Some rapidly changing consumer products, such as color snapshot and slide films, also require standardization. Here the impetus for standardization comes from both camera manufacturers with worldwide markets and traveling consumers. Even the simplest cameras now offer automatic light metering that requires standardized film in order to work properly. Consumers want to buy color film of a known brand and invariant characteristics wherever they go.

VCRs and compact disc players are two cases in which producers influenced consumers around the world to accept a standardized product. In the case of the VCR, at the beginning there were two competing systems, Beta and VHS. Matsushita, who championed VHS, marketed VCRs themselves, produced VCRs for resellers, and licensed the technology. VHS has become the standard format for home videotape. Philips and Sony jointly championed the compact disc player, promoted it jointly, licensed the technology to others, and sold the necessary components to other manufacturers. As a result, the Philips/Sony compact disc is a worldwide standard for recorded music.

Slowly Changing Standardized Products

Producers can standardize industrial products, such as steel and certain petrochemicals and fabrics, because customers' specifications for such products are similar in many countries. Among consumer products, cola beverages seem to be unique in having worldwide appeal. The leading producers – Coca-Cola and Pepsi-Cola – have had little difficulty obtaining consumer acceptance for Coke and Pepsi virtually everywhere they have been available.

Customized Products

While consumer durables such as automobiles and TV sets appear at first inspection amenable to standardization, there are subtle but significant differences in these products across country markets. Automobiles differ in their model names, in trim and headlights, engine sizes, safety equipment and accessories. TV sets must be manufactured to different broadcast standards (e.g., PAL in Great Britain, SECAM in France, NTSC in the US and Japan), and vary in external appearance. The most commonly sold sizes of refrigerators and washing machines in the US are much larger than those most commonly sold elsewhere. This means that, to gain a large share in diverse markets, automobile, TV, and appliance manufacturers must customize to at least some degree.

Differences in consumer packaged goods products across markets are legion. Colgate markets a toothpaste in England that is different from its US offering. Knorr customizes its line of dry soup and sauce mixes to the taste preferences of particular country markets. Even McDonald's does not offer a globally standardized product. Its menu includes beer in Germany and Rendang burgers (an indigenous spiced and stewed beef or buffalo) in Indonesia. And its 'special sauce' varies from country to country.

Machinery sold in the USA tends to be larger than machinery sold in Japan. Japanese firms prefer smaller equipment because factory space is limited and workers are generally smaller than their US counterparts. US firms also prefer machinery with more features. One observer, mixing metaphors in the process, has described US users' preference for machinery with 'lots of bells and whistles', while the rest of the world prefers 'plain vanilla'. Similarly Komatsu's edge over Caterpillar in Asian markets is not due solely to its market proximity or its lower prices; the size and layout of the Komatsu cab fits its generally smaller Asian drivers better than Caterpillar's does.

Customizing is important in slowly changing products as well. As anyone who has traveled internationally can verify, flush toilets are very different across country markets. True, the international class hotels in many countries may install foreign toilets, but it is rare to see anything but the 'national' toilet in any country's private homes.

Finally, chocolate is another example of a customized, slow-changing product. US chocolate bars (Hershey), British (Cadbury), Dutch (Droste), Swiss (Lindt), Mexican (Carols Quinto) and Japanese (Lotte), all taste significantly different. Many chocolate candy producers sell their domestic product multinationally, with some success, but virtually none has achieved the level of penetration in foreign markets that it achieved at home. More often than not, the domestic market-share leader is a specialty product with a small market share in other countries. Consumer taste preferences for chocolate simply differ across countries.

Selecting a Strategy: Identifying the Keys to Competitive Advantage

[Figure 20.2] shows the keys to competitive advantage for each of the product types presented in [Figure 20.1]. Each is discussed below, highlighting the most important elements of a strategy that best captures the competitive advantages available to that particular combination of product/market characteristics. We also look briefly at possibilities for gaining a better advantage by moving the product into a different quadrant, standardizing where everyone else is customizing, or vice versa.

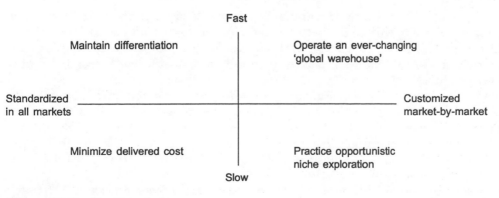

[Figure 20.2] *Strategy choices*

Standardized, Rapidly Changing Products: Maintaining Differentiation

Although firms with products that fall into this category standardize them across country markets, they must at the same time try to differentiate their standardized offerings from those of competitors. Offering, for example, automobile electronics parts or telecommunications products demonstrably better than competitors, is a requirement for continued success. To maintain a product advantage, firms with products falling in this quadrant of [Figure 20.2] must continually improve their products and supplement them with new products whenever possible. Competitive advantage lies in a firm's ability to:

- develop new products more quickly than the competition;
- put them into production quickly;
- produce them reliably and efficiently – and in quantity.

It is essential to locate R&D and production as close as possible to lead markets. New product development and product improvement are, most often, cut-and-try propositions. Success depends on understanding customer needs and an ability to translate those needs into product specifications. Innumerable studies, and the experience of a great many firms, confirm the importance of close and continuous contact with the market in order to anticipate and then successfully develop and commercialize new products. The process is most enhanced when the product developer is in close contact with lead users – those customers whose own needs require technological advances.

German automakers Mercedes Benz and BMW must offer high-performance cars. Fuel injection contributes to performance. Robert Bosch, because of its proximity to Mercedes and BMW's own R&D teams, has managed to develop and maintain a leadership position in fuel injection. Similarly, the Eaton Corporation, working with US producers, has developed a leading position in truck transmissions and powertrains.

Firms should locate their manufacturing plants close to their R&D facilities (this means they will be de facto located close to their lead users). In this way, they can facilitate translation of R&D results into full-scale production and quickly make the changes usually required early in the commercial life of a new product.

Ideally, producers of standardized, quickly changing products should concentrate their manufacturing at the fewest possible locations. They can then take maximum advantage of scale and experience effects, and ensure conformance in manufacture. When concentration is not possible, they must set up mechanisms that ensure dissemination of information from R&D to plant, and from plant to plant.

When designing or upgrading their plants, manufacturers should aim for dynamic flexibility – that is, manufacturing systems that have the flexibility to quickly improve current products and also accomplish quick changeovers to newer, evolutionary products. Such flexibility gives firms the capability to bring innovations to market in the minimum possible time.

Standardized, Slowly Changing Products: Minimize Delivered Cost

Here the key competitive advantage is low delivered cost. But, as we shall see, identifying the manufacturing sites that will produce the lowest delivered cost is not an easy task. Many of these products are mature and are not only standardized from country to country, but differ little from producer to producer. So achieving low delivered cost involves comparing manufacturing costs in different countries with shipping costs from those countries to destination markets. Because demand is relatively stable for many products in this classification, the task is apparently straightforward. In reality, however, it is excruciatingly complicated and full of uncertainty.

[. . .] Uncertainties occur because the relative cost positions of different countries can – and do – change rapidly. [. . .]

Another factor affecting countries' relative cost positions is foreign exchange rates, which fluctuate even on a daily basis, and all too often do not reflect relative productivity across countries. [. . .]

[. . .]

All this adds up to one critical point: the most advantageous cost location can, and likely will, shift. Developing the ability to project sites with potential, and maintaining the flexibility to take advantage of them when they emerge, are an essential part of maintaining the key competitive advantage of low delivered cost.

Customized, Rapidly Changing Products: The Ever-changing 'Global Warehouse'

Most consumer products, both packaged goods and durables, fall into the customized and rapidly changing quadrant of [Figure 20.2]. Global success within this quadrant requires:

- a broad product line;
- constant innovation;
- highly flexible manufacturing;
- quick transmission and adoption of new product ideas across countries.

Markets for these products are highly segmented, and those segments, even if common across countries, are likely to vary significantly in size. Also, because products change so quickly, country customization rather than global standardization is almost always a better choice.

Consumer products usually have high marketing and distribution costs, so it is tempting to standardize products in the hope of saving manufacturing costs, and use the savings to cover marketing costs. But for a firm selling products in this category to adopt such a strategy is risky at best. A standardized version of any product is likely to have only limited appeal in some markets, thereby creating very high unit marketing and distribution costs.

[. . .]

Firms that want to be successful with products that fall in this quadrant might well think of themselves as 'global warehouses' – not edifices that stock physical products, but clearing houses for the collection, storage, exchange, and dissemination of product ideas, needs, and sources. Nestlé, for example, has a 'warehouse' of over 200 products from which subsidiaries can choose. When a Nestlé subsidiary develops a new product for its country market, that product enters the warehouse and becomes available to other subsidiaries that want to manufacture or import it. The warehouse is a coordinating mechanism that encourages product development and sees that the firm, globally, takes maximum advantage of new ideas.

[. . .] Most products in the customized and rapidly changing quadrant are in a continuous state of evolution. Introduction of new models, in the case of durables, and new brands or flankers, in the case of packaged goods, occurs regularly. Firms competing in this sector must develop and maintain a capacity for innovation as a way of life. But maintaining this capacity is much more difficult than in the case of standardized products, because a new product idea can come from just about any country. [. . .]

Ideally, firms should locate R&D units in several countries so as to be exposed to the maximum number of new product ideas. But they also need an integrating and rediffusing mechanism so that they can introduce new products or product improvements into other country markets as quickly as possible – modified, as required, for each.

[. . .] The key to manufacturing also is diffusion rather than concentration. To succeed, firms must support their broad product lines and innovation needs with a manufacturing capability that provides both dynamic and static flexibility. Dynamic flexibility is the ability to quickly put a new product into production, while static flexibility is the ability to easily switch production from product to product, and to economically produce small runs of a large number of products.

A customization strategy works best when manufacturing is located as close as possible to each country market. This facilitates the fast, successful commercialization of new product ideas, and speeds response to demand changes in existing products. The more flexibility – both static and dynamic – a firm can build into its manufacturing, the more production units it can support. The closer the manufacturing/country/market links, the faster the firm's response time.

[. . .] While close national links between manufacturing and marketing are essential, horizontal linkages across countries in R&D, manufacturing, and marketing are equally critical. Without such horizontal linkages, the global warehouse concept simply will not work well. Innovators and producers in one country market must have a means by which they can offer ideas (and product or production capacity) to subsidiaries in other country markets. And individual country subsidiaries need a place to shop for new product ideas and sometimes for sources of products that fill gaps in their existing lines.

Customized, Slowly Changing Products: Opportunistic Niche Exploitation

Here, the global strategy is to find and exploit niches. Products falling in this quadrant will typically have only one, or at best very few, markets in which they can earn a large share, and numerous markets in which they can, at best, gain a small share of niche. Many firms content themselves with being domestic because they do not believe they can profitably operate abroad with low volume. Small volumes offer profit potential only if the firm can obtain a premium price while holding costs down. For these products, the concern is not to develop an explicit global strategy as much as to develop a spirit of curious inquiry. The foreign market opportunities that may exist for customized, slowly changing products are not always easy to spot. Managers must uncover the opportunities and then find ways to use existing institutions and existing capabilities to exploit the opportunities.

Some Swiss chocolate-bar manufacturers, for example, retail their chocolate bars in the USA at prices two to three times those of the leading domestic bar, Hershey's. They are able to hold expenses down because they use an established distribution channel that efficiently performs the required marketing and distribution tasks. They advertise very selectively to a small target audience, and depend for sales on the efforts of wholesalers who place their candy bars with point-of-sale displays selectively in targeted retail outlets.

Changing the Industry's Rules: Standardizing the Customized and Vice Versa

At times a firm might see a potential opportunity to set the rules for a new product line or to change the rules in an existing one. Philips and Sony, for example, established the rules for CD player components by pushing to standardize their system. A firm that considers a rule-changing move must first ensure that it can enforce the rule change and that it will, by changing the rules, improve its relative competitive position.

As a general proposition, moving from customization to standardization makes a business simpler and therefore easier to duplicate. The firm that does a good job of running a complex business well should think long and hard before making the rules of competition in its industry simpler. A firm should try to move its industry from customization to standardization only when it is positive that by so doing it can gain a highly significant, permanent cost advantage. The cost advantage must be large enough to make the standardized product substantially more attractive to consumers than the customized alternative. A better pay-off for such firms, and at the same time a better insulation against a rival that could try to standardize, is to minimize the customization penalty by continually improving the product and by making manufacturing more flexible.

Similarly, the firm that can make a business more complex by moving from standardization to customization also stands to benefit if it can keep the customization penalty low enough. Consumers, after all, buy perceived value, not just price.

Political Constraints on Global Strategies

The worlds of international trade and foreign investment are becoming increasingly constrained by conflicting national interest. All governments, it seems, want to maximize their country's exports and limit their imports. All governments want full employment, and many want to develop high-technology industries because their pay-off is higher than other types of industry. Business firms based in any country want as few competitors as possible in their own back yards, but at the same time want free access to world markets for themselves.

For these and related reasons, there is a political as well as an economic dimension to a global strategy. Governments by their actions influence the location of both manufacturing and R&D. Government regulations of product content, packaging, and labeling affect a firm's ability to standardize globally. Any global strategy, before being adopted, must be tempered by the reality of regulation. A government will be concerned primarily with the economic health of its own country, and will regulate to best serve its national interest, rather than to serve the global strategy needs of foreign firms. Rather than just thinking about global strategies, therefore – even where standardization is indicated – firms must in many cases think in terms of sets of regional or even country strategies.

Notes

[. . .]
8. See, for example, Aaker and Mascarenhas, 1984; Fannin, 1986; Kogut, 1985.
9. See Douglas and Wind, 1987, and Simon-Miller et al., 1986, for summaries of such arguments.

References

Aaker, D.A. and Mascarenhas, B. 'The need for strategy flexibility', *Journal of Business Strategy*, 5(2) (Autumn 1984): 74–82.
Douglas, Susan P. and Wind, Yoram, 'The myth of globalization', *Columbia Journal of World Business* (Winter 1987): 19–30.
Fannin, William R., 'National or global? – Control vs. flexibility', *Long Range Planning* (October 1986): 84–8.
Kogut, Bruce, 'Designing global strategies: Profiting from operational flexibility', *Sloan Management Review* (Autumn 1985): 27–38.
Simon-Miller, Francoise, et al., 'World marketing: Going global or acting local? Five expert viewpoints', *Journal of Consumer Marketing* (Spring 1986): 5–15.

21 Managing Sustainable Development

Frances Westley and Harrie Vredenburg

Management theory, as embodied in such substantive fields as business policy and marketing, has long viewed organizations as single units operating in potentially hostile and uncharted environments. According to this perspective, organizations must minimize threats, maximize opportunities, and manipulate stakeholders for maximum advantage if they are to survive and prosper (Astley, 1984). This view of organizations has shaped theory and practice in management, producing in the extreme a 'conception of managers as pioneers confronting a faceless environment' (Astley, 1984: 533) and exploiting it. Therefore, it is not surprising that collaborative strategies among organizations have received little attention in such a framework.

For various reasons, this competitive framework has been challenged in recent years in theory and practice. Beginning with Emery and Trist's (1965) seminal article, some have argued that cooperation among organizations in similar domains is imperative to control environmental turbulence. Recently, authors have suggested that collaboration among private-sector organizations might, in fact, operate as a new strategic tool – a means of gaining efficiency and flexibility in times of rapid change (Child and Smith, 1987; Kanter, 1989; Miles and Snow, 1984). Empirical studies of linkages among organizations indicate that organizations are much more interconnected than the purely competitive model indicates (Child and Smith, 1987; Granovettor, 1985). Finally, a recognition of the systematic or global nature of many contemporary problems facing public and private-sector organizations and society as a whole has resulted in a normative call for interorganizational, as well as inter-sectoral, collaboration.

Collaborative strategies, which might include a variety of partnerships, strategic alliances and interfirm networks, would seem to be a critical structural innovation, designed to solve the kinds of ill-defined problems that depend on multiple perspectives and resources for resolution (Gray, 1989). On the other hand, the emergence of such collaboration depends on a variety of complex macro- and micro-processes, the dynamics of which are only beginning to be mapped (Gray, 1985, 1989; Kanter, 1989; Waddock, 1989).

We use Gray's (1989: 5) definition of collaboration as a 'process through

Adapted from 'Strategic bridging: The collaboration between environmentalists and business in the marketing of green products', *Journal of Applied Behavioral Science*, 27(1): 65–90, 1991.

which parties who see different aspects of a problem can constructively explore their differences and search for solutions that go beyond their own limited vision of what is possible'. Collaboration is most likely to occur when problems are complex, wide in scope, and beyond the means of single organizations to solve unilaterally. Such situations have been termed *problem domains* (Trist, 1983). Through collaborative negotiations, stakeholders in such domains work to map the boundaries and structures of the domain – a process that has been described as arriving at a 'negotiated order of the domain' (O'Toole and O'Toole, 1981; Gray, 1989). This process has been identified as a critical function of such collaborations as multiparty task forces and community projects, and as a central dimension of collaborative negotiations (Gray, 1989).

This chapter discusses one particular form of collaboration – strategic bridging. It explains why it is a distinctive form of collaboration and identifies the type of context in which it is most likely to be effective. The chapter argues that it is particularly appropriate to attempts by environmental groups and the business community in Canada to collaborate. It concludes with a discussion of the implications for collaborative theory in general and bridging in particular.

Strategic Bridging: A Special Form of Collaboration

Bridging organizations 'span the social gaps among organizations and constituencies to enable coordinated action' (Brown, 1989: 5). Numerous writers have argued that bridging organizations are crucial to contemporary societies. They are essential to establishing cooperative links that help stabilize turbulent environments (Emery and Trist, 1965; Trist, 1983). They are central to the emergence of functional networks that span or link organizations into value-added chains (Lawrence and Johnston, 1988) or PALS (pooling, allying and linking entities), both of which are hailed as alternatives to large hierarchies and as keys to social and technological innovation (Kanter, 1989; Miles and Snow, 1984).

Despite their potential strategic importance, bridging organizations face many potential problems. Essentially, they must find mechanisms to integrate organizations that may be widely disparate in wealth, power, culture, language, values, interests and structural characteristics. The farther apart these organizations are and the more focused the objective of the specific operation, the more difficult the bridging problem. A complicating factor is that, for an organization to qualify for a bridging role, its members must understand the diverse perspectives they are trying to integrate. As long as the bridging organization can continue to integrate these perspectives internally, it can function as a bridge for the organizations. But if any factional contentions arise, they will seriously weaken the organization's bridging ability.

Theoretically, any form of collaboration can be considered a bridge in the sense that, by definition, the bridging process connects entities previously considered separate. It is helpful, however, to define bridging as a distinctive configuration of collaborative negotiation related to, but separate from, such entities as multiparty collaboration (e.g. round tables and task forces), joint ventures, strategic alliances, and mediations.

As described by Brown (1989), bridging represents a distinctive form of collaborative activity. One way it varies from other forms is in the degree of *interpenetration* involved, and in the particular balance between the processes of interorganizational collaboration and intraorganizational commitment building that is determined by that degree of interpenetration. Interpenetration refers to the process whereby stakeholders seeking to collaborate in a problem domain engage in direct or mutual negotiations, pool resources, and/or create or employ a third party as a linking device. By its very name, bridging implies linking. We contend that bridging is characterized by the presence of a third party, which is historically separate and distinct in terms of resources and personnel from the 'island' organizations it seeks to link. In this sense, bridging is unlike joint ventures or multiparty collaborations, which create a third party – such as a joint venture, task force, or project team – by pooling their resources of the island organizations. In such cases, the third party represents the arena and is the communal focus for the collaborative negotiations of all identified stakeholders. Bridges provide no such communal focus. Instead, like mediators, they negotiate bilaterally with key stakeholders.

Unlike mediators, however, bridging organizations enter collaborative negotiations to forward their own ends as well as to serve as a link or brokers among domain stakeholders. Although self-interest is an important motivation for individuals and organizations accepting a mediator role (Touval and Zaltman, 1985), it is important that the mediator does not appear to disputing parties to be placing self-interest over problem resolution in the *process* of mediation (Gray, 1989). Mediators, therefore, do not act as stakeholders in the process of mediation, even when their motivation for accepting the role may be to maintain the status quo or to enhance their position in an emerging order.

Bridging organizations, however, do act as stakeholders. They enter into discrete bilateral collaborative negotiations with stakeholders that direct interaction and exchange, similar to those characterizing negotiations among stakeholders in a joint venture or multiparty project group. In the process, they engage in the incremental creation of a negotiated order that may potentially permit greater collaboration among all stakeholders. In this sense, the bridging organizations act as both broker *and* agent in the problem domain.

This dual role creates a stressful situation for bridging organizations that is not faced by mediators: that of trying to 'sell' negotiation outcomes to their 'home' organizations to secure commitment (Bingham and Miller, 1984; Carpenter and Kennedy, 1988; Gray, 1989). Negotiators in joint ventures and multiparty task forces also face this problem, but because mediators do not act as stakeholders, this problem is considerably reduced. Bridging, as a form of collaboration, in a sense has the worst of both worlds. Like mediators, bridging organizations must engage in multiple negotiations, for no 'communal' vehicle exists to conduct these negotiations. Like negotiators in joint ventures and multiparty round tables, they must secure commitment to these negotiations from their home organizations. In addition, they bring home more than one discrete set of negotiations (although not necessarily simultaneously), which makes the process of commitment more complex and potentially fragile. Figure 21.1 illustrates four configurations of collaborative negotiation and commitment that characterize these different degrees of interpenetration.

As a result, in addition to the difficulties of integrating disparate views which characterize all forms of collaboration (Brown, 1989), bridges face external and internal ambivalence. Constituents who stand to benefit from bridging may be uncompromising in negotiations over values and process; members of the organization may be ambivalent about the importance of the bridging role in relation to other organizational roles and unwilling to commit to the agreements that have been negotiated. These additional strains are a potential structural weaknesses in the bridging organization itself. In multiparty or joint venture collaborations, a breakdown is signalled by the rupture of the negotiations among the organizations; a failure in bridging may also result in the demise of the bridging organization itself.

Types of Bridging Roles

Bridging organizations can adopt a variety of roles. Given the inherent fragility of the bridging role, it is, perhaps, surprising that organizations are willing to accept it. Indeed, many of the bridging organizations identified to date – such as those described by Brown (1989) – are *deliberately designed or mandated* to fill a bridging role. We maintain, however, that it is also possible to accept a bridging role *voluntarily*.

Like many mandated or designed bridges, an organization may volunteer for a bridging role out of a sense of altruism because of its *commitment to problem solution*. For example, a zoo director might volunteer to bring together representatives of national parks and tourism companies (groups with opposing views on wildlife and natural resources) in an effort to protect animals while boosting the economy of the region through tourism. Unlike most mandated or designed bridges, however, a voluntary bridge may also act out of self-interest to defend or improve its own strategic position. For example, a supplier to two competing companies, each of which could benefit from knowledge of the other's activities, may volunteer to serve as an information conduit between the companies and thereby enhance its value to them. In practice, motives are often mixed and may be viewed as points on a continuum. The supplier extends information as a gesture of goodwill; the zoo benefits from the collaboration between the tourism industry and the parks system. Distinguishing among dominant motives, however, is useful for analysing the process involved.

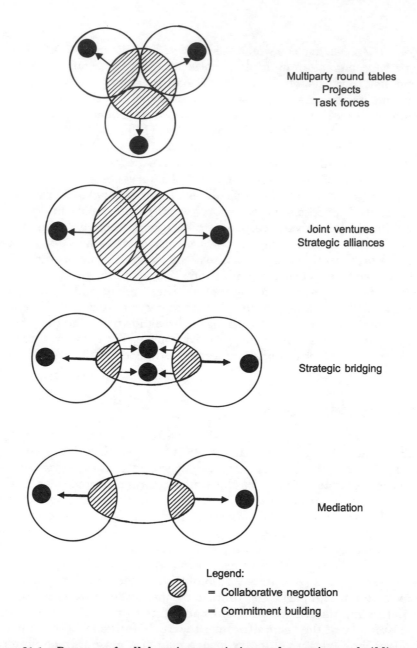

Multiparty round tables
Projects
Task forces

Joint ventures
Strategic alliances

Strategic bridging

Mediation

Legend:
⬚ = Collaborative negotiation
● = Commitment building

Figure 21.1   *Patterns of collaborative negotiation and commitment building*

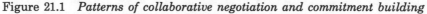

A voluntary bridging organization may, like many mandated bridging organizations, view its role as *transformational* – intending to change social structures and develop a problem domain to make direct collaboration among stakeholders possible in the future. An example is a clinic that takes on outreach activities to bridge the gap between available social services and the needs of elderly patients: it negotiates with service providers and recipients

Table 21.1   *Two types of bridges (based on motivation)*

Egoistic	Altruistic
Voluntary	Designed or mandated
Self-serving	Problem focused
Maintenance oriented	Transformative

directly and hopes that funds and resources will be provided so that eventually it can relinquish this role and other parties can fill it. Voluntary bridges may also be *maintenance oriented* – designed to fill a necessary niche permanently so that the current structure of relationships can simultaneously continue to exist and solve a mutual problem. An example of a maintenance oriented bridge is a lighting company that coordinates relationships among lighting suppliers to consolidate its position with them.

These three distinctions – mandated versus voluntary, problem focused versus self-serving, transformational versus maintenance oriented – cluster into two ideal-typical configurations, which we label *altruistic bridges* and *egoistic bridges* (see Table 21.1). An example of an altruistic bridge is the Savings Development Foundation of Zimbabwe (Brown, 1989). This organiz- ation was designed to act as a bridge among members of the local female population, the Ministry of Agriculture, the Ministry of Community Develop- ment and Women's Affairs, various international donors, and a fertilizer company. Much like a designed or mandated bridge, this group's motivation was to help solve the problem of village poverty by promoting savings and investment in agriculture. The mission was the transformation of the rural economy, and members viewed themselves as a temporary device to aid the development of local autonomy. In contrast, a good example of an egoistic bridging organization is a group of equipment suppliers (Child and Smith, 1987) who aided in a much-needed transfer of design concepts and technical knowledge in the chocolate-making industry. They volunteered for the bridging role out of self-interest: they wanted to increase their value to their customers. Their motives were maintenance oriented in that they profited from a healthy, competitive chocolate-manufacturing industry, and they were prepared to occupy the bridging role permanently if needed.

In sum, strategic bridging shares several characteristics of other forms of collaboration: it has the important social function of creating a negotiated order, it is complex, and it requires the cooperation of previously independent organizations. It differs from other forms of collaboration – particularly many multiparty task forces and joint ventures – in that it links organizations that will not or cannot collaborate directly by means of discrete bilateral negoti- ations. Unlike mediators, however, the bridging organization must also create ongoing intraorganizational commitment.

Despite the difficulty of balancing these demands, strategic bridges elect to play a linking role for altruistic or egoistic motives. In practice, many bridging organizations deviate from these ideal types, mixing motives and missions. This confusion occurred in the case of Pollution Probe and Loblaws (see the case of Loblaws at the end of Part III), and affected the outcome of the collaboration effort.

The Benefits of Strategic Bridging

Despite the challenges, bridging is a distinctive form of collaboration that is particularly appropriate when the willingness of domain stakeholders to collaborate directly, without a bridge, is low. Four factors may lead to an unwillingness or inability to collaborate directly:

- resource or authority restraints – that is, stakeholders may feel they can solve a problem unilaterally (Gray and Hay, 1986);
- ideological or cultural constraints that come into play when core values are at stake and compromise is not considered an acceptable option (Touval and Zaltman, 1985);
- traditional positions of opposition (such as between business and environmentalists);
- legal barriers.

Bridging may be a way around these restraints that prevent stakeholders from coming to the negotiating table or make them unwilling to do so.

Bridging may also occur in situations in which stakeholders are relatively unaware that they have a role in a particular problem domain. They may enter into a subdomain negotiation (for example, green products are a marketing subdomain of the larger sustainable development problem domain) without seeing the implications of the larger context, which are recognized by the bridging organization. This is common when problem domains are underorganized – when 'boundaries of the domain are unclear, shifting, or in dispute [with] the degree of awareness . . . frequently low or nonexistent' (Gray and Hay, 1986). In such domains, collaboration is crucial in organizing the domain so that (a) stakeholders can be identified and develop a common language; (b) norms and values governing ongoing interaction can be established; and (c) authority, responsibility and resources can be allocated. We argue that, of the four forms of collaboration mentioned earlier, bridging is particularly relevant when the domain is underorganized. As a collaborative activity it has a covert, incremental quality compared with the overt and integrated efforts at creating a negotiated order represented by task forces and round tables.

Figure 21.2 plots bridging and a number of other collaborative mechanisms in terms of these two critical dimensions: the degree of domain organization and the degree of willingness to collaborate. When willingness to collaborate is low because of power imbalances or deadlock (Gray and Hay, 1986; Touval and Zaltman, 1985), third-party intervention – such as mediation or bridging – is more likely to occur than multiparty round tables or joint ventures. When the

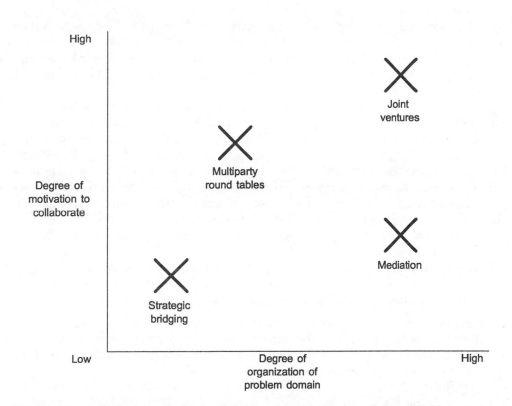

Figure 21.2 *Collaborative form as a function of motivation to collaborate and of organization of problem domain*

domain is also underorganized, conflict is diffuse, nonspecific, and under-organized as well. Bridging is more suitable than mediation in the early stages of domain organization (even before disputes are organized). In underorganized problem domains – in which core value differences and presenting structures such as the articulation of old problem domains are likely to impede communal collaborative negotiations – bridging may be a valuable alternative until further organization of the domain occurs.

In Figure 21.2, the legitimacy of the stakeholders (including third parties) increases toward the upper right-hand corner of the figure. For a joint venture to occur, both parties must clearly acknowledge the capacity and the rights of each other as stakeholders in a well-articulated problem domain (for a discussion of legitimacy in interorganizational collaboration, see Gray and Hay, 1986). The need for mediators, usually accepted only at the point of stalemate, is also clear. Whether the mediator is capable is less certain, and at times this depends on the persuasive power of the mediator. In multiparty collaborations, establishing legitimacy is an important first step; once stake-holders have entered into collaborative negotiations, their legitimacy is further consolidated. In bridging, however, with its incremental, discontinuous collaborations, an individual stakeholder may enter into collaborative negotiations with the bridging organization without ever acknowledging the legitimacy of the bridging organization as a link between it and another stakeholder.

Therefore, as a form of collaboration, bridging may occur *without* the establishment of the clear legitimacy of the bridging organization within the problem domain. In some cases, the lack of recognition may aid bridging organizations by providing a 'corridor of indifferences' (Wrapp, 1976) that provides room for manoeuvre that would not be available to planned collaborations in public arenas (Hiltgartner and Bosk, 1988). Despite this potential advantage, a lack of legitimacy heightens the need for the bridging organization to manage collaborative negotiations with great skill and reduces the likelihood of a negotiated order, which is the optimal result of the collaborative task force.

In the final analysis, success in bridging situations perhaps should be judged less by the consensus achieved regarding a negotiated order and the commitment to implement decisions than by the following:

- the endurance of the organizing links formed;
- the success in advancing the articulation of the problem domain in the form of shared values, terminology, norms for interaction, and mapping of the boundaries of the problem;
- the ability of the bridging organization to secure internal commitment to the bridging activities;
- the ability of the bridging organization to balance its own self-interest with domain concerns.

The Canadian Context of Environmental Concerns

It is argued here that the problem domain that encompasses sustainable development domain is particularly relevant for bridging strategies. It is underorganized, as will be demonstrated below: even the subdomain of green products is poorly understood by stakeholders. Moreover, the traditional enmity between environmentalists and business people has often prevented direct collaboration. This section describes the Canadian context to illustrate these issues.

Historically in Canada, business and environmental groups have maintained their distance from each other. Until recently, most private-sector organizations – except for those subject to governmental regulation or pressure group tactics – have viewed environmental issues as peripheral to their strategic agenda. In response, the best-known national environmental group, Greenpeace, has positioned itself as a watchdog with a mission to uncover and expose destructive industry plans and practices. The result has been a tradition of hostility and mistrust between business and environmentalists, which has made collaboration difficult.

With the advent of the Brundtland Commission in 1986 and the widespread redefinition of environmental problems as issues of sustainable development, a new problem domain was created in which both environmentalists and business were clearly stakeholders. When the environmental crisis was reconceptualized as a domain in which development and economic growth had to be balanced with the need to preserve ecological resources, it became a concern to business and environmental groups alike. The concept of sustainable development thus reframed the issue to make collaboration among businesses, environmentalists and governments a vital aspect of problem resolution. More moderate environmental groups demanded a place in the corporate boardroom. Business responded positively since it needed the support of environmentalists to gain credibility with a sceptical public.

On the other hand, this redefinition created a number of problems. It threatened the more radical environmental groups, who saw sustainable development as an ideological cover for business interests. So, despite the pressure for business and environmentalists to cooperate, continuing structural constraints acted against collaboration. One such constraint was the fear that the concepts of sustainable development and green business could turn environmental groups and businesses into direct competitors. If consumers felt they could protect the environment by 'buying green', their support for watchdog environmental organizations might decline; if they accepted the stringent definitions of the environmentalists, they would not trust most green products and would continue to support the environmentalists' uncompromising stance.

Environmentalists also feared that their nonprofit or charitable status – which allows groups to accept tax-exempt donations and is crucial to the support base of most environmental organizations – could be threatened by a close alliance between business and environmentalists. In addition, the differences in the structure and values of businesses and environmental groups appeared to make collaboration unlikely. The values of most environmental groups – consensus decision-making, love of nature, conservation, anti-consumerism – are not the values of the average private-sector organization, which focuses on profit maximization and growth. It is exceedingly difficult to create common 'institutional thought structures' on the basis of divergent values. Moreover, environmental groups in Canada (as elsewhere) are loosely structured and 'thinly institutionalized', and lack developed internal hierarchy and a central authority. This structure inhibits collaboration, as one policy analyst we interviewed noted:

> This has been one of the problems with the environmental movement [in reaching collaborative accords with business]: they have trouble bringing along their own members. The government and business can be fairly sure that they have the support of their constituencies, but environmental groups being democracies are difficult to control.

As a result, agreements between environmental groups and business are often rejected by the rank and file members, thereby reducing confidence in the process of collaboration.

Finally, the concept of sustainable development framed a problem domain that was highly underorganized. In practice, many groups on both sides had only a hazy notion of their responsibilities in the domain or of the domain's parameters. Considerable dialogue was needed to begin to map out the boundaries and structures of this new problem and to determine the legitimate stakeholders, appropriate language, and interaction patterns. In addition, the emerging domain was plagued with the residues of previous problems, such as conflicts in definitions of environmentalism that predated the notion of sustainable development.

In sum, Canada in 1989 was ripe for the emergence of bridging organizations to span the gap between environmentalists and business. An issue domain had been defined, though it was underdeveloped, which made collaboration a concern for all stakeholders. Yet structural constraints – such as competition for resources, legal and normative guidelines, and value disparities – made direct collaboration difficult. (For an illustration of these difficulties, see the Loblaws case at the end of this part.)

Conclusions

This chapter delineates a special form of collaboration – strategic bridging – using descriptive case study to explore this form's parameters. In it we seek to distinguish this collaborative form from other forms such as multiparty round tables, joint ventures, and mediation. We need to learn more about successful and unsuccessful strategic bridging attempts. Most studies have focused on the collaborative negotiations involved. We suggest that in bridging situations, attention should be paid to the way in which commitment is created in the strategic bridging organization itself.

The strains inherent in the strategic bridging form of collaboration can lead to failure. We speculate that many organizations that are flexible and innovative enough to attempt bridging strategies – such as professional bureaucracies and ad hoc organizations (that is, adhocracies; Mintzberg, 1979) – may be handicapped by the poor ability of their democratic decision-making processes to build internal commitment to a bridging strategy. For example, a business school dean who attempts a bridging strategy between academia and business may fail to obtain commitment from factions in the faculty; and public-sector nongovernmental organizations that attempt bridging strategies have similar structural impediments. A hierarchically organized company, however, such as the lighting equipment manufacturer or the chocolate-manufacturer supplier, may be better able to build internal commitment for a bridging strategy. Further research will, it is hoped, provide more concrete answers to the question of why bridging succeeds in some cases and not in others.

References

Astley, G. (1984) 'Toward an appreciation of collective strategy', *Academy of Management Review*, 9: 526–35.

Bingham, G. and Miller, D.S. (1984) 'Prospects for resolving hazardous waste siting disputes through negotiation', *Natural Resources Lawyer*, 12: 473–9.

Brown, L.D. (1989) 'Bridging organizations and sustainable development', Paper presented at the Conference on Social Innovations in Global Management, Cleveland, OH, November.

Carpenter, S.L. and Kennedy, W.J.D. (1988) *Managing Public Disputes: A Practical Guide to Handling Conflict and Reaching Agreement*. San Francisco: Jossey-Bass.

Child, J. and Smith, C. (1987) 'The context and process of organizational transformation – Cadbury Limited in its sector', *Journal of Management Studies*, 24: 565–92.

Corcoran, T. (1989) 'Activists and business: Strange bedfellows', *Globe and Mail*, 5 July, p. B2.

Emery, F. and Trist, E. (1965) 'The causal texture of organizational environments', *Human Relations*, 18: 21–35.

Goldberg, R. (1989) *Loblaws Companies Ltd.: President's Choice G.R.E.E.N.: Something Can be Done* (Harvard Business School Case No. 9-590-051). Boston: Harvard Business School.

Granovettor, M. (1985) 'Economic action and social structure: The problem of embeddedness', *American Journal of Sociology*, 91: 481–510.

Gray, B. (1985) 'Conditions facilitating interorganizational collaboration', *Human Relations*, 38: 911–36.

Gray, B. (1989) *Collaborating: Finding Common Ground for Multiparty Problems*. San Francisco: Jossey-Bass.

Gray, B. and Hay, T. (1986) 'Political limits to interorganizational consensus and change', *Journal of Applied Behavioral Science*, 22: 95–112.

Hiltgartner, S. and Bosk, C.L. (1988) 'The rise and fall of social problems: A public arenas model', *American Journal of Sociology*, 94: 53–78.

Isaacs, C. (1989) 'Harnessing the profit motive to clean up world pollution – It's faster than government', *Globe and Mail*, 10 July, p. A7.

Kanter, R.M. (1989) 'Becoming PALS: Pooling, allying and linking across companies', *Academy of Management Executive*, 33: 183–93.

Lawrence, P. and Johnston, R. (1988) 'Beyond vertical integration – The rise of the value-adding partnership', *Harvard Business Review*, July–August, 94–101.

Manolson, M. (1989) 'Big business is cashing in on environmental worries while industry keeps polluting', *Globe and Mail*, 10 July, p. A7.

Mcinnis, C. (1989) 'Environment groups face a crisis of identity', *Globe and Mail*, 15 July, p. D2.

Miles, R.E. and Snow, C.C. (1984) 'Fit, failure and the hall of fame', *California Management Review*, 26: 10–28.

Mintzberg, H. (1979) *The Structuring of Organizations*. Englewood Cliffs, NJ: Prentice-Hall.

O'Toole, R. and O'Toole, A.W. (1981) 'Negotiating interorganizational orders', *Sociological Quarterly*, 22: 29–41.

Touval, S. and Zaltman, I.E. (eds) (1985) *International Mediation in Theory and Practice*. Boulder, CO: Westview.

Trist, E. (1983) 'Referent organizations and the development of interorganizational domains', *Human Relations*, 36: 269–84.

Waddock, S. (1989) 'Understanding social partnerships', *Administration and Society*, 21: 78–100.

Wrapp, E. (1976) 'Good managers don't make policy decisions', *Harvard Business Review*, September–October, 91–9.

22 Managing Collaboration

Frances Westley

Organizational activities are shaped by the nature of communication systems. Daily operations are patterned around communications, and the quality of life is influenced by how those communication events are experienced by organizational members. An important aspect of strategy making is its role as a communicative activity: strategy involves the procurement, production, synthesis, manipulation and diffusion of information in such a way as to give meaning, purpose and direction to an organization. This chapter focuses on one subset of strategic communication: the involvement of middle-level managers in strategic systems. It examines three related issues: feelings of inclusion and exclusion experienced by middle managers around strategic issues; the ways in which the dynamics and structure of strategic conversations affect levels of energy among middle managers in relation to strategic initiatives; and the relationship between strategic conversations and the allocation of resources. The term strategic *'conversation'* rather than *'decision'* is used intentionally, since the focus is on the communication between senior and middle management that precedes, accompanies and follows actual strategy decisions.

Strategy and the Middle Manager

Middle managers are rarely the object of research in strategic studies. Strategic sense-making has by and large been treated as the responsibility of top management alone. It is upper management that ought to 'bring together and interpret information for the system as a whole' (Daft and Weick, 1984: 285). This perspective is supported by pointing out that too much equivocality in information impedes action; hence it is efficient for top managers to reduce equivocality so that middle managers may act on clear instructions. It is also viewed as functional to limit the decision-making body to keep the process from becoming unwieldy (Thompson, 1967). As a result, top managers often

Adapted from Frances Westley, 'Middle managers and strategy: The microdynamics of inclusion', *Strategic Management Journal*, 11: 337–51, 1990.

assume the responsibility for scanning the environment, and seldom is that information widely shared (Aguilar, 1967; Leifer and Delbecq, 1978). Top managers' goals and values are taken as unproblematic, and 'strategic planning systems continue to be designed as top-down planning systems with bottom-up information flows' (Shrivastava, 1986: 369). Despite the fact that a growing amount of empirical evidence indicates that middle managers can play a key role in initiating strategic change (Van Cauwenbergh and Kool, 1982; Burgelman, 1983a,b,c; Nonaka, 1988), middle managers are accorded only a supporting role in most normative models of strategy (Shrivastava, 1986).

Such assumptions have resulted in a gap in understanding why some strategies are implemented and others are not; what middle management's role is in this process; and how they view their role. Surveys of middle managers (Kay, 1974; Breen, 1983) indicate that they are dissatisfied with the quality of their communication with top management, which they criticize for being unresponsive and dishonest. They perceive a lack of involvement; a failure of two-way influence; and exclusion from processes they need to understand if they are to advance.

> There appears to be built-in conflict between the role of top executives and the role of middle managers, particularly relating to the sharing of authority. The role of top management traditionally has been one of decision and policy making. There is little or no evidence at this point to indicate management is willing to share more of this influence with middle managers. (Kay, 1974: 21)

Middle managers have also expressed frustration at their exclusion from strategic processes (Levine, 1986), and have experienced resentment about the 'tight control' which top management keep on the strategic agenda (Kelley, 1976) – a situation particularly prevalent in large bureaucratic organizations, but evident even in innovative organizations (Burgelman, 1983a,b,c; Donaldson, 1985).

It is uncertain whether this tight control is in the organization's interests, or whether it is political, having more to do with the status and control needs of top management than with organizational efficiency (Bourgeois and Brodwin, 1984; Shrivastava, 1986). Whatever the reason, it is clear that middle managers' resentment of this tight control has deleterious effects on organizational responsiveness. They can impede the implementation process if they do not perceive cooperation to be in their interests (Guth and MacMillan, 1986), or respond in organizationally dysfunctional ways to perceived powerlessness (Izraeli, 1975). Conversely, when this group is able to exert influence the result may be a more responsive, innovative organization (Ofner, 1985).

How to involve middle managers remains problematic. Formal planning procedures are often actively avoided by middle-level managers who mistrust top management motives for initiating the procedure and who fear failure and exposure if they participate (Lyles and Lenz, 1982: 114). Further, the effects of formal participation in strategic decision-making is mixed (Locke and

Schweiger, 1979) and may result in incremental, disjointed and parochial strategies (Guth, 1976). Senior managers are faced with a dilemma: excluding middle managers from setting the strategic agenda results in demotivation; inclusion, on the other hand, may result in inefficiency. Resolving this dilemma requires a greater understanding of the dynamics of inclusion and exclusion, and their link to energy and motivation.

Strategic Conversations

Microsociologists such as Goffman (1967), Garfinkle (1967) and Cicorel (1975) have long contended that the only truly empirical grounding for social processes lies in micro events. According to these theorists, the notion of organization is a reification. Organizations do not exist *per se*, they are, in fact, only a series of interlocking routines, and habituated action patterns that bring the same people together around the same activities in the same time and places (Giddens, 1984). Similarly, the argument can be extended to the concept of strategy. While strategy is typically viewed at the macro-level as an aggregate of actions, transactions, positions and plans, it is grounded in micro-level actions of individual actors. One mechanism for understanding organizational life is conversation (Collins, 1981). Conversations are discrete, observable events which contain all the elements of social structure. First, they represent a highly ritualistic exchange of rights and obligations. In order to engage in a conversation at all, actors need to agree on certain reciprocities of form, if not of content (Goffman, 1967; Hochschild, 1979; Collins, 1981). Second, conversations contain elements of authority: if they occur between superior and subordinate they potentially enact formal structures of domination. Third, participants must share certain cultural vocabularies or resources for a conversation to occur at all which, in turn, permits participants to sustain the conversation and enact their solidarity.

Conversations thus reflect three elements of social structure: normative structures (legitimation), authority structures (domination), and structures of signification (Giddens, 1984). Participation in conversations also represents a membership ritual. Admission into one conversation has implications for admission into a particular organizational coalition. An individual also may be deliberately excluded from a particular conversation, even if s/he understands the proprieties and the cultural vocabulary because certain interest groups wish to prevent their inclusion in a particular coalition. In short, an understanding of the norms, authority patterns and culture of a given organization may be a *necessary* precursor of full inclusion in a given conversation, but it is not *sufficient*. Inclusion is also dependent on the proclivity of coalition members to sustain solidarity with a given member or to admit a new member.

According to Collins (1981), whether an individual is admitted to a conversation depends in part on his/her perceived social worth which, in turn, is an artefact of that individual's past successes in negotiating membership rituals. The first element of success is admission to the conversation at all. Having been successfully admitted to a conversation, the individual must then negotiate a particular status in the conversation. Any conversation may be mutually determined (co-determined) or it may be dominated by one or the other of the participants. If one person dominates s/he will emerge from the conversation energized at the expense of the dominated individual, who will be de-energized, which reduces the likelihood of action resulting from the conversation and the prospects of the individual dominating the next conversation. An individual may be trapped in a downward spiral of demoralization or, alternatively, an upward spiral of energization. Demoralized and de-energized individuals have less chance of successfully negotiating admission into new coalitions and more chance of being expelled from old coalitions, since their social worth is perceived to be low.

In sum, strategic conversations are the building blocks for coalitions to claim rights to resources and authority. Exclusion from conversations means exclusion from the coalitions which embody organizational routines and hence action; while inclusion coupled with domination or co-determination can produce energy for strategic initiatives.

Middle Managers and Strategic Conversation

With respect to strategic conversations, there are three related dimensions: the dynamics of inclusion in versus exclusion from conversations; the dynamics of domination versus submission within conversations; and the relationship between conversations, their outcomes and the larger context in which they take place, notably the organizational ideology and power balance between coalitions. In the remainder of this chapter, we will examine each of these dimensions in turn.[1]

Exclusion versus Inclusion

Middle managers who feel excluded from strategic processes in their organizations are experiencing exclusion from *particular kinds* of conversations with their superiors. As content, strategy-making discussions correspond to a 'generalized' topic. Strategy is a meaning-generating activity concerned with integrating and interpreting information. As such it is abstracted from specific tactics, policies or operational procedures while being intimately concerned with relating these into an overall pattern. Middle managers are often involved in tactical conversations which, from an information point of view, represent discrete, isolated instructions whose place in the overall picture is not inherently apparent. A wholistic perspective which addresses the 'actual meaning of information' (Nonaka, 1988: 58) is, in practice, reserved for upper management. Since the discussion of strategic generalities is typically emblematic of membership in a top management coalition, admission to them is often carefully controlled. Take the following example.

——————————————— *Example 1* ———————————————

A young woman working in the marketing department of a large multidivisional appliance manufacturer was seen as having high potential and had moved up quickly in the organization. When asked about how strategy was made in her organization and whether strategic goals were clearly communicated she responded as follows:

> The President has these dinners where his direct subordinates report . . . My boss is included, but I have never been invited to one of those meetings where everyone rubs shoulders. Here I am doing research and trying to determine the direction of my department and I'm not included in the meetings where these strategic things are discussed. For a while my boss claimed that they were going to start having communication meetings. That sounded good to me but in practice it never actually happened. That made me angry! I wish he wouldn't dangle these grand illusions in front of me if he's not going to deliver them.
>
> It's not just a question of power access. I feel that by not giving me the necessary information they mishandle my effectiveness. If I'm playing in a small game, my view vis-à-vis that game is small. If they give me a picture of a bigger world, I play a bigger game. Access is part of it.
>
> Take the example of the financial performance of the company. They have these staff meetings where they review with department heads the financial results of the year. I don't get to go to those meetings but when I asked my boss about it he gives me a copy of the figures which is about two inches thick. And I do take them home and read them. But just looking at the numbers doesn't give me the insights. It doesn't give me the total picture. I don't know how they are interpreting those numbers. I take the numbers and read them and try to spot problem areas and then I ask if my interpretations are correct. But it is kind of humiliating to have to go and beg for this kind of information. It makes me feel angry. It makes me feel like shit, like I'm playing in a small world. Requests for information are always brushed off. So I don't have a feeling of ownership and pride. I feel like I've put in a good performance, why don't I deserve to have that information? Why don't I deserve to be party to that inner circle?

This example reveals the relationship between feelings of exclusion and demoralization, as well as the relationship between that exclusion and participation in coalitions. By being prevented from attending certain meetings and participating in certain conversations, this middle manager feels she is excluded from the 'inner circle'. She identifies the authority and property implications of this ('it's not only a question of power . . . they mishandle my effectiveness . . . I'm playing in a small game') as well as the content of the conversations she would like to have. She is searching for strategic generalities, the 'total picture', which makes sense of the specific, particular decisions which are passed on to her as a member of a functional group ('It doesn't give me the total picture . . . I don't know how they are interpreting those numbers . . . I don't know if my interpretations are correct').

This example also illustrates the emotional implications of exclusion. She states her own feelings ('I deserve to have that information . . . I don't feel pride and ownership') and justifications for being included ('I've put in a good performance . . . Here I am doing research and trying to determine the direction of my department'). Her boss, however, will not entertain these definitions, much less allow her to dominate. He 'brushes off' her requests; she has to 'beg' for information. He doesn't acknowledge her claim to the right to feel pride and ownership and the result is that she 'feels like shit'. This manager is excluded from strategic conversation on all three counts: there are no formal conventions, such as the promised communications sessions, recognized by both parties; there is no mutual commitment or solidarity around the conversation; and there is no agreement on significance, meaning or cultural frame for the data because the superior does not share his interpretations. In this particular example, the subordinate perceives the exclusion to be deliberate.

Clearly, these are issues of power and status as well as of efficiency. To the extent that the organization treats strategy making as an elite activity, top managers will be more resistant to including middle managers in strategic conversations. Only middle managers whom they are personally grooming for succession, and hence for admission to their status group, 'need' to be admitted to such conversations. To allow more general access to such conversations and to allow subordinates to dominate or even co-determine such conversations, threatens the boundaries of the status group to which top managers belong. In addition, to relinquish dominance may be perceived as a personal failure to 'think strategically'. By this definition, exclusion is justified because subordinates are incapable of entering effectively into strategic conversation; strategic activity is a status symbol; or politics prevents the inclusion of middle managers even in the interests of championing innovation.

Domination versus Submission

The following two examples illustrate the dynamics of domination versus submission within discrete conversations between subordinate and superior.

Example 2

Ned B., a middle manager, felt that he had been relatively successful in introducing innovation and change. Hired shortly after his company had merged with another appliance manufacturer, this manager felt that his outsider viewpoint helped him to overcome divergent viewpoints of long-standing members of the two parent companies. One such issue concerned the use of the name of the newly merged company (Manufacturing Inc.) over the existing brand names associated with the two separate parent companies. As a sales strategy, Manufacturing Inc. continued to use the original brand names. As an organizational strategy and from a customer service viewpoint, it appeared to Ned (as well as to others) that it would be much more rational to use the name of Manufacturing Inc. Ned's direct superior disagreed, however, as the following anecdote illustrates.

> My boss was very against using the Manufacturing Inc. name in our advertising. He was adamant for five years. There was no explanation for it, and no rationale. Recently I was doing a show and the whole audience was dealers. So underneath the sign I had up I indicated that this was Manufacturing Inc. My manager came up to me and ordered me to take down the sign because it said Manufacturing Inc. So I really lost my temper and I said to him, 'Look, all the audience out there are our dealers and they know we are Manufacturing Inc. This is illogical.' And he turned around and said to me 'It's not the question of using the name or not. I just don't want them to take the easy way out. I want them to think through the process and decide how to present themselves and why . . . decide who they are.' He said he perceived the managers from one of the founding companies as prone to take the easy way out and he felt that they hadn't planned it out and thought out who they wanted to be. In this particular example, I was the person who made things improve. I was put into the organization and I didn't belong to either parent company A or parent company B. I wasn't thought of as one of the crazies from company A, but here I was questioning my boss who was a real company B type. And for the first time he opens up, he essentially gave the ball to me. I was hired by him and yet I challenged him . . . . So I went back and produced a report this thick . . . I really did my homework and they couldn't argue because I beat them at their own game.

Example 3

One of the functions most plagued by these inconsistencies was the consumer service organization. The future of this department was clearly in question and the uncertainty manifested itself to middle managers in terms of what they saw as paradoxical requests to cut manpower to the bare bones while simultaneously expanding the business. Several middle managers had become quite apathetic as a result, but one – Jerry H. – had had quite a different response. Like Ned, Jerry felt he could talk to his boss, that he was connected and not excluded. He mulled over the paradox of growth versus cutbacks and described the following initiative.

> Personally, I feel that opening franchise stores would be a good idea and maybe even eventually franchising technicians. If we franchise the stores we would immediately improve our bottom line drastically because we would have to cut a number of salaried people. In the long run, the cost base gets lower and stays there. Six months ago I talked to my division head about this and he said that

franchising was only an option you looked at when you were resource poor. But then last month I got to thinking that it seemed to me the retrenchment process could be seen as a resource scarcity . . . we were scarce in people. So I did the calculations to see how it would look if we went to a franchise system and I could tell the VP was impressed with my logic. He's taken up the idea with the CEO. I enjoy working with him (the department head). He's a very communicative kind of guy.

Both these examples are in stark contrast to Example 1, in that the managers describe interactions with superiors which made them feel both included and energized. Both middle managers also succeeded in at least partially dominating the conversation. The question remains: how did they do so?

In both examples a similar pattern of interaction may be observed. The subordinate perceives a paradox: in one case, 'how can we have an identity as one company if we represent ourselves to the world as two companies' (associated with the brand names); in the other case, 'how can we grow the business and simultaneously cut costs'. These paradoxes result in the subordinate taking an initiative. The initiative is rejected by the superior, but is treated as a legitimate question. In response, the superior reveals his own interpretation of the situation. This confidence on the part of the superior instills confidence in the subordinate who now sees the resolution of the paradox as a challenge. The subordinate comes up with a new way to define the situation which is accepted by the superior who acts to champion the idea. The dynamic is as follows: paradox → initiative by the subordinate → revelation by superior → challenge to subordinate → innovative response by subordinate → acceptance and championing by superior. Neither subordinate nor superior completely dominates this interchange and the result is a well-researched proposal that addresses the problem.

In both these cases, the superior dominates in terms of framing rules but does not *disallow* the framing rule of the subordinate. They do not claim, for example, that the policy is not illogical (in Example 2) or that cutting costs and improving the bottom line is not important (in Example 3). They merely present their own framing rules and insist they have priority. In finding a solution, the subordinate is free to suggest a solution, as long as it falls within the superior's framing rule. Therefore the superior ultimately dominates the conversation, but allows the subordinate considerable freedom. Through the process the subordinate gains access to the criteria and interpretations which the superior uses to assess strategic initiatives.

The two examples suggest that when superiors enter into strategic conversations with subordinates and allow the subordinate to dominate or at least co-determine some aspect of the conversation, the result is increased energy on the part of the subordinate and the superior. This is achieved through a process of negotiation, the superior articulating his or her framing rules and allowing subordinates to express their own. The subordinate ultimately is given the responsibility of synthesizing the framing rules, overcoming the paradox and creating new meaning. Both the subordinate and the superior are energized and the superior does not experience a loss of control.

Inclusion versus exclusion, and domination versus submission, are two separate but related dimensions. To be excluded is also to experience the ultimate domination, and hence is in itself demoralizing, as in the case of Example 1. To be included and be permitted to dominate should be energizing and give positive results, as in Examples 2 and 3. It is also possible to be excluded from generalized discussions of strategy and nonetheless experience oneself as dominant within one's own coalitions. However, the energy generated would be unlikely to be attached to the strategic ends of the organization, and the energy might instead go into political activity in an attempt to gain more access to authority and property. Finally, it is possible to be included in a generalized discussion, but to be persistently dominated. This would presumably result in some demoralization, unless the dominated individual was sufficiently committed to the same ideology, framing rules and feeling rules of his or her superior so as to relinquish private or separate opinions. In such cases, individuals may become stimulated while still submissive. This may be the case in situations where the subordinate attributes 'charismatic' powers to the superior.

Table 22.1   *Middle managers' response to strategic initiatives based on their relationship to strategic conversation and their role within such conversations*

Role within strategic conversations	Relationship to strategic conversations	
	Included	Excluded
Dominant/co-dominant	Empowered	Political
Submissive	Obedient	Apathetic

The discussion of these two dimensions is summarized in Table 22.1. The 'empowered' cell represents those middle managers, such as the two described in Examples 2 and 3, who experience both inclusion and some level of domination within strategic conversations with superiors. The 'apathetic' cell represents those managers who are excluded and therefore ultimately dominated. The 'political' cell represents those middle managers who are excluded from a top status coalition but who build power bases within functional area coalitions; and 'obedient' are those middle managers who are included but who are unwilling or unable to take initiatives, or to dominate or reframe issues in any way. None of the last three represents an ideal response for an organization. However, complaints about exclusion and demotivation are more likely to come from 'political' and 'powerless' middle managers than from those who are 'obedient'.

The Larger Context

The following discussion illuminates the kinds of dynamics that are likely to produce feelings of inclusion and stimulation around strategic issues among middle managers. These dynamics are embedded in a larger context. To understand the link between the strategic conversations and the strategic process, two concepts must be considered: ideology and coalitions.

Ideology

Hochschild (1979) suggests that all framing rules are ultimately embedded in ideologies. Organizations where one ideology is clearly identified and shared by all members may have little difficulty, in the short run, sustaining energy in all members, because all members will feel included, and framing and feeling rules will be experienced as co-determined. On the other hand, the illustrations in Examples 2 and 3 suggest that some difference of opinion is synergistic and productive. The innovations suggested by the subordinates in these examples depended in part on their effort to synthesize the disparate framing rules with which they were presented – to resolve a paradox. Ideologically driven organizations, by suppressing awareness of such differences or indeed by eliminating such differences, may in the long run sacrifice such innovative potential and responsiveness (Bartunek, 1984; McCall and Kaplan, 1985: 27).

An understanding of the dynamics of strategic conversation gives us a way to conceptualize how such ideologies, through the mechanism of framing rules, influence strategic initiatives and produce the energy needed to fuel activity. It also shows how spirited negotiation allowing co-determination of conversational outcomes, may simultaneously signal the breakdown of ideology and stimulate the creation of new meaning and purpose (Jonsson and Lundin, 1977; Nonaka, 1988). When middle managers gain access to the framing rules of superiors, they are able to negotiate and alter those rules. Each alteration has implications for the web of meaning which sustains organizational activity. As framing rules are redefined, so is ideology; as policies are redefined so is the organizational strategy.

The question of when clarity in organizational ideology stops producing energy and becomes, instead, stultifying and when strategic inconsistencies stop facilitating change initiatives and, instead, frustrate them are addressed in Table 22.2. It shows how the dynamics of strategic conversation suppress or encourage diversity of opinion.

Coalitions

In many organizations, certain coalitions have greater access to resources and greater influence on senior management. It would be logical to assume that if a

Table 22.2   *Relationship between strategic ideology and energy outcomes of strategic conversations*

Strategic ideology clear, uniform, authoritative	Strategic ideology vague, fragmented, lacking authority	
Increased likelihood of strategic conversations occurring	Decreased likelihood of strategic conversations occurring	
↓	↓	
Increased ease of co-determination framing and feeling accepted by all	Increased struggle for domination: framing and feeling rules open to negotiation	
↓	↓	↓
Mutual stimulation energy creation	Suppression of diversity: false unity de-energization	Energy and synergy through resolution of inconsistencies, negotiation
↓	↓	↓
Reinforcement of existing ideology	Gradual erosion of authority of strategic ideology	Change, renewal of strategic ideology

strong coalition and a weak coalition make competing claims, the strong coalition would be more likely to dominate. If this pattern is repeated, a hierarchy of coalitions is produced.

How is this experienced by middle managers? We propose that middle managers who are included in and allowed some dominance in dominant coalitions will not only be energized but also capable of sustaining energy over long periods of time, as their domination would be rewarded by access to resources and authority. In contrast, middle managers who are included and allowed some dominance in weak coalitions only temporarily experience stimulation because the coalition is ultimately unable to influence corporate strategy. In such a situation, the middle manager may become political – trying to either change his or her coalition or displace the top manager in the coalition. A middle manager who is part of a dominant coalition but who is not allowed to influence conversations may derive some energy from membership of that coalition, but is unlikely to sustain this energy in the long run because of his or her submissive role. The manager becomes dependent on coalition 'charity', so to speak, and may be vulnerable to expulsion. Since he or she is unlikely to be able to negotiate admission into a new coalition, the tendency will be to become an obedient member of a powerful coalition. Submissive members of weak coalitions lack power on all fronts (Table 22.3).

Embedding the dynamics of specific strategic conversations within the larger pattern of coalitions helps to explain organizational responsiveness and its relation to patterns of strategic decisions, particularly those pertaining to the

Table 22.3 *Middle managers' (MLM) response to strategic initiatives based on their role within strategic conversations and the status of their coalition in the overall organization*

	Position of MLM's coalition in organization	
Position of MLMs in strategic conversion	Dominant	Submissive
Dominant/co-dominant	Empowered	Temporarily empowered → political
Submissive	Temporarily empowered → obedient	Powerless

allocation of resources. Changes in the dynamics of such conversations – in terms of *who* is included and dominates them, and in the influence of coalitions on the organization – affect the subsequent allocation of resources. In addition, it is important to note that energy created at the level of the individual manager must be sustained by a coalition with access to resources and authority.

Conclusions and Propositions

In closing, we suggest the following propositions concerning the involvement of middle managers in strategic conversations. The *exclusion* of middle managers is likely to increase to the extent that: top managers resist entering into strategic conversations with their subordinates; strategic discussion is formally linked to membership in the top status group; no formal or informal mechanism exists in the organization which allows middle managers to converse cross-functionally around strategic issues; and no one clear ideological perspective dominates – since ideology is implicit and rarely articulated or competing ideologies prevail, the risks of disagreement and misunderstanding on the part of middle managers increases. Middle managers will feel *included* and *energized* about strategic issues to the extent that: middle managers are permitted to dominate a strategic conversation and/or are granted access to the framing rules of the superior; strategic discussions are *not* formally linked to membership in top status groups; formal or informal mechanisms exist, allowing middle managers to converse cross-functionally around strategic issues; the organization is ideologically driven (that is, a single ideology is clearly articulated and widely shared). Finally, middle managers who participate in strategic conversation and are permitted some dominance in these discussions will be more likely to *sustain* high energy levels around strategic issues to the extent that: there is a balance of elites within the organization and not a hierarchy of coalitions; and the organization is not ideologically driven, allowing for negotiation around framing rules due to the presence of competing sets of such rules and ideological perspectives.

In conclusion, middle managers want to be included in strategic conversations because they want access both to powerful coalitions and organizational sense-making. To the extent that the discussion of strategic generalities is not linked to membership in the top status group, and to the extent that there is a power balance between functional coalitions, the motivation for admission to such conversations based on purely political motivations may diminish, leaving only the desire for sense-making. Sense cannot be injected into others as a result of a uni-directional process of communication; it is apprehended only through discourse and response. Strategic conversations, as a process of negotiation, allow for the recombination of information, the mediation of inconsistencies and the co-invention of meaning. If organizations want a middle management group that is responsive, as opposed to paralysed, we need greater sensitivity to how meaning is made in organizations and how to include middle management as actors in that process.

Note

1. The following examples are drawn from interviews, conducted by the author, with middle managers in a large multi-divisional manufacturing company.

References

Aguilar, J. (1967) *Scanning the Business Environment*. New York: Macmillan.

Bartunek, J. (1984) 'Changing interpretive schemes and organizational restructuring', *Administrative Science Quarterly*, 29: 255–372.

Bourgeois, J. and Brodwin, D. (1984) 'Strategic implementation: Five approaches to an elusive phenomenon', *Strategic Management Journal*, 5: 241–64.

Breen, R. (1983) *Middle Management Morale in the 80's*. New York: American Management Association.

Burgelman, R. (1983a) 'A model of interaction, of strategic behavior, corporate context, and the concept of strategy', *Academy of Management Review*, 8(1): 61–70.

Burgelman, R. (1983b) 'A process model of internal corporate venturing in a diversified major firm', *Administrative Science Quarterly*, 28: 223–44.

Burgelman, R. (1983c) 'Corporate entrepreneurship and strategic management: Insights from a process study', *Management Science*, 29(12): 1349–64.

Business Week (1984) 'The new breed of strategic planner', 17 September, 62–8.

Cicorel, A. (1975) 'Discourse and text: Cognitive linguistic processes in studies of social structure', *Versus*, 12: 33–83.

Collins, R. (1981) 'On the microfoundations of macrosociology', *American Journal of Sociology*, 86(5): 984–1013.

Daft, R. and Weick, K. (1984) 'Towards a model of organizations as interpretation systems', *Academy of Management Review*, 19(2): 284–95.

Daft, R. and Lengel, R. (1984) 'Information richness', in B. Staw (ed.), *Research in Organizational Behavior*, vol. 6. Greenwich, Conn.: JAI Press, pp. 191–233.

Donaldson, L. (1985) 'Entrepreneurship applied to middle management: A caution', *Journal of General Management*, 10(4): 5–20.

Garfinkle, H. (1967) *Studies in Ethnomethodology*. Englewood Cliffs, NJ: Prentice-Hall.

Giddens, A. (1984) *The Construction of Society: Outline of the Theory of Structuration*. Oxford: Polity Press.

Goffman, Erving (1967) *Interactional Ritual*. New York: Doubleday.

Guth, W.D. (1976) 'Toward a social system theory of corporate strategy', *Journal of Business*, July, 374–88.

Guth, W.D. and MacMillan, I.C. (1986) 'Strategy implementation versus middle management self-interest', *Strategic Management Journal*, 7: 313–27.

Hochschild, A.R. (1979) 'Emotion work, feeling rules and social structure', *American Journal of Sociology*, 85(3): 551–75.

Hochschild, A.R. (1983) *The Managed Heart*. Berkeley: University of California Press.

Izraeli, D.N. (1975) 'The middle manager and the tactics of power expansion', *Sloan Management Review*, Winter, 57–70.

Jacques, E. (1986) 'The development of intellectual capability: A discussion of stratified system theory', *Journal of Applied Behavioral Science*, 22(4): 361–83.

Jonsson, S.A. and Lundin, R.A. (1977) 'Myths and wishful thinking as management tools', in Paul C. Nystom and W.H. Starbuck (eds), *Prescriptive Models of Organizations*. Amsterdam: North Holland Publishing Company.

Kay, E. (1974) *The Crisis in Middle Management*. New York: American Management Association.

Kelley, G. (1976) 'Seducing the elites: The politics of decision making and innovation in organizational networks', *Academy of Management Review*, 19(6): 66–74.

Leifer, R.T. and Delbecq, A. (1978) 'Organizational/environmental interchange: A model of boundaries spanning activity', *Academy of Management Review*, 3: 40–50.

Levine, H. (1986) 'The squeeze on middle management', *Personnel*, 1: 62–7.

Locke, E.D. and Schweiger, D.M. (1979) 'Participation in decision making', in L. Cummings and B. Staw (eds), *Research in Organizational Behavior*, vol. 1. Greenwich, Connecticut: JAI Press, pp. 265–339.

Lyles, M. and Lenz, B. (1982) 'Managing the planning process: A field study of the human side of planning', *Strategic Management Journal*. 3: 105–18.

McCall, M. and Kaplan, R. (1985) *Whatever It Takes: Decision Makers at Work*. Englewood Cliffs, NJ: Prentice-Hall.

Nonaka, I. (1988) 'Creating organizational order out of chaos', *California Management Review*, 30(3): 57–73.

Ofner, J.A. (1985) 'Middle management: The neglected resource', *Personnel Journal*, 64(12): 14–18.

Pascale, R. (1987) 'The problem of strategy'. Paper presented at the Seventh Annual Conference of the Strategic Management Society, Boston.

Quinn, J.B. (1978) 'Strategic change: "Logical Incrementalism"', *Sloan Management Review*, 1(20): 7–21.

Shrivastava, P. (1986) 'Is strategic management ideological?', *Journal of Management*, 12(3): 363–77.

Starbuck, W. (1985) 'Acting first and thinking later: Finding decisions and strategies in the past', in J.M. Pennings (ed.), *Organizational Strategy and Change*. New York: Jossey-Bass, pp. 336–72.

Thompson, J. (1967) *Organizations in Action*. New York: McGraw-Hill.

Van Cauwenbergh, A. and Cool, K. (1982), 'Strategic management in a new framework', *Strategic Management Journal*, 3: 245–64.

Weber, M. (1978) [1922] *Economy and Society*, edited by G. Roth and C. Wittich. Berkeley: University of California Press.

Weick, K. (1979) 'Cognitive processes in organization', in B.M. Staw (ed.), *Research in Organizational Behavior*, vol. 1, Greenwich, Connecticut: JAI Press, 41–74.

PART III   CASES

General Motors and Electronic Data Systems

On 28 June 1984, General Motors Corporation (GM) – the world's largest automobile manufacturer – paid $2.5 billion for 100 per cent ownership of Electronic Data Systems Corporation (EDS). The acquisition was to form the cornerstone of a GM information processing company and heralded some significant changes for both companies in the months and years to come.

General Motors

The idea to acquire EDS came from Roger B. Smith, CEO of GM since 1981. Smith rose through the GM ranks in the same way as most of his predecessors, through a series of financial positions. After a stint in the Navy and an MBA degree, he had joined GM as a general accounting clerk in 1949. Described as 'bland and colourless, he is a cautious man who even wears a seat belt in his chauffeured limousine'.[1] Despite this persona, his experience running GM's non-automotive and defence group in 1971 had produced a strategic vision that revolved around acquisitions outside the traditional area of automobiles. His aim was to change the strategic focus of the whole company from its 'go it alone' attitude that concentrated on the domestic automobile market to one which emphasized diversification and overseas markets.

> There's been a significant change in corporate culture. The emphasis is on innovation, taking additional risks, and looking at new fields.[2]

The EDS deal came less than three months after GM had purchased a stake in an artificial intelligence company and a quality consulting group. The EDS deal was part of a plan to inject cutting-edge technology into automobile manufacturing as well as provide new revenues from the electronics and data processing business. Smith wanted non-auto operations to contribute at least

---

Case prepared by Professor Cynthia Hardy, Faculty of Management, McGill University, from published materials. Case not to be reproduced without permission.

10 per cent of sales by 1990, more than double the current figure. The emphasis was on data processing, robotics, electronics, factory process control, and computer-aided design and manufacturing. GM had entered into a number of joint ventures with different Japanese automobile manufacturers and, with Fanuc Ltd (a Japanese robotmaker), had set up GMFanuc Robotics Corp. It was hoped that this new company would equip GM with industrial robots to improve quality, and increase productivity. It would also open up new markets by selling 50 per cent of its sales outside GM. Hughes aircraft was acquired in 1985 for $2.7 billion to form the basis of a new subsidiary that would include Delco Electronics and AC Spark Plug's Instrument and Display Systems Group. Another high technology initiative was GM's Saturn Project – a $1 billion programme designed to bring increased productivity to the assembly line with the use of robotics and Japanese-style participatory management. The Union of Automobile Workers (UAW) had been involved in the Saturn experiment and, so far, had been supportive as long as GM promised to transfer or retain workers. The union had not, however, agreed to the company-wide implementation of Saturn's methods.

A number of major changes were, then, occurring in a company that was unused to such proactive, aggressive action. During the 1970s GM had been busy *reacting* to external pressures like pollution controls, safety legislation and Japanese competition, rather than taking steps to render the company more competitive. The attempt to downsize GM's cars had been an expensive and often frustrating experience. Previous diversification efforts had rarely been successful. For example in 1979, GM had sold White Consolidated Industries Inc. – its Frigidaire appliance division – which had been losing $40 million on annual sales of $450 million by making high-quality but over-engineered products. The subsidiary had also lacked financial and management support from GM headquarters. Another cause of GM's inertia was the sheer size of the company. For example, a retreat to discuss major change would involve as many as 900 top executives. GM's policy decisions were the responsibility of a complex committee structure at the most senior levels, where decision-making by consensus prevailed. Some managers argued that these committees were incapable of taking decisions.

> In this type of organization, there are rarely single instants of decision, I frequently don't know when a decision is made at General Motors. I don't remember being in a committee meeting when things came to a vote. Usually someone will simply summarize a developing position. Everyone else either nods or states his particular terms of consensus.[3]

A previous president summed up GM's decision making style as follows:

> Every day you have a problem at the top of the list. My approach is to discuss it with everyone. I also try to hang on and not make a decision until I have all the possible inputs. Then I decide what ought to [happen]. After that I go out and try to sell it. When you arrive at your conclusions you hope it is a majority decision, but it may not be [nevertheless] we must put forward a united front.[4]

In 1980 all these problems had added up to an annual loss, the first since 1921. Smith became CEO the following year with a commitment to shake up the company. He introduced a massive restructuring, which the board approved in July 1984. It was one of the most sweeping changes in GM's 75-year history and reassigned some of the power from the divisions to two new umbrella groups, which were supposed to function as fully integrated operating units. Most of the committee structure remained intact, however, despite Smith's statements concerning a more hands-on approach for his managers and increased authority for middle managers. The restructuring, joint ventures, and acquisitions represented an attempt to galvanize the company into action. Initially, it looked as if Smith had been successful. Profits for 1983 were a record $3.7 billion on sales of almost $75 billion (Table 1).

Table 1   *GM Financial performance 1978–1984*

	Revenue ($000's)	Profit ($000's)
1978	63,221,100	3,508,000
1979	66,311,200	2,892,700
1980	57,728,500	(762,500)
1981	62,698,500	333,400
1982	60,025,600	962,700
1983	74,581,600	3,730,700
1984	83,889,900	4,561,500

Source: *Moody's Industrial Manual*, 1985, vol.1

Electronic Data Systems

EDS had been founded by Ross Perot in 1962. He owned 45.8 per cent of the shares and presided over the company like a general. EDS was a 'paramilitary, macho company with a great esprit de corps'[5] and Perot was a flamboyant character. He was a self-made billionaire, who had once been ranked as the second richest man in the USA by *Forbes Magazine*. His employees were devoted to him. When two employees had been taken hostage and held in an Iranian jail, Perot had hired a former Vietnam commando to free them (an episode that became a bestselling book and a Hollywood film). Shortly after selling EDS to GM, Perot hung Norman Rockwell's *Homecoming Marine* in his office – 'to remind visitors that we used to whip the Japanese regularly'.[6]

Perot promoted a culture that emphasized a team spirit and a spartan regime. Employees remained dedicated despite a rigid code (no beards, no suede shoes, no shoes with tassels, no drinking during the business day), below-average salaries, no overtime pay, no job security, and few benefits. A Calvinist ideology pervaded the firm that required unusual dedication. It encouraged an informal and flexible team approach, nurtured arguments and debate, allowed delegation, and stressed an inextricable link between performance and rewards as evidenced by bonuses that were tied to corporate performance. The result was a highly creative, entrepreneurial 'hands-on', 'can do' culture. Under Perot's leadership, EDS had grown from a $1,000 investment into a billion dollar company in 1984 (Table 2).

Table 2   *EDS Financial performance 1978–1984*

	Revenue ($)	Profit ($)
1978	217,837,000	19,666,000
1979	274,298,000	23,702,000
1980	374,661,000	28,890,000
1981	454,614,000	37,816,000
1982	509,972,000	46,967,000
1983	651,579,000	58,655,000
1984	947,000,000	81,000,000

Source: *Moody's Industrial Manual*: for 1978–80, 1981, vol.1; and for 1981–84, 1985, vol.1.

The Acquisition

Although EDS would contribute over $900 million in revenues to GM – it represented barely 1 per cent of GM sales! Its real potential lay in two main areas: opening up new markets to GM, and unifying GM's data network. The latter offered considerable room for improvement since the losses resulting from redundant and incompatible computer systems were estimated to cost GM up to $600 million a year. Chevrolet's software programs and hardware configurations were different from Pontiac's which were different from Cadillac's. Estimates suggested that GM had as many as 360 different computers, many of which were incompatible. It had 17 Computer Assisted Design and Manufacturing systems alone. Standardizing systems and procedures could save millions of dollars on health benefits alone – GM's medical benefits costs were $2.2 billion a year and 40 million claims were submitted annually. An integrated computer system could also tie offices, dealerships, plants and suppliers into a smooth-working whole instead of the 'islands' of automation that currently existed.

In the longer term, EDS could build a worldwide, state-of-the-art voice, data and video communication network for GM. GM also intended to combine its own capabilities in computerized manufacturing with EDS's programming and marketing prowess to sell a combined package to other manufacturers. Smith wanted 'to create the most technologically advanced computer services company in the world'.[7] EDS could give GM a niche in the rapidly growing computer services business without directly taking on established hardware manufacturers such as IBM (which had only about 15 per cent of the $20 billion services and software industry, in which EDS competed). In addition, the acquisition of Hughes Aircraft offered an opportunity to extend EDS's business into the area of telecommunications.

EDS had developed the skills to design large scale, dispersed computer systems from its earlier work with the government. In 1982, EDS had won a $656 million, ten-year contract from the US army to tie together 18,000 work stations at 47 Army bases with five regional processing centres. The foundation of this system came from the software and communications facilities of its own network, which linked 20,000 terminals with four regional computers. 'EDS approaches these mega-systems as an engineering job rather than a development task'.[8] EDS did not, however, have much experience in either manufacturing or telecommunications. Most of its revenues came from the service industry – such as Blue Cross, banks, airlines, etc. Equally, GM managers had no experience in large-scale data processing systems. They also worked on a completely different time scale. GM worked on a five-year design cycle, while turnaround times in the data processing industry were between 12 and 18 months.

In order to benefit from EDS's expertise and transfer it to GM, EDS was to remain an independent subsidiary and profit centre. Perot had a place on the GM board. A special class (class E) of GM common stock was made available to EDS employees. It was tied to EDS's performance to maintain the loyalty of the personnel. EDS would be responsible for GM's $6 billion data processing budget, which would require the hiring of many new employees to supplement EDS's staff of 13,500. It would also mean the transfer of most of GM's 9,000 computer systems employees, who would become EDS employees. Automating the factory floor would require EDS staff to venture into the plants, where they would encounter a wide range of equipment instead of the IBM-compatible machines with which they were familiar. Another matter that required negotiation were the contracts concerning the work that EDS did for GM (expected to be at least 70 per cent of EDS's total business). EDS worked on a fixed price basis where any efficiencies were rewarded in the form of increased margins to EDS. This pricing strategy normally enabled EDS to secure margins of around 14 per cent. GM, on the other hand, wanted pricing on a cost-plus basis, which would allow EDS margins of less than 10 per cent.

There were, in fact, many issues that still needed to be clarified. The deal, which had been worked out primarily between Perot and Smith, provided very little structure for the new working arrangements. It effectively left EDS personnel free to enter GM with their usual missionary zeal of 'saving GM from itself'.

> We were free to write our own job description, and declared that we would run everything from the largest Cray to the smallest computer, every communications satellite and every telephone handset on every desk.[9]

Perot was the greatest missionary of them all. As GM's performance continued to deteriorate, Perot was quick to criticize. Despite spending $33 billion dollars on new products and factories between 1980–1986,[10] GM profits had continued to decline; a 48 per cent market share in 1978 had fallen to 43 per cent by 1986; production costs that had been $300 a car less than Ford and Chrysler in 1978 were $300 more in 1986; earnings per share fell from $14.27 in 1984 to $8.50 in 1986. Costs remained so high that GM's return on sales was the lowest in the industry. Moreover, Smith's reorganization seemed mired in a bureaucratic morass. To address these issues, GM shut down 11 plants and laid off 29,000 workers. Managers planned to reduce salaried staff significantly over the following three years. The Saturn project was put back a year, and scaled down from $5 billion to $1.7 billion and from 500,000 to 250,000 units. Perot was outspoken on these problems:

> Revitalizing GM is like teaching an elephant to tap dance. You find the sensitive spots and start poking.[11]

He challenged the closure of a GM plant in his home state of Texas. He travelled around the country talking to GM dealers, employees and managers to find solutions. He complained that GM executives were unwilling to admit that the company had problems and argued that all the management procedures were 50 years out of date. His conclusion was that GM was moving neither fast enough not effectively enough to reverse its slide, and he was quick to compare GM unfavourably with EDS:

> The first EDSer to see a snake kills it. At GM the first thing you do is organize a committee on snakes. Then you bring in a consultant who knows a lot about snakes. Third thing you do is talk about snakes for a year.[12]

In some respects Smith agreed with him but, whereas Perot saw these issues as fundamental flaws, Smith saw them as a sign of the transitional adjustments that were inevitable in a company of 800,000 employees.

Questions

- Is GM's acquisition of EDS a good strategic move? For GM? For EDS?
- What problems do you foresee in GM's takeover of EDS?
- What recommendations would you make to deal with these problems?

Notes

1. *Business Week*, 16 July 1984, p. 50.
2. Robert T. O'Connell, director of Worldwide Product Planning, quoted in *Business Week*, 16 July 1984, p. 50.
3. Marketing executive quoted in Quinn et al. (1988): *The Strategy Process: Concepts, Contexts and Cases*, Englewood Cliffs, NJ: Prentice-Hall, p. 439.
4. President quoted in Quinn et al., 1988: 451.
5. Bernard Goldstein quoted in *Business Week*, 16 July 1984, p. 52.

6. Ross Perot quoted in *Business Week*, 6 October 1986, p. 60.
7. Quoted in *Fortune*, 6 August 1984, p. 124.
8. Quoted in *Business Week*, 11 June 1984, p. 44.
9. Quoted in *Fortune*, 24 October 1988, p. 72.
10. Figures quoted in *Business Week*, 15 December 1986, p. 25.
11. Perot quoted in *Business Week*, 6 October 1984, p. 60.
12. Perot quoted in *Business Week*, 6 October 1986, p. 61.

Source Material

'Why GM wants to team up with Ross Perot', *Business Week*, 11 June 1984, pp. 43–4.
'GM moves into a new area', *Business Week*, 16 July 1984, pp. 48–52.
'GM's risky foray into information processing', *Business Week*, 16 July 1984, p. 52.
'Is Perot good for GM?', *Business Week*, 16 August 1984, pp. 124–5.
'Did GM give away the store?', *Business Week*, 15 October 1984, pp. 223–4+.
'How Ross Perot's shock troops . . .', *Business Week*, 11 February 1985, pp. 118+.
'Roger Smith's campaign to change GM culture', *Business Week*, 7 April 1986, pp. 85–6.
'How GM is bringing up Ross Perot's baby', *Business Week*, 14 April 1986, pp. 96–100.
'Ross Perot's crusade', *Business Week*, 6 October 1986, pp. 60–5.
'GM hasn't bought much peace', *Business Week*, 15 December 1986, pp. 24–7.
'Make or break time for GM', *Business Week*, 15 February 1988, pp. 32–50.
'EDS: How sweet it is to have a sugar daddy', *Business Week*, 18 September 1989, pp. 110–11.
'Look out, Roger Smith – Perot is still mad', *Business Week*, 26 September 1988, pp. 108, 113.
'EDS after Perot: How tough is it?', *Business Week*, 24 October 1988, pp. 72–6.

Atomic Energy of Canada Ltd

Atomic Energy of Canada Ltd (AECL) is a crown corporation (state-owned enterprise) that was established in 1952 to develop 'for national benefit, the peaceful uses of nuclear technology'. In 1982, AECL employed 8,000 individuals, primarily in white collar, technical fields. The head office is in Ottawa and the corporation reports to Parliament through the Minister of Energy, Mines and Resources. It relies on government subsidies but also has commercial goals related to the sale of Candu nuclear power reactors. The close connection to government circles and recent debates on the dangers of nuclear power produced a culture that emphasized caution and a low public profile.

> We want to avoid any excessive media attention, and if we do attract media attention we want to be seen to be doing the right thing . . .. We are very defensive regarding the media. I'm not sure that's the right strategy but it's the one we're using right now and it would take a large concentrated effort to do otherwise. (Manager)

In the eyes of AECL managers, it meant that the corporation should be seen to act responsibly and not waste taxpayer's money.

> We're not trying to be the best employer in the world, we're not trying to be the worst – we're trying to be a good employer.

In 1982, AECL was divided into three operating units: Candu Operations, research, and radiochemicals. Candu Operations, based at Mississauga near Toronto, manufactured and sold Candu nuclear power stations in Canada and abroad. In 1982, about 2,500 people were employed there in four employee groups. Two of these groups were unionized: the Society of Professional Engineers and Associates (SPEA), and the Public Service Alliance of Canada (PSAC). The remaining two – the Technical and Administrative groups – were not unionized.

The 1970s had been a productive decade for AECL. The corporation had more than a dozen domestic and foreign contracts. Hiring continued to be a major preoccupation and, in late 1981, new graduates were still being recruited. Most contracts were coming to an end in 1982, however, and no replacement orders had been secured due to a worldwide drop in demand. Senior managers were slow to react to these changing circumstances, and it was only when a tender for a Mexican project fell through that they realized that a workforce of 2,500 could no longer be sustained.

Case prepared by Cynthia Hardy, Faculty of Management, McGill University, based on original research. Case not to be reproduced without permission.

I don't think senior management was ready to face up to the prospect of layoffs at that time. Even though the numbers showed that things were going definitely wrong and we would have to do something, they did not want to think about it. (Manager)

In December 1981, a hiring freeze was instituted. In August 1982, the need for cost reduction measures was announced, and exploratory talks with employee and union groups commenced. On 8 November, the decision to lay off 600 employees in Candu operations was announced. The downsizing announcement came as a shock to employees following, as it did, so closely on the growth of the 1970s.

The thing about the economy came upon us very suddenly. We had had, for so many years, [long term] nuclear projects. We had been accustomed to looking ahead and seeing this horrendous mountain of work. Suddenly here was this huge number of projects that we had been working on beginning to dry up on us. (Manager)

The Human Resources Department was responsible for implementing the layoffs. Policy decisions were a matter for line management and, in particular, the Vice-president (Engineering), with the President's approval. The influence of human resource managers on policy was limited.

It's an engineer's corporation – all the executives are basically baggy pants engineers. Some of them are not very good managers; they are engineers. (Manager)

Human resource managers lacked power to impose decisions on line managers.

[We] tried not to grab a high profile in the sense that 'it's our job and we'll tell them what to do'. That would have been a gross error. (Human Resource Department manager)

AECL operated under the Canada Labour Code, which laid down certain conditions in the event of group termination of employment. (Group termination of employment refers to the dismissal of groups of employees because their jobs have been eliminated due to financial cutbacks, downsizing decisions, etc. The Canada Labour Code distinguishes between this type of termination and the situation where an individual is dismissed for just cause.) The corporation was required to provide sixteen weeks' notice of group layoffs – that is, notice had to be given 16 weeks beforehand that a certain number of jobs would be lost. The specific individuals who would be affected did not have to be named at that point, though they were entitled to two weeks' notice. A Joint Planning Committee had to be set up with representation from management, union and non-union groups to develop a programme that either eliminated the necessity or minimized the impact of the layoffs, and which would help redundant employees find other jobs.[1]

Questions

- What kind of retrenchment (downsizing) strategy would you recommend?
- How would you implement it?

Note

1. Redundancy refers to a redundant position, that is a position that has been eliminated. A redundant employee is the person who has lost his or her job. Redundancies are permanent job losses. Layoffs can be permanent or temporary. In the case of the latter, employees are laid off without pay but may be recalled when economic conditions improve.

Machco's New Finishing Machine

In April 1988, at their annual distributors meeting in Dallas, Texas, a group from Machco stood up and promised to deliver a new manufacturing finishing machine that would 'knock the socks off the market'. A finishing machine is a $300 flashlight-sized, rotary motion tool that runs from several thousand to over 30,000 revolutions per minute, depending on the application. The machine, designed to be held in the hand, is used to finish and polish manufactured pieces in the automotive, machinery or light assembly sectors where everything from furniture to jet engines is made.

Machco is a multi-billion dollar machinery and equipment concern that was founded over 100 years ago. By 1988, the company had grown to three major business segments with eight groups, had 45 plants around the world, and sold everything from huge engines to tiny machined parts. The Production Equipment Business Group sold a variety of small electrically powered machines such as pumps, gauges, drills and special-purpose engines, that are used in industrial manufacturing, assembly and repair processes. The group's manufacturing and engineering functions were located in Springton, a small town in the USA, while Group Headquarters, comprised primarily of the marketing and sales functions, was located near a large city, several hours away by car.

Machco's Production Equipment Group had the reputation of being the 'Cadillac' of small assembly equipment in several segments. As one employee said: 'Production Equipment made godawful gobs of money for years. We had an 80 per cent market share, and there was no pressure to innovate'. However, competition for market share was increasing in many of their business segments, and Machco's bread and butter line of industrial drills was being attacked by a Taiwanese firm that had copied their drill and sold it at a lower price. Customer needs were also changing to demand assembly equipment that operated at closer and closer tolerances. Despite these external changes, the group continued to sell mostly 'me-too' products, and was looked upon as dull and trite by other people in Machco.

Nearly all of the Production Equipment Group's products were sold through industrial distributors, so the top 40 distributors at the Texas meeting represented a large percentage of the overall business. They were sceptical about the announcement, because Machco's finishing machine line was stuck at a distant second in the market, and the Group's last three attempts to

Case prepared by Deborah Dougherty, Assistant Professor, Faculty of Management, McGill University, Montreal. It is based on an actual story, but the company and product have been disguised and some events have been altered in order to highlight issues for teaching purposes. © Deborah Dougherty 1994. Case not to be reproduced without permission.

improve the line had been market failures. Moreover, those improvements typically took three to four years to be developed. As an insider put it:

> Boeing takes ten years to build a new airplane. General Motors takes five years to build a new car. And we take four years to build a new hand-held machine.

But this time Machco met its goal. One year later, in April 1989, at the next annual distributors meeting, they introduced test models of a superior finishing machine called the Hurricane. The Hurricane outperformed the competition in motor performance, ease and comfort of use for the operators, durability and serviceability, all for a comparable price. By July 1989, however, people at the Springton plant were bogged down in manufacturing problems with volume production of the Hurricane. The following discussion helps to explain why.

Developing an Improved Product Innovation Process

In late 1987, Jim Simon, manager of business development for the Production Equipment Group, was challenged by his boss Fred Powers, then director of sales, to devise a way to compress the Group's product development cycle. At the time it was taking three to four years to bring out a new product, resulting in a series of products with poor market response and many missed opportunities. Simon spent several months putting together a new product development process. He included steps that Machco people felt worked well, particularly a multidisciplinary team that took only a year to improve one of their turbine engines. Simon, first, excluded those practices that had caused them problems in the past, such as their 'over the wall' approach in which each function worked separately and then tossed their plan or design over to the next function. Second, he emphasized initial objective setting and multidisciplinary, entrepreneurial teams:

> The second important factor of this development process is that we put a lot of time into defining our objectives upfront . . . You must define what the project has to do, and then create a team to implement it. A team isn't just an engineering group. It isn't just a marketing person. Our team was to be a multi-discipline unit. We felt that if we created a team and made sure they had a clear vision of our objective, we would shorten the development process and we would have a much higher degree of success in the market. That's the key. Know what your objective is, be sure everybody buys in, and then drive for that objective continuously.

Third, the process was to involve the customer closely throughout development, not only during market research.

Getting Started: The Feasibility Study

With these ideas in mind, Jim Simon and Fred Powers selected the finishing machine product line to try out the new process.

> Our finishing machine product line for years had suffered low market share and poor market response. In the last 12 years we've probably redesigned the finishing tool four or five times. It had gotten to the point that it was a joke with our distributors and customers. This was a mature market. But we said if we could go back to the drawing board and come out with a product that was demonstrably better than our competition, we could realize growth at the expense of the competition. (Simon)

The feeling was, if they could not produce the finishing machine in a year they would be unable to do anything in a year.

In late January 1988, Simon sent a memo to the function heads at the Springton plant which outlined these general objectives for the project:

> The Group has determined that its next major development effort (code name Hurricane) will be a line of finishing machines which will enable us to double our market share within three years. The scope of the project will be broad enough to allow product and technology spin-offs into light assembly, automotive after market, and motors markets. In order to accomplish this effort within three years, we have developed a task force structure consisting of a leader from each functional area.

The objectives of the project were to develop a line of finishing machines to double market share within three years; to use modular design for maximum commonality; to use composites where possible; to design the tool for manufacturability and assembly; and that the project should not take longer than one year. All other development projects, unless essential, were to be put on hold. The memo also outlined the preliminary steps in the development process, which included hardware, performance, breadth and price comparisons with the main competitor; market segmentation analyses and visits to a major supplier of accessories; evaluation of international market needs; a benchmark analysis (on quality, margins, purchasing, cost, physical data) with the main competitor; a review of current and preferred manufacturing and cost issues; establishment of technology goals; and analysis of motor requirements.

There was only one hitch at the kick-off meeting: the head of engineering stood up and said that there was not enough manpower available to accomplish a project of this magnitude within a year, given existing commitments. The plan was to develop three machines with different horse-power motors and a variety of accessories and attachments for different market needs (different sanders, angles of heads, etc.). Everyone else was in favour of moving forward.

The Hurricane team was formed on 1 March 1988, and included a person from engineering as project coordinator, and one each from manufacturing, design, and marketing. Jim Simon continued as overall task force coordinator. Working in a multidisciplinary team was new to the Hurricane people:

> We didn't know what we were doing. Some people had read some magazine articles about the multidisciplinary approach, where you take design, manufacturing, and

marketing and put them all in one area and all work together. It was very different from our usual approach. The whole team was responsible to go find out what the market wanted and what the customer needed, and then move the product into design and manufacturing. We never did that before. We had no infrastructure on how it should work. (Team member from engineering)

I have been on new products for about 13 years, but this was different. We were asked to move out of our environment to a whole new location. We were asked to make the move to engineering, to clean out our desks and move our things over. At first I did not like it because I felt I could function better from here. But the move was important because I became part of them. (Team member from manufacturing)

Despite the uncertainties, the team went out together to talk to customers and evaluate market needs. The engineers, who usually did not visit customers, learned a good deal:

We went out and watched the way the finishing machine was used. You'd be surprised at what people did with finishing machines. They don't use them the way they should. It's small so they reach down and inside places where they can't see. One of the big things we found out right away was serviceability. People would say that these things go down all the time, so why don't you make them easier to fix?

The joint visits also helped everyone work out a joint view of what the product should be:

We had a process that gave everyone a common understanding. A lot of times people formulate in their minds different things and expectations . . . Usually, we would let marketing do all the external work and we would do all the internal work. There usually was no major integration of all the functions. (Team member from manufacturing)

Usually the marketing manager would go out to see customers alone, and then stand up and say 'Here's what the customer wants'. No one was prepared to challenge him. With the Hurricane, the team . . . had been in front of the customer, they saw what the customer wanted, and we all had seen the same thing. We could identify durability with Jose in Milwaukee, and safety with Charlie the safety manager at Boeing. This made the difference. It put a face and a name on the application and on what we were trying to achieve. (Team member from marketing)

A group of top distributors were invited to form a distributor focus team and participate on an ongoing basis in the development process.

In our first formal focus meeting, we started the process by asking for all the positive things about the Machco finishing machine. That took about 10 minutes. Then we discussed all the good things about our main competitor. That took about 3 hours . . .. The outcome was that our distributor wanted us to design a machine exactly like our number one competitor. But then we started talking about what the competitor's strategy would be if we offered a product that was equal to theirs but at a lower price. Since they have the reputation and the volumes, they could afford to drop the price. It became clear to our distributors that they were defining a strategy that was going to last about three months before we were behind the eight-ball again. (Simon)

These discussions helped define the product strategy:

One of our philosophies that evolved out of that meeting was that we didn't want to just eke out a victory. We wanted to have something that was demonstrably better. This concept was conveyed to everyone on the team, be it the distributors and the internal people, that we wanted to win and win solidly with something that was demonstrably better and that those competitive features would endure for a considerable length of time. (Simon)

The Hurricane group had coalesced into a real team during these first few months, despite their initial uncertainty about their new working relationships and roles. Simon invested energy in team development activities and included as much fun for the group as he could.

> Jim Simon was more a facilitator . . . He did all of the charts and set the stage for the innovation and for the decision making. We had a lot of meetings at his house. He's the kind of a person who could get the team in a comfortable mode for problem solving and analysis. (Team member)

The team members developed a collegial spirit in which responsibility was shared between them:

> The core team guided the project all the way through. The responsibility came out of the team at different points along the way to take care of different steps . . . The team really created a consensus of what the product should do to be a good product. (Team member)

> When we started the first four months at least, maybe six, we really had no one person in charge. Each guy took his own area and ran with it. We would shift to each area of expertise as we needed to. I think that added to the success, we really didn't have one leader. (Team member)

By May 1988, the team had developed the Project Hurricane business plan and was ready to meet with management for approval to the next stage in their development process. The marketing strategy included meeting specific measurable features in durability, performance, price, reparability, safety, ergonomics, and availability. The design strategy included superior housing, increased motor life, simplified field assembly, improved tool grip, competitive pricing and an application-sensitive breadth of line. The manufacturing strategy included shortened lead times with customers and between engineering and manufacturing, flexibility, and low cost. One especially important insight from all the customer visits was that the machine should be ergonomically sound – that is, safe, easy to use and comfortable, which meant that it needed to run with proper protection and little noise and vibration. They continued to plan for a whole line of products, not just one.

Senior management at Group headquarters provided general support and pushed for the one-year time frame, but they stayed out of day-to-day decisions. Their role in the process was new, too:

> Senior management didn't know any more than we did about what to do, so they stayed out of way and we had a lot of liberty to do things. I made 10 to 12 thousand dollar decisions all the time, selecting the consultants and suppliers, signing final agreements on production dies. Maybe we wasted some money, but we kept the project moving. (Team member)

Designing the New Finishing Tool Product Line

By late May 1988, the Hurricane team had the product concept on paper, but the product itself has not yet become real, at least not for the engineers:

> We realized from the distributors' meeting that it needed 'wow' – it needed things that other products did not have. We knew we wanted higher market share and lower cost, but the technical objectives as far as design was concerned were very vague when we started. There was nothing that said you make it do this. There was nothing concrete. (Engineer)

The team called in industrial design consultants, ID Group, who introduced an entirely new perspective. Machco's traditional approach focused first on the inside features of a machine such as its power, torque or speed, and only then would they think about its outward appearance. ID Group's approach was first to design the outside where the machine connects with the operator's hand to meet the needs for appearance and ergonomics. ID Group also promised concept drawings within three weeks, which was a primary reason they were hired – they could contribute to the Hurricane project's time factor. ID Group reviewed the Hurricane team's market research and carried out some of their own customer visits. In the promised three weeks, they were back with concept drawings:

> We had a meeting with the ID Group people to look at renderings of the finishing machine. They had captured the shape and design of the tool. I remember the winning pick because it stood out like a flashing light.

The design that fit with the product's strategy was very radical for Machco. It featured a D-shaped housing that would fit comfortably into the operator's hand, newly shaped locking levers (the locking lever was supposed to prevent injury from accidental starting, but the lever on Machco's old tool was so uncomfortable that operators removed it), and a flared end to prevent the hand from slipping. It dawned on the Hurricane team that they were faced with the prospect of taking a revolutionary path.

> We had a meeting and we talked about revolutionary versus evolutionary – this crazy shape, this lever, this thing at the end of the machine, versus let's just make a couple small changes and proceed. We got into a huge discussion, because the engineering manager who said the product could not be done in a year was now saying that we had to pick a specific design. I felt that the revolutionary design best met the design criteria but it was so different as to represent a major acceptance risk in the marketplace, a major design risk, and a major manufacturing risk. (Team member)

The team decided to invest most of their resources in the revolutionary design, but also to work along a more evolutionary one until they could be sure they could make it, since it raised two critical problems.

First, to achieve the D shape, the machine's housing had to be made of composites made from plastic. It was a totally new idea in the industry, which might not be acceptable either to a conservative market or a conservative management. The Hurricane team commissioned ID Group to come back in another two weeks with actual models, when they sat down again with the distributors.

> The distributors liked the revolutionary model but they wanted to know how we were going to make it out of steel. We finally said we probably wouldn't make it out of steel, but probably out of the composite like the model. They chewed on that for a while and come back with: 'Good looking machine, and if you make it out of plastic, we won't sell it. We won't bother with it. It will be a disaster.' We were as hard on the fact that if the machine was going to have the new shape, it had to be made out of composite. We said: 'Look, whether it is composite, or aluminium, or whatever, it shouldn't make any difference as long as we are satisfied that our durability objectives were demonstrably met.' We finally got them to agree, but they weren't sure that we were going to be able to produce a demonstrably better composite product. (Simon)

With this grudging acceptance from the distributors, the team then had to convince management.

> We had a design review at Group Headquarters to bring management up on what we had so far, and to report to them that we were going to use composite materials from an outside vendor for the housing. They were concerned because of the perception that plastic housing would be seen as less durable. We had tried to make equipment before with plastic and it had not worked, so management was scared to death. (Team member from manufacturing)

Management wanted 'proof' that demonstrated the composite material was more durable.

> The four of us went back to our motel for the night and we were talking about the problem. We had sample housings made from composites, aluminum and steel. We decided hey, let's tie these on to the back of a car and drag them around. We got some wire from the motel office, tied the three samples onto the bumper of our car, and dragged them around in the motel parking lot. Somebody finally called the police, so the motel operator came out and asked us to stop. The next day we took those three parts into the meeting with management. The composite material looked just fine. The aluminum part was completely obliterated, and the steel part was all banged up. That proved to them and to us that the composite was the way to go.

At this point the company began to work closely with a plastics supplier to incorporate the new material into their design.

The second problem concerned the new shape. The engineers had to redesign the entire tool.

> ID Group designed the outside but not the guts. We had to put together a design that would fit into that new shape. Designing the correct sizes and shapes for all the parts was very difficult. There is a lot going on in there. We did a lot of brainstorming as a group to come up with ideas. We also thought about design for assembly and minimizing the number of parts. (Engineer)

The engineers proposed a one-piece internal shell made of hard-bored steel to house the machine inside the new shape. This shell would represent one-fourth of the finishing machines' total cost, and was very different from anything Machco had manufactured before because it required unfamiliar and complex boring and machining.

To help relieve the conflicts and pressures associated with the work, Simon continued with the team's recreational activities, including a trip to the horse races, a hockey game and several trips to Simon's home, complete with pool, woods and basement basketball hoop. He felt it was important to give the team the time to do something free-spirited and personal rather than formal or structured, as a way to develop trust among the team members.

The Design to Manufacturing Process

To accelerate the design to manufacturing process, the team broke away from the usual practice of waiting until all parts were finalized and fully on paper:

> It wasn't until September or October that we had any design. And that was just on paper – nothing was tested and validated. By this time we did have enough semblance of drawings for different parts to go to manufacturing and to the suppliers to see if they could work with the parts. We didn't do the design all up front. When we got to a point where it looked good on paper we started feeding it to manufacturing. We physically started processing parts right away. (Engineer)

At the same time, manufacturing people had set up special modules to prototype the manufacturing process. So as engineering designed and prototyped parts, the parts went right to the process prototype. The team also made trade-off choices based on time, and continued to combine judgement with documented procedure:

> The major trade-off was time. If you machined every part perfectly that would take forever. So you assume that some parts are right the first time, and make sure you validate the new concepts. It is a balance of analytical work and hardware. We never traded off on quality, but on cost, performance, and time to market. The end date drove a lot of decisions on how we would design the finishing machine.

The team held together throughout the fall.

> Everybody saw the objectives as the team's objectives . . . The team got intimately involved with each step. We went out as an entire team on the plant floor to look at the testing or the quality checks. We all went out together. Before, it was just engineering, not five or six people all doing all of these functional steps. Before, there would be just the one guy. We still had to provide the documents, but the difference with the Hurricane project was the level of manpower. Each functional group now felt that they had a responsibility to contribute. (Team member)

Other functions began to get involved as well, such as purchasing and quality.

> This was the first time we used statistical procedures in developing procedures for quality. After a part was designed, they ran the preproduction right in the shop. Before the Hurricane, a part would go to an industrial engineer who tested it in the lab. The shop guys never had anything to do with testing the tooling. But with the Hurricane, the shop people built the tools, and we ran 25 pieces on each to test the performance and develop quality specs. People in the shop helped a lot because they found problems with the assemblers. We would sit and review the product, review the results from the shop, look at the problem, and we fixed the parts right then and there. (Member of quality control)

Problems with the revolutionary path started to snowball, however, in November 1988. First, the team had to decide on dies for the revolutionary housing even though they did not yet know if they could manufacture the shell. One member described a six-hour meeting in mid-November with fingers pointing everywhere.

> Basically there were two issues involved in this decision over the dies. One was financial and the other was time. At the financial end, we would be putting in additional money and not getting as long a life out of the die. But from the time standpoint, we were potentially gaining about a month on the time frame. A soft die could be reworked easily. So we made the decision to put the extra resources in to help the process. But when we had to invest some big bucks in some molds, and there were some nervous people at Machco, myself included. We really weren't a hundred per cent sure that the direction we were going in was going to be the right one. We hadn't even prototyped the machine. We just had this date in April when we said we would show up with a brand new product.

The outcome of this meeting was that the team and management committed to pick up the pace of the development and to add more resources. According to one team member, they weighed proceeding with the shell against the technical risk in manufacturing and decided to go forward. But the person representing manufacturing recalled the issues a bit differently:

> The shell allowed us to get inside the shape, but the part the engineers designed was impossible. We had to go with it, but we had no idea how to produce it. It called for production methods that we had no experience with, and that hardly anyone else did either. It was a hardened part with an ultra-smooth finish that had to be hard-bored. Traditionally our cylinders are machined, then hardened, and then ground. We went to an outside vendor to grind the part – we machined it soft and then sent it out. We were scared to death. We didn't know if it would work.

The manufacturing problem with the shell raised a more general problem: clashes with established ways of working. First, only a fraction of the shells tried in-house were coming off the line in workable form; the rest were scrap. Machco's Production Equipment Group ran its plant strictly on standard costing, which emphasized high-volume production of standardized parts: any scrap was considered variance for which shop floor people and their managers were penalized:

> We were making scrap in the factory with every one of those parts. It was very difficult for people in the plant to understand that we were taking this risk. There was a lot of scrap. We had so many parts that were just junk. It was a nightmare.

> The high scrap rate was very difficult for the people in manufacturing because they are paid based on piece rate and cycle time, so the more scrap the less they get paid.

Another participant noted problems between the team and the larger manufacturing operation.

The coordination effort was the hard part. Normally they (manufacturing) would take six to nine months to process parts and they didn't need all the pieces to fit together all at the same time. In our usual process we would just throw it over to them and let them take as much time as they wanted. Here, everything was to be done at the same time. All of our GANT charts were all laid out on top of one another. We weren't prepared to handle that.

From a manufacturing perspective, it seemed as if the team was 'nosing in with our parts one at a time, and demanding that they give us priority', while they had all the other product lines to worry about. Meanwhile, senior management continued their hands-off stance, and made no changes in the plant's overall cost system. However, they did share some of the risk by providing the resources that enabled the Hurricane project to absorb the scrap:

Lack of funds was not a problem. Management was willing to support these things and allow us to do what we had to do, but they did not have their eye on us all the time. And especially in the manufacturing end they let us take the risk by building parts that were not fully qualified. That meant we might be machining scrap. That was very different. We never tolerated all those things before.

Field Trials

The Hurricane team forged ahead, as they had agreed to do at the November meeting. Two crucial choices were made. First, they decided to go with an external supplier for the liner for the immediate future, which meant that the part now cost double its original projection, which significantly raised the cost of the finishing machine. They gambled on their ability to figure out how to produce it in-house. Second, they decided to reduce the scope of the project drastically, and come out with only one finishing machine rather than a whole line. They felt it was necessary to produce something in time, and focused on the basic model with the largest market share.

In late January, the team placed about 80 prototypes of the finishing machine in 60 different locations across the country, ranging from heavy to light manufacturing, aerospace and automotive companies. Slowly, the feedback started coming in:

One of the first things that came back consistently was 'It feels great'. The first response that we got was from Caterpillar. Sometimes when you're talking with these customers they don't open up and give you all the information you want. Our distributor and our salesman were out there getting updates on the prototype. They said: 'Well, how do you like it?' and this guy who had been finishing for 16 years and looks like he was a linebacker for the Chicago Bears – big, big guy – said: 'The machine's OK', and this and that, and 'I like it'. Translated, it sounded like 'Big deal!' And as they were walking away he said: 'You know what? I can go home at night and my hands don't hurt any more.' (Team member from marketing)

The April 1989 distributor conference arrived and the Machco team presented prototypes of the new Hurricane finishing machine. Everyone liked it, even the doubters, because it ran smoothly and couldn't be stalled.

The machine was introduced to the market in June 1989 and has met with great success. Initial sales ran 20 per cent above previous levels even though there was only one model, and without the benefit of advertising or structural promotion. The compressed development time and word of mouth alone generated significant interest in the marketplace. It was a stunning achievement for the Hurricane team and the whole Springton plant. They not only produced a demonstrably improved finishing machine that met customer needs, but they also reduced the new product development time by two-thirds, made significant advances in tool design and manufacture, developed new and more effective working relationships with outside vendors, and learned how to work as a team. But the team still had to solve the shell problem, since they still could not manufacture the part in-house and the external part was still costing twice the projected amount. They also had to design the next two finishing tools that were to be part of the new Hurricane family, and add all the accessories to the existing product.

Jim Simon and Fred Powers also wanted to figure out a way to replicate the process. Their original purpose was to devise a system that would enable Machco's Production Equipment Group to have four or five new products moving quickly through the development process at the same time. To make the Hurricane a success the team had overcome, and often crashed through, conventional work practices. They broke rules and routines; they bumped other projects and ruined other schedules; they forced manufacturing people to rework parts; they took risks and made expense decisions that other people were never allowed to do. Simon wondered: 'Could the Hurricane experience be replicated, or was it just a series of lucky breaks?' If it could be replicated, what aspects of the process should be changed? Kept? What changes in the plant's management system or culture, or in the Group's management system or culture, would be necessary before a number of other new product projects could co-exist with the plant's regular work?

Many of the participants had an opinion about these questions:

Manufacturing operations did not view that they were part of the Hurricane team just because one of their people was on the team. We didn't prepare them to share the risks, so as of July they required nothing but perfect designs which are not subject to change. When Hurricane started, engineering shed other projects but manufacturing's load was never reduced.

The project team didn't have sufficient authority to get things done. The rest of the organization didn't accept the team's authority, so the team's decision-making is limited to what the team members themselves control. Hurricane succeeded because there was not a lot of parts. The fewer number of parts helped to downplay the risk of going from engineering to manufacturing this way.

Some of the team members felt they were working above and beyond what others were doing. There was definitely a gap between the hours and level of effort people on the team put in and what the others were doing. It is very frustrating because the work load is much greater in the team environment. People not on a team do not have the visibility, they don't have the eyes on them.

Senior management does not understand that the enormous pressure and lack of compensation for all the hard work affects creativity. People get burned out and turned off if there is no light at the end of the tunnel, and the only thing they have to look forward to is another project. People will fall back into their old ways because it is so much easier to grab what they have already done – use the same tolerances, the same material . . .

Questions

- How did the Hurricane team incorporate market and customer needs into the product's design?
- What types of market–technology knowledge did they develop – or fail to develop?
- Was the development process creative? When?
- What organizing factors were critical to the Hurricane's apparent success?
- How were these processes different from the usual ones at Machco?
- Why did manufacturing drop the ball, or did they?
- What is the relationship between an innovation and the other functions and products?
- Machco decided that the major flaw in their system was that the leadership role on the innovation team was not clearly defined. They changed the process to add a project manager who reported to the head of engineering. In 1990, group managers started three new product efforts, all with the same one-year deadline.
- How do you suppose they did? Why?
- Can you recommend any other changes at Machco to foster innovation?

The Bicycle Components Industry

In April 1991, Valentino Campagnolo was locked in deep thought. For a decade he had been defending the position of his company – Campagnolo – in the bicycle components sector with new products aimed at winning customers from the Japanese industry giant, Shimano. These products had mainly failed, however, and the 1980s had been difficult for the small Italian firm which had enjoyed a reputation far larger than its size. Campagnolo was, without doubt, one of the world's best-known names in cycling, though it made no bicycles – only the components that fitted on to bicycle frames – and it supplied only the very top end of the racing cycle market. The Japanese company, Shimano, had recently made a dramatic impact on the bicycle market. It too produced only components, and yet had achieved a position whereby the Shimano brand sold the entire bicycle: customers were less interested in who built the bicycle than who made its components.

Campagnolo's products were without match when it came to quality. They were also much more expensive than anyone else's but because serious cyclists were known for their loyalty and conservatism, the company had achieved a secure market position. During the 1980s, the quality of Shimano products improved, and the introduction of new and improved components attracted the interest of serious sport cyclists, as well as the larger mass market. So, by the end of the 1980s, while there was no doubt about the quality of its products, questions were being asked about Campagnolo's future.

Valentino had taken over the reins in 1983 on the death of his legendary father, Tullio, and had no intention of letting the company fail. To understand the challenge he faced, it is necessary to put the case in context.

A Brief History of Bicycle Technology

The bicycle is around 100 years old and has changed very little in that time. It is the most efficient way of converting human energy into forward motion. Throughout the early years of the century, small but important technological developments had been made but, since cycles were heavily constructed hunks of steel, they remained uncomfortable to ride for anything but short distances. Gear systems were the key to making bike-riding easier and a number of

Case prepared from original research by D.C. Wilson, N. Gendler and M. Hirst, Warwick University, England. © D.C. Wilson, N. Gendler and M. Hirst 1994. Case not to be reproduced without permission.

companies were involved in this specialized area. Two basic forms emerged that remain to this day. The *hub* system, popularized by Sturmey-Archer in England, works on the principle of a mechanism concealed within the rear hub which regulates the pedalling tension on a single rear sprocket. The *derailleur* system, although less sturdy and requiring regular adjustment, is far more popular since a greater range of gears can be achieved and the mechanism is lighter. Here the chain is shifted between rear sprockets of different sizes using levers, cables and springs. The derailleur system emerged about 25 years after the hub system, in the early 1920s.

While Sturmey-Archer concentrated on refining its hub mechanism, there was strong competition in Europe to bring out the best derailleur system. In 1933 Campagnolo introduced what is known as the parallelogram derailleur, which became the industry standard. The hub gear has hardly changed since 1938 and, until the advent of indexed gears (which allow greater precision in gear selection) in the 1980s, neither had the derailleur.

The continuing technical challenge for bicycle manufacturers is to make bikes lighter and, more recently, more aerodynamic to make them faster and less tiring to use. Much effort has gone into the development of lightweight steels, alloys and carbon fibre. Material such as titanium, fibreglass and metal matrix composites are expected to play a greater role in the future. Component manufacturers have also found that competitive advantage can be derived from introducing lighter and more streamlined parts.

During the early years, the market was dominated by European and particularly British manufacturers. Over 1 million bicycles were sold in the UK in 1935. Cycling grew in popularity for recreational and commuting purposes, particularly between the wars. In the decade following the Second World War, however, prosperity led to an increase in the demand for cars at the expense of bicycles, and annual UK sales of bicycles dropped to below 500,000. A resurgence during the 1960s began in the USA where increased leisure time and disposable income coupled with lighter and more comfortable bikes increased demand. As faster and lighter racing bikes with 10 and 15 speed derailleur gears became available, American demand supported a worldwide industry. Between 1960 and 1975, US sales grew from 4.4 to almost 17 million per year.

From that peak, sales declined to below 10 million in the early 1980s. In the early 1990s they reached 13 million. UK sales were about 2.5 million per year and world sales were somewhere around 100 million per year (about three times as many as the number of cars sold). China made about 40 million, India 8 million, Taiwan 7 million, Europe 12 million and the USA 5 million.

Frame Manufacture

Frame manufacture requires less sophisticated machinery and technological expertise than component manufacture. Consequently there are a large number of players: around 650 bicycle manufacturers in Europe alone, offering over

3,000 brands. At one end are the specialist lightweight hand builders who product a few frames each year, made to order and according to customer specifications. Small factories make bikes to order according to their own designs in quantities of up to 5,000 or 10,000 a year. Larger concerns that make lightweight bikes on a more automated basis in factories may turn out up to 100,000 bikes a year; these are small businesses supplying a portfolio of ready-made rather than custom-built bikes. They tend not to manufacture components at all, so deal directly with component suppliers.

At the other extreme are mass producers such as Raleigh, Schwinn and Giant who are turning out bicycles in the millions. Giant of Taiwan make not only their own brand of cycle but also frames to order for firms known as screwdriver plants, which buy in all parts, including frames, and put them together under their own brand, like manufacturers who provide goods for private labelling by retailers.

Component Manufacture

Until the early 1970s, there were several specialists who made individual components. Stronglight was known for its cranks and chainsets, Sachs and Simplex for their gear systems. Campagnolo, Shimano and Suntour made a range of components. During the 1970s and 1980s there was a significant shake-out as Shimano took control of the market, leaving only four players of any significance in the world. So, while a professional cyclist's bike of the 1960s would have used components from around 13 different manufacturers, today it would be kitted out by one or two suppliers. Shimano is the largest company, selling around 28 million derailleur systems a year – nearly half the 60 million bikes sold use this system. Campagnolo, on the other hand, sells only around 15,000 derailleurs annually.

Shimano's nearest competitor is Suntour, another Japanese firm that produces around 5 million derailleurs per year. Continually in the shadow of its domestic competitor, it has nevertheless made a significant impact on the world cycle market. It supplies a range of components to the same segment as Shimano, competing on the basis of technical innovation. The company has recently grown through a merger with two smaller Japanese firms: Dia Compe and Sakae Ringyo. Sachs-Huret, a European grouping of companies under the Mannesmann group, has grown by acquiring a number of small specialist component manufacturers to become a supplier of all parts. This brand has always suffered from a lack of popularity among consumers and has never managed to achieve a favourable image. Another European player, Mavic, is closest to Campagnolo, aiming components at the enthusiast who wants to build a bike from preferred components. Over the years, it has built up a well-regarded spares distribution system, though it wants to build products that require less maintenance.

Campagnolo's History

The story of Campagnolo SRL is legendary within the world of cycling. Born in 1901, Tullio Campagnolo was the son of a workshop owner in Vicenza, an industrial town near Venice. He took up cycling, and began competing as an amateur at the age of 22. He enjoyed little success, but the experiences led him to believe that there was much potential in making this simple machine more user-friendly, particularly for the sports cyclist. Italians take their sports cycling seriously, almost as seriously as football, and there is a proliferation of small firms in Italy making low volume performance cycles as associated products.

In 1927, Tullio, by now a recognized amateur cyclist, was competing in a cycle race in the Dolomites. When the weather turned to intense cold Tullio was in a good position but one tyre punctured. His fingers were so numb with cold that he could not unscrew the wing-nuts which held his wheel in the frame. As a result of this experience, Tullio Campagnolo developed the quick release skewer which allows wheels and saddles to be removed instantly. It was patented in 1930. Three years later, he patented his first derailleur gear mechanism, the parallelogram design which became the *de facto* standard. By the end of the 1930s he was supplying gears to the top Italian professionals, still making them in his father's workshop and subcontracting to specialist machine shops when needed. He did not take on his first employee until 1940. As the firm's reputation and size grew, Tullio decided to concentrate on the very top end of the sports cycling market. Campagnolo is considered to be the Rolls-Royce and Ferrari of the cycling world rolled into one. A complement of Campagnolo mechanics are always on hand at all of the major races to help the teams with technical assistance and replacement parts.

Technical excellence took the company into other areas during the 1960s and 1970s. Advanced capabilities for working with alloys led to a series of products for motorcycle and auto racing. It then manufactured aerospace products and precision measuring instruments. At this time, although the majority of production was bicycle components, the company was recognized as a high-quality precision engineer. The company has always attempted to remain at the forefront of race cycling technology and today holds around 200 patents. However, foremost in Tullio's philosophy was that each item must be of the highest quality. Legend again has it that once, when touring the factory, he picked up a component to examine it. Finding a blemish he threw it through the nearest window, ordering the rest of the batch to be scrapped.

Until the mid-1970s, virtually all professional cyclists used Campagnolo components. The main competition was among the companies that produced cheaper versions of Campagnolo's products. Campagnolo's emphasis on quality has meant it is not as fast to market with innovations as some of its rivals. Before any product is released it is tested thoroughly for a season or more among professional riders. If any changes are required, further extensive testing is carried out. When, in 1980, aerodynamics became the fashionable way to improve bicycle speeds, Campagnolo was less inclined to jump on the bandwagon than others, and it was not until 1982 that the Victory range was introduced. Even then, company officials were quick to emphasize that it did not mean they were converts to aerodynamics, believing it could save only minute amounts of time. As Silvio Manicardi, sales director at the time, put it:

> There is no way of eliminating the mass that is the rider when considering penetrating the air. Aerodynamics is one of the elements we consider in our designs but it is not the most important. Of greater priority . . . are ways of utilizing new materials, reducing weight and reducing friction.

Today, even Shimano admits that although its Aero series reduced component drag by 20 per cent, it had a negligible effect on speed. Nevertheless, the research involved took component design forward considerably.

Tullio was a man of immense charisma. Employees referred to him with great respect as the Commendatore. 'We work not for the company, but for that man', a security guard once said. Tullio remained in charge until a year before his death in February 1983, when he handed over to his son Valentino, then aged 34.

Shimano's History

The Shimano Iron Works was formed more than ten years before Campagnolo, but did not achieve world recognition until many years later. Shozoburo Shimano was born in 1894 in Sakai, south of Osaka. His talent lay in machinery and things mechanical. At the age of 15 he took on an apprenticeship in a knife-making shop and later at the Takagi Iron works where he learned how to use metal lathes. By the time he was 20, he was a freelance lathe operator, gaining experience in metal technology.

In 1918 Shozoburo started work at what is now the Sakai Bicycle Company where he supervised apprentices in the manufacture of precision components. Bicycles were used for utility purposes at this time. People were not rich enough to cycle for leisure: they rode bicycles because they could not afford cars. Three years later the Shimano Iron Works was founded, initially as a machine repair shop. Within a year, Shozoburo had built the business so that it possessed several lathes, a milling machine and a drill press. With his partner, the firm employed six people and he felt ready to begin making his own products.

Following his experience at the Sakai Bicycle Company, Shozoburo chose to make a bicycle freewheel. At first he had difficulty selling it since quality was inferior to imported models. However, as quality gradually improved, the freewheel became more durable. Shozoburo soon became so confident about the quality of the freewheel that he offered two free replacements for every one found to be defective. Shozoburo also developed ways to improve the production process, such as a system which saved time by not having to turn off the lathes before removing finished items. Thus Shimano was able to produce reasonable quality products at competitive prices and gain access to the important Pacific Rim markets. By 1936 the company was employing 130 operators and, by the end of the decade, it was turning out 100,000 freewheels a month, despite a significant amount of production being turned over to the war effort against China.

The post-war period was good for the company. There was massive demand for new bicycles and for components with which to repair those that had been hobbling along during the war years. Resources were scarce and bicycle makers were given priority over component makers for raw materials. Shozoburo therefore decided to form a bicycle manufacturing company under the management of his eldest son, Shozo. In 1950, the restrictions were lifted and the two companies were merged into one.

Demand for bicycles in Japan peaked in the mid-1950s, after which many of Shimano's customers went out of business. Shimano managed to stave off bankruptcy to enjoy the boom years that followed. As standards of living improved around the world, people turned increasingly to cycling as a leisure activity. Three-speed derailleur gears based on Campagnolo's design were being manufactured in European markets for the leisure sector. The Shimano company saw the beauty of a bicycle that offered the rider appropriate gears for uphill, downhill and flat terrain cycling and quickly went into production with a derailleur of its own.

Shozoburo died in 1958 aged 64, leaving Shozo in control at the age of 30. While some questioned Shozo's experience, others welcomed his enthusiasm and the prospect that new leadership would be an inspiration. He had been successful at managing the bicycle division before he was 20 years old and had been instrumental in saving the company from bankruptcy in the mid-1950s. He also had clear ideas about the potential of the industry.

First, as Japan became richer and motorized transport boomed, Shozo was convinced that wealthy countries would demand bicycles as leisure products. A strand of this vision was to update the domestic distribution system. Nine Shimano Service Centres were set up around Japan to provide marketing assistance to retailers, helping them to manage inventory, product ranges, advertising and general retail skills. Shimano was among the first to offer such a service to their distribution network. As the domestic market picked up, Shimano developed a wider range of products for different cycling sectors including leisure, sport, ladies and children. In 1964 they launched a new derailleur gear, the Skylark, as part of this range-extension process.

Second, Shozo also saw the value of bicycles for basic transportation as well as sports use, particularly in Europe and America. The USA was by now a natural market for Japanese exports, economic links ironically strengthening after the war. As far as the USA was concerned, the Shimano three-speed hub was still relatively unknown compared to the Sturmey-Archer, so Shimano began to market directly to American bicycle manufacturers and slowly achieved recognition for producing reasonable-quality components. New York offices were set up under the leadership of Shozoburo's youngest son, Yoshizo.

Shimano also made an extensive examination of the European market. Different countries in Europe were found to have very different cycling traditions. The French and Italians were keen sports cyclists, Germans preferred more durable, traditional bikes. By the time Shimano was ready to move, during the late 1960s, Shozo had decided on Germany, where the economy was strongest and the demand was for the type of bicycle products that Shimano was already making. The three-speed hub was successful and Shimano began to develop new products for this market. Its reputation spread around Europe and, in 1972, Shimano set up the Shimano Europa offices in Düsseldorf. Today about 60 per cent of Shimano's sales are in Europe.

Shozo also saw the need for technical improvement, both in terms of products and production methods. He began by improving their version of Sturmey-Archer's three-speed hub. By 1960, the company was making 50,000 units a year, many of which were being fitted to Japanese bikes bound for the USA. Within a year Shimano was exporting directly under its own name. Improvements to the production process were also made as a cold forging process was developed. Hot forging, where components are pressed in a softened form, requires significant amounts of labour at the finishing stage because products cannot be hot forged to precision measurements and oxidation in the process leaves the piece looking rough. Cold forging, on the other hand, requires less after-work and produces less waste, though the product is not as strong and durable (which is why Campagnolo continues to hot forge to this day). When the cold forging facility to produce three-speed hubs and freewheels was completed in 1962, production increased by a third, and the use of raw materials decreased by a similar amount. The company continued to develop its production techniques and, by the middle of the decade, capacity had increased tenfold.

By 1970, Shimano was the largest cycle components manufacturer in Japan, though it remained vulnerable to the fashions of the market segments it targeted. As a result, Shimano decided to diversify and chose fishing tackle which used similar technology to the three-speed hub. The move also complemented its aim of offering products that contribute to the health and well-being of the consumer. The company began to think of itself as a manufacturer of outdoor sporting equipment. Today, fishing represents 14 per cent of Shimano's sales; cycle components accounts for 84.5 per cent.

Competing in the European Arena

Tullio Campagnolo was aware of the potential threat from this dynamic new entrant but remained confident of his premier position. In retrospect, some have argued that Tullio was simply too arrogant for his own good, refusing to believe that anybody, let alone a Japanese firm, would ever be able to take away his position as purveyor to the professional circuit. Nevertheless, Campagnolo made an unprecedented move in the early 1970s by introducing a range of components, aimed at a lower segment of the market, named Valentino after the founder's son. Unfortunately, to ensure customers would not switch over, Campagnolo made a far inferior product but priced it highly to defend its image as a top-line producer. The resulting disaster was quickly withdrawn.

In Europe, Shimano realized that they would have to gain the recognition of professional racing teams. Professional racing had been dominated for decades by Campagnolo, but Shimano was successful in entering pro-cycle team sponsoring. In 1973 they backed Flandria from Belgium, the first non-European company to sponsor a continental team. In 1982, Shimano pulled off a major coup by signing the top Italian racer, Francesco Moser, for World Championship road racing. Until this point it was unheard of for any Italian to use anything but Campagnolo. While he was the only member of his team to use Shimano (and he switched back to Campagnolo the following year), the company received extensive publicity. To add to Campagnolo's problems, three of their axles broke in competition during the 1984 season. One was on the bike of Team Renault cyclist Laurent Fignon. The team switched to Simplex in a blaze of publicity causing much embarrassment to Campagnolo. Gradually, during the 1980s, more teams entered into sponsorship deals with Shimano. The World Championship was won by Giani Bugno in 1991 on Shimano and, in the 1992 Tour de France, more teams were using Shimano than any other components supplier, including two Italian teams (Table 1).

Advertising during the late 1970s was designed to demonstrate Shimano's technical advances and send the message that it was producing serious products and exciting innovations. The advertisements were highly informative, with detailed diagrams and explanations. Campagnolo's advertising was less product-oriented, and emphasized the record of racing successes. Not until the 1980s did it include product information.

Shimano also continued with their innovations aimed at making cycling easier and safer, particularly gear-changing technology. Many of these ideas were not original but, nonetheless, Shimano introduced the Positron gear-changing system, the precursor of indexed gears that have become the standard today. Another idea exploited by Shimano was first developed by Campagnolo – the concept of the groupset. The different components that make up a bicycle's mechanical profile (such as chains, gears, brakes and pedals) are designed as a complete ensemble. Each item in the group shares the same product name and styling, and is finished to a particular standard. A parallel can be found in the hi-fi market, where many manufacturers offer complete integrated systems comprising amplifier, cassette player, record player, CD player and tuner. The idea never really worked for Campagnolo, whose customers were more interested in buying individual components. Shimano took the groupset idea a stage further and marketed its products to manufacturers as a completely interdependent product. Since Shimano offered a wide range, manufacturers could source components for any price level of bike, saving them time and effort compared to buying components from a variety of suppliers.

Table 1 *1992 Tour de France teams and component usage*

Components	Team	Nationality
SHIMANO	Castorama	France
	Tulip	Belgium
	Panasonic	Netherlands
	TVM	Netherlands
	Ariostea	Italy
	Gatorade	Italy
	Festina	Spain
	Motorola	USA
CAMPAGNOLO	Z	France
	Postobon	Colombia
	Telekom	Germany
	PDM	Netherlands
	Carrera	Italy
	MGBoys-GB	Italy
	Banesto	Spain
MAVIC	RMO	France
	Lotto	Belgium
	Clas-Cajastur	Spain
	ONCE	Spain
SUNTOUR	Buckler	Netherlands
	Amayer	Spain
SACHS-HURET	Helvetia	Switzerland

To make the concept work, Shimano had to demonstrate the superior performance of its integrated system. The Uniglide chain, introduced in 1977, improved gear-shifting performance. The following year, the idea was extended with the Dura-Ace and 600 series of race components. In this way Shimano achieved a high profile among consumers. As Shimano's reputation grew with its innovations, the brand of the bicycle became less important than the brand of the components: children were asking for a bike with Shimano gears, not a Raleigh or Schwinn.

Shimano also took advantage of the new market created by mountain bikes. The craze started on the west coast of America, when a crowd of ageing hippies caused a sensation by racing old roadsters down mountains. The bikes were sturdy machines with stiff frames and wide wheels converted from ordinary leisure bikes. Shimano watched events with interest and worked with the small MTB (mountain bike) frame builders to develop a series of components especially for this specialized form of cycling. The first serious offering – the Deore XT groupset – was introduced in 1982.

Campagnolo, along with other European players, watched from the sidelines. Only in 1988 did Campagnolo introduce the Euclid off-road groupset.

We wanted to see if it was only a momentary thing, or if it was going to last a long time, before we got involved . . .. The first mountain bikes have been gradually transformed into competition machines. It goes without saying that where there is competitive cycling there is Campagnolo. (Company spokesperson)

By the end of 1989 the Centaur and Olympus ranges were added, but Campagnolo's late entry meant that Shimano became *the* name for mountain bike components, and enabled the Japanese company to stay well ahead of the field in terms of innovation.

During the 1980s, people became more concerned with the environment and health. Bicycles addressed both of these issues: they represent an environmentally friendly mode of transport for the city as well as being excellent for fitness. They are also a good way to experience nature and enjoy the countryside. Shimano picked up on all of these issues to promote both cycling and the company as an environmentally friendly organization. They also invested in production methods and materials technology to minimize ecologically compromising side effects.

Comparing the Companies

The two companies had adopted very different approaches. Shimano began by making low-end components sold to Original Equipment Manufacturers (OEMs). Campagnolo, on the other hand, had targeted competitive cyclists. The effect of these different approaches became clear. By the 1980s, Shimano components were fitted to the majority of bikes being built. The OEMs liked the ability to buy complete groupsets and the customers demonstrated a preference for Shimano, the 'trendy' name to have. Campagnolo was the brand in the locked-glass cabinet of the specialist shop.

New Product Development

Although thought of as highly innovative, Campagnolo had introduced nothing radically new since the parallelogram derailleur. In the 1990s, the company is rarely the first to market with innovations, though it often develops its own versions of products that are better than the original. Campagnolo continues to produce even the most obscure parts to maintain its excellent reputation for after-sales service.

> Frankly I'm a Campagnolo fan. The quality is good, not always perfect, but good to work with and easy to strip down . . .. There is an international guarantee with Campagnolo material. If I see a Campagnolo man on a race and I have some faulty components, I know he will change them.

This is an expensive strategy and Campagnolo cannot afford to introduce new products on a regular basis: its Record group has remained virtually unchanged for over 20 years.

The company also endeavours to use standard gauges and sizes when designing products so that the customer is not dependent upon it for replacement parts like bolts, while Shimano tends to use non-standard sizes. In order to achieve the same or better quality for its products, Campagnolo will spend a great deal of time in development so that the result is based on standard parts.

Sensing the competitive threat from Shimano, Campagnolo launched a new budget groupset in 1978 called the Gran Sport, which was about a third of the price of its more expensive products. Learning from its mistakes with the Valentino, Campagnolo ensured quality was up to standard: materials were the same as for more expensive products like the Nuovo Record group, only the finish was different; even the design was very similar. The Gran Sport enjoyed some commercial success but was replaced in 1984 by the Victory range. In turn, the Victory was phased out and replaced by the Xenon group in 1989. The Xenon was launched to compete with the hugely successful 105 budget racing groupset from Shimano. Both were priced around the £200 mark but the Xenon was made of cheap materials, rather as the Valentino had been in the 1970s. It was withdrawn in 1991 leaving only three Campagnolo ranges: the flagship Record, the Chorus, and the Athena.

Shimano had quite a different strategy, driven by the need to keep up with demands for new products from ordinary cyclists. When Shimano introduced indexed gears in the early 1980s, it woke the industry up from decades of R&D lethargy. Indexed gears had a profound impact on mountain bike sales. To keep people interested in cycling Shimano found it necessary to continue bringing out products that interested and excited the consumer. Shimano's most recent innovation was the dual control lever (known as STI) – a system where the gear shifting lever is integrated into the brake lever. It has attracted a great deal of interest among professional cyclists. A year later in 1991, Campagnolo introduced their own version, Ergopower, which was considered to be superior to Shimano's offering. The concept has had such an impact that all major components manufacturers had their own versions by 1992.

Production Methods

Quality is extremely important to Campagnolo. Raw materials are purchased according to tight specifications. They are then pressed and forged by approved suppliers. Every item is then X-rayed. An item will be rejected if any flaw whatsoever is discovered. Minor components such as screws are often bought in and checked by a separate department. Computer controlled machinery is used to manufacture articles in-house. Every sixth piece is checked for conforming to specifications and the machine is automatically adjusted where the output begins to drift from that specification. For hubs, Campagnolo designed and made their own machinery, not being able to find anyone who could supply them with a tool that met their needs. The firm examines every broken component that is sent back to them. Campagnolo expects items to last for at least ten years, and it has been known for wheel hubs to be replaced after eight or ten years of use because they were found to have been below standard when fractures were examined under a microscope.

Many operations are still done by hand. Rear gear mechanisms, for example, is a six-stage process requiring six people. Pedals, likewise, has five people. Chainsets are assembled by hand with a permitted tolerance of 0.1 mm. To ensure the necessary strength, Campagnolo sends products to its own heat treatment department before they are polished and anodized. In addition to its quality measures, Campagnolo has a laboratory where metallurgy tests are carried out on products to assess their durability under extreme use or conditions.

A great deal of money was invested in new machinery and processes during the latter half of the 1980s. By 1989 Campagnolo had replaced 90 per cent of the plant at its main factory. Computer technology was introduced, though sales director Alberto Angeletti emphasized that it did not mean that Campagnolo was about to become a mass producer. He argued that the quality systems would not allow production capacity to be increased by much.

Shimano has always invested heavily in R&D. At each stage of the company's success the majority of the profits were invested into new ideas and processes. An important aspect of the R&D programme has concerned production methods. One industry observer said:

> Going back twenty years, Shimano's approach has been one that sees production as paramount. Ease and economy of production is paramount. Campagnolo is more likely to say: 'Hang the cost, ultimate quality is paramount'. Twenty years ago Campagnolo's approach gave them a far superior product, but now production technology is such that Shimano's adequate quality is better than you need anyway, in terms of durability. A good example is Shimano's use of cold forging. If you really want the ultimate strength and durability out of a product you've just got to heat forge it. Campagnolo does this. But the Shimano one is perfectly adequate; you'll never break it. Hot forging is a lot more expensive: it's a more involved process, it leaves you with a lot more post-forge machining to do. When you cold forge something you can do it very fast . . . you don't necessarily have the best quality, but for cycling purposes you have perfectly adequate quality.

As Shimano sees it, there are two aspects to new product development. Yoshizo Shimano explained in a recent interview:

> We have two types of designer, the artistic designer who is responsible for the overall look, and the industrial designer who is responsible for function, durability and technical excellence.

Hans von Vliet, Shimano's European Marketing Director, said that Shimano does not see the same potential for innovation for the 1990s as there was in the 1980s. In consequence, Shimano would be placing greater emphasis on aesthetic developments.

Service and Distribution

Shimano's exposure to the US market had given them a very different perspective on how the supply and support of consumer durables should be met. In North America, labour is expensive while capital is cheap. As a result, a disposable culture emerged where repair became a thing of the past: products were cheaper to replace than to fix. When Shimano began to concentrate on the European markets it found that this concept met with some resistance among serious cyclists who were used to maintaining their components. At first, Shimano was not interested in supporting a repairs system – the company wanted to sell a new model rather than keep old ones going. In 1992, however, Shimano set up a number of regional maintenance and support centres within approved dealers in the UK. This move is aimed only at the high-end customer since the vast majority of Shimano's customers are unlikely to repair their bikes.

Because of its policy on repair, Shimano operated a spare parts service considered to be very poor by the retail sector. Complaints about the difficulty of getting spare parts for Shimano were legion, and there was even speculation that the supply of spares was controlled to influence price. Between 1989 and 1990, UK manufacturers were waiting as long as nine months for deliveries. Kozo Shimano, grandson of the founder, said the reason for slow delivery was simply the inability to keep up with the demand. Despite its claims to be playing fair, Shimano did lose some anti-trust disputes in the USA, where the company was found guilty of withholding products to fuel demand.

There is little doubt that bicycle manufacturers are uncomfortable with the current situation. They feel locked into buying their components from Shimano though they do not want to. They know that they will sell fewer bikes if they are not Shimano equipped, so they hope that one of the other manufacturers will be able to introduce a range of components that will capture the public's imagination in the way that Shimano did. One leading manufacturer feels that Shimano was beginning to dictate aspects of frame design so that frames would conform to the needs of the components. The purchasing manager in another firm complained of unreliable deliveries and errors in the processing of orders. He said:

> I could show you a book of faxes and communication between us and Shimano. They make so many fundamental errors and it's so difficult to keep track of them ... They're very arrogant because they have the market cornered.

Some of the blame for poor parts service in the UK has been aimed at its distributor, Madison Cycles. It has been suggested that Madison does not have the resources to carry a wide enough inventory of Shimano spare parts. Shimano introduced Electronic Distribution Information (EDI), whereby retailers linked to the distribution point receive faster support. Of course, this electronic link makes retailers more dependent on Shimano since the EDI system monitors stock control and locks in the retailers to Shimano's system. Shimano's distributors have also found it difficult to manage their stocks because Shimano introduces updated products so regularly. Wholesalers, and particularly manufacturers, must order products based on forecasts made six to nine months before they are required. Manufacturers are not able to fit last year's products on to new bikes, so, it is not uncommon for them to unload old designs on to large retailers and mail order houses, sometimes at a loss.

Campagnolo's distribution system is more traditional, operating an agency network throughout the world except in Japan, which is managed directly from Italy, and the USA, which has its own Campagnolo stocking branch. The number of agents employed depends on the amount of business done in each country. For example, in Italy there are five agents, while in the UK there is only one agent.

Conclusions

Valentino Campagnolo is faced with important strategic decisions to make. His company is rapidly losing ground against Shimano, which is not only dominating the entire industry but is also number one in Campognolo's chosen niche and well ahead of the rest of the market in terms of innovation. Campagnolo has improved its innovation over recent years but is still behind Shimano. Campagnolo has also been the subject of much rumour. A number of Italian newspapers have been speculating about a take-over by Benetton, the clothing firm. One financial paper has written that Campagnolo were in desperate need of investment. These rumours were denied and Emilio Bosoni, the publicity manager, announced that Mr Campagnolo did not intend to sell the company.

Questions

- Compare the strategies adopted by Campagnolo and Shimano. What is the impact of both national and organizational culture in the formation of these strategies?
- Why has Campagnolo had difficulties in countering Shimano? What strategic alternatives are open? What can Valentino do to exploit the global market?
- Why has Shimano been so successful? Should Shimano change its strategy?

Loblaws' G.R.E.E.N Line

Dave Nichol, President of Loblaws' International Merchants subsidiary, had just returned from Europe. During his stay in Britain he had observed that several retail operations, including Tesco's, Sainsbury and the Body Shop, had successfully introduced 'green' products to their stores. As no food retailer in Canada was yet selling green products, Nichol decided to capitalize on what he perceived to be a huge untapped market. Loblaws started developing the G.R.E.E.N. line.

Loblaws Companies Ltd is a holding company whose subsidiaries are engaged in food retailing and wholesaling in Canada and, to a limited degree, in the USA. Some of its main subsidiaries include Loblaws Supermarkets Ltd, Central Canada Grocers Inc., Atlantic Wholesalers Ltd, Westfair Foods Ltd, Loblaws International Merchants, and the National Tea Company in the USA. In 1989, Loblaws had total sales of $8.42 billion (Canadian) in more than 300 retail stores and various wholesale outlets with about 1,200 franchised accounts and 12,000 independent accounts.

Nichol had become the President of Loblaws' Ontario division at the young age of 35. A native of Ontario with an MBA from Harvard, he had been hired by Loblaws in 1972. In 1978, he had helped change the fortunes of the company by the introduction of no name 'generic products'. The generic branding innovation had created a great deal of consumer interest because it addressed the desire for plainly packaged, less expensive versions of common grocery products. The high-profile advertisements, using Dave Nichol as spokesman, and the distinctive yellow packaging, attracted media publicity which helped establish Loblaws as the generic product's innovator. Although other supermarket chains copied Loblaws, Loblaws retained the lion's share of the business because it had been the first one in the market, and consumers had come to associate its name with generic products. By 1989, Loblaws carried over 2,200 generic products, whose retail margins were 15 per cent more than manufacturers' brands.

By the early 1980s, however, the generic products branding strategy had reached maturity, and Loblaws was looking for a new retail branding idea to attract and hold consumers. In 1984, a line of products labelled 'President's Choice' was introduced by Nichol, to appeal to the upscale end of the market. These products were developed with an eye for the 'high quality at a realistic'

This case is based on the paper 'Marketing the environment: The strategic alliance of business and environmentalists', by Frances Westley, McGill University, and Harrie Vredenburg, University of Calgary. It was written by Paul Rossman under the supervision of the authors, 1990. © F. Westley and H. Vredenburg 1994. Case not to be reproduced without permission.

price. Like their 'no name' predecessors, they were immediately successful, and by 1987 the two lines accounted for 21 per cent of warehouse volume and 30 per cent of Loblaws' total grocery sales.

The G.R.E.E.N. line would be the third such initiative, and Nichol thought that it could be even more successful than the first two branding innovations.

The G.R.E.E.N. Initiative

Background research was first conducted into the state of the environment, and Canadian consumers' perceptions about environmental issues (Table 1). The environment was ranked as the most important issue facing Canada. The same survey conducted in the USA found that more than three times the number of Canadians as Americans held the environment as their primary concern (Table 2). Loblaws then initiated its own in-house surveys which showed that 69 per cent of customers were at least 'quite concerned' about the environment, and 93 per cent were at least 'somewhat concerned'. Another survey indicated that 92 per cent of their customers would pay 47 cents more for environmentally friendly products and 65 per cent of Loblaws' customers would be at least 'somewhat likely' to switch supermarkets to buy environmentally friendly products (Table 3).

Nichol realized that marketing green products would be significantly different from marketing either the No Name or President's Choice lines: environmentalism was a much more sensitive issue. Some consumers would undoubtedly question Loblaws' motivation in introducing green products. Nichol felt that he would need to have a strategy to give the G.R.E.E.N. line credibility: he would have to convince consumers that Loblaws was not exploiting the environment, but providing consumers with products that were less harmful. Some companies in Europe had received product endorsements from environmental groups to legitimize the environmental value of the products and overcome any mistrust of business motives in the minds of consumers. Nichol felt that this would be a worthwhile strategy to look into. Friends of the Earth and Pollution Probe seemed to be two groups that were positioned appropriately within the environmental industry for product endorsements.

After a preliminary meeting with Friends of the Earth, the environmental group sent a letter to Dave Nichol outlining ten products that they thought could be considered environmentally friendly. Most of the products were on supermarket shelves already, but could be used as alternatives to environmentally harmful products. Baking soda and concentrated lemon juice, for example, could be used instead of harmful cleaning agents. Vinegar, low-energy light bulbs and an organic rose food were other examples. Friends of the Earth encouraged Loblaws to help educate the public by promoting the alternative uses of these products. After another talk with the environmental group,

Table 1 *Environmental statistics*

- Canada produces approximately 5 million tons of hazardous waste each year, 80% of which enters the environment untreated. There are approximately 10,000 old dump sites, containing decades of toxic, untreated chemicals, the four biggest on the American side of the Niagara River alone are threatening the drinking water of 7 million Canadians and 1 million Americans downstream. The cleanup cost of these dumps is estimated to be from $11 billion to $100 billion.
- About 20% of industrial waste enters sewers and landfills directly.
- Every year 300 million tons of topsoil disappear, and organic matter is being destroyed 10 times faster than it's being produced.
- Every three years the world's population increases by about 275 million – about the size of the United States and Canada.
- The earth's protective ozone layer is being chemically eroded by chlorofluorocarbons (CFCs) and other damaging chemicals. As it thins, the ozone layer loses its ability to filter out the sun's ultraviolet rays, increasing skin cancers, cataracts, and other medical problems.
- The greenhouse effect. Over the next 50 years, scientists predict an average temperature increase of up to four degrees Celsius – larger than any climate change since the dawn of mankind. Melting icecaps will cause sea levels to rise and impact vegetation.
- Each year more than 11 million hectares of tropical rain forests are destroyed. Over 30 years, that adds up to a land mass the size of India. Since trees absorb carbon dioxide, deforestation abets the global warming trend.
- Deforestation causes species loss. Over the past 200 million years, the average annual rate of species extinction has been one every year or so. The present rate is more than 50 species a day.
- Tree roots act as pumps bringing ground water to the earth's surface, so deforestation also stimulates desertification. Every year more than 6 million hectares of land become desert. Within three decades a new desert the size of Saudi Arabia will form.

Source: *President's Choice G.R.E.E.N.: Something Can Be Done.* Case study, Harvard Business School, 1989.

Table 2 *Consumer environmental survey results*

The most important problem facing the country today:

Canada		United States	
Pollution/Environment	17%	Drugs/Alcohol	18%
Unemployment	10	Deficit	16
Free trade	9	Social/Moral	6
Deficit/National debt	9	Homeless/Poverty	6
Social/Moral	9	Pollution/Environment	5
Inflation	5	Economy	5

Source: President's Choice G.R.E.E.N.: Something Can Be Done. Case study, Harvard Business School, 1989.

Table 3   *Loblaws customer survey*

Concern with environment
32%   extremely concerned
37%   quite concerned
24%   somewhat concerned
 5%   not very concerned
 2%   don't care

	Purchasing environmentally friendly products	Switching supermarkets for environmentally friendly products
Very likely	49%	20%
Somewhat likely	43	45
Not too likely	2	24
Not at all likely	4	10

Source: President's Choice G.R.E.E.N.: Something Can Be Done. Case study, Harvard Business School, 1989.

Nichol felt that he could probably persuade Friends of the Earth to endorse, or at least recommend, some or all of the products they had suggested.

Nichol took a different approach with Pollution Probe. Instead of soliciting suggestions from them, he approached them directly and asked them if they would endorse an environmentally friendly fertilizer. Colin Isaacs, the executive director of Pollution Probe, seemed willing to talk about it, so Nichol thought that, if handled correctly, he could get the fertilizer endorsed by the environmental group. If he were able to get one endorsement, Nichol felt that he could probably obtain endorsements of other environmentally friendly products.

The G.R.E.E.N. Line

Instead of simply relabelling a few products and promoting them differently (as Friends of the Earth had suggested), Nichol was interested in developing a whole new *line* of environmentally friendly products, as a branch of the President's Choice brand. There was no shortage of products that could be made environmentally superior to what was on the market now, though both Loblaws and environmental groups admitted that there was no such thing as a product that was not, to some extent, harmful to the environment. Nichol thought that Loblaws could make a meaningful contribution to the well-being of society by providing consumers with the option to buy products that were *less* harmful than what was currently available. Loblaws could help consumers to 'take a step in the right direction'. Many styrofoam disposable plates, for example, were no longer made with ozone depleting CFCs. They were not as 'environmentally friendly' as reusable plates, but if consumers were going to use disposable plates, it would be better to use ones that had not contributed to the depletion of ozone. It would be a step in the right direction. The same could be said of disposable diapers, napkins, coffee filters and other paper products: they could all be made from pulp that had not undergone a chlorine bleaching process. Such products would not create the harmful dioxins and furans that current products did: another step in the right direction.

Nichol also saw a large segment of the market that was becoming increasingly health-conscious. He thought that it might be profitable to add 'body-friendly' products to the G.R.E.E.N. line, which would include low calorie, high fibre, low fat and low cholesterol foods.

As Nichol pursued the endorsement of environmental groups in order to give credibility to the new product line, he concentrated on Pollution Probe.

Pollution Probe

Pollution Probe had been founded 21 years earlier by Donald Chant, and had initially been associated with the University of Toronto. At that time there were only a handful of environmental groups in Canada and very little institutional awareness. From 'finger pointing', Pollution Probe had gradually started to work with business to achieve sustainable change. From the beginning it had not been opposed to accepting donations from corporations: in 1988 7 per cent of the organization's $1.4 million budget came from business contributions. The organization's attitude toward business as well as toward other environmental groups had generally been one of cooperation. For 20 years Pollution Probe had sought access to the boardrooms of the nation; first to implement policy, and second to raise money.

The process of moving into the boardrooms had been accelerated by the appointment of Colin Isaacs to the position of executive director in 1983. Isaacs was clear about his objective, and the role he saw for Pollution Probe: 'working together with companies is a very important part of the role of the environment group today'. Not all members of Pollution Probe, however, were totally in accord.

In 1989, the staff of Pollution Probe numbered approximately 30 people, who managed the office and a large canvass operation of volunteers. Decisions in the organization were traditionally made by consensus and there was little hierarchy. After a major downturn in the organizational fortunes in 1985, and a subsequent series of layoffs, the staff unionized. A period of rapid growth then occurred, during which Pollution Probe launched an innovative door-to-door campaign, and the budget grew from $350,000 to $1 million in revenues in the space of three years.

Isaacs felt that with the sudden growth, the structure had become unwieldy.

> The executive director had no authority. Authority rested with all the staff and as all the staff were getting to be thirty people it was impossible to run weekly meetings . . . they were a zoo. The staff were functioning as a group of independent entrepreneurs; we were paying their salaries, but they were doing what they wanted. The only formal decision-making body was the weekly staff meetings, but that structure couldn't hold anyone accountable.

Isaacs brought in a consultant and the staff were subsequently reorganized into three teams: a coordination and communication committee, which was essentially an administrative unit; an environment and society committee; and a development committee. The three committee heads and the executive director formed the executive committee, theoretically facilitating the process of decision-making.

The reorganization had not, however, been entirely successful. Staff/board relationships had always been less than cordial and, with 'Colin Isaacs acting as the only conduit between the staff and the board', the reorganization had been experienced as a further exclusion by many of the staff. They resented what they called Isaacs' 'management style' and the 'process' he employed to reach his ends. In addition, there remained an ideological split in the organization between what Isaacs described as 'a radical philosophy of social change', and a more 'mainstream' philosophy which advocated 'looking for environmental improvement in existing structures' – including cooperation with business. As a result, many employees were suspicious of Pollution Probe's relationship with Loblaws.

The Endorsement Process

When Loblaws initially approached Pollution Probe to endorse the fertilizer, the latter refused to do so unless some of the ingredients were changed. Pollution Probe's offer to help develop an organic fertilizer was accepted, and eventually a suitable fertilizer was developed and endorsed.

Loblaws continued approaching Pollution Probe with ideas for environmentally friendly products, and asking for their endorsement. The fertilizer, however, was the only product that Pollution Probe used its expertise to help develop, although it endorsed seven products: fertilizer, topsoil, disposable diapers, sanitary napkins, recycled motor oil, non-phosphate detergent, and automatic dishwashing detergent. For these endorsements it was agreed that Loblaws would pay Pollution Probe a 1 per cent royalty fee. It was estimated that these royalties would eventually amount to $75,000, with an additional $75,000 accruing from Loblaws' sale of G.R.E.E.N. sweatshirts and T-shirts (which were not endorsed by Pollution Probe, but from the sale of which Loblaws would donate one dollar per item to the environmental group).

The G.R.E.E.N. line also included two products endorsed by Friends of the Earth: baking soda and an organic rose food. The 90 other products in the line

Table 4 *List of President's Choice G.R.E.E.N. products*

Bathroom tissue	'Green' baby wipes	Ecover fabric conditioner
Phosphate-free laundry detergent	Ecover 100% biodegradable laundry powder	Turkey frankfurters
Diapers	Low acid coffee	Slim and Trim cat food
All-purpose liquid cleaner with Bitrex	Green maxi pads	Natural fertilizer
High fibre corn flakes	'The Virtuous' canola oil	Ecover 100% biodegradable toilet cleaner
Foam plates	'The Virtuous' cooking spray	Ecover 100% biodegradable wool wash
Just Peanuts peanut butter	Green T-shirt/sweatshirt	Ecover floor soap
Smart Snack popcorn	Ecover dishwashing liquid spray cleaner with Bitrex	100% natural rose food
Biodegradable garbage bags	Laundry stain remover with Bitrex	Green panda stuffed toy
Hi-performance motor oil		Green polar bear stuffed toy
Automatic dishwasher detergent	Baking soda	Norwegian crackers
'The Virtuous' soda cracker	Drain opener with Bitrex	Turkey, whole frozen
Swedish chlorine-free coffee filters	Boneless and skinless sardines	Gourmet frozen foods (low-fat)
Cox's Orange Pippin apple juice	Green oat bran	Cedar balls
	Flavoured raisins: lemon, cherry, strawberry	All natural dog biscuits
White hulless popcorn	Low ash cat food	'If the World Were PERFECT Water'

Source: President's Choice G.R.E.E.N.: Something Can Be Done. Case study, Harvard Business School, 1989.

were not endorsed by environmental groups. They included 'body friendly' products – fruit-injected raisins, 'just peanuts' peanut butter, and lean meat. The products could be justifiably sold under the G.R.E.E.N. label according to Loblaws' philosophy which equated environmentalism with health and well being. The environment and food were linked – if people should be avoiding chemicals and impurities in the atmosphere because they are bad for them, then they should also avoid eating those same chemicals and impurities in food (see Table 4).

The Challenge

The products were launched in June 1989, without any more than the usual media fanfare. However, national attention was captured on 5 July 1989, when Greenpeace called a press conference and demanded that Pollution Probe remove its endorsement of the G.R.E.E.N. organic fertilizer. Greenpeace director Michael Manolson produced independent lab results that indicated the presence of extractable organic halides in the fertilizer. The presence of these chemicals, argued Greenpeace, could indicate the presence of various toxins, including dioxins. Under no circumstances could the fertilizer be considered environmentally friendly.

Greenpeace

Greenpeace is very different from Pollution Probe. It has never accepted corporate donations, and instead relies on donations, memberships, and grants from Greenpeace International. It proudly accepts the label of environmental watchdog and sees itself as an activist organization. Key to the Greenpeace movement has been a relatively unstructured, highly committed, elite band of activists ready to risk personal danger in support of various causes, from nuclear testing in the South Pacific, which brought the organization into being in the late 1960s, to the protection of whales and seals. Due to the dramatic nature of many of these demonstrations, Greenpeace had always secured a significant amount of media coverage, though they were generally considered to be a 'fringe' movement. During the 1980s, the increasing environmental awareness, coupled with environmental disasters like Bhopal and Chernobyl, affected both media and public perceptions. Media coverage became much more positive and contributions and membership soared.

Pollution Probe director Colin Isaacs responded that the fertilizer had been tested for dioxins and found acceptable, but the incident cast somewhat of a shadow over the launch of the G.R.E.E.N. products. This shadow was deepened by another attack from the Consumers' Association of Canada, which argued that the advertising of the G.R.E.E.N. products verged on being misleading. Loblaws and Pollution Probe withdrew neither product nor endorsement. The whole case raised considerable media discussion about the advisability of joint ventures between environmental groups and business, as well as the rift in the previously apparently cooperative environmental movement.

While Greenpeace questioned only the fertilizer at the initial press conference, it became evident that the critique was more generalized. Michael Manolson, executive director of Greenpeace, stated that the objection was one of principle: 'The environmental crisis is not a challenge for marketers to come up with clever ways to sell products.' In an article published in the *Globe and Mail*, Manolson stated:

> Loblaws' pitch to the consumer is that 'something can be done' and by implication, it is the consumer who should be doing it. Meanwhile the company makes more money and fools us into thinking that by buying such products as high-fibre corn flakes we are doing something to save the planet. But Loblaws may be lulling us into a false sense of accomplishment. Because in the meantime, industries, the real polluters, continue to pollute.

Greenpeace felt the real issue concerned the definition of a 'green' product:

> Greenpeace says that there are some basic questions that need answers. Who is checking up on things? What is a green product? Loblaws has not identified or published what criteria is used in determining which products made it into the green line. What's to stop any retailer from labelling any product environmentally friendly? . . . Honest green consumerism is a positive response to the environmental crisis. But where is the bottom line? Is saving our world almost as important as making money? It is just as important? Or is it even more important? (Manolson)

The Consumers' Association of Canada also attacked the definition of 'green', pointing out that disposable diapers take about 300 years to break down in a landfill site. Such attacks seemed to indicate a mistrust of Loblaws' dealings with Pollution Probe, and a feeling that the endorsements were lending more credibility to the line than it deserved.

It was also common knowledge that many members of the Pollution Probe's staff had not been in favour of the endorsements – especially the disposable diapers. Many resented the process that Isaacs had used in putting the endorsement deal together. Traditionally, decisions were made largely by staff consensus, but because of Loblaws' insistence on confidentiality and speed, the staff members of Pollution Probe had not been told what products were being endorsed until just before the line was launched.

Within a few days of the G.R.E.E.N. line being launched, Pollution Probe's board established a committee to review the criteria and policies for future endorsements. They decided to let the diaper endorsement lapse at the end of the year. Colin Isaacs was excluded from this committee. He immediately resigned.

The Rebuttal

Isaacs repeatedly denied in the media that his resignation was tendered as a result of the controversy over Pollution Probe's endorsements:

> The timing is frankly purely coincidence, except for the fact that the debate over this program has crystallized in my mind some uncertainty as to whether the board was or was not backing me to the extent that I believe was necessary.

Loblaws defended the products in the G.R.E.E.N. line. They argued that all was the result of a misunderstanding. The disposable diapers, for example, were made from fluff pulp, and did not use any pulp that was bleached at a chlorine mill. The advantage of these diapers over the regular disposable diapers was that not as many trees were used in their production, and no dioxins and furans were produced from a chlorine bleaching process. The Loblaws advertisements stated that cloth diapers were more environmentally friendly, but if one had to use disposable diapers for some reason, then the G.R.E.E.N. diapers were the best from an environmental standpoint. Loblaws maintained that Greenpeace's objection to the fertilizer was not legitimate, and again was the result of misunderstanding. A component of the fertilizer was pulp mill sludge, but Loblaws and Pollution Probe were careful to make sure that no sludge was used from pulp mills that used a chlorine bleaching process. The dioxins that Greenpeace said could be present were only produced at mills that use a chlorine bleaching process. So, clearly there could be no problem with the fertilizer; and Pollution Probe's tests had confirmed that the fertilizer was environmentally friendly. Another misunderstanding about the G.R.E.E.N. line concerned the 'body friendly' products. Loblaws argued it did not claim that fruit-injected raisins or high-fibre flakes were environmentally friendly: they were 'body friendly' (see Table 5).

Conclusion

Loblaws' introduction of the endorsed G.R.E.E.N. line was both hailed in the press as a brilliant visionary environmental breakthrough, and condemned as a typical business move designed only to make a quick profit from a hot trend. Patrick Carson, the Vice-president of Environmental Affairs of Loblaws, thought that Loblaws had done well: they had proven that cooperation between business and environmentalists was possible; they had provided environmentally friendly and body friendly products not previously available; and they had done it through a profitable business venture.

At the other extreme, conservative commentators from the business world took the incident as an example of why the apparent advantage to be gained by such endorsement was not worth the cost:

> One fundamental issue is whether any company should get into bed with advocacy groups whose methods, objectives, beliefs, ideologies and philosophies may be inhospitable to business in general, but whose activities may otherwise improve a company's sales and profits ... the synergy is largely superficial. The only true common element is money, which both the companies and the advocacy groups believe they will get more of if they cooperate. Sometimes, money can hold partnership together. But when the cooperation involves linking two different segments of society – profit-making and advocacy groups – the association is doomed to be troubled and anxious. (T. Corcoran, in 'Activists and business: Strange bedfellows', *Globe and Mail*, 5 July 1989, p. B2).

Questions

- What motivated Loblaws to create the G.R.E.E.N. line and how successful was it from a marketing perspective, and from a broader societal viewpoint?
- What motivated Pollution Probe and Greenpeace? Could Loblaws have predicted the reactions of these groups to product endorsements?
- Pollution Probe tried to play an intersectoral 'bridging' role between the business and environmental industries? Were they successful? Why, or why not?

Table 5   *An open letter to Canadian consumers about President's Choice*
G.R.E.E.N. products

Over the last year, while travelling the world looking for new products, I was astounded at the level of consumer interest in environmentally friendly products. For example, the best-selling book in England last year was an environmental handbook ranking retailers and their products.

Back in Canada, I noticed that every public opinion poll indicated that the environment was the number one concern of Canadian consumers – confirming what my mail had been telling me for at least a year.

Convinced that this concern was genuine, the Insider's Report team met with the executives of many of Canada's leading environmental groups and asked them what products they would like to see us create that would in some way help to reduce pollution. Their guidance was the genesis of the G.R.E.E.N. 'Environment-Friendly' product program and in many cases we actually worked with these groups to develop specific products which they then felt confident in endorsing.

At the same time we also began development of 'Body-Friendly (low calorie, high fibre, low fat, low cholesterol, etc.) products under the G.R.E.E.N. label. This Insider's Report highlights the first wave of our new G.R.E.E.N. Product Program.

Here are a few points of clarification about the program:

1. With few exceptions, President's Choice G.R.E.E.N. products are priced at, or below, the price of the national brand to which they are alternative.
2. We do not intend to censor products that some may feel are 'environmentally unfriendly'. We see our role as providing a choice so you may decide for yourself.
3. Protecting the environment is a young and, therefore, imprecise science. As a result, not all groups agree on what the best products are to help control pollution. For example, some advise us to use paper pulp trays for eggs while others say recyclable, ozone friendly foam trays made with pentane instead of chlorofluorocarbons (CFCs) are a better solution. We accept the fact that it is inevitable that not all environmental groups will agree with all of our President's Choice G.R.E.E.N. products.
4. Some may accuse us of being 'environmental opportunists'. WE SEE OUR ROLE AS PROVIDING PRODUCTS THAT PEOPLE WANT. That's why we created No Name products when Canada's food inflation was running at 16%. That's why we created President's Choice when demand for superior-quality products arose. And that's why we've created G.R.E.E.N. products when the overwhelming concern of Canadians is the environment.

    We invite you to read about our new President's Choice G.R.E.E.N. products in this Insider's Report and decide for yourself whether or not they fill a real need in our society.
5. A number of our G.R.E.E.N. products are products that we've carried for years (such as baking soda). Putting them under the G.R.E.E.N. products label was in response to environmental groups who chided us by saying, 'You have a number of products in your stores right now that could help fight pollution but you have to bring them to your customers' attention and then explain how to use them.'

We acknowledge that we are not environmental experts and we readily admit that we do not have all the answers. However, we feel strongly that these products are a step in the long journey toward the solution of our enormous environmental problems. If G.R.E.E.N. products do nothing more than help raise the awareness of the need to address environmental issues NOW, and give Canadians hope that SOMETHING CAN BE DONE, then in the end, they will have made a positive contribution.

David Nichol
President,
Loblaws International Merchants

Source: President's Choice G.R.E.E.N.: Something Can Be Done. Case study, Harvard Business School, 1989.

Conglom Inc

> We invest in good quality businesses, which provide essential services and goods to industry and the consumer and thereby obtain an improving return for our shareholders in terms of earnings per share and dividend growth. There are only 50 executives in our Central Headquarters concentrating on financial and strategic management, leaving operating company management with clear responsibility for running their business. (Chairman's 1987 report)

Formed in 1957 Conglom Inc was, by 1987, a group of some 50 companies with total annual sales of over £2.5 billion and pre-tax profits of £260 million. Most of its growth had come from acquisitions. The Chairman's report indicated that Conglom's strategy rested on the existence of a small corporate group that focused on the financial and strategic control of existing businesses, while leaving operating units with the responsibility of running their individual businesses. In fact, this recipe was judged to be the 'secret' of Conglom's success.

In 1979 Conglom made a hostile but ultimately successful bid for the Electric Light Bulb Co. (ELB). The bid, launched in May, was finalized on 22 December 1979 at a cost of £105 million. Two days later a team of three people from Conglom arrived at ELB.

The Electric Light Bulb Company

ELB had a turnover of £172 million with factories in the UK, Europe, Africa and the Far East. Over 60 per cent of its turnover came from goods manufactured in the UK. The company consisted of two divisions: ELB (UK) and ELB (International). The two divisional boards reported to the ELB Main Board, which was located in London, together with senior management from the UK division and a research centre. The company was run by a group of 60-year-olds who had worked their way through the various functions of the UK operations and who maintained a strong, centralized control over the company.

There were five main production centres in the UK as well as a series of smaller, specialized units which employed some 6,000 people. Factory managers

Case prepared by Professor Cynthia Hardy, Faculty of Management, McGill University, from published sources. All material and quotes taken from John Roberts, 'Strategy and accounting in a UK conglomerate', *Accounting, Organizations and Society*, 15(1/2): 107–26, 1990. Names are disguised. Case not to be reproduced without permission.

were organizationally separated from the Main Board by five hierarchical levels which represented a lengthy, tortuous and sometimes political chain of command. In addition, board members would often take a personal interest in individual factories by securing information from factory managers on costings and particular product runs.

Within the UK, ELB enjoyed a near monopoly and, with increasing demand, sales and profitability had grown by an annual 10 per cent during the late 1960s and early 1970s. This market dominance allowed cost increases to be easily passed on to customers with the result that the attention of the Main Board was almost exclusively on the achievement of high volume production to service growing international demand. The factory managers were, as a result, under considerable pressure to concentrate on volume regardless of cost. There were costing systems within the factories but in practice the managers were not held accountable for them. Factory accounts were produced centrally, but their accuracy was often contested.

> Our clerks fed all sorts of raw data up the line to Head Office and that all got accumulated with everybody else's *ad hoc* information. They crunched the old sausage machine and miraculously spewed one grand profit and loss account for the whole of the UK. Then they tried to analyse it and split it up by factories. But of course when they gave it back to us, we didn't recognize any of it as our own. And of course the timescale to produce all that was quite long so by the time we got it, it was out of date! (Factory manager)

In any event the arguments over the validity and accuracy of factory accounts were irrelevant since volume, not costs, was the central pivot of accountability within ELB.

Between 1973 and 1977, competition started to heat up when a foreign company introduced more expensive but longer-lasting light bulbs into the UK. Moves to develop a similar product were blocked by Main Board members who believed that the company's strength lay in its traditional products. As a result, UK sales started to decline. Some of the slack was taken up by foreign markets, especially in Africa, though political developments in 1977 threatened this source of income. At this time, a number of Main Board members retired. The new Board embarked on a new strategy emphasizing divisionalization, a long-life product, and a worldwide brand. Both ELB (UK) and ELB (International) were split into smaller, separate divisions to cover European and Worldwide markets and Head Office was increased by about 100 employees to service them. The development of a long-life product was finally sanctioned in 1979. The creation of a worldwide brand involved the harmonization of several local brand names and was fiercely opposed by local and regional managers.

In the mid-1970s, company performance began to decline: from profits of £31 million on sales of £172 million in 1975, to £17 million on sales of £240 million in 1978. The share price fell from its peak of 200 pence to 53 pence at the time of Conglom's bid.

The Acquisition Team

The acquisition team from Conglom included a group executive, a lawyer and an accountant. They commissioned a business audit from a firm of chartered accountants which detailed the profit and loss situation. Ready by February 1980, it was used for the financial restructuring of the business, which included the sale or closure of many overseas operations, particularly in Africa and the Far East. The European operations (together with some valuable patents and technology) were sold off in 1982 to the main competitor. British operations were left largely intact. A market survey was also commissioned since the sale of the overseas operations had rendered the worldwide brand strategy obsolete, and a new strategy was required.

Conglom's management argued that the sale of overseas operations was necessary because it could not afford to sustain loss-making units for very long.

> Well, very simply, Conglom had paid £100 million for those assets and unless one was going to get earnings out of them that were going to give a reasonable return on that then it would have been a bad acquisition for Conglom . . . What we knew was that the Group had been weakened by poor management which had led to losses in a number of areas which had to be put right. Otherwise it could have pulled down the whole of Conglom. So the only thing we wanted to make sure we didn't do, was to make sure we didn't throw the baby out with the bath water. I suppose you're in a fairly high risk area there because at that stage your knowledge is fairly scant. (Michael Briggs, accountant on the Conglom acquisition team)

The most contentious decision was the sale of the European operations, which was approved by corporate management before the acquisition team had time to assess the European market strategically.

Conglom justified it by saying the risk associated with such a competitive market was not worth it.

> I think what we felt was that even if we put a lot of effort into these companies, and even if we had a chance of doubling their profits, we were still only going to go from something like £1 million to £2 million. The whole thing would have been a major review job and easily a year could have gone by, consumed a lot of energy and time for which the upside was what looked, superficially anyway, fairly limited. (Michael Briggs)

They also argued that this strategy also had the advantage of relieving the acquisition team, which had limited time and resources, of a lot of potential problems simply by removing a whole level of strategic complexity from the business.

> Two years on it is regarded by people here as a stroke of genius because it enmeshed the competition in a whole lot of problems in Europe and therefore has taken their eyes off the UK. (Conglom manager)

Corporate managers were convinced that ELB managers understood their actions, but ELB managers were worried that by taking a short-term view, Conglom was destroying strategic opportunities.

When they sold Singapore and South Africa, to some extent that was understandable. Because of the tremendous losses that these places were making, it would have needed too much management effort to get it right, but when they sold Europe I was making plans for another billet. I thought then and still think now, with hindsight, that it was a disaster. (ELB manager)

You immediately shut the door on the one area where you could sell your high cost product, in a high cost market, a very high margin market. Not only that, but having decided to sell the business, they sell it to the major bloody competition! (ELB manager)

By pursuing their strategy and disregarding any contrary views from ELB managers, Conglom's managers also sent a strong message concerning the conditional and limited nature of ELB's membership of Conglom's managerial elite.

Conglom's actions clearly indicated that it wanted to avoid highly competitive markets and, instead, intended to concentrate on the UK market where they had domination and price leadership. Its primary concern was, then, the return on its capital. It was not concerned with how that return was achieved and made a virtue of maintaining a distance from its operating divisions. The Chairman made a point of never visiting them and corporate concern was focused wholly on the acquisition strategy and the return that operating units yielded.

The biggest strength that we have is that we have a Parent Board that is completely divorced from the operating companies and therefore they're not emotionally involved in making light bulbs or making them in a particular way. They're more involved in what is the return coming out of bulbs and if the return isn't as good in bulbs as we could get in something else then maybe we should get out of bulbs. And so, if ELB's results began to slow down, even if all the changes were in ELB managers' minds for the sake of the future – alarm bells would start ringing. If they rang just for the local management then they'd say that there are very necessary steps that we've got to take because of their emotional commitment. But there's one more body behind them, if you like, firing bullets. (Conglom manager)

Conglom indicated to ELB managers that it was willing to leave operating divisions to carry out their own business strategy but only as long as those units met their financial obligations and served corporate concerns. By leaving unit managers alone, it was easier to hold local management accountable for the financial consequences of their actions. If divisional performance was strong, managers were allowed greater autonomy. When things turned bad, however, the reverse was true.

We have undoubtedly taken a very strong stand with them [Conglom] over one or two things that we have wanted to do. And clearly you are in a position to do that when you are producing a very high profit level and a very high return on capital. Come the day when profits start to go down, then the rules of the game or the emphasis may change slightly. (ELB manager)

Corporate–Unit Relations

Conglom's financial priorities were embodied in a whole series of rules and practices that shaped contact between operating units and corporate headquarters. An annual budgeting cycle required units to show consistent, annual improvement in return on capital employed and, if possible, profits. Budget proposals were initiated by the CEO and Financial Director of the individual unit in collaboration with the unit's Financial Controller at corporate headquarters. Final proposals had to be approved by Conglom's Chairman and Finance Director, however, in discussions at which unit management was not present. A quarterly reporting cycle then tracked the progress of actual performance against budget. The capital appropriation programme required central authorization for any expenditure over £1,000. An unwritten rule meant that investments with a payback of over 4 years were unlikely to be sanctioned. The 'rules' were so well known that unrealistic proposals were rarely put forward by unit managers, even if they were crucial to the long-term viability of their unit.

> It is a wicked system actually because it leads to a very substantial commitment by the management of the division because they know that what they want to do is not meeting with approval or enthusiasm. But the Chairman is able to look me or my Chief Executive in the eye and say 'All my people up here are saying that we shouldn't do it, so how can you do this to me?' And if we agree to it, how can I be certain when all the figures say it won't work. Can you squeeze more out of it! And he'll either squeeze a greater commitment financially or he'll get an enormously strong commitment to what has been promised . . . It's really putting the skids under the people who are planning to spend the money and it's effective – very effective – and it concentrates the mind something wonderful. (ELB manager)

Such procedures thus drew divisional management on to corporate ground by forcing them to consider financial returns.

The salaries of the CEOs and Finance Director in the operating units were linked directly to the budgeting system, enabling them to earn 25–40 per cent above their basic salary. Conglom's acquisitions provided career opportunities for this echelon of senior divisional managers. Share options of up to four times salary were also offered to senior unit managers.

> Of the companies we take over, we generally find that senior management might have a share option of say £20,000 if they're lucky, whereas we're talking of something like £100,000. The influence this has is to get them to identify with Conglom, not so much that they can influence the Conglom problem, but that they recognize the contribution the company makes to Conglom and also they might find it difficult to understand some of Conglom's regulations like over capital expenditure. Once they became shareholders in Conglom they began to look at these things with shareholders' eyes. It is easier then for them to be more amenable to the kind of things we are trying to do. (Conglom manager)

Corporate headquarters appointed the CEO and Finance Director of each operating unit. Finance Directors often started their financial career as a Financial Controller at corporate headquarters where they monitored the performance of a particular operating company. In this way, young accountants learned the ways of senior managers. If successful, they were then promoted to Finance Director in an individual unit where they were no longer responsible to corporate headquarters, but to the CEO of the unit. The risk from Conglom's point of view was that their interests would shift accordingly.

> What happens inevitably with anyone who leaves the Conglom Office and works for a division is that after a while you go native. (Ex-Conglom manager)

The extent of this 'disloyalty' was reduced by the extensive socialization that these individuals received at headquarters and by a dotted line relationship they had to the corporate Finance Director.

The Turnaround Team

The sole surviving ELB Main Board Director – Ray White, the Chairman of the UK division – was given permission to move ELB's Head Office from London to its main production site in north-west England to reduce costs. For a while it seemed that Conglom was grooming White to take over as CEO of ELB but, in August 1980, Conglom bought United Industries, in which they had owned a 20 per cent stake for some years, and moved its CEO – Bill Thornton – over to ELB. Thornton came in with a lot of the less palatable decisions – particularly the sale of the European operations – having already been taken. Thornton's job was, then, to defend the UK market, which was in an irreversible decline. For the first six months he retreated behind closed doors with the team he had brought with him and Michael Briggs (previously the accountant on the acquisitions team, and now the Finance Director).

Thornton relied heavily on the market audit that had been commissioned. It questioned some key assumptions, namely the belief that economies of scale were derived from production. Instead, it suggested they lay in marketing and distribution: the protection of market share depended on the possession of a distribution network and on the firm's ability to fund media advertising. Both factors created significant barriers to entry for firms with a market share below 15 per cent. ELB had an established van sales distribution network but only a very low advertising budget. A second assumption to be questioned was the inherent profitability of the UK operations: if competition was to increase, as it had overseas, ELB would face a collapse – not a decline – of UK sales caused by the substitution of long-life products, since ELB was still without one.

The turnaround team decided to try and slow the loss of ELB's market share. In October 1981, a long-life light bulb was launched; the following year the existing line of products was rationalized, and plans to increase marketing were made.

> Prices are more stable and higher in the UK than in Europe but the brand is tighter and we maintain that through advertising. Marketing as a process is about

establishing and maintaining market imperfections, to establish that your products are so different in character from lower end offerings that they cannot be considered as similar. Its not coincidental in the least that we have the best product because only if we start with some valid technical claim that you then advertise intensively, can you keep prices high and the competition low, and so feed the cycle. (ELB marketing director)

The problem was: how was ELB to fund an expensive advertising strategy that would not increase sales but only slow down the decline?

> The advertising report suggested we'd slow the decline but we wouldn't reverse it. I mean it wouldn't be going up – it would be going down at a slower rate and only with an injection of something like £5 million into advertising. I was saying 'where is all the money for advertising coming from?' (Bill Thornton)

Thornton knew that if he was to be successful, he would have to find a solution that would fit with the goals of the parent company. He decided against approaching Conglom for the funding for increased marketing. Conglom had made it clear that it did not want to become involved in the operating decisions of its divisions, much less provide large amounts of money. Instead, Thornton decided to reorganize ELB to cut costs *ahead* of the decline in volume and thus release funding internally, which could be used to increase advertising and slow down the decline in sales. His plans were announced to ELB managers in March 1981. They revolved around decentralization through the creation of profit centres.

Thornton cancelled the plans to relocate ELB headquarters in north-west England even though they were only three weeks away and many of the key staff had bought houses, and new staff from the area had been hired. Conglom, although somewhat startled, backed Thornton. Houses were sold, staff recalled, and new hires laid off. Thornton believed that a decentralized structure would be more effective for realizing the cost savings upon which his strategy depended. Each factory would be treated as a separate profit centre selling to a reorganized trading division. The factory managers who previously had been separated from central management by several layers of hierarchy would become Factory Directors reporting directly to Thornton.

In the meeting of March 1981, strict performance criteria – which meant holding costs constant in the face of both the decline in sales and inflation – were imposed. Any factory failing to meet them would be rationalized and its operations folded into a successful factory. The message was very clear – Factory Directors would be held accountable on the basis of the information they provided to ELB headquarters. They would no longer be able to wrangle over its accuracy and would have to learn how to be financially literate, since it would be on the basis of financial measures that they were to be judged. Managers were worried about their ability to meet these standards.

> [W]hat had happened previously was that as volume had gone down costs had gone up. Now all of a sudden volume was going to go down and costs weren't [supposed to be] going to go up at all. But it was clear what he intended, there was no ambiguity about it, but I was very apprehensive that we'd achieve it. (Manager)

It would, however, mean a repatriation of a lot of power to these managers.

> By working for the Chief Executive all of a sudden you felt as though you were going to belong again. It's a totally different world. Bear in mind that before I'd had no financial involvement and no involvement in volume decisions. Now I had control of the factory again. I had financial controls. The ball was in my park. (Manager)

A vital element of the decentralization involved the redesign and implementation of a decentralized accounting information system based on the factories. Michael Briggs, the new Finance Director, with only a handful of staff was charged with creating such a system in less than six months. Suddenly, the accounts payroll clerks in the factories would have to become accounting managers responsible to the Factory Directors for producing the accounts on the basis of which their performance would be judged. To the surprise of most of those involved they survived the transition, and within nine months a rudimentary but satisfactory set of decentralized accounts was being produced. It was subsequently refined to revolve around four key ratios: profit to sales, sales to capital employed, sales to inventory, and sales to working capital. On the basis of these systems, productivity gains of 30 per cent were achieved in the first year and 8 per cent per annum in subsequent years. Return on capital employed rose from 11 per cent in 1979 to 90 per cent in 1986. The Factory Directors were happy with the selection of the ratios which, they felt, allowed them to take a somewhat longer-term view.

> Once you set up trend analysis of ratios then it puts the whole discussion about a particular cost on a totally different plane. So instead of looking at one month and saying 'Too bad, in the month of May we were £200 behind budget' or they say 'It was the cold weather' or 'It was because we made a few more bulbs', which all puts it on a superficial short-term basis. If you can actually put them into a ratio form you have a much longer timescale.

Thus the Factory Directors were relatively happy with the changes: they gained more authority and were better able to initiate change in their factories. So, although their collective and individual survival was at stake, at least they had some control over it.

In many respects, Thornton's plans mirrored the relationship between Conglom and its divisions – financial controls coupled with autonomy, as long as performance was satisfactory. However, Thornton could not afford the degree of isolationism and compartmentalization that prevailed among Conglom's acquisitions. Whereas Conglom's divisions were self-contained businesses, ELB's future depended on the ability of the factories to work together. Without some centralizing force, the creation of strong local teams in the individual factories would jeopardize the performance of ELB.

> With a highly decentralized, profit motivated, bonus incentive set up, you could easily get – and I've seen vague snatches where I could see that under a different regime – we could have got anarchy. (Manager)

Building cohesion was particularly important in ELB because of the loss of corporate identity following the takeover by Conglom.

The one that we're weak on is superordinate goals. What's it's all for? Is it to make the Chairman richer, which isn't a superordinate goal that many people can identify with? Is it to make us all richer employees? I don't think that one's very useful because you're in the area then of is it going to be fewer higher paid guys or more lower paid guys? . . . (Bill Thornton)

Thornton was deciding what he could do to revive a collective identity and establish a strategic vision for ELB.

Questions

- Analyse the forms of control used by Conglom and Bill Thornton. What sources of power underlie them?
- How can Bill Thornton ensure the Factory Directors subscribe to a collective vision? Provide an action plan to help him achieve his goals.

Index